36: *British Novelists, 1890-1929: Modernists,* edited by Thomas F. Staley (1985)

37: *American Writers of the Early Republic,* edited by Emory Elliott (1985)

38: *Afro-American Writers After 1955: Dramatists and Prose Writers,* edited by Thadious M. Davis and Trudier Harris (1985)

39: *British Novelists, 1660-1800,* 2 parts, edited by Martin C. Battestin (1985)

40: *Poets of Great Britain and Ireland Since 1960,* 2 parts, edited by Vincent B. Sherry, Jr. (1985)

41: *Afro-American Poets Since 1955,* edited by Trudier Harris and Thadious M. Davis (1985)

42: *American Writers for Children Before 1900,* edited by Glenn E. Estes (1985)

43: *American Newspaper Journalists, 1690-1872,* edited by Perry J. Ashley (1986)

44: *American Screenwriters,* Second Series, edited by Randall Clark, Robert E. Morsberger, and Stephen O. Lesser (1986)

45: *American Poets, 1880-1945,* First Series, edited by Peter Quartermain (1986)

46: *American Literary Publishing Houses, 1900-1980: Trade and Paperback,* edited by Peter Dzwonkoski (1986)

47: *American Historians, 1866-1912,* edited by Clyde N. Wilson (1986)

48: *American Poets, 1880-1945,* Second Series, edited by Peter Quartermain (1986)

49: *American Literary Publishing Houses, 1638-1899,* 2 parts, edited by Peter Dzwonkoski (1986)

50: *Afro-American Writers Before the Harlem Renaissance,* edited by Trudier Harris (1986)

51: *Afro-American Writers from the Harlem Renaissance to 1940,* edited by Trudier Harris (1987)

52: *American Writers for Children Since 1960: Fiction,* edited by Glenn E. Estes (1986)

53: *Canadian Writers Since 1960,* First Series, edited by W. H. New (1986)

54: *American Poets, 1880-1945,* Third Series, 2 parts, edited by Peter Quartermain (1987)

55: *Victorian Prose Writers Before 1867,* edited by William B. Thesing (1987)

56: *German Fiction Writers, 1914-1945,* edited by James Hardin (1987)

57: *Victorian Prose Writers After 1867,* edited by William B. Thesing (1987)

58: *Jacobean and Caroline Dramatists,* edited by Fredson Bowers (1987)

59: *American Literary Critics and Scholars, 1800-1850,* edited by John W. Rathbun and Monica M. Grecu (1987)

60: *Canadian Writers Since 1960,* Second Series, edited by W. H. New (1987)

61: *American Writers for Children Since 1960: Poets, Illustrators, and Nonfiction Authors,* edited by Glenn E. Estes (1987)

62: *Elizabethan Dramatists,* edited by Fredson Bowers (1987)

63: *Modern American Critics, 1920-1955,* edited by Gregory S. Jay (1988)

64: *American Literary Critics and Scholars, 1850-1880,* edited by John W. Rathbun and Monica M. Grecu (1988)

65: *French Novelists, 1900-1930,* edited by Catharine Savage Brosman (1988)

66: *German Fiction Writers, 1885-1913,* 2 parts, edited by James Hardin (1988)

67: *Modern American Critics Since 1955,* edited by Gregory S. Jay (1988)

68: *Canadian Writers, 1920-1959,* First Series, edited by W. H. New (1988)

69: *Contemporary German Fiction Writers,* First Series, edited by Wolfgang D. Elfe and James Hardin (1988)

70: *British Mystery Writers, 1860-1919,* edited by Bernard Benstock and Thomas F. Staley (1988)

(Continued on back endsheets)

British Mystery and Thriller Writers Since 1940 First Series

Dictionary of Literary Biography • Volume Eighty-seven

British Mystery and Thriller Writers Since 1940 First Series

Edited by
Bernard Benstock
University of Miami

and

Thomas F. Staley
University of Texas, Austin

A Bruccoli Clark Layman Book
Gale Research Inc.
Detroit, New York, Fort Lauderdale, London

Advisory Board for
DICTIONARY OF LITERARY BIOGRAPHY

Louis S. Auchincloss
John Baker
William Cagle
Jane Christensen
Patrick O'Connor
Peter S. Prescott

Matthew J. Bruccoli and Richard Layman, *Editorial Directors*
C. E. Frazer Clark, Jr., *Managing Editor*

Manufactured by Braun-Brumfield, Inc.
Ann Arbor, Michigan
Printed in the United States of America

Library of Congress Cataloging-in-Publication Data

British mystery and thriller writers since 1940, first
   series / Bernard Benstock and Thomas F. Staley, eds.
      p. cm. – (Dictionary of literary biography; v. 87)
   "A Bruccoli Clark Layman book."
   Includes index.
   ISBN 0-8103-4565-X
   1. Detective and mystery stories, English–Dictionaries.
2. Detective and mystery stories, English–Bio-bibliography.
3. Novelists, English–20th century–Biography–Dictionaries. 4. English fiction–20th century–Bio-bibliography. 5. English fiction–20th century–Dictionaries. I. Benstock, Bernard. II. Staley, Thomas F.
PR888.D4B68 1989
823'.087209091–dc20
                                                89-12021
                                                CIP

Contents

Plan of the Series

The advisory board, the editors, and the publisher of the *Dictionary of Literary Biography* are joined in endorsing Mark Twain's declaration. The literature of a nation provides an inexhaustible resource of permanent worth. We intend to make literature and its creators better understood and more accessible to students and the reading public, while satisfying the standards of teachers and scholars.

To meet these requirements, *literary biography* has been construed in terms of the author's achievement. The most important thing about a writer is his writing. Accordingly, the entries in *DLB* are career biographies, tracing the development of the author's canon and the evolution of his reputation.

The purpose of *DLB* is not only to provide reliable information in a convenient format but also to place the figures in the larger perspective of literary history and to offer appraisals of their accomplishments by qualified scholars.

The publication plan for *DLB* resulted from two years of preparation. The project was proposed to Bruccoli Clark by Frederick G. Ruffner, president of the Gale Research Company, in November 1975. After specimen entries were prepared and typeset, an advisory board was formed to refine the entry format and develop the series rationale. In meetings held during 1976, the publisher, series editors, and advisory board approved the scheme for a comprehensive biographical dictionary of persons who contributed to North American literature. Editorial work on the first volume began in January 1977, and it was published in 1978. In order to make *DLB* more than a reference tool and to compile volumes that individually have claim to status as literary history, it was decided to organize volumes by topic, period, or genre. Each of these freestanding volumes provides a biographical-bibliographical guide and overview for a particular area of literature. We are convinced that this organization—as opposed to a single alphabet method—constitutes a valuable innovation in the presentation of reference material. The volume plan necessarily requires many decisions for the placement and treatment of authors who might properly be included in two or three volumes. In some instances a major figure will be included in separate volumes, but with different entries emphasizing the aspect of his career appropriate to each volume. Ernest Hemingway, for example, is represented in *American Writers in Paris, 1920-1939* by an entry focusing on his expatriate apprenticeship; he is also in *American Novelists, 1910-1945* with an entry surveying his entire career. Each volume includes a cumulative index of subject authors and articles. Comprehensive indexes to the entire series are planned.

With volume ten in 1982 it was decided to enlarge the scope of *DLB*. By the end of 1986 twenty-one volumes treating British literature had been published, and volumes for Commonwealth and Modern European literature were in progress. The series has been further augmented by the *DLB Yearbooks* (since 1981) which update published entries and add new entries to keep the *DLB* current with contemporary activity. There have also been *DLB Documentary Series* volumes which provide biographical and critical source materials for figures whose work is judged to have particular interest for students. One of these companion volumes is entirely devoted to Tennessee Williams.

We define literature as the *intellectual commerce of a nation:* not merely as belles lettres but as that ample and complex process by which ideas are generated, shaped, and transmitted. *DLB* entries are not limited to "creative writers" but extend to other figures who in their time and in their way influenced the mind of a people. Thus the series encompasses historians, journalists, publishers, and screenwriters. By this means readers of *DLB* may be aided to perceive litera-

---

ture not as cult scripture in the keeping of intellectual high priests but firmly positioned at the center of a nation's life.

DLB includes the major writers appropriate to each volume and those standing in the ranks immediately behind them. Scholarly and critical counsel has been sought in deciding which minor figures to include and how full their entries should be. Wherever possible, useful references are made to figures who do not warrant separate entries.

Each DLB volume has a volume editor responsible for planning the volume, selecting the figures for inclusion, and assigning the entries. Volume editors are also responsible for preparing, where appropriate, appendices surveying the major periodicals and literary and intellectual movements for their volumes, as well as lists of further readings. Work on the series as a whole is coordinated at the Bruccoli Clark Layman editorial center in Columbia, South Carolina, where the editorial staff is responsible for accuracy of the published volumes.

One feature that distinguishes DLB is the illustration policy—its concern with the iconography of literature. Just as an author is influenced by his surroundings, so is the reader's understanding of the author enhanced by a knowledge of his environment. Therefore DLB volumes include not only drawings, paintings, and photographs of authors, often depicting them at various stages in their careers, but also illustrations of their families and places where they lived. Title pages are regularly reproduced in facsimile along with dust jackets for modern authors. The dust jackets are a special feature of DLB because they often document better than anything else the way in which an author's work was perceived in its own time. Specimens of the writers' manuscripts are included when feasible.

Samuel Johnson rightly decreed that "The chief glory of every people arises from its authors." The purpose of the *Dictionary of Literary Biography* is to compile literary history in the surest way available to us—by accurate and comprehensive treatment of the lives and work of those who contributed to it.

                                                                    The *DLB* Advisory Board

Foreword

British mystery writing underwent as significant a series of changes during the early years of World War II as it did during World War I, but with certain differences. In the earlier period, vestiges of the adventure tale, already a feature of mystery fiction, became increasingly persistent as the war generated greater enthusiasm for action and personal combat. Mystery writers were prompted by patriotism and profit to satisfy an appetite for espionage literature in a reading public no longer concerned about anarchists and other "foreign" radicals but eager to uncover German spies under every bed and along every part of the English coast. Already endemic—an early example being Erskine Childers's *The Riddle of the Sands* (1903)—espionage fiction, having burgeoned during World War I with such novels as John Buchan's *The Thirty-Nine Steps* (1915), reached epidemic proportions during the 1930s, becoming an important subgenre of its own at least with the first Eric Ambler novels. The epidemic has persisted undiminished from World War II through the cold war years, even increasing since the success of John le Carré, whose first spy novels evolved from detective novels.

Although the adventure component retained its dominance in the American genre of realistic, violent crime-and-detection stories, it faded significantly between the wars during the Golden Age of British detective fiction. Crafted by such female writers as Agatha Christie, Dorothy L. Sayers, and Ngaio Marsh, the British detective story became more narrowly defined, more formal, and more literary. In the 1920s and early 1930s, when the detective genre assumed a specific, even a rigid, form, "rules" were agreed upon which insisted on fair play in the detection process. As these rules were codified, and detection was made to depend on available evidence, identifiable clues, and acceptable motivations, the format solidified into the "genteel puzzle," the unraveling of which was now the dominant factor. Suspense and atmosphere, action and characterization were generally sacrificed for the purity of the puzzle itself (as in Christie's 1943 novel, *Five Little Pigs*). The familiar manor-house settings, the upper-class characters, a comedy-of-manners tone, and overliterary writing styles all contributed to narrowing the applicability of the genre to the world of the 1930s. The "classic" detective novels reflected an image of England at odds with the reality of the Depression years, the extremities of right- and left-wing politics, and the developing fears of a new world war. Their insulation against historic events may be a factor in their persistent popularity. No less than the Sherlock Holmes stories, their ancestors, they continue to attract new readers and reverential dramatic adaptations; and their authors' names are invoked in advertising blurbs for another generation of "Queens of Mystery Writing."

Nonetheless, the traditional type of detective, usually a serial figure who dominates the fiction through the force of personality or even idiosyncrasy, a Holmes or Poirot or Wimsey, has fared least well during the past three decades. Other kinds of thrillers, suspense novels and crime novels, including the psychological thriller and of course the spy story, have attracted a wider reading public at the expense of the "pure" detective novel.

The backlash against the highly restrictive format of genteel-puzzle fiction did not take a recognizable form until after the war, which in some ways "liberated" the genre, allowing it to develop along diverse lines, challenging the homogeneity of that format. The new thrillers were actively in competition with—and often indistinguishable from—serious works of literary fiction. In particular, a strong sociological perspective, at times even quite political, influenced crime literature, describing and analyzing an England caught between traditional and progressive modes of behavior, the changes wrought by the advent of the welfare state, the new permissiveness, the disruption of conventional family life, and most recently such problems as unemployment, drugs, and racism.

The role of the detective, in England often given over to the amateur gentleman rather than—as in America—to the professional policeman or the private investigator, underwent changes as well. Police procedurals became more frequent, although rarely with the focus on forensics and technology that became obsessive in the American variant, and chief inspectors of either Scotland Yard or a constabulary outside London found themselves and their immediate family members the nuclei of serial detective fiction. The genre, in effect, has become far more domesticated, and in many instances the family conditions of the police official parallel those of the victims and suspects, so that plot situations are intricate and charged with dramatic irony. In addition, complex and perverse sexual relationships are part of the interpersonal complications both inside and surrounding the crimes; homosexuality and even incest are important subjects in crime fiction, as psychologically determined characterization has become the major emphasis. (Since the 1960s, as in the Golden Age, in British detective literature some of the strongest reputations belong to women writers, particularly P. D. James and Ruth Rendell.) In apparent contrast to detectives whose professional and personal problems are determinedly contemporary are "historically-distanced" detectives, such as Ellis Peters's medieval monk-detective and Peter Lovesey's Victorian police sergeant. Yet they, too, are observed with minutely scrupulous attention to realistic detail.

The degree to which British mysteries in the contemporary era have responded to Continental anti-detective-novel influences may appear minimal, but some aspects of that perverse variant have become important. French and Italian novels especially have confused the detective with the criminal, have allowed crimes to go unpunished, have resisted the conclusive ending in which all loose ends are tied up and poetic justice realized, a tendency toward indeterminacy that has been prevalent since the antinovel of Alain Robbe-Grillet in the 1950s. As many new writers of mysteries in England reacted against the limitations of the genre itself, they have also moved away from the "well-made" plot format, the artifices that had their field of play in the puzzle, the neat distinction between good and evil, and the insistence that the values of societal norms be upheld, particularly in plot resolutions. These crime novels have moved closer to investigating real sociological problems in contemporary Britain, and although often with the familiar elements of humor and horror, more often with new insights into human behavior and social conditions.

—Bernard Benstock and Thomas F. Staley

Acknowledgments

This book was produced by Bruccoli Clark Layman, Inc. Karen L. Rood is senior editor for the *Dictionary of Literary Biography* series. Charles Lee Egleston was the in-house editor.

Production coordinator is James W. Hipp. Systems manager is Charles D. Brower. Art supervisor is Susan Todd. Penney L. Haughton is responsible for layout and graphics. Copyediting supervisor is Joan M. Prince. Typesetting supervisor is Kathleen M. Flanagan. William Adams, Laura Ingram, and Michael D. Senecal are editorial associates. The production staff includes Rowena Betts, Anne L. M. Bowman, Nancy Brevard-Bracey, Joseph M. Bruccoli, Teresa Chaney, Patricia Coate, Marie Creed, Allison Deal, Holly Deal, Sarah A. Estes, Brian A. Glassman, Cynthia Hallman, Susan C. Heath, Mary Long, Ellen McCracken, Kathy S. Merlette, Laura Garren Moore, Sheri Beckett Neal, and Jack Turner. Jean W. Ross is permissions editor.

Walter W. Ross and Jennifer Toth did the library research with the assistance of the reference staff at the Thomas Cooper Library of the University of South Carolina: Lisa Antley, Daniel Boice, Faye Chadwell, Cathy Eckman, Gary Geer, Cathie Gottlieb, David L. Haggard, Jens Holley, Jackie Kinder, Marcia Martin, Jean Rhyne, Beverly Steele, Ellen Tillett, Carol Tobin, and Virginia Weathers.

Dictionary of Literary Biography • Volume Eighty-seven

British Mystery and Thriller Writers Since 1940 First Series

Dictionary of Literary Biography

Ted Allbeury

(24 October 1917-)

Michael J. Tolley
University of Adelaide

BOOKS: *A Choice of Enemies* (New York: St. Martin's, 1972; London: Davies, 1973);

Snowball (London: Davies, 1974; Philadelphia: Lippincott, 1974);

Palomino Blonde (London: Davies, 1975); republished as *Omega-Minus* (New York: Viking, 1975); republished again as *Palomino Blonde* (New York: Harper & Row, 1983);

The Special Collection (London: Davies, 1975);

Where All the Girls Are Sweeter, as Richard Butler (London: Davies, 1975);

Italian Assets, as Butler (London: Davies, 1976);

Moscow Quadrille (London: Davies, 1976);

The Only Good German (London: Davies, 1976); republished as *Mission Berlin* (New York: Walker, 1986);

The Man with the President's Mind (London: Davies, 1977; New York: Simon & Schuster, 1978);

The Lantern Network (London: Davies, 1978; New York: Mysterious, 1987);

The Alpha List (London: Hart-Davis, MacGibbon, 1979; New York: Methuen, 1979);

Consequence of Fear (London: Hart-Davis, MacGibbon, 1979);

Codeword Cromwell, as Patrick Kelly (London: Granada, 1980);

The Twentieth Day of January (London: Granada, 1980);

The Lonely Margins, as Kelly (London: Granada, 1981);

The Other Side of Silence (London & New York: Granada, 1981; New York: Scribners, 1981);

The Reaper (London & New York: Granada,

Ted Allbeury

1981); republished as *The Stalking Angel* (New York: Mysterious, 1988);

The Secret Whispers (London: Granada, 1981);

All Our Tomorrows (London & New York: Granada, 1982);

Shadow of Shadows (London & New York: Granada, 1982; New York: Scribners, 1982);

Pay Any Price (London & New York: Granada, 1983);

The Judas Factor (London: New English Library, 1984; New York: Mysterious, 1987);

No Place to Hide (London: New English Library, 1984);

The Girl from Addis (London & New York: Granada, 1984);

Children of Tender Years (London: New English Library, 1985; New York: Beaufort, 1985);

The Choice (London: New English Library, 1986);

The Seeds of Treason (London: New English Library, 1986; New York: Mysterious, 1987);

The Crossing (London: New English Library, 1987).

OTHER: "Memoirs of an Ex-Spy," in *Murder Ink: The Mystery Reader's Companion*, edited by Dilys Winn (New York: Workman, 1977), pp. 164-168.

PERIODICAL PUBLICATION: "It's the Real Thing," *New Statesman* (1 July 1977): 27.

As a writer of spy fiction Ted Allbeury has always relied on that apparently easy air of authenticity which comes from experience. Like several other leading British mystery authors, among them Somerset Maugham, Ian Fleming, and David John Moore Cornwell (John le Carré), Allbeury was himself a spy. He served in the British Intelligence Corps from 1939 to 1947, rising to the rank of lieutenant colonel. He described his experience in a pleasantly humorous vein in an article in *Murder Ink: The Mystery Reader's Companion* (1977). Unlike the Guy Burgess-Donald Maclean-Anthony Blunt stereotype, Allbeury was not recruited from Oxford or Cambridge; rather, he was one of the first "grammar school" volunteers. Accordingly, his forte is not the world of le Carré's Smiley, a top professional "control" who makes the large decisions, but that of the subordinate agent, operating in the no-man's-land between the superpowers, as much exposed to betrayal by his masters as by his colleagues or the ever-deceitful enemy. Allbeury has produced some of the chilliest, most depressing endings since the Berlin Wall claimed its archetypal victim. In *Twentieth-Century Crime and Mystery Writers* (1980) he has said of his endings that they are deliberately sad: "I believe that all wars have sad endings for both losers and winners, and that those who are concerned with espionage and counter espionage tend to have sad endings even in peace

time." H. R. F. Keating, the author of the brief assessment there of his work, comments that "Allbeury is a writer who can handle suffering, make us feel the deep misery of tragedy, and even, because he is a writer, a novelist, make us realize that the tragedy is a part of a greater whole. There are not many others in the suspense field who can do this." In a blurb for the 1979 Mayflower edition of Allbeury's *The Lantern Network* (1978) mystery writer Desmond Bagley is quoted. Of Allbeury he says, "I've been reading all his stuff and am most impressed. He has had personal experience in the Intelligence racket and it shows—the books are authentic and most exciting."

Theodore Edward le Bouthiller Allbeury was born in Stockport, England, the son of Theo and Florence Bailey Allbeury. He attended schools in Birmingham, England. After the war Allbeury worked in advertising. In 1964 he cofounded the public relations and marketing firm of Allbeury Coombs and Partners. On 13 May 1971 he married his third wife, Grazyna Felinska.

In a list of acknowledgments forming a preamble to his fourth novel, *The Special Collection* (1975), Allbeury spoke about the unknown person whose action caused him to begin writing espionage novels: "I must start with the person who kidnapped my small daughter Kerry in November 1970 so that to this day I don't know where she is. It was in this desert of unhappiness that I started on a book which became *A Choice of Enemies*. My business partner and friend Roger Coombs read it, and sent it to the man who became my first literary agent, Peter Janson-Smith. He liked it and offered it to Derek Priestley of Peter Davies Ltd. He bought it immediately and encouraged me to write more, and his constant encouragement and helpful advice led to *Snowball, Palomino Blonde* and now this book."

Allbeury's first novel, *A Choice of Enemies* (1972), establishes a narrative pattern that he often uses: characters are first presented in a World War II field of action, then recalled years later for the main story. First-person narrator-hero Ted Bailey (the close similarity to the author's name quite properly suggests numerous autobiographical elements in the book) is seconded after the war to MI 6 to run (from the west side of the border) a successful line-crossing and espionage operation within East Germany. The operation is blown; on crossing over to check, he is captured and violently interrogated by the Russians,

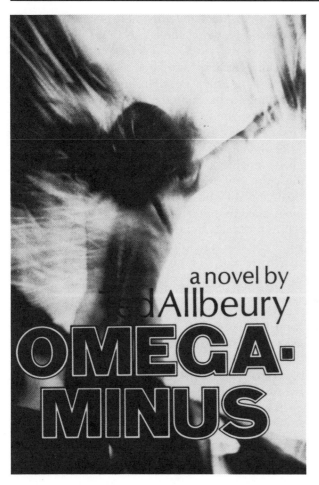

Dust jacket for the American edition of Allbeury's third novel, originally published in England as Palomino Blonde

but he does not give away any secrets, though he is inevitably under suspicion after his escape. His main associate has been an American, Joe Steiner (in charge of all Russian intelligence covering military matters), and previous to the secondment Bailey had the fortune to arrest a Belgian double agent, Louis Berger. Bailey returns to civilian life. He marries his childhood sweetheart, from whom he is divorced after two years, falling in love with a warmer woman called Sally, who dies before the divorce goes through. He next has a long unhappy affair with a married woman, Lara, an alcoholic who eventually goes back to her husband, taking with her their child, Samantha (Sammy), but abandoning her some years before she herself dies. Bailey tries but fails to discover the whereabouts of his beloved Sammy. He works successfully in advertising until, fifteen years later, he is forced out of his job in order to work against Berger, who has found a way to send sensitive industrial informa-

tion to Russia by tampering with British and American computers. Bailey's main helper is a warm, friendly CIA man named Bill Autenowski. Joe Steiner is one of those running the operation. Bailey has a boat on the Thames, as does Berger; while investigating Berger's boat, on which sophisticated transmitting equipment is concealed, Bailey is surprised by a Russian agent but manages to kill him. He uncovers the computer plot (an occasion for Allbeury to give readers some up-to-date, if now elementary, technical information) and prepares to arrest Berger, who then reveals he has control of Samantha, who is in Warsaw. Bailey defects to Poland, quoting E. M. Forster to justify his action: "If given a choice of betraying my country or betraying a friend, I hope I'd betray my country." Once in Warsaw, however, he falls in love with a liaison officer who looks like Audrey Hepburn, Grazyna Kujawska. She returns his love and is prepared to flee with him back to the West while Bailey makes a last-ditch attempt to thwart Berger. Samantha is left behind with her fiancé under protection arranged by Steiner. Autenowski comes across to help in the escape, which is effected after an exciting siege on a farm near the border.

The narrative style in *A Choice of Enemies* is too clipped in the beginning but is otherwise highly characteristic of vintage Allbeury. The hero's background in working-class Birmingham, used here to set him against the typical "Oxbridge" breed of spy, derives from Allbeury's own. Bailey's wretched domestic life after the war, combined with a successful business career, is a pattern only more fully developed in Allbeury's mainstream novel, *The Choice* (1986). Bailey is given an ability to detect lies in others which is associated with a sensitivity at odds with his ruthless killing ability; Allbeury's heroes often have a hard shell and a soft interior. As a spy Bailey has "a touch of the 007s" but is much closer to the Len Deighton model. The master spies are experts in cruel manipulation of the weaknesses of agents, whatever side they are on, though authorial bitterness about this does not obtrude as in some later Allbeury novels. The heavy satire found in *All Our Tomorrows* (1982) against British social and political values as reflected in BBC and ITV news and documentaries is only lightly adumbrated here in chapter 18.

Snowball (1974) encompasses violence, treachery, and eroticism but renders their extremes palatable; there is frequent and bloody killing. The British-Polish hero, Tad Anders, is a hard man who finds love against his will when he has to employ a gorgeous French woman, Marie-Claire Foubert, to infiltrate a group plotting against the security of Britain and Western Europe. The highly elaborate scheme is to soften up Western Europe by securing widespread disaffection with America. The French think the scheme is their idea (although that is only a part of the plan), the KGB think it is their idea (bigger, but still only a part), but it is really a Red Army plan: they think they can sweep to the English Channel in a few days if it works. As a basis, the plot involves revealing that America and Canada would have made a deal with Hitler if England had fallen. The whole elaborate plot is neatly defused by the British counterespionage network, headed by Anders, with the help of a top KGB man, but in the process individuals are killed, including the French woman, for whose death Anders takes a savage vengeance (for which he is dismissed from full-time work). Allbeury uses neat, short chapters, easy to follow, for his narrative. Anders becomes something of a series character, being used in a subordinate role in *Palomino Blonde* (1975; published in the United States as *Omega-Minus*) and, much later, as the hero of *The Judas Factor* (1984).

The main British spy-hero in *Palomino Blonde* is Ed Farrow, who is in charge of an investigation into the interest shown by American and Russian agents in a rich inventor, James Hallet, a lustful middle-aged man who has discovered a new weapon. The CIA assign Kristina, a blonde Danish girl with a Russian mother, to investigate him. Hallet would like to divorce his wife and marry her, but she is kidnapped and tortured in the Polish embassy in London, which leads to a big scandal. This novel has a downbeat ending: in spite of Farrow's efforts Hallet is killed, as is a Russian agent who tries to abduct him, and relations between the various national factions are strained. Kristina survives, much saddened. The narrative seems too fragmented at first, before the characters and the story's main outlines are established, and one feels little sympathy for those involved. It is implausible that the British would give Hallet quite so much latitude; he might have gotten his secret away to Russia. On the dust jacket of *Omega-Minus* Len Deighton calls the work "truly a classic of espionage fiction."

The first part of *The Special Collection* concerns the adventures of the hero, Stephen Felinski, as a British agent in Hanover in World War II. In the second part he is recruited for a counterespionage campaign which proceeds along lines roughly similar to those in Allbeury's two previous novels. There is a Russian plot to neutralize Britain (and so Europe) by fomenting strikes and other destabilizing activities, before launching an attack on the United States. As in earlier books, the plot involves the kidnapping of a girl in order to put pressure on a man, and Allbeury's introductory note, already quoted, explains much, including his reticence in describing the emotions of the victims involved, the serious treatment of the consequences of the kidnapping, and the bitter ending. Here, as it happens, Felinski's fiancée is rescued efficiently, although a good Russian agent sacrifices himself needlessly, as it turns out, for his friend's sake in exchange for her.

The Only Good German (1976; published in the United States as *Mission Berlin*, 1986) is a good, if depressing, thriller. Most of the story is seen (in sympathetic third-person narrative) through the eyes of the hero, David Mills, an intelligence officer in World War II who, twenty years afterward, is brought back into Germany to contact a man he helped during the war and (as it happens) to confront once again a German he arrested. His team destroys a complicated KGB attempt to create havoc that will look as if it were perpetrated by West Germans against Russia. However, an error of judgment causes the death of Mills's old friend, Otto Munsel, and another error of judgment causes Mills to marry Munsel's nymphomaniac daughter, Jutta. She leaves him, and he commits suicide.

In the mid 1970s Allbeury produced two books under the name of Richard Butler, *Where All the Girls Are Sweeter* (1975) and *Italian Assets* (1976). Their hero, Max Farne, is a boat salesman who had fought alongside Italian partisans during World War II. One of these partisans, Gianni Podoni, has become a wealthy Mafioso. In *Where All the Girls Are Sweeter* Farne becomes embroiled in a scheme to provide money for a new Fascist leader and calls on Podoni to help him avenge the murder of a woman with whom Farne was having an affair. Podoni is killed in the process, and *Italian Assets* concerns the hunt for Podoni's hidden treasure, a large quantity of heroin. Podoni's two lieutenants, Franceschi and Carlo Lunghi, have divided his operations, but Franceschi, pressured by the Mafia, threatens Carlo with the death of his ward, Podoni's daughter Gabby, if Carlo does not find the treasure. Carlo decides that only Farne can help, through

Chapter 7

It took Erich Linden three days to get to Magdeburg, about 70 kilometres from the Zone border. He made for the church near the main square. In the dawn its stained-glass windows but otherwise it was still intact. There were half a dozen women sitting on benches near the altar. and A priest was reading a prayer and the women mumbled responses. Linden stood at the back of the church and eventually the priest walked down the aisle with the women. When the women had left Linden spoke to the priest and asked him if he knew where there was a room he could rent.

'Where have you come from?'

'From Berlin, father.'

'Do you have papers?'

'No, father.'

The priest glanced at Linden's hair which had been dyed black. 'Where were you, my son?'

'A conscript.'

'There's an officer coat you're wearing.'

'I took it off a dead man, father. If I didn't take it the Russkis would have taken it.'

'Is it very bad in Berlin?'

'Berlin's finished, just rubble and corpses.'

The priest sighed. 'There is a lady, Frau Hartman who has an old house in Einbeckstrasse. Number 57. Tell her Father Brimer sent you. I believe she has a room you could rent.'

'Thank you, Father.'

'God bless you.'

The priest turned away abruptly as if his blessing had become a ritual that he no longer believed in.

Frau Hartman was in her fifties with the big staring brown eyes of someone permanently alert for where the next blow would come from. She looked at his face for a long time and then said, 'How can you pay for the room. Not Reichsmarks.'

'I can pay ten cigarettes a week.'

She closed her eyes, moving her lips and Linden guessed that she was trying to work out the black-market value of her cigarettes. When she opened her eyes she said, 'For twelve I can do it. Weekly in advance. If you ever get caught don't come back again.'

The room was quite large, with a single bed, a wardrobe, wash-basin and stand and a small bed-side table. It was on the top floor and was rather damp because the roof had been covered with a tarpaulin because when the roof-timbers were in place, the roof tiles were gone.

Page from the manuscript of Allbeury's current work in progress with the tentative title of "Another Place, Another Time"
(courtesy of the author)

his past knowledge of Podoni. Farne rapidly develops such a great, lustful attraction toward Gabby that he has sufficient incentive to make the attempt. She in turn has a calf love for Farne. Murder and mayhem follow, and the most unusual feature of the story is an interesting stand-off at sea between Farne and the Italian navy and police, who wish to arrest him for murder in international waters. *Italian Assets* rises some distance above the potboiler level through its detailed, thoughtful expertise about boats and Italy. The hero ends up in a sexually murky area, on holiday with both Gabby and her mother; he has previously slept with both of them, separately.

In *Moscow Quadrille* (1976) an interesting situation is given heavy injections of eroticism, and violence is confined for the most part to the end of the book. The British ambassador to Russia, a Scot named Sir James (Jamie) Hoult, is about to become special adviser to the British prime minister, so the KGB takes steps to corrupt him. The first woman they employ for the purpose fails, but the second is his own choice, a beautiful big-busted blonde, named Yelena, half his age. However, Yelena used to be the mistress of Krasin, a professional actor and the man who passes her on to Hoult. Hoult divorces his French wife, Adèle, and marries Yelena. He supplies the Soviets with some information but refuses to give them what they really want, a list of agents and fellow travelers about to be purged, so Krasin arranges to kidnap Adèle, with whom he is personally friendly. His plot fails, and Adèle becomes Krasin's lover when she persuades him to seek asylum with her. Hoult attempts to rescue her, but he and Adèle are shot by a KGB assassin, leaving Krasin back again with Yelena. Krasin appears again in *The Alpha List* (1979).

The Man with the President's Mind (1977) employs two unfeasible but plausible ideas: the Russians train a man to react in the same way as the American president and plan to take over Berlin, using as a simple unsettling first step the removal of the Berlin Wall. The plot fails because two of the principal parties to it, feeling betrayed, go over to the Americans. Ivan Slanski, the nominal leader of the team, a sensitive man, defects after being pushed aside by Boris Panov, representing the military who are crazy enough actually to want World War III. Andrei Levin defects because he hears that his girlfriend, Clodagh Maria Kevan, has been killed once she became redundant. Allbeury gathers together the strands of the action slowly, then has a violent, cynical end-

ing; there are, however, some playful elements in the book. The sequence of Levin's escape (he thinks he is near the Chinese border but is actually in New York State) is reminiscent of a famous episode in Deighton's *The Ipcress File* (1962).

The Lantern Network is perhaps not a good title, as the story concerns individuals rather than an organization. Its central concern is with the difference between those sometime traitors who put people first and those monsters who put party first (specifically the Communist party). The story is in three parts. Commander Nicholas Bailey of Special Branch visits a reclusive man named Walters, who is known to have made contact with the KGB in Paris. As soon as questioning begins, Walters cuts his own throat. Part 2 begins to explain why Walters has killed himself by taking readers back in time to the French Resistance in Périgueux near Bordeaux and telling the story of a local leader, Englishman Charles Parker (known as Chaland), who marries a co-worker, Sabine, but is caught by the Gestapo soon afterward and believed executed; the likely betrayer is a Communist leader, Bonnier, who was arrested at the same time. This part of the story is much like other such war stories, but telling points of irony are made, establishing a pattern. For instance, Parker warns his wireless operator, Toinette, not to form close relationships with anyone; she ignores the advice and is betrayed and tortured. Parker does not follow his own advice when he falls in love; as a result he betrays many people, under torture. At the end of part 2, Allbeury draws a parallel between the Bonnier type and the Russians, who let the Germans crush the Polish uprising rather than come to their aid: "The people who organized risings could do the same again some day against their new masters. It was better if their deaths were chalked up to the Germans." In part 3 Bailey goes to Périgueux and establishes that Walters was really Parker, not dead but forced by Bonnier to become a traitor for fear that his wife, Sabine, would have her life ruined. However, Bailey falls in love with Sabine's daughter, which compromises his investigation. He keeps the truth to himself, finding that like Parker he must live alone rather than become involved with the woman he loves, and he kills Bonnier. Bailey discovers that Parker had fought simply for the love of France: he had no politics. Parker's popularity had made him a nuisance to Bonnier, who wanted all the credit for Resistance work to go to his party.

The Alpha List is solidly rooted in Midlands working-class values. The first-person narrator-hero, David Marsh, is pulled from a liaison job in Berlin to investigate and, later, interrogate his boyhood friend, now a Labour M.P., Charlie Kelly, who knows about the Alpha list, which comprises those of the old-boys'-network type who will be saved (at a price) should Britain be bombed in a nuclear war. Out of disgust Charlie helps the KGB (though, actually, they already know plenty about it and, frankly, do not much care). The corruption and ruthlessness of a British master spy, Sellars, and especially of a lying minister, Parker, are set against the lower-class decency represented by Marsh and Kelly, as is the sexual perversity of Harrap, an unlikable spy, and the abuse of sexual attractiveness by Aliki, an MI 5 girl set to watch Marsh. The Russian spies are no more pleasant, for they have no sense of Britain's special value. It comes down to what help an individual can give to his friend; Marsh helps Kelly escape to Russia, though at the cost of his own life. There is a strong element of autobiographical feeling in the novel, not only in the Midlands background but in the pleasanter surroundings near Lamberhurst, Kent, where the interrogation of Kelly takes place and where Allbeury himself was living at the time of writing the novel. Although the novel has a depressing ending, its tone is for the most part fairly cheerful.

Consequence of Fear (1979) takes its title from critic Cyril Connolly. The consequence of fear is hate, here that of Yuri Galitsyn for all Germans after he was forced at the age of thirteen to watch his mother being raped and murdered during World War II. His hatred helps to mar a well-laid plot in the novel's shocking climax. The novel features one of the author's best ideas, that of a big explosion of nuclear waste in Russia which was covered up for a time, despite hundreds of deaths, until the information is leaked to the West. As with several other Allbeury novels the hero's wartime experience results in his reactivation when an old acquaintance surfaces years afterward. Boyle was an intelligence agent in the war who controlled Otto Lemke, who is now an East German sports journalist known as Otto Müller. Müller leaks the information that the Russians caused the explosion deliberately in order to understand more than the Americans the effects of a nuclear war. Müller will deal only with Boyle, who in the meantime has become a

top prosecuting solicitor and is about to be made a judge. Müller meets Boyle in Moscow and passes on part of his evidence. Boyle is arrested by the KGB and interrogated by Galitsyn. At this stage of the novel, one tends to feel interested in the story but disengaged from the actors. However, Boyle's dilemma develops him into an interesting character as his ability to judge is tested by Galitsyn, who tries to persuade him that the explosion was an accident. Boyle finds a friend in a Soviet dissident, Panov, who helps him interview people purporting to be witnesses to the explosion. Galitsyn's idea is that Boyle, who would otherwise be killed along with Müller, should go to Berlin for the evidence and return home to discredit his source. However, the CIA, ignorant of the details, decides that Boyle has been "turned" and must be killed. In the end, Galitsyn kills Müller in a fit of rage against Germans, and Boyle is shot by the CIA. All goes for nothing, and readers are left with no certainties: the status quo of the cold war continues.

Allbeury used the pseudonym Patrick Kelly for two books published in 1980 and 1981, *Codeword Cromwell* and *The Lonely Margins*. *Codeword Cromwell* is basically a tragic story of thwarted love and betrayed heroism. The title refers to a code word issued twice in late 1940 to warn of a possible imminent invasion of Britain. The hero is Max von Bayer, a "noble" young German of the old school, who was a riding champion before the war, when he fell in love with Sadie Aarons, the too-young daughter of a Jewish professor at King's College, Cambridge. Her father, Moshe, refused to allow him to propose to Sadie. Thereupon Max becomes a fanatical German patriot, SS man, and warmonger and is enlisted by a mysterious Nazi officer, Otto Kästner, to keep a watchful eye on the plans for Operation Sealion (the planned invasion of Britain after Dunkirk). When the invasion comes to nothing, Max draws Kästner into helping him run his own small invasion, with radar and air stations as the targets. He puts together a team of five civilians; predictably, they have some success, but the affair ends messily, and Max is killed. Before he dies, he asks to see Sadie, but she is already dead from a bombing raid on London, and her father can offer him only a meager consolation, the words of "Loch Lomond." The team has been betrayed by German leaders and its members branded as traitors for acting on their own initiative.

The Lonely Margins is another grim World War II story, but far from routine and in fact one of Allbeury's finest and bleakest novels. It is divided into three parts, of which only the first concerns the war. Part 2 concerns the investigation made in 1957 by the leading character, James Harmer, now a police chief superintendent, as to why he was betrayed, which ends with his murder of Carter, his SOE (Special Operations Executive) control. Part 3 concerns the subsequent police investigation, Harmer's trial, acquittal, and suicide.

Harmer's parents were dour people who cared nothing for him, and all the "love" he got was from prostitutes until he met Jane Frazer, who is half-French, half-Scottish and acts as his wireless operator on a strange World War II mission to Paris where he has gone to observe an SOE cell, Seagull, ostensibly because it may have been infiltrated. Harmer and Frazer are not supposed to contact the cell, but the demoralized group contacts them, and Harmer decides to run it; however, a radio message from Carter insists that he abandon Seagull, and the whole group is arrested by the Gestapo. Harmer is tortured severely but maintains silence throughout interrogation and survives Buchenwald. Before his arrest he had made love to Jane and had bought her an engagement ring, but he had not given it to her. For him the greatest joy in life had been visiting her home at Christmas and feeling welcomed and loved by her family. She had saved him from becoming a zombie (her own term), but after the war he reverts, becoming extremely successful as a police detective but having no private life. Accidentally he meets Jane again (he did not know she had survived), and they resume their friendship, but her experiences have left her frightened even of being touched by a man. He discovers that all the group think he betrayed them but also discovers that Seagull was in fact blown by Carter. Harmer (this time) gives Jane an engagement ring, says his final farewell, and goes after Carter, who has become a rich banker. When confronted, Carter is quite unrepentant; the Seagull affair had been a distraction to enable preparations for the Allied invasion of France to proceed smoothly. Harmer executes him by exerting pressure behind his ear and dumps the body in a nearby wood. He then takes leave from his job and simply waits upon events, reading the work of Blaise Pascal. His own police force puts together sufficient evidence to arrest him, but when this happens Harmer refuses to speak and stays mute throughout his trial, using the same techniques as he had under torture in France. This time he is, in a sense, lucky: it works. The trial of a man who stands "mute of malice" raises interesting points of law. Harmer speaks only to Jane's father. When he kills himself afterward it is because he cannot touch those who gave Carter his orders.

Allbeury makes readers feel great sympathy for the hero and heroine of *The Lonely Margins*. Both are very likable in their simplicity and integrity, especially as their relationship develops. Allbeury's expertise is everywhere apparent, notably in the account of interrogation methods, all of the SOE detail, weaponry, legal knowledge, and the unusual trial. There is a weakness in the plotting of the early sequence, when Harmer seems too confident of his own ability and ignores his radio instructions to withdraw, but a tragic hero must have some hubris.

The Reaper (1981; republished in the United States as *The Stalking Angel*, 1988) is unique in Allbeury's work in having a woman as its leading character. It is a well-paced thriller which concerns a vengeance mission undertaken by an "ordinary" young German woman, Anna Simon, after four ODESSA agents kill her husband in a countermove against Israeli efforts to bring Nazis to judgment. The seeds of her implacability are sown when her parents, the Woltmanns, cut short her college education because they decide they have spent enough on her. She found love with Paul Simon, and when she discovers from her father-in-law why he was killed and by whom, she trains to be an assassin with a former CIA agent, Hank Wallace. She kills one ODESSA man in the United States and another in Amsterdam. However, before she can pursue the third, in Croydon, he is already alerted to her, and she is being hunted by him, as well as by the police and by Wallace, who doesn't know what is going on but wants to help her; he falls in love with her. Wallace kills the Croydon man, who would have been beyond Anna's capabilities, and the two together stalk the last killer, the most difficult target of all, in Portugal, followed by a Dutch policeman, who has already met Anna and wants to help her. Wallace kills the policeman before he can speak to Anna and dispatches the final target, also, overriding Anna's insistence that she shoot him herself. Wallace then leaves her. Although they have become lovers, he decides that they have no secure future together. Wallace believes (there is an epigraph from Galatians) that

Dust jacket for the first American edition of Allbeury's 1978 novel (courtesy of Otto Penzler)

Dust jacket for the first American edition of Allbeury's 1979 novel

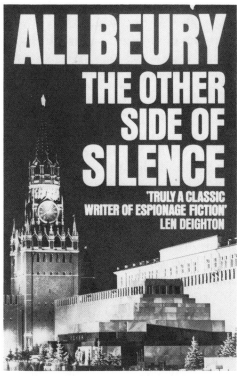

Dust jacket for the first American edition of Allbeury's 1981 novel whose title is taken from George Eliot's Middlemarch *(courtesy of Otto Penzler)*

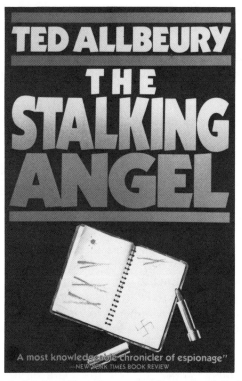

Dust jacket for Allbeury's seventeenth novel, originally published as The Reaper *(1981) (courtesy of Otto Penzler)*

such killing extorts a price; his is to give up Anna so that she can find a future entirely free of the violent past.

The title of *The Twentieth Day of January* (1980) refers to the date on which a newly elected U.S. president takes office. Just before the election a British agent, James MacKay, finds reason to suspect that the man likely to be elected, Logan Powell, has a Communist, Andrew Dempsey, for his campaign manager. He takes his knowledge to the CIA and becomes involved in a difficult, but very smoothly recounted, investigation. The main CIA investigator, Peter Nolan, becomes the novel's principal hero, as the situation demands that he do most of the work. Throughout, the agents must have an eye on the rules of the game, particularly the Fourth and Fifth Amendments, which concern rights of privacy and freedom from unlawful arrest. This does not stop them from searching, phonetapping, and abducting suspects, but they have to be careful. They uncover a sordid story of corruption which separates one man from another on the basis of their attitudes toward sexual partners. People are killed, but there is little direct danger to Nolan and MacKay. There is a moment of sad humanity after Nolan visits, as an unpleasant but necessary duty, the utterly indifferent brother of a murdered agent. There is also an odd erotic leitmotiv, the movement of a man's eyes from a well-endowed woman's breasts to her knowing face; this occurs on four occasions, the first three setting up the last, which is clearly intended to be humorous. In it the eye movement is interrupted by a news story about what actually happened on the twentieth of January. (This trick of erotic description can be found in other books by Allbeury, for instance, *The Girl from Addis*, 1984.)

The title of *The Other Side of Silence* (1981), based on a phrase from George Eliot's *Middlemarch* (1871-1872), concerns the silence of those who have gone across to the enemy. The book's premise is that English traitor Kim Philby, aged sixty-eight, wishes to return to his homeland, and the British government needs to know why in considering whether or not to accept him. Johnny Powell, of the Milord Committee that monitors Philby's movements, is asked to make the decision. He patiently unravels the truth, Allbeury adding much historical material in italics. This is a mystery novel which happens to concern espionage, but it is not at all a thriller, although it contains a murder victim ("Milord," who recruited Philby for the Russians). The novel is a compassionate study of character, especially of Philby, who was recruited by both sides and trapped into treason and defection, and of Powell, a sensitive orphan who can love others who need help but is afraid to marry. As elsewhere, Allbeury also exposes the cynical use and abuse of individuals by those in power who put state or politics first. The Russians and British unions and politicians are portrayed as amoral. Burgess and Maclean figure prominently as characters. Desmond Bagley is quoted on the dust jacket as saying it is "the best novel of espionage" he has ever read. It is noteworthy that in his praise of Jock Haswell's *Spies and Spymasters* (in a 1977 *New Statesman* review), Allbeury asked any reader who ever fancied trying to write a spy story to "look at the picture of Philby on page 165 and write 1,000 words on what you see."

Around the time *The Secret Whispers* (1981) was published, Allbeury's Patrick Kelly titles were released; it may have been one of them originally. It begins with an SOE story and then jumps to Nikita Khrushchev's era. It is one of Allbeury's better (and most bitter) novels, in which men are used for information and women are used for their bodies. At the end the hero, David Miller, is shot by one of his own colleagues because he cannot be taken out of East Berlin at the same time as the man he is helping to defect, and he is too valuable to be left behind. The defector had been turned by Miller during the war and used to send misleading radio messages; afterward he goes back to Germany as a double agent and becomes a West German politician under the name of Otto Becker. He becomes even more useful to the British SIS when he defects to East Germany and becomes a deputy minister of internal affairs. Unfortunately, Lowrey, a sergeant, who was supposed to shred his papers at the end of the war, keeps two very damaging letters and decides to blackmail Becker when he sees his face on television. Lowrey runs a seedy London nightclub and has a friend, Laufer, another club owner, in West Berlin, to help him. Lowrey decides to marry one of Laufer's young blondes, Heidi, who foolishly tells a local police officer about the blackmail attempt; all three are picked up by the SIS and presumably killed. Meanwhile, the East Germans become alarmed, and Miller has to bring out Becker at short notice. Gisella Harting is used cruelly, being persuaded to defect to East Berlin on a promise of marriage which will never be honored, after she herself has served as a double agent. Another kind of blackmail used is emotional: Miller's mother-in-law employs the feigning of a weak heart against her daughter, Penny; when Penny turns at last against this tyranny, readers are given one of the few satisfying moments in the novel.

In most of Allbeury's novels Russian threats are averted, though at great individual cost. Allbeury must have decided that a stronger warning was needed, and so he produced a prophetic fiction, *All Our Tomorrows*, in which Russia actually invades Britain. In the *Times Literary Supplement* for 10 December 1982, T. J. Binyon remarked that the book "seems in some ways to be more of a tract than a novel," but the story of how the Russians are ousted is still "all very gripping stuff." The political part of the novel, which is heavily satirical, is hard to swallow in its exaggerated account of anarchy in the streets uncontrolled by a farcical Parliament, of Russian stupidity, and Gallic perfidy. British prime minister Cooper is forced into an unlikely surrender (and an even more unlikely lapse of memory in reciting the Lord's Prayer at a moment of crisis). The account of the British resistance under occupation is credible and exciting until it becomes obvious how easily the Russians will collapse (it is crucial that the British have American assistance). The utopian ending, whereby Britain becomes a republic on the American model, is unrealistic, although there are shrewd realistic touches. The form of the book gives Allbeury an opportunity to say harsh things about his pet peeves: lying politicians, over-tolerant democracy (even as it is instanced in the BBC practice of giving equal time to both sides in any dispute), and Russian brutality in applying power. He is highly convincing on the ugly nature of Russian-style communism. The heroes in the story are not overplayed and are warmly conceived: they include the principal resistance leader, Harry Andrews, who is a means of counteracting racist tendencies through his love for the daughter of a Pakistani grocer; a Scot, Jamie Boyle, whose wife, Jeanie, encourages the attentions of a Russian (Boyle has the Russian killed and finds it hard to forgive his errant wife); and an upright unionist leader, Joe Langley. This and his mainstream novel, *The Choice*, are Allbeury's only works of substantial length (more than three hundred pages). Moderation is one of his virtues and should not be neglected in measuring him against le Carré and Deighton.

In *Shadow of Shadows* (1982) George Blake's story has to be understood by the hero, British agent James Lawler, after a hitherto compliant defector, Anatoli Petrov, suddenly clams up in his debriefing for fear that the same will happen to him as happened to Blake. Blake's story is tied to the Lawler-Petrov one by another thread, an unknown double agent whose identity it behooves Lawler to learn, since he could be in danger from him. As so often happens in Allbeury's books, women become crucially involved. Petrov has had to leave his wife, Maria, behind in East Germany and acquires a look-alike substitute, Siobhan Nolan. Petrov and Lawler are physically alike, too, an odd motif. Siobhan becomes Lawler's woman (and eventually his wife), when Petrov is persuaded to trust his interrogators on condition that Maria is brought out to him, a task which is undertaken successfully by Lawler.

Pay Any Price (1983), its title from John F. Kennedy's inaugural address, is one of Allbeury's best cynical exercises. The plot concerns the hypnotizing of innocents for use as assassins or in other ways. One such, readers are told, was Lee Harvey Oswald, while another was Jack Ruby; the killing of the Kennedys is attributed to a conspiracy between the Mafia (especially Jimmy Hoffa) and the CIA. However, the main story centers on the abuse of two British innocents, George Walker and Debbie Shaw. Walker is hypnotized while in the army when he visits a dentist. Shaw, a nightclub singer, is caught because she is strongly attracted to the hypnotist, Anthony Symons, who uses his skill as a pianist for his cover. Symons is a psychopath who enjoys his work for the CIA. When he and another psychiatrist, Petersen, are moved to a house in Northumbria after the Kennedy murders, they are used by the SIS. Shaw is made to kill an IRA man. The trouble is that, despite posthypnotic blocks, the experiences Walker and Shaw have undergone start to "leak," giving them moments of disorientation. Unfortunately for them, they come to the attention of a decent MI 6 agent, James Boyd, who knows some of the CIA people involved. Boyd becomes indignant when he learns the truth, partly because he sympathizes with the sorrow of one of his informants, Shaw's boyfriend, a stage hypnotist called Stephen Randall, who diagnosed her problem and encouraged her to see a specialist, as a consequence of which she spends the rest of her life in a mental hospital on government orders. Boyd makes the error of confiding in his superior, Cartwright, who puts national interests ahead of private ones and so connives at the murder of Boyd. Boyd had interrogated Symons, who in turn is killed by a CIA assassin. This theme of individuals subjected to "higher" ends is familiar from earlier novels but is given more sophisticated treatment here than in, say, *The Lantern Network*.

In *The Judas Factor* Tad Anders of *Snowball* and *Palomino Blonde* is recalled for a story deriving from the real-life murder of a man in London by the poisoned spike of an umbrella. Tad is sent after the KGB assassin, Burinski, not to kill him but to bring him back for questioning. However, the job is too hastily planned, and Tad is betrayed to the KGB, who torture him in an unsuccessful interrogation. He is released in exchange for a Russian scientist. While recuperating, he gets to know Burinski, whom he despises, and also Burinski's wife, Inge, a freethinking East German, of whom he approves. The SIS boss, Sir Arthur French, kidnaps Burinski using a full team, and Tad is sent to question him. Burinski agrees to talk, provided that Inge and his child are rescued; on the promise of this, they proceed. However, French never intends to keep the promise, and, when he understands this, Tad takes it on himself to escort Burinski back to Germany. There, however, Burinski is simply murdered.

Tad, no longer formally employed by the SIS, runs a seedy London nightclub; when he commits misdemeanors he is neither cast off nor allowed to resign. He also has a love problem, having to choose between two girlfriends. He is strongly attracted to Judy, a spoiled aristocratic type, already married, who reminds him of his lost love, Marie-Claire. However, a young woman of working-class origin (and very conscious of it), Candy Price, loves him better than Judy, and readers are glad to see them set on the road toward marriage at the end of the story. Allbeury deals sensitively with both women and their very different parents. A theme, used elsewhere in his fiction, of the value of being accepted without question in rightly conducted, unsnobbish homes, is presented through Candy's experience in the home of Tad's immediate SIS contact, Peter Nicholson. Despite their somewhat shabby treatment of Tad, the SIS men come out more favorably than usual in Allbeury's fiction.

No Place to Hide (1984) has an interesting story featuring a sensitive assassin, Johnny Rennie. He works for the SIS, who are treated cynically. The end of the story is presented at the beginning: Rennie is established on a farm in Vermont but must take out insurance so that he will not be harassed by his former bosses. He is living

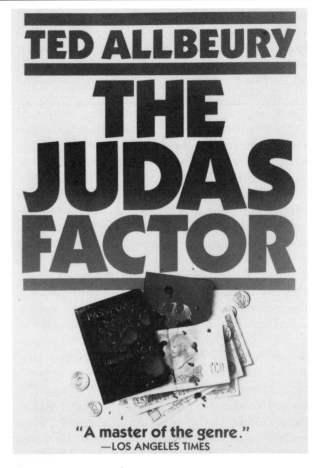

Dust jacket for the first American edition of Allbeury's 1984 novel, which features Tad Anders, a protagonist he also uses in Snowball and Palomino Blonde (courtesy of Otto Penzler)

with a much younger woman, Joanna de Vries, whom he has met in Amsterdam.

In the main story, told in retrospect, he rescues her from drug addiction. Rennie is sent to free a colleague, Mason, who has been captured by Palestinian-style terrorists. There is a rich Arab involved in their plot, Khalim Said, and Rennie is instructed to kidnap Khalim's daughters in order to have pressure put on the terrorists. This works but turns out to have been needless as well as hurtful: one of the daughters loses her sanity, and Khalim's wife, Gabriella, blames her husband for the abduction and breaks up the marriage. When Rennie, influenced partly by Joanna's antiestablishment values, tries to dissociate himself from these events, he is punished, first by harassment, then by a threat to his own daughters (he is divorced). At that point, Rennie resigns: he finds that he is on the point of being committed to a mental institution by his bosses for questioning their authority. The cold-blooded control, Paynter, and the liaison, Fredericks, are hard to credit, but the victims in the novel are treated with great sympathy. Allbeury also makes some telling points about the rationale for counter-espionage activities.

The Girl from Addis is a considerable departure from Allbeury's usual run of spy thrillers, being set in Ethiopia and concerning the love between a cameraman-spy, Johnny Grant, and a Somali beauty, Aliki Yatsou. The first-person narration by Grant is lyrical and warm, although the story is exciting and includes grim details (the girl is kidnapped and suffers multiple rape; Grant's revenge is as brutal as that of Tad Anders in *Snowball*) before the happy ending. The ending is itself interesting, perhaps reflecting Allbeury's disaffection; Grant and Aliki find they cannot bear to live in Britain and exile themselves to Somalia.

Typically for Allbeury the first phase of the story is set in World War II, when Grant's work as an agent gives him the necessary knowledge and contacts for him to be enlisted in the present day, using the cover of his job as a successful fashion photographer. The British want information about a stockpile of Russian weapons which they believe will be used against Somalia as the beginning of a push to take over Nairobi. Complications ensue when Grant falls in love with Aliki, the mistress of the top local Russian, Panov, and she turns out to be the daughter of a woman who had helped him during the war. He beats up Panov when the Russian tries to abduct her from a hotel in Addis Ababa and keeps Aliki with him when he goes to survey and blow up the Russian weapons near the Somali border. However, although he is warned by an old enemy, Jonnet, who is sick of the Russians, Grant does not have the sense to send Aliki to the safety of London; she is abducted, and he rescues her in a violent climax. The scene in which Grant kills Panov is remarkably vicious for a "nice" British hero. Description of the hill country near Addis Ababa is enthusiastic, although it is perhaps unfortunate that Grant describes Aliki's nude, prostrate body as "like a freshly opened box of Dairy Milk."

In *Children of Tender Years* (1985), as in *No Place to Hide*, the virtues of the SIS agent-hero are used against him by his masters. Because his character dictates that, after he has solved a major international problem, he should file a low-key, deceitful report, Jacob Malik is deemed unreliable; yet he had been chosen for the job be-

cause his masters knew he would react in this way. From the epigraph which gives the novel its title (children of tender years were to be "invariably exterminated" in Nazi camps) to the last paragraphs, this is a horribly chilling book, even for Allbeury.

Malik, a Pole, is a survivor of Auschwitz, thanks to his mother's prostitution of herself in the camp, where eventually she is killed. Malik can never tell his father about his mother's heroism, and when, at the beginning of the story proper, his father dies, he is completely alone. The SIS sends him to West Germany purportedly to investigate a bout of anti-Semitic slogan-painting which, he is told, is thought to be Soviet-inspired. Actually he is sent to find and destroy five nuclear missiles which (along with five others in Israel) are being held in private hands by rich Jews who plan to use them as a threat against the Russians should they ever invade either West Germany or Israel. He is given only one assistant, Heinz Fischer, a young German who is ignorant of the real situation. Malik is terrified of Germans, so that when Fischer's musical family shows kindness to him he overresponds. He and Lisa, Heinz's sister, fall in love, and he takes her to Israel, so she can consider it as a possible future home for them. A Mossad agent, David Levy, teams with him to destroy the German weapons, by putting pressure on their owners. Unfortunately, this results in the murder of two of the German conspirators, including a friend of the Fischer family. Heinz, already upset by Malik's killing of a minor figure after an interrogation (because he could not be allowed to inform the others involved), is so outraged by this that he threatens to tell Lisa. Malik is shattered, realizing that his dreams of marrying Lisa are over. Fischer is murdered as "unreliable," and readers are left at the end with few hopes that Malik's life will be spared. There are some implausibilities in the story (for instance, it is not likely that Bonn or Israel would need to call in London to solve their internal problems), but it serves once again to illustrate the inhumanity of master spies and the wretched plight of agents whose starved affectionate impulses can be turned against them.

Allbeury's mainstream novel, *The Choice*, is much illuminated when considered in relation to his earlier fiction, which often shows a greater interest in the civilian lives of the protagonists than in their active service. As one reads the novel, one keeps expecting the hero, David Collins, to be recruited for some work of counterespionage.

Basically, the author takes the situation of James Harmer, the hero of *The Lonely Margins*, but restricts his postwar life to business, marriage, and adultery. The title refers principally to a choice given David by his aggrieved wife, Mary (Hawkins), who does not love him, when she discovers that he has a mistress, a younger woman, his secretary, Sally Major. David has an hour to decide whether to give up Sally or leave home. Part 1 relates the previous events. Part 2 hypothesizes what might happen should he stay with Mary. Part 3 shows what future he might have should he choose Sally. In both cases, readers find that the essential choice was made for David before he was born, when his father was killed in the war and his mother decided, out of resentment, not to love her husband's baby. David never overcomes his loveless childhood. A failure at school, he blossoms later under encouragement, first in the army, then in business. Unfortunately, he marries a woman too like his mother, one capable of narrow, unyielding resentment which she begins to exert against him as soon as he leaves their working-class childhood environment in Birmingham to extend his career. His business life with an advertising agency is full; his home is loveless (apart from his relationship with his son, Jimmy, whom he neglects somewhat); he responds to the unselfish love shown him by Sally. His job takes him to New York, but Mary has no wish to go with him. When she acquiesces, she soon divorces him in favor of a wealthy Long Island neighbor. David then falls prey to a wealthy swinger, Dolly Jones; he is too square to enjoy her promiscuous dope-swapping parties and thinks she has given them up when she marries him, as does her father, Casey Jones, who gives him a partnership in his business. However, Dolly has not changed her habits; the marriage ends abruptly. He returns to London but finds no work available to a man over fifty and commits suicide on learning of Casey's death.

Choosing Sally would have been better eventually. His guilt causes him to lose his creativity, and when Sally leaves him, promising to remain "in cold storage" for a year, he has a nervous breakdown from which he is restored only through the kindness of a colleague, Trevor Amis, who suggests he might have a better future as a photographer than as a business executive. David has the ability to appeal to people at a level denied almost all others in his profession, the secret of his success in advertising. His new career stabilizes him for a time, but a jealous business manager, Carmen Friedman, who has worshipped him "from afar," wrecks the career after David falls in love with a rich model, Penny Goodhew. He is rescued only by an out-of-the-blue commission to do a set of photographs of Birmingham. He teams with a young journalist, Patsy Thatcher. The close of the project, however, precipitates another emotional crisis, from which Patsy rescues him. He cannot bear to be left friendless; fortunately she responds and eventually marries him. They live happily for ten years on the same street where he grew up as a child. Part 3 of the novel has a moving ending.

With *The Choice*, Allbeury may have effectively worked out of his system the characteristic life pattern which has informed so many of his novels. This pattern, reiterated so often, enabled him to express his anguish about the constrictions of modern life. His most recent novels, *The Seeds of Treason* (1986) and *The Crossing* (1987), convey a more affirmative mood, though readers should not expect it to be one of shallow optimism.

Papers:
Allbeury's manuscripts are held in the Mugar Memorial Library, Boston University.

Desmond Bagley

(29 October 1923-12 April 1983)

Gina Macdonald
Loyola University in New Orleans

BOOKS: *The Golden Keel* (London: Collins, 1963; Garden City, N.Y.: Doubleday, 1964);
High Citadel (London: Collins, 1965; Garden City, N.Y.: Doubleday, 1965);
Wyatt's Hurricane (London: Collins, 1966; Garden City, N.Y.: Doubleday, 1966);
Landslide (London: Collins, 1967; Garden City, N.Y.: Doubleday, 1967);
The Vivero Letter (London: Collins, 1968; Garden City, N.Y.: Doubleday, 1968);
The Spoilers (London: Collins, 1969; Garden City, N.Y.: Doubleday, 1970);
Running Blind (London: Collins, 1970; Garden City, N.Y.: Doubleday, 1971);
The Freedom Trap (London: Collins, 1971; Garden City, N.Y.: Doubleday, 1972); republished as *The Mackintosh Man* (New York: Crest, 1973);
The Tightrope Men (London: Collins, 1973; Garden City, N.Y.: Doubleday, 1973);
The Snow Tiger (London: Collins, 1974; Garden City, N.Y.: Doubleday, 1975);
The Enemy (London: Collins, 1977; Garden City, N.Y.: Doubleday, 1978);
Flyaway (London: Collins, 1978; Garden City, N.Y.: Doubleday, 1979);
Bahama Crisis (London: Collins, 1980; New York: Summit, 1982);
Windfall (London: Collins, 1982; New York: Summit, 1983);
Night of Error (London: Collins, 1984; New York: St. Martin's Press, 1986);
Juggernaut (London: Collins, 1985; New York: St. Martin's Press, 1987).

OTHER: "A Matter of Mouths," in *Winter's Crimes*, edited by Hilary Watson (London: Macmillan, 1976), pp. 9-35;
"The Circumstances Surrounding the Crime," in *I, Witness: True Personal Encounters with Crime by Members of the Mystery Writers of America*, edited by Brian Garfield (New York: Times Books, 1978), pp. 151-165;

Desmond Bagley (photograph by Howell Evans)

John Wynne, *Crime Wave,* introduction by Bagley (London: Collins, 1981; New York: Riverrun, 1981).

PERIODICAL PUBLICATIONS: "My Old Man's Trumpet," *Argosy* (January 1957);
"Writing Action Fiction," *Writer,* 86 (May 1973): 11-13;
"Modern Backgrounds for Today's Novel," *Writer,* 94 (October 1979): 18-21;
"An Old and Honorable Profession," in "How I Write My Books," compiled by H. R. F. Keating, *Writer's Digest,* 63 (October 1983): 29.

At the time of his death in Southampton, England, Desmond Bagley was one of the most highly paid thriller writers in the world, with twenty million copies of his sixteen novels in print in twenty-three languages, in large print, in braille, and on tape. A film of *The Freedom Trap* (1971), released in 1973 as *The Mackintosh Man* by Warner Bros., starred Paul Newman and Dominique Sanda and was a box-office success. Mystery writer Reginald Hill (*Twentieth-Century Crime and Mystery Writers*, 1980) praises Bagley as "more consistently lively than [Hammond] Innes, less mechanical than [Alistair] MacLean" and argues that "action, authenticity, [and] expertise" are what make his books "outstanding in their field." He is one of the finest thriller writers because of his scrupulous but balanced attention to detail, his exciting use of first-person narration to plunge the reader into action and motive, and his sense of moral outrage and moral culpability. Bagley's international settings are enriched by vivid and pertinent descriptions of place, custom, and local interest; his technical information is vital to the plot and is carefully researched and detailed. He depicts natural disasters, political and economic sabotage, third-world revolutions, sea and air adventures, and treasure hunts. His themes range from the incompetence and inhumanity of international espionage to the search for personal identity to the danger of wounded vanity to tribal Africa.

Born in Kendal, Westmorland, England, the son of John Bagley, a miner, Desmond Bagley was brought up in Blackpool in a theatrical boardinghouse. He began work at age fourteen as a printer's devil and tried a variety of jobs until transferring to an aircraft factory at the start of World War II. After the war he traveled to South Africa, working his way south through Europe and the Sahara, stopping for a year each in Uganda (1947), Kenya (1948), and Rhodesia (1949), finally reaching Durban, South Africa, in 1951, having covered territory from the Mediterranean to the Cape of Good Hope. In Durban he wrote radio programs on scientific subjects for the South African Broadcasting Corporation (1951-1952). He was editor of the house magazine for Masonite in 1953. Between 1958 and 1962 he served as film critic for the *Rand Daily Mail*, Johannesburg, and contributed to the *Johannesburg Star*, among other newspapers, in particular writing book, theater, concert, and record reviews. On 2 September 1960 he married Joan Margaret Brown, and during the first two years of their marriage he worked as scenario writer for Filmlets, a Johannesburg subsidary of 20th Century-Fox. During this time he experimented with the short-story form, but with little success. Intrigued by both still and motion photography, Bagley and his wife took advantage of their African location to photograph animals in the wild (both fervently opposed game hunting). As a consequence, his stories of African adventures abound in interesting details about the habits and patterns of wildlife. After the success of his first novel, *The Golden Keel* (1963), Bagley returned to England and lived with his wife in Totnes, Devon, for twelve years. They next moved to Guernsey in the Channel Islands, where Bagley continued to pursue his writing and his other interests (computers, mathematics, military history, and international friendships). They bought a Georgian house, acquired a dog and cats, and entertained a stream of visitors. He died in 1983. His wife completed the manuscripts of his last two novels.

Over the years Bagley recrossed the Sahara, visited Australia, New Zealand, Canada, the United States, and Europe (especially the Scandinavian countries, Greenland, and Iceland), and toured Antarctica (polar bases and the South Pole itself) as a guest of the United States Navy. His settings range the world: the Pacific Ocean (*Night of Error*, 1984); the Mediterranean (*The Golden Keel*); the Andes (*High Citadel*, 1965); British Columbia (*Landslide*, 1967); an island in the Caribbean (*Wyatt's Hurricane*, 1966); an ancient Mayan city in the Mexican jungle (*The Vivero Letter*, 1968); Middle-Eastern deserts and poppy fields (*The Spoilers*, 1969); the ice fields of Iceland (*Running Blind*, 1970); rural Ireland and Malta (*The Freedom Trap*); Norway (*The Tightrope Men*, 1973); the avalanche country of New Zealand's South Island (*The Snow Tiger*, 1974); Scotland's Cladach Duillich (*The Enemy*, 1977); the Sahara (*Flyaway*, 1978); Texas and the Bahamas (*Bahama Crisis*, 1980); the oil-rich African state of "Nyala" (*Juggernaut*, 1985); and Los Angeles, New York, London, and Kenya (*Windfall*, 1982). His treatment of place always suggests the in-depth perceptions of one who has lived and worked in an area and knows it intimately. For example, in *Running Blind* he discusses the local Icelandic motor sport of driving into a crater and trying to get out the hard way, takes readers on a camper's tour of the countryside, and confronts villains along with deadly geysers, impassable torrents, and slick lava. In *The Tightrope Men* he describes the Scandi-

Dust jackets for the first British editions of four of Bagley's early novels (courtesy of Otto Penzler)

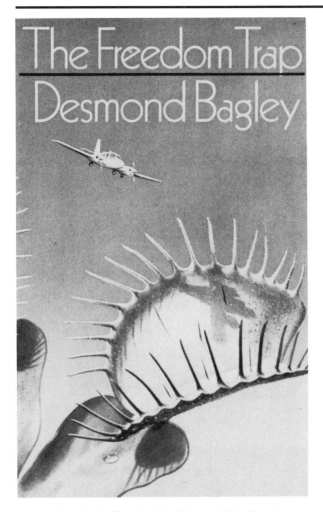
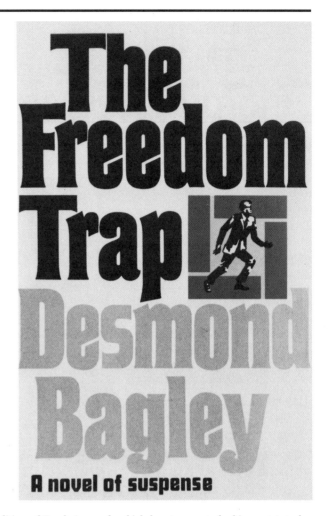

Dust jackets for the first British edition and the first American edition of Bagley's novel, which has proven to be his most popular work (courtesy of Otto Penzler)

navian tradition of the sauna–with the hero unknowingly having vodka substituted for water. In *Flyaway* a camel breeder among the Tuareg teaches the protagonist about desert beauty, desert lore, and desert survival, as well as ancient ruins and even more ancient customs, rivalries, and courtesies. In *Windfall* one learns about African tribal, racial, and religious differences, the animal life of the Nairobi National Game Park, and the Rift, the "biggest geological scar on the face of the earth." Bagley's knowledge of natural phenomena is equally impressive: jungle insects, fevers, flora and fauna (*The Vivero Letter*); the causes and behavior of hurricanes (*Wyatt's Hurricane*); earthquakes (*Landslide*); volcanoes, hot pools, and river fords (*Running Blind*); avalanches (*The Snow Tiger*); and shifting desert sands (*Flyaway*). His technical detail is convincing and ingenious, with his books incorporating short dissertations on such varied topics as computer-

managed farming for optimum profit, archaeological methodology, and Mayan architecture (*The Vivero Letter*); compasses, aerodynamics, and security systems (*Flyaway*); the history and efficiency of the swagger stick and large hotel plumbing systems (*Bahama Crisis*); undersea mineral deposits (*Night of Error*); clay mineralogy (*Landslide*); laser beams projected by X rays (*The Tightrope Men*); guns and their characteristic virtues and limitations (*Running Blind*); the theory, construction, and practical application of the medieval crossbow (*High Citadel*); boat design and construction (*The Golden Keel*); hot-air balloons and satellites (*Windfall*); transport rigs and raft design (*Juggernaut*); and model railway systems, computer programs, and genetic research, particularly DNA splicing (*The Enemy*). *The Spoilers* is packed with telling statistics on every area of drug distribution and abuse. *The Snow Tiger* provides an impressive scientific analysis of the conditions of snow and ice that precipitate avalanches and a detailed account of standard procedure for safety tests and for rescue operations; *Wyatt's Hurricane* does the same for hurricanes. The technical information not derived from personal knowledge Bagley has acquired by going to the experts, as he said in a 1979 article in the *Writer*. For example, for *The Spoilers* he contacted the president of the Royal Pharmaceutical Society to find out about the manufacture, use, and abuse of heroin from the poppy fields of Thailand to the streets of London, while for *The Enemy* he went to the president of the Royal College of Physicians to learn about genetic engineering. For *The Snow Tiger* he read a monograph on snow dynamics by Malcolm Mellor, secretary of the International Commission on Snow and Ice.

Bagley's images are clever, varied, and highly visual. Characteristic are comments such as "He had bled like a cow in a Moslem slaughterhouse" (*Running Blind*) and "The track of my wanderings over Algiers if recorded on a map, would have resembled the meanderings of a demented spider" (*Flyaway*). His images derived from nature are particularly vivid. For example, he describes the islands in *Bahama Crisis* as being "white anted" and explains that when termites (South African white ants) have attacked a wooden house, it will still look solid but one blow will collapse it all into a heap of powder. In *Flyaway* he describes a villain as a "financial shark" for whom "snapping up a profit is . . . as mindless a reflex as when a real shark snaps up a tasty morsel." A rebellious employee in *Juggernaut* cocks his arm back "like a cobra about to strike," and his companions compare their fate (trapped in an ever-changing civil war) to "living inside a kaleidoscope . . . being shaken by some gigantic hand." Bagley's dialogue is at times ironic: "I'm the man from the Prudential," his hero says "pleasantly" to the Russian whom he had once castrated by accident and who is now out for revenge: "How's your insurance, Vaslav?" (*Running Blind*). He enjoys making learned allusions to history and literature, showing a particular affinity to Shakespeare's *Hamlet* and *Macbeth*. In *Juggernaut*, remembering Polonius's advice to Laertes about friendship ("Grapple them to thy soul with hoops of steel") inspires the construction of a raft from empty barrels and steel hoops cut from them. In *Bahama Crisis* Bagley alludes to Henry II's conflict with Thomas à Becket when Fidel Castro asks his revolutionary soldiers, "Who will rid me of this turbulent island?" In *Windfall* Bagley re-

lates the Masai name *Naivasha* and its English translation, *Hell's Gate*, to the entrance to Dante's *Inferno* and quotes Cardinal Richelieu and Samuel Johnson about politics and morality. He also enjoys the occasional pun: in *Flyaway* a deserter in the Sahara, queried, asks, " 'Aint that what a desert's for?"

Bagley preferred to let his plots develop from character, focusing on action and motivation in a generally straightforward, chronological narration. He followed strict office hours (an eight-hour day five days a week) because he believed hard work, not inspiration, produced novels. He would write from three to five thousand words a day on a first draft, then would totally rewrite. In "An Old and Honorable Profession," in *Writer's Digest* (October 1983), he talked about his technique, arguing that his research was largely unconscious–close observation of people and places. For example, in 1963 he had had an idea for a story about an avalanche; his search for information led him to the Antarctic and the South Pole; he talked to snow and ice scientists and toyed with ideas for twelve years. Not until the 1970s had he learned enough for his ideas to coalesce. Though he might have used only ten percent of the information thus garnered, Bagley felt the painstaking research was necessary to lend authority to his writing. His retentive memory allowed him to avoid note taking and synopses. As he said, his usual pattern was to postulate "What if . . . ?" and then to let the plot grow "organically like a tree," with complications and denouement emerging on a day-to-day basis.

Bagley's books usually involve men who have suffered a physically or psychologically crippling experience (for example, a dead wife or brother, a missing father, or betrayal by trusted colleagues) and must learn once again to come to grips with life. Bagley contrasts cynics with idealists, and weak men, selfish and dangerous, with the self-sacrificing and the courageous. His emphasis is on deeds, not words, proving the man. In *High Citadel* the heroine glibly argues that fear is the human predicament and then learns what real fear can do when a survivor of a Korean prisoner-of-war camp recounts the torture that he endured without yielding and his fear of recapture. Usually the battle against hostile nature is as important a feature of his books as the battle against hostile humans. In *The Vivero Letter*, for example, one of the archaeologists points out that "the forest is the enemy in Quintana Roo" and argues that they will "have to fight it" to find their lost city, as indeed they do. *Flyaway* includes selections from the diary of a stranded pilot who struggled to survive in the Sahara and whose skeletal remains are near his downed plane.

Another recurring Bagley pattern is for a quiet, unassuming man, with a civilized veneer, to discover that one can try to fight force with intelligence, but that ultimately the primitive can only be overcome by resorting to primitive means. In *The Vivero Letter* the protagonist charges the main villain with a machete and chops him to pieces. In *The Spoilers* the antidrug task force uses methods as deadly as their prey, and those members unwilling to do so die as a result. In *Running Blind* a man who quit the secret service because he deplored the needless violence stabs a man to death, shoots another through the kneecap, cracks the skulls of several others, and ends up killing even more in order to protect his innocent fiancée. In *Windfall* a mild-mannered scientist turns his hot-air balloon burner into a flame thrower and nearly burns a man to death. Bagley's heroes are coolheaded, calm, collected, and very stubborn; they do not like to be pushed around, and attempts to discourage their efforts merely spur them on. When government agents try blackmail, Bagley's heroes do not crumble before authority but instead go on the offensive, fight back, and at times even threaten to smash and personally ruin the smug agents in charge. They feel a kinship with and a respect for others who are competent and self-aware and are willing to learn from them. They are free from racial prejudice, responding to their fellowmen as individuals, not as representatives of race or class.

Bagley's villains, on the other hand, may be educated, but they are amoral, self-centered, and greedy. Some are hotheaded and others coolly calculating, but they are always willing to betray their fellows and kill without qualms. They are people without pity, and Bagley, sparing them no pity, delights in their dying in gruesome ways–burned alive, buried alive, their heads blown off, their bodies smashed by rampaging "juggernauts" or chomped in half by angry hippos. His secret agents are cold, ruthless men who kill on order without questioning why, even if the assigned target is a friend. His mobsters depend on gangs to overwhelm their opposition and are capable of piracy on the high seas and gun battles on land. His revolutionaries have lost all sight of humanity in particular in their obsession with humanity in general. In *Juggernaut*, for example, a Marxist African general uses a shotgun to

blow off the head of an innocent bystander, and his companions boot a convulsing man off a rig, break his neck, and shoot him for good measure.

Though posthumously published, *Night of Error* was written in 1962. Bagley, dissatisfied with it, never finally revised it, but he did jot down notes for changes that have been incorporated into the published version. The book's fast-paced narration, its wealth of technical detail cleverly used, and its exciting action with the protagonist contending with sea and storm as well as a gang of villains are characteristic of Bagley, but obviously, as reviewer T. J. Binton notes (*Times Literary Supplement*, 30 November 1984), it is not Bagley at his best. Its protagonist, Mike Trevelyan, an oceanographer, expounds on wind and sea and minerals as he and his friends, a group of former commandos backed by an American millionaire, search for an immense treasure in mineral deposits. The only clue to its seabed location came from Mike's dead brother, Mark, the black sheep of the family. *Night of Error* shares with Bagley's *The Golden Keel* a love of the sea and its mysteries.

The Golden Keel is as sensitive to the moods of the sea as a Hammond Innes novel. In fact, Bagley gives credit to Innes's inspiration by having one of the characters remark that the action is like "a Hammond Innes thriller." His discussions of sailing and sailing vessels are not just knowledgeable but reflect a love of the sea and of sailing that gives the book a power beyond its spectacular fights and hair-raising chases. In the *New York Times Book Review* (3 May 1964) Anthony Boucher, speaking of the book's tense, suspenseful plot, claims that *The Golden Keel* "moves like nothing" he has read "since the last Gavin Lyall." The plot grows out of the real-life disappearance of Mussolini's fabulous personal treasure when the Allies invaded Italy and chaos ensued. Bagley's protagonist, Pete Halloran, a South African boat builder who, like Bagley, "travelled from England to South Africa by road, across the Sahara and through the Congo," recounts a barroom encounter that led to a daring project to steal away Mussolini's lost treasure from its hiding place in an Italian lead mine. Motives are mixed. Two of those involved simply want personal wealth, one wants to return the funds to loyal partisans, and Halloran is simply "ripe for mischief." Together the four have the ingredients for a successful venture: funding, the secret of the mine, knowledge of how to get it past customs, and how to fence it. Halloran devises a method first for removing the gold bullion from the mine and then for secreting it from the country–disguised as the keel of his own specially designed boat. But there are the additional problems of violent outside interference and a traitor in the ranks. The project founders, but Halloran regains his sense of balance, finds love, and starts anew. Of Bagley's early efforts, this is clearly his best. It established his reputation, and its profits, together with those from *High Citadel,* enabled him to return to England.

High Citadel begins with the political hijacking and forced landing of a nonscheduled passenger plane carrying home the former president of a South American republic, his niece, and an aide. Amid the towering peaks of the Andes, passengers must first survive a crash landing, then make a perilous descent from sixteen thousand feet, only to find themselves trapped by a hostile, armed, Communist force intent on preventing a democratic coup by executing the former president and any potential witnesses. Reviewer T. V. O'Hara (*Best Sellers,* 1 March 1965) finds the dialogue "thick," the characters "artificial," and the story "muddled," but most critics agree that, despite stock situations, Bagley's tale is certainly action packed and at times highly original. Unusual characters include a professor of history who has specialized in medieval warfare. He designs a crossbow and then a trench mortar to use against trained guerrilla fighters with machine guns. While most of the motley group wait, battling their fears, holding off the enemy, and learning compassion and cooperation, three set off over the Andes to bring help. The cold, the ice glare, and the oxygen-low atmosphere take their toll as inexorably as the traitor in the camp and the enemy in wait across the river. The book ends with an exciting aerial dogfight and the resounding lines from Shakespeare's *Henry V* about "we few, we happy few" who shared wounds in a significant battle.

Landslide focuses on a geologist whose survey for a rich but unscrupulous family precipitates a gradual recovery from amnesia suffered years before. As his memory returns so, too, does his realization of chicanery. There is arson, attempted murder, a devastating landslide, and a burst dam–all amid the timberland of British Columbia. The reviewer for the *New York Times Book Review* (16 July 1967) argued that the book "has the simple appeal of the old pulps where men were men, women blushed, and you could tell a villain by his sneer."

Dust jacket for the first British edition of Bagley's 1978 novel (courtesy of Otto Penzler)

In *Wyatt's Hurricane,* a disaster story, a British meteorologist, Wyatt, correctly plots the path of a force-ten hurricane, one that carries with it fifty-foot tidal waves, but he has a difficult time convincing naval officers and a militaristic Caribbean island dictator that the hurricane must be reckoned with. While the president of San Fernandez Island plots strategy and the chief military weather officer tries to make the storm follow naval regulations, Hurricane Mabel stops a revolution, deflates an egocentric American author, and blows Americans out of a base they have rented for a pittance for more than fifty years. The first half of the book sets up Wyatt's warnings and incorporates detailed information about the nature and qualities of hurricanes, while the last half demonstrates the protective measures Wyatt advised and the violence of raw nature on the rampage. Critics found the book to be mildly entertaining but considered it too much of a "weather report" to be an effective novel.

Shortly after the protagonist of *The Vivero Letter,* London accountant Jeremy Wheale, overhears his date describe him as "a grey little man in a grey little job," he finds himself coolly handling the discovery of a dead man and a dying brother, appalled by a more primitive world in which sudden death is a shocking commonplace. He stirs up rival archaeologists competing for a golden Mexican tray which has been in his family for generations, learning of the de Viveros family who owns the key to Uaxuanoc, a lost city in Yucatán. Wheale discovers that the double plates serve as mirrors that together reveal a map, and he sets out on an expedition to confirm these findings. When the Mafia gets involved and a helicopter is sabotaged, he spends a week being chased through the jungle, then hides out in a cave within a cenote. Ultimately he is forced to call upon the primitive in himself, trade violence for violence, and massacre in order to save.

The pattern of a quiet man forced to extreme action also dominates *The Spoilers.* A guilt-ridden millionaire film tycoon, whose daughter dies from a heroin overdose, decides to try to make up for his indifference and save other men's sons and daughters by declaring war on drug peddlers, not just the pushers on the streets but the large-scale international suppliers. He calls on Nicholas Warren, a London drug specialist who had treated his daughter, and challenges him to act on his knowledge by organizing an expedition to the Middle East to track down and eliminate big-time dope runners. It is Warren who proves to be the real power, choosing for his companions a professional soldier, a torpedo expert, a gambler and con man, a hot-shot reporter, and a psychiatrist, and acting decisively and effectively: "He was tired of fighting the stupidity of the public. . . . If the only way to run his job was to turn into a synthetic James Bond, then a James Bond he'd be." This team follows two slender clues (two names and a place) and baits a trap that leads to an underground Kurdish lab in Iran, then an opium farm in Iraq and one hundred million dollars in heroin. The novel ends with an exciting sea battle off the coast of Lebanon. *The Spoilers* lectures a good bit about the statistics and patterns of drug addiction, but it captures the sense of waste, anguish, and ruthlessness that is a part of the drug scene.

Running Blind, a spy thriller, has been praised for its splendid use of terrain and its

Photograph of Bagley riding a camel in the sub-Sahara used on the dust jacket of the first American edition of Flyaway *(photograph by Joan Bagley)*

richly inventive plotting. Alan Stewart, a British intelligence agent called out of voluntary retirement to be a messenger boy, perhaps because he speaks Icelandic and knows the terrain, learns that the mysterious electronic component he is supposed to deliver to an unknown pickup man is not as innocent as it seems. He is nearly killed en route to his destination inside Iceland and has to use his *sgian dubh,* the black knife of the Highlander, to save himself. Russian and American agents tail him and shoot at him, and his fellow agents bug, blackmail, and try to kill him, but ultimately he exposes a double agent and a double-blind situation and saves his own and his girl-friend's lives.

The Freedom Trap, better known by its American republication title, *The Mackintosh Man* (1973), is the fast-moving tale of a clever scheme to expose a criminal and political railroad for smuggling men out of Britain. The plot's success hinges on Owen Stannard, alias Rearden, a counterintelligence agent brave enough and clever enough to go totally underground: to commit a crime (a diamond robbery), be genuinely sentenced to prison, and play the game to buy his freedom. The hitch is that only Stannard and his lone-wolf superior, Mackintosh, know the true story, and if Mackintosh dies, Stannard may never be believed. Their plan works to an extent, and "Rearden" is sprung from prison, together with a top Russian spy. Both are passed along an underground route to Ireland. But there Stannard's cover is blown, and he must not only break free but chase down the organization which freed him and prove their guilt and his innocence, a task made more formidable by his accusations against a respected and popular millionaire M. P. However, aided by Mackintosh's daughter, he chases the villains down in Malta. This is clearly one of Bagley's most exciting and credible works, and certainly his most popular.

The Tightrope Men has a brilliant opening: English director of industrial films, Giles Denison, wakes up in a Norwegian hotel suite suffering from amnesia, a week of his life gone, his face altered by plastic surgery, and his mind tinkered with–a looking-glass experience. Louis Finger of the *New Statesman* (25 May 1973) praises its "luxurious care for tiny details," its treble crosses, and its puzzles within puzzles and argues that it comes close to being a "convincing political parable." Newgate Callendar of the *New York Times Book Review* (12 April 1973) finds the writing "stiff " and the "basic situation completely unbelievable." Indeed, the action is elaborately plotted, with Denison persuaded by British intelligence agents to act as a decoy to fend off Czech and Russian agents vying with the British for the discovery of the father of the British government scientist whom Denison now resembles. The plan proves difficult to maintain, however, when the daughter of the scientist shows up and Denison becomes enamored of her. Bagley toys with the idea of incest, though of course Denison is not really her father. The final phase of the plot involves some very clever bluffing on the Russian side and the blackmail of a high-ranking spy. On the question of justice the book is unequivocal: "no man can expect justice in this world; if he does then he's a fool. . . . Come; let us enjoy the sunshine while we may."

The protagonist of *The Snow Tiger,* Ian Ballard, a highly skilled manager and administrator, goes back to the scene of childhood embarrassments and confronts the bullies who unfairly labeled him "coward," proving himself a responsible adult and the bullies even more irresponsible than they had been as children. He is a quiet, self-effacing hero who accepts the internal and external challenges with discipline and control. His story is told in the third person–mainly through

Dust jacket for the first American edition of the last novel published before Bagley's death in 1983

an investigation by the New Zealand Commission of Inquiry into an avalanche disaster. The commission blames human error: it points out the harm in stripping the mountainside of trees, cutting hay and leaving it in the fields to form a slick icy coating, ignoring the warnings of a snow scientist and of Maori lore, not setting up snow barriers at a mine's mouth, and not following regulations for construction of support structures. The inquiry ultimately vindicates Ballard, but more important, the legal procedure provides him a forum in which to prove his abilities as a mature, competent, responsible adult. The book is remarkable for the realistic and detailed description of the avalanche exploding in savage fury, the grotesque images of human suffering (for example, men pressed against hot stoves, cut into pieces by shattered glass, mangled and battered and broken, then buried alive in depths up to sixty feet), and the portrait of a psychopath whose insane acts had been excused for far too long as boyish pranks.

The Enemy is a bitter story of government agencies pressuring geneticists to experiment with gene splicing in *Escherichia coli* bacteria without proper controls and containment—"self-interest masquerading as patriotism." The title is shortened from the adage, "We have met the enemy, and he is us." E. E. Rehmus in the *New York Times Book Review* (9 April 1978) calls *The Enemy* Bagley's best book by far, smoothly written, accomplished, "as pleasant a few hours of escape" as one can encounter. There is a gripping plot, direct action, convincing characters, and impressive technical details. The protagonist, financial consultant and professional agent Malcolm Jaggard, having fallen in love with Penny Ashton, the elder daughter of a rich industrialist, finds himself caught up in espionage and intrigue when her sister has acid thrown in her face and her father and his manservant disappear. Jaggard's search for his prospective father-in-law uncovers a religious fanatic obsessed with genetic research, a Russian defector—an atomic scientist and a theorist—and secret agencies as devious as those found in the fiction of John le Carré. Jaggard is an interesting hero, a man with a private income that allows him to be flippant and even rebellious toward superiors, a man capable of deep compassion who can share Ashton's anguish at his daughter's injury, but also a realist, a close observer of human behavior who is physically and mentally adept at survival. He is a good intelligence officer who finds himself morally outraged by the dangerous and inhumane connivings of his superiors. Jaggard finally unlocks the key to Ashton's research and discoveries—an elaborate model railway system that is really a complex computer program that could revolutionize genetic research.

In *Flyaway* Max Stafford, security chief of a growing private agency, finds himself drawn into a missing-person investigation that sends him searching the Sahara for traces of a 1930s air wreck, the key to attempted murder and peculiar financial manipulations within his own firm. A cruel beating to warn him off only heightens his curiosity. The main interest of the novel is Stafford's discovery of the reality of the desert—"in Atakor, in Koudia, in the air, in the Tenere, on the Tassili"—that affects him so profoundly that, even amid the "hurrying crowds of Londoners," he has "an awful sense of loss." He undertakes his trek in a battered Toyota Land Cruiser, on camel, and on foot as he enters "killer country"—"a jumble of lava fields and the protruding cores of volcanoes for as far as the eye" can see. He learns to deal efficiently not only with thirst and heat and desert men but with "civilized" sharks anxious to earn their "contract" fees and cover up a long-hidden murder. His discoveries in the desert give him the edge he needs to save his company and punish a "financial shark" back home. This book clearly builds on sentiments and observations from Bagley's own trek across the Sahara in his youth; details are concrete, graphic; the explanations seem born of personal experience. In fact, Bagley appears on the dust jacket of the first edition decked out in full Tuareg regalia. Readers are left ultimately with a sense that men and their dramas have been played out on the desert sands for centuries. T. J. Binyon, reviewer for the *Times Literary Supplement* (22 September 1978), called *Flyaway* "a very solid, immensely professional piece of work, each carefully researched detail falling into place in the narrative with the precision of a well-engineered machine."

Bahama Crisis is narrated by Tom Mangan, a white Bahamian, proud of his family heritage and his region and proud of using his securities corporation to help build the Bahamian economic base. A rich man with ingenious but sensible ideas for business expansion, Mangan finds himself the object of a concerted effort to destroy him and the economy he so strongly supports. A chain of disasters occurs designed to injure tourism, the islands' main economic base: rioting in the streets of Nassau, Legionnaires' disease at local hotels, arson at the Fun Palace, shredded luggage from a sabotaged airport carousel, and an exploded oil tanker in the sound producing an oil slick that fouls the beaches. When his friends are murdered or badly injured and Mangan's second wife is kidnapped, raped, and tortured, and their baby is lost in the process, he has had enough. Though he, too, is kidnapped and threatened with torture and death, he responds violently, brutally, effectively, rescues his wife, and exposes the Texas-based syndicate and Cuban revolutionaries who are plotting to destabilize and undermine a sound capitalist economy. Though Bagley's Texans talk more like Tennesseans and his description of a Texas financial empire headed by a Scottish clan is unrealistic, the chase scenes are exciting and the puzzles challenging.

Bagley returns to a past hero, Max Stafford, in *Windfall*. Stafford remains firmly established as the head of the successful private intelligence and security operation. Through his friendship with his client from *Flyaway,* Stafford finds himself involved with a question of inheritance. A New York private investigator sent to find a missing heir is fired under peculiar circumstances and pursues answers to England and to a fake heir. When Stafford hires him to continue his investigation, they end up at an unusual "agricultural installation" in Kenya with strong security measures and a satellite, supposedly for monitoring animal migration patterns. There they must deal with British, American, South African, and Kenyan intelligence agents, some charming and responsible, some vicious, dangerous, and irresponsible. Critics found the plot weak and padded, but his story-telling skill is obvious. For example, there is a double plot, one an ordinary scam, the other a more devious game of espionage. There are fine descriptions of Kenya–its terrain, its wildlife, its mixture of races, cultures, sects, and customs–but Bagley's depiction of South African "dirty tricks" is at the heart of the action.

Juggernaut, like *Windfall* a tale of Africa, focuses on troubleshooter Neil Mannix's dedicated efforts to move a 550-ton transformer across a land erupting into civil war. As he and his colleagues learn firsthand the stupidities, brutalities, and evasions of war, they find themselves transporting wounded and dying civilians, nuns, and a medical team from danger center to danger center, followed in procession by hundreds of devotees who regard the transformer as a symbol of protection and hope. Realistically fearing a massacre and shocked by their company plane being shot down, their supporters bombed, their friends needlessly and cold-bloodedly murdered, they begin to use their technical expertise and Western ingenuity to fight back. The portrait of an amoral maverick is particularly well drawn; of him the protagonist remarks: he was "intelligent, sound in military thinking and utterly without fear. . . . he might be a useful man to have about

in a war, but perhaps on the first day of peace he ought to be shot without mercy." *Juggernaut* assesses values. It demonstrates the selfishness, heroism, and basic humanity of mankind.

Bagley's adventure novels employ an effective combination: vivid details of place; convincing technical discussions by experts; admiration for rugged, competent individualists as opposed to company men; mild-mannered heroes up against difficult odds (gangs, agencies, and nature itself); an array of colorful minor characters; and plots that twist and turn to keep even the most jaundiced reader intrigued. His style is straightforward, direct, usually with a first-person narrator who plunges readers into the action and compels attention. Bagley warns about man's need to respect nature's power and, in his technological expansion, to consider its laws. He is critical of racist dismissal of whole peoples on the basis of something so insignificant as color, and enjoys surprising the racists in his audience by getting them involved with, admiring, and caring for a character who only at the end is revealed to be non-Aryan. He finds cultural and individual differences the spice of life. He disapproves of any organization that threatens the individual and that forgets man's humanistic obligation to his fellowman, and of any nation that makes terrorism and violence its weapons. He approves of taking strong measures to fight poverty, intolerance, and violence. The casual reader may be surprised to discover how much he learns from a Bagley novel. They are always consummate entertainments and educational experiences. Bagley teaches moral values as well as technical information but never loses sight of the need to engage his reader through plot and action.

Interview:
Deryck Harvey, "A Word with Desmond Bagley,"
     Armchair Detective, 7 (August 1974): 258-260.

Edmund Crispin
(Robert Bruce Montgomery)
(2 October 1921-15 September 1978)

David A. Christie

BOOKS: *The Case of the Gilded Fly* (London: Gollancz, 1944); republished as *Obsequies at Oxford* (Philadelphia & New York: Lippincott, 1945);

Holy Disorders (London: Gollancz, 1945; Philadelphia & New York: Lippincott, 1946);

The Moving Toyshop (London: Gollancz, 1946; Philadelphia & New York: Lippincott,1946);

Swan Song (London: Gollancz, 1947); republished as *Dead and Dumb* (Philadelphia: Lippincott, 1947); republished again as *Swan Song* (New York: Walker, 1980);

Love Lies Bleeding (London: Gollancz, 1948; Philadelphia: Lippincott, 1948);

Buried for Pleasure (London: Gollancz, 1948; Philadelphia: Lippincott, 1949);

Frequent Hearses (London: Gollancz, 1950); republished as *Sudden Vengeance* (New York: Dodd, Mead, 1950);

The Long Divorce (London: Gollancz, 1951; New York: Dodd, Mead, 1951);

Beware of the Trains (London: Gollancz, 1953; New York: Walker, 1962);

The Glimpses of the Moon (London: Gollancz, 1977; New York: Walker, 1978);

Fen Country (London: Gollancz, 1979; New York: Walker, 1980).

OTHER: *Best SF: Science Fiction Stories*, 7 volumes, edited, with introductions, by Crispin (London: Faber & Faber, 1955-1970);

Best Detective Stories, 2 volumes, edited, with introductions, by Crispin (London: Faber & Faber, 1959, 1964);

Best Tales of Terror, 2 volumes, edited by Crispin (London: Faber & Faber, 1962, 1965);

Cyril M. Kornbluth, *The Syndic*, introduction by Crispin (London: Faber & Faber, 1964);

The Stars and Under: A Selection of Science Fiction, edited by Crispin (London: Faber & Faber, 1968);

Edmund Crispin (photograph courtesy of Victor Gollancz, Ltd.)

Outwards from Earth: A Selection of Science Fiction, edited by Crispin (London: Faber & Faber, 1974).

PERIODICAL PUBLICATION: "Edmund Crispin," as Robert Bruce Montgomery, *Armchair Detective*, 12 (1979): 183-185.

Edmund Crispin enjoyed an active and diversified career. He is known primarily as the creator of Gervase Fen, amateur detective as well as Oxford professor of English language and literature. But Crispin was also an anthologist, chiefly of science fiction, an author of film scripts and radio plays, and, after 1967, a mystery-fiction reviewer for the *London Sunday Times*. Crispin's real name was Robert Bruce Montgomery, and as Bruce Montgomery he was a pianist, organist, conductor, and composer not only of background music for films but also of serious music. He described himself in a partly autobiographical sketch in the *Armchair Detective* (1979) as "a lazy person essentially, and of a sedentary habit." (All Crispin quotes are from this article unless otherwise stated.) He had chosen professions requiring effort, an audience, and a certain amount of public recognition, yet he called himself in *World Authors* (1975) "a person temperamentally requiring a good deal of solitude." Such paradox is characteristic of Crispin's life. In the *World Authors* profile he championed middle-class values, but he created, in Fen, a character whose eccentricity and occasional offensiveness constitute an affront to middle-class propriety. He became a political Conservative, yet in *Buried for Pleasure* (1948) he depicted Labourites and Conservatives as equally foolish and self-interested and proposed apathy as the only reasonable response to politics.

Crispin was born 2 October 1921 at Chesham Bois, Buckinghamshire; his mother and father were Scottish and Irish, respectively. He attended the Merchant Taylors' School, where lameness prevented his participation in athletics, and began writing and composing as compensation for this lameness. Crispin went from Merchant Taylors' School to St. John's College, Oxford, where he studied modern languages (and earned, in his words, "an ignominious Second") and held several music positions. He was in the habit of discussing literature with John Maxwell, who, at one of their meetings, expressed surprise at Crispin's never having read John Dickson Carr. Crispin, who characterized himself as "an intellectual snob in those days," believed detective stories to be unworthy of his attention. However, he agreed to read *The Crooked Hinge* (1938) and was so taken with the book that he decided to write a mystery of his own. The product of that decision is *The Case of the Gilded Fly* (1944; published in the United States as *Obsequies at Oxford*, 1945); in April 1942, in the process of writing the book, he adopted the Crispin pseudonym and created Gervase Fen.

He had planned to enter civil service eventually, but with the success of his novel, he altered his plans. He taught at a public school in Shrewsbury in 1943. In 1945 he left teaching to live in Devon as a full-time writer and composer. From 1945 to 1953, he published seven more Gervase Fen novels and a collection of short stories, all but a few of which concern Fen.

Then, however, he "lay fallow," as he put it. He turned to film music and until the 1970s wrote little other than book reviews. *The Glimpses of the Moon* (1977), the last Fen novel, marked the end of Crispin's fallow period. *Fen Country*, a volume of short stories, appeared posthumously in 1979. Crispin married late in his life, and died on 15 September 1978.

Why Crispin stopped writing for a time is suggested by a change in literary objectives that one can trace in his work. The books can seem formulaic (the *London Times* goes as far as to say in Crispin's obituary [18 September 1978], "all the Edmund Crispin novels followed the pattern of the first"), but actually are not. The earlier novels are for the most part mysteries enlivened by an absurd humor, and in each of these Crispin concerns himself primarily with a different method of detection. Gradually other concerns, a more sophisticated use of humor, for instance, or the development of distinct, multifaceted characters (as opposed to characters who are possible murderers, but little more), assume increasing importance, but mystery remains the primary focus of each book. However, the later books might be described as novels that are built around mysteries. They have as their foci, by turns, political satire, character study, or social comedy, and mystery becomes less important from book to book.

In *The Case of the Gilded Fly* an actress in Oxford for the rehearsal of a new play is murdered. There is no shortage of suspects; the actress was despised not only by the repertory company of which she was a member, but also by almost everyone she knew outside of the company, and almost no one has a convincing alibi for the time the murder was committed. Investigation by motive would therefore be entirely profitless. Fen learns the identity of the murderer by an examination of the physical evidence: the position and condition of the body, the room in which the crime was committed, the gun found in the room, and a ring found on the victim's finger, but known not to belong to her. Crispin established himself with *The Case of the Gilded Fly* as a fair-play mystery novelist–that is, one who provides the clues necessary for the solution of a mystery, then challenges the reader to solve it. As Fen tells one character, "You've had all the facts that I've had; more, you've had a lot of them at firsthand; they give you everything you want. Do you honestly

THE MOVING TOYSHOP

a new

detective story

by

EDMUND CRISPIN

author of

THE CASE OF THE GILDED FLY,

HOLY DISORDERS

Dust jacket for the first British edition of Crispin's 1946 mystery novel, the third featuring his series character, amateur detective Gervase Fen (courtesy of Otto Penzler)

mean to tell me you still don't know what this is all about?" This challenge is issued as much to the reader as to the particular character and forms the basis of one's enjoyment of the book.

Fen can be frustrating company. He is "habitually rude to everyone." He is tempermental, his most common mood being "an excessively irritating form of boisterous gaiety." His mercurial temperament tends "not unnaturally to get on people's nerves." Yet his behavior seems more refreshing than unpleasant; he believes that "we are all becoming standardized and normal," and his eccentricity is a way of opposing this tendency. He is accompanied by an old friend who serves as his foil; his eccentricity is thus accentuated, but so are his wit and intelligence. (Various old friends serve this purpose in most of the books.) Finally, he practices "a sort of unconscious amoralism, since he was always so interested in what people were doing, and why they

were doing it, that it never occurred to him to assess the morality of their actions."

Holy Disorders (1945), another fair-play mystery, finds Fen in a place called Tolnbridge, investigating the murders first of a cathedral organist, then of the precentor of the cathedral. Fen chooses to investigate and solves the murders by examining the alibis of all involved. Readers are privy to his interviews of the suspects; they learn, as he does, that Nazi spies are operating out of Tolnbridge, and that the murders and spying are probably connected. Fen gives a list of alibis and related facts and says that this list should indicate the identity of someone who is connected with the murders, who may be the actual murderer, and who is almost certainly the leader of the spy ring. An organist of Fen's acquaintance, one Geoffrey Vintner, is invited to fill in for the organist who was murdered. Vintner is, however, warned against traveling to Tolnbridge, presumably by the original organist's attackers. He makes the trip anyway, sharing his train compartment with several people, three of whom also are going to Tolnbridge. Vintner selects an empty seat, and after adjusting some baggage overhead, finds on his seat a letter containing a second warning. One might reasonably presume, and indeed it occurs to Vintner, that one of the compartment's occupants, probably one bound for Tolnbridge, placed the letter and is therefore connected with the murders and spying. Thus three promising suspects are established. The incident is not a mere red herring, for one of the passengers proves to be involved with the murderous spies, and late in the book Fen concedes that that passenger must have been the one who delivered the second warning. Yet Fen ignores the incident, and a limitation of the fair-play genre is consequently illustrated. The reader is given everything he needs to know to solve the mystery in one particular way (in this case by alibi), but he is not given (indeed cannot be given, as he must follow the author's train of thought) the freedom to investigate in any other way. By including this incident and another like it, Crispin seems to acknowledge a limitation of, and to express a certain dissatisfaction with, the genre in which he worked.

The Moving Toyshop (1946) and *Swan Song* (1947; first published in the United States as *Dead and Dumb*, 1947) are better than his first two mysteries in that plotting, setting and character development are handled with more depth. *The Moving Toyshop* concerns a murder that is "impossible" in itself and is complicated greatly by

Dust jacket for the 1980 American republication of Crispin's 1947 novel first published in the United States as Dead and Dumb

the disappearance not only of the body but also of the scene of the crime. Fen solves the mystery by first identifying the suspects, whose names were disguised according to a literary puzzle, and then employing a process of elimination. Similarly, *Swan Song* concerns a seemingly impossible crime: a singer is hanged in his dressing room at an Oxford opera house under circumstances in which the murderer apparently could have neither hidden nor escaped. A second, also apparently impossible murder is committed. Fen solves the mysteries by reconstructing the methods employed and determining that "the method of each murder indicated the murderer beyond question." In *The Moving Toyshop* what begins as a methodical investigation degenerates rapidly into a series of progressively more fantastic chase scenes. In one, Fen finds himself first singing, both badly and without invitation, in an Oxford University choir, then hitching a ride with a truck driver who gives gratuitous and ill-formed

opinions of D. H. Lawrence. In later chases, groups of drunken Oxford undergraduates pursue suspects into a nude bathing club and a carnival. Although humor is used to define Fen's character (for instance, he occupies his few placid moments playing games such as "Awful Lines from Shakespeare" and "Detestable Characters in Fiction"), it is used also to define a world in which absurd occurrences are not surprising, in which people conduct themselves in bizarre ways. By placing Fen firmly in a world as eccentric as he is, Crispin gives his character legitimacy. In *Swan Song* Fen first appears in the sixth chapter. Until then, the story is largely of theatrical life, and more particularly of two characters, Elizabeth and Adam Langly, who meet and marry in the first chapter. Over the course of the book the Langlys are depicted as growing gradually more distant, reaching an emotional crisis, then achieving a reconciliation. By contrast, in *The Case of the Gilded Fly* a similar couple is treated far more superficially; they fall in love, plan to marry, never disagree, and even manage to inherit a good deal of money, almost as if they had been plucked from a fairy tale. The mystery is the more important element of *Swan Song*, but the Langlys' marriage is developed not only for its bearing on the mystery but also for its own sake.

In *Love Lies Bleeding* (1948) Fen solves the murders of two public-school masters and a woman by a combination of methods. The suspects' alibis, the movements of key figures, and the physical evidence yield facts that fall into place with the discovery of a motive: possession of a lost Shakespeare manuscript. The solution, therefore, is quite complex, and although Fen says "the case was unusually plain and straightforward," he is the only character who thinks so. The book is noteworthy as a display of Crispin's talent for suspenseful writing. One subplot concerns Fen's attempt to learn what has become of, and if possible to rescue, a schoolgirl who has been kidnapped and may have been killed. The search leads him deep into a forest, where he has an unexpected confrontation with the murderer. That he is led to this confrontation by an unusually malevolent bloodhound named Mr. Merrythought in no way decreases the excitement of the episode. Fen changes appreciably over the course of the first five books. In *Love Lies Bleeding* he says of his *Moving Toyshop* days that "I was irresponsible and carefree in those days. . . . I've sobered up quite a lot since then." This proves to be the case. He is still eccentric, still moody, and still witty. Yet he was indiscriminately rude before, and now saves his outbursts for those, like Mr. Taverner in *Love Lies Bleeding*, who deserve them.

Buried for Pleasure, unlike its predecessors, contains two distinct main plots. One, of course, has to do with murder. A woman who has been blackmailed dies after eating poisoned chocolates. A detective investigating her death is also killed, and a third murder is attempted. When given the details of the first murder, Fen is told that a logical implication of those details leads to "a certain conclusion," which proves to be nothing less than the murderer's identity. Because Fen grasps that implication (whether or not the reader does), he knows immediately who committed the crime. The second murder, and the attempted third, are committed to cover up the first, and therefore are committed by the same killer. Fen investigates to establish proof, and to explode an erroneous theory advanced by the police. Although the investigation requires intricate and satisfying deduction, there is a sense that the basic problem, the murderer's identity, has been solved all along, and this has the curious effect of downplaying the importance of the murder plot.

The second plot, in which Fen stands for Parliament, seems therefore all the more important. Fen chooses to run more to escape the routine of his professorship than from any political conviction; his strategy, which is to avoid if possible committing himself to any position on any issue more specific than the evils of party politics, is suggested to him by his agent. He grows disenchanted quickly ("to woo them politically was like trying to discuss the binomial theorem with a broom") and begins to fear that he may win. To forestall this possibility, he delivers, at the climax of his campaign, a speech calculated to lose votes. He is as insulting as only Fen can be and advises the electorate to avoid voting altogether as an affront to the politician's "sordid trade." The satire reaches its conclusion when Fen's speech has the unintended effect of earning him just enough votes to win. The extra-mysterious elements of the Fen books up to *Buried for Pleasure* are connected with, and secondary to, the murder plots. Characterization is an important element in *Swan Song*, for instance, but the mystery dominates the book, and the characters' importance to that mystery is greater than their importance as characters. In *Buried for Pleasure* the two plots exist entirely independently of each other. Moreover the political plot is in no way secondary to the murder plot. *Buried for Pleasure* marks

Dust jacket for the first American edition of Crispin's 1977 Gervase Fen mystery, which appeared twenty-six years after the previous Gervase Fen mystery

a turning point in Crispin's writing; hereafter mystery will become less, and other elements more, significant.

In *Frequent Hearses* (1950; published in the United States as *Sudden Vengeance*, 1950) a film actress kills herself, and her death is followed by the murders of those who drove her to suicide. The investigation is conducted principally by Detective Inspector Humbleby of Scotland Yard, a character who was introduced in *Buried for Pleasure* and who reappears in many of the short stories. However, "in hastening the killer's final revelation nothing that Fen or Humbleby could do was of any avail," and perhaps as a consequence Humbleby's investigation consists mainly of identifying and attempting to protect the potential victims while awaiting unexpected developments. Fen is left out of not only much of the investigation but also much of the book and solves the mystery only to find that Humbleby and the police, acting on one of Fen's suggestions, have solved it independently. One has the sense of a mystery that resists, for a time, any attempt to solve it and that finally can be solved as well by an ordinary, methodical police investigation as by Fen's deductive method. For these reasons and because he is so often absent, Fen is much less the controlling influence here than in the earlier books; indeed, the story's main interest rests not in how the mystery is solved but in how the characters react to it. Thus a portrait of one of the potential victims reveals, in a subtle way, his concern for the threat to his life. There is a suspenseful episode in which a character chases the killer into a maze in which both become lost. (This episode is more successful than the similar one in *Love Lies Bleeding*, if only because the reader could reasonably expect Fen to come safely out of the earlier episode, but cannot know what to expect in the case of a character whom Crispin need not keep alive.) The killer even is given a chance to explain himself. In a letter to Fen he gloats over his crimes but unwittingly reveals that they have driven him to lunacy.

Anonymous letters sent to residents of a small village, a suicide prompted by one of the letters, and a murder are the mystery elements in *The Long Divorce* (1951). As usual, Fen investigates and, as usual, the reader is given the information necessary to solve the mystery before it is explained. Yet the mystery is of only secondary importance, and this is emphasized by the nature of Fen's investigation. For the first time, he works entirely in secret. He uses a pseudonym, is often absent from the book, and is unconnected with the formal investigation undertaken by the local police. With the real investigation occurring somewhere in the background, the reader is concerned more immediately with two of the characters. Helen Downing is a doctor whose practice is failing. She is unable to compete with another doctor principally because her competitor is a man. She is, consequently, in debt. She becomes engaged to the local police inspector, although their acquaintance has been brief. When she inherits the suicide victim's money, and becomes a suspect in the murder case as well, she finds that she cannot afford to trust fully the man she loves, and that neither can he afford to trust her. Penelope Rolt is a girl whose father is hated by most of the village. She loves her father but experiences a normal adolescent resentment of him. He is a natural suspect as the author of the anonymous letters and is implicated also in the two

deaths. She is uncertain of his innocence and is ashamed of her lack of trust. The story deals with questions of love and trust and centers on the emotional crises suffered by Downing and Rolt; the mystery serves as a catalyst that brings each crisis to a climax.

After the publication in 1953 of a short-story collection, *Beware of the Trains* (comprising fairly straightforward fair-play mysteries), Crispin ceased production of fiction for a quarter-century. He may have stopped writing because he had exhausted the limits of the fair-play mystery. Each of his books contains an intricate but solvable puzzle, but his writing certainly developed to reflect an interest in characterization. Fen is first defined by being placed solidly in his Oxford environment in *The Moving Toyshop*, then other characters receive gradually more extensive treatment. With *The Long Divorce*, Crispin brought his development of the genre as far as it could go. Before it characters helped to advance the mystery, but here mystery helps to define the characters. Thus for Crispin to continue in the genre would be only to repeat himself. This is perhaps why, when he began to write again, he planned books that would "embrace crime stories of every possible kind, from armchair detection through spy fiction and humor to atmospheric horror stories."

Why he began to write fiction again is an easier question to answer; he "was beginning to run out of money, and went back to writing Crispin novels, the first [and as it happened, last] of them being *The Glimpses of the Moon*." Such a motivation induced him to some extent to follow the old formulae. There is, of course, a mystery: most of the body of a local, much-disliked farmer is found hacked to pieces, and the head keeps turning up in unlikely places. A second body receives a similar treatment. The mystery again is deliberately de-emphasized: Fen seems remarkably uninterested, the local police seem very stupid, and even Fen is embarrassed to discover that a sack he's been carrying about for the better part of a day contains the head of one of the victims. Once again characterization is important: in this case, a great many eccentrics are brought to life to produce a comic portrait of English rural life.

There is one important difference between *The Glimpses of the Moon* and the earlier Fen books. Although Crispin came out, especially in *The Moving Toyshop*, rather strongly against those who conspire to murder, he maintained in his earlier books the amoralism he attributed to Fen. In

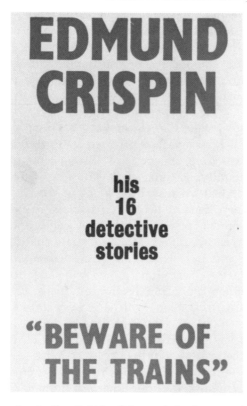

Dust jackets for the first British edition and the first American edition of Crispin's 1953 collection of mystery stories in which Gervase Fen does not appear (courtesy of Otto Penzler)

Dust jacket for the first American edition of Crispin's 1979 collection of twenty-six mystery stories which feature Gervase Fen

The Glimpses of the Moon there are definite judgments. Fen's opinions of, for instance, some characters who hope to sabotage a hunt, or for that matter, of government-run business or African politics, indicate that Crispin had become a political Conservative, and indeed something of a parallel exists between Fen and his creator. Fen was at first indiscriminately rude. When Fen first appeared, Crispin was, by his own admission in *World Authors*, "a prig and an intellectual snob." Fen becomes more interested in what people do, and why; Crispin's gradually more precise characterizations indicate that so was he. Crispin produced a series of effortlessly funny, genuinely perplexing mysteries. Moreover, he successfully developed the genre to reflect his own interests.

References:

Jacques Barzun, "In Memorium: Edmund Crispin," *Armchair Detective*, 12 (Winter 1979): 13;

Barzun and Wendell Hertig Taylor, Preface to Crispin's *Buried for Pleasure*, in their *A Book of Prefaces to Fifty Classics of Crime Fiction, 1900-1950* (New York: Garland, 1976), pp. 37-38;

Erik Routley, *The Puritan Pleasures of the Detective Story* (London: Gollancz, 1972), pp. 162-164;

William A. S. Sarjeant, "Edmund Crispin: A Memorial and Appreciation," *Poisoned Pen*, 3 (May-June 1980): 3-10;

Sarjeant, "Obsequies about Oxford: The Investigations and Eccentricities of Gervase Fen," *Armchair Detective*, 14 (1981): 196-209.

Len Deighton

(18 February 1929-   )

Gina Macdonald
Loyola University in New Orleans

BOOKS: *The Ipcress File* (London: Hodder & Stoughton, 1962; New York: Simon & Schuster, 1963);

Horse under Water (London: Cape, 1963; New York: Putnam's, 1968);

Funeral in Berlin (London: Cape, 1964; New York: Putnam's, 1965);

Action Cook Book: Len Deighton's Guide to Eating (London: Cape, 1965); republished as *Cookstrip Cook Book* (New York: Geis, 1966);

Où est le garlic; or Len Deighton's French Cook Book (London: Penguin, 1965); revised as *Où est le garlic; or French Cooking in 50 Lessons* (New York: Harper & Row, 1977); revised and enlarged as *Basic French Cooking* (London: Cape, 1979);

Billion-Dollar Brain (New York: Putnam's, 1966; London: Cape, 1966);

An Expensive Place to Die (London: Cape, 1967; New York: Putnam's, 1967);

Len Deighton's London Dossier, with contributions by Adrian Bailey and others (London: Cape / Penguin, 1967);

Len Deighton's Continental Dossier: A Collection of Cultural, Culinary, Historical, Spooky, Grim and Preposterous Fact, compiled by Victor Pettitt and Margaret Pettitt (London: Joseph, 1968);

Only When I Larf (London: Joseph, 1968); republished as *Only When I Laugh* (New York: Mysterious Press, 1987);

Bomber (London: Cape, 1970; New York: Harper & Row, 1970);

Declarations of War (London: Cape, 1971); republished as *Eleven Declarations of War* (New York: Harcourt Brace Jovanovich, 1975);

Close-up (London: Cape, 1972; New York: Atheneum, 1972);

Spy Story (London: Cape, 1974; New York: Harcourt Brace Jovanovich, 1974);

Yesterday's Spy (London: Cape, 1975; New York: Harcourt Brace Jovanovich, 1975);

Twinkle, Twinkle, Little Spy (London: Cape, 1976); republished as *Catch a Falling Spy* (New York: Harcourt Brace Jovanovich, 1976);

Fighter: The True Story of the Battle of Britain (London: Cape, 1977; New York: Knopf, 1978);

Airshipwreck, by Deighton and Arnold Schwartzman (London: Cape 1978; New York: Holt, Rinehart & Winston, 1979);

SS-GB: Nazi-Occupied Britain, 1941 (London: Cape, 1978; New York: Knopf, 1979);

Blitzkrieg: From the Rise of Hitler to the Fall of Dunkirk (London: Cape, 1979; New York: Knopf, 1980);

Battle of Britain (London: Cape, 1980; New York: Coward, McCann & Geoghegan, 1980);

The Orient Flight: L. Z. 127-Graf Zeppelin, by Deighton, as Cyril Deighton and Fred F. Blau (Maryland: Germany Philatelic Society, 1980);

XPD (London: Hutchinson, 1981; New York: Knopf, 1981);

The Egypt Flight: L. Z. 127-Graf Zeppelin, by Deighton, as Cyril Deighton, and Blau (Maryland: Germany Philatelic Society, 1981);

Goodbye, Mickey Mouse (London: Hutchinson, 1982; New York: Knopf, 1982);

Berlin Game (London: Hutchinson, 1983; New York: Knopf, 1984);

Mexico Set (London: Hutchinson, 1984; New York: Knopf, 1985);

London Match (London: Hutchinson, 1985; New York: Knopf, 1986);

Game, Set & Match—comprises *Berlin Game, Mexico Set*, and *London Match* (London: Hutchinson, 1986);

Winter: A Berlin Family 1899-1945 (London: Hutchinson, 1987; New York: Knopf, 1987);

Spy Hook (London: Hutchinson, 1988).

MOTION PICTURES: *Only When I Larf*, screenplay by Deighton, Paramount, 1968;

Oh! What a Lovely War, screenplay by Deighton, Paramount / Accord, 1969.

TELEVISION: *Long Past Glory*, ABC, 17 November 1963.

Len Deighton, circa 1984 (photograph by Paul Kavanagh)

OTHER: *Drinks-man-ship: Town's Album of Fine Wines and High Spirits*, edited by Deighton (London: Haymarket, 1964);

The Assassination of President Kennedy, edited by Deighton, Howard Loxton, and Michael Rand (London: Cape, 1967);

How to Be a Pregnant Father, edited by Deighton and Peter Mayle (London: Stuart, 1977);

Tactical Genius in Battle, edited by Deighton and Simon Goodenough (London: Paidon, 1979).

PERIODICAL PUBLICATION: "Even on Christmas Day," in "How I Write My Books," compiled by H. R. F. Keating, *Writer's Digest*, 63 (October 1983): 26-27.

Len Deighton is a celebrated spy-thriller writer and military historian whose fiction is innovative and convincing. His novels are well crafted and entertaining. He has been called "the Flaubert of contemporary thriller writers" (Michael Howard, *Times Literary Supplement*, 15 September 1978) because of his carefully detailed and complicated backgrounds, his intriguing digressions, and his layered levels of perception. His works are consistently popular, and yet critical response to them has been oddly mixed, ranging from high praise to deep contempt with little middle ground, perhaps because of his comic departures from the standard patterns of the genre and his unwillingness to opt for either the fully serious or the fully popular. Graham Greene, W. Somerset Maugham, and Dashiell Hammett have been named his mentors and Ian Fleming's James Bond the reverse of his reluctant and not-so-debonair heroes. His works have always been characterized by a painstaking attention to detail, both technical and otherwise; a concern with the illusions that obscure reality; and the depiction of the double-and-triple crosses of espionage. Consistent in them is a disdain for the pretensions and snobbery of "old boy" networks, Oxford and Cambridge graduates, and upper-class English society in general. Deighton's works critically and closely examine the ethics and morality of the shadowy world of espionage. At the same time they investigate–with humor and forgiveness–the nature of man, the experiences, the values, the loyalties, and the betrayals that make him what he is. Deighton has a sound understanding of human behavior. His characters are usually well rounded, his plots intricately developed though elliptic and challenging, and his concerns sophisticated and humanistic. His most recent works are stylistically much better than his first.

Leonard Cyril Deighton was born in Marylebone, London, England, on 18 February 1929, of Anglo-Irish parentage. His father was a chauffeur, and his mother was the cook of Campbell Dodgson, the keeper of prints and drawings at the British Museum. Deighton attended Marylebone Grammar School, playing hooky to attend plays and visit museums whenever possible. During World War II he dropped out of school to act as a messenger for his father's first-aid post. At seventeen he was conscripted into the Royal Air Force, serving two years as a photographer. While working for the Special Investigation Branch, he developed interests that eventually led to his becoming an expert with rifle and pistol, an experienced frogman, a pilot (though not a legally qualified one), and an authority on weaponry and aircraft. Upon being demobilized he took a veteran's grant to study for three years at St. Martin's School of Art, London, and later he entered the Royal College of Art, from which he graduated in 1953 as a commercial artist. He has been an illustrator for advertising agencies in London and New York. Always curious and willing to try out new areas, Deighton has held a number of quite diverse jobs, including railway lengthman, assistant pastry cook (Royal Festival Hall, 1951), manager of a gown factory (Aldgate), waiter (Piccadilly), teacher (Brittany), co-proprietor of a glossy magazine, magazine artist, travel editor for *Playboy* magazine, news photographer, B.O.A.C. steward (1955 to 1956), syndicated cooking columnist, founder of a London literary agency, scriptwriter, and motion picture producer. He married Shirley Thompson (an illustrator) in 1960. He has resided longest in London, though he spends several months of each year at a residence north of Los Angeles and has an isolated farm near the mountains of Mourne in Ireland.

Inevitably Deighton's experiences are reflected in his novels. While a producer he developed an affinity for the cinematic style that characterizes his novels. As B.O.A.C. steward he traveled widely, from Hong Kong to Cairo, employing his layovers to explore new places and to read extensively. Even his knowledge of Communist countries and their bureaucracy derives from personal experience. According to Hugh Moffet in an interview for *Life* (25 March 1966), Deighton was at one time "hauled into police barracks in Czechoslovakia when he neglected to renew his visa." Another time, in Riga, Latvia, when he was unable to find a map of the city, he drew one–risking the possibility of search and seizure. He has personal knowledge of such diverse locales as Havana, Casablanca, Tokyo, Berlin, Cuernavaca, and Anchorage. He knows gold smugglers in Bangkok and counts as friend a military attaché from behind the Iron Curtain. He has experienced a hurricane in New York and a typhoon in Tokyo, claims to have hunted alligators in the New York sewers, and to have been taken into custody in East Berlin. He has watched blue movies in pre-Castro Cuba and accompanied Los Angeles cops as they kicked their way into a narcotics dealer's apartment. Deighton has fallen into Hong Kong harbor and been a crew member on a burning airliner.

Deighton is self-deprecating about his work. He told Moffet in the *Life* interview that he only began writing "for a giggle" while traveling with his wife in France in 1960 and wrote much of *The Ipcress File* (1962), his first novel, while on that vacation. A chance conversation with Jonathan Clowes, a literary agent, at a cocktail party sometime later led him to submit the manuscript to publishers. In an interview with Edwin McDowell in the *New York Times Book Review* (21 June 1981) he claimed he began by writing spy books because he did not know enough about police procedure to write detective fiction: "So I wrote my first books the way people would write science fiction, because they gave me much more latitude to invent situations. In a *Tatler* interview (4 November 1964) he expressed an "interest in narration and in the pattern of events" that lead to "a good, bold pattern, a geometric shape" but disclaimed any real ability as a writer. In a *Writer's Digest* article about his method of composition (October 1983) he deplored his lack of formal training, claiming to have "evolved a muddled sort of system by trial and error." He has said he prefers "the initial dynamic vulgarity" to any pretensions to art, though his latest works have been both polished and literary. Although a number of his novels have made the best-seller lists in England and America, Deighton asserted he was more interested in "a strong rapport from a small number"

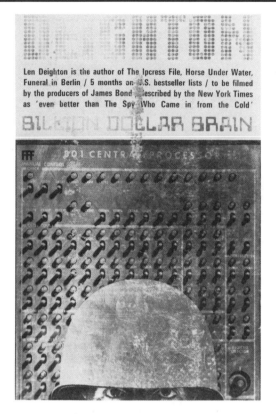

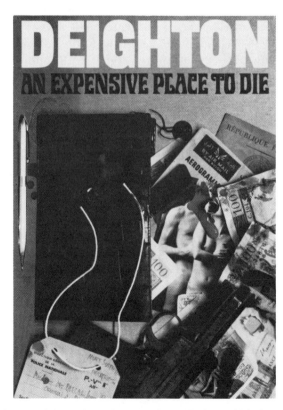

Dust jackets for the first British editions of three of Deighton's early spy thrillers which share the same unnamed agent-narrator
(courtesy of Otto Penzler)

than in widespread notoriety. His method is careful, meticulous, "characterized by an agonizing reappraisal of everything" he writes and a difficult discarding of "thousands and thousands of words." His writing builds on personal experience, travel, and interviews with experts, supplemented by painstaking research. For *Fighter: The True Story of the Battle of Britain* (1977) and *Blitzkrieg: From the Rise of Hitler to the Fall of Dunkirk* (1979) he visited the place where the German spearheads crossed the Meuse River, so as to be able to match the current season with that of the actual event. For *Horse under Water* (1963) he practiced scuba diving, and for *Billion-Dollar Brain* (1966) he learned to pilot helicopters and even flew with the U.S. Air Force on a simulated dropping of an atomic bomb off the coast of Britain. To assure historical accuracy he finds the people involved in real situations and either interviews them or corresponds with them. He keeps a notebook of observations, conversations, and images, draws maps and sketches as guidelines for description, and forces himself to write seven days a week, even on Christmas. Each novel usually requires six to eight drafts and continuous, year-round work. Often he has several projects in progress and has never completed a book in less than five years. An important project might take as long as nine years. *Declarations of War* (1971; published in the United States as *Eleven Declarations of War*, 1975), a quickly written book, resulted from family conditions (living in hotels and temporary accommodations while house hunting) that made a longer work impossible. *Bomber* (1970), in contrast, involved a monumental effort both of research and travel, gathering maps, charts, movies, and recordings of interviews, taking about "half a million words" in notes, all color-coded in loose-leaf notebooks by topic and planned final use, keeping straight the many characters who were physically and psychologically similar because of the nature of their work and the fact that they all had to reflect the vocabulary, background, and mental attitudes of 1943. For a book (which has never been completed), about how the fighter pilots of the air war in Vietnam compared with those of previous wars Deighton spent weeks at air bases in England and Germany. His dedication to his craft has involved experimentation and a willingness to take chances with new approaches, ones that do not always work but that further his understanding. As Pete Elstob points out in *Books and Bookmen* (December 1971) he develops with each new book, trying "for more subtlety, for more convincing, more substantial characters."

Deighton makes use of all his experiences in his fiction. Typical is the way he builds on his expertise as a cook and as a writer of cookbooks detailing the secrets of French cuisine, an expertise possibly cultivated by his mother. In *The Ipcress File* the protagonist prides himself on being a connoisseur of fine foods, discussing the merits of fresh mushrooms over canned, carefully selecting Normandy butter, garlic sausages, fresh salmon, and *pommes allumettes*, and savoring vichyssoise rich with fresh cream and the "mellow," "earthy" flavor of leek. In his trilogy *Berlin Game* (1983), *Mexico Set* (1984), and *London Match* (1985) food defines the man and the culture, and reveals prejudices, values, and temperaments. British food is played off against French food, German food, and Russian food. In *Mexico Set*, for example, the protagonist, Bernard Samson, a cynical, experienced professional agent with fixed loyalties, is in marked contrast to his immediate superior, Dicky Cruyer, an amateurish dilettante who dabbles and samples culture with no real depth of feeling. The difference in their personalities and abilities is summed up in their reaction to Mexican food. Samson is knowledgeable and culturally oriented but knows what he likes and cautiously sticks to it; "I have a very limited capacity for the primitive permutations of tortillas, bean mush, and chilis that numb the palate and sear the insides from Dallas to Cape Horn," he quips, and he claims to "never really trust drinking water anywhere but Scotland, and I've never been to Scotland." Cruyer, in contrast, prides himself on sampling market food, trying *surtido* and *carnitas* with various *salsas*, marinated cactus, and tortillas, lecturing on their virtues as the more culturally knowledgeable Samson quietly points out that it is pork ear and intestine he is consuming with such gusto. As Cruyer, with cultivated condescension, pedantically explains the differences in chilis, while mistaking "cayenne for one of the very mild *aji* chilis, from the eastern provinces," Samson silently watches and relishes Cruyer's reactions to the fiery pepper. Samson can merge with an alien population, lose himself in the crowd, and, because of his sensitivity and caution, survive. Cruyer alienates the locals, rushes headlong into disaster, and does not have a clue to the subtleties around him.

Deighton's novels are crammed full of minutiae–technical data, statistics, and references to documents, training manuals, and memos–that lend authenticity and realism to his descriptions and leave the reader feeling he has learned something about an area of expertise. His control of the specialized jargon of spying, flying, and computer operations is impressive and convincing. The need to incorporate interesting tidbits gathered while researching his books finds release in his early works in the form of footnotes explaining the current jargon of espionage and appendices on such diverse topics as Soviet military districts, privately owned intelligence units, the recipe for a powerful cocktail, advice on handling unfamiliar pistols and tapping telephones, the prices currently fetched by Indian hemp, poisonous insecticides, the Abwehr (Nazi military intelligence), the Official Secrets Act of 1911, Soviet and French security systems, and the composition of neutron bombs. His scholarly apparatus can become a vice when it dominates the main text at the expense of plot, theme, and characterization. *Bomber*, powerful though it is, exemplifies this problem. Throughout it are banal conversations, stilted and unconvincing because they function only to detail masses of information; for example:

> "I've never seen a LaG3, but its newest variant is the La5FN. It's got fuel injection, a 1,650-h.p. motor, and the exhaust gases–carbon dioxide and nitrogen–are passed into the fuel tanks as a precaution against incendiary bullet hits. It's got two cannons with supplementary rockets. . . . It's a good plane."
> "How fast?" asked Kokke.
> "I got nearly 400 m.p.h. out of it at 15,000 feet."
> "That's fast," said Beer.
> "But what can it do at higher altitudes?" asked Kokke.

Paul West believes Deighton loads his books with data "not to create plausibility, but because he seems to like data for data's sake" (*Book World*, 27 September 1970). He finds Deighton's obsession with digressive detail "infuriating" and "stultifying"; for example, Deighton tells readers of *Bomber* that the price of training a Lancaster crew would be enough to send them all to Oxford or Cambridge for three years and that the cost of maintaining a single bomber totaled 120,000 pounds in 1941, though of course a central point throughout *Bomber* is the wastefulness of war. T. J. Binyon in the *Times Literary Supplement* (13 March 1981) is disturbed by what he calls "the re-

dundant adverbial and adjectival clutter" that sacrifices literary quality for documentation.

Deighton certainly makes no claim to being a stylist; he used metaphors and literary allusions sparingly in his first efforts and rarely strove for the poetic touch. His prose, however, has always been serviceable. One difficulty may be that critics often judge Deighton in terms of the traditions of the genre when in fact most often he works against the genre, using it, parodying it, transforming it to suit his own purposes.

Mexico Set illustrates the way Deighton works in information he wants to share with the reader, while integrating it into the progression of his novel. In it Samson's friend, Werner Volkmann, delivers a brief dissertation on why Mexico is ripe for revolution: " 'Look around; two-thirds of the Mexican population–about fifty million people–are living at starvation level. You've seen the *campesinos* struggling to grow crops in volcanic ash or rock, and bring to market half a dozen onions or some such pathetic little crop. You've seen them scratching a living here in the city in slums as bad as anywhere in the world. Four out of ten Mexicans never drink milk, two out of ten never eat meat, eggs, or bread. But the Mexican government subsidizes Coca-Cola sales. The official explanation is that Coca-Cola is nutritious.' Werner drank some of the disgusting coffee. 'And now that the IMF have forced Mexico to devalue the peso, big U.S. companies–such as Xerox and Sheraton–can build factories and hotels here at rock-bottom prices, but sell to hard-currency customers. Inflation goes up. Unemployment figures go up. Taxes go up. Prices go up. But wages go down. How would you like it if you were Mexico?' " Such details obviously give Deighton an opportunity to express a moral outrage he personally feels, and, within the context of *Mexico Set*, they function to make the point that the KGB agent the British all assume has subversive intelligence business in Mexico has obviously not been briefed by his diplomatic service; the inevitable conclusion is that he is there for some other purpose than what London assumes.

The Ipcress File combines humor and suspense in a taut story of betrayal and survival, establishing a pattern and a sensibility that has remained Deighton's hallmark throughout his literary career. It depicts a deceptive world of antagonism and secret hatreds sugared over with the polite and ambiguous catchphrases of upper-class social manners. Deighton's world of espionage is one of bureaucrats and civil servants, com-

Deighton, circa 1967

peting for power and prestige, deceiving and betraying one another, and institutionalizing incompetence. It is a world of "old boy" networks in which rank and class, attendance at the right schools, and use of the right accent count for more than intelligence, competence, or loyalty. The result is a collection of self-centered dilettantes–lisping homosexuals, senile eccentrics, bumbling idiots–engaged in ambitious interdepartmental games that lead to serious betrayals. There is trickery and deceit on every hand, and loyalties and values are readily subverted by power and money. The interoffice intrigues are often as complex as those dealing with the enemy abroad.

The nameless protagonist of *The Ipcress File*, so effectively played by Michael Caine using the name Harry Palmer in the 1965 Universal Films production, is a cunning, versatile, adaptable rebel, one convinced of his skills and arrogant enough to treat his superiors with a measure of roguish disrespect. He is a cynical, competent professional. Anthony Boucher finds him "completely of the 1960's" (*New York Times Book Review*, 10 November 1963). Robert Spector of *Book Week* (17 November 1963) calls him a modern "picaro" through whom Deighton satirizes and parodies "modern espionage agencies" and "the fictional techniques of Ambler, Fleming, and Greene." The nameless agent-narrator is the mainstay of Deighton's early works, appearing in

Horse under Water, Funeral in Berlin (1964), *Billion-Dollar Brain* and *An Expensive Place to Die* (1967), among others, his aliases shifting with time and place. He is a loner, an outsider with only one or two friends (who are usually not fully reliable), a man beset by danger and intrigue on all sides, from enemy and colleague alike. If the KGB does not entrap him, then the incompetence, malevolence, or perverse ideology of an ally might well achieve the same effect. In *The Ipcress File* he asks, "what chance did I stand between the Communists on one side and the Establishment on the other–they were both outthinking me at every move." In *Funeral in Berlin* a quote from Einstein sums up the dilemma of Deighton's heroes: "If I am right the Germans will say I was a German and the French will say I was a Jew; if I am wrong the Germans will say I was a Jew and the French will say I was a German."

Unlike the suave, debonair, upper-class super agent created by Ian Fleming, Deighton's hero is street-tough, self-educated, and independent, a man of irreverent quips and surprising strengths. He is impudent and fallible but a survivor, highly skilled and highly trained. Like Deighton he lacks a classical education but is worldly, brash, and insolent. He has a cheeky working-class rudeness and uses his superior knowledge of gourmet food, locale, and language to goad his superiors. He knows how to do his job far more competently than those around him, which also irritates his supervisors. Thus, he wages the class battle with wit and charm, and the ideological battle between the superpowers with deep-rooted moral and physical resources. Unyielding professionalism and personal integrity help him survive the deception and the treachery that are the essence of his world. When Ross tests "Harry's" reliability by pretending to offer him stolen information, "Harry" is insulted:

> You're prepared to sell information. But you won't sell it to anyone who really wants it, like the Russians or the Chinese, 'cos that would be unsporting, like pinching knives and forks from the mess. So you look around for someone on your side but without your genteel education, without your feeling for social niceties about who it's nice to sell information to.... You've got the nerve to sell something that doesn't belong to you to someone you don't like....

He chokes on his Tio Pepe, and returns to his assignment; "even if I don't get the Minister's certificate of Good Housekeeping doing it," he shouts as he rushes away. Ultimately, in Deighton's work there is the sense that there is no national honor, only the personal honor of a few individuals who dare to stand up against the faceless majority of self-seeking hypocrites who run the spy agencies on both sides of the Iron Curtain.

His protagonist, to some extent, reflects Deighton's interest in Dashiell Hammett. Deighton has him read and quote from Hammett. In fact, the first-person narrator of Deighton's early works tells his story with patterns like those Hammett uses in *The Continental Op* (1945): a series of seemingly disconnected episodes, vividly related and packed with action. The unified pattern is only visible in its entirety at the end of the game (discussed in "Cloak without Dagger," *Times Literary Supplement*, 8 February 1963). This approach has irritated critics who decry the loose, episodic sequences as baffling, enigmatic obfuscation, but beneath the seeming chaos there is almost always a brilliantly executed design.

In Deighton's early works the protagonist is a young man, new to the espionage game, a pawn in the hands of his superiors as well as a pawn of competing agencies. In his later works the protagonist is middle-aged, entering his forties and experiencing the disillusionment inevitable from thwarted ambition, constant betrayal, and a knowledge that incompetent amateurs are still playing games with his life and the lives of

those around him. He is a man who has more in common with a middle-aged KGB agent than with his own people, a man for whom seeing through illusion has become so much a way of life that he instinctively mistrusts his own prejudices and reexamines his most cherished allies with the realistic knowledge that ultimately one's closest companions remain to some degree strangers, and that the patterns of an incompetent are more to be trusted as predictable and manageable than those of an intelligent equal who can catch one by surprise. In *Mexico Set* the high ranking amateurs, both British and Russian, turn a standard exercise in defection into a near disaster, and the two professionals from London Central and the KGB share disdain at that unprofessional behavior and admire their mutual caution:

> "I had no intention of going up there all on my own. The blinds were down; narrow stairs, crowded bar. It didn't look healthy. What happened?"
> "Nothing much," I said. "Moskvin's a deskman, isn't he?"
> "Yes," said Stinnes. "And I hate deskmen."
> "So do I," I said feelingly. "They're bloody dangerous."

In *London Match* a section head framed by the KGB turns to Samson for assistance, though the two have always been at odds, and explains his trust in terms much like those expressed by the surviving head agent at the end of *The Ipcress File*: "You're an egomaniac. You're cynical and intractable. You're the only son of a bitch in that Department who'd take the rest of them on single-handed." As expected, Samson has in mind a clear-cut plan that will expose the KGB scheme, prove his and his associates' innocence, and remedy certain of his personal problems as well. Throughout these works the protagonist remains morally superior to those around him, not because he is any less self-interested, but because he has no illusions about himself and does not disguise his personal motives behind the stodgy and hypocritical guise of principle, ideology, or patriotism. He is loyal to his friends, his family, and himself. At the end of *London Match* he concocts a sophisticated scenario that will save London Central great embarrassment, thwart a devious KGB plot that has already greatly upset the structure and balance of his agency, and vindicate his superior, who has been erroneously labeled a mole by ambitious fellow intelligence officers. Those who know Samson's record assume his real motive is

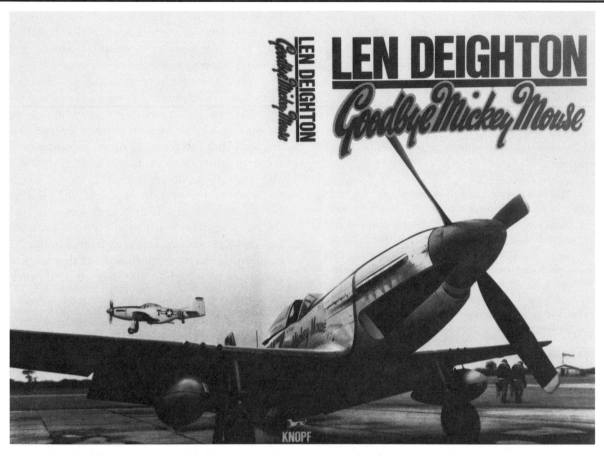

Dust jacket for the first American edition of Deighton's 1982 novel set in England during World War II

to rescue a childhood friend who has long assisted him unofficially on various assignments. Those privy to his secrets, in turn, know that his most pressing motivation is to make sure Fiona Samson, his wife and nemesis, understands she dare not ever take their children from him. This is not to say that he no longer believes preventing tyrannical regimes from overpowering individuals is not important; he is simply distrustful of all government bureaucracy.

The Ipcress File was an immediate commercial success, praised by critics, serialized in the *London Evening Standard*, and declared a best-seller in England, France, and the United States. According to *Current Biography Yearbook 1984* its sales "topped 2.5 million" in a mere three years. It concerns the mass abduction of British biochemists (eight in six weeks) by a free-lance dealer in information, code-named Jay, who supposedly masterminded the successful escapes from England of Guy Burgess and Donald Maclean. The story begins with surveillance in a Soho coffeehouse, moves on to a rescue in Beirut and a nuclear test on a Pacific atoll, and ends with a brainwashing

in an unknown locale. As it does so it exposes the weaknesses of the CIA, Scotland Yard, and MI 5, among others. The hero works for an organization called WOOC(P) and claims to be "in a very confusing business." Boucher concludes that the "spasmodic pointlessness" of much of the action is "part of Deighton's picture of what espionage is really like" (*New York Times Book Review*, 10 November 1963).

Horse under Water, about attempts to salvage Nazi-forged currency from a German submarine sunk off the coast of Portugal, is one of Deighton's weaker efforts and was not considered worth reprinting until after the success of his other works. The protagonist from *The Ipcress File*, at an earlier stage in his career, finds himself caught up in deep-sea diving, blackmail, and the heroin traffic (the "horse" of the title), topics to which Deighton devotes whole chapters. As usual there are plots within plots, a plethora of details, and, as Boucher calls it, "the crisp, precise indirection of Deighton's prose" (*New York Times Book Review*, 14 January 1968). Richard Boeth (*Book World*, 4 February 1968) finds the character

Dust jacket for the 1984 first American edition of the first volume of the trilogy which also includes Mexico Set *and* London Match

of "cartoon" quality and the plot merely a series of "elaborate charades," and Richard Schickel (*Book Week*, 1 May 1966) finds the novel lacking in "literary craft." Nonetheless, there is a subtle tension that unifies and propels the action, and the complexities of the plot do not unravel until almost the final page. At the close of the book all that is left of the hero is to seek consolation in the arms of an admiral's daughter.

On the *New York Times* best-seller list for twenty weeks, Deighton's third novel, *Funeral in Berlin*, was filmed by Paramount in 1966, again starring Caine. The book sold more than forty thousand hardcover copies by its second year in print. Called by Sergeant Cuff a "sure-footed, and thoroughly adult espionage number" (*Saturday Review*, 30 January 1965) and by Boucher "a ferociously cool fable of the current struggle between East and West" with "a plot very nearly as complex and nicely calculated as that of 'The Spy

Who Came in From the Cold'" (*New York Times Book Review*, 17 January 1965), *Funeral in Berlin* tells of a Russian scientist supposedly smuggled out of East Berlin in a coffin with the aid of Colonel Alexeyevitch Stok, a sympathetic, clever, but not too trustworthy Russian master spy. It moves from London to Prague and from the Franco-Spanish border to Berlin–the prototype of the cold war, a dangerous, divided city where multiple sets of spies watch "the watchers and the watched." The seemingly haphazard plotting, unified by obscure chess game images, comes together at the end, and the elusive conversations ultimately lead to intriguing revelations. There are gruesome deaths, including a traitor stabbed in the back by a display case of drills and another consumed by his own Molotov cocktail amid celebratory fireworks. The protagonist-narrator, code-named Kadavar, is skewered in the palm with a shish kebab stick and seduced by a red-headed Israeli spy named Samatha Steel. It is the world of "the expendable hero" in which one must make "plans upon the basis of everyone being untrustworthy."

Billion-Dollar Brain, produced by United Artists in 1967 and once again starring Caine, went into its fifth printing in the United States in 1966, its first year in publication. Julian Symons in his *Mortal Consequences: A History–From the Detective Story to the Crime Novel* (1972) says of Deighton in *Billion-Dollar Brain* that "there is something almost lyrical about his re-creation of the dangerous and transitory lives of agents, as well as something sharp and knowing"; Symons describes *Billion-Dollar Brain* as having a plot "as intricate as the lock of a good safe," and he praises in particular the "characterization of the clownish double agent Harvey Newbigin," the "wonderfully vivid picture of the shooting of Harvey in the snow outside the Russian Train," and the "evocation of General Midwinter's dotty neo-Fascist organization in Texas." The story's action occurs worldwide: London, Helsinki, Leningrad, Riga, New York, and San Antonio. General Midwinter, a reactionary Texan, and his sexy Scandinavian agent, Signe Laine, recruit the unnamed protagonist into Facts for Freedom, their huge, private, international espionage organization at whose heart is the horrifying menace, a giant computer, the "billion-dollar brain" of the title. The organization is dangerous to all governments, and its head, Midwinter, is maniacal in word and deed and Napoleonic in ambition. The story features the bumbling George Dawlish, the unnamed cynical British protagonist, his pragmatic friend Colonel Stok, and the neurotic, driven American agent, Newbigin, "an unstable man in a high-pressure world." The hero becomes more and more disillusioned with space-age machinery, fearing that "it's only a matter of time before machines are pressing buttons to call people." He joins with KGB Colonel Stok in his musings on the similarity of their worlds. Christianity and Marxism both postulate a life of hard work rewarded by a paradise either for the individual or the future, both fear a loss of faith, the "abandoning of principle for the sake of policy," and both seek "an economic miracle." Stok sums up their situation:

> You must imagine, English, that there are two mighty armies advancing toward each other across a vast desolate place. They have no orders, nor does either suspect that the other is there. You understand how armies move—one man a long way out in front has a pair of binoculars, a submachine gun and a radiation counter. Behind him comes the armor and then the motors and the medical men and finally dentists and generals and the caviar. So the very first fingertips of those armies will be two not very clever men who, when they meet, will have to decide very quickly whether to extend a hand or pull a trigger. According to what they do, either the armies will that night share an encampment, exchange stories and vodka, dance and tell lies; or those armies will be tearing each other to shreds in the most efficient way that man can devise. We are the fingertips.

The protagonist calls Stok "an incurable romantic," but it is clear from the context that the description is accurate. This is a story of those "fingertips" meeting with very disastrous potential. There are surprise targets in a shooting gallery, murder in bed with a hat pin, and cat-and-mouse games on every side, but ultimately both sides lose out. At the end the hero concludes that the case will never be over, that "it's like a laboratory experiment where some poor bloody mouse is infected and everything is normal for one hundred generations and then they start bearing offspring with two heads." Thinking of the story's action, he concludes that the usual "path to hell" for agents is not betrayal for the sake of an ideal, but in response to immediate problems:

> They do the things they do because they want a new car or they fear they'll be fired or because they love a teen-age girl or hate their wife,

or just because they want to get away from it all. There was no sharp motive. There never is, I should have known that, just a ragged mess of opportunism, ambition and good intentions that go wrong.

An Expensive Place to Die, with a title derived from a quote by Oscar Wilde about the cost of dying in Paris, has been praised for its tight construction, crisp prose, fast action, and vivid scenes. It continues Deighton's focus on dangerous and misleading cold-war games. Jack Nessel (*Book Week*, 7 May 1967) places it "somewhere between Fleming's bizarre exaggeration and le Carré's gray understatement." In it a CIA operation to leak information on nuclear fallout to the Chinese, coupled with plans to explode a Chinese hydrogen bomb, could produce a catastrophe that the nameless protagonist is made personally responsible for preventing. Deighton explores the seamy underside of Paris with its hallucinogenic drugs, its institute for sex research, and its rejects, perverts, and social misfits: "Paris is a woman with too much alcohol in her veins. She talks a little too loud and thinks she is young and gay. But she has smiled too often at strange men and the words 'I love you' trip too easily from her tongue. The ensemble is chic and the paint is generously applied but look closely and you'll see the cracks showing though." There is blackmail, murder, and an especially gory climax. The wary protagonist must deal with a melancholy French police-inspector from the Sureté Nationale with octopuslike contacts and a too knowing habit of analysis, a sadistic Chinese agent who recites poetry, a talented but destructive Englishman, a fascinating woman who is playing both ends against the middle, and Monsieur Datt, "a puppet master" who operates a brothel on Paris's Avenue Foch. He sells information on his influential clients to the highest bidder and identifies "thuggery with capitalism." The protagonist is interrogated while under the influence of LSD and suffers muscular pain induced by acupuncture but somehow manages to come through unscathed, though those around him are not so lucky.

Deighton's sixth novel, *Only When I Larf* (1968; published in the United States as *Only When I Laugh*, 1987), filmed by Paramount (1968) and starring David Hemmings, Richard Attenborough, and Alexandra Stewart, is a comedy thriller about three confidence tricksters—Bob Appleyard, Silas Lowther, and Liz Mason—

exploring exotic territory for the pleasure of a good con. A ménage à trois binds the three as they operate with skill and style to gain thousands of dollars, until their final falling-out. The point of view shifts from one to the other, with each at some point assuming the narrative "I."

Bomber, subtitled *The Anatomy of a Holocaust*, is a powerful and moving account of the devastation, destruction, tragedy, capriciousness, and irreversible vicissitudes of war. Edward Weeks (*Atlantic Monthly*, December 1970) rightly sums up the book's theme: "the devastation of machines and the decent powerless to bring them to a halt." John Sutherland (*London Review of Books*, 19 March 1981) asserts it is "probably the best and certainly the most accurate popular novel about the Second World War in the air." Michael Howard (*Times Literary Supplement*, 25 September 1970) labels it a "dispassionate record of horror," admirable in moral purpose and in technical detail, research, and reconstruction, though a bit ponderous and occasionally tedious. Paul West (*Book World*, 27 September 1970) praises it as "first-rate imaginative reporting . . . done with obsessive care" to "convey as well as anything written by an Englishman what it feels like to fly, to crash, to bomb, to be bombed, to be conscious that you are experiencing the first of your last sixty seconds of life as you fall without parachute." The format is an alternating pastiche of action and perspective from both sides of a fictional World War II bombing raid directed at the heavy industry of the Ruhr valley but by error centered on the quiet town of Altgarten, Germany, 31 June 1943. The novel sympathetically renders the worries and suffering of human beings on both sides of the struggle: British Lancaster bombardiers, German night fighters and aircraft crews, support forces at Little Warley and at Kroonsdijk, and, most significantly, the townspeople of Altgarten. It captures their fears, their prejudices, their innocence, and their guilt and transforms into human terms the impersonal terrors of war. It also provides an ironic tension as the scene moves from a Spitfire reconnaissance team to a historical discussion of a thirteenth-century village, from preparations for a bombing raid to discussions of lovely sunsets, from an unexpected revelation of love to six hundred pounds of explosive annihilating the would-be lovers. Endorsing the book's theme, the father of one of the British crew members, a Mr. Cohen, notes that "There is a common mistake made by historians: to review the past as a series of errors leading to the perfect condition that is the present time"; what Deighton so graphically illustrates is that for the errors of war there is no remedy because only by the prevention of war can devastation be prevented. *Bomber* ends with a field report: "It doesn't look like anywhere. It doesn't look like anywhere," and the official military sentencing of the German and British scapegoats. Ultimately Deighton's depiction of a village transformed by war is so realistic and so horrifying that even the most rabid of anti-Germans cannot help but feel compassion. It shows havoc wreaked on a world that, as one of his characters points out, "it's taken . . . old men so long to put together." Quoted on the dust jacket, William McPherson criticizes the novel as "overlong, overpopulated and underedited," but "despite its gross faults the final impact of *Bomber* stuns. I have never been in a war but having just read *Bomber* I felt shell shocked and battle-fatigued, and I was moved beyond tears."

Close-up (1972) departs from Deighton's established repertoire to focus on the Hollywood film industry, portraying the life and associates of British movie star Marshall Stone as his ex-wife's husband, Peter Anson, writes Stone's biography. The *Times Literary Supplement* (16 June 1972) reviewer finds Deighton doing what he does best, "reporting, lucidly, and readably, on what his imagination sees," in this case "a business so obsessed with surfaces he can exploit his eye for what one might (reluctantly) call the 'furniture' of the world." In his *Writer's Digest* article Deighton called *Close-up* one of the best books he had ever written, perhaps because "it was a safety valve," something he did "instead of murdering certain people." Douglas Dunn of the *New Statesman* (2 June 1972) called the novel "an earnest demolition job . . . an old-fashioned expose" which "leaves no stone unturned" as it grinds "down every falsity of an industry obsessed with itself." Deighton captures the essence of the motion picture industry: the narcissism, the insecurity, the cynicism, the hypocrisy, the back-stabbing, the pandering to youth and to profit, all beneath a gaudy and hyperactive exterior. Its cast of characters includes a movie mogul who enjoys playing with people's lives; a legendary agent out for his percentages; a blackmailing producer; and a leading man who demands a million dollars for each picture, fawning admiration, and satisfaction of his every whim and desire–a world of predators and victims. As the biographer proceeds about his work he uncovers scandals and a

Dust jacket for the first British edition of Deighton's 1987 novel

world of cutthroat competition where ratings are rigged and people are bought and sold as easily as books and films.

In *Spy Story* (1974) Deighton returns to the spy format, telling of British secret agent Peter Armstrong, recently hired by a joint Anglo-American naval warfare committee to aid a defecting Russian admiral, a task which necessitates worldwide travel and, at one point, participation in a "hair-raising" nuclear submarine battle beneath the Arctic icepack. Despite Pearl Bell's denunciation of the work as "an impenetrable lemon" (*New Leader*, 19 January 1976), the *Times Literary Supplement* (3 May 1974) reviewer called *Spy Story* "a vintage Len Deighton thriller" with "an overall impression of richness," "too laconic for an old-fashioned cliffhanger" but embodying "a sort of dispassionate cerebral excitement which, like the polar ice itself, is nine-tenths sub-

merged and all the more menacing for that." Roderick MacLeish of the *Washington Post Book World* (17 September 1974) praised its atmospherics, noting particularly "the bone-buckling cold and interminable rain of the Highlands . . . [and] the hushed, lifeless world of ice, emptiness and stars that looks as if they would break from the sky while submarines, with the power to incinerate the world, play tag miles below." The story revolves around the insanity of a NATO think tank located in north London, one plotting global strategy on computers, in this case war games in the Arctic. A cocky, sardonic U.S. Marine Corps colonel named Schlegel chooses Deighton's unnamed narrator as his personal assistant, as he puts into play the strategies played out by the computer. The hero, named Patrick Armstrong, is a typical work-Deighton protagonist, another reluctant spy, at odds with the world of unintelligent intelligence, a bit despairing, cynically detached and disenchanted, fumbling but decent–a survivor. The game begins at a Scottish loch where nuclear submarines have their home and ends aboard one such sub, beneath the polar ice cap. In between, Armstrong finds his flat and himself duplicated down to the last detail, and he is propelled into an East-West power play that involves Colonel Stok. He is sent on a trek across the arctic ice pack, suffering from snow blindness and concussion, and carrying on his back his injured, dying companion–all because of a computer's theoretical concern with German reunification. The novel was filmed in Great Britain in 1976.

Yesterday's Spy (1975) moves from the French Riviera to Bonn and south again in a fast-paced story of the complex deceptions of espionage. The protagonist, Charlie, is sent after an old friend, who saved his life in the war: Steve Champion, a retired British agent with a distinguished record with the French Resistance but now suspected of a double game involving atomic shells, a game dangerous to Eygpt and thereby to Britain. To rewin Champion's trust and prompt him to betray his position, Charlie pretends to be ousted from his agency in disgrace and left desperate and bitter. The protagonist must face the discovery that the past is not what it seems and that an old friend is just as much a stranger as the unknown man on the street–and perhaps more dangerous. The final confrontation takes place in a mine shaft beneath a chemical plant with bullets ricocheting "like a drunken steel band at Mardi Gras." Robin Winks in the *New Republic* (13 December 1975) finds the novel "a story written to the attitudes, the manners, the very style of the 1960s in which he won his audience" so that "it is Deighton who is truly Yesterday's Spy."

Twinkle, Twinkle, Little Spy (1976; published in the United States as *Catch a Falling Spy*) also involves a defection, this time of a Soviet scientist, a flying-saucer fanatic and a developer of a new maser. He is aided both by an American, CIA major Michael Mann, and a nameless British agent, but this time the abrasive CIA agent is the protagonist, and the operation is American, not British. This change in focus reduces to some extent the effectiveness of the tale, for, despite the fact that the English might well consider Deighton's work American in nature, his treatment of Americans is almost always slightly askew, a little overdone and never on target. Nonetheless, the focus on political stupidity and duplicity is typically Deighton. The action catapults from New York to France, back to America again, and finally to a clandestine communications satellite tracking station in the Algerian Sahara. The story contains a number of red herrings, a baroque plot, and multiple potential villains, from a disgraced CIA agent to a reactionary American tycoon. There are karate chops, explosions, hijacking, a lesbian relationship (London controlled), and the murder of a U.S. senator, and readers are left with the discouraging impression that everyone is using everyone else.

SS-GB: Nazi-Occupied Britain, 1941 (1978), a Book-of-the-Month Club alternate selection, speculates in a very convincing way about what might have happened had Britain lost World War II. Set in London in November of 1941, it draws on Deighton's wide-ranging knowledge of military history, and it is crammed with details about the German army, London geography, the SS, and British art treasures. It describes England enthralled, King George a prisoner in the Tower of London, Scotland Yard controlled by an SS-Gruppenfuhrern, and the Germany Army and the SS torn by rivalries so fierce that sabotage as a means to power and authority is inevitable. P. S. Prescott (*Newsweek*, 19 February 1979) calls *SS-GB* "A superlative muddle which might have become chaotic," but which, thanks to Deighton's competence, "compels belief," while Michael Howard (*Time Literary Supplement*, 15 September 1978) admires its "counter-factual situation" while deploring its "unnecessarily . . . confused" plot. Most of Deighton's novels, like this one, tend to be more concerned with ideas and action than with charac-

terization, a fact that is perhaps the root of the critical controversy surrounding much of his efforts. Inevitably the portrait of German interservice rivalries (Gestapo, Wehrmacht, SD, Abwehr, SS, Geheime Feldpolizei) and the details about military protocol, insignias, uniforms, and policies are so lovingly recorded, so credibly conceived, as are the imaginative and speculative touches about a conquered England in which German army bands play "Greensleeves," cathedral ruins attract American visitors, and a fast-trade in devalued antiques keeps Wehrmacht personnel on leave spending, that the fictive plot, which should be the center of reader interest, seems a minor concern.

Captain Jamie Farebrother and Lieutenant Z. M. "Mickey" Morse, American pilots fighting in World War II Europe in *Goodbye, Mickey Mouse* (1982), alternate between arresting and realistic aerial combat and love scenes with two English women, Victoria Cooper and Vera Hardcastle, respectively. In this novel Deighton departs from the witty byplay and moral vision of his earlier works to attempt, as Peter Andrews of the *New York Times Book Review* puts it (14 November 1982) "a straightforward commercial novel" about a meddlesome general and his effect on the lives and loves of his subordinates. Critical opinion is greatly divided over this book, with most rejecting the dialogue as stilted, the characters as two-dimensional, and the plot as lumbering and incoherent, but a few finding the love scenes as skillfully handled as the combat scenes and the work overall effective entertainment.

In *XPD* (1981) a compromising and potentially destructive World War II document has for forty years been stamped XPD, meaning expedient demise (sanctioned murder) to ensure total secrecy. Part of a Nazi treasure hoard confiscated by American GIs, it exposes a clandestine face-to-face meeting between Winston Churchill and Adolf Hitler in a Belgian bunker in June 1940 to discuss the possible surrender of England. Once stolen the document sets in motion a ruthless and desperate battle between secret agents from Great Britain, the United States, Germany, and Russia. However, unlike the historical invention of *SS-GB*, here Deighton weighs down his novel with heavyhanded documentation to suggest that the postulated meeting did in fact take place and argues that, if the facts were admitted and Churchill thereby discredited for considering surrender–yielding land and sea to Germany and giving vast reparations–"it would mean the

Dust jacket for the first British edition of Deighton's 1988 thriller, the first volume of his second trilogy featuring secret agent Bernard Samson

end of the Tory party," world outrage against Britain, and the collapse of the pound sterling, conclusions *Times Literary Supplement* reviewer T. J. Binyson (13 March 1981) finds difficult to accept. John Sutherland finds *XPD* building on many of Frederick Forsyth's techniques, including "the rapidly changed international setting, the dead-pan reportage style, the cut-out characters, the stress on insider's knowledge and terminology, familiar to the author, alien to the average reader" and admiration for the "front-line men" (*London Review of Books*, 19 March-1 April 1981). Despite vicious critical attack, *XPD* was a Literary Guild alternate selection whose first printing ran to sixty-five thousand copies and which became a best-seller in both England and America.

Deighton's trilogy, *Berlin Game*, *Mexico Set*, and *London Match*, reflects the changes in his ap-

proach. Still oblique and ironic, with a sense of humor and disillusionment and a sensitivity to "manners," his writing has become more serious, more credible, more fully developed, and even more adept at innuendo than his earlier work. There are more metaphors and more allusions. Bernard Samson cites *Hamlet* and makes Oscar Wilde-like assertions. For example, in *London Match* he says, "The tragedy of marriage is that while all women marry thinking that their man will change, all men marry believing their wife will never change. Both are invariably disappointed." "What rot," remarks his listener. These three novels share overlapping characters that readers come to know in greater depth as the series progresses and as they see them in changing circumstances and from different perspectives. Readers learn, as do the characters themselves, that initial impressions may be deceptive but that beneath the cover-ups and the social games is an essence of the person that to some degree can be known and that can form a basis for predicting behavior or attitudes with some degree of success. Samson's immediate supervisor, Dicky Cruyer, for example, may change styles and fads, but he remains lazy, incompetent, and self-convinced. Whatever he says will be glib, a neat theory, but totally superficial and totally at odds with reality, for he is insensitive to people, place, and atmosphere, revels in a geopolitical drama that calls "for maps and colored diagrams," and seems more often "a clown" than "the cool sophisticate that was his own image of himself." He achieves competence only in his methodology for rising on the political ladder of the "old boy" network by undercutting his personal opposition—he keeps little cards with short résumés of what he estimated to be his acquaintances' and contacts' wealth, power, and influence.

In *Berlin Game* a leakage of sensitive intelligence information suggests the presence of a high level KGB mole who threatens the continued success of an undercover intelligence-gathering operation and its key intelligence source, Dr. Walter Von Munte, code-named Brahms Four. Munte is a highly placed official in the Deutsche Notenbank, in on the money exchanges between East and West but now frightened by a secret control change and personal knowledge of a traitor who could destroy him. The protagonist, Samson, is an honorable, competent professional surrounded by opportunistic upper-class "twits." One of these may be having an affair with his luscious, wealthy, aristocratic wife, Fiona, who is a fellow agent adept at computer operations. Samson grew up in Berlin, which he considers home, and has a set of close allies from his childhood days whom he trusts and values far more deeply than he does any of his British associates. His friends include Werner Volkmann, a competent Berliner with tough, self-made rules and a yen for espionage, one who "instinctively sees things in people that you and I have to learn about," but who is on the outs with British intelligence. Another friend is Tante Lisl, a brave old woman whose hotel once hid a Jewish family (Werner's) from the Nazis for the whole of the war. Samson is in his forties, obsessed with aging and feeling too tired and too well known to attempt undercover intelligence work. But he is the only one in his department with a jaundiced enough view of human nature to be able to ferret out the traitor. More importantly he is the only one Munte trusts to bring him across the Berlin Wall. Twenty years before Munte had saved his life ("I owe him . . . I know that and so does he. That's why he'll trust me in a way he'll trust no one else. He knows I owe him").

Frederick Busch in the *Chicago Tribune* (18 December 1983) names *Berlin Game* among Deighton's best efforts, the writing "pungent," the characters "persuasive," the information "authentic feeling," and the social perceptions "right." Julian Symons in a *Times Literary Supplement* review (21 October 1983) calls it "a masterly performance," though critical opinion in general has been unjustifiably lukewarm, perhaps because one needs to read the three works together to appreciate the subtlety and complexity of Deighton's achievement. The plot turns on intricate psychological maneuverings, sexual misalliances, an allusion to Nikolay Gogol's *The Government Inspector* (1836), and a handwritten report that betrays identity.

Mexico Set begins with Werner and his wife, on vacation in Mexico, spotting a known KGB agent, and with Samson being sent to follow up. Under suspicion because of Fiona's defection, Samson must prove his loyalty by doing the seemingly impossible–persuading a successful KGB agent, Major Erich Stinnes, to "enroll," a specialized term Samson says "could mean a lot of things, from persuaded to defect to knocked on the head and rolled in a carpet." The agency's reasoning is that Stinnes, whose real name is Nikolai Sadoff, is the only one who can tell them who is reliable and who is not and which operations have been successful and which have been failures.

Deighton, circa 1988 (photograph by Mark Gerson)

Samson moves from Mexico to London, Paris, Berlin, and the East-West border, making apt observations about culture and place. He is aided by Werner and obstructed by Werner's young, beautiful, unfaithful, money-hungry wife, Zena, as well as by the distrustful amateurs of his own department who fear the Russian will expose their past mistakes. In fact, the internecine office warfare and the machinations for manipulating the senile director-general almost give the game to the Russians, and Samson, insubordinate with just cause, finds himself continually placed in incriminating positions, his strategy undermined, his scenarios disastrously interfered with. At the very end of the novel, however, his competence, professionalism, and an understanding of the weaknesses of his support and the strengths of his opposition allow him to perform his directive and thereby to some extent clear his name. Samson seems to win this set.

London Match, the final set before a new match begins, completes the trilogy about loyalty and deception and the politics of espionage, and exposes what seems to be the final twists in the game of wits between Samson, Fiona, and the KGB. The *New York Daily News* calls it a "stylish, complex story, told at disarmingly slow speed"; Hans Knight of the *Philadelphia Inquirer* finds Deighton anticipating real events in his fiction with "uncanny" accuracy; and John Barkham of

John Barkham Reviews praises Deighton for his "superior characterization" and for "a degree of sophistication rarely found in such thrillers." As the KGB defector from *Mexico Set* is debriefed and his information checked against other sources, detail after detail suggests that there is a second KGB agent still active in London Central. The bureau suspects Samson, the loving husband of a defector, but is willing to accept another scapegoat if the circumstantial evidence will fit. Only Samson himself, depending on old friends and old alliances instead of his own department, figures out the multiple-crosses played by the KGB, ferreting out planted misinformation and arranged "deaths," seeing through the hypocrisies of his associates, and unravelling the complex scheme to turn London against its own. His children are threatened and his old associates murdered, but he manages, amid all this, to begin a new romance of enduring quality and to field a backhand that ends the game–for the moment. Samson sums up at the end:

> The willingness to break rules now and again is what distinguishes free men from robots. And we spiked their guns, Werner. Forget game, set, and match. We're not playing tennis; it's a rougher game than that, with more chances to cheat. We bluffed them; we bid a grand slam, with a hand full of deuces and jokers, and we fooled them ... Okay, there are wounds, and there will be scars, but it's not game, set, and match to Fiona. It's not game, set, and match to anyone. It never is.

A 1989 television production, *Game, Set, Match*, does a credible job of capturing the essence of the books in twelve episodes.

Deighton's *Winter: A Berlin Family 1899-1945* (1987) is his most disturbing, most serious, most compelling work to date. It is a study of the authoritarianism, the patriotism, and the religious and economic fervor that were both the strengths and the weaknesses of wartime Germans. To answer the question of how German citizens could accept and participate in Nazi atrocities Deighton follows the rise and fall of a German-Austrian family from the days of the kaisers to the fall of Berlin and the Allied occupation. The elder Winter, with his Jewish mistress in Vienna and his American wife in Berlin, expands his growing banking empire by investing in zeppelins before World War I, thereby assisting in the step-by-step buildup of the German war machine. His sheltered sons, Peter and Pauli, attend proper mili-

tary academies and move into elite and competing branches of the army, one flying spy missions over England aboard his father's new craft and the other trapped in the no-man's-land of trench warfare. In the Weimar years Peter stands firm for the standards of old Germany, while his brother is drawn deeper into the vortex that would become Hitler, anti-Semitism, the SS, and blitzkrieg.

An ignorant and rowdy peasant youth, Fritz Esser, who saves the two Winter boys from drowning, exploits Pauli's gratitude to rise quickly in politics, first on the left, then on the right. He becomes one of Hitler's intimates, assigned to handle the dirty work of the regime. Peter's and Pauli's American mother closes her eyes to the steady changes occurring around her until it is too late. Their father continues to amass wealth by investing in aircraft production. Pauli himself, his hands physically untouched by blood, is nonetheless responsible for many of the horrors perpetuated by the Nazi party, for it is his advice that reveals legal loopholes that allow confiscation of Jewish property, internment, and deportation, and his suggestions that help produce the terrifying efficiency of the camps. Deighton makes the reader understand and even sympathize with Pauli, who denies the consequences of his acts and continues a bourgeois life-style without feeling guilt or self-incrimination. He also illuminates the conflict between duty and honor of the traditionalist Peter, who must survive in a world in which honor takes second place. In one ghastly sequence Pauli saves his Jewish sister-in-law by unknowingly placing his illegitimate Jewish half-brother from his father's Viennese romance in a cattle-car headed for the death camps in her stead. Later, when that same sister-in-law dies, Peter grudgingly joins the American forces to help them bring down the country that has been his life's joy but that has destroyed what he held most dear. Most novels about World War II make the American and British liberators heroes, but Deighton, providing a German perspective, makes them seem fanatical and abrasive. After the war, as the brothers meet in a bitter life-and-death struggle at the Nuremberg trials, both must confront the realities of what they were and what they have become. This final sibling confrontation takes readers deep inside the German mind to the extent that Deighton must indicate that the opinions expressed by his characters are not necessarily his own. The ultimate question raised by the novel is whether anyone could completely honor his values if placed in the same situation as Peter or Pauli.

Spy Hook (1988), the first in an espionage trilogy to be entitled "Hook, Line, and Sinker," returns to the British Secret Service agent who untangled the maze of *Game, Set & Match:* the cool, cynical, would-be detached Bernard Samson. For so long the London Central "dogsbody who got the jobs that no one else wanted," Samson now possesses dangerous and confounding information about a huge in-Service financial scam. This information leads him to move secretly back and forth from London to Washington, D.C., from a heavily guarded California estate, to the south of France, East and West Germany, and the home of the Secret Service's Berlin Resident. The old crew (Bret Rennselaer, Dicky Cruyer, Frank Harrington, Lisl Hennig, and Werner Volkmann) are playing out their private games once more, as is Ingrid Winter, a relative of the Berlin Winters of Deighton's *Winter.* Fiona Samson is also intricately involved in action that leaves one puzzling over new twists and turns in an ever more complicated sequence. While Samson's associates begin to suspect him of paranoia, he begins to understand that, though he has "enough enemies without looking for more," some of his closest associates may be involved in the most damaging security breach yet. *Spy Hook,* dealing with places and characters the author knows intimately, gives the reader Deighton at top form: the book is riveting, suspenseful, masterful.

Deighton's short stories, *Declarations of War,* read like genuine fragments of history, realistic stories of the experiences and dramatic confrontations of soldiers, whether in South American revolutions, world wars, the Vietnam conflict, the American Civil War, or potential colonial uprisings. They are tightly plotted, dramatic tales with moral twists aimed at making readers reconsider their perceptions and their judgments, at making them accept, as does Deighton, the humanity of the soldier but reject the inhumanity of the war in which he is engaged. "Winter's Morning," for example, captures the beauty and the dangers of a dawn patrol as recounted by a World War I flying ace, Major Winter, who downs two enemy planes but at the cost of his youthful flight assistant; the major wins the reader's sympathy and only at the story's close reveals his German identity. In another story a munitions salesman to a South American country in the thralls of revolution so successfully demonstrates his wares that he escapes imprisonment and winds up a gen-

eral. In other of these stories a general losing a paper war means a real loss of command, a young British World War I pilot rushes home (across the English Channel) for his birthday, a colonel and a corporal (now civilians) recall a night spent trapped in a farmhouse by German tanks, and a British flight officer denied a medical leave becomes a hero in order to gall the hard-nosed, noncombat doctor who refused him. Whatever the situation, these stories succinctly and effectively capture the sentiments and interaction of men at war. Peter Elstob in *Books and Bookmen* (December 1971) ranks these stories with those of Stephen Crane in their haunting and realistic depiction of men in battle.

Deighton's nonfiction treats particulars of World War II with the same attention to detail and accuracy and the same expertise as does his fiction. Based on meticulous research and personal interviews, *Fighter: The True Story of the Battle of Britain* is a careful, incisive, and gripping account of the planes, personalities, inventions, and strategies that decisively changed the war. It is impressive in its technical discussion of the history and development of the aircraft used by English and by Germans, and in its detailed and specific analysis of aircraft strength and limitation. It is also impressive in its sensitivity to the organizational structures and to the personality conflicts and motivations behind the scenes, as well as to national and individual psychology that affected strategy and day-to-day results. Its dramatic rendering of fighter action and its balanced analysis of both German and English perspectives earned praise from both sides of the channel. *Blitzkrieg* is more rambling and anecdotal and as a result less effective than *Fighter.* Building on some new sources, Deighton traces the idea, planning, and realization of blitzkrieg, recounting the how and why of the German victory of 1940, particularly focusing on the influence of industrial change on the German war machine and the interaction of technology and personality. D. E. Showalter in *Library Journal* (15 May 1980) found it oversimplified and lacking synthesis, but John Keegan in *New Statesman* (14 September 1979) praised it for "some gems of research and some arresting conclusions." Deighton argues that the attack on Poland in September 1939 was too conventional to be really called a blitzkrieg. He outlines the development of military communications, tanks, and air power, praises the German military emphasis on individual initiative, and concludes that German failure to annihilate the British troops at Dunkirk was a "fatal flaw" that limited German chances for final success. *Airshipwreck* (1978) plainly and graphically through text and photographs gives a brief record of the natural and man-made hazards faced by lighter-than-air dirigibles and the heroism of their crews when faced with calamity. Extensively researched, it is a tribute to the perseverance and ingenuity of those dedicated aviation experimenters.

Throughout Deighton's canon there is an attempt to make readers see events from a new perspective, to present opposing ideologies, and to debunk sacred cows. This is clear from the way Churchill in particular receives the brunt of his attack. In *SS-GB* Churchill is in part responsible for the German success and is shot early in the book; in *XPD* he behaves more like a whipped dog than a tenacious bulldog, submitting to Hitler's every demand, betraying tradition and honor. Deighton's attempt to disorient and suggest new perspectives is also clear from the sympathetic portraits of some Germans and Russians who are humanized and who, for all their faults, are at times more admirable than the English or Americans for whom readers would traditionally root. The Russian KGB officer in *Funeral in Berlin* (and several other Deighton novels), Colonel Stok, is a likeable, jaded professional who finds irritating the naïveté, prejudice, and mindlessness of his associates, particularly the Stalinists. He tells amusing jokes that mock his own system, and only he and his British counterpart, the protagonist, are able to really determine what is going on. In fact, the protagonist finds Stok's outwitting Western intelligence amusing and says, "Stok and I are in the same business—we understand each other only too well." Samson finds the same affinity with his opposite number, Stinnes. While the enemy at times proves as upright as the protagonist there is often disdain for commanding officers in Deighton's work. Samson's tirades are directed as much against the public-school aristocrats, who learned to enjoy physical discomfort but who depend for self-identity on "some grand illusory image" they have of themselves or who arrogantly consider personal satisfaction of greater importance than country or duty, as against the duplicitous Soviet opposition.

One might, with time, forget Len Deighton's plot, the details that created the suspense, the host of characters, and even the main point of an individual work, but what stays with the reader is a vivid image of Berlin and clandestine East-West relationships, of the Deighton protagonist, his wit, his irreverence, his competence, his disillusionment. One also remembers the attitudes central to Deighton's canon: a disdain for self-serving, amateurish games of the top-level "authorities," admiration for the competence and humanity of the men of the rank and file, a horror of war and the machinery of war, a sense of the basic humanity of men on both sides of the political barriers, and a deep-seated awareness that all is never what it seems and that one must look closely and think carefully with the mind, not the heart, to find the reality behind the illusion—and even then still be wrong.

Interviews:

"Interview: Len Deighton," *Tatler* (4 November 1964);

Hugh Moffet, "Hot Spy Writer on the Lam," *Life*, 60 (25 March 1966): 84-86;

Edwin McDowell, "Behind the Best Sellers," *New York Times Book Review*, 21 June 1981, p. 34.

References:

Fred Erisman, "Romantic Reality in the Spy Stories of Len Deighton," *Armchair Detective*, 10 (April 1977): 101-105;

Constantine Fitzgibbon, "Len Deighton's Cold New View," *Spectator*, 228 (8 April 1972): 546;

H. R. F. Keating, *Whodunit?: A Guide to Crime, Suspense and Spy Fiction* (New York: Van Nostrand, 1982);

"Men Who Throw Cold Water on Hot Spies," *Vogue* (July 1965): 94-95;

Edward Milward-Oliver, *The Len Deighton Companion* (London: Grafton, 1987);

Lars Ole Sauerberg, *Secret Agents in Fiction: Ian Fleming, John le Carré and Len Deighton* (New York: St. Martin's, 1984);

Julian Symons, *Mortal Consequences: A History—From the Detective Story to the Crime Novel* (New York: Harper, 1972).

Colin Dexter

(29 September 1930-   )

Bernard Benstock
University of Miami

BOOKS: *Liberal Studies: An Outline Course*, by Dexter and Edgar Geoffrey Rayner, 2 volumes (Oxford: Pergamon, 1964; New York: Macmillan, 1964);

Guide to Contemporary Politics, by Dexter and Rayner (Oxford: Pergamon, 1966);

Last Bus to Woodstock (London: Macmillan, 1975; New York: St. Martin's Press, 1975);

Last Seen Wearing (London: Macmillan, 1976; New York: St. Martin's Press, 1976);

The Silent World of Nicholas Quinn (London: Macmillan, 1977; New York: St. Martin's Press, 1977);

Service of All the Dead (London: Macmillan, 1979; New York: St. Martin's Press, 1980);

The Dead of Jericho (London: Macmillan, 1981; New York: St. Martin's Press, 1981);

The Riddle of the Third Mile (London: Macmillan, 1983; New York: St. Martin's Press, 1984);

The Secret of Annexe 3 (London: Macmillan, 1986; New York: St. Martin's Press, 1987).

OTHER: "Crosswords and Whodunits–A Correlation Between Addicts," in *Murder Ink*, edited by Dilys Winn (New York: Workman, 1977), pp. 447-450;

"Evans Tries an O Level," in *Winter's Crimes*, edited by George Hardinge (London: Macmillan, 1978; New York: St. Martin's Press, 1978);

"At the Lulu Bar," in *Winter's Crimes*, edited by Hardinge (London: Macmillan, 1982; New York: St. Martin's Press, 1982).

Although the "New Wave" of British detective fiction began early in the 1960s–in which a group of young writers brought the world of the fictional mystery closer to the world of sociological reality, and the literary structure of their novels closer to the narrational techniques of post-World War II fiction–Colin Dexter arrived somewhat late on the scene, with *Last Bus to Woodstock* (1975). Nor has he been as prolific as his immediate predecessors, Ruth Rendell, P. D. James,

Colin Dexter (courtesy of the author)

Nicolas Freeling, and Peter Lovesey. The seven novels published between 1975 and 1986 are carefully crafted, of uniform length (the 250 pages or so quite standard for "mature" examples of the genre), and consistent in style, tone, atmosphere, and intellectual level. If not quite as successful or accomplished as those four forerunners, Dexter is surely, as Dylan Thomas once classified himself, the best of the second rank.

Norman Colin Dexter was born on 29 September 1930 in Stamford, Lincolnshire, and was locally educated until entering Christ's College, Cambridge, in 1950, where he took his degree in classics. As he says of his writing in *Twentieth Century Crime and Mystery Writers* (1985), "My English style *ought* to be adequate. . . because in my youth

55

I studied the Classics." He received his B.A. in 1953 and his M.A. in 1958 and has worked in various aspects of the academic profession throughout his career, writing his detective fiction as a second vocation. He was an assistant classics master at Wyggeston School in Leicester and at Loughborough Grammar School, then senior classics master at Corby Grammar School in Northamptonshire. From 1966 Dexter has been employed by the Oxford Delegacy of Local Examinations and utilizes the Oxford environs and even his workplace for his crime novels. "I am lucky that I lived in Oxford," he has commented, "in which city all my books are set. It is a place that many know, or at least would like to know, and I take much pleasure in describing it." As well known as it is, Dexter has succeeded in putting Oxford—and the North Oxford area in particular—on the literary map.

To most readers of Colin Dexter's books his major accomplishment is the creation of his particular detective hero, Detective Chief Inspector Morse of the Thames Valley Constabulary of Kidlington, Oxon. It is easy to overemphasize Morse's peculiarities—even eccentricities—yet the development of his personality has been painstakingly achieved by the balancing of his all-too-human and perverse characteristics. At times his seediness is similar to the seediness of a Graham Greene character, his bluster and swagger similar to John Mortimer's Rumpole of the Bailey, but always there is an element of the pathetic to counterbalance the braggadocio. Morse's vulnerable and remarkable character unfolds serially from book to book, so that eventually there are no mysteries about him—except for his given name.

Hardly a Morse case develops without someone asking him his given name (often it is a woman who is sexually attracted to him and even in bed with him), but Morse remains evasive throughout: at the end of *Service of All the Dead* (1979) he promises, "I'll tell you afterwards." Even his devoted assistant, Sergeant Lewis, seems unable to put a first name to Morse (in *The Silent World of Nicholas Quinn* [1977] Lewis muses that he "never thought of Morse as having one," a signal that calls attention away from the fact that nowhere in the seven novels is Lewis's full name ever revealed). A search in the telephone directory in *Service of All the Dead* reveals his initial as E., and in *The Dead of Jericho* (1981) the full reading is "Morse, E. The Flats, Banbury Road," which makes him a neighbor of Norman Colin Dexter. The police surgeon in *The Riddle of the*

Dust jacket for the first American edition of Dexter's 1975 first novel

Third Mile (1983) even speculates on "Eric" or "Ernie"—but to no avail.

The dossier on E. Morse builds slowly, text by text, even though the force of his personality is felt immediately and is sustained throughout. In *Last Bus to Woodstock* he is seen doing a crossword puzzle, and each book includes this momentary respite from his case. In *The Dead of Jericho* Lewis has picked up the crossword habit as well—although he uses the *Daily Mirror*. (Dexter is himself a master in compiling as well as solving crossword puzzles, for three years the national champion in the Ximenes clue-writing competitions.) Morse drives a Lancia ("He's had a Lancia ever since I've known him," Lewis comments in *The Riddle of the Third Mile*, but it is Lewis who is particularly fond of fast driving, despite his otherwise staid and conventional personality). Readers learn from the first novel that Morse had been an undergraduate at Oxford, but it is not until the sixth novel that the story of his "dark, disastrous days" at St. John's College unfolds, the love affair that disintegrated and destroyed his academic chances: in his fourth year he failed Greats and left the university. Yet his interest in his chosen subjects–history, logic, and philosophy–in strange ways shape Morse's thinking. His status as a bachelor, dreamily romantic and sexually cynical, is given its foundation in the failed affair. In *Last Seen Wearing* (1976) Morse is in his mid forties; in *Service of All the Dead* he is forty-seven; in *The Dead of Jericho* he has just turned fifty; in *The Riddle of the Third Mile* he is fifty-two. But it is in *The Secret of Annexe 3* (1986) that the fullest description of fifty-four-year-old Morse is given–greyish hair and balding, still somewhat slim but getting fat, more barrel-chested than stomached, but nonetheless attractive to women. (His blue-gray eyes are noted in *The Silent World of Nicholas Quinn*).

A loner, Morse moves through a world of crime–murder cases that he eventually solves, but not without many mistakes. It is a world that includes desirable women in an ostensibly sexually permissive society. He lusts after these women, and in turn is admired and even accosted by several of them. In some cases he accepts or is accepted, and in others he finds reasons for refusing offers that might compromise him. But more often opportunities evaporate through postponement or bad timing, adding to the mood of nostalgic sadness and personal disappointment that pervades the later novels in particular. His foibles are of course legion. His bad temper is often vented on his subordinates for their mistakes (although he readily forgives his own) or for just being there when he needs a scapegoat. Usually it is Sergeant Lewis who gets the brunt of it, but Lewis is both in awe of Morse and genuinely fond of him and has no trouble in discounting Morse's outbursts, despite Morse's frequent inability to apologize. In *The Dead of Jericho* a young detective constable incurs Morse's wrath for incompetence, and at the end of the book he quits the police and joins the army, with no remorse from the chief inspector. The rookie had early acknowledged that "people said what an eccentric, irascible sod he could be; they also said that he'd solved more murders than anyone else for many leagues around, and that the gods had blessed him with a brain that worked as swiftly and as cleanly as lightning." The opinions of Morse's superiors corroborate this "balanced" evaluation, although it is conceded that he has been passed over for promotions, without his caring very

much about these bypasses. "I've got a private income," he responds to the assistant county commissioner, "and a private harem," neither of which either of them believes. Morse seems content enough with his shabby existence, living with his mother's furniture. Chief Inspector Bell of the Oxford City Police, with whom Morse comes close to a rivalry in *Service of All the Dead* ("they were old sparring partners"), has developed an admiration and fondness for his colleague from the Thames Valley Police: " 'If you can help me in any way,' said Bell quietly, 'I'll be grateful–you know that, don't you?' " Superintendent Strange shares Bell's confidence in Morse: "Strange had known Morse for many years and had marveled many times at the exploits of this extraordinary and exasperating man." Unlike other unorthodox police officers, such as Nicolas Freeling's Piet Van der Valk, Morse incurs the wrath but the genuine admiration of his superiors despite his unorthodoxy.

The relationship between the chief inspector and the sergeant, which begins with their first case together in the first novel and sustains itself as a working relationship throughout Dexter's books, has come under scrutiny as the traditional Holmes-Watson/hero-sidekick pairing of opposites, the latter a foil for the dominant intellect of the former. To a certain degree this relationship exists for Morse and Lewis, yet the reversals are frequent and comic, especially when the hardheaded and skeptical Lewis quietly deflates many of Morse's wild flights of fancy theorizing. Of all fictional detectives Morse is the one who most often violates that sacrosanct standard of not theorizing before the facts. When Morse is at his most despondent, a basic characteristic of his personality when the case is not progressing well, he invites himself to the Lewis household for the basic British meal that Lewis loves, eggs and chips. More often, Morse sulks over his pints of beer (pubs are his natural habitat, and pints are invariably in the plural). When Lewis is his drinking companion, either to listen to the fanciful new solution enthusiastically narrated by his chief or to share his frustrations, he often finds that he has to pay for many of the rounds, Morse being conveniently forgetful when it comes to paying.

The major area of contention between the two detectives is Morse's maddening insistence on complicating an investigation ("he always had to find a complex solution to everything," Lewis complains), while Lewis himself assumes, on the basis

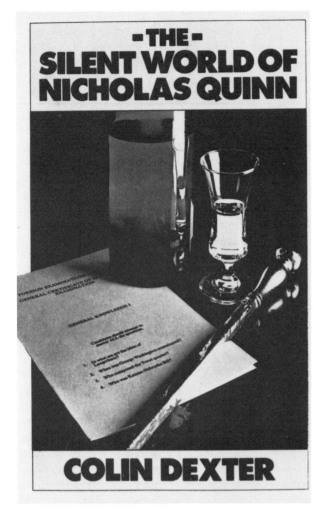

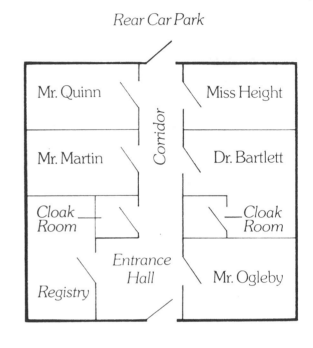

The Foreign Examinations Syndicate
Ground Floor Plan

Dust jacket and frontispiece from the first American edition of Dexter's 1977 novel about the murder of a deaf faculty member of the agency which tests foreign candidates for Oxford University

of his years of police experience, "that few of the criminals themselves had sufficiently intelligent or tortuous minds to devise the cunning stratagems that Morse was wont to attribute to them." In effect, the difference in approach mirrors the differences between Morse's tortuous mind and Lewis's relatively simple mind. Morse's mind *invents*, and although Lewis's "reality" overturns those inventions throughout the text, it is fanciful invention that triumphs at the conclusion. Not that Lewis ever loses his confidence in Morse, although even in his "simplicity" he hedges his bets. "Morse didn't seem quite the man he had been, one way or another," he muses in *The Silent World of Nicholas Quinn*, "but Lewis knew from previous experience that it wouldn't be long before something happened. Something always happened when Morse was

around." In *The Riddle of the Third Mile* Morse admits to himself that his fondness for Lewis is based on their opposite personalities, suggesting the extent to which Lewis *completes* Morse's own psyche and that together they function as a combined entity: "Lewis was so totally unlike himself. . . . placid, good-natured, methodical, honest, unassuming, faithful, and (yes, he might as well come clean about it!) a bit *stolid*." On the other hand, Lewis has his own evaluation of his companion: "Morse was his hero, and always would be. But even heroes had their momentary weaknesses, as Lewis had so often learned." Morse's fallibility becomes undeniable in *The Secret of Annexe 3* when Lewis discovers evidence Morse had overlooked, and despite his attempts at first to bluster his way out of it, Morse comes to admit his failing and Lewis's success, and he actually apologizes and expresses his gratitude.

Dust jacket for the first American edition of Dexter's 1979 novel, in which he continues to develop the personality of his fictional detective Morse (courtesy of Otto Penzler)

Morse's fallibility provides many of the comic touches in the Dexter novels, but it also has greater ramifications for the changes being made in the characteristics of the genre. In the postmodern literary era the antidetective novel has received a great deal of critical attention, particularly in Europe, particularly as it challenges the "closed" aspects of traditional detective fiction and the overly determined situations that evolve in the crime plot. Not that Dexter reaches the extremes of the indeterminate and inconclusive facets of the antidetective novel, or even the elliptical patterns of the *roman nouveau* of the 1950s, but the possibilities for any cohesive solution falling apart are always operative in Dexter's work—at least until the final resolution. From the beginning of *Last Bus to Woodstock* Morse's self-advertised "grand design" disintegrates under scrutiny, and Morse has to admit, once he has actually succeeded in solving the murder, "I've taken

one or two wrong turnings, as you know, Lewis." Every Morse case has its wrong turnings, even to the extent of bringing in a suspect and making an actual accusation, only to have Morse watch his grand design crumble and the suspect released. Several "complete" analyses can be fabricated by Morse in any one case, and there is an instance in which he allows a suspect to be released only to have to rearrest the same person at the end–the flaw in the original argument later redressed. With hardly any capacity for humility Morse is given to blustering through the weakest points of his arguments, especially in the face of Lewis's stolid intransigence. At the end of *The Riddle of the Third Mile*, even with a completed case, Morse is confronted with Lewis's skepticism during the reconstruction ("Are you making some of it up, sir?") and retorts: "Of course I bloody am! But it fits the clues, doesn't it? And what the hell *else* can it do?"

Morse's uniqueness as a fictional detective lies in the influence of his particular temperament not only on the tone of the fiction but on each individual case he undertakes, putting the stamp of his personality on each venture. The peculiarity of his own philosophical bent colors the situation and runs counter to established norms, and he occasionally tries to bring himself in line: "Why not go with the evidence, Morse," he addresses himself, "and fling your flimsy fancies aside?" As his own most confounding critic he complains, "Why, oh, why, just for once in a while was he not willing to come to terms with the plain, incontrovertible facts of any case?" (although it is to the reader's delight that he never does). Lewis bemoans the situation in which Morse took "the most prodigious leaps in the dark . . . utterly blind to the few simple facts that lay staring him in the face." Yet by *The Riddle of the Third Mile*, the sixth book, the verdict is that Morse's approach to a case, although "unorthodox, intuitive, and seemingly lazy," nonetheless results in proving him to be "an extremely capable administrator." What shapes Morse's attitudes and interests becomes known as the canon matures: in *The Silent World of Nicholas Quinn* he quotes one of the few sources for his philosophical development, criminologist Hans Gross: "No human action happens by pure chance unconnected with other happenings. None is incapable of explanation"; in *The Riddle of the Third Mile* he reaffirms his belief in the proposition that "the wider the circle of knowledge the greater the circumference of ignorance"; and in *The Secret of Annexe 3*

Dust jacket for the first American edition of Dexter's 1981 novel which takes place in the Jericho section of Oxford

he confides to Lewis that it is amazing "what feats of logic the human brain is capable of. But sometimes life eludes logic–and sometimes when you build a great big wonderful theory you find there's a fault in the foundation." Throughout his career he continues to knock against hard facts he would prefer to ignore and insists on imaginative conceptualizations for which he has no factual bases, yet to Lewis's admission of his own religious convictions, Morse confesses to being an unbeliever.

The most astonishing aspects of Morse's "liabilities" begin to become part of the fabric in *Last Bus to Woodstock* when he offhandedly admits to an ignorance of the law, and by *The Silent World of Nicholas Quinn* he even more blithely tells Lewis that he has no interest in pathology, constantly asking why forensic science is incapable of informing him accurately of the time of death (mutual irascibility with the police pathologist becomes a constant motif in his cases, sometimes

over several drinks in the local pub). By *The Silent World of Nicholas Quinn*, the third book, it is also obvious that Morse is nauseated by the sight of blood and terrified of heights, characteristics that are mentioned thereafter, as when in *Service of All the Dead* he quickly drives away from a road accident. He has no compunction about admitting his "inadequacy and cowardice" and what he terms "chronic acrophobia." He also admits to being afraid of the dark. By *The Riddle of the Third Mile* the self-diagnosis includes "incurable acrophobia, arachnophobia, myophobia, and ornithophobia." But heights, spiders, mice, and birds are not nearly as frightening to him as his most prevalent horror: "Morse also suffered from necrophobia: and had he known what awaited him now, it is doubtful whether he would have dared to view the horridly disfigured corpse at all." The comic portrait of Chief Inspector Morse, that "towering, if somewhat eccentric, genius," hardly matches those of the great fictional detectives. Added to the portrait are his excessive smoking and frequent excessive drinking, so that at the beginning of *The Riddle of the Third Mile*, at age fifty-two, he swears off food, drink, and cigarettes, "virtually total abstinence . . . urgently demanded by stomach, lungs, and liver alike"–but to no avail. His addiction to the music of Richard Wagner is harmless, however, and is shared by his creator, Dexter.

The reader's fascination with the character of E. Morse is paralleled with a fascination for the intricate webs of criminal and sub-rosa events that form the plots of Dexter's mysteries. A basic impression of the very ordinary world, the middle-class English environment of Oxford and suburban environs, dominates, along with aspects of the working-class elements of the area. But the lives of the inhabitants contain the secrets of clandestine involvements and concealed desires, so that the surface crime that brings the Thames Valley police into the investigation defies solution; that everyone has something to hide complicates the search for the murderer. *Last Bus to Woodstock* concerns the brutal murder (and possible sex-murder) of a scantily clad female hitchhiker, whose companion at the bus stop fails to identify herself. Several young women are likely possibilities for the companion, but Morse is frustrated by their refusal to be honest with him. Illicit love affairs have been in progress prior to the murder–and essentially independent of it–and a sexually disturbed young mechanic was the first to discover the body. Insisting that various people are lying does not help Morse overcome his basic obstacle; he has earmarked the wrong liar. The web of affairs between Oxford dons (Lonsdale College is Dexter's Oxford locus for various plot situations) and secretaries or barmaids complicates the case, even as crossword enthusiast Morse decodes an innocuous letter, pointing toward one of the affairs but not necessarily the pertinent one. The grisly deaths of a husband and wife, each of whom had confessed to the murder, bring matters to a head, and Morse apprehends the woman murderer–an attractive young woman he had admired, who confesses that she has fallen in love with him–as she is taken away to stand trial.

It is the disappearance of a Kidlington schoolgirl that provides the central mystery in *Last Seen Wearing*, but the case is several years old when Morse and Lewis are forced into reopening it. The original investigator had died in an accident. Not only is the case predated, but the opening scene of the novel predates the girl's disappearance by another year and involves the sexual adventure of a schoolgirl and a candidate for the headmastership of the school. Independent scenes in which many of those involved act out their life situations are frequent in the Dexter novels, so that reconciling such independent knowledge of the dramatis personae with the police proceedings undertaken by Morse and Lewis becomes the problem for the reader. In this case Morse is determined to prove that the girl is dead (he is of course wrong), and he becomes more obstinate in his assumption as the fruitless investigation continues. The murder of a member of the school faculty eventually makes the novel an authentic *murder* mystery, and the missing girl now has the distinction of being considered either a murder victim or a murderer. The convoluted sexual adventures of several of the school staff and the possibility of identity changes (the mistress masquerading as the deposed wife) provide the Dexterian complications. Morse bumbles and blusters to a resolution, and yet *Last Seen Wearing* ends inconclusively with the missing person once again missing and perhaps too clever ever to be found. Morse "solves" the case, but the case remains open.

The Silent World of Nicholas Quinn locates the action in a Foreign Examinations Syndicate in North Oxford, a locus close to Dexter's own workplace, and a floor plan of the building is offered to the reader. The jealousies and personality clashes of the staff of the academic syndicate, as

well as secret love affairs, provide motivations for secrecy, if not necessarily for murder. The plot hinges on the hiring of a virtually deaf replacement faculty member, and it is his ability to read lips in a situation where dangerous information is exchanged that leads to his death. The long delay before his body is discovered allows for innumerable complications as to the time of death and the veracity of various alibis; a fire drill at the syndicate also allows for suspects to be unaccounted for at a crucial time. Notes and letters, coded and elliptical, give the crossword-trained Morse further opportunities to utilize his talent, and duplicated stubs from a sex-exploitation Oxford cinema have Morse in and out of the place– as apparently were several of the suspects (Morse had an on-duty opportunity to visit a Soho sex show in *Last Seen Wearing*, and here he takes advantage of just such an opportunity, even dragging the prudish Lewis along). The possibility that the case revolves on cheating at the examinations, dismissed as impossible by the staff, leads to the solution of the murder–and the cover-up murder. Morse solves the case, and the syndicate goes out of business, but the beautiful woman who had been a suspect never succeeds in making Morse aware of her passion for him, and the novel ends inconclusively along those lines.

In various ways *The Silent World of Nicholas Quinn* is the least characteristic of the Dexter novels. Little of the seediness of the first two carries over; the mood is rather relaxed and even refined; the situation less hectic, perhaps because the setting derives so apparently from Dexter's familiar office; and even Morse is somewhat subdued. By contrast *Service of All the Dead* comes close to being Gothic and rather atmospheric. The setting is an Oxford church, and petty pilfering from the collection plate serves as the gambit leading to death. The opening section, "The First Book of Chronicles," discloses the churchwarden is stealing church money to bet on horses, his wife is involved with the church organist who also is seducing one of his music students, while the vicar, who is presumed to be homosexual, has a brother who turns up as a local vagrant– and threats of blackmail are overheard in the church. Morse wanders into the church (and the case) quite by accident, curious about the murder of the churchwarden several months earlier and the disappearance of his wife and the organist. The suicide of the vicar brings the case to a climax. Although the Oxford city police have the case, Inspector Bell gets the flu, and Morse finds

Opening manuscript page for a short story by Dexter published in 1987 (courtesy of the author)

himself deputized, taking Lewis along with him—making official Morse's unofficial obsession with the case, as well as with the alluring parishioner he interrogates. Whether those who are missing are alive or dead, whether the suicide was murder, problems of identity and sexual liaisons—these become part of the familiar Colin Dexter pattern. Even the actual identity of the vicar's corpse becomes problematic, and the multiple conspiracies within the church produce Dexter's most complex plot, one requiring multiple restatements and trial questions (the last section is titled "The Book of Revelations"). Morse's amorous success is hinted at by the title of the penultimate section, "The Book of Ruth."

Morse's romantic interests provide the entry into *The Dead of Jericho*, and the existence of a Jericho Street in Oxford provides Dexter with a region of concentration that he can impose on the map of that city and eventually remove once the case is concluded: "the curious visitor will no longer find Canal Reach marked upon the street map, for the site of the narrow little lane in which Ms Scott and Mr Jackson met their deaths is now straddled by a new block of flats." And the biblical Jericho also provides such epigraphs as "A certain man went down from Jerusalem to Jericho"—in a text in which each chapter is headed by quotations, usually short ones, pithy and ironic. But the basic atmosphere of the novel is the very ordinary world of both the rundown sections of the city and its cultural life, with Morse attending lectures on literature and publishing at the Clarendon Press Institute. The suicide of Anne Scott, with whom Morse has been having an affair, and the death of her voyeuristic neighbor take place within the jurisdiction of the Oxford city police, with Inspector Bell in charge of the investigation, while Morse for most of the book is not only a mere onlooker, but something of a suspect. Constable Walters arrests Morse as he leaves the dead woman's apartment house, a mistake that contributes to his decision to leave the police force. But Bell is eventually promoted out of the case, and the better detective takes it over—although in effect he is told that he is being passed over for promotion since the new position involves a skill in public relations. The placid world of Oxford reveals sexual infidelities past and present, teenage drug overdoses, blackmail, voyeurism and pornographic magazines, striptease performances (the latter two engaging Morse's excessive interest), as well as suicide and murder. Multiple maskings of identity confuse

the complex situations as family members contribute to the cover-ups. Despite his numerous misjudgments of evidence and even the admission that it was his own fingerprints that led him astray, Morse solves the sordid case and returns to the North Oxford party in hope of meeting another Ms. Scott.

As the locus of the plot situation in *The Dead of Jericho* proves to reside in the past of the characters, so it does in *The Riddle of the Third Mile*. But in the latter case the past event, cowardice and death at the battle of El Alamein, Egypt, some forty years earlier, is offered as the opening chapter of the text. And as *The Dead of Jericho* centered on the interchanging of two brothers, *The Riddle of the Third Mile* centers on twin brothers revenging the death at El Alamein of their third brother. Several members of the faculty of Lonsdale College, Oxford, figure prominently; the disappearance of one of them coincides with the finding of a dismembered and unidentifiable, drowned corpse. The disparate worlds of Oxford's "dreamy spires" and Soho sex shops allow for the skillful Dexter touch, as he works the two against each other for comic and ironic possibilities. Morse's personal preoccupation in this investigation is an abscessed tooth, and his major faux pas is breaking the news to the widow of her husband's death. The reappearance of the "dead" husband severely disconcerts the "widow," but the husband had a twin brother of course. Several murders later, Morse solves the series of crimes, and academic politics prove to have been even more lethal than vengeance that smoldered for forty years.

Dexter's extraliterary flourishes involve the headnotes affixed at the beginning of chapters in *Last Seen Wearing* and *The Dead of Jericho*, (which will reappear in *The Secret of Annexe 3*). Alternately, *The Riddle of the Third Mile* uses for headnotes statements of plot-argument, short and succinct and tongue-in-cheek. "In which we have a tantalizing glimpse of high-class harlotry" is the first "tantalizing" epigraph, while even more characteristic of the author's comic style is "In which those readers impatiently waiting to encounter the first corpse will not be disappointed, and in which interesting light is thrown on the character of the detective, Morse." Also operative in *The Riddle of the Third Mile*, in which an obvious villain who manages a Soho topless bar reads the *Köchel* catalogue, is a momentary allusion (and an apparently gratuitous one) to James Joyce's *Ulysses*, signaled by the comment in an anonymous letter written by one of the Lonsdale dons: "a devastatingly lovely woman–a Siren fit to beguile the wily Ulysses himself." On an Underground train Morse sits next to a brunette who is reading *Ulysses*, but neither she nor the book has any relationship to the murder case. Yet, when interviewing the "widow," Morse compares her with "Molly Bloom in *Ulysses*." Such literary red herrings add to the comic "asides" of the Dexter novels, and nowhere with more absurdity than in *The Dead of Jericho:* Morse has determined that the Oedipus tale holds the clue to the Jericho deaths and narrates the tale to an incredulous Lewis, even to the extent of insisting that "if there was one man guilty of Anne Scott's death, that man was Sophocles." Sophocles, however, is soon exonerated as the more hardheaded attributes of Chief Inspector Morse uncover the real events. For someone who shamefacedly admits that he more frequently reads the *Daily Mirror* than the *London Times*, Morse has his cultural moments.

Early in *The Secret of Annexe 3* the reader is promised "a murder planned with slow subtlety and executed with swift ferocity." The introductory scenes involve marital infidelity presumably discovered and leading to revenge killing (Dexter has often included sexual motivations throughout his murder mysteries). *The Secret of Annexe 3*, however, multiplies the possibilities of sexual alliances and misalliances as it is located at a New Year's weekend hotel festivity, particularly in the not-quite-completed annex wing of the hotel. The four rooms populated for the costume party by three couples and a no-show single set the stage for the "impossible" murder with all the familiar characteristics of the genre: the locked-room, snow on the unfinished grounds revealing

no footmarks, the convenient disguises, the false names on the hotel register, and the various illicit affairs producing an ample number of motives. The reader attempts to trace the information of the opening scenes through the actual murder event, as Morse tries to trace the real identities of the participants in the three occupied rooms–and even the unoccupied one. *The Secret of Annexe 3* is as much a comedy of sexual misadventures as a murder mystery, and, as is often never far from the surface in a Dexter novel, the genre of the "thriller" is being gently spoofed while it is nonetheless being deftly manipulated. Throughout the seven novels the comic vies with the grotesque, pathos with the tragic, within an effective evocation of the mundane. The surface realities of ordinary life consistently color the criminal situations without impinging on the careful artifice of the usual murders and the bumbling but brilliant methods of investigation undertaken almost in spite of himself by Chief Inspector E. Morse. Needless to say, no villain ever threatens the life of the investigating detectives; no one assaults him or even causes him to run or chase, on foot or in his Lancia. Sedentary Morse is outside the action, an armchair detective whose chair is most often in a pub, and the activity of his little gray cells is chaotic and off-center much of the time, while his hair turns gray and thins. The basic norm in the Dexter novels is best characterized by the epigraph to chapter 14 of *The Riddle of the Third Mile*: "Preliminary investigations are now in full swing, and Morse appears unconcerned about the contradictory evidence that emerges."

Reference:
Art Bourgeau, *The Mystery Lover's Companion* (New York: Crown, 1986), p. 135.

Peter Dickinson
(16 December 1927-   )

T. R. Steiner
University of California, Santa Barbara

BOOKS: *Skin Deep* (London: Hodder & Stoughton, 1968); republished as *The Glass-Sided Ants' Nest* (New York: Harper & Row, 1968);

The Weathermonger (London: Gollancz, 1968; Boston: Little, Brown, 1969);

Heartsease (London: Gollancz, 1969; Boston: Little, Brown, 1969);

A Pride of Heroes (London: Hodder & Stoughton, 1969); republished as *The Old English Peep Show* (New York: Harper & Row, 1969);

The Devil's Children (London: Gollancz, 1970; Boston: Little, Brown, 1970);

The Seals (London: Hodder & Stoughton, 1970); republished as *The Sinful Stones* (New York: Harper & Row, 1970);

Emma Tupper's Diary (London: Gollancz, 1971; Boston: Little, Brown, 1971);

Sleep and His Brother (London: Hodder & Stoughton, 1971; New York: Harper & Row, 1971);

The Dancing Bear (London: Gollancz, 1972; Boston: Little, Brown, 1973);

The Iron Lion (Boston: Little, Brown, 1972; London: Blackie, 1983);

The Lizard in the Cup (London: Hodder & Stoughton, 1972; New York: Harper & Row, 1972);

The Gift (London: Gollancz, 1973; Boston: Little, Brown, 1974);

The Green Gene (London: Hodder & Stoughton, 1973; New York: Pantheon, 1973);

The Poison Oracle (London: Hodder & Stoughton, 1974; New York: Pantheon, 1974);

Chance, Luck & Destiny (London: Gollancz, 1975; Boston: Little, Brown, 1976);

The Lively Dead (London: Hodder & Stoughton, 1975; New York: Pantheon, 1975);

The Blue Hawk (London: Gollancz, 1976; Boston: Little, Brown, 1976);

King and Joker (London: Hodder & Stoughton, 1976; New York: Pantheon, 1976);

Annerton Pit (London: Gollancz, 1977; Boston: Little, Brown, 1977);

Dickinson, circa 1975 (photograph by John A. Williamson)

Walking Dead (London: Hodder & Stoughton, 1977; New York: Pantheon, 1977);

The Flight of Dragons (London: Pierrot, 1979);

One Foot in the Grave (London: Hodder & Stoughton, 1979; New York: Pantheon, 1979);

Tulku (London: Gollancz, 1979; New York: Dutton, 1979);

City of Gold and Other Stories from the Old Testament (London: Gollancz, 1980; New York: Pantheon, 1980);

The Seventh Raven (London: Gollancz, 1981; New York: Dutton, 1981);

A Summer in the Twenties (London: Hodder & Stoughton, 1981; New York: Pantheon, 1981);

The Last House-Party (London: Bodley Head, 1982; New York: Pantheon, 1982);

Healer (London: Gollancz, 1983; New York: Delacorte, 1983);

Hindsight (London: Bodley Head, 1983; New York: Pantheon, 1983);

Death of a Unicorn (London: Bodley Head, 1984; New York: Pantheon, 1984);

Giant Cold (London: Gollancz, 1984; New York: Dutton, 1984);

A Box of Nothing (London: Gollancz, 1985; New York: Delacorte, 1988);

Tefuga (London: Bodley Head, 1986; New York: Pantheon, 1986);

Merlin Dreams (London: Gollancz, 1988; New York: Delacorte, 1988);

Perfect Gallows (London: Bodley Head, 1988; New York: Pantheon, 1988);

Eve (London: Gollancz, 1988; New York: Delacorte, 1989).

OTHER: *Presto! Humorous Bits and Pieces*, compiled by Dickinson (London: Hutchinson, 1975);

"Superintendent Pibble," in *The Great Detectives*, edited by Otto Penzler (Boston: Little, Brown, 1978), pp. 175-182.

Following traditions of donnish wit, romance, and scientific interest represented variously by G. K. Chesterton, H. G. Wells, and Michael Innes, Peter Dickinson has written among the most imaginative and bizarre detective novels of the 1970s and 1980s. His specialty has been to place exotic, imagined worlds next to the everyday world of conventional detective fiction, and then to carry the play of investigation freely from one to the other. At Dickinson's best his invention not only renews the genre but makes it thoughtful in ways seldom found in the work of other detective writers.

Peter Malcolm de Brissac Dickinson was born in Livingstone, Northern Rhodesia (now Zambia), in 1927. His father, Richard Sebastian Willoughby Dickinson, assistant chief secretary of the Rhodesian colonial government, was the second son of Baron Dickinson, barrister, royal commissioner, and MP, who was one originator of the League of Nations. Dickinson's eldest brother has succeeded to the barony, and Dickinson himself is an "honourable." The family has included British peers and high military officers, social groups often presented in his novels. After Dickinson's father's death in 1935 the family re-

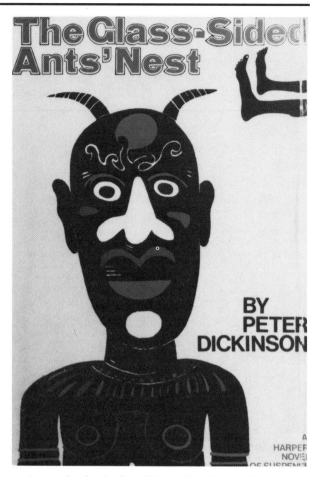

Dust jacket for the first edition of Dickinson's first novel

turned to England, where Dickinson was educated at preparatory school (as fictionalized in *Hindsight*, 1983), Eton, and King's College, Cambridge (exhibitioner in classics, B.A., 1951). In 1953 he married Mary Rose Barnard, daughter of Vice-Admiral Sir Geoffrey Barnard; the couple had four children.

From 1952 to 1969 Dickinson was assistant editor and a crime-fiction reviewer for *Punch*. Publishing his first book at forty, he since has been a prolific writer of esteemed children's books and detective fiction. *Skin Deep* (1968; published in the United States as *The Glass-Sided Ants' Nest*) and *A Pride of Heroes* (1969; published in the United States as *The Old English Peep Show*) each won the Crime Writers' Association award for the best mystery of the year; Dickinson has also received other writing honors. From 1978 to 1980 he chaired the management committee of the Society of Authors.

Dickinson's detective fiction is very much that of a man of letters. He uses to advantage his wide interests and knowledge, ranging from anthropology to antique clocks, railroading to the history of the British empire. During much of his career Dickinson has been a "Farceur," to use Julian Symons's term (in *Bloody Murder: From the Detective Story to the Crime Novel*, 1972) for the school of facetious inventors within Golden Age detective fiction. *Skin Deep*, for example, envisions a community of New Guinea aborigines living in inner London; *The Green Gene* (1973) presents an Orwellian Great Britain in which a servant underclass of green-skinned Celts revolts against its Saxon masters. Comparable in inventiveness, though less strange, is *King and Joker* (1976), built on the hypothesis that Prince Eddy, the eldest son of the future Edward VII, did not die in 1892. It then pictures the realm of an imagined contemporary successor, "King Victor II." Also, Dickinson's novels usually allude to history, especially to the passing of a Britain dependent on empire. Often they exploit his insider's knowledge of the British upper class.

Readers sometimes have wished that Dickinson's detections, which tend to be slender or marginal, were up to his otherwise evident imaginative strength. Superintendent Jimmy Pibble, the series detective who appears in the early novels, is little involved in Scotland Yard procedures or other kinds of detection; and the detective novels without Pibble tend to emphasize procedure even less. Pibble is a detective "greying toward retirement." He is described as "not at all James Bondish . . . , unsexy, easily browbeaten, intelligent, fallible." Despite Pibble's success with "kooky cases," he remains something of a cipher, and his competence as a detective often appears oblique and tardy.

In *Skin Deep*, the first Pibble novel, Dickinson seemed to announce that strangeness would be his distinction as detective writer. Within the closed circle of the New Guinea tribe that provides the setting for the story, exotic social and religious practices prevail. For example, all the members of the tribe are named "Ku." Dickinson employs the tribal milieu not only for its exoticism but also because non-Western mores alter or compound the problems of detection. Dickinson works with parallels of detection and anthropology. The drama of social life, as anthropology constantly demonstrates, is various and subtle; by contrast, police investigation "plunges in, a jagged Stone Age knife, to probe delicate tissues of people's relationships." For the detective to construct the true milieu of a crime is "like trying to reconstruct a civilization from three broken pots and a

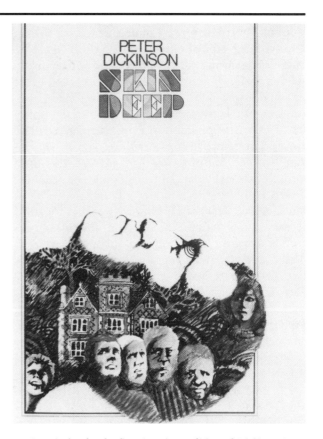

Dust jacket for the first American edition of Dickinson's first novel

seven-inch lump of baked clay." The murder and final detection depend only marginally on this exotica, and Dickinson's striving for the unusual can seem strained; but much of the investigation within a society both primitive and sophisticated is intellectually absorbing. In *A Pride of Heroes* Dickinson makes an aristocratic milieu exotic. The titular heroes are an admiral and a general, coholders of their ancestral estate, "Herryngs" (probably a sly reference to "red herrings," the false leads of detective fiction). The great home is exotic because of its original eighteenth-century form, complete with a lion pit and pornographic carvings, and because it has been made into a representation of "Olde England" for tourist expectations. The next Pibble novel, *The Seals* (1970; published in the United States as *The Sinful Stones*), is mostly revelation of the power mania within an isolated religious community. On the Hebridean Clumsey Island, in a demented version of Dante's *Purgatorio*, bodies literally are bent, humbled before God. A helicopter chase late in the book indicates how much more *The Seals* inclines toward adventure than classic detection. *Sleep and His Brother* (1971) is distinguished by the invented milieu of a hospital for "cathypnics," children marked by a distinctive eye-ring for growing sluggishness and early death. The murder is committed very late, and once again there is little deduction. The villain, unmasked but because of limited evidence unpunished, is an egomaniacal doctor-scientist, a villain favored in detective-story tradition and by Dickinson. In *The Lizard in the Cup* (1972), the most densely atmospheric of the Pibble novels, the closed scene of the crime is a fictional Ionian island, Hyos. Here Dickinson weaves together Greek natives and Anglo-Saxon intruders, extremes of poverty and plutocratic opulence, secularism and religious monasticism. Pibble's detective task is to learn who plans to assault his patron, Thanassi Thanatos, an Onassis-like multimillionaire first introduced in *Sleep and His Brother*. The investigation is made particularly complicated because he has to deal with a variety of criminal situations involving international terrorists and members of the Mafia, the drug trade, planned assaults by professional hit men, and private betrayals. The actual attack, a sudden fusillade that wounds Thanatos and kills others, and its detection are developed late and then perfunctorily. Indeed, the book gets its form mostly from developing beforehand the red herrings of potential suspects: Thanatos's odd associates; his mistress, a beautiful American terrorist in disguise who arouses Pibble's waning sexuality; two drunken monks; and a colony of British and American expatriates. Yet, despite the profuse invention and the glitter of Thanatos's life-style and Mediterranean scenic beauty, this prolix novel is the most difficult of the Pibble novels to get through.

By contrast the last Pibble, *One Foot in the Grave* (1979), which appeared after a seven-year interval, economically integrates detective convention, human interest, and depth of theme. After the untimely death of Pibble's wife, the superintendent goes into a funk that is followed by a life-threatening illness. While recuperating in a swank sanatorium paid for by Thanatos, he confronts his own death wish. Just as Pibble is about to commit suicide, he stumbles on a corpse, and the familiar situation forces him back into life and, what is for him synonymous, detection. Since illness and age have impaired his mind, he cannot remain in proper detective fashion focused on the matter at hand but in reverie and dreams shuttles back and forth over his entire career. He meets the heroes and the demons of his

past and comes to recognize that as detective and man he is grounded in both moral principle and the thrill of detection. By absorbing himself in the murder investigation–and a love interest with his nurse–he regains the will to live.

In these early books Dickinson the "Farceur" indulges his love of words and wordplay. Sometimes it is schoolboy frivolity, as in the name "Clumsey Island," in the etymology of "Hyos" (Greek for pig), and in the negative implications (however effective) of the name "Jimmy Pibble." Sometimes, however, Dickinson's verbal wit merits closer attention. Are readers invited to regard *Skin Deep*, in which nearly all the apparent suspects are named "Ku," as outrageously implying a new detective genre, the "Ku-dunit?" To be more serious: the name "Thanatos" in the last three Pibble novels refers to death or, more specifically, to the Freudian death instinct and points to the formal necessity of death in detective fiction. The character could be seen as a metaphorical "patron" of this type of fiction.

With the exception of *One Foot in the Grave*, no Dickinson novel since *The Green Gene* has used a conventional detective investigator; scientists and amateurs have replaced Pibble. Despite Dickinson's claim in 1980 that he tries "to write proper detective stories," most of his later books employ little actual detection, and in the instance of *A Summer in the Twenties* (1981), none at all. Typically, the late novels present a murder, but it functions much more as a narrative device than as a springboard for investigation. One frequent focus of Dickinson's books published in the 1970s was science or pseudoscience–the mathematics of *The Green Gene* and the psychology of *The Poison Oracle* (1974) and *Walking Dead* (1977)–bearing out Dickinson's own description of his books in *Twentieth-Century Crime and Mystery Writers* (1985) as "science fiction with the science left out." Politics has figured in nearly all of the later books, especially scrutiny of the emergent third world, as in *The Green Gene, Walking Dead*, and *Tefuga* (1986).

Dickinson's recent mystery books manifest a growing absorption with the history of twentieth-century Britain, especially as it seems to impinge on his own history. Thus, he has moved from an early, tenuous connection to the traditional detective story, to greater freedom as "Farceur," to a more sober, historical mode of detective fiction. Speaking of *Hindsight*, Robin W. Winks talks about Dickinson's "ever deepening personal nostalgia," and indeed the latest books have a dis-

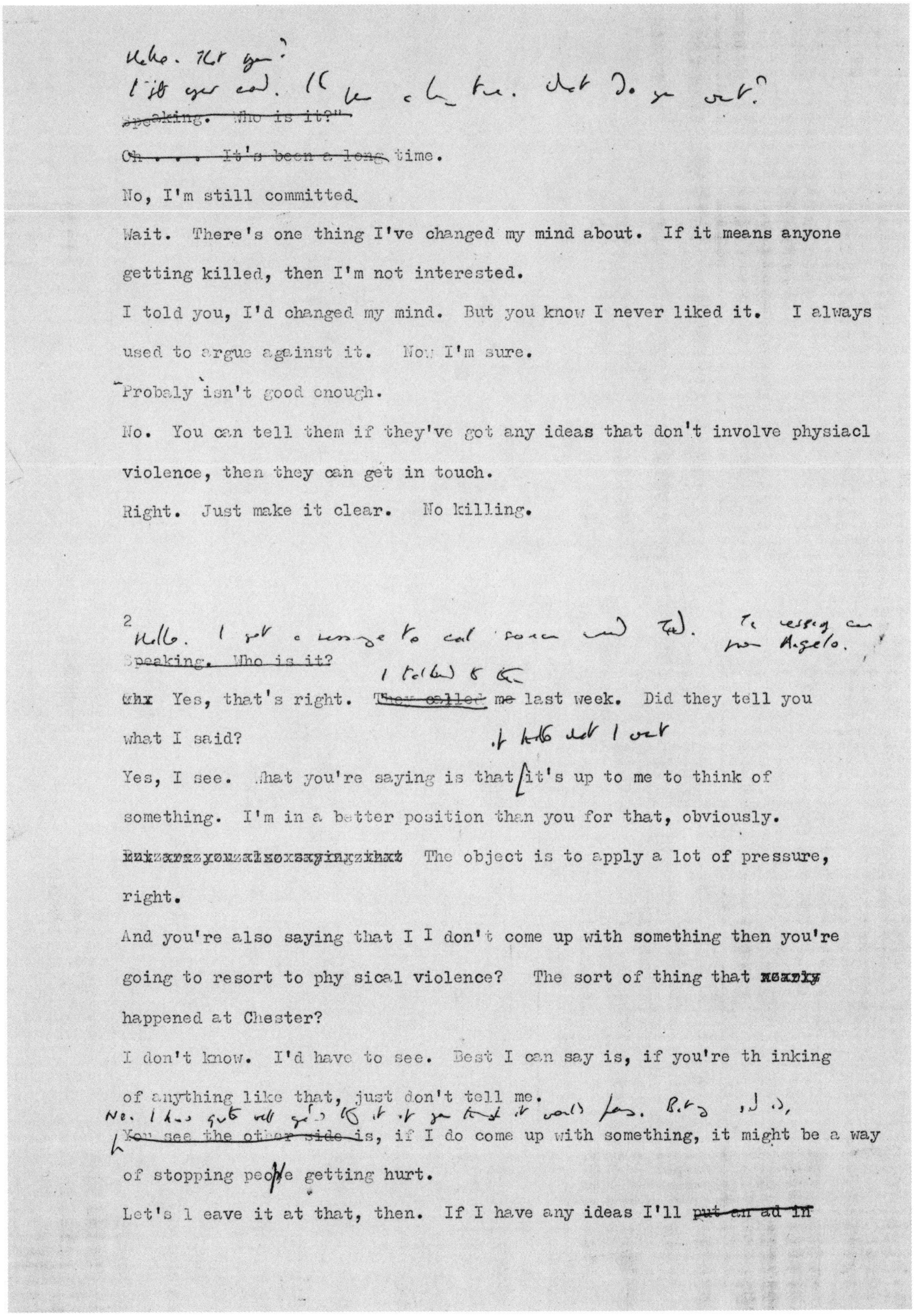

[handwritten: Hello. Is that you?]
[handwritten: I'll call you back. If ... the ... but do you want?]

~~Speaking. Who is it?"~~

~~Oh . . . . It's been a long~~ time.

No, I'm still committed.

Wait. There's one thing I've changed my mind about. If it means anyone

getting killed, then I'm not interested.

I told you, I'd changed my mind. But you know I never liked it. I always

used to argue against it. Now I'm sure.

Probaly isn't good enough.

No. You can tell them if they've got any ideas that don't involve physiacl

violence, then they can get in touch.

Right. Just make it clear. No killing.

2 *[handwritten: Hello. I ... a message to call some ... and tell. Te message ... for Angelo.]*

~~Speaking. Who is it?~~ *[handwritten: I told ... the]*

~~Whx~~ Yes, that's right. ~~They called~~ me last week. Did they tell you

what I said? *[handwritten: it told me I ...]*

Yes, I see. What you're saying is that /it's up to me to think of

something. I'm in a better position than you for that, obviously.

~~Kxixxrxzyxxxxxxxxxxxxxxxxxxxx~~ The object is to apply a lot of pressure,

right.

And you're also saying that I I don't come up with something then you're

going to resort to phy sical violence? The sort of thing that ~~nearly~~

happened at Chester?

I don't know. I'd have to see. Best I can say is, if you're th inking

of anything like that, just don't tell me.
[handwritten: No. I ... got all ... if it if you told it ... has. But ...]

~~You see the other side~~ is, if I do come up with something, it might be a way

of stopping people getting hurt.

Let's l eave it at that, then. If I have any ideas I'll ~~put en ad in~~

Corrected typescript for Dickinson's current work in progress, "Skeleton-in-Waiting" (courtesy of the author)

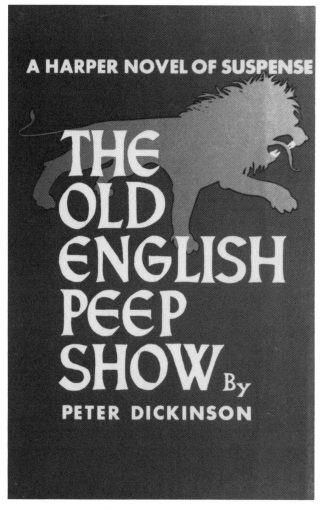

Dust jacket for the first American edition of Dickinson's 1969 novel, which under its English title, A Pride of Heroes, *won the Crime Writers' Association's Gold Dagger Award as the best crime novel of the year*

tinct personal character. *Hindsight* seems to originate in what Winks calls "schoolboy reminiscence," and *The Last House-Party* (1982) reminisces about prewar country-house life. The Honourable Thomas Sankey of *A Summer in the Twenties* (which takes place in the year before Dickinson's birth) is a railroading buff like the author and perhaps may be read as his alter ego. In *Death of a Unicorn* (1984) Lady Margaret Millett provides another "honourable" character, who, like Dickinson, began writing for a London magazine in the early 1950s and eventually became a successful popular writer. *Tefuga* is set in colonial Nigeria, an analogue to the colonial scene in which Dickinson had his origin. The best of these works bear out Earl F. Bargainnier's general estimate (in *Armchair Detective*, Summer 1980) that Dickinson "cram[s] . . . the formula,

without its either exploding or collapsing. He plays with the conventions, stretching and twisting them, but never allowing them actually to break." With none of his early excess and strain, with more restrained style, his latest detection novels synthesize detection, fictionalized autobiography, history, more profound self-reflexiveness, and substantial ideas, approaching at times the conceptual density of Borges and other postmodernist writers of detective fiction.

Hindsight dramatizes the detective author's process of creation. With indicators such as first-person narration and a shared first initial, Dickinson encourages readers to identify the novelist Paul Rogers with himself, Rogers's "book" with his own. At the start of the novel Rogers is fortuitously redirected to think about his prep school days, forty years earlier, when World War II was beginning. As he pieces together the past, he begins to conceive that what then had been regarded as an accidental death was actually murder. He decides to make a detective novel from this boyhood memoir. As he tries to shape the material, he finds problematic both the validity of his "memories" and the unity of his novel, which resists the synthesis of personal "truth" and conventional detective plot. *Hindsight* combines two kinds of detective novel: a straightforward whodunit that sequentially presents the antecedents, commission, and solution of a murder and a mystery that could have been called, after Agatha Christie's 1942 thriller, *Murder in Retrospect*, in which the problems of detection are compounded by time's ceaseless consumption of both material clues and witnesses' memories. By the conventional standards of the whodunit, as Rogers notes about his own novel, the "death comes later in the book than is normal in the genre," and the solution comes prematurely; but that seems of little importance since the book is much less concerned with classic detection than with how and why Rogers, the "writer," makes detective stories out of personal material, and with metaphysical themes of "serious" novels: time, history versus fiction, and the validity of imaginative truth.

More subtle in execution and more moving than *Hindsight* is *The Last House-Party*, which uses a favorite scene of Golden Age detective stories, the great country house that encloses a circle of acquaintances. Like *Hindsight* the novel is a double narrative of present crime and detection and of retrospection. In its 1930s setting and typical third-person narration, as well as in its essential faithfulness to convention, it is even closer than *Hindsight* to the Golden Age mystery. Despite its complexity, the book may be structured with little strain as a whodunit: "In June 1937 who raped seven-year-old Sally Quintain and set fire to the clock tower of Snailwood Castle?" Nevertheless, *The Last House-Party* puts to question the Golden Age detective novel, especially its conventions of time and narrative. Report, reminiscence, and documents from the past are substantial in themselves and are not merely instruments for providing clues. The quiddity of a particular time in history, ignored or, at most, ornamental in Golden Age fiction, is a principal meaning here. The plot does not point unwaveringly to a conclusion. In one formal particular only does it seem identical with the conventional novel. *The Last House-Party* does end with a detection, al-

though by that time readers have been led to regard the mere satisfaction of curiosity as trivial.

The mystery which initiates *The Last House-Party* is common in detective fiction: Has a rightful heir returned, and what is the possible claimant up to? In 1937 the rapist and arsonist had been identified as one possible heir of Snailwood, Vincent Masham, who then had fled and had never been heard from again. Although supposed dead, if alive Masham would be the heir of Snailwood. Now forty and more years later it may be that he has returned in the altered guise of a clockmaker. The role of detective is taken by a grown-up Sarah (Sally) Quintain, ironically the latest holder of Snailwood, which she inherited long before from her stepfather, Masham's cousin. Skeptical that Masham committed the crimes and actuated by a sense of justice, Sarah tries to exonerate and to identify him. Ironically it happens that Masham, who has indeed returned, *was* the criminal, though the revelations are held back until the last page. *The Last House-Party* has depth of character and, even more, of theme well beyond that of Golden Age detective novels. Neither Sarah nor Masham is moved by the typical motives of detective fiction–greed, envy, or revenge–but by generosity and humbleness. Sarah and Masham are ideal contrasting public-school types, the silent athlete and the voluble leader. Their intimate, mutually supportive bond is hardly expressible or even fully understood by either. They, like Snailwood itself, represent the passing of an imperial England that for all its faults produced manly character and virtues.

The cast of characters gathered by the dazzling Countess of Snailwood for the 1937 house party represents a microcosm of the Anglo-European-Mediterranean world as the 1930s careened toward World War II and the end of empire. To see sparks fly, the countess brings together Jew and Arab, Fascist and anti-Fascist, the masters of British politics and the lords of the press. As the reader seeks whodunit, the crimes must be studied for possible public motivation as well as private. Brooding over the action at Snailwood Castle is a central metaphor: an elaborate old clock in the castle tower presents a dance of the seasons, a Christian knight beheading a Saracen and Father Time with his scythe pursuing all. It is a *Totentanz*, implying the "last party," the mortality of "Old" England, of 1930s Europe, of all human beings. In burning the tower Masham had attempted symbolic destruction of the time and world that had mismade him into a child rapist.

Dickinson's resolution of the mysteries is especially satisfying. The criminal is revealed only by suggestions; Masham has struggled over the years for reform and expiation; he himself is made to invoke time. In the book's finale Masham patches up the clock so that one last time it can strike noon and tell its conventional narrative. This time, however, he makes the Saracen conquer the Christian knight to compliment the new owner of Snailwood Castle, an Arab prince to whom the British had condescended at the last house party, now about to become the savior of Snailwood, which the penniless British no longer can maintain. Thus, the last expiation is historical and political, an apology to a former client from the old empire.

In *The Last House-Party* Dickinson's sophistication is at its rich but controlled best. In some of his other books, unfortunately, it has produced a displeasing strangeness, overcomplexity, and archness. Like Chesterton, the distinctive idea man of classic detective fiction, Dickinson has tended by the brilliance of his invention and style often to promise more than he achieves. Sometimes, as Winks urges, "there is less going on in the end than there appears." It is not only the "less learned reader" who is put off by the "heavy-going" of Dickinson's "formidable intelligence," as H. R. F. Keating notes in *Twentieth-Century Crime and Mystery Writers*, but anyone who reads for pleasure. Nevertheless, intelligence, learning, and fecund invention fed by them are his distinctive strengths: the best Dickinson novels provide not only the tonic of novelty but also much to delight in, to learn from, and to think about.

References:

Earl F. Bargainnier, "The Playful Mysteries of Peter Dickinson," *Armchair Detective*, 13 (Summer 1980): 185-193;

Robin W. Winks, "The Devon Deception," *Book World-Washington Post*, 18 December 1983, p. 7.

Elizabeth Ferrars
(Morna Doris Brown)
(6 September 1907-   )

Mary Helen Becker
Madison Area Technical College

BOOKS: *Turn Single*, as Morna MacTaggart (London: Nicholson & Watson, 1932);

Broken Music, as MacTaggart (London: Nicholson & Watson, 1934; New York: Dutton, 1934);

Give a Corpse a Bad Name (London: Hodder & Stoughton, 1940);

Remove the Bodies (London: Hodder & Stoughton, 1940); republished as *Rehearsals for Murder* (New York: Doubleday, Doran, 1941);

Death in Botanist's Bay (London: Hodder & Stoughton, 1941); republished as *Murder of a Suicide* (Garden City, N.Y.: Doubleday, Doran, 1941);

Don't Monkey with Murder (London: Hodder & Stoughton, 1942); republished as *The Shape of a Stain* (Garden City, N.Y.: Doubleday, Doran, 1942);

Your Neck in a Noose (London: Hodder & Stoughton, 1942); republished as *Neck in a Noose* (Garden City, N.Y.: Doubleday, Doran, 1943);

I, Said the Fly (London: Hodder & Stoughton, 1945; Garden City, N.Y.: Doubleday, Doran, 1945);

Murder Among Friends (London: Collins, 1946); republished as *Cheat the Hangman* (Garden City, N.Y.: Doubleday, 1946);

With Murder in Mind (London: Collins, 1948);

The March Hare Murders (London: Collins, 1949; Garden City, N.Y.: Doubleday, 1949);

Hunt the Tortoise (London: Collins, 1950; Garden City, N.Y.: Doubleday, 1950);

Milk of Human Kindness (London: Collins, 1950);

Alibi for a Witch (London: Collins, 1952; Garden City, N.Y.: Doubleday, 1952);

The Clock That Wouldn't Stop (London: Collins, 1952; Garden City, N.Y.: Doubleday, 1952);

Murder in Time (London: Collins, 1953);

The Lying Voices (London: Collins, 1954);

Enough to Kill a Horse (London: Collins, 1955; Garden City, N.Y.: Doubleday, 1955);

Elizabeth Ferrars, mid 1970s (The Scotsman Publications, Ltd.)

Always Say Die (London: Collins, 1956); republished as *We Haven't Seen Her Lately* (Garden City, N.Y.: Doubleday, 1956);

Murder Moves In (London: Collins, 1956); republished as *Kill or Cure* (Garden City, N.Y.: Doubleday, 1956);

Furnished for Murder (London: Collins, 1957);

Count the Cost (Garden City, N.Y.: Doubleday, 1957); republished as *Unreasonable Doubt* (London: Collins, 1958);

Depart This Life (Garden City, N.Y.: Doubleday, 1958); republished as *A Tale of Two Murders* (London: Collins, 1959);

Fear the Light (London: Collins, 1960; Garden City, N.Y.: Doubleday, 1960);

Sleeping Dogs (London: Collins, 1960; Garden City, N.Y.: Doubleday, 1960);

The Busy Body (London: Collins, 1962); republished as *Seeing Double* (Garden City, N.Y.: Doubleday, 1962);

The Wandering Widows (London: Collins, 1962; Garden City, N.Y.: Doubleday, 1962);

The Doubly Dead (London: Collins, 1963; Garden City, N.Y.: Doubleday, 1963);

The Decayed Gentlewoman (Garden City, N.Y.: Doubleday, 1963); republished as *A Legal Fiction* (London: Collins, 1964);

Ninth Life (London: Collins, 1965);

No Peace for the Wicked (London: Collins, 1966; New York: Harper & Row, 1966);

Zero at the Bone (London: Collins, 1967; New York: Walker, 1968);

The Swaying Pillars (London: Collins, 1968; New York: Walker, 1969);

Skeleton Staff (London: Collins, 1969; New York: Walker, 1969);

The Seven Sleepers (London: Collins, 1970; New York: Walker, 1970);

A Stranger and Afraid (London: Collins, 1971; New York: Walker, 1971);

Breath of Suspicion (London: Collins, 1972; Garden City, N.Y.: Doubleday, 1972);

Foot in the Grave (Garden City, N.Y.: Doubleday, 1972; London: Collins, 1973);

The Small World of Murder (London: Collins, 1973; Garden City, N.Y.: Doubleday, 1973);

Hanged Man's House (London: Collins, 1974; Garden City, N.Y.: Doubleday, 1974);

Alive and Dead (London: Collins, 1974; Garden City, N.Y.: Doubleday, 1975);

Drowned Rat (London: Collins, 1975; Garden City, N.Y.: Doubleday, 1975);

The Cup and the Lip (London: Collins, 1975; Garden City, N.Y.: Doubleday, 1976);

Blood Flies Upwards (London: Collins, 1976); published as *Blood Flies Upward* (Garden City, N.Y.: Doubleday, 1977);

The Pretty Pink Shroud (London: Collins, 1977; Garden City, N.Y.: Doubleday, 1977);

Murders Anonymous (London: Collins, 1977; Garden City, N.Y.: Doubleday, 1978);

Last Will and Testament (London: Collins, 1978; Garden City, N.Y.: Doubleday, 1978);

In at the Kill (London: Collins, 1978; Garden City, N.Y.: Doubleday, 1979);

Witness Before the Fact (London: Collins, 1979; Garden City, N.Y.: Doubleday, 1980);

Designs on Life (London: Collins, 1980; Garden City, N.Y.: Doubleday, 1980);

Frog in the Throat (London: Collins, 1980; Garden City, N.Y.: Doubleday, 1980);

Experiment with Death (London: Collins, 1981; Garden City, N.Y.: Doubleday, 1981);

Thinner than Water (London: Collins, 1981; Garden City, N.Y.: Doubleday, 1982);

Skeleton in Search of a Cupboard (London: Collins, 1982); republished as *Skeleton in Search of a Closet* (Garden City, N.Y.: Doubleday, 1982);

Death of a Minor Character (London: Collins, 1983; Garden City, N.Y.: Doubleday, 1983);

Something Wicked (London: Collins, 1983; Garden City, N.Y.: Doubleday, 1984);

Root of All Evil (London: Collins, 1984; Garden City, N.Y.: Doubleday, 1984);

The Crime and the Crystal (London: Collins, 1985; Garden City, N.Y.: Doubleday, 1985);

I Met Murder (London: Collins, 1985; Garden City, N.Y.: Doubleday, 1986);

The Other Devil's Name (London: Collins, 1986; Garden City, N.Y.: Doubleday, 1987);

Come to Be Killed (London: Collins, 1987; Garden City, N.Y.: Doubleday, 1987);

A Murder Too Many (London: Collins, 1988; Garden City, N.Y.: Doubleday, 1989).

OTHER: *Planned Departures*, edited, with an introduction, by Ferrars (London: Hodder & Stoughton, 1958);

Crime on the Coast and No Flowers by Request, includes contributions by Ferrars, Dorothy L. Sayers, and others (London: Gollancz, 1984; New York: Berkeley, 1987).

Elizabeth Ferrars, who is known in the United States as E. X. Ferrars, has been entertaining readers on both sides of the Atlantic with traditional mystery novels and short stories since 1940. In 1980 she received a special Silver Dagger Award from the Crime Writers' Association, an organization which she cofounded in 1953, for writing "no less than 50 outstanding crime books." In *Murder Must Appetize* (1975) H. R. F. Keating places her among "that quite large and much-to-be-thanked band of crime authors who were writing in the good old days and are writing still in today's yet better ones." In a statement that represents Ferrars's typical work, the domes-

Dust jackets for the first British editions of two of Ferrars's novels from the 1940s (courtesy of Otto Penzler)

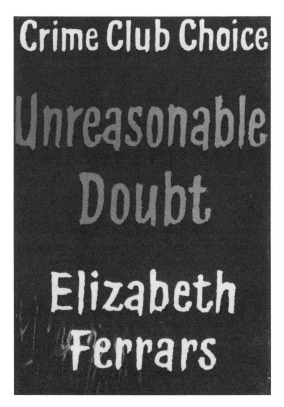

Dust jacket for the first British edition of the novel published in the United States as Count the Cost *(courtesy of Otto Penzler)*

Dust jacket for the first British edition of Ferrars's thirtieth novel (courtesy of Otto Penzler)

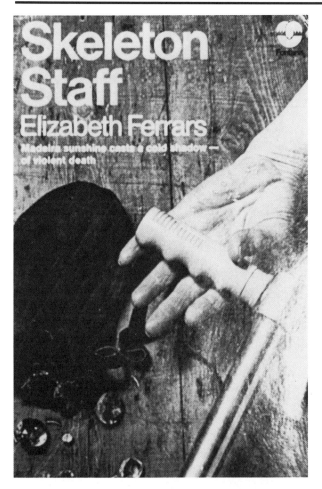

Front cover for the first British paperback publication of Ferrars's 1969 novel (photograph by Hilde Adler)

tic mystery, a character in *The Small World of Murder* (1973) says, "Murder's generally an intimate sort of thing. It happens in a small world, a little shut-in world of violent feelings."

Ferrars, whose real name is Morna Doris MacTaggart, was born in Rangoon, Burma, on 6 September 1907, the daughter of Peter Clouston and Marie Ferrars MacTaggart, and was taken to England at the age of three. She attended Bedales School in Petersfield, Hampshire, from 1918 to 1924, then studied at University College, London, from 1925 to 1928, the year that she received a diploma in journalism. During the 1930s she wrote two novels under her own name: *Turn Single* (1932) and *Broken Music* (1934). When she decided to try her hand at detective fiction, she chose a pseudonym for what she thought might be her only effort in the genre, planning to keep it separate from her "serious" work. Ferrars, her mother's maiden name, was preceded by Elizabeth, a name she liked. Her American publish-

ers, believing they had too many women on their list, asked her to use initials. She has said that she chose "X" as a middle initial "just to be awkward," but when pressed, has claimed it stands for Xavia, or Xantippe (the name of Socrates' wife).

In her first five mysteries Ferrars features detectives Toby Dyke–formerly a journalist–and his companion George. Dyke is in his thirties, tall, well built, swarthy and dark haired, with slanted eyes and a beak of a nose. George is his opposite: older, fair, short, and plump. His last name is never disclosed, but he claims various names beginning with *P* (Pinkerton, Prendergast, Posslethwaite, Poppenheimer, and so on). George's history is never revealed, though there are hints that he may be a reformed criminal (his picture is on file at Scotland Yard, but that could be the case if he is a retired policeman). Toby Dyke is in the limelight and accepts credit for solving their cases, but George is seen to be by far the better detective.

Ferrars's first crime novel, *Give a Corpse a Bad Name*, was published in 1940, the year that she married botanist Robert Brown, whose career took the couple to many universities and research institutions, as well as to meetings and conferences in foreign countries. The novel, which was praised in the *Times Literary Supplement* (3 February 1940) as a "first-rate story" and reprinted by Collins in 1981, was an auspicious beginning. Set in Devonshire, it contains an amusing cast of eccentrics. Fortyish Anna Milne, a successful author of pseudonymous fiction whose would-be son-in-law, also a writer, envies her, has run over and killed a man on her way home from the badminton club. The police know that the deceased was very drunk at the time of his death, but they do not know who he was. Toby Dyke and George observe the local constable searching for clues and decide to aid in the investigation. Sir Joseph Maxwell, the local squire, identifies the body as his son, but his wife adamantly disagrees. When it transpires that the dead man is in fact Anna Milne's estranged husband and Toby Dyke begins to receive anonymous letters, George's sleuthing skills are put to the test.

The second and third books featuring Toby Dyke and George are *Remove the Bodies* (1940; published in the United States as *Rehearsals for Murder*, 1941) and *Death in Botanist's Bay* (1941; published in the United States as *Murder of a Suicide*). *Remove the Bodies* opens with a very scared young woman visiting Toby and begging to stay the

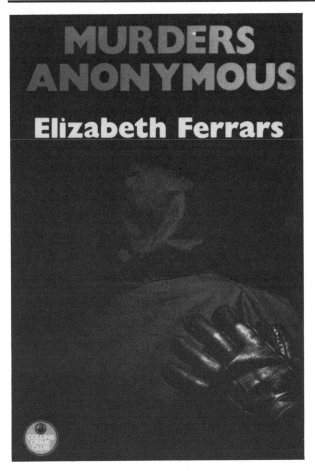

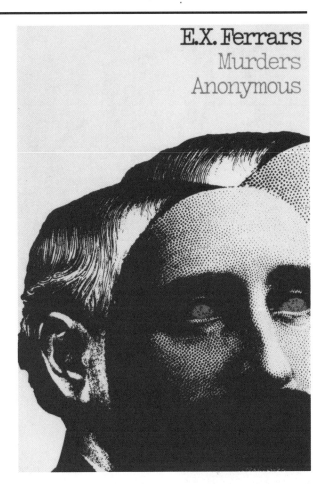

Dust jackets for the first British and first American editions of Ferrars's 1977 novel, published during her tenure as chairman of the Crime Writers' Association

night. The next day, after she has borrowed money and departed, Toby tells George how kind-hearted she is, and how frustrating, adding that he has often felt like murdering her. Later that day Toby learns that she has indeed been murdered–with strychnine. The *Times Literary Supplement* reviewer claimed that had the book "not been designed as a detective story it might have become a psychological study of serious pretensions. Unlike those authors who boast of being psychological–she never uses the word–Miss Ferrars has come nearer to deserving this label for her mystery than any novel of the kind for a long time past." *Death in Botanist's Bay* has among its characters several eccentric botanists and a writer of romantic fiction. Edgar Prees, curator of the herbarium at Asslington Botanical Gardens, is found dead, but it is not clear if his death is murder or suicide. Ferrars pokes fun at psychologists with her portrayal of Dr. Vanedden, a Ph.D. from an obscure American university and a most unappealing personage, who of-

fends everyone with his unwelcome psychological analyses of character. He is called "a damned, hypocritical little charlatan" and a "bogus little weasel."

The last two Toby Dyke and George books are *Don't Monkey with Murder* (1942; published in the United States as *The Shape of a Stain*) and *Your Neck in a Noose* (1942; published in the United States as *Neck in a Noose*, 1943). *Don't Monkey with Murder* is an amusing book set in a remote village inhabited by rather degenerate folk. Toby and George answer an urgent summons to East Leat to save Irma, who turns out to be a chimpanzee. Irma is only the first primate to be killed–the others are human. Isaac Anderson (*New York Times Book Review*, 19 July 1942) wrote that while George "turns up the evidence necessary to convict the murderer . . . , all the credit goes to Toby. George, apparently, is satisfied to be the man behind the man who is supposed to have done the work. Modest chap, this George. You'll like him." Ferrars, however, tired of Toby Dyke.

Dust jacket for the first American edition of Ferrars's only short-story collection

His final appearance is in *Your Neck in a Noose*, set in the country and at a London boardinghouse in Carberry Square, a neighborhood she would employ in several subsequent books. Toby's last adventure is overcomplicated and not particularly memorable.

Other early books by Ferrars use World War II as background. Kay Bryant returns to Little Carberry Street after the blitz and finds her old lodgings gone in *I, Said the Fly* (1945), a good story told in a flashback. There is a clever juxtaposition of the nursery-rhyme fly in "Who Killed Cock Robin?" and the fly invited into the spider's parlor. The heroine must keep the nursery rhymes straight to understand a clue to the killer's identity. In *Murder Among Friends* (1946; published in the United States as *Cheat the Hangman*) a cocktail party is interrupted by the alarming news of a murder in a neighboring apartment. Ferrars, who is known for her domestic murders, tells a good story of private passion and vengeance against the backdrop of air raids and blackouts. The killer confesses to wishing for the outbreak of war: "I wanted a disaster so enormous and overpowering and impersonal that my own personal feelings and troubles and problems and miseries would disappear in all the crashing and banging! They don't [disappear] of course." *Hunt the Tortoise* (1950), set in a village in southern France, is directly concerned with the aftermath of the war. A young woman journalist returns to a hotel she had loved nine years earlier, trying to recover from an illness and from the loss of her fiancé, who was killed in Italy. More of a thriller than most of Ferrars's novels, this one concerns the smuggling of refugees.

Ferrars departed from her usual narrative style in *With Murder in Mind* (1948), which consists of a young woman's conversations with her analyst: a "preliminary discussion" followed by ten sessions. The result is somewhat tedious. Booksellers, bookbinders, and book collectors figure in her next novel, *The March Hare Murders* (1949), which Elizabeth Bullock (*New York Times Book Review*, 30 October 1949) called "a good, absorbing mystery novel."

If one were to divide Elizabeth Ferrars's books into periods–early, middle, and late, for example–*Milk of Human Kindness* (1950) might be selected as the first of the middle period, for in it she has perfected the domestic murder mystery. In the novel the "milk" is definitely sour. Norman Rice, seemingly the mildest of men, is bitter and malevolent, particularly toward his former wife, Susan, and her second and third husbands. The first-person narration by Marabelle Baynes, Susan's sister, is humorous and emphasizes the "domestic" motif: at the beginning Susan's dirty dishes are piled up in the kitchen, and at the end the same dishes are finally washed by her current husband. *Milk of Human Kindness* is one of the titles not yet published in the United States and one her American fans would enjoy.

Two of Ferrars's novels were published in 1952. *The Clock That Wouldn't Stop* features a middle-aged lady who writes an advice column for a London newspaper and believes herself to be an astute judge of character. Less perspicacious than she thinks, she is accused of using special knowledge of a crime for purposes of blackmail. *Alibi for a Witch* is an intricate puzzle set on the southern coast of Italy. The reviewer for the *New York Times Book Review* (21 December 1952) wrote that the "picture of English expatriates in Italy is interesting; the plot, in which the same

American-edition dust jacket for one of Ferrars's novels featuring the characters Virginia and Felix Freer

man is apparently murdered twice, is highly ingenious; but the characters are cold and exceedingly talkative." Loquacious characters are common in Ferrars's books; the point at which their talkativeness becomes excessive depends on the taste of the reader or critic.

Her novel *Murder in Time*, which was published in 1953, explores a murder at a house party at which one of the guests observes: "The company was as ill-assorted as if he [the host] had deliberately collected it for the purpose of achieving a social disaster." In *The Lying Voices*, which was published in 1954, the lying voices are dozens of clocks which tell neither the right time nor the time of a murder committed in the same room. Equally unreliable are the statements made by the various characters in this puzzle novel. Justin Emery, back in England after six years in Australia and having nothing much to do, pays a visit to an old friend in the village of Fallow Corner and stays on to solve several murders (the outsider who noses about until he solves a crime is a protagonist whom Ferrars will

use repeatedly). There is arsenic in the lobster patties at a small party in *Enough to Kill a Horse* (1955). A mild-mannered professor of genetics discovers the truth of the rather complex plot, the solution of which turns on an obscure bit of scientific trivia.

Ferrars published two novels in both 1956 and 1957. In *Always Say Die* (1956; published in the United States as *We Haven't Seen Her Lately*) a young woman tries to find her elderly aunt, who seems to have met with foul play. Leo Harris (*Books and Bookmen*, April 1956) wrote that "bags of clues, red herrings, personal relationships, motives and even allergies bedevil the would-be solver. Miss Ferrars uses the Christie technique of shoving great clues under your very nose disguised as idle chit-chat or semi-relevant description." A writer and a scientist at an agricultural research station are characters in *Murder Moves In* (1956; published in the United States as *Kill or Cure*). *Furnished for Murder* (1957) is set in a small community. *Count the Cost* (1957; published in Great Britain as *Unreasonable Doubt*, 1958) is an intriguing tale of stolen Greek coins. Though a few scenes are set on the French Riviera, most of the story unfolds in an English village containing a museum in a thirteenth-century house. Ferrars embellished her plot with details such as Mr. Tolliver's prize onions at the village fete.

Two of Ferrars's novels focus on family problems. *Depart This Life* (1958; published in Great Britain as *A Tale of Two Murders*, 1959) is a complicated story about an unfortunate group of people manipulated by a vicious blackmailer who is finally murdered. Marvin Lachman called the book a " 'soap opera' in the pejorative sense . . . , [for it is] basically about domestic quarrels and problems, with occasional interludes of mystery. There is seemingly endless dialogue, much of it repeated for what appears to be padding." *Fear the Light* (1960), like *Depart This Life* a story of family difficulties and illicit love affairs, is more interesting. The family in the novel has had several distinguished members, including an eighteenth-century scientist whose letters, if they could be found, would be valuable. Several people are trying to get their hands on them, including an American professor who, fearing the letters may have been destroyed, says: "You are certainly acquainted with those conscienceless women who throw things away simply because they don't care for litter. Have you ever thought of all the history that's been sacrificed to the mere habit of neatness of some brainless housewife, reaching

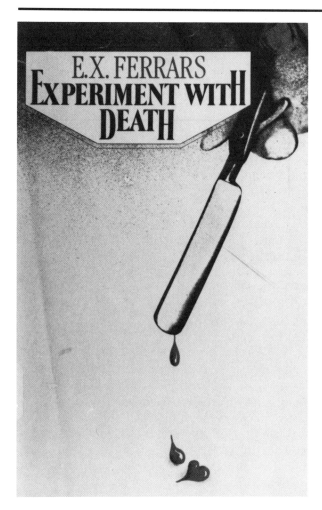 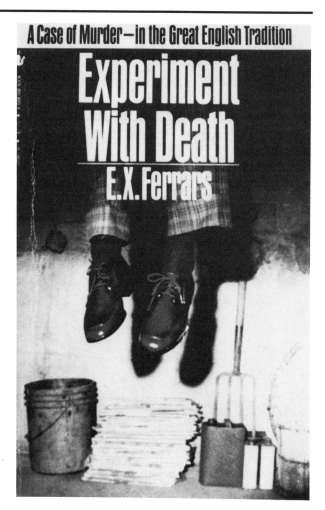

Dust jacket and wrapper for American editions of one of the many novels Ferrars set amid a community of scholars

out with her broom and duster to deprive the future of its heritage?"

In the 1960s Ferrars was a consistent producer of fine mysteries. *Sleeping Dogs* (1960), featuring a writer who does a story about a housekeeper tried for murdering a child, and *The Busy Body* (1962; published in the United States as *Seeing Double*), which has an especially intriguing opening, are exemplary Ferrars novels. *The Wandering Widows* (1962), set on the island of Mull off the western coast of Scotland, is an ingenious tale about swindlers who prey on gullible women. Theft and murder among family and neighbors are the principal problems in *The Doubly Dead* (1963), but Paul Hardwicke, a character who is writing a book on biology for young people, provides considerable humor as he muses about modern education. Anthony Boucher (*New York Times Book Review*, 16 June 1963) praised the book, calling Ferrars "one of England's steadily most reli-

able pros." *The Decayed Gentlewoman* (1963; published in Great Britain as *A Legal Fiction*, 1964) is an excellent mystery about a stolen Rubens painting. Colin Lockie, a botanist from the University of Edinburgh, in London to read a paper to the Royal Society, receives a puzzling message from a childhood friend and tries to discover the location of the painting. Boucher (*New York Times Book Review*, 22 December 1963) called this book the best he had read by Ferrars, "a fine high-spirited adventure-romance which manages to hold you breathless without (for most of its length) introducing a corpse or any other overt violence," and said that she is "a consistently admirable craftswoman who combines neat puzzles with a fine feeling for people." *Ninth Life* (1965), set in the West Country hamlet of Dexter Abbas, concerns a crime reporter, a bookseller, and a rare copy of Robert Hooke's *Micrographia*. A British woman vacationing in Greece is protagonist in *No*

Peace for the Wicked (1966). Unbeknownst to her, she is in possession of industrial diamonds and is caught up in an ingenious smuggling scheme. The reviewer for the *Times Literary Supplement* called the novel "an amiable holiday story set on a Greek island, with confusions ever more–perhaps–too unfounded, and murder included."

Zero at the Bone (1967) has received more criticism, both favorable and unfavorable, than most of Ferrars's work. The novel's title is taken from a poem by Emily Dickinson. Susan Lyne, a zoology student from the University of London, is visiting her sister and brother-in-law in the country. People in the area keep falcons, and considerable information about falconry is worked into the story. Jacques Barzun and Wendell Hertig Taylor were very negative about the novel in the introduction to *A Catalogue of Crime* (1971), while not actually mentioning it by name. They used it as an extreme example of what they call the *Had I But Known* (HIBK) tale: "Since the modern psychological novel has devoted itself to exploring the abnormal and oddly alarming, no great originality was needed to raise the emotional pitch of the girlish murder story another notch and make HIBK into EIRF [*Everything Is Rather Frightening*]." They claim further that "in this same story of vague frights and frustrated passions, it turns out that the only two attractive and sensible people in the book are the murdering desperadoes: this is a subversive attack on the fundamental decencies." They do allow that the story was written "by a formerly solid writer." The book was praised by Leo Harris (*Punch*, 15 November 1967), who said that it is a "pity [that] 'feline' is thought uncomplimentary; it perfectly describes Miss Ferrars' sinuous, gentle sheathed-claw manner. Comparison with Jane [Austen] is not unjustified. Neat trickery, well-concealed and well-decorated with country characters, peregrine falcons, and even an escaped python." Allen J. Hubin (*New York Times Book Review*, 15 September 1968) wrote that *Zero at the Bone* "comes closer to the classic detective novel than any reviewed here of late. . . . Attractively offbeat characterizations add zest to the tale. The essential clue hangs in full view, ripe for plucking–but Miss Ferrars sneaks us by it adroitly."

Zero at the Bone was followed by *The Swaying Pillars* (1968), the title of which is symbolic of the crumbling social order in a former British colony in Africa. The domestic problems of a British family unfold against the background of revolution. A small child is kidnapped, and the kidnapper is

eaten by a crocodile, a fate well suited to the crime and to the setting. This novel is discussed at length by Susan Baker in her essay on Ferrars in the book *And Then There Were Nine: More Women of Mystery* (1985). Baker contrasts the author's use of an exotic setting with Agatha Christie's use of archaeological sites and Ngaio Marsh's tales set in New Zealand and concludes that the novel makes a perceptive sociological comment: "*The Swaying Pillars* finally questions the ability of *any* society to restrain the violence intrinsic to its members; were social order 'natural,' it wouldn't require such extensive foundations to remain intact. . . . The social order functions moderately well as long as people behave themselves, but it is utterly inadequate to restrain, contain, or expel wickedness when it erupts into violence, as it sometimes will. For Ferrars, the veneer of civilization is real and to be valued, but it is fragile."

The next few books by Ferrars–set in Madeira, Scotland, the English town of Helsington, and even on a trip around the world (*The Small World of Murder*)–are fine examples of her domestic murder mysteries. Set in Madeira, *Skeleton Staff* (1969) is as much romantic melodrama as murder mystery, with the numerous characters' histories related in detail. The local police chief, Raposo, is an interesting character who reappears in *Witness Before the Fact* (1979). In the latter novel Peter Corey, a writer of children's books about "Edward Otter," goes to Madeira to check up on his old friend Alec Methven, only to discover he has been murdered. On his way home, Peter decides that he has finished with Edward Otter. Another novel set in Madeira is *Breath of Suspicion* (1972), which, unusual for Ferrars, is a story of spying. A spy escapes to the island and writes a successful thriller which is made into a film. His alias appears in the list of credits, leading to his discovery and murder–a clever and ironic touch.

The Seven Sleepers (1970), set in Scotland, has so many characters that it is a struggle to keep them straight–though it transpires that the effort is unnecessary. When a young man is asked to come to Edinburgh on family business, he learns that his late grandfather had seven wives, six of whom died mysteriously. The reviewer for the *Times Literary Supplement* (11 June 1970) called *The Seven Sleepers* "a pretty plot and an amusing tale . . . ; the morbid gaiety never flags."

The pleasant village of Royden Saint Agnes near the town of Helsington is the setting for *A*

Ferrars in the 1980s (photograph by Rosemary Herbert)

Stranger and Afraid (1971), which introduces Inspector Ditteridge, a character Ferrars was to use again. Holly Dunthorne, a doctoral student at London University, arrives in the village to visit her aunt and to see the Meridens, a lively group Holly has always wished was her own family. The aunt is murdered, and the Meridens prove not to be such a happy family after all–adultery, blackmail, and murder are among their activities. Ferrars is quite skilled at depicting the thoughts of her protagonists. The unspoken thoughts as well as the conversations in this book are amusing, and she pokes fun at writers (the literary scholar, a playwright, and a "happy little hack" who writes love stories for women's magazines). Ditteridge also investigates in *Foot in the Grave* (1972), set in Helsington itself. Ferrars returned to Helsington for *Alive and Dead* (1974) and *Blood Flies Upwards* (1976; published in the United States as *Blood Flies Upward*, 1977). *Alive and Dead* features two delightful characters: Martha Crayle, age fifty-five, who volunteers at an agency for unwed mothers; and her boarder Mr. Syme, age sixty-seven, who is writing a history of medieval Helsington and who says Martha "suf-

fers from a pathological trust in the human race." In *Blood Flies Upwards* Allison Goodrich, whose husband has gone on a botanical expedition, gets a job as housekeeper for the Eckersalls, who live near Helsington. Allison's sister Sally had worked for them before she disappeared, and Allison hopes to discover what happened to her. The neighborhood is decidedly strange: an escaped convict lives nearby, and next door there are two peculiar old women who come over to borrow treacle after midnight.

Scientists and university faculty are frequent participants or spectators in murder mysteries by Ferrars. Typical is *Hanged Man's House* (1974), which is set in a small community containing the Martindale Research Station. Horticultural research is carried out at the station when the scientists are not busy committing murders and disposing of bodies. Charles Gair, the director, dies from a fall but is strung up by the deputy director to symbolize execution. A mummified body is found in a cupboard in Gair's cellar. Perhaps in this book Ferrars is symbolizing how stultifying, even deadly, the atmosphere can be in some academic environments. The *Times Literary Supple-*

ment reviewer (25 January 1974) calls *Hanged Man's House* "one of Elizabeth Ferrars' better-made books, nicely unified, nicely ratiocinated, with a pleasant detective and a potential mate for him." In *Murders Anonymous*, published in 1977, the year Ferrars took over the chairmanship of the Crime Writers' Association, Matthew Tierney, a professor of molecular biology, goes to stay with his sister and brother-in-law following the murder of his wife, Kate. He has an alibi for the time of Kate's death but is being blackmailed by the real killer. *Experiment with Death* (1981) is set at the King's Weltham Institute of Pomology, a scientific organization whose director is murdered. All sorts of personal problems of staff members are exposed, including alcoholism, drug selling, and wife beating. Dr. Emma Ritchie, who researches the effects of carbon dioxide on apple storage, is an attractive character who, through an understanding of her colleagues and their families, discovers the truth.

In her recent books Ferrars has created several recurring characters. *Last Will and Testament* (1978) introduces the charming-but-separated couple, Virginia and Felix Freer. Now working as a physiotherapist in the town of Allingford, Virginia is surprised by the arrival of Felix. Although pleasant company, a good cook, and quite domesticated, he is also a con man, and Virginia fears that any gift he brings is stolen. Nevertheless, after the death of an elderly friend and several murders in the neighborhood, she is glad enough that he is there. Virginia, visiting friends Helen and Andrew Boscott, is surprised when Felix arrives at their house in *Frog in the Throat* (1980). Her pleasure in his company is mixed with dread of what new complications he may bring into her life. They attend a cocktail party and meet two sisters who write popular novels under the name Carola Fyffe. One sister is murdered, but Felix solves the crime through creative intuition about as quickly as the police solve it through more conventional methods. Virginia and Felix are wedding guests at the second marriage of an old friend, Gavin Brownlow, in *Thinner than Water* (1981). They had also been present at his first wedding. The groom's father, who did not attend the wedding, is found murdered when the Brownlow family returns home. Felix tries to figure out who is responsible, while Virginia prides herself on preventing him from stealing a Steuben owl he fancies. Felix and Virginia are invited to a farewell party for a friend in *Death of a Minor Character* (1983). The party is held in their

old neighborhood, Little Carberry Street, a London setting Ferrars used in earlier books. Given their history, it is remarkable that any of their friends would invite both Virginia and Felix to the same party: murders ensue, and old crimes are revealed. Virginia is invited to Sunday lunch by Ann Brightwell, a former patient who has inherited some valuable paintings in *I Met Murder* (1985). When Virginia reads in an obituary that Sara Noble, a famous actress and cousin of Ann's, has died "peacefully," she immediately considers the alternative, then thinks: "I had a feeling that this was getting rather close to Hegel. I am very ignorant of philosophy, but I was fairly sure that some good, solid German had stated that anything you say must imply its opposite." A reviewer in the *New Yorker* (18 August 1986) wrote: "Degas is quoted, a French painting is admired, and a quiche is consumed, but the title of this slight, tidy mystery alludes to a poem by Shelley, and the character who solves it–Felix Freer, a petty thief and chronic liar who commutes between a Fox & Grapes and a Rose & Crown; who is not above sharing his estranged wife's roof, joint of lamb, and tea when it suits him; and who compares their alliance unfavorably with that of the Macbeths–is English to the core."

Andrew Basnett, a retired botany professor, was introduced in *Something Wicked* (1983). While his London apartment was being redecorated he decided to stay in his nephew's cottage in the village of Godlingham and work on his book about Hooke, the seventeenth-century natural philosopher. A blizzard cuts off power to the village, and a murder is committed. Although eager to go home, Andrew solves the crime. Andrew combines traits of Ferrars and her husband: "Robert, like Andrew, walks around the house in his socks and I'm the one who, like Andrew, endlessly memorizes and quotes bad verse" (*Publishers Weekly*, 25 October 1985). Invited to spend a quiet Easter at the home of his old friend Felicity Silvester in *Root of All Evil* (1984), Andrew finds his hostess murdered. In *The Crime and the Crystal* (1985) Andrew is spending the Christmas holidays in Australia with a former student when a murder is committed on Christmas Day. Andrew, who acts as a catalyst as much as he detects, gets the facts out in the open. In *The Other Devil's Name* (1986) Andrew, wearing a dressing gown and socks but no shoes, answers his door one morning to find his old friend and colleague Constance Camm, who asks his advice. Once again he gets involved with murder. In *A Murder Too Many* (1988) he attends a scientific meeting at a university where he had taught as a young man. A friend confides his worry that an innocent man may have been sent to prison for murder, and the old man reluctantly questions various people who (somewhat surprisingly) answer his questions. After much fretful cogitation he figures out who committed the murders and why. In each book he makes no progress on his study of Hooke, tearing up as many pages as he writes. Ferrars may have observed this habit in others, but certainly it cannot be one of hers.

Over the years Ferrars has written numerous short stories which have appeared in *Ellery Queen's Mystery Magazine* and have been included in anthologies such as *Winter's Crimes*. Nine of her stories, first published between 1940 and 1976, have been collected in a volume entitled *Designs on Life* (1980). She contributed two chapters to the collaborative, round-robin story *Crime on the Coast and No Flowers by Request* (1984), which first appeared as a serial in the British *News Chronicle*, and is the editor of a collection of stories called *Planned Departures* (1958).

Ferrars has produced an impressive collection of crime novels and short stories. Called traditional–probably because of the settings, the upper-middle-class characters, and the civilized reticence about sex and violence–Ferrars's books differ substantially from those of Golden Age authors such as Marjorie Allingham, Agatha Christie, Dorothy L. Sayers, or Ngaio Marsh. In the classic mystery, society is stable and, at least among the privileged classes who populate the stories, crime is an aberration which must be exorcised. In Ferrars's books things do not return to normal when a criminal is caught; her characters are changed by the intrusion of murder into their lives. Baker declares that "Ferrars finally creates a rather grim world, and her books leave a reader uneasy and wary rather than comfortably reassured. For this reason, Ferrars–more than Christie or Sayers–should be seen as a significant predecessor of the new generation of female British mystery writers, such as P. D. James and Ruth Rendell." It is significant that Ferrars began publishing crime fiction in the 1940s, two decades after the Golden Age began. While some of her characters would fit comfortably into stories by those other writers, Ferrars has a darker–and no doubt more realistic–view of human nature. Murder is catastrophic and has consequences that change lives.

Ferrars's characters are developed in greater depth than in many other writers' crime fiction. She is highly skilled in detailing the personal quirks, preferences, and opinions of her protagonists. Sometimes she is criticized for creating characters that are "too ordinary"–though her characters are neither dull nor uninteresting. Many of her readers are undoubtedly rather ordinary themselves and can identify with her fictional creations, who seem more amusing than reality. Another criticism compares her stories with soap opera, but this is not accurate since the majority of her books are carefully and cleverly constructed, unlike the open-ended stories found in television serials.

Ferrars has chronicled the times and places she knows best: London in the years preceding World War II, the war years, and the decades that follow; English villages, Bloomsbury, Madeira, and Australia. She is especially known for the social settings she evokes so skillfully. Frequently her characters are members of research institutions and universities, extended families, friends in small communities, or journalists or writers of one sort or another. Her understanding of human nature shows in her characters who are believable because they embody the complex and confusing mixture of good and evil found in real people. Although she writes about the darker side of human nature, she does so with humor and a finely developed irony.

A gentle satirist of many of the institutions of her society, Elizabeth Ferrars has been entertaining a large audience for almost half a century. In quantity and in quality, her work establishes her as one of the outstanding writers of mystery fiction today.

References:

Susan Baker, "E. X. Ferrars," in *And Then There Were Nine: More Women of Mystery*, edited by Jane S. Bakerman (Bowling Green, Ohio: Bowling Green University Popular Press, 1985), pp. 146-167;

Rosemary Herbert, "The Cosy Side of Murder," *Publishers Weekly* (25 October 1985): 20-32;

H. R. F. Keating, *Whodunit?* (London: Windward, 1982), p. 157;

Marvin Lachman, "It's About Crime," *Mystery FANcier* (January-February 1984): 17.

Ian Fleming

(28 May 1908-12 August 1964)

Joan DelFattore
University of Delaware

BOOKS: *Casino Royale* (London: Cape, 1953; New York: Macmillan, 1954); republished as *You Asked for It* (New York: Popular Library, 1955);

Live and Let Die (London: Cape, 1954; New York: Macmillan, 1955);

Moonraker (London: Cape, 1955; New York: Macmillan, 1955); republished as *Too Hot to Handle* (New York: Permabooks, 1957);

Diamonds Are Forever (London: Cape, 1956; New York: Macmillan, 1956);

From Russia, with Love (London: Cape, 1957; New York: Macmillan, 1957);

The Diamond Smugglers (London: Cape, 1957; New York: Macmillan, 1958);

Dr. No (London: Cape, 1958); republished as *Doctor No* (New York: Macmillan, 1958);

Goldfinger (London: Cape, 1959; New York: Macmillan, 1959);

For Your Eyes Only: Five Secret Occasions in the Life of James Bond (London: Cape, 1960); republished as *For Your Eyes Only: Five Secret Exploits of James Bond* (New York: Viking, 1960);

Thunderball (London: Cape, 1961; New York: Viking, 1961);

The Spy Who Loved Me (London: Cape, 1962; New York: Viking, 1962);

On Her Majesty's Secret Service (London: Cape, 1963; New York: New American Library, 1963);

Thrilling Cities (London: Cape, 1963; New York: New American Library, 1964);

You Only Live Twice (London: Cape, 1964; New York: New American Library, 1964);

Chitty-Chitty-Bang-Bang (3 volumes, London: Cape, 1964-1965; 1 volume, New York: Random House, 1964);

The Man with the Golden Gun (London: Cape, 1965; New York: New American Library, 1965);

Octopussy, and The Living Daylights (London: Cape, 1966); republished as *Octopussy* (New York: New American Library, 1966).

Portrait of Ian Fleming by Amherst Villiers used as the frontispiece to a 1963 limited edition of Fleming's twelfth James Bond novel, On Her Majesty's Secret Service

MOTION PICTURE: *Thunderball*, screenplay by Fleming, Kevin McClory, and Jack Whittingham, United Artists, 1965.

OTHER: Herbert O. Yardley, *The Education of a Poker Player*, introduction by Fleming (London: Cape, 1959), pp. 7-9;

Hugh Edwards, *All Night at Mr. Stanyhurst's*, introduction by Fleming (London: Cape, 1963), pp. vii-xx;

"The Property of a Lady," in *The Ivory Hammer: The Year at Sotheby's*, by Frank Davis and others (London: Longmans, Green, 1963; New York: Holt, 1964);

"Introducing Jamaica," in *Ian Fleming Introduces Jamaica,* edited by Morris Cargill (London: Deutsch, 1965; New York: Hawthorn Books, 1966).

PERIODICAL PUBLICATIONS: "Raymond Chandler," *London Magazine* (December 1959): 43-54;

"James Bond's Hardware," *Sunday Times* (London), 18 November 1962, pp. 18-22.

Ian Fleming was the creator of James Bond, the most popular hero of espionage fiction in the late 1950s and the 1960s. Bond, whose name still suggests a certain type of spy-hero–sophisticated, sexy, glamorously dangerous–is particularly well known because of the James Bond film series, which exaggerates the guns-gadgets-and-girls aspect of Fleming's original stories.

Ian Lancaster Fleming, the second son of Valentine Fleming and Evelyn Beatrice Ste. Croix Rose, was born in the elegant and expensive London district of Mayfair. His birth certificate describes his father's occupation as "of independent means"; his paternal grandfather, who had founded the prosperous London banking firm of Robert Fleming and Company, was a multimillionaire. Fleming's mother's family claimed descent from John of Gaunt, fourth son of King Edward III and founder of the royal house of Lancaster–hence Fleming's middle name.

Fleming was nine years old when his father, who was then a major in the Oxfordshire Hussars, was killed by a German shell at Gillemont Farm in Picardy, France. Valentine Fleming's will left his entire estate to his wife in such a way that she could, if she wished, disinherit any of their sons, and during her lifetime she had absolute control over all of the income from her late husband's fortune. As a result, Ian Fleming, who survived his mother by less than a month, coveted but never enjoyed the luxury of inherited wealth. Throughout his life he associated with wealthy and class-conscious people, in part because of family connections but largely by choice. Perhaps because he had less money and less leisure than many of his friends, he made a point of stressing quality, exclusiveness, and singularity in clothing, food, wine, and recreational activities. James Bond's much-discussed snobbery and his some-

what eccentric epicureanism derive primarily from this source.

Fleming's formal education began when, at the age of eight, he was sent to Durnford School on the Isle of Purbeck, near Corfe Castle. Its headmaster, Tom Pellatt, placed great emphasis on the cult of physical toughness, which was to become an important part of Fleming's self-image and a primary characteristic of his fictional hero. The boys at Durnford School bathed naked in a cold natural pool every morning, ate large quantities of unpalatable food, bullied one another, played rough games, and roamed freely around the countryside. Academic work was not stressed, and Fleming was, in any case, uninterested in it.

After five years at Durnford, Fleming was sent to Eton, where he continued to do mediocre academic work. His performance at team sports, which were an important part of life at Eton, was uneven because of his erratic and unsocial behavior and because his desire to display ruggedness and courage gave his play a kamikaze quality which was sometimes breathtaking but often ineffective. However, he consistently excelled in field sports such as racing and hurdling, and in 1925, at the age of sixteen, he won almost every event in the school competition: the 220-yard, quarter-mile, half-mile, and mile races, the hurdles, the long jump, throwing the cricket ball, and the steeplechase. In 1925 and again in 1926 he was Victor Ludorum (Champion of the Games).

Despite his athletic accomplishments Fleming's personal eccentricities brought him into conflict with his housemaster, E. V. Slater, who was old-fashioned in his ideas and abrupt in his manner. Slater was annoyed by Fleming's use of strongly-scented hair oil and by his habit of eating late breakfasts at a local inn. At a time when British schoolboys were expected to be keen, lively, and straightforward, Fleming affected to be bored, languid, and Byronesque. Finally he enraged Slater by keeping a car, which was forbidden, and a mistress, which was insupportable. Mrs. Fleming was persuaded to remove him from Eton a term early to send him to study with a Colonel Trevor, who specialized in helping boys to "cram" for the Sandhurst entrance examination.

Mrs. Fleming's decision to send Fleming to the Royal Military College (now the Royal Military Academy) at Sandhurst rather than to Oxford was based partly on his academic mediocrity and partly on his evident need for discipline. She was anxious to see all of her sons settled in respect-

Telegrams : " Guinpen, Piccy, London."
Telephone : Regent 1998

GROSVENOR STREET

23 CONDUIT STREET, LONDON, W.1.

Ian Fleming Esq.,   18th June. 1935.
    118, Cheyne Walk,
        CHELSEA.   S. W. 3.

To Elkin Mathews Ltd.
Booksellers
Directors : A. W. Evans, Hon. R. E. Gathorne-Hardy, H. V. Marrot, P. H. Muir, Camilla Washington

The Earl of Cranbrook   NET

EINSTEIN	Uber einen der Erzeugung u. Verwandlung.	5	5	-	
"	Einheitliche Feldtheorie.		10	-	
"	Riemann-geometrie mit aufrechterhalting.		10	-	
"	Einheitliche Feldtheorie v. Gravitation.		18	-	
"	Allgemeine Relativitatstheorie.		18	-	
"	Zur einheitlichen Feldtheorie.		10	-	
"	Neue Moglichkeit f. eine einheitliche Feldtheorie.		10	-	
"	Ather u. Relativitatstheorie.		18	-	
"	Die Grundlage der allgemeinen Relativitatstheorie.	1	5	-	
		11	4	-	
	Less 10%	1	2	5	10 1
CLIMATE:	Vol. 111. Oct. 1901. No. 9.	1	10	-	
ANGELL:	The Great Illusion	1	10	-	
ANSTEY:	Vica Versa	3	10	-	
PLIMSOLL:	Our Seaman	1	10	-	
RUSSELL:	The Atlantic Telegraph	2	-	-	
JANE:	All the World's Airships	4	-	-	
CONDITIONS:	of Peace	5	-	-	
KIPLING:	Rewards and Fairies	1	10	-	
"	Barrack-room Ballads	1	10	-	
ELIOT:	The Waste Land	4	10	-	
MACKENZIE:	Extraordinary Women	1	1	-	
"	Vestal Fire		12	6	
BATESON:	Mendel's Principles of Heredity	1	5	-	
CURIE:	Theses.	8	10	-	
"	Recherches	1	5	-	
GRAY:	The Early Treatment of War Wounds		3	6	
RONTGEN:	Eine neue art von Strahlen	2	-	-	
EHRKICH & HATA:	Experimental Chemotherapy of Spirilloses.		4	6	
MOORE:	Omnibuses & Cabs		16	-	
ACCUM:	Practical Treatise on Gas-light	1	10	-	
LETTER:	to a Member of Parliament from W. Murdock	1	10	-	
PITMAN:	Dhonography	2	-	-	
STRACHEY	Eminent Victorians	3	-	-	
GOEBEL:	Friedrich Koenig	1	15	-	52 2 6
					£ 62 4 1

Invoice for books purchased by Fleming for his western civilization collection (courtesy of Lilly Library, Indiana University, Bloomington, Indiana)

Goldeneye, Fleming's home in Oracabessa, Jamaica, where he wrote his novels

able positions in life, and she thought that a prestigious regiment would be the best place for him. After passing the entrance examination creditably, Fleming was enrolled as a gentleman cadet. Predictably, he responded well to the physical training and poorly to the discipline. He was finally caught climbing over the Sandhurst wall after an evening with a girl in Camberley and was severely disciplined. He decided that army life was not congenial to him and declined to take up his commission.

During the summer before his entrance into Sandhurst, Fleming had visited the Tennerhof, an experimental educational community located in Kitzbühel, in the Austrian alps. The Tennerhof was run by Ernan and Phyllis Forbes-Dennis, who attempted to put into practice the psychological theories of Alfred Adler in dealing with troubled young adults. They also provided a sophisticated and challenging academic program. After leaving Sandhurst, Fleming returned to the Tennerhof for a year. There he dramatized himself as a romantic young Englishman who, having quarreled with his commanding officer over a point of honor and given up a promising military career, was in terrible disgrace with his wealthy and influential family. His looks, charm, and reputation made him a favorite with the Austrian girls; in fact, his amorous affairs almost led to his explusion from the Tennerhof, where the conservative Forbes-Dennises were appalled to learn of his behavior. After a tearful scene of repentence, however, he was allowed to remain.

At the Tennerhof, Fleming became an avid mountain-climber and skier, partly for the sake of the exercise and partly because he loved danger and tests of endurance. He also succeeded in setting for himself an academic goal which

stretched his abilities and thereby held his interest: preparing for the Foreign Office examination. Phyllis Forbes-Dennis, who wrote fiction under her maiden name, Phyllis Bottome, also encouraged Fleming to develop his skills as a creative writer. The only extant Fleming story from this period, "Death on Two Occasions," has never been published.

After a year at the Tennerhof, Fleming went to Munich to live with a German family and to attend lectures at the University of Munich. His German improved, and he began to study Russian. From Munich Fleming went to Geneva, where he studied at the University of Geneva and improved his French. In 1931 he was one of sixty-two candidates who sat for the ten-day Foreign Office examination. He claimed, later in life, that he had ranked seventh in a year when there were only five vacancies; in fact, there were three vacancies, and Fleming ranked twenty-fifth.

While he was at the University of Geneva Fleming became engaged to a French-Swiss girl named Monrique de Mestral. However, Fleming's mother felt that the girl was not a suitable match for her son, and, since Fleming's failure to qualify for a position in the Foreign Office had left him without the means to support a wife, the engagement was broken. Family influence and his own appearance and bearing helped Fleming to secure a position at Reuters news agency, but because he was being trained he received only a nominal salary of three hundred pounds a year. This meant, of course, that Fleming was forced to live with his mother in her Chelsea home. After the independence that he had enjoyed abroad Fleming found this a difficult adjustment to make, and his lifelong determination to acquire enough money to live as he liked became stronger.

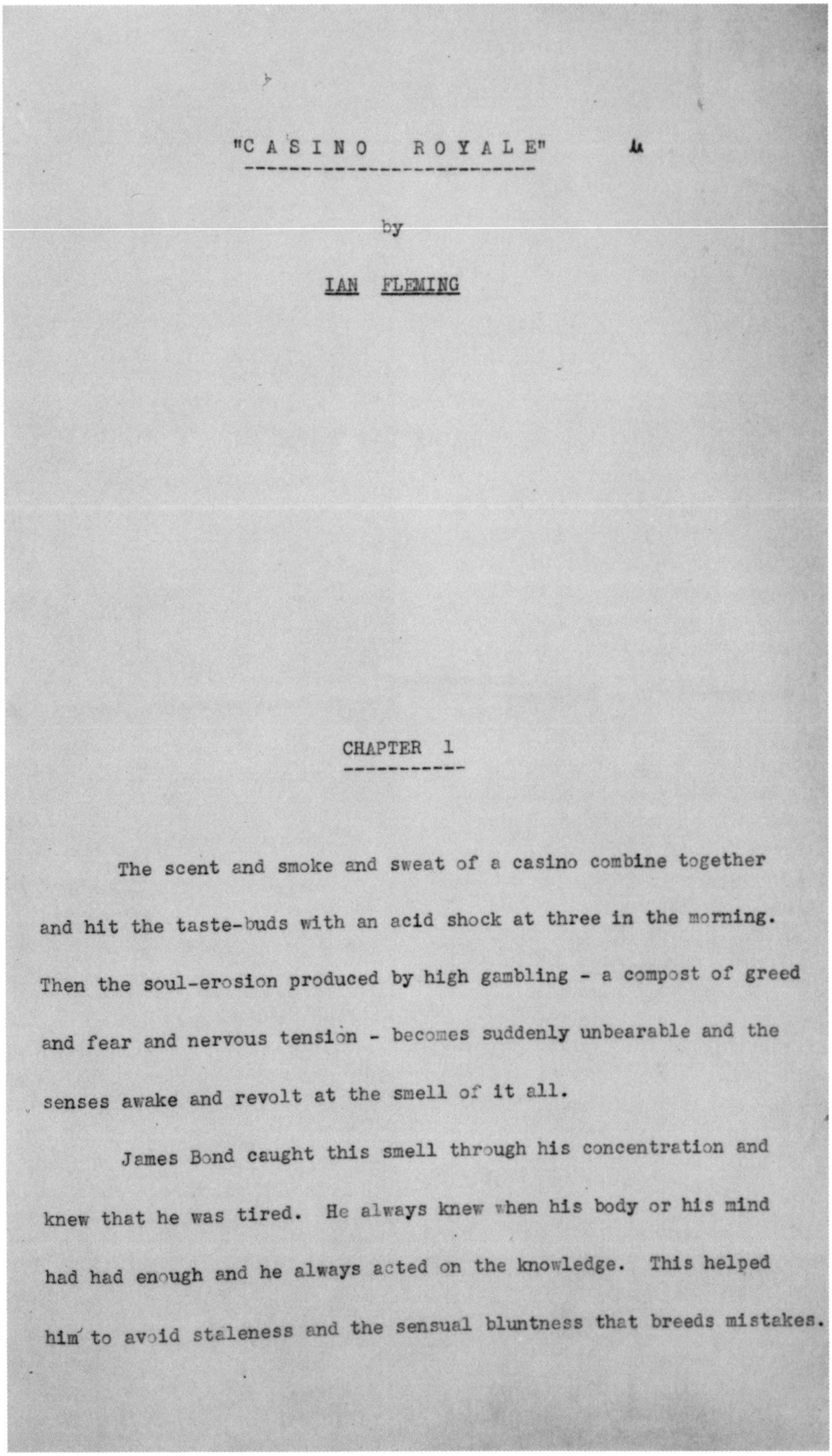

"C A S I N O   R O Y A L E"

by

IAN FLEMING

CHAPTER 1

The scent and smoke and sweat of a casino combine together

and hit the taste-buds with an acid shock at three in the morning.

Then the soul-erosion produced by high gambling - a compost of greed

and fear and nervous tension - becomes suddenly unbearable and the

senses awake and revolt at the smell of it all.

James Bond caught this smell through his concentration and

knew that he was tired. He always knew when his body or his mind

had had enough and he always acted on the knowledge. This helped

him to avoid staleness and the sensual bluntness that breeds mistakes.

Typescript page from Fleming's first novel, Casino Royale *(courtesy of the Manuscript Division, Lilly Library, Indiana University, Bloomington, Indiana)*

The highlight of Fleming's brief career (1931 to 1933) at Reuters was his assignment to cover the Moscow trial of six British engineers, employees of the Metropolitan-Vickers Electrical Company, who had been accused of espionage and sabotage. Fleming's knowledge of the language allowed him to converse with Russian nationals, and, in addition to doing a creditable job of covering the trial, he acquired firsthand information about Moscow which was to be useful in a later assignment. He also requested an interview with Joseph Stalin, who sent him an autographed letter of refusal which became one of his most treasured possessions.

In 1933 Fleming's grandfather, Robert Fleming, died. Ian Fleming, believing that his father had, perhaps unintentionally, done his sons an injustice in leaving all of the income from his fortune to his widow, assumed that Robert Fleming would rectify this injustice by bequeathing some of his own wealth to Valentine's sons. However, Robert Fleming left his entire fortune of three million pounds in trust for his widow. It was then to pass to his surviving son, Valentine's brother Philip. Shortly after the reading of his grandfather's will Fleming was offered the post of assistant-general manager of the Far Eastern division of Reuters at a salary of eight hundred pounds per year. Knowing that his salary as an employee of Reuters would never be a great deal higher and that no inherited income was forthcoming, he refused on the grounds that "I wouldn't be able to keep up with the Joneses of Singapore." He left Reuters in order to take up a career in business, which he hoped would prove to be more remunerative. His first position was with a firm of merchant bankers, Cull and Company. Two years later he joined a firm of stockbrokers, Rowe and Pitman, as a junior partner. His income suddenly rose to over two thousand pounds annually, and he was able to afford a home of his own.

Fleming's first home was a converted Baptist chapel on Ebury Street, which he decorated in gray, dark blue, and black. He began to entertain quite frequently, particularly a group of friends to which he gave the title *Le Cercle gastronomique et des jeux de hasard*. He also began to collect books, encasing them in expensive black boxes with which he lined the windowless walls of the converted nave which served as his living room. Percy Muir, a noted expert on rare books, located for Fleming first editions of works which introduced significant new discoveries in sci-

Dust jacket designed by Fleming for the first British edition of Casino Royale

ence, medicine, and the history of ideas. The Ian Fleming Collection of 19th-20th Century Source Material Concerning Western Civilization, which is now in the Lilly Library at Indiana University, includes such works as a copy of Madame Curie's 1903 doctoral dissertation on the isolation of radium and a copy of Sigmund Freud's *Die Traumdeutung* (1900; translated as *The Interpretation of Dreams*, 1913).

Fleming was a noted womanizer. He attributed his ruthlessness with women to his mother's domineering nature and, in particular, to her refusal to allow him to marry Monrique de Mestral. Others thought that he never actually knew a woman in any but the carnal sense. John Pearson's 1966 biography of Fleming quotes one of his mistresses who says that "he looked on women just as a schoolboy does, as remote, mysterious beings. He could never hope to understand them, but if he was lucky he felt he might occasionally shoot one down." Fleming's attitude toward women is surely one of the reasons for the uneven quality of James Bond's relationships with the female characters in his novels.

In 1939 Fleming was given an opportunity to interrupt his routine as a junior partner at Rowe and Pitman for the purpose of accompanying a British trade mission to Russia and Poland. Ostensibly, Fleming was covering the event as a representative of the *London Times;* in fact, he was preparing a report for the Foreign Office on anything he observed that might help the British assess Russia's potential usefulness as an ally in the war which was now imminent. Fleming was chosen for this assignment because of his knowledge of Russian, his experience as a journalist, and the insights and acquaintances he had acquired during his previous visit to Moscow. This assignment, in turn, helped to bring about one of the most important events of his life: his appointment as personal assistant to the director of Naval Intelligence during World War II.

Adm. Sir Reginald Hall, director of Naval Intelligence during World War I, had employed as his personal assistant a former stockbroker, Claude Serocold, whose experience had made him invaluable as a complement to the career military men around him. Hall suggested to Adm. John Godfrey, the new director of Naval Intelligence, that he should look for someone with a similar background to serve as his own personal assistant. Godfrey consulted the governor of the Bank of England, Montagu Norman, who undertook an intensive but confidential survey of the records of promising young men in London's business world. Norman finally suggested only one candidate, Fleming. Godfrey, having interviewed Fleming, had him commissioned as a lieutenant in the Naval Reserve and assigned to the Department of Naval Intelligence. Fleming was later promoted to commander, the rank that he eventually assigned to James Bond.

In 1941 Fleming accompanied Godfrey to the United States for the purpose of establishing relations with the American intelligence services. In New York he met Sir William Stephenson, "the quiet Canadian," who became a lifelong friend. Stephenson allowed Fleming to take part in a clandestine operation against a Japanese cipher expert who had an office in Rockefeller Center, and Fleming later embellished this story and used it in his first James Bond novel, *Casino Royale* (1953; republished as *You Asked for It,* 1955). Stephenson also introduced Fleming to

Fleming, circa 1954

Gen. William Donovan, who had just been appointed Coordinator of Information and who later became director of the U.S. Office of Strategic Services. At Donovan's request Fleming wrote a lengthy memorandum describing the structure and functions of a secret service organization, and parts of this memorandum were later included in the charter of the OSS. In appreciation, Donovan presented Fleming with a .38 Police Positive Colt revolver inscribed "For Special Services." Fleming later wove a number of fantasies around this weapon, suggesting that the services for which he had received it had been of a violent character.

Fleming visited North America again later in the war to prepare a report on Stephenson's training school for secret agents located in Oshawa, Ontario. He took part in the training course himself and did extremely well. One of his assignments was to swim underwater at night to a derelict vessel moored in a lake, attach an inactive limpet mine to its hull, and escape without being seen. The story of that swim, suitably embroidered, became one of the most important scenes in Fleming's second Bond novel, *Live and Let Die* (1954). He also succeeded in planting a dummy bomb in the Toronto power station under the eyes of guards who had been warned that this "attack" was to take place. Other trainees from Stephenson's school tried to sneak into the power station and failed. Fleming telephoned the managing director for an appointment, representing himself as a member of a British engineering firm, and walked in–and out–without question.

At the end of the training course, Stephenson told Fleming that the intelligence services had located a spy in a Toronto hotel, and ordered him to burst into the hotel room and shoot the spy without giving him a chance to draw his own gun. The occupant of the hotel room was actually a former member of the Shanghai Water Police who made a profession of surviving such attempts on his life. The presence of a live target and the use of live ammunition gave the exercise the verisimilitude necessary to allow Stephenson to determine which of his trainees were capable of killing a man in cold blood. Fleming was not. He got as far as the landing outside the hotel room, but, after a long pause, he turned and left. Stephenson and Fleming's fellow trainees were very amused and not very sympathetic, and Fleming found the experience intensely embarrassing. After the war he occasionally confided to one or another of his friends (as a matter of great secrecy) that he had once had to kill a man in the line of duty. The circumstances surrounding this alleged killing varied considerably, although the discrepancies were never noted during Fleming's lifetime because the friends to whom he told the story kept it in confidence. Most of these fantasies eventually appeared in the Bond books, along with the central fantasy of a man who, licensed to kill in cold blood, dislikes doing so but always succeeds.

One of Fleming's most exciting assignments during World War II was the command of Number 30 Assault Unit, which he called "My Red Indians." It was modeled on a German unit under Obersturmbandführer Otto Skorzeny, which went into captured areas with the first wave of troops and gathered up all available intelligence materials. As the Allies advanced across North Africa and then across Europe, he determined the nature and location of intelligence material and directed his commandos to it. On the whole the unit carried out its tasks so well that it was eventually removed from Fleming's control and placed under the direct command of Adm. Sir Bertram Ramsay.

In 1944 Fleming was sent to Kingston, Jamaica, to attend a conference. He was accompanied by his friend Ivar Bryce, who had a home in Jamaica. The weather was miserable, but in spite of the rain Fleming was so enchanted with Jamaica that he asked Bryce to find him a piece of land on which to build a house. Bryce located a suitable place on the bay at Oracabessa, and after the war Fleming built a house which he called Goldeneye. It was there that he wrote the James Bond novels.

After his discharge from the Navy in 1945 Fleming returned to journalism as manager of the foreign news service for the Kemsley (later Thomson) newspapers, including the *London Sunday Times*. Before accepting Kemsley's offer, however, he insisted on a guarantee of a two-month paid vacation so that he could spend January and February of each year at Goldeneye. Fleming remained in this position for most of the rest of his life, although his power and prestige gradually declined through the 1950s because of internal economy measures and because of the inability of his foreign news service to compete with organizations such as UPI, AP, and Reuters. In 1953 Fleming also became "Atticus," a post once held by an earlier writer of espionage fiction, John Buchan. As Atticus he wrote a weekly column of more or less sophisticated gossip.

In 1946 Fleming, experiencing pain and a sensation of tightness in his chest, visited a cardiologist. Two years later, he suffered a recurrence of the chest pain along with kidney trouble. He was smoking between sixty and seventy cigarettes a day and drinking inordinate quantities of gin. Despite his gradually failing health Fleming remained physically active, particularly during the part of the year that he spent in Jamaica. He greatly enjoyed underwater swimming, and he took a personal interest in the fauna in the bay at Oracabessa. He called one unusually friendly octopus Pussy Galore, a name which he later gave to a character in *Goldfinger* (1959).

Fleming's Jamaican property was very beautiful, with a large garden, a private beach, and an unobstructed view across the bay, but the house itself was uncomfortable. At Goldeneye Fleming combined his penchant for physical ruggedness with a desire for expensive singularity which bordered upon eccentricity. For most of the time that he owned the house it had no telephone and no hot water, and the living room had a blue concrete floor which the native servants polished with slices of orange, with the result that the resi-

Fleming with a copy of the American edition of his first novel (photograph by Maurey Garber)

dents' bare feet were always sticky. A narrow banquette ran around three sides of the dining room table, cutting into the diners' thighs, and the food was abominable, although Fleming always insisted that it was delightfully plain Jamaican cooking.

In 1946 one of Fleming's guests at Goldeneye was Anne Rothermere, née Charteris, granddaughter of the eleventh Earl of Wemyss and wife of Fleming's friend Viscount Esmond Rothermere. She and Fleming had carried on a casual romance before and during the war, but during her visit to Goldeneye they began to feel seriously attracted to one another. They continued to meet, and in 1951 Viscount Rothermere sued for divorce, naming Fleming as co-respondent. His wife did not contest the action. When Fleming went to Goldeneye for his annual holiday in January 1952 she went with him to await the final divorce decree.

The period of waiting which Rothermere and Fleming endured at Goldeneye that winter was, naturally, a time of great tension. She found relief in painting. Fleming, who had been talking

for years about writing what he called "the spy story to end all spy stories," finally decided to try it. For three hours every morning and for two hours every afternoon he interrupted his Goldeneye routine of swimming and sunbathing to record the first adventure of James Bond, namesake of a well-known ornithologist whose *Birds of the West Indies* (1936) was one of Fleming's favorite books.

Fleming chose this rather plain name because, admiring W. Somerset Maugham's Ashenden stories and the novels of Graham Greene and Eric Ambler, he originally intended to write realistic espionage fiction centering around the type of featureless gray protagonist that those authors often used. However, his vivid imagination and love of the dramatic, combined with the self-imposed pressure of producing a new Bond novel every year, led him into giving Bond a number of personal idiosyncracies and into placing him in thoroughly improbable situations. As a result, his books never approached those of Maugham, Ambler, and Greene in realism, depth, or complexity. He wrote, not for the sake

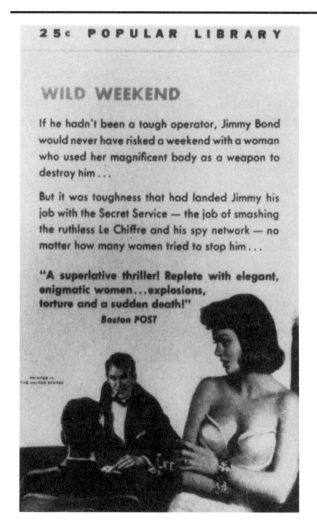 

Front and back covers of the first American paperback edition of Casino Royale

of making thematic statements or contributing to the development of a genre, but for the sake of entertaining himself and his readers and making a great deal of money. However, it is hardly fair to conclude, as some critics have done, that Fleming's work has no merit at all. The James Bond novels are, unquestionably, popular formula fiction rather than great—or even good–literature, and at their worst they are improbable, repetitive, and abominably structured. However, at their best they are entertaining, spectacularly imaginative, and highly readable. A reviewer for the *Daily Telegraph* (26 April 1955) observed that Fleming's third novel, *Moonraker* (1955; republished as *Too Hot to Handle*, 1957) was "A fantastic piece of nonsense. I didn't believe a word of it. But I couldn't put the book down until it was finished."

Because Bond's physical appearance is modeled on Fleming's own–a tall and lean man with black hair, gray eyes, and high cheekbones–and because his adventures include romanticized versions of events in which Fleming is known to have participated, the question of Fleming's identification of Bond with himself, or with an idealized concept of himself, naturally arises. In some respects Bond does externalize Fleming's drives and fantasies: he enjoys the finest food and drink, makes love to the most beautiful and affectionate women, and defeats the most fiendish villains. On the other hand, Bond is unquestionably a fictional creation, consciously and deliberately developed, whom Fleming manipulated according to the requirements of his plots and, later, in response to critical observations and popular demand. Bond's accomplishments do reflect a vivid wish-fulfillment fantasy that arose, to some extent, from his experiences; but, as Fleming's fan mail suggests, similar fantasies are equally vivid in the minds of many readers. Fleming knew

["yebionna mat!" The gross obscenity was a favourite
with General G. His hand slapped down on the desk.
CHAPTER SIX. [DEATH WARRANT

~~Bondih~~ General G's hand slapped down on the desk. 'Comrade,

there certainly is 'a man called Bond' as you put it' His voice
'James Bond. (he pronounced it 'Jems)
was sarcastic. ∧ 'And nobody, myself included, could think of this

spy's name! We are indeed forgetful . No wonder the Intelligence

Apparat is under criticism.'

    General Vozdveshensky felt he should def~~end~~ himself and his

department. 'There are countless enemies of the Soviet Union,

Comrade ˇeneral' he protested. If I want their names, I send to ~~the~~ The
Central Index
~~Records Department~~ for them. Certainly I know ~~this~~ the name of this

/Bond˙. He has been a great trouble to us at different times. But
                                        --names of
today my ~~name~~ mind is full of other names/~~of~~ people who are

causing us trouble today, this week. ~~One cannot remember~~ I am

interested in football, but I cannot remember the names of every

foreigner who has scored a goal against the ~~D~~ Dynamos.'

    ~~Nikitin was not to be cowed~~ 'ˇou are pleased to joke, Comrade!.

said ˇeneral G to underline this out of place comment, ~~but~~ 'This
                                      for one
is a serious matter and ˇ/admit my fault in not remembering the
                notorious
name of this ~~famous~~ agent. Comrade Colonel Nikitin will no doubt

refresh our memories further, but I recall that this Bond had

at least twice frustrated the operations of SMERSH. That is'

he added ~~quickly~~,' before I ~~became~~ assumed control of the

Department. There was this affair in France, at that Casino town.

The man Le Chiffre. An excellent leader of the ˇParty in France.

Hefoolishly got into some money troubles. But he would have got

out of them if this man Bond had not interfered. ~~I had to make~~

I recall that the Department had to act quickly and liquidate ~~him~~

the Frenchman. The executioner should have dealt with the Englishman

at the same time , but he did not. Then there was this negro of

ours in ˇarlem. A great man -- one of the greatest foreign agents

we have ever employed, and with a vast network behind him. There

was some business about a treasure in the ˇaribbean, I forget the

details. ~~But~~ This Englishamn was sent out by the Secret Service

and smashed the whole organisation and killed our man. It was a

great reverse, and again my predecessor should have proceeded

Revised typescript page for Fleming's fifth James Bond novel, From Russia, with Love, *one of his favorites among his books
(courtesy of the Manuscript Division, Lilly Library, Indiana University, Bloomington, Indiana)*

that, and he exploited it consciously and skillfully. As a result, although the Bond novels romanticize incidents from Fleming's life and dwell on wish-fulfillment fantasies, the autobiographical and psychological elements in these books are quite deliberate and, for the most part, superficial.

Among the romanticized autobiographical incidents in Fleming's first novel is an epic baccarat game between Bond and the villain, Le Chiffre, which was suggested by an occasion during World War II when Fleming, visiting Lisbon with Godfrey on navy business, tried to defeat a group of Portuguese gamblers at baccarat. In the real-life game the Portuguese soundly beat Fleming, but that was, of course, one of the details that he altered when he turned the event into fiction. Other adapted real-life events in *Casino Royale* include Bond's number, 007, which is based on a classification system formerly used by Whitehall to designate top-secret documents. The scene in which two Bulgar assassins blow themselves up in an attempt to murder Bond is based on an identical failure on the part of two assassins who tried to murder Franz von Papen in Ankara during World War II, and Bond's killing of a Japanese cipher expert is based on the much less violent operation in which Fleming had participated in New York in 1941.

Shortly after he finished *Casino Royale* Fleming and Anne Rothermere were married in the town hall at Port Maria, Jamaica, with Noel Coward as principal witness. The next day Fleming flew to New York with his wife and the completed typescript of his novel. A few months later he gave the typescript to a friend, William Plomer, an author and one of the readers for Jonathan Cape, who passed it along to other readers. They liked the book, and it was scheduled for publication in the spring of 1953. About this time Anne gave birth to a son, Caspar.

Fleming made a number of changes in the typescript before the book was published, particularly in the style. He divided compound sentences into simple ones and replaced general terms such as "the middle of the week" with specific terms such as "Tuesday." He also eliminated some of the more obvious clichés; for example, he replaced "or I'll eat my hat" with "if I'm not mistaken." Far fewer changes of this kind were necessary in the typescripts of the later books, but he did have to make changes in the typescripts of all his books to correct at least some of his numerous errors of fact. In *Casino Royale*, for example,

he had to substitute "Marchall headlights" for his original reference to "Chagall headlights." The most significant changes involved the celebrated torture scene in which Le Chiffre attacks Bond's private parts with a carpet beater. No one who read the typescript was absolutely sure what effect such treatment would have in reality, but they felt, understandably, that it was rather lively stuff for a book which was to be published by a reputable and respected firm. Even after Fleming had toned it down by changing some of the language and by substituting a knife for the pair of rusty scissors with which Le Chiffre originally threatened Bond, that scene provoked a great deal of discussion. The real arguments about sadism in the Bond books, however, did not begin until after the publication of *Dr. No* (1958).

The reviews of *Casino Royale* were generally good both in Britain and in the United States; for example, one reviewer described Fleming as "a kind of supersonic John Buchan" (*Listener*, 23 April 1953), and another said that "If Bulldog Drummond had had brains, this is the kind of work he would have done" (*Harper's*, May 1954). Fleming persuaded Jonathan Cape to give him a higher royalty on his next book, and he observed with delight that his royalty–although not, of course, his advance–was equal to Ernest Hemingway's. He also began to investigate the possibility of a film sale. Although he enjoyed writing the Bond books, at least for the first few years, his intention was to make the fortune which had, so far, eluded him.

As Fleming planned his second novel, *Live and Let Die*, he began consciously to perceive and interpret events in terms of their suitability for use in his books. During a plane trip to Jamaica in 1953, for example, he made notes which became the source for the account of Bond's plane trip in the novel. On occasion he deliberately set about having an adventure so that he could describe it in one of his books, as he did when he and a close friend, Ernest Cuneo, made a round of the major Harlem nightclubs so that Fleming could use them as background for some of the scenes in *Live and Let Die*. However, although these Harlem scenes are highly entertaining in themselves, they have little to do with the plot, and Fleming's indulgence in this kind of interpolated set piece was to become one of the weakest points in the structuring of his novels.

Live and Let Die contains no scene of torture as vivid as the one in *Casino Royale*, but it does help to establish the trend of mayhem in Flem-

Fleming's library in his home at Sevenhampton, near Surndon, which contained his collection of nineteenth- and twentieth-century source material concerning western civilization (courtesy of the Lilly Library, Indiana University, Bloomington, Indiana)

ing's books by having Bond commit far more acts of violence than he does in the earlier story. For example, at one point in the novel, Bond's American associate, Felix Leiter, is dropped into a shark tank. His body is returned to Bond, bloody and maimed, with a note saying, "He disagreed with something that ate him." Bond retaliates against the author of this biting satire by kicking him into the same tank and listening to the grunts of the sharks as they hit. This type of poetic justice, which is a common characteristic of earlier thriller literature written by such authors as Buchan, Edgar Wallace, "Sapper," and Leslie Charteris, occurs frequently in Fleming's novels.

Although Fleming had not yet succeeded in making a film sale by the time *Live and Let Die* was published, when he wrote his next novel, *Moonraker*, he visualized it in terms of a screenplay. He later used this cinematic perspective as an excuse for the episodic quality of the novel, explaining in an unpublished 1956 letter, "I originally thought of this book as a film and the reason why it breaks so badly in half as a book is because I had to more or less graft the first half

of the book onto my film idea in order to bring it up to the necessary length." In fact Fleming was never at his best in handling the transitions between the dramatic episodes which are the strength of the Bond books–he simply stuck them together with the literary equivalent of scotch tape and chewing gum. *Moonraker* is actually one of his better-constructed novels, but, as his letter indicates, even here he had structural difficulties. The first half of the book concerns an epic bridge game between Bond and the villain, Drax, which resembles both the baccarat game in *Casino Royale* and the round of golf that Fleming would incorporate into his seventh novel, *Goldfinger*. The game itself is suspenseful and colorful, but it has nothing to do with the rest of the novel except to suggest that, since Drax cheats at cards, he is probably capable of other forms of skulduggery. Further, the tension which builds up between Bond and Drax during the game makes it difficult to believe that Bond's boss, who is present at the game, would choose Bond, rather than one of the other three operatives considered for the assignment, to investigate

Dust jacket and front flap from the 1954 first British edition of Fleming's second James Bond novel

the death of a security officer assigned to Drax. The second half of the book, which Fleming refers to in his letter as "my film idea," concerns Drax's threat to drop a rocket on the center of London. Ironically, by the time *Moonraker* was made into a film in 1978 this plot was out of date, so that the film owes almost nothing to Fleming's original idea.

By the time *Moonraker* was published, the Bond books had begun to achieve modest popular success in both the United States and Britain, and this growing popularity was fostered by the first of the elaborate advertising campaigns which came to be associated with the Bond books. In the United States, for example, Macmillan ran full-page color advertisements showing a cordial bottle with "Moonraker" on the label and lines like "The sensational new 100 proof spinechilling concoction," and "WARNING. Take dosage only in sitting, prone, or supine position. If apathy continues, consult your psychiatrist." In part as a result of this campaign, *Moonraker* was reasonably successful commercially, although the Bond stories were still far from the height of their popularity.

Encouraged by the success of *Moonraker*, Fleming continued with his plan of writing an an-

nual Bond novel, and he continued to draw much of the material for these novels from his own experiences and those of his friends. He acquired some of the source material for his fourth novel, *Diamonds Are Forever* (1956), from a former schoolmate, Philip Brownrigg, who was then a senior executive with De Beers, the world's largest diamond corporation. Brownrigg supplied Fleming with factual information about diamond mining and smuggling, and Fleming added to it the gadgetry and glitter which were becoming increasingly important in his books. He also included in *Diamonds Are Forever* episodes which take place in Saratoga, New York, where Fleming had attended horse races with his friends Bryce and Cuneo. Other episodes take place in Las Vegas, Nevada, which Fleming and Cuneo, who appears in the book as a heroic taxi driver named Ernie Cureo, had visited for the specific purpose of allowing Fleming to use it as one of the settings for this book.

Fleming's use of all of this source material makes *Diamonds Are Forever* one of his most self-indulgent and loosely structured books. For example, because he had been fascinated by the mud baths which he had visited at Saratoga, he included in *Diamonds Are Forever* a graphic descrip-

Dust jacket designed by Fleming for the first British edition of his third James Bond novel

tion of Bond's experience in a coffin full of smelly, 110 degree mud; this scene, like many of Fleming's set pieces, has little to do with the rest of the story. The same is true of much of the information that Fleming provides about the pipeline of stolen diamonds that Bond has been sent to investigate. Furthermore, Fleming made the error, which he was to repeat in a few of his later novels, of providing no clear-cut villain to serve as a focal point for the action. The Spang brothers are hackneyed gangster types who seldom appear in the story and whose actions, like Bond's, are exciting in themselves but often unrelated to what is supposed to be the main story line.

Despite its serious structural flaws, *Diamonds Are Forever* was reasonably successful commercially because, although much of it is neither logical nor probable, most of it is exciting. It also includes an interesting variety of settings, such as a restored Western town, in which Bond engages in an uncharacteristic fistfight, and a luxurious Victorian train on which Bond is kicked insensi-

ble by a pair of gangsters who ceremoniously don football boots for the purpose.

Although his first four books were by no means commercial failures, after he wrote *Diamonds Are Forever* Fleming became discouraged with the Bond series and acutely discontented with the comparatively small financial returns he was receiving. Therefore, when Gregory Ratoff offered him six thousand dollars for the film rights to *Casino Royale*, Fleming accepted because he could see no possibility of a better offer in the immediate future. As a result, this is the only Bond book which cannot be used by the production company which now owns the film rights to the other titles and to the Bond character. The film of *Casino Royale*, released in 1967 by Columbia, is a spoof of the more conventional Bond films, which were by that time well established. It features David Niven as an aging Bond and Woody Allen as his nephew, Jimmy Bond.

Fleming's discouragement with reference to Bond was lightened to some extent by the appearance at Kemsley House of a Russian who claimed to have firsthand information about an organization called Smiert Spionam (SMERSH), which Fleming had heard about in the late 1940s and used in *Casino Royale* and *Live and Let Die*. This information was apparently inaccurate, but Fleming made good use of it in depicting Bond's Russian adversaries in his next novel, *From Russia, with Love* (1957). He also heightened the verisimilitude of the story by inserting an author's note beginning with the characteristically offhand assertion, "Not that it matters, but a great deal of the background to this story is accurate," and including the exact address of SMERSH headquarters in Moscow.

Fleming was given the opportunity to collect further material for *From Russia, with Love* when Sir Ronald Howe, assistant commissioner of Scotland Yard, arranged for him to attend the conference of the International Police Organization (Interpol) in Istanbul. The Interpol conference itself was of little interest to Fleming, but he was fascinated by Istanbul. He became friendly with a Turkish businessman, Nazim Kalkavan, who showed him around the city. Kalkavan, who provided the inspiration for Bond's friend Darko Kerim in *From Russia, with Love*, made a remark which Fleming paraphrased in the novel as, "But I am greedy for life. I do too much of everything all the time. Suddenly one day my heart will fail. The Iron Crab will get me as it got my father. But I am not afraid of The Crab. At least I shall

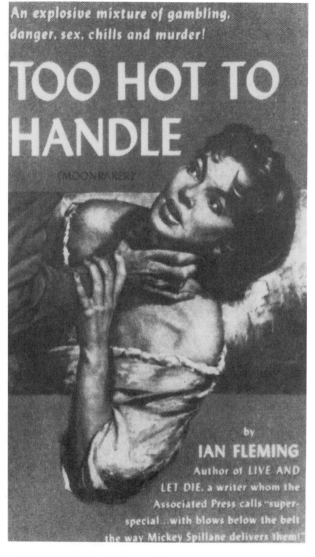

Front and back covers for the first American paperback edition of Moonraker

have died from an honourable disease. Perhaps they will put on my tombstone 'This Man Died from Living Too Much.'" Fleming, who had his own recurrent problems with the "Iron Crab," found in this attitude an affirmation of the kind of life he had chosen and a justification for the kind of death he expected to meet as a result.

From Russia, with Love is one of Fleming's best novels, in part because it is more carefully structured than most of his other books. There are a few interpolated scenes, such as one in which girls are fighting in a gypsy camp, but on the whole the individual events in the story fit together comparatively well. Its basic premise—that the Russian Secret Service wants to ruin Bond's reputation by filming him in bed with a female

Russian agent and then killing them both—is somewhat farfetched, but within the world of the Bond books it is by no means impossible.

The characterizations in *From Russia, with Love* are also better than those in Fleming's earlier novels. Fleming never came anywhere near creating such realistic characters as Ambler's Arthur Abdel Simpson or John le Carré's George Smiley, primarily because most of the action in the Bond novels takes place because of the requirements of the plot. However, Darko Kerim, who has a rudimentary philosophy of life and a rather eccentric sense of humor, is one of Fleming's best characters, and, although none of his female characters is really well-rounded (in the literary sense), Tatiana Romanova is one of the most charming.

Dust jacket designed by Fleming and Richard Chopping for the first British edition of From Russia, with Love

During his period of discouragement following the publication of *Diamonds Are Forever*, Fleming had considered killing Bond off, and, although he decided against it, he concluded *From Russia, with Love* with a scene in which Bond, stabbed with a poisoned blade which had been concealed in the toe of a villainess's boot, crashes to the floor. This ending naturally aroused a great deal of comment, as it was meant to do. Iain Hamilton, a friend of Fleming's, wrote him a jocular letter of protest (unpublished): "I have said harsh words about this fellow in the past but, by George, you can't go and let an ugly old trollop kick him to death with an absurdly poisoned boot. This won't do at all." In a letter of 1 May 1957 Fleming replied, "Surely a man can have a dose of Fugu poisoning (a particularly virulent member of the curare group obtained from the sex glands of the Japanese globe fish) without at once being written off. Pray spare your tears." A more public explanation appeared in the newspapers in the form of a medical bulletin from Sir

James Molony, physician to the British Secret Service in Fleming's books, declaring James Bond to be alive and well and recovering from a dose of Fugu poisoning. As the high-powered advertising campaign for *From Russia, with Love* got under way, the bulletins from Sir James were accompanied by entries in the "Personals" sections of various newspapers, addressed to characters in the story: one such advertisement, addressed to Bond himself, warns him that "Rosa Klebb may have poisoned knife blade concealed in toe of shoe. Look alive."

From Russia, with Love received glowing reviews, many of which not only assess this particular novel, but also comment on the growing importance of Bond as a popular hero. These reviews discuss in some detail the wish-fulfillment aspect of the character, particularly his professional and amatory prowess and his enjoyment of an exciting and at times luxurious life-style untouched by inflation, taxes, or mass-produced shoddy goods. As these reviews suggest, Fleming was by now committed to writing formula-based escapist fiction which included certain elements that the public had come to expect: emphasis on expensive brand-name products; feminine capitulation (immediate or eventual) to Bond's charms; Bond's survival of fiendish tortures, deadly perils, acts of God, and assorted other unpleasantries; exotic, or seemingly exotic, settings; and the presence of outrageously ugly villains with grandiose schemes for world domination.

Following the success of *From Russia, with Love*, the *London Daily Express* offered Fleming fifteen hundred pounds per book for permission to publish Bond's adventures in comic-strip form. Despite the advice of friends who feared that this might cheapen Bond, Fleming agreed. He also agreed to write his first non-Bond book, an account of the work of the International Diamond Security Organization (IDSO), which had been formed by the Diamond Corporation to discourage smuggling. Although some of the material that Fleming collected was suppressed for reasons of industrial security and personal privacy, *The Diamond Smugglers* became a very successful series in the *London Sunday Times* before being published in book form in 1957. The success of *The Diamond Smugglers* led to a second nonfiction series for the *London Sunday Times*, based on travels financed by the newspaper, describing and commenting on famous or exotic places. Some of the material that Fleming collected for these essays served as the basis for his descriptions of the set-

James Bond sets up a golf match with Goldfinger on a manuscript page inserted into the typescript of Goldfinger *(1959)*
(courtesy of Lilly Library, Indiana University, Bloomington, Indiana)

Fleming and Belgian mystery writer Georges Simenon (courtesy of Lilly Library, Indiana University, Bloomington, Indiana)

tings in his later novels, and the essays themselves were collected in book form as *Thrilling Cities* (1963).

By the time Fleming left Jamaica with the typescript of *From Russia, with Love,* he had already decided on the setting for his next book, *Dr. No.* Fleming's friend Bryce had invited him to accompany an expedition whose purpose was to assess the well-being of a colony of flamingos on Inagua Island in the Bahamas. In addition to exploring the marshy island, Fleming had talked with a member of the expedition, Dr. Robert Murphy, about the guano harvests of South America, where bird droppings are collected for fertilizer. Fleming later combined his impressions of Inagua with what Dr. Murphy had told him, filtered it through his imagination, and created in the fictional island of Crab Key a suitable setting for the sinister Dr. No. The plot, in which a thoroughly up-to-date villain uses a privately-owned island as a base for deflecting American missiles

fired from Turks Island, came from a television script which Fleming had written for an abortive NBC series.

The most controversial scene in *Dr. No* is one in which Bond, imprisoned by Dr. No, seeks escape through a tunnel prepared to test the endurance of Dr. No's victims up to the moment of their supposedly inevitable demise. Having been knocked down by an electric shock and burnt, screaming, in a heated segment of pipe, Bond mashes twenty giant tarantulas into a "writhing, sickening mess of blood and fur," crawls over the pulped tarantulas and stops to catch his breath before tumbling headfirst down a shaft and being knocked unconscious when he hits the sea at 40 MPH. He clings to a convenient cable strung across the inlet, in which, recovering consciousness just in time, he watches the fish eat his blood until a fifty-foot squid tries to eat the rest of him. Some reviewers felt that this episode was unacceptably violent. Then, recalling scenes of bloodshed in the earlier Bond books, these reviewers protested against Fleming's romanticized view of mayhem in general. These were not by any means the first objections to the violence in Fleming's books, but they were the first signs of a comprehensive attack.

The two most influential blasts at Fleming's work in general which were provoked by *Dr. No* were Paul Johnson's "Sex, Snobbery and Sadism" in the *New Statesman and Nation* (5 April 1958) and Bernard Bergonzi's "The Case of Mr. Fleming" in *Twentieth Century* (March 1958). These writers expressed disapproval not only of the violence, but also of the gambling, drinking, sexual permissiveness, and materialism found in the Bond books. Other critics, maintaining that the Bond stories were highly entertaining tales of adventure which ought not to be taken too seriously, deplored the narrow-mindedness of the objectors. All this controversy, of course, did no harm to the sales of Fleming's books, and he continued to include the disputed elements in his fiction.

One aspect of the argument over the violence in the Bond books concerns the question of whether it is relieved by humor. Fleming himself often expressed disingenuous surprise at the seriousness with which some critics took scenes which he regarded as funny, although he could hardly have failed to recognize the extent to which he made use of "inside" jokes which are incomprehensible to anyone unfamiliar with the real-life people and events that Fleming parodied. Some of the humor in the Bond novels, however, is more general; for example, Fleming used a number of rather adolescent sexual puns, including M's telling Bond, in reference to a jeweler's loop, "Don't push it in. Screw it in" (*Diamonds Are Forever*), and a genealogist's telling him that the Bond family's coat of arms features three golden bezants (balls), to which Bond replies, "That is certainly a valuable bonus" (*On Her Majesty's Secret Service,* 1963). Other examples of humor in the Bond novels occur in conjunction with the violence itself: these include the note attached to Felix Leiter's shark-mauled body; Dr. No's startling demise under a twenty-foot heap of guano; and Bond's reference to his assignment in *From Russia, with Love* as "pimping for England." Even Fleming's grimmest book, *You Only Live Twice* (1964), includes a scene in which the lobster that Bond has been served by his well-meaning Japanese host flips over and wanders off across the dinner table, prompting Bond to exclaim, "Good God, Tiger! . . . The damn thing's alive!" Despite

Fleming and his wife, January 1962 (Wide World Photo)

these examples, humor is certainly not as important in Fleming's stories as it is in thrillers written by such authors as "Sapper," Buchan, and Charteris, and it is unquestionably much less important here than it is in the Bond films. As the torture scenes in *Casino Royale* and *Dr. No* suggest, the infliction and the endurance of pain play an important part in the Bond novels, but it is hardly fair to define them, as some critics have done, as utterly humorless orgies of sadomasochism.

As a means of escaping from the controversies surrounding his books and from the increasingly unpleasant problems that he was encountering at this time in his position on the Kemsley newspapers, Fleming often spent weekends in or near Sandwich so that he could play the Royal St. George golf course. As he played, Fleming worked out an imaginative, if dishonest, way to defeat a villainous opponent at golf. This scheme became the basis of a preliminary encounter between Bond and the villain of Fleming's next novel, *Goldfinger*. Letters which began to arrive as soon as the book was published pointed out that the stratagem Fleming had devised would not work in real life, and that in any case it was not nearly so creatively reprehensible as the novel sug-

Dust jackets for the British editions of Fleming's tenth and eleventh James Bond novels

gested. One of Fleming's friends, for example, wrote to tell him that they would not raise an eyebrow at that sort of thing at *his* club. Nevertheless, the golf game in *Goldfinger* is one of the best known and most popular scenes in the Bond novels, and it became an equally successful sequence in the filmed version of the story. Unfortunately, however, the novel itself is one of Fleming's poorest, and the effectiveness of the golf scene in the first half of the story makes the ineffectiveness of the main plot line even more glaringly apparent.

One of the central weaknesses of *Goldfinger* is that it lacks plausibility, even by the undemanding standards of Fleming's usual style. For example, Goldfinger, knowing who Bond is and hating him because of his triumph in the golf game and because Bond has discovered that Goldfinger cheats at cards, wants Bond, for no convincing reason, to be his assistant. Further, Goldfinger's plot to infiltrate Fort Knox is described in excruciating detail, a type of error into which Fleming, to do him justice, seldom fell. Most important, although Fleming often repeated such situations as

fights in moving vehicles, the sexual surrender of previously unresponsive women, and castration-fantasy tortures, in *Goldfinger* he carried such repetitions to the point of self-parody. The book does include a few original and entertaining elements, such as the character of Oddjob (a squat Korean bodyguard who kills people with his hat and eats pet cats), but these are not sufficient to compensate for its shortcomings. The reviews of *Goldfinger,* although they were not entirely negative, were the worst that Fleming had ever received.

Even before these reviews appeared, Fleming, discouraged, exhausted again, and suffering from chest pains, sciatica, and kidney trouble, decided that he could not face the prospect of writing another novel. His next book, *For Your Eyes Only* (1960), is a collection of five short stories. He had already written one of them during his most recent trip for the *London Sunday Times,* and he adapted three of the others from plot outlines that he had developed for an abortive James Bond television series for CBS.

Dust jacket for the British edition of Fleming's eleventh James Bond novel, which takes its title from a haiku by Matsuo Bashō: "You only live twice: / Once when you are born, / And once when you look death in the face"

One of the stories in *For Your Eyes Only*, "Quantum of Solace," is presented in the form of a narrative told to Bond by a dinner host; it concerns the breakup of a marriage because of the failure of each of the partners in turn to provide the other with a necessary minimum of comfort: a "quantum of solace." Each of the other four stories in the book is based on the kind of adventure which would ordinarily have formed one of the more striking scenes in a Bond novel. Such scenes readily presented themselves to Fleming's imagination, and by using the short-story form he spared himself the effort of working out any more than the separate, disconnected episodes. Reviews of *For Your Eyes Only* were generally polite, but it was clear that Fleming was running out of ideas and energy.

Finding the production of his annual Bond book increasingly difficult, Fleming was more anx-

ious than ever to make a film sale which, he felt, would bring him the kind of financial reward that he had long hoped for. He was therefore delighted when Bryce, who had become acquainted with a talented young producer, Kevin McClory, proposed a three-way collaboration on a film: Fleming would provide the character of Bond and help to write the script, Bryce would put up the money for the film, and McClory would produce and direct it. Accordingly, Fleming and McClory worked together on a story outline, and Jack Whittingham, a well-known British scriptwriter, was brought in to work on the screenplay. The final draft therefore incorporated the work of Fleming, McClory, and Whittingham. Fleming eventually decided to terminate his association with McClory and Whittingham and to sell the film rights to the character of Bond to an established film company. However, he assumed that he had the right to use as the basis for his next novel the story that he, McClory, and Whittingham had produced. McClory disagreed, and when *Thunderball* (1961) was about to be published he brought his case to court, claiming that the novel was based on a film story to whose development he had made substantial contributions.

On 25 March 1961 Fleming attended a hearing at which the court, because of the investment which Jonathan Cape had already made in printing *Thunderball* and in advance publicity, permitted the publication of the book. However, the court made it clear that its action did not prejudice McClory's pending suit in any way, and two years later McClory was awarded the film rights to *Thunderball* as well as substantial damages paid by Fleming's codefendant, Bryce. Three weeks after the 1961 hearing, Fleming attended a conference at the headquarters of the Kemsley—now Thomson—newspapers, in the course of which he had his first major heart attack. He was taken to the London Clinic, where he made a surprising recovery. He amused himself during his convalescence by writing a children's book, *Chitty-Chitty-Bang-Bang* (1964-1965), which was based on stories of a magic car that Fleming had told his son. *Chitty-Chitty-Bang-Bang* was later made into a film.

Because of his physical condition, Fleming was ordered to limit himself to three ounces of hard liquor a day. Appalled, he wrote to a friend in the Ministry of Agriculture, Fisheries, and Food to ask what liquor has the highest alcohol content per ounce. His friend recommended Green Chartreuse (102 proof), followed by Benedictine and Yellow Chartreuse (74 proof) and then by whiskey, brandy, and rum (70 proof). However, as he began to feel better, Fleming gradually returned to his former drinking habits as well as to his heavy smoking.

Despite the *Thunderball* suit and his heart attack, not everything that happened to Fleming in 1961 was unpleasant. Sales of his books increased noticeably after *From Russia, with Love* was included in a list of President Kennedy's ten favorite books. Arthur Schlesinger has since claimed that Kennedy was not in fact a great admirer of the Bond books, but, true or not, the publicity had its effect. More importantly, Fleming finally made the film deal that he had been thinking about for so many years. Harry Salzman, a Canadian producer, had taken out an option on the film rights to the Bond books, but he had been unable to secure the backing of a major film company. Another producer, Albert Broccoli, became Salzman's partner and succeeded in negotiating a contract with United Artists. Fleming was guaranteed a minimum of one hundred thousand dollars per film, but because of the great commercial success of the Bond series, his profits were actually much higher. Broccoli and Salzman formed a company, Eon Productions, and planned to begin their series with *Thunderball.* However, because of McClory's pending suit, they filmed *Dr. No* instead. The 1962 film was a success, and they went on to make *From Russia, with Love* (1963) and then *Goldfinger* (1964). Fleming read the scripts, made suggestions, and was present during some of the filming, but the films themselves were in the hands of Broccoli and Salzman. Although Fleming felt that he had incorporated humor into his books, chiefly in the form of tongue-in-cheek exaggerations, the producers wanted a broader kind of humor, and they began using the one-liners and send-ups which have become hallmarks of the Bond films.

Fleming enjoyed much of the humor in the Bond films, but he was pained by jokes which detract from Bond's status as a British gentleman. In reading the script of the third Bond film, *Goldfinger,* for example, he objected to a scene in which Bond, looking into a woman's eyes, sees in them the reflection of an assailant approaching with a blackjack. At the last moment Bond swings the girl around so that it is she who is coshed. "Bond," wrote Fleming in the margin, "wouldn't do this to a girl!" Nevertheless, this film, which features the first of the famous Bond cars and a great deal of sophisticated gadgetry and stunt

work, was even more popular than the first two had been. Many students of the Bond films date the beginning of the Bond-film cult from the release of *Goldfinger,* and it certainly became the major commercial success that Fleming had long hoped for. Ironically, he never enjoyed the profits from this film, which was released in the year of his death.

Despite the *Thunderball* hearing, his heart attack, and the film deal, Fleming had his next novel ready for publication in 1962. *The Spy Who Loved Me* is significantly different from the other Bond novels because it is narrated by the heroine, Vivienne Michel; Bond does not even appear until more than halfway through the book. The major events of this story–Vivienne's early sexual traumas, her encounter with Bond, and their lovemaking–follow a pattern which can be found in almost every Bond novel, but the emphasis on the heroine becomes the controlling factor in this one. *The Spy Who Loved Me* is, in fact, a woman's love story, and a surprisingly perceptive one, although it suffers from overwriting and outrageous sentimentalism. Predictably, however, Fleming's audience was disappointed by the absence of a major villain, a world-threatening conspiracy, and the trappings of the good life. Even reviewers who thought that *The Spy Who Loved Me* was a reasonably good novel in itself protested that it was not what readers expected a Bond story to be. *The Spy Who Loved Me* was, and remains, Fleming's least popular novel.

His publishers' apprehensive reception of the typescript of *The Spy Who Loved Me* had led Fleming to anticipate the negative reaction that the book received, so even before it was published he had begun working on a more traditional Bond novel which would, he hoped, achieve the kind of success that some of the earlier Bond stories had achieved, and, to some extent, it did. Despite the undereffectiveness of its villain and a few tediously lengthy digressions into genealogy and biological warfare, *On Her Majesty's Secret Service* is the best book that Fleming produced after *Dr. No.* It includes several exciting chases, such as a ski scene which became an important sequence in the filmed version of the story; a love affair which is serious enough to terminate, briefly, in marriage; and the brand-name products and opulent settings which had become hallmarks of the Bond novels. The villain's machinations and Bond's love affair relate to one another only tangentially, but by this time Fleming's readers had become so accustomed to the epi-

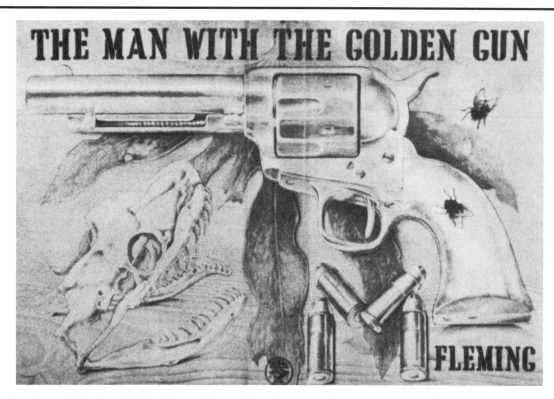

Dust jacket for the 1965 first British edition of the twelfth and last James Bond novel. Fleming died after completing the first draft, which was prepared for publication by another hand.

sodic quality of his plots that very few reviewers even mentioned it. The reviews of *On Her Majesty's Secret Service* were better than Fleming's reviews had been for five years, and its sales, boosted by the publicity regarding President Kennedy's enjoyment of the Bond books and by the success of the first two Bond films, were excellent. When Pan Books put out the paperback edition, they printed one million copies and had to print more a few months later.

Shortly before the publication of *On Her Majesty's Secret Service*, Fleming left England for Japan to collect background material for his penultimate novel, *You Only Live Twice*. In part because of his own failing health, he was particularly fascinated by what he perceived as the Japanese preoccupation with death, and *You Only Live Twice* is filled with death-oriented scenes and imagery. Although there is no shortage of deaths by violence in Fleming's earlier novels, those were the deaths of people who did not want to die; in this book Fleming displays an obsession with death itself which is carried to the point of morbidity.

Fleming's excessive concern with death is most evident in his depiction of the villain of *You Only Live Twice*, a nightmarish figure whose scheme is the least adequately motivated and the most macabre in the entire Bond series. With no thought of world domination or of wealth, he creates a garden for suicides solely to give himself the pleasure of furnishing others with the opportunity to destroy themselves by means of poisonous plants, a pirahna pool, or steaming fumaroles. Fleming's state of mind also affected the character of Bond, who, even in *On Her Majesty's Secret Service*, seems older, more subdued, and more tired than he does in the earlier novels. In *You Only Live Twice* Bond is reflective and even poetic, quoting the haiku verse from which the novel takes its title: "You only live twice: / Once when you're born, / Once when you look death in the face." He is also less tough and more sentimental than ever before. *You Only Live Twice* is imaginative and eminently readable, but it is, in comparison with the earlier Bond novels, a depressed and tired story written by a depressed and tired man.

Fleming went to Goldeneye as usual in January of 1964 to work on what was to be his last novel, *The Man with the Golden Gun* (1965). He found the book almost impossible to write, partly because he could no longer work for long periods of time and partly because, although he would not yield to his illness by failing to pro-

Christopher Lee (left) and Roger Moore (right) as James Bond in a scene from the 1974 film, The Man with the Golden Gun
(United Artists)

duce his annual book, the joy had long gone out of his writing. Not surprisingly, *The Man with the Golden Gun* is the least original of Fleming's novels. It includes, among other repetitions, a fight on a train which derives from similar scenes in *Diamonds Are Forever* and *From Russia, with Love* and the device of having Bond gain access to the villain by being employed by him, as he does in *Goldfinger* and *On Her Majesty's Secret Service*. It also includes the use of a dossier like those in *Casino Royale* and *Live and Let Die,* providing not only factual information about the villain, but also a pseudo-sophisticated psychological analysis which is not entirely serious: in this case, the suggestion that Scaramanga became a hired killer because of a traumatic childhood experience involving the shooting of a bull elephant in heat.

In addition to being repetitious *The Man with the Golden Gun* is even less plausible than Fleming's other novels. It relies heavily on coincidence, and the characters often indulge in unaccountable behavior. For example, Bond, who has killed innumerable adversaries, including some who, like the crane operator in *Dr. No* and the

night guard in *On Her Majesty's Secret Service,* never even saw him coming, repeatedly refuses to kill Scaramanga under circumstances which he regards as unsporting. The novel culminates in a wildly improbable scene in which Bond agonizes over the fact that he is duty-bound to kill Scaramanga, who, wounded and apparently unarmed, eats a raw snake and then recites a Roman Catholic prayer for the dying–in Latin. Fleming undoubtedly wrote this scene, as he wrote many others, with tongue-in-cheek; however, because of the weakness and unevenness of the novel as a whole, this scene comes across as painfully poor melodrama masquerading as suspense.

Fleming was very dissatisfied with *The Man with the Golden Gun,* and he intended to edit it heavily. However, on a rainy summer day, despite a bad cold, he insisted on attending a committee meeting at the Royal St. George golf club. The next day he suffered a hemorrhage, and that evening he was taken to nearby Canterbury Hospital, where he died shortly after one o'clock in the morning of 12 August 1964, at the age of fifty-

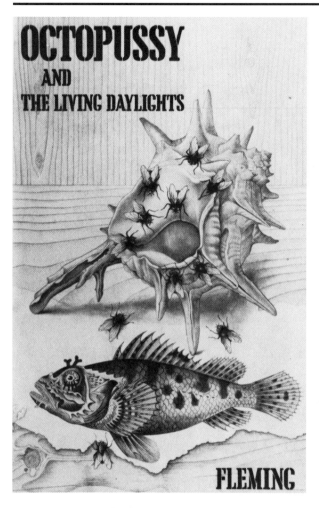

First British edition of Fleming's last book

six. His last recorded words were an apology to the ambulance attendants for having inconvenienced them.

The Man with the Golden Gun was published posthumously, followed by *Octopussy, and The Living Daylights* (1966), two short stories which resemble those in *For Your Eyes Only.* The paperback editions of this book also include "The Property of a Lady," a short story which had appeared in Sotheby's annual report for 1963. Shortly after Fleming's death, Glidrose Productions, the company which controls the James Bond copyright, commissioned Kingsley Amis (under the name of Robert Markham) to write an original Bond novel, *Colonel Sun* (1968). More recently, Glidrose commissioned John Gardner to write *Licence Renewed* (1981) and *For Special Services* (1982). Eon Productions, now controlled not by Broccoli and Salzman but by Broccoli alone, has filmed almost all of Fleming's original titles and Gardner's first Bond book. Chiefly because of the popularity of

the Bond films, James Bond Fan Clubs are active in the United States, Great Britain, and Canada, holding annual conventions and selling such items as film posters and models of the Bond cars and guns.

Eighteen years after Fleming's death, critical opinion regarding the quality of his books and his own importance in the field of espionage fiction is radically divided. The following observation by Amis, originally published shortly after Fleming's death, still reflects the viewpoint of his supporters: "Ian Fleming has set his stamp on the story of action and intrigue, bringing to it a sense of our time, a power and a flair that will win him readers when all the protests about his supposed deficiencies have been forgotten. He leaves no heirs." Fleming's detractors, on the other hand, view his work as ephemeral and hopelessly inferior. As Leroy L. Panek writes, "No publisher today would even consider printing *Casino Royale,* and if it were not for the films, James Bond would mean as little to the contemporary consciousness as, say, Okewood of the Secret Service. It is, then, historical accident which has made a public figure of a muddled hero created by a third-rate hack." There is very little moderate opinion on the subject; whatever its other shortcomings, at least Fleming's work does not inspire indifference. Nevertheless, the truth is probably somewhere in the middle. Fleming's books are superficial, implausible, and erratically structured, and they have unquestionably been overshadowed in popularity by the Bond films, which are even more superficial, implausible, and erratically structured. On the other hand, Fleming's work is, for the most part, imaginative, readable, and, most important, outrageously entertaining. Fleming himself remarked in an interview quoted by Amis that he was in "the business of getting intelligent, uninhibited adolescents of all ages, in trains, aeroplanes and beds, to turn over the page."

Interview:

"Interview: Ian Fleming," *Playboy,* 11 (December 1964): 97-106.

Bibliography:

Iain Campbell, *Ian Fleming: A Catalogue of a Collection* (Liverpool: Iain Campbell, 1978).

Biography:

John Pearson, *The Life of Ian Fleming* (London: Cape, 1966; New York: McGraw-Hill, 1966).

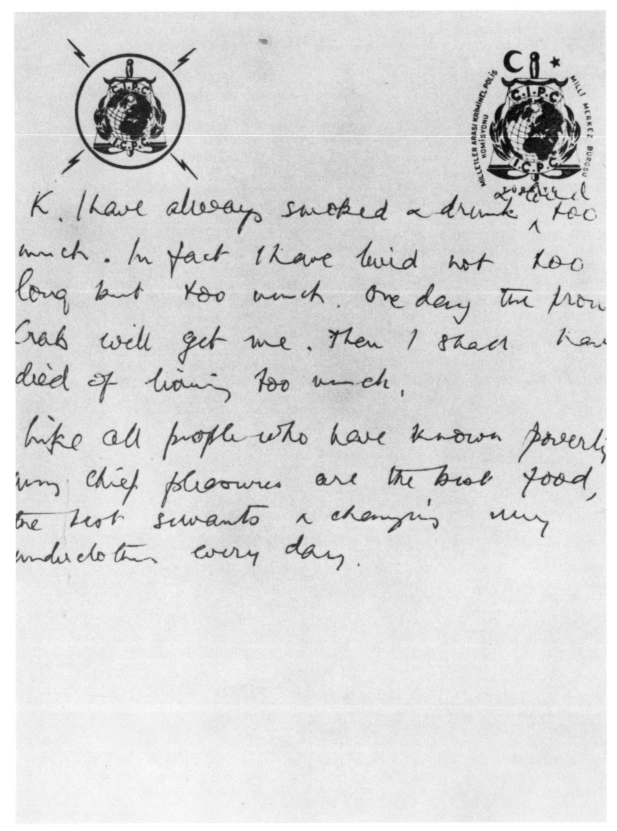

Note by Fleming in which he accurately predicts his death from "the Iron Crab"–heart disease (courtesy of Lilly Library, Indiana University, Bloomington, Indiana)

References:

Kingsley Amis, *The James Bond Dossier* (London: Cape, 1965; New York: New American Library, 1965);

Mary Wickham Bond, *How 007 Got His Name* (London: Collins, 1966);

Ann S. Boyd, *The Devil with James Bond* (Richmond, Va.: Knox, 1967; London: Collins, 1967);

Ivar Bryce, *You Only Live Once: Memories of Ian Fleming* (London: Weidenfeld & Nicholson, 1975);

Oreste del Buono and Umberto Eco, eds., *The Bond Affair,* translated by R. A. Downie (London: Macdonald, 1966);

Richard Gant, *Ian Fleming: The Man with the Golden Pen* (New York: Mayflower-Dell, 1966);

John E. Gardner, *Ian Fleming's James Bond* (New York: Avenet, 1987);

Sheldon Lane, ed., *For Bond Lovers Only* (London: Panther, 1965);

Percy Muir, "Ian Fleming: A Personal Memoir," *Book Collector,* 14 (Spring 1965): 24-33;

Leroy L. Panek, *The Special Branch: The British Spy Novel, 1890-1980* (Bowling Green, Ohio: Bowling Green University Popular Press, 1981);

Eleanor Pelrine and Dennis Pelrine, *Ian Fleming: Man with the Golden Pen* (Wilmington, Del.: Swan, 1966);

Lars Ole Sauerberg, *Secret Agents in Fiction: Ian Fleming, John le Carré and Len Deighton* (New York: St. Martin's, 1984);

O. F. Snelling, *007 James Bond: A Report* (London: Holland, 1964; New York: Signet, 1965);

Lycurgus M. Starkey, *James Bond: His World of Values* (Nashville: Abingdon, 1966);

William Tanner, *The Book of Bond or Every Man His Own 007* (London: Cape, 1965; New York: Viking, 1965);

Colin Watson, *Licence to Kill* (London: Eyre & Spottiswoode, 1971), pp. 233-251;

Henry A. Zeigler, *Ian Fleming: The Spy Who Came In with the Gold* (New York: Duell, Sloan & Pearce, 1965).

Papers:

Correspondence, typescripts, interview notes, annotated copies of Fleming's books, and Fleming memorabilia are at the Lilly Library, Indiana University. Additional material is owned by Glidrose Productions.

Ken Follett

(5 June 1949-)

Andrew F. Macdonald and Gina Macdonald
Loyola University in New Orleans

See also the Follett entry in *DLB Yearbook 1981*.

BOOKS: *The Big Needle*, as Simon Myles (London: Everest, 1974); republished as *The Big Apple* (New York: Kensington, 1975);

The Big Black, as Myles (London: Futura, 1974);

The Big Hit, as Myles (London: Futura, 1975);

The Shakeout (Lewes, U.K.: Harwood-Smart, 1975);

Amok: King of Legend, as Bernard L. Ross (London: Futura, 1976);

The Bear Raid (Blandford, U.K.: Harwood-Smart, 1976);

The Modigliani Scandal, as Zachary Stone (London: Collins, 1976); as Follett (New York: Morrow, 1985);

The Power Twins and the Worm Puzzle: A Science Fantasy for Young People, as Martin Martinsen (London: Abelard-Schuman, 1976);

The Secret of Kellerman's Studio (London: Abelard-Schuman, 1976);

Paper Money, as Stone (London: Collins, 1977); as Follett (New York: Morrow, 1987);

Capricorn One, as Ross (London: Barker, 1978; New York: Fawcett, 1978);

The Heist of the Century, by Follett and René Louis Maurice (London: Fontana, 1978); republished as *The Gentlemen of 16 July* (New York: Arbor House, 1980);

Storm Island (London: Macdonald & Jane's, 1978); republished as *Eye of the Needle* (New York: Arbor House, 1978);

Triple (London: Macdonald & Jane's, 1979; New York: Arbor House, 1979);

The Key to Rebecca (New York: Morrow, 1980; London: Hamilton, 1980);

The Man from St. Petersburg (London: Hamilton, 1982; New York: Morrow, 1982);

On Wings of Eagles (London: Collins, 1983; New York: Morrow, 1983);

Lie Down with Lions (London: Hamilton, 1985; New York: Morrow, 1986);

The Pillars of the Earth (New York: Morrow, 1989).

PERIODICAL PUBLICATIONS: "Books that Enchant and Delight," *Writer*, 92 (June 1979): 9-11, 29;

"Model Rules for Socialists Under Cover," *New Statesman*, 113 (10 April 1987): 8, 10.

Ken Follett began his career as a fiction writer while working for the *London Evening News*. He produced a series of mysteries and thrillers (two for children) under various pseudonyms until he felt he had learned enough and written well enough to author under his own name. His early works are, as he told *DLB Yearbook 1981* (1982), intentionally "very racy, with a lot of sex," but by writing them Follett gained the skill to write the novels which have made his fame and fortune: *Storm Island* (1978; published in the United States as *Eye of the Needle*), *Triple* (1979), *The Key to Rebecca* (1980), and *The Man from St. Petersburg* (1982). Robert Lekachman (*Nation*, 26 April 1980) aptly designates Follett's forte as "the variation upon history," and Michael Demarest (*Time*, 3 May 1982) labels him "an expert in the art of ransacking history for thrills," for each of his best works grows out of news stories and historical events. Cinematic in conception, they follow a hunter-hunted pattern that leads to exciting chase scenes and games of wit and brinkmanship. His treatment of his women characters is always interesting and unique.

Born in Cardiff, Wales, on 5 June 1949, the son of Martin and Lavinia Follett (the former an internal revenue clerk, now a teacher of tax inspectors), Kenneth Martin Follett attended University College, London, where he received a B.A. in philosophy in 1970. While still at university, on 5 January 1968, he married Mary Emma Ruth Elson, who worked as a bookkeeper to help put Follett through school. The Folletts have a son, Emanuele, and a daughter, Marie-Claire. Follett began his career in journalism as rock-music columnist for the *South Wales Echo* from 1970 to 1973. Then he became a crime reporter for the *London Evening News* (1973 to 1974), an editorial

Ken Follett

director for Everest Books Ltd., London (1974 to 1976), and deputy managing director for the same company (1976 to 1977). He has been a full-time writer since 1977. He occasionally contributes to *Writer*. The family resided in Surrey, England, until 1980 when they moved to Grasse, France, to avoid the taxes resulting from being in the 83 percent tax bracket.

Follett is a popular writer. He relies but little on metaphor and allusion and broadens the scope of his works beyond the specific facts and the series of coincidences only to play around with popular psychology, albeit at times with feminist or romantic trappings. Sometimes his psychology is off the mark. The German spy in *Storm Island*, for example, is categorized as a man "chronically incapable of feeling safe," one who "understood, in that vague way in which one sometimes understands the most fundamental things about oneself, that his very insecurity was the reason he chose the profession of spy; it was the only way of life which could permit him instantly to kill anyone who posed him the slightest threat.

The fear of being weak was part of the syndrome that included his obsessive independence, his insecurity, and his contempt for his military superiors." One wonders at this analysis, which would seemingly fit an extroverted man of action better than a closed, controlled, disciplined, deep-cover spy. The Jewish spy in *Triple* moralizes about the ethical ambiguity of his position: "it did not seem possible to live honorably. Even if he gave up this profession, others would become spies and do evil on his behalf, and that was almost as bad. . . . He had long ago decided that life was not about right and wrong, but about winning and losing. . . . Justice and fair play never entered into it." The Mossad has no reputation for this agonizing that is such a feature of British spy fiction; the sentiments seem misplaced and in the context of the novel, serve only as window dressing. A. J. Mayer (*Newsweek*, 29 September 1980) argues that "Follett is no literary stylist," though "his clean, purposeful prose is more than adequate to the demands of his tightly plotted fast-moving story." He can become distracted from his central focus and lapse into the sentimental. At times he rushes to press without proper editing to eliminate repetitiveness and wordiness.

At its best, Follett's prose is lean and driven. His forte lies in setting up a chain of events in chronological sequence. The theft scene in *The Key to Rebecca* is a classic; the master spy and villain Wolff creates a diversion for the theft of a British Army briefcase by shouting "thief " and pointing at a small, running boy. Pandemonium ensues:

The crowd from the bus stop, the acrobats' audience, and most of the people in the cafe surged forward and began to attack one or another of the drivers–Arabs assuming the Greek was the culprit and everyone else assuming it was the Arab. . . . Someone picked up a chair from the cafe and hurled it into the crowd . . . the waiters, the kitchen staff and the proprietor of the cafe now rushed out and began to attack everyone who swayed, stumbled or sat on their furniture. Everyone yelled at everyone else in five languages. Passing cars halted to watch the melee, the traffic backed up in three directions, and every stopped car sounded its horn. A dog struggled free of its leash and started biting people's legs in a frenzy of excitement. . . . [T]he fight engulfed the cars [of drivers who had stopped to watch the fun] . . . men, women and children, Arabs and Greeks and Syrians and Jews and Australians and Scotsmen, jumped on their roofs and fought on their hoods and fell on their running boards and bled all over their paintwork.

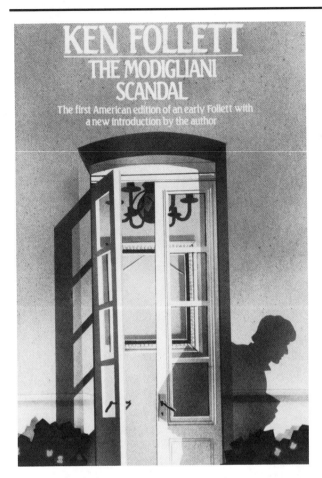

Dust jackets for the first American editions of two novels published in England under Follett's pseudonym Zachary Stone

Somebody fell through the window of the tailor's shop next to the cafe, and a frightened goat ran into the souvenir shop which flanked the cafe on the other side and began to knock down all the tables laden with china and pottery and glass. A baboon came from somewhere.... A horse broke free ... a woman emptied a bucket of dirty water into the melee. Nobody noticed. At last the police arrived.

Follett's ideal, set forth in his 1979 essay "Books that Enchant and Delight," is a compromise between the serious and the popular, the "plot, story, excitement sensation, and the world outside the mind" that he believes serious writers too often ignore merged with the "graceful, powerful prose" and more complex "character development" that mass-market writers fail to take time for.

Follett's early novels share the faults he attacks in mass-market writing, but his later ones strive for more attention to character and motivation and an avoidance of stock responses (his villains are sometimes so sympathetic that one finds

oneself rooting for Nazi spies and assassins); yet there remains a sense of calculation and an eye on mass readership in, for example, his conscious appeal to the female readership in his portrayal of weak women rising to heroism and saving the day. His first novel, *The Big Needle* (1974), was quickly turned out under the pseudonym Simon Myles to pay car repair bills after the birth of Marie-Claire in 1973. It reflects its origins: sensationalist, racy, short. It is the story of a vengeful father, horrified by the heroin overdose of his seventeen-year-old daughter and determined to mete out punishment to the drug dealer who set her on her downward course. As his daughter lies comatose, his search for vengeance takes him into the human hell of the world of the addict: "The place stank. There were empty bottles of cheap wine all over the filthy floor and about a dozen prone bodies scattered around them. In a corner, a girl wearing only a pair of green silk trousers opened one eye." When his Jamaican lover is raped to warn him off, the protagonist has double cause. "Bitter, vengeful and ruthless," he

292

looking at pictures.'

'You were with a man.'

Papa said: 'Oh, <u>no</u>. Charlotte, what <u>is</u> all this?'

'He's just somebody I met,' Charlotte said. 'You wouldn't approve of him.'

'Of course we wouldn't approve!' Mama said. 'He was wearing a tweed cap!'

Papa said: 'A tweed cap! Who the devil is he?'

'He's a terribly <u>interesting</u> man, and he understands things - '

'And he holds your hand!' Mama interrupted.

Papa said sadly: 'Charlotte, how vulgar! In the National Gallery!'

'There's no romance,' Charlotte said. 'You've nothing to fear.'

'Nothing to fear?' Mama said with a brittle laugh. 'That evil old Duchess knows all about it, and she'll tell everyone.'

Papa said: 'How could you do this to your Mama?'

Charlotte could not speak. She was close to tears. She thought: I did nothing wrong, just held a conversation with someone who talks sense! How can they be so - so brutish? I hate them!

Papa said: 'You'd better tell me who he is. I expect he can be paid off.'

Charlotte shouted: 'I should think he's one of the few people in theworld who can't!'

'I suppose he's some Radical,' Mama said. 'No doubt it is he who has been filling your head with foolishness about suffragism. He probably wears sandals and eats potatoes with the skins on.' She lost her temper. 'He probably believes in Free Love! If you have - '

'No, I haven't,' Charlotte said. 'I told you, there's no romance.' A tear rolled down her nose. 'I'm not the romantic type.'

Page from the typescript for The Man from St. Petersburg *(courtesy of the author)*

finds the big dealer, breaks through his defenses, and destroys him in an exciting chase scene that has since become the hallmark of a Follett novel. *The Shakeout* (1975) and *The Bear Raid* (1976) are mediocre spy stories from the period of the mid 1970s, unique only in their focus on industrial espionage.

The Modigliani Scandal (1976), however, is a cut above Follett's other early fiction. Set in the London art world, it involves a search in Paris and in Italy for a lost, hashish-inspired Modigliani painting. In the introduction to the 1985 Signet reprint of this work Follett claims that he was "trying to write a new kind of novel, one that would reflect the subtle subordination of individual freedom to more powerful machinery." He admits that this goal was invisible to everyone but himself, but he agrees that the novel was rightly praised as "sprightly, ebullient, light, bright, cheery, light (again), and fizzy." *The Modigliani Scandal* is a classic caper novel, the kind that focuses on myriads of characters dashing around romantic European locations in search of a big score. The story is precisely the kind that has underpinned dozens of movies over the last twenty years, films that are amusing, refreshing, a bit amoral and risqué, likeable, and ultimately quite forgettable.

Dee Sleign is a young British art-history student living in Paris with her American boyfriend. When she accidentally discovers the existence of the Modigliani painting done under the influence of hashish, she sees the possibility of an academic and financial coup. Dee incautiously tells an art-dealer uncle and an actress friend about her discovery, and the less-than-reliable uncle sets a private detective after the masterpiece, while the actress lets the news leak to a desperate gallery owner and involves a cockney gangster and a safecracker in a related subplot. This subplot about the forgeries of a failed artist and his art-teacher friend is eventually integrated seamlessly into the main plot as "experts" prove unable to tell real masterpieces from redundant forgeries. The humor comes from the polished and mostly privileged characters using art and artists as their main chance, betraying others and corrupting themselves not for the love of beauty but for monetary leverage, reputation, and academic or social success. Chance indeed rules their fates, just as Follett claims in his introduction, but it is chance contrived by the author when he creates an incestuous, narrowly focused society in which

everyone is somehow connected with everyone else and no one is free of some character flaw.

Follett's big break came in 1978. The highly acclaimed *Eye of the Needle*, a Literary Guild selection and winner of the 1978 Edgar Award from the Mystery Writers of America, was in fact (thanks to a carefully conducted marketing campaign) on the best-seller list weeks before its actual publication. Follett's motivation remained monetary; having attended a sales conference held by Futura Publications, distributors of Everest Books, Follett was asked by Anthony Cheetham, Futura's managing director, to write an adventure story related to World War II. After a night on the town he wrote a three-paragraph summary, which the managing director lost; Follett recalled it when sober, received a commission, and wrote the book in three months. *Eye of the Needle* sold five million copies worldwide, and was adapted for the screen by Stanley Mann and released by United Artists in 1981.

Peter Prescott (*Newsweek*, 7 August 1978) called *Eye of the Needle* "rubbish of the very best sort," "a triumph of invention over convention," characterized by a "remarkable pace," an "astute use of violence," a "sense of particular environments," and "occasionally felicitous prose." Richard Freedman (*New York Times Book Review*, 16 July 1978) said it is "a thriller that really thrills, on both the visceral and intellectual levels." Robert MacLeish (*Book World-Washington Post*, 2 July 1978) labeled it "a great flight-and-pursuit novel" and found its plot equal to a Frederick Forsyth novel and its writing of a quality with John le Carré. He called it "quite simply, the best spy novel to come out of England in years," and compared Follett's development of the title character to Wilkie Collins's handling of Count Fosco in *The Woman in White* (1860) since in both the villain is made more sinister by being portrayed as "a whole man . . . like us."

Eye of the Needle gives a convincing image of wartime life-styles, sensibilities, and attitudes. It tells of a German spy in England, Heinrich von Müller-Güden (alias Henry Faber) code-named "Die Nadel" (The Needle). A few weeks before D-Day he discovers that the military forces gathered in East Anglia are really a ruse (skeleton barracks, wooden planes and ships), carefully faked to make German intelligence believe the invasion will be at Pas de Calais instead of Normandy. To ensure credibility, he determines to deliver the information and photographic evidence in person. But British intelligence is onto him, and he is pur-

THE SMALL BOYS came early to the hanging.

It was still dark when the first three or four of them
sidled out of the hovels, quiet as cats in their felt boots.
A thin layer of fresh snow covered (the little town) like a new coat
of paint, and theirs were the first footprints to blemish its
perfect surface. They picked their way through the huddled
wooden houses and along the streets of frozen mud to the market
place, where the scaffold stood waiting.

The boys despised everything their elders valued. They
scorned beauty and mocked goodness. They would hoot with laughter
at the sight of a cripple, and they would stone to death a wounded
animal. They boasted of injuries and wore their scars with pride,
and they reserved their special admiration for mutilation: a boy
with a finger missing could be their king. They loved violence;
they would run miles to see blood shed; they never missed a
hanging.

One of the boys piddled on the base of the scaffold. Another
mounted the steps, stood on the platform, put his thumbs to his
throat and slumped, twisting his face into a grisly parody of
strangulation: the others whooped in admiration, and two dogs
came running into the market place, barking. A very young boy
recklessly began to eat an apple, and one of the older ones punched
his nose and took his apple. The young boy relieved his feelings
by throwing a sharp stone at a dog, sending the animal howling
home. Then there was nothing else to do, so they all squatted
in the porch of (the church) waiting for something to happen.
Candlelight flickered behind the shutters of the stone houses
around the square, the homes of prosperous craftsmen and traders,

Page from the first draft typescript for Pillars of the Earth *annotated by Follett and by his agent, Al Zuckerman (courtesy of the author)*

It begins with a curse, a song, and a hanging

and it builds into a magnificent adventure no reader will ever forget.

Ken Follett, the author of six #1 bestsellers, now takes a brilliant new turn in his extraordinary career to evoke one of the most flamboyant and fascinating periods in human history: England in the Middle Ages.

THE PILLARS OF THE EARTH takes the reader back to that turbulent era of intrigue and treachery—a time of civil war, famine, religious strife, and battles over royal succession. It was also a time when man's greatest skills and aspirations were expressed in the building of a magnificent cathedral at Kingsbridge.

Against this richly imagined backdrop, filled with the ravages of war and the rhythms of daily living, Follett draws the reader irresistibly into the intertwined lives of his characters—into their dreams, their labors, their loves: Tom, the Master Builder; Aliena, the Noblewoman; Philip, the Prior of Kingsbridge; Jack, the artist in stone; and Ellen, the woman from the forest who casts the curse. From humble stonemason to imperious monarch, each character is wonderfully alive.

At once a sensuous and enduring love story, and an epic that shines with the fierce spirit of a passionate age, THE PILLARS OF THE EARTH is without doubt Ken Follett's masterpiece.

$400,000 Marketing Campaign
- In-store: August 30 • Pub date: September 7 • National print advertising • National radio advertising • Advance reading copies • Press kit • ABA display • 12-copy floor display • Carton stickers • National author tour and autographings • National coop
- First printing: 400,000 • A Dual Main Selection of the Literary Guild
- Price: $22.95 • ISBN: 0-688-04659-2

ABA Autographing: Meet Ken Follett and get a signed galley of THE PILLARS OF THE EARTH. Please note that quantities will be limited.   **William Morrow**

Publishers advertisement from the 19 May 1989 issue of Publishers Weekly

sued across England and Scotland by Percival Godliman, a professor of medieval history turned intelligence officer, and Fred Bloggs, a Scotland Yard detective acting for MI 5. For both Godliman and Bloggs work has become a substitute for living; the war has simplified life and provided clear-cut, comfortable issues. On his way to rendezvous with a German submarine Faber shipwrecks on Storm Island off the coast of Aberdeen, Scotland, and is taken in by David and Lucy Rose and their son, Jo, the only other island inhabitant being an aged shepherd. After seven years of celibacy in England, Faber (as he is usually called in the novel) is caught up in a torrid affair with Lucy Rose. She responds to Faber because David Rose, embittered by the loss of both legs in a car accident on their wedding night, has given up on life and love and has immersed himself in debilitating self-pity. Lucy's vulnerability breaks down Faber's defenses, and readers learn he is a man who is charming, witty, ingenious, and disdainful of the German high command and the National Socialist party. He tells her that he is so appalled by the need to take human life that he vomits in response, and that he once gave false information to save St. Paul's Cathedral from bombing. He is fearful, tense, and incredibly lonely, plagued with nightmares about betraying himself by using German sentence construction and wearing swastika-adorned socks. Faber is genuinely human, a man to be recognized, understood, and reckoned with; yet he ruthlessly kills both David and the shepherd when they threaten his mission. The final showdown, as Bloggs and Godliman close in, is between Faber and Lucy, both torn between love and duty.

Triple, Follett's second best-seller, earned him $2.5 million dollars and a three-book, 3 million-dollar deal with New American Library. It took nine months to write. *Triple* builds on the 1968 shipboard heist of two hundred tons of uranium that speculation suggested provided the Israelis the raw material to produce thirty atomic bombs. In the novel Follett fictionalizes from an Israeli point of view how they hijacked the uranium and thereby gained nuclear capability. The story begins at Oxford where three of the protagonists are students (David Rostov, later a Soviet intelligence officer; Yasif Hassan, a Palestinian who becomes a triple agent for Egyptians, Soviets, and the fedayeen; and Nathaniel [Nat] Dickstein, a cockney Jew, later an immigrant to Israel and a highly successful though reluctant spy). The story then skips to their reunion at the home of Stephan Ashford, professor of Semitic literature, where they are joined by a wartime friend of Dickstein, Mafia don Al Cortone, a former GI. Dickstein and Hassan are stunned to meet Suza Ashford, their host's daughter, for she is the embodiment of her Lebanese mother, whom both men loved. Ironically, the group meet again in competition after they learn Egypt is building a nuclear reactor in the western desert. To the Israelis the uranium heist seems necessary for survival. To the others it is an opportunity for power or for propaganda not to be neglected. Israel's Mossad, the Soviet KGB, Egypt's General Intelligence, the fedayeen, and the Mafia jockey for control of the uranium. Dickstein and Cortone team up, joined by Suza Ashford, with whom Nat falls in love. But Dickstein's cover is blown, his steps are anticipated, his movements are traced, and one expects his objective to be thwarted ("You wouldn't think we were the chosen people, with our luck," his ally quips), yet he is tenacious and resourceful, and with aid from Suza (whom the Israelis suspect is an Arab spy) somehow muddles through so he can return to his vineyards a respected hero.

Robert Lekachman (*Library Journal*, 1 November 1979) found this book a disappointment, full of activity but lacking real action, elaborately plotted but overly sentimental. Michael Demarest (*Time*, 5 November 1979) lauded Follett for processing a news story "into one of the liveliest thrillers of the year," for his effortless ranging "from an Israeli kibbutz to the intricacies of Euratom

Follett, late 1980s (photograph by Terry O'Neill)

and the shipping world," and for the craft and detail of his set piece in which Dickstein's men, the fedayeen, and the Soviets battle for the freighter with its cargo of uranium.

Despite its technical failures, *Triple* deserves praise for looking at both sides of the Arab-Israeli conflict. It makes readers feel sympathy for the human motives of Mossad agent and PLO terrorist, even as they deplore the human consequences of these motives. The book suggests the complexities and moral ambiguities of Middle Eastern politics: the Palestinian who understandably wants to revenge his loss of nation and dignity but who knows it is wrong to betray old friends and endanger lives, and the Israeli who must act when his country needs him but who, as a romantic, is disturbed by the need to deceive and who would prefer to tend his garden. Though *Triple* finally comes down rather firmly on the Israeli side through sympathy for Dickstein, readers can appreciate the motives of PLO outrage and extremism. If an understanding of and a tolerance for paradox and ambiguity is a defining characteristic of both civilized behavior and literary art, then the novel's attempt to balance motives by humanizing villains and questioning the heroics of its protagonist qualifies the book as literary. Ambiguity alone does not make literature, however; technique must interact with authorial intention, and here *Triple* is wanting.

The Key to Rebecca had a first printing of one hundred thousand copies, was subsidized by the leading book clubs, and serialized in several magazines. Follett took a year to write the novel, and his care is reflected in the quality of its prose and characterization. It is based roughly on accounts of Erwin Rommel's 1942 North African campaign. Rommel's Afrika Korps, within fifteen miles of Alexandria, was able to outmaneuver British forces superior in weapons and in numbers, thanks to a wily and effective spy. A 1980s legal suit by Leonard Mosley charged Follett with plagiarizing the exploits of German spy John Eppler as depicted in his *The Cat and the Mice* (1958) and, though the suit was voluntarily dropped, it is clear that Eppler was the model for Alexander Wolff. Set in Cairo, *The Key to Rebecca* includes a plausible portrait of Anwar-el-Sadat as a young Egyptian army officer who is one of the leaders of the Egyptian nationalist movement. The nationalists prefer the Germans to the British, but only if the Germans enter as allies not conquerors. In Lieutenant Colonel Reggie Bogge the novel satirizes the British pukka sahib, a man who spends his time polishing his cricket ball, deriding natives, and closing his eyes to awkward and dangerous possibilities. Through Major William Vandam, a military intelligence officer who must deal with Nazi sympathizers on a daily basis, Follett editorializes anachronistically: "We're not very admirable, especially in our colonies, but the Nazis are worse. . . . It is worth fighting. In England decency is making slow progress; in Germany it's taking a big step backward. Think about the people you love, and the issues become clearer." Vandam is charged with tracking down a Nazi spy code-named Sphinx, Berlintrained, desert-tested, who has called attention to himself by killing an Assyut corporal suspicious of his cover. The spy is revealing crucial British secrets to Rommel's army. In the process of his investigation Vandam falls in love with Elene Fontana (née Abigail Asnani), an Egyptian Jew of questionable virtue with whom he baits his trap. Meanwhile, Alexander Wolff, the Nazi spy who has trekked across the vast and blazing Sahara–alone–to infiltrate Egypt, uses his own sexual relationship with Sonja, a notorious belly dancer who revels in kinky sex aboard her houseboat on the Nile, to gather British secrets, particularly battle plans crucial to the defense of Tobruk and Mersa Matrûh. As Rommel's forces move nearer victory, British and Egyptians search frantically for Wolff's code book (for very different reasons).

Vandam comes closer to the elusive Wolff and the key of the title (a marked copy of Daphne du Maurier's *Rebecca* [1938], the basis of Wolff's code and that of the real German spy, Eppler). Tension builds; coincidences abound; and the reader is treated to an incredibly comic staged theft, an even more incredible motorcycle chase through blacked-out Cairo, and a harrowing race with a speeding train before the final climax in the desert.

The Key to Rebecca contains evocative descriptions of wartime Cairo, with its restive and hostile population, its fleshpots, and its ancient charms. The descriptions of the desert and nomadic life convince the reader Follett has special knowledge of the subject. He plays off against each other the life-styles of desert wanderers and jaded Cairenes, of British officers and of the king of the Cairo pickpockets so as to create a highly credible portrait of a complex society. Readers learn about World War II history, Arab culture, colonialism, spying and spycatching, the motives of settlers wishing to go to Palestine before Israel existed, the difficulties of being a widowed father, and a half dozen other subjects without the least strain or interruption of narrative. Years later the reader can dredge up entire scenes and a particular sense of the characters.

All the main characters of *The Key to Rebecca*, female and male, heroes and villains, are memorable and individualized, just quirky enough to persuade readers of their reality. The main contrasts in the novel are between the two relationships–both initially exploitative, but one finally transformed by love–between Vandam and Wolff, one dogged and decent, the other a cruel psychopath, and Sonja and Elene, both voluptuous, one obsessed with physical gratification and manipulated by sex to act as spy, the other willing to use her beauty to fight Nazis. The female characters are the most interesting, for while they perhaps do less in terms of plot than their male counterparts, they are psychologically more complex, playing pivotal roles simply by being who they are. Demarest, in his *Time* review (29 September 1980), called Follett "the most romantic of all the top espionage thriller writers" and admired his understanding and sensitive portraits of "the women who come in and out of his cold": "When the belly dancer and the courtesan appear onstage, Rommel seems almost irrelevant."

The Man from St. Petersburg, a Literary Guild and a Reader's Digest Condensed Books selection, is set in London in the spring and summer of 1914 as Europe edges toward the brink of war, and is another historically plausible tale, this time of an anarchist assassin's determined plot to eliminate a Russian envoy to Britain who can involve Russia in the coming war on the English side. First Lord of the Admiralty Winston Churchill persuades the Earl of Walden, his own good friend and a father figure for the young Russian Prince Orlov during his student days at Oxford, to host the prince in London and to assume negotiations for an Anglo-Russian treaty to insure a second front for Germany when war does finally break out. This act makes Orlov the target for Feliks Kschessinsky, the terrorist from St. Petersburg who proves to have unexpected ties with the Waldens. T. J. Binyon (*Times Literary Supplement*, 4 June 1982) described Kschessinsky as "a fiercely independent loner, sexually irresistible, who bends women to his will and uses them to further his plans." Most critics found this novel less suspenseful than Follett's earlier successes but admired its effective sense of character and setting and more controlled and polished style. Personal tragedy is bound in with world tragedy, and emotional and sexual entanglements (between husband and wife, lover and mistress, father and daughter) are played out against the backdrop of historical events. Despite images of political unrest in Czarist Russia and of the suffragette movement in Georgian England, Follett's focus is on the coming-of-age of young Charlotte Warden, an overprotected daughter of the elite plunged into the realities of working-class life, sexual encounters, and betrayal.

The plot of *The Man from St. Petersburg* is heavy on coincidence and larded with operatic climaxes which strain credibility. The ending, for example, apart from a neat twist involving the young Winston Churchill taking charge of events, has the experiences of mother and daughter paralleling each other so neatly that parental reaction–get thee to a convent–is virtually identical over a twenty-year span. During a heroic rescue of the ingenue from a flaming bedroom, the fire seems to burn only the appropriate character–the others are blackened and blistered but emerge intact. Yet next to the melodrama readers get sharp and memorable portraits of London at the apex of its imperial splendor, and a fine sense of how and why it was all about to end so suddenly. The choice of the naive, eighteen-year-old Lady Charlotte Walden as the focus of change is perfectly appropriate: the age of willful Victorian innocence was disintegrating daily be-

fore the onslaughts of feminism, socialism, and anarchism. Follett's conceptualizing of this change in characters and larger events is precise and persuasive, but deserved a better working out of plot and situation.

Lie Down with Lions (1985) follows the changes in a romantic triangle composed of a 1960s radical turned CIA spy, an idealistic young Englishwoman, and a treacherous young French doctor. Ellis Thaler is the CIA man, a thirty-four-year old poet manqué who lives undercover in Paris as he tries to capture a KGB bankroller of terrorist operations. He has entered the world of fellow travelers by exploiting his relationship to Jane, a linguist and translator who embraces every leftist group the French capital can provide. Ellis falls in love with Jane, but their relationship is destroyed when his cover is blown, and she realizes he has used her to spy on her friends. In reaction she marries Jean-Pierre, supposedly an idealistic volunteer with *Medecins pour la Liberté*, an organization which provides doctors for Afghanistan, but in fact he is a deep-cover Soviet operative who intends to spy on the Afghan freedom fighters.

Jane and Jean-Pierre set up shop as nurse and doctor in a primitive Afghan village. Jane, who has a baby even though she is dissatisfied with her relationship with the psychologically fragile and manic-depressive Jean-Pierre, is unaware of his attempts to betray Masud, the Afghan rebel leader who may unite all the competing Afghan groups under a unified and effective command. Then, Ellis, bored after more than a year at a Washington desk job and anxious to see Jane again, volunteers for a mission to Masud on behalf of the U.S. president, who wishes to trade weaponry for promises of Afghan unity. Jane discovers her husband's treachery when Ellis arrives and is reunited with Ellis even as Jean-Pierre is unmasked. This "false climax" is followed by a patented Follett chase scene into Nuristan and the mountain passes of the Hindu Kush. As usual there are twists enough to keep the most jaded thriller reader turning the pages.

Follett's milieu is impressively detailed and persuasive in its rendering of Afghan society. The clash of two cultures, of Jane's liberated Western confidence and the male chauvinism of the Islamic peasantry among whom she lives and works, is wonderfully precise and informative. Follett's sympathies are with his female characters in the main; most of the males, even the Western ones, remain slightly one-dimensional. Jane is a fully realized character but curiously seems to lack imagination and will when she most needs them. Her attractiveness as a character palls when Follett's plot has her submit to her childishly obsessive and shallow husband, mothering him as he wishes in spite of his beating her, his betrayal of her friends to Russian execution, and his inability to confront the truth. Are readers to see Jane as a sympathetic, liberated female character or as a satiric portrait of the excesses and dishonesties perpetrated by the personally warped in the name of the women's movement? Jane often fails to act when it is most crucial that she do something; she bows to the most egregious Afghan chauvinism, yet insists on formal male-female equality at the most wildly inappropriate times, in the middle of the night on a slippery mountain trail somewhere in the Hindu Kush, for example, Russians in pursuit and Siberian exile be damned. Jane seems to act as a smug cliché of the shrewish wife when she tells Ellis he should have handled a situation "better." Jane's failure to save their small party from Russian capture is motivated by a sentimentality so rank as to make Follett's motives suspect; she cannot blow up some Russians,

> "Because they are so young . . . and innocent . . . because it would have been murder. But most of all . . . Because they have mothers," she said.

Such bathos calls into question readers' previous sympathies toward Jane, and, if intentional, makes her portrait inconsistent with her earlier good sense and stability. If unintentional, then Follett's sense of character surely fails him in these episodes, just as it does with other female characters in his weaker works.

Lie Down with Lions provides good examples of the critics' main complaints about Follett, that he is an exciting and engaging writer but sometimes sloppy and manipulative. For example, in *Lie Down with Lions* readers sometimes get a sudden look at all the stage machines creaking into place to create an effect. Five chapters before the conclusion the main issues of the plot have been settled, long before the obligatory Follett chase starts; Afghan rebel unity seems assured and the survival of hero and heroine, while emotionally crucial, is only a minor sidebar as far as world politics is concerned. Then readers suddenly and clumsily hear from the villains that Ellis Thaler is the top CIA agent in the world and that his escape will jeopardize the entire operation. All this

is news to the reader, who has regarded Ellis as competent but slightly woolly and who has assumed the CIA requires its operatives to confirm agreements with headquarters, just as traveling salesmen check in with their managers from time to time. Yet Ellis has no way of contacting the agency, there are apparently no other operatives in Afghanistan, and no one seems to have considered what he should do to ensure the agreement if his personal survival is in jeopardy. These are not the marks of a top agent, but this lack of competence does serve Follett's plot needs admirably. The enslavement of character and situation to the needs of plot also mars Follett's weaker books such as *Triple* and *The Man from St. Petersburg*; in both of which an irritating and unfathomable lack of competence is required to keep things moving.

On the Wings of Eagles (1983), taking advantage of American bitterness over the Iran hostage crisis, is a nonfiction account of Texas industrialist H. Ross Perot's successful rescue of two senior corporate executives from Tehran. Imprisoned during the 1979 anti-American and revolutionary movement, the executives escaped during a mob attack on the prison (assisted by the rescue team) and trekked across hostile territory to meet Perot in rural Turkey. According to Sanford Silverburg (*Library Journal*, August 1983) this book "captures the anarchy of the Iranian revolution, the ineffectiveness of the American embassy there, and the boldness of one prominent American entrepreneur." It is well researched and creates rich images of Iran. Follett's latest novel is *The Pillars of the Earth* (1989).

Follett's performance has been somewhat uneven. His most successful works have dealt with World War II, perhaps because he requires a wide backdrop and world-shaking events to justify the tumultuous passions he instills in his characters. A positive feature of these books is his humanizing of his villains, of Faber in *Eye of the Needle*, Wolff in *The Key to Rebecca*, and Feliks in *The Man from St. Petersburg*. All are well rounded and complete, with credible motives and understandable passions–if anything, they are sometimes so sympathetic that they jeopardize the reader's relationship with the hero. Here Follett has achieved his goal of giving the mass-market thriller some of the characteristics of more serious literature. Yet his less successful books tend to indulge the mass-market conventions that he criticizes, losing the necessary balance between plot, character, and conception that works so well in *Eye of the Needle* and *The Key to Rebecca*. Given more care with plot and more careful integration of character and conception, Follett might yet lay claim to the title of the best writer of thrillers, as well as to being one of the most popular.

Interviews:

Carol Lawson, "Behind the Best Sellers: Ken Follett," *New York Times Book Review*, 16 July 1978, p. 24;

Fred Hauptfuhrer, "Out of the Pages: When It Comes to Cliff-Hanging, Ken Follett Has, at 29, Clawed into Competition with le Carré," *People*, 10 (25 September 1978): 107-108, 110;

Barbara Isenberg, "No Cheap Thrillers from Follett Pen," *Los Angeles Times*, 1 October 1980, VI: pp. 1, 5.

References:

John M. Baker, "Ken Follett," *Publishers Weekly* (7 January 1986): 54-55;

Thomas Lask, "Publishing: The Making of a Big Book," *New York Times*, 12 May 1978, III: p. 26;

Donald McCormick, *Who's Who in Spy Fiction* (London: Elm Tree Books / Hamilton, 1977), pp. 76-77.

Frederick Forsyth

(1938-)

Andrew F. Macdonald
Loyola University in New Orleans

BOOKS: *The Biafra Story* (Harmondsworth: Penguin, 1969; New York: Penguin, 1969); revised as *The Making of an African Legend: The Biafra Story* (Harmondsworth: Penguin, 1977; New York: Penguin, 1977);

The Day of the Jackal (London: Hutchinson, 1971; New York: Viking, 1971);

The Odessa File (London: Hutchinson, 1972; New York: Viking, 1972);

The Dogs of War (London: Hutchinson, 1974; New York: Viking, 1974);

The Shepherd (London: Hutchinson, 1975; New York, Viking, 1976);

The Devil's Alternative (London: Hutchinson, 1979; New York: Viking, 1980);

No Comebacks: Collected Short Stories (London: Hutchinson, 1982; New York: Viking, 1982);

The Fourth Protocol (London: Hutchinson, 1984; New York: Viking, 1984);

The Negotiator (London: Bantam, 1989; New York: Bantam, 1989).

Frederick Forsyth, late 1970s (photograph by Coutts Photography, Dublin)

Frederick Forsyth is certainly among the best contemporary writers at capturing the heart and soul of organizations at work. While most crime novels pay necessary attention to police procedure and the motivation of chief and underling, few writers risk the minute concern with the organizational dynamics and the massive amount of detail which truly represent the way organizations do, in fact, operate. The actions of large numbers of people working in concert involve numerous subcategories of specialized knowledge, each with its own nomenclature and special emphasis; the relationship of these groups is what determines what gets done, whether it is apprehending assassins, buying illegal weaponry, or acquiring a perfectly legal driver's license. It is surely no exaggeration to say that organizations largely create the texture of modern life; yet few novels, crime-oriented or otherwise, shed much realistic light on their operation. This is Forsyth's

forte, with the added bonus of precise technical description, worthy of a science writer, of how things work, ranging from the construction of a special rifle (*The Day of the Jackal*, 1971) and improvised car bombs (*The Odessa File*, 1972), to gunrunning (*The Dogs of War*, 1974) and the innards of oil tankers (*The Devil's Alternative*, 1979), to the assembly of miniature nuclear bombs (*The Fourth Protocol*, 1984).

Forsyth was born in Ashford, Kent, in 1938 and educated at Tonbridge School, where he studied French and German. He joined the Royal Air Force in 1956 and served as its youngest fighter pilot at age nineteen before entering a career in journalism. From 1958 to 1961 he was a reporter for the *Eastern Daily Press*, first in Norwich and later in King's Lynn, Norfolk; in 1961 he was a Reuters correspondent and traveled between London, Paris, and East Berlin, serving as bureau chief in the East German capital because of his knowledge of languages; next he acted as a BBC radio reporter in London between 1965 and 1967, an assistant diplomatic correspondent for BBC Television in 1967, and a free-lance journalist in Nigeria in 1967 and 1968 after his pro-Biafran coverage offended Sir David Hunt, British high commissioner in Lagos.

His coverage of the Biafran war led to his one work of nonfiction, *The Biafra Story* (1969; revised as *The Making of an African Legend: The Biafra Story*, 1977). Upon the publication of *The Day of the Jackal*, his first novel, he received the Mystery Writers of America Edgar Allan Poe Award (1971). He married Carrie (a model) in 1973 and has two sons, Stuart and Shane. He and his family presently reside in St. John's Wood, London. Forsyth told J. Bonfante in 1971 that he had no literary ambitions but to be merely a commercial writer whose intent was to sell copies and make money. He claims that *The Day of the Jackal* was born of his need "to ease a financially embarrassed position."

Forsyth's background as a fighter pilot, journalist, world traveler, and speaker of several languages is reflected in *The Shepherd* (1975), a finely crafted short novel about a modern jet pilot, lost and in trouble, guided to safety by a ghost airplane from World War II, but is put to best use in his major novels, all written in a terse journalistic style. Journalistic writing at its best is concrete, immediate, and immensely well informed. A reserved authorial persona confines himself to precise, thorough description about how illegal actions and transactions are managed. His journalistic style is enhanced by the verisimilitude that comes from using real people, places, and events in the immediate background; the ultimate effect is less that of fiction than of a fictional projection into the lives of the real makers of history, not the great leaders but their lieutenants, details about whom never make the front page.

Forsyth's interest is in the individual's relationship to the organization. In his suspense thrillers a man of action in his thirties (in his forties in later works), a consummate professional, is pitted against an establishment, bureaucracy, or organization. The hero, a maverick who succeeds by cutting through standard procedure and who as a result often has difficulty in fitting in, lives up to his own high professional standards. Forsyth suggests that it is the lone professionals, whether opposed to the organization or part of it, who truly create history, but a history represented only

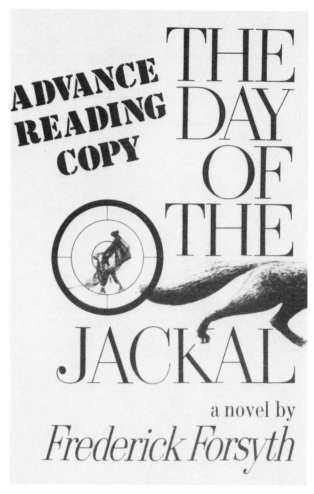

Pre-publication copy of Forsyth's first novel, which sold six million copies within three years of publication (courtesy of Otto Penzler)

palely on the front pages of newspapers. The public is given palatable fictions while the real story is known only by a few professionals who act in concert with their foreign opposite numbers. Forsyth's scenes shift back and forth from the hero to the organization; a collision course is set up early, and the action gradually quickens to the inevitable confrontation. The main characters travel constantly: if their movements were represented on road maps, the opponents would begin in widely separated locations, zigzag with increasing rapidity across the map, sometimes, ironically, crossing paths, and then finally head inexorably toward one another for the denouement as the masterminds quietly manipulate affairs to their liking. As Forsyth cuts from one seemingly unrelated event to another, his technique begins to suggest a hidden pattern governing great events, a pattern not always obvious even to the participants, much less to newspaper readers, who receive only a sanitized version of current history. Inexorable characters and events meet in a satisfying and credible conclusion.

Forsyth's early style is a model of clarity and simplicity, reflecting a journalist's discipline operating at its best in a fictional setting. Sentences are spare, lean, and Hemingwayesque, constructed mainly in a subject-verb-object order, with a minimum of modification and subordination. Some passages could be used to teach technical description, for example, the construction of the bomb in *The Odessa File:* "It was a simple bomb he made. First he emptied the tea down the toilet and kept the can only. In the lid he jabbed a hole with the handle of the wire clippers. He took the nine-foot length of red wire and cut a ten-inch length off it."

The effect of detail invites the reader into the world of the expert, establishing credibility and making the nonexpert a partner and an insider. Forsyth's disciplined style is more than simple restraint, the resisting of the tempting melodramatic adjective or adverb. Rather, it constitutes a point of view, a "transparency" of style that allows the reader a view of plot and character apparently untrammeled by authorial guidance.

Forsyth's imagery, in accordance with his style, is restrained and functional, often serving readers' visual understanding rather than attempting to shape their emotions. For example, in *The Dogs of War* the supports of a pier that had crumbled away are described as "sticking up like broken teeth," and in *The Odessa File* a dead man's face reminds Peter Miller, the protagonist, of "the shrunken skull from the Amazon basin he had once seen, whose lips had been sewn together by the natives."

In his more recent work Forsyth seems to allow himself more latitude with picturesque imagery. For example, in "Sharp Practice," a story from *No Comebacks* (1982), someone is said to be "as harmless as a calf in the byre," and in "A Careful Man," a story from the same collection, a character looks at a pile of money "with the indifference of a satyr observing a virgin." Yet his imagery still serves theme, hardly ever calling attention to itself unduly, and never functioning as simple ornament. For example, in *The Fourth Protocol* most of the imagery has the utilitarian function of characterizing the general secretary of the Communist party of the Soviet Union. He blinks "rarely, and then slowly, like a bird of prey" and nods "like an old lizard." His "hooded eyes

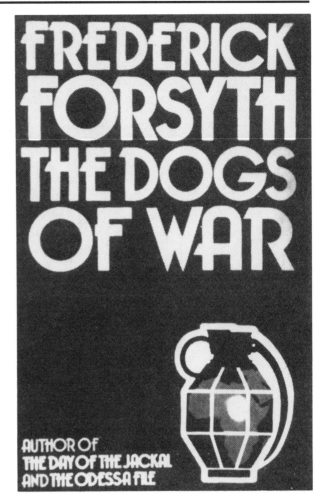

Dust jacket for the first edition of Forsyth's third novel (courtesy of Otto Penzler)

brooded behind the glittering glasses." The style remains otherwise spare and laconic, with understatement Forsyth's only indulgence (for example, "Anyone stopping those four [nine millimeter machine-gun] rounds will speedily feel very unwell").

The Day of the Jackal, based on actual attempts to assassinate French president Charles de Gaulle, was written in thirty-five days. It won immediate acclaim and sold six million copies in three years. Stanley Elkin (*New York Times Book Review*, 15 August 1971) found Forsyth's "implausible villain, a professional assassin whose business card might well read 'Presidents and Premiers My Specialty,'" not only plausible but so professional "that even saintly readers will be hard put not to cheer this particular villain along his devious way." The book opens with a factual account of de Gaulle's signing of the document that made Algeria independent. Forsyth then shows

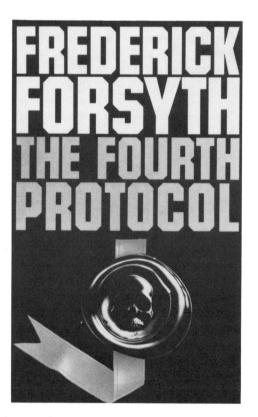

Dust jackets for the first editions of Forsyth's three novels published from 1975 to 1984

readers that right-wing former colonists might well want to attempt to assassinate him, and thus he makes his fictitious account of the assassination attempt seem like a "reconstruction" of a real event. In fact, as Forsyth told Bonfante, the description is so precise and plausible because "everybody in the book is based on somebody . . . not my close friends, just people I've come across or deliberately went after when I was researching. I used old contacts to find people like the Armorer, who told me how to pick up a certain kind of gun, and the Forger, who told me all about false identity cards. Eventually I got to a couple of killers" who "will do a job anyplace, anytime if the price is right." Drawing on his experiences as a Reuters correspondent in Paris and interviews with his technical consultants–assassins, a passport forger, and an underground armorer–Forsyth contrasts the professional and amateur; the professional assassin with an OAS amateur terrorist, the professional gun maker with the amateur forger, the professional detective with political appointees. Only the true professionals are capable of appreciating the subtlety and thoroughness of fellow professionals, since each pays close attention to trivial details, checks remote angles and contingency plans, and deals with situations intellectually rather than emotionally. Thus only Charles Lebel, the French police official who tracks the potential assassin, is capable of keeping up with the Jackal's calculated attempt to assassinate de Gaulle, and both men know it. Lebel's task is to identify an assassin known only by his pseudonym; the Jackal's is to penetrate a tightening police dragnet. The alternating points of view become an intricate chess game as each professional begins to recognize the skills of the other, until the combat ends, quite literally, on a personal level. Forsyth has rejected attempts to identify his fictitious creation with a real assassin, the "Corsican" or the "Scottish Rhodesian" whom he consulted. As he told Bonfante, "No, my Jackal is a superkiller, a human computer. He's quite a bit better than the ones you'll find actually operating around the place. I've put this to the ones I know, and they've said, 'Well, we could do that too.' But they haven't." Deservedly Forsyth's best-known book, *The Day of the Jackal* is both a treatise on police procedure and a testimony to the power of a determined individual. *The Day of the Jackal* has been translated into eleven languages. A successful film was made by Universal Pictures in 1973

with Fred Zinnemann directing and Edward Fox playing the Jackal.

The Day of the Jackal established a highly successful formula, one repeated by Forsyth and a host of other writers. Critics praised its powerful effect (adjectives like "riveting" and "gripping" are common), with some minor cavils at his language. Elkin, for example, talks about his "graceless prose style which shapes up as a lot of *recitatif* and very little aria." Forsyth's novels ever since have been criticized for what they don't do more than for what they actually attempt, but he refuses to rank his work as belles lettres. Yet with each subsequent book, commentators have complained about elements of the formula as faults rather than as essential parts of Forsyth's approach. Michael Crichton (*Saturday Review*, 9 September 1972) found that the subject matter of *The Odessa File* had "too many reverberations, too many profound moral questions, to fit comfortably in a suspense-novel format." He added that the "use of real background in this instance often seems exploitative in a disagreeable way." While Forsyth's historical narration and technical expertise are irreproachable, in *The Odessa File* his "exposed wires of plot" and "dialogue's lumber" help "sour" and "discolor" the "moral urgency" of the book's absorbing facts, according to Richard P. Brickner of the *New York Times Book Review* (5 November 1972). *The Odessa File* follows the attempts of Peter Miller, a highly competent German crime reporter, to uncover and track down a former SS concentration camp commandant in the face of an official and unofficial conspiracy of silence. (The commandant is based on a real person, Captain Eduard Roschmann, who is rumored to be now living in South America.) Miller's investigative expertise serves him well until he runs up against the professionalism of the Odessa (the organization of former SS) and of the anti-Nazi underground. As in *The Day of the Jackal* an individual must penetrate an organization determined to stop him, though here, of course, the moral positions are reversed. Miller's motives for his lonely mission are personal, but the reader is given an exposé of Nazi power in postwar Germany, and the contest begins to assume a larger meaning. Also, as in *The Day of the Jackal*, individual determination proves a worthy adversary to the efficiency of a political machine. To prepare this book, an interesting mix of fact and fiction, Forsyth interviewed Nazi-hunter Simon Wiesenthal, and, in his foreword, confirmed that Odessa really does exist and does aid former SS officers. Columbia Pictures released a film version in 1975 starring Jon Voigt.

If Nazi-hunting bothered some as the setting for docudrama, Forsyth's next book was even more controversial, although *The Dogs of War* breaks his pattern somewhat since no hunt or chase is involved. The book seems to demonstrate a larger concern on Forsyth's part for political systems. Based on his experiences as a correspondent during the Nigerian civil war, it concerns the efforts of a brilliant mercenary leader, Cat Shannon, to topple a corrupt, Idi Amin-like African tyrant on behalf of Sir James Manson (wealthy director of a British mining company), who has discovered and covets a mountain of platinum in the tyrant's country. Shannon and a handful of mercenaries are engaged to install a puppet government which will turn over mining rights to Manson, but the values of the professional mercenary and the amateur king-maker ultimately conflict, and the situation evolves into a contest between Shannon and the company, with results highly satisfactory to the reader who pulls for the underdog. Shannon's motives at first seem purely financial, on a moral par with those of his employer, yet his final actions prove otherwise. The book was controversial not only because of the subject matter but also because of events associated with it. A *London Times* article (25 October 1974) accused Forsyth of financing a coup, paying two hundred thousand dollars to equip, arm, and supply mercenaries to oust President Francisco Marcias Nguema of Equatorial Guinea under the guise of a coastal oil survey. The apparent goal would have been to provide Biafrans with a new homeland. Although the coup failed because of undelivered weapons and an investigation by suspicious Spanish authorities, Forsyth does seem to have been involved to some degree. Having first denied allegations, he finally admitted (*Newsweek*, 1 May 1978) making inquiries and investments that were misunderstood to get inside information about the logistics of starting a coup. Critics such as Donald Goddard (*New York Times Book Review*, 14 July 1974) have attacked the book as less skillful than *The Odessa File*, more of a chess game than a realistic portrait of human action and interaction. (A film released by United Artists in 1981 also received less critical acclaim than the previous two films of Forsyth novels.) They also find the book distasteful for racial and moral reasons: condescending toward black Africans in its assumption that a handful of Europeans could deal with palace guards

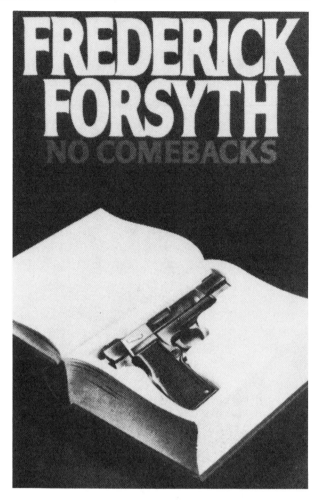

Dust jacket for Forsyth's only short-story collection

and a back-up army totaling close to five hundred men, patronizing in its description of black-African behavior, and overtly sympathetic with mercenaries. A general criticism by Valentine Cunningham (*New Statesman*, 20 September 1974), one reflecting in part the standard objection to Forsyth's method, is that Forsyth, like Daniel Defoe, is "besotted on the detailed processes of capitalist enterprise." Large sums of money effect a "kind of hypnosis" in the reader which is "corrupting" since "you're encouraged to believe that with money all things are possible . . . enviably acceptable and proper."

The Devil's Alternative attempts to raise the question of how world terrorism might lead to world war, even given good intentions on the part of most involved. The vision is somewhat darker than in Forsyth's earlier works, in which a moral choice was possible. Here, both governments and individuals in a shrinking world face "devil's alternatives"; that is, somebody must get hurt, no matter which alternative is chosen. A subsidiary point concerns the vulnerability of oil supertankers, portrayed as floating bombs, unprotectable by land-based security organizations; the seizure of a supertanker automatically transcends national interests, for every coastline threatened by a spill must be defended in a chaos of overlapping jurisdictions.

The Devil's Alternative represents a somewhat new direction for Forsyth, for he includes geopolitics and national leaders as well as his typical lone wolves working for and against the system. The shift is a natural one, given Forsyth's canon. The book hypothesizes what happens when a lone wolf meets a person who has mastered a massive bureaucracy. The last scene of *The Devil's Alternative* suggests that the two roles have more in common than one might think, an answer that is important to an understanding of global political events.

The Devil's Alternative was found by Marghanita Laski (*Listener*, 10 January 1980) to be "competent and well-informed" but "laborious." Adrian Karatnycky (*New Leader*, 7 April 1980) criticized Forsyth's "careless and inaccurate" descriptions of nationalist dissident groups in the Soviet Union, while misunderstanding Forsyth by claiming he "invents" guns that "emit sounds powerful enough to stun an opponent"—elite antiterrorist squads have used such weapons for years. A common element in all the criticism is a refusal to accept Forsyth's docudrama formula for what it is, but rather to assume it should be more conventionally "fictional."

No Comebacks is a collection of ten short stories, three of which were originally published in *Playboy*, loosely grouped around the idea of the title story of actions being taken with finality and irreversible decision. The collection is surprising and delightful, for most of the protagonists are well developed, and Forsyth reveals an unexpected wit and a deft, O. Henry-like skill at ironic final reversal. Yet the main themes of individual against organization, or the supercompetent hero pitting himself against evildoers, of the fascination with how things are done, whether the hiding of funds from Inland Revenue or the hijacking of cognac, remain the same. Forsyth's common theme of defying the establishment is broadened in that some of his protagonists are middle-aged or elderly, in that their defiance includes arranging the comeuppance of a shrewish wife and wreaking revenge on an arrogant journalist. The plots turn, not on apocalyptic events, but rather on the small victories and defeats that create the texture of everyday life for the ordinary person. As such, they come closer to more "serious" literature than the world-shaking plots of his long novels.

The stories offer great variety. "No Comebacks" itself is about an arrogant industrialist, of the type first met in *The Dogs of War*, who hires a hit man to eliminate his competition for the love of a woman. As in the novel the industrialist learns that Forsyth's professionals often behave in unpredictable ways. "There Are No Snakes in Ireland" includes Forsyth's most unusual hero, an Indian medical student studying in Ireland and working as a day laborer. The student's revenge on a bully is ingenious and also in accord with a long British literary tradition concerning exotic Indian fauna, yet (even so) nothing works out as planned. (The Irish stories reflect Forsyth's tax exile in Ireland in the late 1970s, when he lived near Dublin with his Irish wife.) "The Emperor" is a fishing yarn with a final and satisfying twist. (Forsyth himself fishes in the Indian Ocean yearly.) "There Are Some Days . . . " makes sense of the kind of news story one sometimes finds so puzzling: How can a meticulously planned robbery be so stupidly muffed in its outcome? The title of "Money With Menaces" refers to the legal definition of blackmail, with the villains completely underestimating the nature of their prey, a Forsyth-type hero in his later years. "Used in Evidence," set in Dublin, creates an intriguing hero, Chief Superintendent Hanley, a former rugby star who charges hard at a solution to an apparent twenty-year-old murder, only to have it evade him. The final twist so neatly defines the pressure created by an almost perfect interpretation of the facts that the story might well serve as required reading for students in any of the interpretive professions. "Privilege" is about the revenge taken by a small businessman on an arrogant journalist; the story made an excellent short film for Irish television (shown in the United States in March 1984). As a former journalist with characteristic strong-mindedness, Forsyth comes down firmly on the side of the underdog victimized by the establishment. "Duty" is the kind of horrific tale one hears from veteran travelers who discover their most embarrassing nightmares coming true as, for example, when their train compartment companion pulls out the pictures of himself in an SS uniform, only this version has an Irish twist. "A Careful Man" returns to a classic Forsyth protagonist, the supercompetent mature

- 217 -

pedestrians and came through the doorway into the foodfare
shop like a tornado. The telephone was on the cash desk,
next to the register, behind which stood Mr Patel.

'Those kids are stealing your oranges,' said Quinn
without ceremony. At that moment the phone rang. Torn
between a telephone call and stolen oranges, Mr Patel
reacted like a good Gujerati and ran outside. Quinn
picked up the handset.

The Kensington exchange had reacted fast, and the
enquiry would show they had done their best. But they lost
several of the forty seconds through sheer surprise, then
they had a technical problem. Their 'lock' was on the
flash-line in the apartment. Whenever a call came in to
that number, their electronic exchange could run back up
the line to establish the source of the call. The number
it came from would then be revealed by the computer to be
such-and-such a booth in a certain place. Between six and
ten seconds.

They already had a lock on the number Zack had
used first, but when he changed booths, even though the
kiosks were side-by-side in Dunstable, they lost him.
Worse, he was now ringing another London number into
which they were not tapped. The only saving grace was that
the number Quinn had dictated down the line to Zack was
still on the Kensington exchange. Still, the tracers had
to start at the beginning, their call-finder mechanism
racing frantically through the 20,000 numbers on the
exchange. They tapped into Mr Patel's phone fifty-eight
seconds after Quinn had dictated it, then got a lock on
the second number in Dunstable.

'Take this number Zack,' said Quinn without preamble.
'What the hell's going on?' snarled Zack.
'Nine-three-five: three-two-one-five,' said
Quinn remorselessly. 'Got it?'
There was a pause as Zack scribbled.

'Now we'll do it ourselves, Zack. I've done a
runner on the lot of them. Just you and me, the diamonds
against the boy. No tricks, my word on it. Call me on
that number in sixty minutes and ninety minutes if there's
no reply first time. It's not on trace.'

Corrected typescript page for The Negotiator *(courtesy of the author)*

businessman who pits himself against a government and dishonest individuals. A highly recommended 1985 videotape was filmed for Irish television with Dan O'Herlihy and Cyril Cusack. Finally, "Sharp Practice," another Irish tale, focuses on con men playing on their victims' greed to outwit the law even when caught dead to rights.

Forsyth's short stories reveal a gentler and more "literary" sensibility than the hard-driving, masculine persona of the longer novels. However allegedly pecuniary Forsyth's motives for writing his more successful works, the short stories show a determined sympathy for the vulnerable little man and an almost nostalgic championing of traditional fair play. In spite of their abbreviated length the stories for the most part showcase fully rounded characters in relatively realistic situations, facing problems which are often quite modest and ordinary. The stories thus offer a more domestic and limited perspective on the themes that inform the longer novels.

While James Campbell (*New Statesman*, 30 April 1982) feels a "Forsyth story exists for its detail alone" and these details "choke" the short story form, most critics find the stories "diverting" and highly enjoyable, and perhaps most surprisingly given the grimness of the novels, sometimes very funny (see Mel Watkins, *New York Times Book Review*, 9 May 1982 and Margaret Cannon, *Maclean's*, 14 June 1982).

The title of Forsyth's *The Fourth Protocol* refers to a secret agreement by the original nuclear powers not to introduce miniature and portable nuclear weapons onto the soil of an enemy. When technological capability coincides with political opportunity, the temptation for the Soviets becomes too great, and a plot is set in motion so secretly that even the KGB is unenlightened. In typical Forsyth fashion the scene jumps from location to disparate location as seemingly unrelated events begin to coalesce into a related pattern, albeit one invisible even to the participants. The action moves from London's upper-crust society to London's underworld, from Moscow to South Africa, from Glasgow to the airports of Europe. A jewel theft and the patriotism of an irritated jewel thief provide keys to the violation of the fourth protocol, but no one, not even the nominal hero John Preston, has all the answers until the end. Preston is a dogged intelligence agent similar to Lebel from *The Day of the Jackal*, but here Forsyth depicts a middle-aged man rendered obsolete by the political machinations of

Publisher's advertisement from the 31 March 1989 issue of Bookseller

the shallow bureaucrats around him, officials who have lost the spirit of their enterprise even as they practice its superficial appearances. Forsyth's supercop is unappreciated by everyone except another old-school type nearing retirement, Sir Nigel Irvine, head of MI 6. The Russian secret services also reward the most able political manipulators rather than their best operatives, and readers are left with a fictional world like that of John le Carré in which the shadowy politics within intelligence agencies on both sides of the Iron Curtain take precedence over the simple interests of the nations they defend.

Preston is forty-six years old, divorced, and nearing burnout in his job. Like all of Forsyth's supercops he is a master at setting in motion complex investigations involving public records and a team of special agents, yet he yearns for the excitement of the chase in the field. There is a distinctly sour note to Preston's life. His prey, Major Valeri Petrofsky, is a typical Forsyth villain, single-minded and completely committed, and it is this contrast between the two characters and the book's heavy political orientation that is the major difference between *The Fourth Protocol* and Forsyth's earlier novels.

Although Forsyth's adventure works have always had a definite political cast (that has been a subtext that informed readers' enjoyment of their escapist surface), they have remained relatively objective in their depiction of hero and villain. *The Day of the Jackal* encouraged readers to admire the Jackal's competence and daring even as they deplore his goal of assassinating de Gaulle; certainly part of the appeal of the book is the glimpse into the mysterious workings of the OAS and its assassin. *The Odessa File, The Dogs of War,* and *The Devil's Alternative,* on the other hand, all pick safe enough targets for their villains: Nazis, rapacious capitalists, mad dictators, and irresponsible terrorists have few defenders among the reading public. *The Fourth Protocol,* however, depicts the British Left as the tool, however unwitting, of Soviet imperialism, as a left-wing takeover of the Labour Party makes Britain a ripe candidate for Soviet satellite status. The book posits an unusual ideological position for adventure or spy fiction, and as such makes a far harsher criticism of the Left than his previous novels; yet Forsyth maintains it throughout, with antinuclear weapons protesters and other leftist groups being held in "disgust and contempt" even by the Russian agent: "He sighed as he thought of the speedy way his own country's MVD troops would deal with this march before handing over the ringleaders to the lads in the Fifth Chief Directorate for an extended question-and-answer session down at Lefortovo." Forsyth's first novel set on English turf is also his most politically controversial.

Reaction to *The Fourth Protocol* has naturally taken some partisan turns. Walter Clemons (*Newsweek,* 3 September 1984) called it a "Tory boy's book" with "childish pretensions"; if the "mere idea of the defeat of Margaret Thatcher doesn't make your conservative spine tingle," then the "urgency" of the book disappears. Michiko Kakutani (*The New York Times,* 30 August 1984) said the premise of the book was "silly" and the denouement "predictable," while Peter Maas (*New York Times Book Review,* 2 September 1984) pointed out that only intelligence officials come off well in the book, with politicians on both sides either foolish or corrupted. Roderick MacLeish (*Book World,* 26 August 1984) said *The Fourth Protocol* was Forsyth's "best book so far." Jane Stewart Spitzer (*Christian Science Monitor,* 7 September 1984) said the plot "unfolds like a cabbage . . . leaf by leaf " in a "suspenseful" manner.

With *The Negotiator* (1989) Forsyth continues his "building-block" format, this time to focus on a political kidnapping set in the 1990s. British prime minister Margaret Thatcher has a cameo-role: in the book she is "an extremely humane lady, far more than her five immediate male predecessors . . . able to stay cooler than any of them under pressure" but "far from immune to tears" as she weeps for her ineffectual ally John Cormack, president of the United States, whose son has been kidnapped from Oxford. The focus of the book is on the negotiations for the son's release and the security-service rivalry that affects them. Interwoven with this central plot is a multinational oil scheme designed to force an American invasion of Saudi Arabia and the installation of a puppet monarchy by murdering the entire Saudi royal family (six hundred princes) and allowing an Islamic fundamentalist to take control. Meanwhile, the Soviets plan to take over Iran, Western capitalists and Soviet militarists join forces to block a comprehensive American-Soviet disarmament treaty, and the pro-Pentagon vice-president threatens to invoke the 25th Amendment to rid the nation of President Cormack. Quinn, a seasoned Vietnam veteran and the negotiator of the title, works for the kidnapped youth's release, only to be thwarted by American traitors and an incompetent FBI. Throughout the book Quinn arrives moments too late, finding the president's son killed at the moment of his ransoming and various villains assassinated just as he is on to them. Ultimately, with assistance from a female FBI agent, Quinn tracks down the murderers of the president's son and exposes the powers behind them.

Christopher Hawtree, in the *Spectator* (6 May 1989), finds the first ninety pages of *The Negotiator* "the worst that Forsyth has written," with jets lumbering to and fro and "leaden-laden" and "wooden" world figures engaging in political analysis that reads like it was taken from the British tabloid the *Sun.* Hawtree finds the Middle East oil subplot clumsy, the love interest unexciting, and the "catalogue of statistics" overwhelming. What bothers Hawtree most about the novel is what makes many Forsyth readers come back for more: the sense of immediacy, of an insider's view of world affairs, of all-too-human world figures. There are details that give a sense of thorough research and a plot that leaps from scene to scene and place to place but inexorably connects the loose threads. Forsyth demonstrates his understanding of the intricacies of hostage negotiations and of the best ways to transport huge amounts of money as well as his ability to effectively capture a sense of place. As Harry Anderson in *Newsweek* (24 April 1989) says, the weaknesses of the novel are "almost beside the point," for Forsyth delivers a "string of unsettling climaxes." The book's tension and the brutal plot twists make it "a comparative rarity: a completely satisfying thriller." Martin Morse Wooster in *Wall Street Journal* (12 April 1989) agrees, concluding that "*The Negotiator* confirms Mr. Forsyth's position as one of the world's best thriller writers."

A writer who has sold more than thirty million copies of his books can certainly afford to indulge some tendentious political jawboning, whether his critics approve or not. A far more interesting literary question than whether Forsyth is correct about the British Left or the American Right concerns the future of the modern docudrama genre, one which Forsyth has a legitimate claim to having helped develop and popularize. The docudrama form, of course, is the fictional side of the marriage of fiction and journalism which was popular in the 1960s with such books as Truman Capote's *In Cold Blood* and Norman Mailer's experiments with fact and the novel form. While many writers elected to write journalism using the devices of fiction, others, like Forsyth, chose fiction made realistic by the conventions of journalism. Certainly none of Forsyth's imitators have duplicated his precise technical description nor his fast-moving cinematic plots, yet readers can expect to see more blending of jour-

nalism and literature into one of the most popular literary forms of our times.

Interview:

Paul Levy, "Down on the Farm with Frederick Forsyth," *Wall Street Journal*, 18 April 1989, p. A22.

References:

B. A. Bannon, "Story Behind the Book: *The Day of the Jackal*," *Publishers Weekly*, 200 (9 August 1971): 34-35;

J. Bonfante, "Some Bloody Critics Check Out the Jackal," *Life*, 71 (22 October 1971): 77;

"Britain's Shy Spy Master at Work," *World Press Review*, 34 (May 1987): 61;

D. Butler and A. Collings, "The Forsyth Saga," *Newsweek*, 91 (1 May 1978): 44;

"Day of Frederick Forsyth," *World Press Review*, 27 (March 1980): 61–interview with F. O. Giesbert;

David Howard, "Frederick Forsyth," *Book and Magazine Collector*, 63 (June 1989): 4-10;

"A Profile in Intrigue," *People*, 22 (22 October 1984): 87-89;

Erick Sauter, "Spy Master," *Saturday Review*, 11 (July-August 1985): 38-41;

Joan Smith, "Who's Afraid of Frederick Forsyth?," *New Statesman*, 115 (15 January 1988): 24-26;

Peter Wolfe, "Stalking Forsyth's Jackal," *Armchair Detective*, 7 (May 1974): 165-174.

Dick Francis

(31 October 1920-   )

Gina Macdonald
Loyola University in New Orleans

BOOKS: *The Sport of Queens: The Autobiography of Dick Francis* (London: Joseph, 1957; revised, 1968; New York: Harper, 1969; revised again, London: Joseph, 1974);

Dead Cert (London: Joseph 1962; New York: Holt, Rinehart, 1962);

Nerve (London: Joseph, 1964; New York: Harper, 1964);

For Kicks (London: Joseph, 1965; New York: Harper, 1965);

Odds Against (London: Joseph, 1965; New York: Harper, 1966);

Flying Finish (London: Joseph, 1966; New York: Harper, 1967);

Blood Sport (London: Joseph, 1967; New York: Harper, 1968);

Forfeit (London: Joseph, 1969; New York: Harper, 1969);

Enquiry (London: Joseph, 1969; New York: Harper, 1969);

Rat Race (London: Joseph, 1970; New York: Harper, 1971);

Bonecrack (London: Joseph, 1971; New York: Harper, 1972);

Smokescreen (London: Joseph, 1972; New York: Harper, 1973);

Slay-ride (London: Joseph, 1973); republished as *Slayride* (New York: Harper, 1974);

Knock Down (London: Joseph, 1974); republished as *Knockdown* (New York: Harper, 1975);

High Stakes (London: Joseph, 1975; New York: Harper, 1976);

In the Frame (London: Joseph, 1976; New York: Harper, 1977);

Risk (London: Joseph, 1977; New York: Harper, 1978);

Trial Run (London: Joseph, 1978; New York: Harper, 1979);

Whip Hand (London: Joseph, 1979; New York: Harper, 1980);

Reflex (London: Joseph, 1980; New York: Putnam's, 1981);

Twice Shy (London: Joseph, 1981; New York: Putnam's, 1982);

Dick Francis (photograph by Mary Francis)

Banker (London: Joseph, 1982; New York: Putnam's, 1983);

The Danger (London: Joseph, 1983; New York: Putnam's, 1984);

Proof (London: Joseph, 1984; New York: Putnam's, 1985);

Break In (London: Joseph, 1985; New York: Putnam's, 1986);

A Jockey's Life: The Biography of Lester Piggott (London: Joseph, 1985; New York: Putnam's, 1986);

Bolt (London: Joseph, 1986; New York: Putnam's, 1987);

Hot Money (London: Joseph, 1987; New York: Putnam's, 1988);

The Edge (London: Joseph, 1988; New York: Putnam's, 1989);

Straight (London: Joseph, 1989; New York: Putnam's, 1989).

OTHER: "Dead Cert," in *Best Racing and Chasing Stories*, edited by Francis and John Welcome (London: Faber & Faber, 1966), pp. 86-101;

"The Midwinter Gold Cup," in *Best Racing and Chasing Stories 2*, edited by Francis and Welcome (London: Faber & Faber, 1969), pp. 143-151;

The Racing Man's Bedside Book, edited by Francis and Welcome (London: Faber & Faber, 1969);

"The Gift," in *Winter's Crimes 5*, edited by Virginia Whitaker (London: Macmillan, 1973), pp. 104-130;

"Nightmares," in *Ellery Queen's Searches and Seizures*, edited by Ellery Queen (New York: Davis, 1977), pp. 141-149;

"The Day of the Losers," in *John Creasey's Crime Collection 1980*, edited by Herbert Harris (London: Gollancz, 1980).

PERIODICAL PUBLICATION: "Can't Anybody Here Write these Games? The Trouble with Sports Fiction," *New York Times Book Review*, 1 June 1986, p. 56.

Author of twenty-eight novels, which have been translated into nearly two dozen languages and which have sold more than twenty million copies, Dick Francis is unequaled at making horseracing come alive. In fact, Philip Larkin (*Times Literary Supplement*, 10 October 1980) calls his novels "brilliant vignettes," and admirers such as John Welcome (*London Magazine*, March 1980) point out that in his work "one can hear the smash of birch, the creak of leather and the rattle of whips." He asserts that no one can touch Francis at capturing the "tragedies and occasional triumphs," "the seductive beauties" of the track, and infusing them with a significance beyond their domain: "a microcosm of the contemporary world." Julian Symons has argued (*New York Times Book Review*, 29 March 1981) that what Francis does best is to capture the "thrills, spills and chills of horse racing." His prose is lucid, his plots ingenious, intricate, and carefully conceived. His dialogue captures the nuances of class and region as he throws together the echelons of equine sports: owners, trainers, jockeys, stable lads, bookmakers, and touts.

His basic formula is predictable: competent stoics, out of love or loyalty or a sense of fair play and decency, are forced to come to terms with a hidden evil, one at first only suspected but then clearly defined by injury or death. His heroes must face physical pain or psychological trauma and must summon up their inner strength, their resilience, and their sheer grit to unravel the mystery, save their friends, prove themselves, or simply defeat evil. His villains are always motivated by greed or insanity, or, as in *Break In* (1984), both. Despite his standard approach, Francis's works are never the same. His plots remain fresh, unexpected, solid. They move forward briskly, with an admirable sense of timing, and are lent variety by his interweaving of racing and other concerns: mining, photography, banking, computer science, aviation, accounting, art, antiques, yachting, private investigation, acting, and the wine business. Francis's books are not simply novels of suspense, but, as Edward Zuckerman has so aptly called them (*New York Times Magazine*, 25 March 1984), "novels of character and manners."

Richard Stanley Francis was born on 31 October 1920 at Coedcanlas, his maternal grandfather's farm near Tenby, Wales. His father, George Vincent Francis, who had been a professional steeplechase jockey before World War I, was later manager of W. J. Smith's stables at Holyport, near Maidenhead.

Francis learned to ride at age five and showed horses at age twelve. He vowed at age fifteen to become a professional jockey and helped race, train, transport, and show horses for his father, first at Holyport, then at the family stables near Wokingham. During much of World War II he was an airplane mechanic. In the later years of the war he flew fighter planes, troop-carrying gliders, and Wellington bombers for the Royal Air Force. After the war he returned to racing, first as an amateur (tacitly taking under-the-table "gifts" from grateful owners), then as a professional. The conflict between amateurs and professionals, which he personally experienced, provides tension in many of his novels. Standing five feet, eight inches tall and weighing 150 pounds, Francis was too large to ride in flat races and so made the steeplechase his specialty. After riding seventy-six horses to victory during the 1953-1954 racing season, he won the title of champi-

Dust jacket for the first American edition of Francis's novel set in Moscow

on jockey. The same year he began riding for Elizabeth, the Queen Mother.

Francis had long been a devotee of detective fiction, in his youth reading Arthur Conan Doyle, Nat Gould (a pre-World War I English racing writer), and Edgar Wallace. In maturity he began to read writers such as Alistair MacLean, Desmond Bagley, Gavin Lyall, and Michael Underwood, all writers who competently capture a world of expertise. But Francis never considered writing until forced to retire from steeplechasing at age thirty-six. He had just before suffered an unusual incident at the Grand National, when Devon Loch, the Queen Mother's horse, perhaps frightened by the roar of the crowd, fell on its stomach ten strides from the winning post–and that after clearing the last fence of the grueling four-and-a-half-mile course. Losing the race remains a sore spot, with Francis's nightmare that of being remembered as the man who lost the

Grand National in so spectacular a way. Shortly after, Francis had a horse fall on top of him, kick him in the stomach, and break his wrist. His doctor recommended retirement. Until that time he had had an illustrious career as a jockey, having ridden 350 winners and having served as the Queen Mother's first jockey. However, as Francis himself points out in a 1983 *Writer* interview, after age thirty-five "the human body doesn't allow you to bounce back" from falls "thirty or forty times a year at forty miles an hour," the average for most steeplechase jockeys.

After the agent son of a friend of his mother had encouraged him to write his autobiography, and then the sports editor of the *London Sunday Express* had persuaded him to try his hand at covering the track, Francis finally decided to try to make a living as racing correspondent and did so, working for the *Sunday Express* for sixteen years. The position allowed him to move in familiar circles, but the difficulties of walking "a fine edge" in dealing with one's friends and acquaintances as "raw material" that the racing correspondent-hero of *Forfeit* (1969) complains about clearly reflect Francis's feelings. Consequently, while still a correspondent, Francis decided to attempt mystery writing to help pay for the education of his two sons and improve the family finances. He has turned out a novel a year ever since. Francis feels that journalism taught him a crisp, disciplined style that, together with his own obsession with precision and timing, has made his novels terse, fast-paced, and solid. Nonetheless, racing remains his first love. When Sid Halley, in *Whip Hand* (1979), quotes a former champion who took thirty years to get over his yearning for racing, it is probably Francis speaking of his own sense of loss. At the track he takes pleasure in watching the tactics of jockeys; at home he works out those tactics on paper. As he pointed out in the interview with Zuckerman, "Having a book on the best-seller list is very nice, but there's nothing nicer than jumping over large fences on a good horse and looking through his pricked ears for the next ones."

Francis claims his method is to think of a plot by midsummer, do his research in the fall, and start writing around 1 January when the family goes to Fort Lauderdale, Florida; he does his first draft in longhand, then reads it aloud on tape, types it up, and submits his manuscript by late April. He discusses his plots a good deal with his wife, Mary Margaret Brenchley, whom he married in 1947. She researches new fields of exper-

Dust jacket for the first American edition of Francis's 1979 novel featuring the one-handed ex-jockey, Sid Halley, who was introduced in Odds Against *(1965).*

tise, makes suggestions about details and credibility, and helps him with the final editing. Sometimes he does not know how he will end his story until he actually sits down with his exercise book and starts writing. Since the early 1970s he and his wife have traveled around the world for his research, once going to Australia for a promotional campaign that produced *In the Frame* (1976) and later to Johannesburg, South Africa, to judge the National Horse Show, see a gold mine, and visit a game reserve (the basis for *Smokescreen*, 1972). A trip to see the fjords of Norway produced *Slayride* (1973; published in the United States as *Slayride*, 1974); a visit to Moscow, a city he observed with distaste, led to *Trial Run* (1978). Travel in America spawned *High Stakes* (1975), which takes place in part in Florida, and *Blood Sport* (1967), a tale of kidnapping, which is set in London, New York, Kentucky, Las Vegas, and California (Francis took a Greyhound bus cross-country to see the lay of the land). A meticulous

writer, he prides himself on his accuracy and claims, in fact, to have made only one error since beginning his publishing career, miscalling the London School of Music the London College of Music. His works incorporate experiences from his own life, though he claims never to have had any sinister dealings at the track, only a half-hearted attempt at a bribe made by a bookmaker who wanted him and his brother to stop a horse. He agreed with Brigette Weeks that his heroes "are all very similar" because, although their characters are built up "out of a number of people," they are like someone he would like to meet or be like himself; they are male because he feels unable to place himself "in a woman's mind."

Francis's novels combine the best of the classical and the hard-boiled detective fiction traditions: 1) country truths with city vice; 2) ratiocination with personal involvement; 3) an unquestionably upright, genteel hero of sound principles who is tough, hard-boiled, cynical, and down-to-earth, capable of violence, and mistrusted by the police; 4) an objective search for a pattern of clues amidst red herrings and a carefully reasoned elimination of suspects with a personal motivation for seeking justice, a crusade in which the search involves questions of loyalty and personal betrayal and ends with personal solutions; 5) offstage deaths with active violence and a physical confrontation between investigator and criminal. The combination of the two traditions is part of what gives the Francis adventure novel its power and appeal. Though the particulars change from novel to novel, the Francis hero is basically the same: a seemingly common man who proves himself uncommon. He may be upper class or working class, but he always reflects a mixture of the values of both classes, yet is not totally a part of either world. He values decency, hard work, competence, practicality, and amiability, and is contemptuous of snobbery, hypocrisy, and bullying. He is often an amateur rather than a professional, riding more for the joy of the sport than for the income, and his choice of vocation or avocation involves physical labor and hobnobbing amicably across class barriers. He does not particularly care about power or prestige; he judges men by who they are and what they can do, not by money or class. He is self-disciplined and resourceful, introspective, and usually in his thirties. He is also a loner (for example, the hero in *Enquiry* [1969] is said to have eyes that are "dark and sort of smiley and sad and a bit withdrawn"), but in spirit he is allied with other men of principle. He instinctively protects the weak and the innocent. What one of the characters says about the protagonist in *Slay-ride* applies to all Francis heroes: "Give him one fact and he guesses the rest."

Francis's hero's interest in crime grows out of his personal sense of moral outrage. In *Flying Finish* (1966) he is appalled by the cold-hearted villainy of throwing men out of planes in mid flight, just because they *might* know too much, and disturbed that his friend, a decent man, believes the best of everybody, "even with villainy staring him in the face," all because of his "illogical faith in human goodness." In *Dead Cert* (1962) he approves of a retired sergeant-major who, when faced by murderous thugs demanding protection money, not only effectively protects himself and his family but organizes the community, helping them train guard dogs and hiring a judo expert to protect the children on their way to school. In *Slay-ride* he is angered by the callous beating of a scared and pregnant young woman and sympathizes with a guilt-ridden youngster who kills to save himself and who is deeply wounded by his father's ruthlessness. He also mourns a treacherous friend who betrayed him and nearly destroyed him. In *In the Frame* he wants "to smash in the heads of all greedy, callous, vicious people who cynically devastated the lives of total strangers. Compassion was all right for saints. What I felt was plain hatred, fierce and basic." This anger leads him to spend money and effort, travel halfway around the world, and face near death to help a friend; he criticizes the modern attitude that "anyone who tries to right a wrong" is "a fool" who would be much better off not meddling, not getting involved, not accepting moral responsibility, and asks, when "I see the hell he's in" and know "there's a chance of getting him out," "how can I just turn my back?"

Francis's villain is a social climber, a ruthless person who wants money, rank, and title, but lives in too flashy a fashion so all seems overdone. He is impeccably turned out. His car is expensive and garish. He bears a pretentious name such as Trevor Deansgate, Ivor den Relgan, Hedley Humber, or Quintus. He values possessions more than people. He is rather a snob and either seems too good to be true (like the "golden boy" of *Smokescreen*) or has shady associates who reflect his true nature. Sometimes his greed drives him mad, and the animal behind the facade takes over. Like the villains of the Conan Doyle stories, he exists by way of contrast with the detective-hero and is sometimes a cruel, sadistic bully (like Grimsby Royden in "The Adventure of the Speckled Band"), driven by greed, jealousy, and an inherent evil. The description of Kraye in *Odds Against* (1965) is typical: "Even though I was as far as he knew an insignificant fly to swat, a clear quality of menace flowed out of him like a radio signal. The calm social mask had disappeared along with the wordy, phony surface personality." What lies beneath is the dangerous, sadistic, amoral villain—"the boa constrictor" behind the guise of "grass snake."

The Francis hero, on the other hand, is loyal, honorable, self-aware, and at times self-sacrificing, a man who values friendship and who desires to stand on his own merits; but he is also a man who knows what he wants, even if it does not meet the conventional social expectations. He will do all he can to win the love of the girl he finds attractive, but he has a strong sense of fair play and will not gain an unfair advantage over a rival by telling the girl's parents he is wealthy or a lord. His powers of close observation and deduction are highly developed, but his reasoning often involves instinctive leaps of the imagination; for example, the hero of *Dead Cert* is said to have "an unerring instinct for smelling out crooks." He may be tortured by self-doubt and insecurities and openly deny his heroic instincts, but beneath his quiet, nondescript exterior is an inner core that is tough, resilient, and undefeatable. In *Flying Finish* the hero is described as "ice on a volcano," and his friends agree. Often the hero's brush with villainy results from his kind heart. He is capable of enduring extreme physical punishment and not only surviving but being able to laugh at it. In *Rat Race* (1970) he braves it out: "I've been bruised before and I've broken my collar-bone before. It doesn't last long!" But he adds ruefully to himself that it was indeed highly "unpleasant" while it lasted, though he can feel better about personal damage if he inflicts a little himself: "They took with them some damaged knee cartilage, aching larynxes, and one badly scratched eye."

Francis's setting is usually peaceful, rural, idyllic, his central character in tune with nature and animals. He eulogizes the glories of taking racehorses for their morning exercise, the simple pleasures of unity of man and beast, the wind in one's hair, and the sun on one's back. His descriptions of the racetrack reflect a classical view of nature as controlled and tamed, with white picket

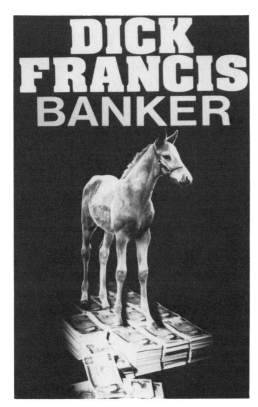
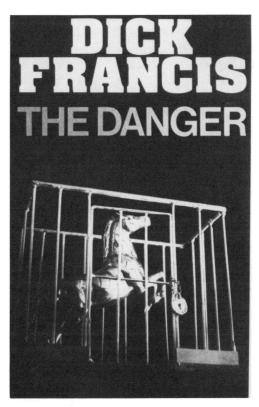

Dust jackets for the first editions of three of Francis's many books set in the world of horse racing

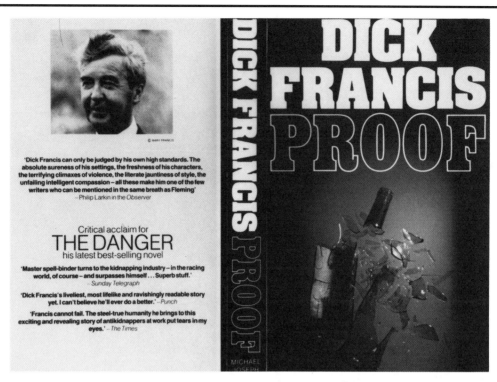

Dust jacket for the first edition of Francis's 1984 novel

fences, manicured turfs, and well-groomed horses. The stables usually are near a city but far enough out for the air to be fresh and invigorating. Within the setting, city men, greedy and corruptible, may betray these rural values with blackmail, bribes, threats of violence, and foul play, fixing bets and fixing races. In doing so they force authority to control everyone's freedom. *Whip Hand* looks behind the beauty and ritual of the track to capture the bleaker side: "People ready to bribe, people with the ready palm. Anguished little hopefuls and arrogant big guns. The failures making brave excuses, and the successful hiding the anxieties behind their eyes. All as it had been, and was, and would be, as long as racing lasted."

Francis builds on both English and American detective traditions in his focus on justice. In *Dead Cert* Alan York allows Uncle George to commit suicide rather than be placed in an insane asylum or be dragged through a homicide trial that would be injurious to and painful for his family. He also punishes the dishonest jockey, Sandy, for guilt by complicity when the law cannot touch him, tossing him off his horse in mid race, to be bruised, battered, and broken. In *Rat Race* Matt Shore, who has once before broken air-flight regulations to deliver needed supplies to impoverished Latin American refugees, now breaks them

again to rescue Nancy, noting that he always told himself to stay out of trouble but never listened: "I had just broken two laws and would undoubtedly be prosecuted again by the Board of Trade. I wondered if I would ever learn to keep myself out of trouble." In *Forfeit* James Tyrone, intoxicated by whiskey forced down his throat, fuzzily thinks, "Got to stop him smashing up our lives, smashing up other people's lives." Someone, somewhere, had to stop him, and Tyrone does so, causing a car wreck that kills the key villains. He feels guilty when sober but realizes that his deed has ended crimes that the law would have had trouble confirming.

Another Francis hallmark is his emphasis on the intrinsic and extrinsic rewards of competence and skill that go beyond class barriers. For Francis, the best man is one who is well rounded and versatile; he can move with ease among all classes, knowing that competence, not class, makes the man, and that a man should ultimately be judged on what he is as an individual, not on what his origins are. In *Trial Run* someone describes the hero as looking like "one of those useless la-di-das in the telly ads," but he performs with the reflexes and coolheadedness of a professional. In the majority of Francis's books his characters demonstrate competence in racing. They are able to recognize their horse's potential despite appearances. Because they know the horse, the course, and the psychology of racing, they can get the best performance from an animal, no matter what its quirks. They also know how to fall and how to deal with injuries both to horse and man. But usually they are also competent in other areas as well. If they are pilots, they fly with mechanical precision, understanding the versatility and the limitations of the aircraft. They know flight patterns and navigational devices beyond a simple mechanical ability with instruments so that even under primitive conditions they can maintain a high level of precision. Such familiarity with their machinery is so much a part of them that they can recognize intuitively when anything is amiss. In *Rat Race*, for instance, Matt senses a bomb on board the plane because the slight weight has been enough to alter the way the plane feels in flight. Francis's boatmen are easy masters of their boats and their situations. The painter in *In the Frame* knows that "if you mix flake white, which is lead, with cadmium yellow, which contains sulfur, . . . you get a nice pale color to start with, but the two minerals react against each other and in time darken and alter the picture." Clearly for Francis, competence involves understanding one's limits as well as one's potential, so one can recognize when someone else is a better jockey, a better aviator, or a more astute businessman. Such competence also involves a process of character building. As men learn to handle unexpected situations and are forced to develop physical and mental strength and agility to deal with every possibility, they are also forced to make moral decisions, to develop a code of loyalty, and to learn to listen to their inner voice.

However, as one might expect, Francis's focus on competence also means a focus on the realities of a profession rather than the idealized public view of it. Hence, while Francis does show readers the winner and all his glory, he also emphasizes that there are more losers than winners, that winning is not always a comfortable experience, that being a jockey is a hard, demanding job. He portrays trainers having to endure criticism from owners and jockeys, owners being duped by unscrupulous trainers or jockeys, and jockeys being used by owners and trainers. He also demonstrates the high potential for physical injury in horseracing, a potential that, as a steeplechase jockey, he learned about firsthand. He has broken his back, arm, and wrist once each, his nose five times, his collarbones about six times

each side, and his ribs uncountable times. He also has cracked his skull and crushed some vertebrae and has had horses throw him, kick him, and fall on top of him. According to Zuckerman, he once won two races and rode in ten others with an untreated broken arm; he just couldn't be bothered by doctors.

A Francis novel depends on contrasts between the competent and the incompetent. Some of his upper-class figures are naive, simplistic, bumbling dabblers, who judge on superficial appearances. His university professors (like Chaner in *Rat Race*) are out-of-date, unreliable men trying to sound like a combination of Marx and a Liverpool street punk. In fact, whenever a character resorts to polysyllabic diction and spouts unintelligibly about the nature of the universe, he should be immediately suspected of ignorance, pretension, and perhaps villainy. Francis's villains often become criminals because of their inability to thrive honestly. The experienced, competent pilot is contrasted with the capable beginner and the flashy but unskilled incompetent (easily recognized by his bad landing and poor attitude). The successful female horse trainer, who wins male admiration, is played off against the woman who is incompetent at love and incompetent at dealing with a man's world. Competent crooks who almost get away with fraud and murder are set against incompetent ones who cannot hang on to money, who try too many scams at once, and who make too many mistakes, though often all are denigrated as limited. "The worst vandals are always childish," says the hero of *Enquiry*. The naive and trusting endanger themselves and those around them and are foils to those whose sense of instinct comes from knowledge and experience.

Cynicism is absent when Francis treats romance. His heroines may differ in physical appearance or social background, but they immediately win the hero's attention and heart. They always have an inner fire that sets them apart from other women and a compassion that involves them in others' problems. They are always competent at what they do but often are vulnerable in some way, whether it be due to disease or injury, difficult relatives, a recent bereavement, or merely an inability to speak English. Their vulnerability brings out hidden strengths in the heroes. In *For Kicks* (1965), for example, the trusting and innocent young daughter of an English lord unwittingly destroys the hero-spy's cover, but he knowingly sacrifices his own safety to protect her.

Often there are other weak, vulnerable, but sympathetic characters in the background, such as a sister with leukemia, a brother who is an alcoholic, a youngster ignored by parents, an older woman helpless in the face of economic or physical threats, a husband who mourns his dead spouse, a simpleminded stable lad.

The language of a Francis novel is straightforward. He enjoys parallel series, mainly in sets of threes, such as "gentle, generous, and worried," or "bribed, bludgeoned, or blackmailed." He employs the terminology of specialized fields, but with explanations, so that the reader shares in the expertise of the characters. Occasionally there are biblical allusions, such as the hero sowing the wind and reaping the whirlwind (*Dead Cert*). He also uses Shakespearean references. In *Blood Sport*, for example, the hero, who contemplates suicide but always puts it off because of obligations, not fear, remarks, "I haven't a horse. Nor a Kingdom to give for one." Francis enjoys word games and crossword puzzles and frequently employs puns. The title *For Kicks*, for example, plays on the protagonist's motive in acting and the physical beating he must endure, kicked for kicks, while the title *Break In* refers to both the training of a young horse and a burglary, and the title *Proof* means both evidence and percentage of alcohol.

The narrative voice in a Francis novel is always first person, the point of view of his central character. It is this first-person perspective that hurtles the action forward, that infuses it with a sense of moral concern, that adds wit and compassion. It is also difficult to control, for the problem is always how to reveal the heroic character of the protagonist without making him seem egotistical, how to suppress conclusions in order to hold suspense without leaving the reader feeling cheated. Francis has learned to do this well. His opening lines are always clever attention getters.

Francis's techniques and themes have undergone continual development. His first novel, *Dead Cert*, which got an advance of three hundred pounds sterling (about seven hundred dollars at the 1960s exchange rate), made Francis's reputation as a mystery writer and set the pattern which has made him famous. Many still consider it his best work, though there is clearly competition for the title. Its hero, self-effacing but tenacious and unrelentingly compelled to face danger for the sake of right, is based on a real person whom Francis knew. In fact, Francis reports that he had to be very careful to keep his charac-

ter fictitious because his tendency was to copy him too closely from his real-life model. A surreal quality dominates much that is memorable: "the mingled smells of hot horse and cold river mist," an isolated string of riders, severed from reality by a "silent, surrounding whiteness" and suddenly the thrashing legs of a fallen champion. The satiric treatment of class snobbery, the contrasting portraits of casual friendships, and the underlying concept of illusion hiding reality raise *Dead Cert* above the level of pulp fiction and give it seriousness and depth without losing the excitement and pleasure of the mystery genre.

Nerve (1964), which was selected to be a *Reader's Digest* condensed book, is a study of character under pressure. It begins with the suicide of an aging jockey. The rest of the book unravels the motivation and despair behind that act. Rob Finn, the protagonist, the tone-deaf son of a musical family, is a beginning jockey, enough of a neophyte to be elated when asked to be a second-string rider: "Give me a horse and a race to ride it in, and I don't care if I wear silks or . . . pajamas. . . . I don't care if I don't earn much money, or if I break my bones, or if I have to starve to keep my weight down. All I care about is racing . . . , racing . . . and winning, if I can." But after six of his mounts in a row have made a showing far below their usual capabilities, a fact that has outraged owners, considerably diminished his reputation, and led to accusations of lost nerve, he begins to understand the perspective of the suicide victim and decides to take action. He uncovers a calculated destruction of jockeys, then doctored sugar cubes, and finally a jealousy and a hatred that explain who and why. But before he makes the final discovery, he is hung on harness hooks, doused with icy water, and left to freeze in a cooler. Only sheer determination helps him overcome seemingly impossible odds. Here the motive of the villain is not profit but revenge and madness, and interest for the reader comes more from the psychological study of the hero than from the villain's exposure.

In *For Kicks* a restless young Australian, Daniel Roke, forced by his parents' death into giving up his career dreams and devoting himself to providing and caring for his young siblings, is by chance offered an opportunity to play stablehand in England in order to investigate a new, undetectable stimulant for racehorses. Feeling like a "dull, laborious prig" caught in a prosperous trap (managing a stable), and sick of being sensible, Roke agrees. He cultivates a cockney accent,

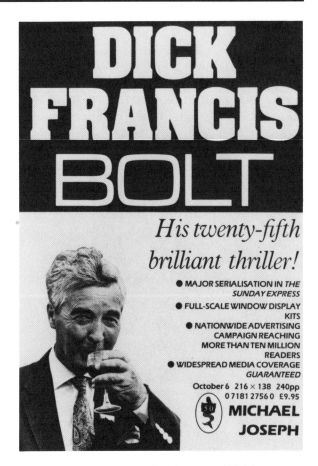

Dust jacket for the first edition of Francis's 1986 novel and publisher's advertisement from the 23 August 1986 issue of Bookseller

changes clothes and hairstyle, grows sideburns, and begins to behave in a shifty, insolent way to insinuate himself among the rougher sort. Francis brings the phrase "clothes make the man" to life as he shows the hero's precipitous decline from gentleman to down-and-outer on the make. Here the "aggressive egalitarianism" Francis so admires in Australians meets the English class structure at its most rigid; Roke must restrain his rebellious instincts and submit for awhile in order to overthrow the most abusive of class offenders: the clever, well-born psychopath whose bullying aggression is dismissed as high spirits and the climbing money-men who make up for their own insecurities by their snobbery and their wanton spending. His ruse works. While experiencing a Dickensian life of torture, humiliation, and servitude in the worst of stables, Roke methodically studies the facts, follows them to their logical conclusions, and tests a chain of assumptions step by step. In a violent and terrifying sequence of events he solves the case, uncovering Pavlovian conditioning carried out in a most sadistic way,

only to find himself jailed for murder. Again, despite the Holmesian pattern of ratiocination and the suspenseful climax, character and class conflict provide the main interest, as Roke discovers the strengths and weaknesses that make him what he is by instinct: a democratic man and a born hunter.

Odds Against and *Whip Hand* share a protagonist (the first time Francis had written two books about the same character), Sid Halley. Francis wrote the screenplay of the television version, "The Racing Game," and was delighted with Mike Gwilym's performance as Halley. However, in his interview with Weeks he rejected any plan to write another Sid Halley book because he prefers to build characters as he plans plot, so that "If I started with a ready-made character like Sid, I should be lost." (Jockey Kit Fielding's appearances in *Break In* and *Bolt* [1986] signal that Francis has had a change of opinion.) A champion jockey turned detective after losing his hand in a racing accident, Halley is nearly killed in the first few pages of *Odds Against;* his father-in-law tries to revive his interest in life and help him regain his self-confidence by involving him in a plan to save the racetrack at Seabury from a particularly underhanded and fraudulent management takeover, one strengthened by seeming accidents: tanker collisions, collapsed drains, stable fires, and exploding boilers. Halley's strategy is for his father-in-law to denigrate him so the villains will grossly underrate him–to their dismay. As Halley plays sleuth, he learns to trust his instincts and accept his inner wounds–in part by helping a young woman with a scarred face do the same. By not accepting personal defeat, he turns the villains' secret connivings against them and saves a track whose executives had too easily accepted defeat. Both *Odds Against* and *Whip Hand* treat the humiliation of the handicapped and the shattering viciousness of class snobbery with sensitivity and grace.

In *Whip Hand* several top racehorses, brilliant two-year-olds, prove undistinguished as three-year-olds and die young from heart problems. Halley, pursuing a new career as private investigator and building his growing reputation for tenacity and cleverness, is indirectly called in on the case by his estranged, embittered former wife. Aided by his cheerful, irreverent sidekick, Chico Barnes, Halley links the horses' poor performance to a deadly, artificially induced swine disease. In the process he is caught up in an exciting balloon race presided over by a true eccentric and spends a good deal of time adjusting to the wonders and limitations of his new mechanical hand. The book effectively captures the two key tensions of the Francis novel: the excitement of a horse race as the rider feels the ripple of muscles, "the striving bodies, uniting in one . . . the balance . . . the stretching brown neck, the mane blowing in my mouth, my hands on the reins," and the fear of physical injury as the villain tries to humiliate and break his victim. Francis waxes eloquent about the "feeling of oneness with horses" and the passion for winning; but he also captures the human cost: divorce, injury, the wrench of loss when dreams must be discarded. In this book Halley is paralyzed by fear for his remaining hand: "All the fear I'd ever felt in all my life was as nothing compared with the liquefying, mind-shattering disintegration of that appalling minute. It broke me in pieces. . . . And instinctively, hopelessly, I tried not to let it show."

Flying Finish on the simplest level is about a scam to take advantage of a tax loophole by transporting the same racehorses and brood mares

Dust jacket for the first American edition of Francis's 1987 novel about racing and family strife

back and forth by air–under false papers, a scheme adopted wholeheartedly by other, more sinister thugs, who transport defectors East for a fee. But the novel's real interest is in Henry Grey, soon to be Lord Grey. He sickens of friends and opportunities that exist only because of his rank and of women who pursue him for title and wealth, and he seeks to prove himself as a man. He throws over an easy office position for a laborer's job (managing horse air transport) and races horses for a cut of the winnings. He finds his beloved in Italy, a working woman who has never heard of his family or title. The real test of Grey's manhood comes when he discovers he was hired because it was assumed he would be lazy and unobservant; his competence and hard work make him too aware of inconsistencies in flights and horses transported, too curious about the disappearance of acquaintances who covered the same territory. He is a threat to a lucrative and illegal business. Attempts to distract his attention by playing on his sense of fair play, his class guilt, and his fear of pain fail, and when the villains move in to eliminate him, he draws on all his knowledge and resources to withstand pain, puzzle out a method of coping, and rescue himself and his friend. The emphasis is on his options, step-by-step, and the psychology that motivates him to react as he does. He has no qualms about brutally destroying the sadistic thug who tortured him, nor about taking off in a plane in which he had never trained. He may feel the weakness seeping into his limbs and shiver from exhaustion and fear; he may reject his choice as childish and vainglorious; but he somehow finds the strength and determination to face impossible odds and take the right action–for his country, for his friend, and for himself.

The protagonist of *Blood Sport* is a world-weary bachelor, an active intelligence officer, skilled in European languages, perceptive about human motives and human weaknesses, and artful at placing bugs, breaking and entering, and arranging "accidents." He hurtles himself fearlessly into investigation and action, half in love with death. He dives into dangerous waters to save a drowning man and survives being sucked through a weir; he guides a nervous horse along a narrow ledge in the dark, heedless of its terrifying height; he faces would-be murderers without giving ground: "You will not, whatever you do, recover the horse," he says into the barrel of a rifle. His skill at deductive reasoning and intuitive leaps of the imagination is Holmesian in nature, as too is his skill at collecting and interpreting statistics and facts. He always acts with care and caution, setting up a timed schedule, arranging minute details, even counting and collecting each of the shells expelled from his Luger, though his friend lies dead beside him. Those around him often accuse him of reading their minds because of his uncanny sensitivity to their secrets and emotions. He is a hunter, most at home with other hunters. His challenge in *Blood Sport* is to recover first one, and then two more, thoroughbred studs stolen over a ten-year period. Against all odds, he does so, tracing clues overlooked by others, first in England, then in Kentucky and Nevada, until they lead first to a dude ranch, then to a reputable stud farm. Along the way he uncovers blackmail, fraud, and murder. But it is the protagonist himself, not the mystery, exciting though its unraveling may be, that makes *Blood Sport* one of Francis's finest efforts. The hero is detached enough to admire the artistry of his opponent, realistic enough to realize when

prosecution is impossible, and cold-blooded enough to know how to reap vengeance without consulting the police or breaking the law. A naive young girl on the verge of womanhood helps both the protagonist and the wife of his employer come to terms with that "gray-black octopus," depression, whose "tentacles" reach out and suck "into every corner of the spirit until" life becomes "unbearable" and death seems "the only possible relief."

Forfeit builds on family trauma. Francis's wife, who contracted polio in 1949 while pregnant with their first child, was in an iron lung for five weeks. Out of that experience, Francis produced the character of Elizabeth, a lovely young woman, much in love, her life ahead of her, suddenly stricken by polio, ninety percent paralyzed, permanently confined to an iron lung. Her husband's attempts to cope with his physical needs, with his guilt, and with his love form a key part of this work. He is James Tyrone, a writer for the *Sunday Blaze*, turned sleuth when a fellow writer dies "accidentally" from a fall. The dead writer's past record and his notebooks tell of blackmailing bookmakers, encouraged by a South African mobster, playing with people's lives and finances. Investigation uncovers daughters threatened with rape and sons threatened with kidnapping to pressure owners into withdrawing horses from running and to force newspaper reporters into giving controlled tips. After his veiled hints in an aggressive exposé and his steps to hide a famous racehorse for its protection, Tyrone is savagely beaten, then blackmailed for adultery, but he doesn't take aggressive action until the villains trick his mistress and endanger his helpless wife. In the novel's resolution Tyrone not only routs the villains but comes to terms with his own weaknesses.

Enquiry, as its title suggests, centers on an official inquiry into race fixing, but the panel is rigged and the evidence manufactured. The accused are at first too shocked to defend themselves; facing financial ruin and social ostracism, one contemplates suicide, while the other determines to fight back. The odds may seem hopeless, but protagonist Kelly Hughes is ready to redeem his reputation "or die in the attempt." And he almost does so, from carbon-monoxide poisoning and multiple dislocations–hip, knee, and ankle. He methodically traces the faked evidence and intentional errors to their multiple sources, checks out old enemies (vindictive bookmakers and jealous jockeys), and faces hostility and abuse

Dust jacket for the first edition of Francis's 1988 novel in which a security operative for the British Jockey Club disguises himself as a railway waiter

with aplomb. This is a novel about courage and the human will. The situation tests friendships and men's willingness to stand up to authority and power. It is also a novel about class. Lord Ferth, an aristocratic racing patron, is stunned to find a jockey who attended university and who can talk eruditely of the history of politics and about the nature of aggression. Ferth learns to face the fact that justice should not depend on good manners and that "men in power positions" are not "infallibly truthful." The snobbish daughter of a moneyed trainer learns to concentrate on character, not accent, and to see that judging people "by their voices" and origins is wrong; she must, for the first time, deal with another class, throwing off "the fetters" in her mind and the "iron bars" in her soul. In the process she learns to love a man for who he is and what he is. When Hughes asks her, "Would you consider coming down to my level?," she responds, "Are you speaking literally, metaphorically, intellectually, fi-

nancially, or socially?," but later she discovers that mean-spirited, "kinky" blue bloods are really inferior to "gutsy," considerate, strong-hearted men of working-class origins.

Rat Race was not very popular with the critics, who found it a bit disappointing because of the negative attitudes of its protagonist, Matt Shore, but it is a convincing study of a man who has almost given up on life. Condemned by the Board of Trade for humane but illegal acts, divorced, disillusioned, he has lost his sense of joy in his work and has tried to practice stoic detachment by cutting himself off from human emotions. He chauffeurs the wealthy racetrack crowd but feels contempt for most of them. The novel is interspersed with brief, satiric portraits of aristocrats. Shore sees his battle for dominance over a rival company as nature's "pecking order" at work and himself as a rat "trapped on a treadwheel" going in circles. And yet his virtues shine through. His humane act was smuggling food and medical supplies to starving refugees. He is competent and careful–a man who knows his business well. Despite his self-admonitions not to get involved, his automatic tendency toward deduction, coupled with intuition and instinct, help him get passengers off a flight before a bomb explodes, deal kindly with a leukemia victim (twin sister of the heroine), talk Nancy (the heroine) down when her airplane's electric system is sabotaged, and ferret out motives and villains so that, at the close of the book, he has rediscovered himself and his values and has learned to love again.

Bonecrack (1971), set at a prestigious racing stable in Newmarket, is a briskly paced story of syphilitic-induced megalomania that gains tension from a conflict of generations. The hero, a sober-minded businessman, Neil Griffon, a former antique dealer turned accountant-troubleshooter for small companies in financial difficulty, returns to the home he had left fourteen years before to manage his father's stables while the old man recovers from a car accident. His relationship with his father is antagonistic and competitive, with the old man never forgiving his son for attaining his freedom and making a success of his life on his own. He resents his son's assistance in his time of need and does his best to undermine his son's efforts and thereby prove to the world his own superiority. His son, in turn, finds that managing a stable and training horses is a pleasurable, instinctive skill he thought he had lost. This father and son relationship is contrasted to that of an Italian-Swiss mobster, Rivera, who gives his spoiled only child everything in order to curtail the son's freedom and to maintain his own ascendancy. When the son decides to become a champion jockey, the father kidnaps Neil Griffon to force an arrangement, breaks the legs of Griffon's horse to prove his threats are real, and ultimately tries to murder the stable's leading jockey to make way for his son. But he does not count on Griffon's competence and courage, for, while seeming to partly acquiesce, Griffon quietly collects evidence that could damn Rivera and ruin his son's career chances. He teaches the mobster's son that success as a jockey cannot be bought but must be won by hard work, determination, self-control, clear thinking, and talented horsemanship; forces him to recognize in others skills he has not yet honed; chides him when he fails for want of trying; praises him when he demonstrates real care, and thereby uses him as a pawn in his struggle to save his own father's stables and diminish Rivera's power. Griffon's girlfriend remarks that "anything which smells of challenge is your meat and drink," and Griffon rises to the occasion.

Illusion becomes reality in *Smokescreen* as an initial movie take–the hero handcuffed to the steering wheel of a tiny sports car in the blazing desert heat–is played out for real in the scorching sun of Kruger National Park, South Africa: six days without food or water, only a growing rage and a will to survive. The protagonist, Edward Lincoln, "Linc" for short, is a successful actor. An experienced stuntman and a close observer of human nature, he works hard at turning out a professional performance. A family man, he also works hard at being a good husband and parent. His explosive temper is usually indulged only "on behalf of someone else." Linc can handle snobs and fans with equal finesse. At the request of a terminally ill family friend he agrees to investigate the unexpected losing streak of a group of thoroughbred flat racers in South Africa. After two murder attempts disguised as accidents (one his being knocked out in a gold-mine shaft shortly before a scheduled blast), he realizes he has been lured to the killing ground by a deceptively charming man, "cold and ruthless as ice," one more savage than the beasts around him. The descriptions of South Africa, the discussions of the controversies of apartheid, the carefully contrasted characters, and the portrait of a good man who must protect the weak by exposing the dangerous beast beneath the civilized fa-

cade mark this book as an interesting and effective variation on Francis's traditional concerns.

The protagonist of *Slay-ride*, British investigator David Cleveland, in Norway to find and vindicate a missing jockey accused of grand theft, finds his small boat intentionally overturned and himself left to drown; later he is knifed and his car is bombed as he uncovers murder and then an oil stock swindle. Readers get a British view of Norway: shock at the cold, at horse races that are literally in the dark, at liquor licensing laws "madder . . . than Britain's." The book is well worth reading for the final image of a man, bound to a sleigh, flying though space, down to his death in a cold, Nordic sea.

The refrain of *Knock Down* (1974; published in the United States as *Knockdown*, 1975) is "Bash me, I bash back," the words of Jonah Dereham, a former steeplechaser turned bloodstock agent, whose toughness and honesty in a basically dishonest business make him the object of a concerted campaign to turn him crooked or break him. Here Francis captures the inner workings of a business that functions on the basis of reputation and trust and hence is open to wholesale manipulation and dishonesty. The sales-ring scenes are convincing, as are the "ruthlessness, rudeness, and rows" behind the scenes. The book is a straightforward exposé of the nasty reality behind the shining facade of bloodstock sales. Dereham is advised that there is no place left for the individualist, that one must join the firm or forge an agreement, and that bucking the system is passé, that business is a Darwinian world in which "invaders" single out the strong to overcome so that the weak will then submit quietly. Critics complained of the multiple plot threads, but Francis does carefully interweave them as they move inexorably toward a final confrontation. Bound together with webbing to keep his shoulder from dislocating, a plight Francis still shares, Dereham finds himself the object of an unrelenting series of attacks. First he is mugged, then forced to sign away a sales slip for a new purchase. Later a horse worth seventy thousand pounds is loosed from his stable at night and is nearly killed. An attempt to steal Dereham's next purchase only fails by chance. His brother, an alcoholic, is fed liquor, the family stables are burned down, and lies and rumors are spread to reduce his clientele. But the villains have chosen the wrong man to try to break; Dereham is outraged, not only by the personal attacks, but by the viciousness of men who demand kickbacks and then en-

Dick Francis, late 1980s (photograph by Mary Francis)

force their demands with rumors that drive down prices, turning a business that is built on dreams into a swindle. His counterattack conclusively exposes past swindles and makes use of the villains' own key tool: rumor.

The fact that the hero in *High Stakes* is a toy manufacturer new to racing (having only recently acquired a string of racehorses) provides an excuse for Francis to teach newcomers about the racing scene, but most particularly about the multiple fiddles a crooked trainer has at his command, especially collusion between trainer and bookmaker to their mutual profit. It begins with the neophyte, Steven Scott, giving his trainer the sack and, as a result, immediately having his prizewinner stolen and his name besmirched in the press. With no legal remedy possible he enlists carefully chosen friends to help him go after the criminals. Using a Florida look-alike, they exchange nag for champion and thereby set a trap that elicits a confession, undoes the villains, and vindicates Scott.

In the Frame begins with a violent and seemingly senseless murder, the after-product of a burglary: "a harmless girl, come to harm." The police clearly suspect the husband, who is so in shock that life has lost all meaning for him. The cousin, Charles Todd, determines to prove them wrong and does so, tracking down a series of coincidences that lead to Australia, art fraud, and international burglary. He discovers "a mobile force of thieves shuttling containerfuls of antiques from continent to continent, selling briskly to a ravenous market." The "supermarket" villains chat amiably with middling wealthy tourists about their art collections back home, sell them a genuine painting, substitute a fake, then recover the lot in a carefully planned burglary. To unravel the web of this monolithic spider, Todd joins forces with an old school friend, a mad artist, being with whom was "like a toboggan run, downhill, dangerous, and exhilarating." Together they flush out the villains, gather their evidence (breaking and entering and absconding with it), and, before finally letting the police in on the action, nearly get themselves maimed or killed. The setting allows Francis to explore cultural differences, as he captures the unique and elastic diction of Australians, explains the origins of Australian male chauvinism (two-thirds of the best seats in the members' stands reserved for males only, a division that has since been removed), praises Australian wines, and provides precise images of Australian cities.

Risk (1977) is dedicated to the memory of Lionel Vick, a professional steeplechase jockey and certified accountant, who obviously inspired Francis's portrait of the main character Roland Britten. Britten is an amateur steeplechase jockey, enamored of racing but well aware of his limitations, a rider who, in a run of luck, gives a good horse its head and wins time and again—to the consternation of dishonest trainers and bookmakers. Because he is an honest man, he is beset by enemies who are angered by his unwillingness to take bribes, both as jockey and as accountant, and by his instinctive ability to recognize a swindle or a fiddle, no matter how artfully disguised. When he is kidnapped and imprisoned in dark, isolated quarters, first below deck on a sailboat, later in a covered van, he begins to consider who among the felons and frauds he has exposed might want not simply revenge but freedom of action to perpetuate another fraud. Britten's knowledge of bank accounts, stables, and training yards means a wide field of possibilities, but the list of suspects narrows when his partner joins the action. This book has powerfully rendered portraits of men and women making the most of life's challenges: a quiet, unobtrusive man coping with the terrors of total darkness, isolation, seasickness, and despair finds he is made of "sterner stuff " than he believed; a dowdy, middle-aged headmistress finds the courage to save a life, investigate a crime, and explore her potential as a woman; a young girl learns to see behind the facade, admit her father's weakness, and make her own life without him.

In *Trial Run* Randall Drew, a Warwickshire gentleman farmer, banned from racing because he wears eyeglasses, is recruited by British Intelligence to go to Moscow to determine whether or not it is safe for a member of the royal family, an equestrian aiming for the Olympics, to attend. Drew is disturbed by the cold, the food, the queues, the regimentation, the inherent suspicion, the carefully controlled faces, and the daily fear and harshness of life in Moscow; yet as a repu-

table horseman, he gains acceptance and respect that make him a fearful antagonist, and, in battling a terrorist plot to embarrass both the British royal family and the Russian regime, he gains common cause with Russian patriots. This book laments the social, political, and economic conflicts that warp one's youth and transform disturbed youngsters into weak, irresponsible adults bent on striking out at authority–no matter what the cost to others.

Reflex (1980), a Book-of-the-Month-Club selection, whose initial hardback edition sold eighty-five thousand copies, marked a breakthrough in Francis's popularity, and deservedly so, for it is one of his finest efforts. Paperback rights sold for $440,000. Since *Reflex* (the title of which refers to camera type as well as to an involuntary response), Francis's novels have automatically been best-sellers in America. In the novel Philip Nore, a disillusioned, aging jockey and amateur photographer, stumbles on a blackmailing scheme built on corruption and murder and unwittingly sets himself up as the next target. Nore's mother, disowned by her own mother for stealing her young lover, had passed her son from friend to friend until she eventually died of a heroin overdose. Nore's much despised grandmother wants him to find a sister, Amanda, whom he never knew existed, so the sister can inherit the fortune the grandmother wishes to keep out of the hands of her homosexual son and her illegitimate grandson. Nore, instead, gets caught up in investigating curious negatives left by a skilled but seemingly amoral photographer, negatives that suggest blackmail and murder. The description of Nore's process of discovery through his photographic skill is excellent. Ultimately his investigation interlocks with the search for his sister and for his parentage so that, in dealing effectively with the foibles and vices of others, he stops a heroin dealer (among other wrongdoers), regains his self-respect, and acquires a sense of family and roots. This book is an especially powerful study of the influence of one man on another, as Nore learns "his [own] mind, his intentions, his beliefs," solves "his puzzles," and fires "his guns."

In contrast to *Reflex*, his next novel, *Twice Shy* (1981), is one of Francis's weakest efforts, possibly because the evil characters are not deeply evil. They are a father and son team, both minor thugs, and as such unworthy of the hero's effort. The novel is also weakened by being split into two parts, separated not only by fourteen years, but by different protagonists, so character development is much more limited than is usually possible in a full-length novel. In the first half a young physicist, Jonathan Derry, discovers that a cassette of Broadway music handed him by a friend is really a computer program for a handicapping system that works. When his friend is killed in a boat explosion and his wife has a nervous breakdown, Derry, instead of using the cassette to make a fortune for himself, seeks to trace the tape's rightful owners to return their property. As a result his wife is kidnapped, and a rescue scene ensues. At this point the book leaps forward to after Derry's departure to California, when his racing-enthusiast brother, William, assumes the burden of the tape and finally ends the train of violence. The final image of the villainous son, permanently brain-damaged, is pathetic and dissatisfying. In Francis's other novels the villain has been warped but intelligent, weak and incompetent in some areas, but highly skilled in others. In this novel there is a sense of not merely ineptitude but limited mental capabilities. It is as if Francis has brought together all his usual ingredients for mystery and adventure but has somehow lost the moral thread that gives them strength and substance.

In *Banker* (1982) the first-person narrator-hero is Tim Ekaterin, thirty-two years old, an alert, sharp-minded banker on his way up in his family's famous London firm. He is skilled at managing enormous sums of money and at making correct decisions about risky loans. The novel covers a span of three years in which the world of thoroughbred racing and merchant banking are interwoven. *Banker* begins with Tim's immediate superior stepping into the courtyard fountain and hallucinating paranoid fantasies–the result of an overdose of medication for Parkinson's disease. Tim considers the proposition of a reputable stud-farm owner, Oliver Knowles, who wants a five-million-pound loan to buy a star-quality racing stallion, Sandcastle. As the plot advances and Sandcastle's foals are born deformed, readers learn a great deal about investments, horse disease, stud-farm management, pharmacology, and herbal lore. This plot has been called one of Francis's most intricate, for it involves two murders, the solution to which rests on a bottle of shampoo, several tightly spun subplots concerning office politics, a sixteen-year-old would-be murderer, a miracle worker who restores dying horses to health, and Tim's quiet passion for his ailing boss's wife. Unlike the typical Francis hero, Tim Ekaterin has never experienced physical

pain and is "unconvinced" of his own mortality until he finds himself locked in a stall with a crazed horse, its forelocks crashing down so close they brush his hair. Francis's method in formulating this book is typical of his most recent pattern. Approached by a fan, Jeremy H. Thompson, a UCLA professor of pharmacology, Francis was intrigued by the professor's knowledge of drugs that were safe for people but fatal for horses (a reversal of his method in *Trial Run* where drugs safe for horses kill humans); during the same general period, an important banker in a nearby box at the Cheltenham race meeting suggested a merchant banking focus. After extensive research, aided by London banking officials, he produced *Banker*.

In *The Danger* (1983) Andrew Douglas, star operative for a British antikidnapping agency, travels the world recovering kidnap victims in some way connected with the racing world. He recovers three victims in the novel: the jockey daughter of a rich industrialist, the three-year-old son of a racehorse owner, and the senior steward of the Jockey Club of England. As self-effacing "consultant," Douglas liaises with overanxious police, who are willing to sacrifice the victim to capture the criminal; with relatives torn by grief and then later resentful of the disruption of their lives and the crippling ransom that decimates their finances; and with the victims, who endure physical and psychological injury. Francis is particularly skillful in showing the psychological state of the kidnap victims. In the first case police interference almost costs the life of the victim; in the second Douglas and a friend trace clues to a boat house and effect a rescue; but by the third, Douglas has so narrowed the field, postulating a kidnapping crime lord with racing connections, that he himself is kidnapped and learns the hard way the truths of his training manual. The final descriptions of hunter and hunted share the detail of Geoffrey Household's classic treatment of the same subject in *Rogue Male* (1939).

Proof (1984), the story of a wine merchant enlisted by police to detect fraudulently labeled wines, was derived in part from Francis's thirty years of discussing wine with his brother-in-law Dick Yorke and local merchant Margaret Giles, visits to the Australian wine regions in the Barossa Valley, and an awareness of the notorious European wine-fraud scandals of the 1970s. Tony Beach (a grieving widower, son and grandson of war-hero jockeys, and owner of a liquor store), while catering wine at a training farm, witnesses a horse van plunge down a hill into a tent filled with wealthy imbibers. The plot leads directly to an explanation of this bizarre incident. *Proof* is well researched and gives readers a sense of the day-to-day business of a British liquor store and describes French vintages and Scotches, but it has limited dialogue, no love interest, and less memorable action and fewer values than most Francis novels. Beach, in aiding the police, must deal with hijacking, murder, and a near drowning. Nevertheless, his self-doubts seem strained and the final discovery of his idealized father's humanity too predictable.

Francis's *Break In* and *Bolt* return to the track. Steeplechase jockey Kit Fielding, a dour loner but a trusted friend of a princess whose horses he races, is the central character of both books. In *Break In* he enlists royal assistance to discover the motive for a scandal sheet attack on his twin (Holly) and her beleaguered husband, Bob Allardeck, a horse trainer near bankruptcy, but in the end he unravels the threads of a complex plot himself. In *Bolt* he returns the royal goodwill, however, by providing the strength to help Princess Casilia and her family stand up to the blackmail, threats, and violence that are part of a would-be business takeover by a power-mad arms merchant. In traditional Francis style both books include vivid descriptions of English steeplechase racing, romance beset by class differences, telling comments on lineage and class, and conspiracies based on unbounded ambition. The misuse of the press and the inhumanity of loan sharks dominate *Break In*, while the villainy of arms merchandising and the irrationality of revenge dominate *Bolt*. The intricate plot of *Break In* involves the seething hatred of feuding clans (Fielding vs. Allardeck), the telepathic bonds of twins, character assassination, illegal wiretaps, break-ins, bribery, and sabotage. The book opens with a tough race in which Fielding struggles body and soul against a truculent brute of a horse with winning style; it concludes with an even tougher competition in which Fielding employs the skills of mass-media video splicing to bridle an embittered brute of a man whose winning style depends on the destruction of others. The feud continues in *Bolt* but with a nastier edge that forces Fielding to go beyond the law to safeguard those he loves. To force the princess and her husband to sign over their company, the arms merchant, who believes "every conscience has its price," tries acid, a near-fatal push off a second story, and a bomb to frighten and compel, while his vengeful coun-

terpart arranges for their champion horses to be put down with a "bolt," a so-called "humane killer." Fielding proves his "capacity for endurance" and his nerve, as he sets himself up as bait and turns the villains' own weapons against them.

Hot Money (1987), extending a pattern begun in *Break In* and *Bolt*, emphasizes family relationships, a topic always of concern to a Francis hero but one often left undeveloped as the alienated protagonist moves away from his family group to form new connections, whether romantic or convivial. Here the hero, Ian Pembroke, does the opposite, rebuilding his relationship with his estranged father, Malcolm, and acting as the only common bond between his father's three living divorced wives and his seven children and their assorted spouses: an embittered clan, few of whom have much in common beyond a pressing need for their sire's money. Horse racing is only a background concern, with Ian a jockey and with Malcolm learning to enjoy the sport, as father and son deal with murder plots, their own somewhat prickly relationship, and the pain of knowing that some blood relative wishes one or both of them dead. Francis's achievement here lies in showing that unhappy families are not all alike; this one is riven by the disagreements and contrary ambitions of a varied set of people, all recognizably Pembrokes, yet with genetic predispositions twisted and rearranged by personal history and circumstance. As a result, *Hot Money* is one of Francis's finest novels.

Tor Kelsey of *The Edge* (1988) is another of Francis's quietly competent, resilient heroes whose performance continually dumbfounds his associates. Despite an inherited fortune, Kelsey chooses the challenge of the security operative game, working undercover for the British Jockey Club to anticipate trouble and moving with ease between classes. He enjoys the comfort money can buy but relies on the day-to-day strains of a working man's toil to give his life meaning. His forte is his ability to blend chameleon-like with his environment, and in the course of the novel he masquerades as a wealthy horse owner, a congenial actor assisting with a staged murder, and a self-effacing waiter on The Great Canadian Transcontinental Mystery Race Train. Doing so allows him to thwart a disgruntled railway saboteur, salvage the honor and the horse (but not the insane son) of a troubled racing family, and trap a deceptively charming blackmailer (Julius Apollo Filmer) who brutishly thrives on wielding power through threats, intimidation, and violence. A broken shoulder blade does not stop Kelsey from making the case against the "slippery" Mr. Filmer cast-iron by allowing himself in his role as innocent waiter to be knocked out in front of significant and vocal witnesses.

Francis had in progress for over ten years a biography of English jockey Lester Piggott but had agreed not to publish it until that eleven-time British flat-racing champion had given up the sport. When Piggott retired in 1985, *A Jockey's Life: The Biography of Lester Piggott* was published. Piggott is in certain respects the model of the Francis hero, a man who has striven against difficulties, who has devoted his life to racing, who for Francis sums up the ideals of the sport of kings.

Through time the Francis novel has lost its early focus on sadistic physical violence, and, although there is still violence, the later books concentrate more specifically on psychological stress—emotional conflict and self-doubt. The hero is less a man who can endure torture than one who has the strength to face self-doubt, fear, and human inadequacy and still endure and thrive. His later books strive more for a psychological study of a just and decent man than for a dramatic presentation of heroic action. They also try to teach readers about different places and different fields, about bearing one's crosses and showing moral fortitude and courage. There is a world-weary, stoic quality to his heroes that is part of Francis's statement about dealing with life. His journalist understands that the story he fights to piece together for Sunday will light fires and wrap fish and chips on Monday. His actor realizes that there is really little significant difference between the first take and the fifty-first take and that the "realism" of the movie theater fails to even approximate reality. His books' compelling action keeps Francis at the top of the best-seller list, but as Barry Bauska (*Armchair Detective*, July 1978) points out, while his work remains "splendidly readable," he has evolved into "less a writer of thrillers and more a creator of literature."

Francis's popularity and success in England and America is not hard to account for. Besides the obvious fact that he is a first-rate novelist, one who has mastered all the technical tools of his craft, his underlying theme is a successful blend of old-world tradition and elegance and new-world innovation and energy. Francis marries the British ratiocinative detective tradition with Chandleresque loners who suffer massive physical punishment or deep inner stress in the pursuit of truth. The corruptions of the city and of excessive, self-indulgent wealth (themes in many American hard-boiled works) contrast with the calm decencies of English country life.

Francis's heroes make the ultimate accommodation to the new democratic realities. The world of horse racing provides a fine metaphor for a class-divided society whose different levels must nevertheless cooperate if common goals are to be attained. In *Slay-ride*, when Arne asks Cleveland, "Do you know so many rich people?," after Cleveland has just rejected a wealthy man's rudeness as atypical, Cleveland replies: "Meet them every day of the week . . . ; they own racehorses." In *Break In* Fielding rises above money and class to mix easily with touts and princesses, chatting companionably with stockboys and fellow jockeys as well as with the blue bloods on whom his business depends. As Francis continually emphasizes, racing needs the efforts of stable lads as well as millionaires, of photographers and drivers as well as jockeys. Yet the material rewards—such as they are for the majority of participants—are distributed with gross inequality, as a few profit hugely, while large numbers sacrifice their efforts for minimal rewards. Francis's emphasis on the nonmaterial benefits of the racing life, the almost sensual descriptions of everyday activity, help justify and rationalize the material inequities. There is a sense of belonging in his books, a sense of loyalty to racing that is akin to patriotism. Francis's heroes offer the hope so necessary to stability of the racing world or society in general, the hope generated by the intrinsic rewards of competence.

Since Francis's heroes are defined by their ability to perform under pressure with a high degree of efficiency, if not grace, the blending of the hard-boiled and the ratiocinative traditions of mystery writing in his work can be said to have a political end. The future belongs to the competent. The new technocrats will transcend impoverished backgrounds, limited education, and formerly forbidden careers. The class system will be smashed, not by Marxist posturing or by class struggle, but by applied knowledge. Democracy will consist of a middle ground—rather like a race meeting—where elevated and humble will mix amicably in the pursuit of profit and fun, and where the star players will reap the rewards for their competence in proportion to their suffering and devotion. Francis is not the first writer to see life as a horse race, but his vision is certainly the most complete and thoroughly rendered.

Interviews:

"Dick Francis," *New Yorker*, 45 (5 March 1969): 29-30;

Deryck Harvey, "A Word with Dick Francis," *Armchair Detective*, 6 (May 1973): 151;

Brigette Weeks, "Writing Mystery Novels," *Writer*, 96 (August 1983): 11-12;

Edward Zuckerman, "The Winning Form of Dick Francis," *New York Times Magazine*, 25 March 1984, pp. 40, 50, 54, 60-62.

References:

Pete Axthelm, "Writer with a Whip Hand," *Newsweek*, 97 (6 April 1981): 98;

Melvyn Barnes, *Dick Francis* (New York: Ungar, 1986);

Barry Bauska, "Endure and Prevail: The Novels of Dick Francis," *Armchair Detective*, 11 (July 1978): 238-244;

Ronald Blythe, "Literary Lairs: Ronald Blythe on the Realm of the British Writer," *Architectural Digest*, 42 (June 1985): 98-103;

Robert Cantwell, "Mystery Makes a Writer," *Sports Illustrated*, 28 (25 March 1968): 76-78;

J. Madison Davis, *Dick Francis* (Boston: Twayne, 1989);

Judy Klemesrud, "Behind the Best Sellers," *New York Times Book Review*, 85 (1 June 1980): 42;

Jack Newcombe, "Close-up: Jockey with an Eye for Intrigue," *Life*, 66 (6 June 1969): 81-82;

"Riding High," *Forbes*, 117 (15 April 1976): 100;

Alvin P. Sanoff, "Finding Intrigue Wherever He Goes," *U.S. News & World Report*, 124 (28 March 1988): 56;

Michael N. Stanton, "Dick Francis: The Worth of Human Love," *Armchair Detective*, 15 (Spring 1982): 137-143.

Nicolas Freeling
(3 March 1927-)

Carol Shloss
West Chester University

BOOKS: *Love in Amsterdam* (London: Gollancz, 1962; New York: Harper & Row, 1963); republished as *Death in Amsterdam* (New York: Ballentine, 1965);

Because of the Cats (London: Gollancz, 1963; New York: Harper & Row, 1964);

Gun before Butter (London: Gollancz, 1963); republished as *Question of Loyalty* (New York: Harper & Row, 1963);

Valparaiso, as F. R. E. Nicolas (London: Gollancz, 1964); as Freeling (New York: Harper & Row, 1965; Harmondsworth: Penguin, 1971);

Double-Barrel (London: Gollancz, 1964; New York: Harper & Row, 1965);

Criminal Conversation (London: Gollancz, 1965; New York: Harper & Row, 1966);

The Dresden Green (London: Gollancz, 1966; New York: Harper & Row, 1967);

The King of the Rainy Country (London: Gollancz, 1966; New York: Harper & Row, 1966);

Strike Out Where Not Applicable (London: Gollancz, 1967; New York: Harper & Row, 1968);

This Is the Castle (London: Gollancz, 1968; New York: Harper & Row, 1968);

Tsing-Boum: A Novel (London: Hamilton, 1969); republished as *Tsing-Boom!* (New York: Harper & Row, 1969);

Kitchen Book (London: Hamilton, 1970); republished as *The Kitchen: A Delicious Account of the Author's Years as a Grand Hôtel Cook* (New York: Harper & Row, 1970);

Over the High Side: A Novel (London: Hamilton, 1971); republished as *The Lovely Ladies* (New York: Harper & Row, 1971);

Cook Book (London: Hamilton, 1972);

A Long Silence: A Novel (London: Hamilton, 1972); republished as *Auprès de ma Blonde* (New York: Vintage, 1979);

Dressing of Diamond (London: Hamilton, 1974; New York: Harper & Row, 1974);

What Are the Bugles Blowing For? (London: Heinemann, 1975); republished as *The Bu-*

Nicolas Freeling, early 1970s

gles Blowing (New York: Harper & Row, 1976);

Lake Isle (London: Heinemann, 1976); republished as *Sabine* (New York: Harper & Row, 1977);

Gadget (London: Heinemann, 1977; New York: Coward, McCann & Geoghegan, 1977);

The Night Lords (London: Heinemann, 1978; New York: Pantheon, 1978);

The Widow (London: Heinemann, 1979; New York: Pantheon, 1979);

Castang's City (London: Heinemann, 1980; New York: Pantheon, 1980);

One Damn Thing after Another (London: Heinemann, 1981); republished as *Arlette* (New York: Pantheon, 1981);

Wolfnight (London: Heinemann, 1982; New York: Pantheon, 1982);

The Back of the North Wind (London: Heinemann, 1983; New York: Viking, 1983);

No Part in Your Death (London: Heinemann, 1984; New York: Viking, 1984);

A City Solitary (London: Heinemann, 1985; New York: Viking, 1985);

Cold Iron (London: Deutsch, 1986; New York: Viking, 1986);

Not as Far as Velma (London: Deutsch, 1989; New York: Mysterious, 1989).

Nicolas Freeling has written several books on life in the kitchens of the great hotels of Europe and several novels of suspense, but his reputation rests on three series of European detective novels. Each series is structured around a single detective: in Holland, Police Inspector Piet van der Valk hunts down crime; in Strasbourg, Piet's widow, Arlette, takes up investigation through a private "help" bureau; and in an unnamed town located in central France, Henri Castang continues to explore the disruptive behavior that often characterizes contemporary European culture. Freeling has an acidulous wit, and his writing is alternately suave and concerned, dispassionate and involved. His trademark has always been the close observation of human character, and through the years he has been recognized as having the stature of Georges Simenon and the depth and variety of John le Carré. "Nicolas Freeling," remarked the *Fort Worth Morning Star-Telegram* in a typical comment, "is the undisputed King of a rainy country of his own–a realm of detective fiction where irony is biting, the satire [is] funny, and the backgrounds scintillat[ing]."

Knowledge of Freeling's private life is anecdotal. He was born in London on 3 March 1927 but spent his early years in "Le Croisic on the Loire estuary, and later in Saint-Malo and later still in the town of Southampton," as he says in the autobiographical *Kitchen Book* (1970; published in the United States as *The Kitchen: A Delicious Account of the Author's Years as a Grand Hôtel Cook*). His father was a country man, "from a landowning squirearchy kind of family"; his mother was "an aristocratic personage who, like Jessica Mitford, thought that electricity was a gift of God and needed no payment." The family struggled with finances; in 1939, Freeling's father died. Remembering his father's love for pigeon pie, for hanging roasts, and for fishing, he decided while still a boy that he wanted to work in a hotel as a chef. He apprenticed first at "one of the most gilt-edged houses in France," went next to the Hôtel des Pyramides in Paris, and then, in search of higher wages and more responsibility, to the Hôtel Atlantic in Belleplage, an example of the late Victorian grand hotel. Around 1954

he went to England, where he married, and then wandered restlessly around Northern Europe for several years. It was during this time that he decided to become a writer and "went about this with the incompetence that characterizes all young men who want to be writers: any job not actually in a kitchen seemed a step in the right direction."

The right direction eventually came. In 1961 Freeling created his first detective, Piet van der Valk, and, with *Love in Amsterdam* (1962; republished as in the United States as *Death in Amsterdam*, 1965), began the series of ten Dutch mysteries that established his reputation as a crime writer of the first order. Technically these books fall into the category of "police procedure," for Van der Valk is an inspector of the Amsterdamse Recherche who gradually works his way up the ranks to chief inspector and then commissaire. Van der Valk is crude, flamboyant, idiosyncratic, and generally known as a bad policeman. He is committed to avenging crimes against the state, but he does not believe that bureaucratic methods are effective. Time and again he violates orderly procedures, offends his superiors, and damages his own chances for promotion; yet he is recognized for an ability to solve mysteries that have eluded other, more conventional investigators. Using intuition, gossip, and hunches about human motivation as his guides, constantly curious, always breaking for well-cooked (and lovingly described) lunches with his French wife, Arlette, he plods along, letting criminals "simmer" like well-cooked soups, until some psychological insight allows him to understand the crime. He succeeds because he is immersed in community life without being lulled into unexamined habits of mind. For these reasons all of Freeling's Van der Valk books are rich in the description of character and vivid in the evocation of places and ways of life in the Netherlands.

In *Love in Amsterdam* Van der Valk is asked to find the murderer of Elsa de Charmoy, a middle-aged woman who had lived alone, supporting herself by making clay figurines. A former lover, Martin, stands accused of the crime. It is only Van der Valk's belief in Martin's innocence that leads him to pursue the investigation, for the examining magistrate is satisfied with the arrest. Trusting in the accused man's essential honesty, Van der Valk leads Martin through the psychological mazes of his past affair, through his meeting with Elsa during World War II, his friendship with her when she was a young wife and

Nicolas Freeling: biog. elements.

          My father was a countryman, of a family of landed
squires in Norfolk. I lost him of heart-failure when aged only ten:
it is one of my great regrets. My mother came of a line talented,
amusing, and mostly drunk, going far back in English history. I am
thus English on both sides. I was born in London but brought up in
France. I had a vagabond youth, with little education and that patchy.

  The first element of stability in this existence was military service
at the close of the wartime period (1945-7). The second was twelve
years in hotels & restaurants, which taught me to work with my han s:
the beginnings of craftsmanship. The experience replaced schools and
universities. Midway through this period, I married a Dutch woman of
great strength of character. It could be called a final formative
element. Of this (only) marriage have been born four sons & one
daughter, between 1955 & 1966. Two were born in England, two in
Holland: one in France: this illustrates a continuation of vagabondage.

  It could be said that stability was reached in 1960 when I wrote my
first novel. Initial success allowed me to quit hotels and become a
full-time writer. I view my first ten books, from 1960-70, as another
apprenticeship. This covers the 'van der Valk' series based on my life
in Holland.

In 1964 I went to live on the borders of France and Germany; a broader
and more varied terrain for exploration. This Rhineland country has
been 'mine' ever since. In 1966 I bought a farmhouse in the Vosges
countryside, which has been my base to this day, and where my days
will end. The 'death of van der Valk', for which I have been much
reproached, simply reflects the need to seek a wider frame of reference
in fiction, and the turning of a page in my life. The 'Castang' books
beginning in a narrowish French background have expanded to a wider
European frame of reference to keep pace with an enlarged vision. The
present (e.g. 'next') Castang book is the last to be set in France.

Autobiographical statement by Freeling (courtesy of the author)

2./   NF: 'critical elements'.

Series writing obeys the wish of a readership which likes to read of what it already knows: this is important commercially to a writer with no resource beyond writing-earnings. It also allows what I have called expansion: development and enrichment of central characters from book to book. I can thus cite with approval the well known opinion of Georges Simenon; the wish that he should be judged only on the entire body of his output.

At the age of sixtytwo, having started writing only at the age of thirtythree, and feeling after thirty-odd books that I am just beginning to learn something of what it is all about, I would underline my opinion that whatever critical assessment may be made of my work until now should be regarded as provisional.

While I live, I write. Living implies both growth and decay. I should hope that it were not yet possible to point to a moment where the second begins to outweigh the first.

It is my further settled conviction that the socalled mystery genre is no more than a minor mannerist offshoot of the larger and longer crime-writing tradition. This genre, whose legitimate ambition is to entertain, is well suited to a minor mannerist talent. I believe, nonetheless, that it should be possible to any writer of some energy to disregard the sillier among the restrictive conventions governing the genre.

Nicolas Freeling. Grandfontaine, June 1989

Barry Foster as Van der Valk in the Thames Television series based on Freeling's novels

mother, his sexual obsession, and his disillusionment when, after eight years, he realizes that her love had grown sour and corrupt.

Taking Martin out of jail, Van der Valk forces him to enter Elsa's flat on the Josef Israelskade: "I think that the secret of all of this . . . lies here in this street, in this house. It all springs from here. In this room I can smell the hanky-panky. . . . This is a question of character. Her character. She was a secretive woman. Everything she did, when she could make it so, was underhand, designed to deceive and to mislead." Never wavering from his assessment of Elsa's character, Van der Valk decides that the drama, the scheming, the rages, and the need for reconciliation that had characterized her affair with Martin would not have ended after he married Sophia Ter Laan. He posits another lover for Elsa and persists until a trap ensnares the unknown killer.

Freeling's first Dutch novel established a characteristic mode of writing: the heart of the book is a series of disclosures about the intimate details of someone's life which Van der Valk pursues almost as if he were a lover. Martin notices the erotic nature of this bond: "He sounded as though he had a personal grievance against Elsa. He too, thought Martin, has come under the spell." Each of the subsequent Van der Valk

books explores another aspect of Dutch private life.

In *Because of the Cats* (1963) Van der Valk assumes a new police role in a department called "Zeden en Kinder-Politie" (Morals and Children). Having passed examinations and earned a diploma, he takes on the youth culture of Amsterdam, using all of his patience; his friendliness; his lazy, joking manners; and his talent for creating confidence to deal with truculent teenagers. He is challenged to identify a gang which seems unusually calculating, professional, and vindictive. The boys have frequently robbed homes, but they come to Van der Valk's attention at the point when they bind a husband, rape his wife, and leave as their only "clue" the remark that "the cats won't like it."

Making a private assessment of the character of the gang, Van der Valk focuses his investigation on Bloemendaal aan Zee, a prosperous, modern suburb whose bourgeois citizens have lots of money but little time for their children. In their parents' absence, these teenagers have turned to a kind of neo-Nazism which is instigated and supported by Hjalmar, the owner of a local nightclub, the Ange Gabriel. Under his guidance, the Ravens, along with their girlfriends, the Cats, smoke dope, engage in orgies, and, as a mark of their superiority to bourgeois proprieties, rob and pillage apartment houses. In their desperation to maintain a closed ring of secrecy the girls kill Kees van Sonneveld, the group member whom they suspect might talk. In the night, they entice him out to the sea with his new scuba, lure him into making love with Hannie Troost, and drown him in the act.

Van der Valk elicits this bizarre and sordid tale by sheer force of character and by an underhanded ploy of his own: he introduces one of the Ravens, Erik Miehle, to a Russian prostitute, hoping that the boy's experience of mature love with a woman will break his allegiance to the gang. It does. Between the boy's story and the confession of Hannie Troost, the truth emerges. Van der Valk's interaction with the "criminals" is once again intense, empathetic, erotic: "He had just broken her [Hannie]; he felt as though he had raped her. The struggle had been like an act of love."

Gun before Butter (1963; published in the United States as *Question of Loyalty*) involves Van der Valk in a double plot and a case of double identity. When he understands how two seemingly disparate stories converge, he has solved the mystery. The first story is about a young girl, Lucienne Englebert. She is the daughter of Arnolf Englebert, who is a superb musician, a renowned symphony conductor, and, in private life, a womanizer. His death leaves Lucienne with few resources. Proud and idealistic, she disdains most of the options open to young, uneducated women and chooses life as an auto mechanic in Brussels rather than sit in a Dutch office as a typist. Van der Valk meets her at several key points in her life and then loses track of her.

The second story is a murder: a man is found stabbed to death in a sparsely furnished house in the Apollolaan in Amsterdam. Since he is unknown to his neighbors and carries no identification Van der Valk is forced into a series of shrewd guesses. Eventually he pieces together the picture of a secret and obscure life: the dead man is Meinard Stam, a man of wealth, with no identifiable profession, who had also been a sportsman and nature lover. In addition to the house in Amsterdam, Stam had rented a hunter's cottage in Tienray near the Belgian border. Van der Valk is stalled until he guesses that a wealthy man who had lived near the border could have been a smuggler. This is the case; the deceased had smuggled butter and had assumed the identity of Stam in order to do so. In his other, legitimate life, he had been Gerard de Winter, a forty-

Dust jacket for the first edition of Freeling's penultimate novel featuring Piet van der Valk

four-year-old Belgian hotelier who was married to a woman named Solange.

Establishing the double identity of the victim brings Van der Valk no closer to his murderer. For this he returns to the Apollolaan house and to the kind of psychological investigation on which his reputation rests. He focuses on two objects: an original painting by an artist named Breitner and a white Mercedes coupe which had been abandoned in front of the house: they are both objects that show discrimination and taste. When an art dealer traces the Breitner painting to Brussels, Van der Valk knows that the answer to the murder lies in Belgium, not Holland, and when he reencounters Lucienne Englebert at a gas station in Brussels, he intuits a relation between the two lives: Lucienne is the kind of woman who could have bought the Breitner painting; she would have appreciated the Mercedes coupe. His hunches prove to be correct: Lucienne had fallen in love with Stam and had stabbed him when she learned of his duplicity. She tells Van der Valk the story of her decision to let Stam love her, their lives together in the hunter's cottage, and her sense of betrayal: the daughter of a man who had had several lovers, she would not herself participate in a similarly sordid situation. Van der Valk appreciates her integrity and shields her from further investigation. Looking back, he calls the whole affair "The Diamond-cutters": "He saw each character as a diamond, that cuts others into facets, and is itself cut and throws out light and sparks and strange fires." *Gun before Butter* received England's Crime Writer Award and, in 1965, the Grand Prix de Roman Policier.

Double-Barrel (1964) initiates one of the most interesting of Freeling's speculations about the relation of public and private life and the role of gender in the process of detecting crime. Van der Valk and his wife, Arlette, are sent to Drente, a poor province in the northeast corner of Holland, to discover the reason for a series of seemingly unmotivated suicides. Initially Arlette is simply part of Van der Valk's cover: "If you are to be the complete, convincing, colourless if intelligent state functionary, you need a wife to do the housekeeping." But eventually she assumes a primary role in the investigation. As much as Van der Valk prides himself on being able to penetrate the lives of strangers, he remains puzzled by what he finds in Zwinderen. Arlette eventually provides the key to the mass hysteria and Calvinistic zeal that have marred the industrial development of the area: " 'Well, one feels a strong hostility to the outsiders. . . . There's a hatred, almost, of all this progress.' " Listening to his wife's analysis of everyday life, Van der Valk comes to see that all the women who received anonymous threat letters were locals who had married leaders of industry. From this composite image of the victims Van der Valk is able to piece together a psychological portrait of the murderer. She turns out to be a very religious spinster who resented the betrayal of traditional Dutch values that these progressive marriages represented to her.

In the course of discovering the frustrated woman's identity, Van der Valk speaks frequently with an elderly man who had at one time been suspected of being the murderer. Mr. Besançon, a Jewish survivor of World War II, provides Van der Valk with interesting conversations during an otherwise boring investigation, and it is he who initially gives Van der Valk the idea which leads him to discover Miss Burger's identity: " 'What happens' " Besançon asks, " 'to civil servants . . .

who come to the conclusion that their government has betrayed them? They commit treason.' " As Van der Valk comes to see, Miss Burger has been an excellent example of such a civil servant: an administrative assistant to the mayor, seemingly devoted to her work, she had nonetheless felt betrayed by the government's support of modernization. Van der Valk's gratitude for this insight is not uncomplicated, for he asks himself how a lonely and ailing Jewish man could have such knowledge. Following his intuition and sensing some unexplained guilt in the man, he posits an accurate theory about Besançon's real identity: he is impersonating a Jew and is not the victim of World War II atrocities but the perpetrator of them. Besançon is really SS Lieutenant General Heinrich Müller. This double recognition accounts for the title of the book, and, on a textual level, for Van der Valk's promotion to the rank of chief inspector at the book's conclusion.

In *Criminal Conversation* (1965), when the police receive an anonymous letter accusing a Dr. Hubert Van der Post of killing an artist named Cabestan, Van der Valk is bored enough to look into the matter himself. Once again eschewing a police mentality, he investigates by engaging Dr. Van der Post in a series of private discussions in which he hopes to elicit an expression of guilty knowledge. Initially masquerading as a patient, he enters the doctor's consulting room only to reverse their roles, to act as a diagnostician to the doctor whom he sees as having become a murderer because of deep wounds to his self-esteem.

Van der Post is a skillful opponent who gives away nothing that could serve as concrete evidence. Instead, Van der Valk deduces his guilt simply from his willingness to engage in conversation and to persist in his relation to an investigator. In the course of their talks, Van der Valk discovers that Van der Post has taken to living in Cabestan's bohemian digs; he uncovers his affair with a wealthy banker's wife, as well as an abortion that he has given to her daughter. He posits an elaborate set of relations among the characters under investigation: "Doctor has mistress, mistress has daughter, daughter knows painter, painter knows–presumably–Doctor's wife, painter blackmails Doctor." But no diligence gives him any concrete grounds for prosecution.

The second half of the book is narrated from the criminal's point of view. Breaking his convention of third-person narration with direct dialogue, Freeling writes in the form of a diary that the doctor addresses to Van der Valk, a dialogue which he begins because he has seen that the policeman is himself capable of illegality. Initially the doctor says, "I have no hunger to confess, to be caught." But his diary, which traces his childhood, his student days, his early loves, and finally his marriage to a cold patron of the arts, eventually yields up his frustration, rage, and sheer jealously of Cabestan for living out a bohemian life-style and for having an affair (or so he imagines) with the beautiful daughter of his current mistress.

This diary dramatically reveals parts of the doctor's mind which remain hidden from Van der Valk. But in the course of writing down these confessions, Van der Post realizes that the policeman is the only person who cares enough about him to ferret out his motivations and to discover why he would feel compelled to kill another human being. It is the closeness of adversaries; but since it is the only intimacy that exists in Van der Post's life, he turns himself in. " 'He's realized, I think,' said Van der Valk soberly, 'that I'm the only [friend] he's got.' "

In *The King of the Rainy Country* (1966) Van der Valk experiences the cosmopolitan world of very rich Europeans who have no sense of the boundaries which usually guide conduct among ordinary Dutch families. Because his criminal investigations have always been unorthodox, he is not entirely surprised when he is detached from his normal duties and asked to find a missing person, Jean-Claude Marschal. As Mr. Canisius, who initiates this search, explains, Jean-Claude is forty-three; heir to the Sopexique, a French multinational corporation, married, and without any known scandals. While Canisius offers no clues or theories about the disappearance, he does make it clear that Van der Valk must safeguard the health, property, and good name of the family. With nothing more to go on than a hefty expense account from Sopexique, Van der Valk visits Jean-Claude's home and office to construct a hypothesis about what such a man might pursue and what might cause him to leave his home without any notice. Marschal's distant and elegant wife, Anne-Marie, gives him some sense of the claustrophobia that wealth and property can foster, and an old army record gives him a list of places that had once figured in Marschal's past. When Stössel, an old police buddy in Cologne, comes up with another missing person–a young "Tanzmariachen" (carnival princess)–he has a "crazy idea" that the two missing-person cases are related. Van der Valk's investigation takes him to

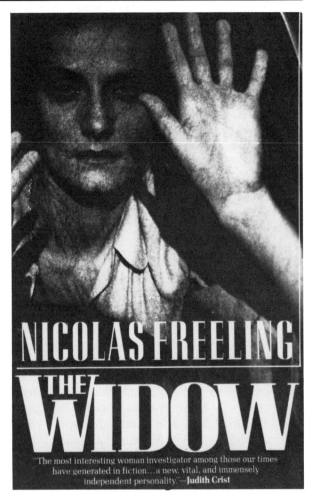

Dust jacket for the first American edition of the novel that continues the Van der Valk series with Piet van der Valk's widow Arlette as the featured detective

Cologne, where he continues to work idiosyncratically; he makes his next move when he discovers (through Stössel's telex) that an elegant and assured man had bought a large quantity of ski equipment and then two first-class tickets to Innsbruck. The name on the check is "Ney," and Van der Valk, seeing that this is the name of one of Napoleon's marshals, knows immediately that this is the kind of romantic gesture that Marschal would make. He goes first to Innsbruck and then to Strasbourg in pursuit and finds Jean-Claude and the missing girl together in bed, both killed by Jean-Claude's Mayerling pistol. As he waits for the local gendarmerie Van der Valk reads Baudelaire's poem: "I am like the king of a rainy country: rich–and impotent: young–and very old."

The mystery does not end with the discovery of Marschal's body, for Marschal's wife is convinced that he had been hounded to death by

Canisius, the very man who had instigated Van der Valk's search. When Van der Valk discovers that Marschal's rifle is missing, he guesses that Anne-Marie is trying to take justice into her own hands and follows her to Biarritz. True to form, Van der Valk remarks that "[h]e was a fool and an amateur, but this had to be done in an amateurish way. He was going against a woman with a rifle . . . with his bare hands." For being an amateur, he is rewarded as an amateur: Anne-Marie, mistaking Van der Valk for Canisius, shoots him and then kills herself with a high-speed Mauser cartridge. *The King of the Rainy Country* won the Mystery Writers of America Edgar Allan Poe Award in 1966.

Strike Out Where Not Applicable (1967) takes the recovering Van der Valk, now a commissaire, to Lisse, a town between Haarlem and Leiden, at the heart of the Dutch tulip country. In celebration of their new status, Van der Valk's wife, Arlette, takes up horseback riding at Francis La Touche's stable, and she is the one who alerts her husband to the death that he is later called to investigate. Bernhard Fischer, the owner of a provincial restaurant, "Im Weissen Rössl," has been killed while riding. The death, thought first to be from the kick of a horse, is questioned by a young local doctor who cannot believe that a horse could kick at such an angle.

In the course of his investigation Van der Valk discovers the hidden desires and tensions of the people who ride at the stable: Marguerite, Fischer's widow, is found to be a cool and extraordinarily competent business woman who does not miss her husband either as an intimate companion or as a business partner. She is loved, secretly, by her assistant, Saskia Groenveld, who is a lesbian. Marguerite is in love with Mr. Matthew, an English diplomat from The Hague, to whom she gives a picture of herself riding a horse. As Van der Valk proceeds, he uncovers other secret passions: Janine Zwemmer, a rich, pretty wife of a famous bicyclist, is lonely, unable to bear children, and snubbed by the local people for having "new" money. In her desolation, she turns to a young painter, Dickie Six, with whom she has a brief affair. Van der Valk discovers the two of them meeting secretly in the sand dunes at night and is able to rule out Janine's guilt and finally to elicit a confession from the painter.

The intensity of feeling between the police and the criminal and between the criminal and his victim is similarly explored in Freeling's next Van der Valk book, *Tsing-Boum: A Novel* (1969). He extends his exploration of the psychology of investigation with the use of "penal marriage" as a central metaphor. *Tsing-Boum* is a book about the relationship between a husband and wife, between two former lovers, between public and private life, and between present-day Holland and Vietnam during its war with France. It is filled with unexpected attachments, and it takes Van der Valk to a new level of involvement with the subjects of his investigation. In *Double-Barrel* he relied on his wife, Arlette, to help penetrate the tranquil surface of a small provincial town. Here, Arlette, who is French, provides the key to his understanding of a French woman, Esther Marx, who, after a dull but blameless existence as a housewife, is found dead in her flat of machine-gun wounds.

Tsing-Boum marks an attempt by Freeling to move his fiction away from the purely personal to a wider political arena. In the foreword he gives readers an "aide-mémoire," reminding them of the events that happened at Dien Bien Phu in Vietnam in 1954, during the French occupation. He quotes from various press reports and eyewitness accounts of the time, which show the mood of the French forces changing from confidence to total panic. Freeling's intention is clearly to locate Van der Valk's current criminal investigation in a larger historical context and to show the ways in which individual lives can be caught up and shaped by events that are of vast national or international significance.

In his efforts to discover why Esther Marx should be the victim of homicide, Van der Valk is driven back into French political and military history, for he rather quickly discovers that she had been a military nurse in Vietnam. Knowing that she had also had an illegitimate child (a girl named Ruth, whom he and Arlette eventually adopt), Van der Valk posits that the child's father is someone who was also in Vietnam and sets about finding members of the old Indochina group who might know his identity.

His search leads him first to Marseilles, where he learns that Esther had loved a Lieutenant Laforêt, and then to Clermont-Ferrand, where a Colonel Voisin fills him in on the details of their romance: Laforêt, a paratrooper, had deserted the army during the Dien Bien Phu offensive, and Esther had shot him when she discovered his cowardice. She had been tried in court but had been exonerated by the testimony of other military personnel who perjured themselves to give her a self-defense plea. The soldier had recovered, and though Van der Valk cringes at raking up old enmities, he has little doubt that Laforêt is involved in Esther's death.

It is Arlette who pieces together the more recent dimension of Esther's past. Esther's daughter, Ruth, tells her that she and Esther had made a trip to a flying school in Belgium, where they had met a man who argued with her mother. Arlette realizes grimly that this flier must be Ruth's "unknown" father, and she cries when she imagines what Van der Valk must do: go to Belgium to arrest Ruth's father for killing her mother.

A dramatic ending prevents this from happening: Laforêt–now known as Mr. Bos–takes his business partner, Conny Desmet, up in a private plane and dies in the attempt to parachute out of it. Van der Valk returns to Arlette and decides to adopt Ruth–a move that is a symbolically appropriate ending to his "intimacy" with Esther Marx. The child represents the fruit of the "penal marriage" between a good investigator and the victim of crime.

Over the High Side: A Novel was published in 1971 (published in the United States as *The Lovely Ladies*). In 1972 Freeling's final volume of the Van der Valk series, *A Long Silence: A Novel*, was published (published in the United States as *Auprès de ma Blonde*, 1979). *Over the High Side* is not colored with political or social issues. Van der Valk travels to Ireland to untangle a murder and finds himself in the familiar situation of teasing out the intrigue and malice behind seemingly placid, bourgeois lives. The book begins with the fatal stabbing of an elderly man, F. X. Martínez. The man had a young wife who called him "Vader" and three daughters by a previous marriage who lived with him in Belgrave Square, Dublin. A threefold coincidence convinces Van der Valk that the solution to this death lies in Ireland: a car parked illegally outside the Martínez flat is registered to Denis Lynch, a young Irishman; a pair of eyeglasses at the Amsterdam Lost Property Office comes from a Dublin optometrist; and the daughters continue to live in Ireland after the death.

Denis Lynch's guilt is almost immediately apparent: he is the son of a wealthy Irish senator, a friend of the Martínez sisters, and a tourist in Amsterdam at the time of the old man's death. He has continued his travels but disappears when his father, an honorable man who is determined to discover the truth, flies to Rome to find him. Van der Valk knows that he has discovered the murderer, but he cannot discern any motive for the boy's passion. While waiting for some sign of the young man, he decides to become better acquainted with the sisters. Stassie Flanagan interests him the most, for she is the sexiest of the sisters; and he imagines that Denis Lynch was once her lover. Still with no evidence in hand, he receives a poison-pen letter, a shove into the street which results in a broken collarbone, and a visit in his hotel room by Stassie, who seduces him. Van der Valk knows that he is onto something, but he is still working in the realm of intuition.

A good hunch leads him closer to actual evidence: asking how a teenage boy could "disappear" most easily in Europe, he comes upon the idea of a yacht, and then locates a wealthy young Irishman's boat that had been harbored in the Mediterranean. Denis is on it and headed home. A rendezvous in Cork brings the suspect to hand, and Van der Valk has only to understand the boy's motive for killing. Finally he sees that Anna Martínez, the young wife in Amsterdam, had been in a position analogous to Stassie's: both were bored and sexually available young wives of older men; and while Denis had once accepted that Stassie would never be free to be his, he could not accept the same from Anna. Her husband had to be eliminated.

While *Over the High Side* has as much psychological insight as Freeling's other novels, one can sense in it a tightening or a resistance to the material itself. It is as if Freeling realized with this book that he had played out the possibilities of police procedure in relation to contemporary Dutch society and could go no further with it. It is not, then, altogether surprising that Van der Valk should die in *A Long Silence;* this book completes the series in several ways. Van der Valk, who has always succeeded because of tremendous powers of empathy with the victims of crime, finally joins the victims completely, in death. And Arlette, who has always acted as a female helping figure, supporting, encouraging, and inspiring Van der Valk in the use of talents that are usually considered feminine, assumes his role as detective: by her knowledge of her husband's character, she will find his murderers.

At the point of Van der Valk's death, Freeling breaks his customary narrative stance in order to speak in the first person: "It was at this point that I found myself involved in this story. I must explain myself: the writer is of course always 'involved' but he detaches himself as much

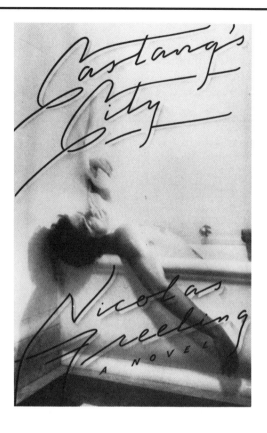

Dust jackets for the first American editions of three of Freeling's Henri Castang novels

as possible." Freeling continues to explain that he and Van der Valk were friends, that they had met when he, working as a cook in a Dutch restaurant, had gotten arrested for taking home food. Van der Valk had shown him kindness while he was in jail and later had taken him home for one of Arlette's famous meals. She had, he explained, come to see him when she needed help in deciphering her husband's notebooks. Still in the character of writer and friend, Freeling observes that he is no detective but he did "contribute something to her detective work."

The last section of the book is written from Arlette's perspective. After moving to France and trying to forget that Piet van der Valk was assassinated, she realizes that she cannot rest without first attempting to find his murderer. She returns to her old neighborhood in Amsterdam, where Old Mother Counterpoint, a piano teacher; Trix and Willy, the butchers; and Hilary and Dan De Vries, a young couple, join her in piecing together clues to Van der Valk's death from his police notebooks. Together they form a theory about Van der Valk's last investigation: references to a stolen watch; a boy, Richard Oddinga; a man referred to as "B"; another called "Louis"; and a bit of poetry ("stripped tree of the false apples, Neil's son of woeful Assynt") lead them to look for a jeweller in the Leliegracht. There Arlette discovers a sex shop, "The Golden Apples of the Hesperides," which, by coinciding with Van der Valk's snippet of poetry about false apples, convinces her that she has stumbled upon the right place and the right assailants.

The book plays out a series of moves that Arlette and her neighbors use to "squeeze" Richard Oddinga, Larry Saint, and Louis Prins, for these neighbors share Van der Valk's opinion that justice must be carried out privately if it is to be carried out at all. But at the point where violence would be required to harm Larry Saint, they all back away from the use of bombs or guns. Instead they go to the police, who, for all their lack of imagination, are finally seen as the only appropriate vehicle of justice: "the police; we all thought them useless but I mean, it's the best one can do."

In ending the Van der Valk series Freeling remained true to the themes and social attitudes that informed his work from the beginning: the bureaucratic methods of the police are shown to be ineffective in discerning crime; Van der Valk is successful to the extent that he forsakes official procedures and relies on his own intelligence.

Arlette, having nothing but her own intuition and the collective efforts of her neighbors to help her, succeeds almost immediately in her investigation.

Considering the esteem in which his Dutch novels were held, Freeling's decision to kill Piet van der Valk and to begin two new series of mysteries was remarkable. With his detective laid to rest, however, he was able to explore different cultural issues with two new detectives. Through Arlette, Van der Valk's French widow, he looked at life from a feminine, "unofficial" point of view; through Henri Castang, a policeman in a provincial French town, he continued to write about the interaction of police bureaucracy and private life.

Arlette van der Valk reappeared in *The Widow* (1979). Eight years after Piet's death, she marries an English sociologist, Arthur Davidson, whose work with the Council of Europe had brought him to Strasbourg. At his suggestion, Arlette opens an advice bureau to help people with personal problems that are not easily classifiable as legal, financial, or medical in nature. Three people immediately ask for help: a young, struggling mother whose husband has deserted her; an adolescent girl, Marie Line Siegel, whose relatives have threatened to institutionalize her if she does not leave her current boyfriend; and a very distracted man, Albert Demazis, who is run over by a train before he can bring himself to explain his full trauma to Arlette. In the course of the novel Arlette sorts out the problems of all her clients, but it is Demazis's death that provides most of the drama in her own life: in investigating his problems, she unwittingly infringes on the operations of a professional narcotics ring. She is kidnapped, marked with a "croix de vaches," that is, with razor slashes on her palms, and then attacked on the street. The police, who have realized that she can act as bait for these men, watch and protect her so that Arlette is saved from death and the criminals are found.

Arlette's unprofessional life as an investigator is marked by more melodrama than Piet van der Valk's had been: she is hounded by the press, harassed by the police, shot at in her car, almost raped by a client's husband, and stands helpless while her home is damaged by a bomb. Many people are upset by her snoopiness. Her value to Freeling lies directly in her amateur status: "Was she the cops or the social worker or the Ministry of Education? No? Then something governmental, departmental, municipal? Neither? Then . . .

what ... was she?" As a woman in private life, she knows things that are incapable of formal or legal proof; she can penetrate the areas of personal life that evade professional scrutiny.

She continues to pursue similar activities in *One Damn Thing after Another* (1981; published in the United States as *Arlette*), where several strands of life in Strasbourg are woven together by Arlette's genius for finding creative solutions to dreary problems: Xavier Marchand comes to her after he has lost his job, his social position, and his wife. A businessman without imagination, he languishes until Arlette realizes that his marketing talents would benefit another of her clients, a disillusioned officer who wants to leave the police judiciare and to start his own woodworking business. This man, Subleyras, later does Arlette a good turn when the son of another client, Madame Solange Bartholdi, robs an illegal pelt from a fur dealer who had shot and killed his brother. Subleyras, together with Xavier and Arthur Davidson, breaks into the furrier's shop under cover of darkness and disguises the signs of previous entry in order to protect the boy. With these problems taken care of, Arlette is free to address a more exotic call for assistance: at the request of Madame Hervé Laboisserie, the wife of a French Foreign Service official, she travels to Argentina in search of Gilles, the Laboisseries' missing son. In Buenos Aires she goes directly to see a commanding general and succeeds only in having herself arrested, jailed, and kept in solitary confinement. Having made the point that Europeans must not assume Argentinian authority to be beneficent, the general releases Arlette and leads her to the missing boy. In talking with Arthur later, Arlette ruminates about the Amnesty International reports which had previously claimed that ten thousand people had simply vanished at the hand of the current regime.

The Arlette series of mysteries allowed Freeling to explore some biases implicit in the Van der Valk novels, where Piet's unorthodox behavior had always triumphed over traditional bureaucratic procedures. The books were well received. *Newsweek* remarked, "Nicolas Freeling ... has given the detective story new dimension much as John le Carré has done for the spy novel." The *New York Times Book Review* considered, "Freeling is the only major crime writer who can, for all his individuality, be classed with Simenon," and the *St. Louis Post-Dispatch* claimed, "Mr. Freeling is rapidly outwriting the few au-

Dust jacket for the first American edition of the first novel by Freeling which does not feature any of his series detectives

thors who have been good enough to be in his class."

Henri Castang lives in France; he is younger than Van der Valk, less introverted, but still "a bit of an original." The police in France have different procedures; and Castang's city has its own flavor; but Freeling continues to write with his own distinctive "signature": crime provides the occasion for examining human character. Castang is introduced in *Dressing of Diamond* (1974). The book takes its title from a poem written by French novelist Albertine Sarrazin, who was a "half-Arab illegitimate child brought up by the Assistance Publique, first adopted and then rejected by a French bourgeois family ... and a prostitute at fifteen and engaged in an armed hold-up at sixteen." In prison she became a writer. The scrap of verse which prompts the theme of Freeling's novel was written in 1958:

Peace of mind suits me
As soft white velvet hands become a man,

As on half-healed wound a dressing–
A dressing of diamond.

The "wound" inflicted in Freeling's book is the seemingly unmotivated kidnapping of an eight-year-old child, Rachel Delavigne. Her mother, Colette, is the children's court judge, who at twenty-seven is one of the youngest judges in France; her father, Bernard, is an executive in the dairy business. When Colette and Bernard return home after work and realize that Rachel is not to be found in any of her customary places, they telephone Henri Castang, "an O.P.A. or adjunct officer of police in the S.R.P.J., or Regional Service of Police Judiciare." Castang is small, wiry, usually clad in tweed jacket and whipcord trousers, with beautifully polished shoes and clean fingernails. Discreet, direct, kind, he helps the Delavignes understand the probable nature of the crime–"more often stupidly aggressive than violently psychopathic"–the usual steps for making a search, and the publicity that will be the consequence of initiating a police procedure. Colette, who is in the unusual position of being able to launch a police action without, of course, being able to instruct her own case, decides to ask the procureur de la republique to intervene on her behalf. Besson, who is immediately sympathetic ("What after all is more to us than a child?"), calls in all the resources of the state and imposes secrecy on everyone concerned. He asks Castang, already involved as a friend, to lead the criminal investigation.

In the course of finding Rachel (she has been kidnapped by a peasant family which had once quarreled with Bernard over picking fruit in the country and had later suffered because Colette, in her capacity as judge, had punished their son), Castang is forced to reflect on the nature of the Delavignes' bourgeois existence and to see how their values, assumptions, and class prejudices have wounded the peasant family. Since they have tried to redress their pain by taking the child, the wounding is mutual; no one, except Rachel, is without blame. In Freeling's characteristic style, a world is created around the victims and criminals so that crime, rather than being a mystery, is the logical outgrowth of the damage and resentments of contemporary European life. Castang's own private world is revealed as fully as Piet and Arlette van der Valk's had been: he is married to Vera, a Czech gymnast who has suffered damage to her legs through a

serious fall and who uses a wheelchair. Like Arlette, her counterpart, she is an outsider–both by birth and by virtue of being an artist–and she retains a strong woman's sense of values: her soups, sympathy, and conversation ballast Castang, who returns to the safety of his home after the trials and risks of each day on the police force.

Each of Freeling's subsequent Castang novels develops the world which is introduced in *Dressing of Diamond*: Castang grows in skill and is promoted; Vera recovers the use of her legs and eventually bears two children; Colette remains a friend; and Commissaire Richard, Castang's superior, emerges as a fuller and more sympathetically portrayed character.

What Are the Bugles Blowing For? (1975; published in the United States as *The Bugles Blowing*, 1976) brings Castang to meet the president of the French Republic, who has to decide whether to grant mercy to a man who has been given the death penalty. Several months earlier, Castang had been called to the telephone by a man who announced quietly and factually that he had just killed his wife, his daughter, and "a man." Going to Gilbert La Touche's home, he found three naked bodies. La Touche said he had arrived home unexpectedly and had found his wife and his daughter in bed with David, a Jewish artist. As Castang waited for the technical crew to arrive, the oddities of the case began to appear: La Touche, far from being distraught, was tranquil, courteous, and neatly dressed. He was obviously extraordinarily wealthy, lived in a "hôtel particulier," and was the republic's inspector of finance–a man who would have highly placed friends. He had none of the overt signs of temporary insanity that one would expect in a crime of passion. Since Castang had no search to conduct, his time was spent in gathering information that would explain La Touche's act: gradually he discovered that the wife was frequently unfaithful and the daughter also known to be promiscuous. A second daughter, Victoria, was a drug addict. When she was killed during his search for her, Castang wondered briefly if there might be a link between the La Touche family and various Arab liberation groups; but neither in this, nor in the painter's Jewishness, could he discern any covert political motives. He finally comes to understand that La Touche, sickened by his family's values and by his own acquiescence in the effete lifestyle of the rich and privileged, has killed as a desperate act of manhood, and he is prepared to die as a consequence. After consulting personally with Castang, the president decides not to cancel the death penalty.

In *Lake Isle* (1976; published in the United States as *Sabine*, 1977) Castang undertakes his first independent homicide investigation when Richard sends him to Souley, a small, thriving, walled town where Sabine Lipschitz has been killed. This elderly woman had been a rich widow, owner of a property that had gained value as the town emerged as an historically important site. She had once come into the city to seek the protection of the police against the increasing harassment of her adopted son, Gerard, and his wife, Janet. Neither Richard nor Castang had considered her complaints to be serious until her death. At that point they began to suspect that someone had plotted her demise, and Castang is faced with establishing proof that more than hippie vandalism is involved.

Like *Dressing of Diamond*, *Lake Isle* is organized around a literary referent. Here William Butler Yeats's poem "The Lake Isle of Innisfree" shapes Castang's imagination as he explores the hidden schemes and alliances that motivate Sabine's neighbors in Souley. An old friend of Vincent and Sabine's, an artist named Miss O'Brien, refers to the poem in passing as she tries to describe the nature of the couple's life together. "He looked forward to retiring. Had it all planed. . . . He was going to cultivate that lovely great garden. And there'd be a bottle of white wine down the well to cool, and it would all be the Lake Isle of Innisfree."

As Castang looks into the affairs of Sabine's son and daughter-in-law and the dealings of various land developers in the area, "lake isle" becomes his way of identifying the meaning of property to the French bourgeoisie. "These lake isles: they glowed in the mind. Long years painfully worked for. Persistent mirage needing money, money, money. Always slipping out of reach. What would one not do to grab and hold the magic dream? . . . Anything. Yes. Murder."

Having identified the type of person who would want Sabine's property–someone short of cash, hounded by creditors, with an eye to restoring lost fortunes–Castang is able to sort through the local population and to find the particular man whose circumstances and desires coincide with the type. M. Barde lives ostentatiously in a country manor with formal French gardens, a stable, an expensive automobile and a uniformed maid whom he beds. Since he lives without the income to sustain this establishment, Castang posits that he could have made some kind of a deal with Sabine's vituperative and greedy daughter-in-law. "Who actually hit the old lady is for a jury to decide." Castang leaves Souley before anyone is brought to trial, content to leave dreams behind and to appreciate what actually grounds him in life: Richard and the job; Vera and their flat.

The Night Lords (1978) brings Castang three murders in quick succession. In the course of finding the authors of these crimes, Castang and Vera (who is three months pregnant with their first child) have an occasion to reflect on the general function of police, whom one of Castang's associates, M. Bianchi, calls "Les Seigneurs de la Nuit"–the night lords. The name, Venetian in origin, causes Castang to think about the nature of night, of darkness, of civilization as a thin patina spread over a vast history of "crime, vice, folly . . . ignorance, disease, fear."

No matter what thoughts he may share with Vera, Castang's tasks are tedious, immediate, and not without a certain black humor. The first case in the novel requires his most extensive attention: someone has dumped the naked body of a young woman into the boot of a Rolls Royce which belongs to an English high court justice, Sir James Armitage. Summoned to the parking lot of Thomases–one of France's three-star restaurants–Castang finds a British family filled with outrage and incredulity: who could have played such a foul joke on them? Castang takes down preliminary testimony from the judge; his wife, Rosemary Armitage; and their two grown children, Patience and Colin. He lets them proceed on their holiday while he attempts to establish the young woman's identity. He is hampered by the international nature of the crime, for the British consul tries immediately to dissociate the judge from the death and to pressure Castang to think of the body's discovery as an unfortunate coincidence. As stubborn and independent as Van der Valk had been, Castang continues his inquiry, reconstructing the previous stages of the judge's trip, tracing backward until he finds someone who had actually met the deceased woman (later identified as Laetitia Toth, a journalist from England). Still without irrefutable evidence, Castang again gathers the judge and his family for questioning, putting pressure on Colin (whom he knows had slept with the woman) and appealing to the judge's sense of the honor of his own profession. Unexpectedly, Vera plays a role

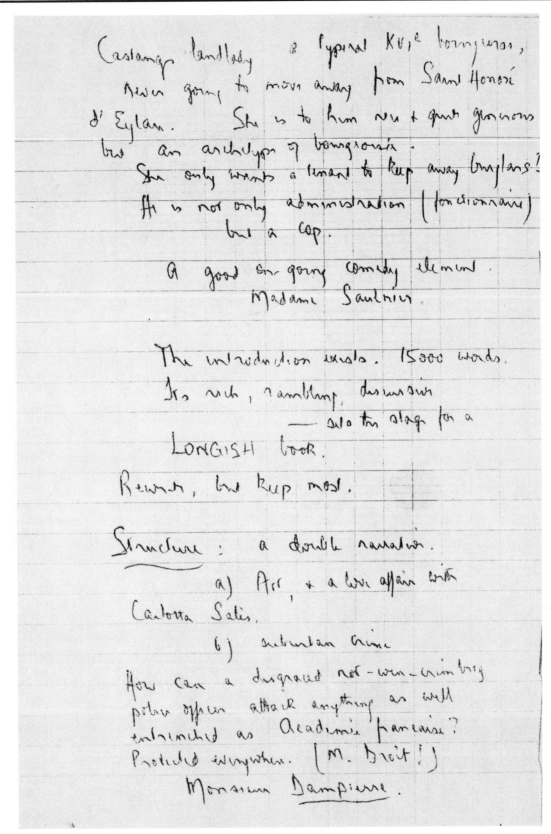

October 1988 notes described by Freeling as "jottings" on "the initial notions of character" in the "work notebook" for his novel in progress, "Reeds and Wild Cherry Trees" (courtesy of the author)

Elements of suburban crime.
Incest. Child Abuse. Not even 'crimes
in the code! The man who shoots his own son
thinking him a burglar!

Friendship: Dr. Denis. The judge Maurice
Manuel Revel.

Structural element: the child Sabine.
Daughter of restaurant owners.

The secrecy of the Fr. bourgeoisie.
Avarice & parsimony.
Authoritarian.
Hatred of proletariat, socialist, left-wing.
Distrust even of own family.

Spectator was I? Police officer asked 'If your child was
raped, would you treat it as police matter, or as
family? His reply: family, but many policemen
would disagree.

Little town in the Val de Marne: Villiers-Combray.
(Centre stays the same (Fr. intense conservatism)
despite explosion of population.

'Monde' (Pouvot-Delpech) "On sort de Modiano convaincu
que nos moindres instants pourraient
ressembler à un roman policier".
BUT THEY ARE A R.P. — IMBECILE!

172

in Armitage's confession: meeting her in the city's Jesuit garden, Armitage discusses day, night, and the power of darkness. When he says, " 'What I have not understood is why she hated me . . . and sought to entrap me,' " Vera gently suggests that he go to the police, to her husband who has enough imagination to understand the traumatic nature of his experience. The novel ends with his confession of a nighttime killing and with the story of a bizarre young woman, enamored of violence, filled with contempt for the British aristocracy, who had seduced him in his Rolls Royce and then pointed a pistol at him.

Having found the other murderer—a pathetic local man named Goltz, who had killed a concierge and a tramp when they threatened to interrupt his real-estate schemes and who then wounds both Castang and Bianchi in the course of their investigation—Castang returns as usual to Vera, his touchstone of simplicity and trust, and to the marriage which he pits against the mendacity of the outside world.

In the foreword to *Castang's City* (1980) Freeling assures his readers that the city in which Castang operates is fictional: "A reviewer once said that it just had to be Toulouse. . . . It isn't, and nor is it Strasbourg. Inevitably it has features of both: numerous French cities are ancient regional capitals; seats of powerful dukes, and even kings. With palaces, Gothic cathedrals, Renaissance and classical buildings. . . . Castang's city is imaginary." In this book Castang continues to grow not only in terms of the cases he is faced with professionally but also in his relations to Vera and to the values she represents. Vera bears the child conceived in *The Night Lords*, and Castang sees clearly how life and death form the two poles of his existence. On the job, he is once again charged with ferreting out the intrigues and hidden connections of well-placed people in the community. Early in May, Commissaire Richard bundles him into a squad car headed toward the scene of an assassination: Etienne Marcel—municipal councillor, adjunct mayor, and general man-about-town—has been murdered by a barrage of bullets in the Cours La Reine. Terrorism is suspected. Richard takes on the task of looking for political and/or financial motives; Castang is assigned to the personal side of Marcel's life. His investigation is hampered by a second death in the family: Didier, Marcel's oldest son, is found electrocuted in his bathtub. Shortly afterward, Marcel's widow, Noelle, tries to commit suicide. Convinced by this time that deaths recurring within

one family point to crimes authored in the larger family circle, Castang dismisses the idea of terrorism and probes until he finds a cadre of townsmen—a group of marginal, weak-minded, and disgruntled men—who have carried out both the killings under the direction of a wealthy wine-grower, Maresq. The link between the family and the group is provided both by the younger son, Thierry, who hangs out in billiard rooms and private airports with them, and by Magali, Marcel's married daughter, who plays wife-swapping games with Maresq in his country villa.

The privacy that Castang has so carefully maintained with his wife is threatened in Freeling's next book, *Wolfnight* (1982), when Vera is kidnapped and held hostage by a Fascist group. Castang, who has been promoted to senior officer of serious crimes, enters into this unprecedented circumstance by beginning an investigation into a car accident reported by M. Marc Vibert, a politician, a well-known public figure, and someone who is being groomed, it is rumored, for the presidency of the republic. Vibert had waited seventeen hours to report the accident, which has seemingly claimed the life of the other passenger, Viviane Kranitz. Castang, with Watergate and Chappaquiddick on his mind, realizes that the inquiry will have political consequences, and he sees the noose drawing closer when he discovers that Madame Kranitz, whose body is still missing, has been both a political advisor and a lover to Vibert. While searching Kranitz's apartment he finds the address of Alberthe de Rubempré, who interests him because she lives near the scene of the accident. Rubempré turns out to be a beautiful woman of immense wealth and extraordinary taste. Her right-wing, extremist tendencies have led her to think money can buy anything, including Castang's allegiance. When Kranitz is found assassinated and Rubempré leaves town without warning, he knows there to be more than coincidence involved, but he has no legal leverage to bring Rubempré back from Germany. At this point, Richard, remembering his days in the French Resistance, decides to circumvent the law: weaving a web of false identities, he, Castang, and Orthez kidnap Rubempré and bring her back to a prison cell for interrogation. They are convinced that she holds the key to understanding the relation between Vibert, right-wing political extremists, and Kranitz's death, but they have not reckoned on the vindictiveness and treachery of their foes. Castang returns to his flat one afternoon to find

Orthez knocked unconscious, Lydia, the baby, in hysterics, and Vera gone: kidnapping-for-kidnapping.

Nothing in Castang's life is as important as Vera; public service has been made possible for him by her good judgment, honesty, and straightforward conduct. Enraged that a supposedly professional matter should invade his home, Castang decides that the time for being professional has ceased: taking Rubempré from her cell, he drives her to a deluxe country hotel, where he presents himself to his adversaries as a private, aggrieved man who wants, with no repercussions, to trade one woman hostage for the other.

A chagrined Richard covertly surrounds Castang with a support staff, and before Vera is rescued an exotic band of paratroopers has jumped into the garden of Rubempré's estate. It is she, intoxicated by money and power, who has killed Kranitz, and she is carted off to face trial while Castang, Vera, and Richard return to Judith, Richard's wife, who has been keeping Lydia, the baby.

The bonds between Richard, Castang, and their wives are strengthened in *The Back of the North Wind* (1983). At work, Richard and Castang (now promoted to commissaire) face crimes of increasing barbarity: the decayed, mutilated body of a young girl is found in a swamp on the outskirts of the town. Working with a trusted colleague in pathology, Castang learns that she had been sexually violated, then butchered, and her flesh eaten before being disposed of in the swamp. The enormity of this perversion is too great for Castang to understand: he finds the assailant, a Japanese Buddhist, very quickly but can make no connection between the Buddhist respect for the sanctity of life and the motives of the person who had so brutally massacred Lonny van Barneveldt.

Richard next gives him the files of two unsolved homicides: a middle-aged man of blameless habits had been found bludgeoned to death in his car near the railroad station; in another location, a middle-aged woman had been found dead in her car, killed by a sharp blow from behind. Castang posits a connection between the two deaths and imagines some kind of narcotics or prostitution hustle as a motive. Setting up surveillance equipment at the railroad station he notices a very pretty, very young girl "working" the crowd. He and his colleagues, Maryvonne, Liliane, Orthez, and Lucciani, set up a trap, catch the girl's accomplice, but by a series of blunders

Freeling, from dust jacket of Cold Iron *(photograph by Helen Pask)*

let the ringleader escape. The ringleader, Thérèse Martin, aged fourteen years, seven months, is eventually picked up at a long-distance truckers' cafe. Although Castang has solved this case as neatly as the other, he is similarly perturbed by a culture that can produce children who kill people with no provocation.

His reflections on the corruption he must deal with as a police officer lead him inevitably back to Vera. The Castangs have moved from their flat in town out to a little cottage with a walled garden, and Vera has taken time from her homemaking to become better friends with Judith, Richard's shy, awkward Spanish wife. Together the women decide to revolutionize police thinking. In their talks and private reflections, "the back of the north wind"–a phrase Richard learned in the mountains of England–becomes a code for imagining a different kind of culture where violence is abhorred and mutual well-being is a collective goal. In this book it remains an elusive ideal, for Richard and Judith's home, a lovely place with gardens built into a hillside, is destroyed by an incendiary bomb–the result an investigation into the dealings of Aldo de Biron, a politician who had tried to support his political aspiration with a corrupt secret police network.

Castang's work takes him to Munich, Germany, and Dorset, England, in *No Part in Your Death* (1984), which is divided into three parts. Because he was wounded in trying to discover who had set fire to Richard's house, Castang had expected to be retired on a small pension. Instead Richard showed his gratitude by making him chief of staff. His new position makes him the logical choice to represent the S.R.P.J. at an international congress on police procedures. Taking Vera and three-year-old Lydia, Castang prepares to speak and to listen to papers while his family sightsees in Bavaria. Their disparate activities are unexpectedly joined when Vera shields an unknown young woman from people pursuing her on the street. Annoyed at the stranger's intrusion into her holiday, but prompted by a sense of personal responsibility, Vera learns that Birgit Rennemann is a Norwegian woman of loose, bohemian habits who is married to a German man of excellent background. Birgit's unorthodox behavior has led her in-laws to question her ability to raise children and to push her toward a psychiatric imprisonment. Vera thinks the woman distraught, but certainly not insane, so she takes her to Castang. Although his judgment of Birgit coincides with Vera's, Castang counsels her to submit to psychiatric examination as a way to win back her freedom most effectively. This brief interference in the Rennemanns' affairs leads to an inordinate amount of trouble, for the German authorities trace Castang's history on German soil back to the illegal abduction of Alberthe de Rubempré. Although Castang had been following Richard's orders in kidnapping Rubempré, and although his meeting with Birgit Rennemann had been fortuitous, the two incidents lead the German police to suspect him of having terrorist connections. Briefly kidnapped and interrogated, Castang is freed just in time to watch the now crazed Birgit shoot her mother-in-law. What part, he asks, did I play in this death?

An assessment of personal responsibility underlies Castang's investigation into the drowning of Marlene, the wife of his good friend Roger Riderhood. Castang drives out to find his friend's house in disarray, the river swollen by storms, and Roger in a drunken stupor. As the storm abates and Roger sobers up, Castang learns that he had been jealous of Marlene's supposed infidelities with two village men, but neither Castang nor Commissaire Richard can assign irrefutable blame for pushing her into the river. No one is arrested, but Castang leaves Roger's house feeling as contaminated by this crime as he had felt in Germany.

The final episode of this book occurs in England when another friend, Geoffrey Dawson, asks Castang to help with an investigation into the supposed suicides of two young French people staying in Dorset. Castang is dubious, but once again he responds to the needs of friendship. Together he and Dawson discover the web of intrigue that led the two youths to their deaths: with family money, Anne-Marie Bontemps and her lover, Daniel Cardenal, had bought a sailing boat. They had been asked, while at Saint-Malo, a French port, to deliver a parcel to England. Full of student rebelliousness and idealism, living out a rejection of corrupt bourgeois values by their life on the sea, they had no idea that they had been asked to smuggle guns. At a Christmas dinner in Dorset at the home of one of the racketeers, they had learned what was concealed on their boat and had been offended. They were then killed by an overdose of barbiturates. Agatha Margindale, a wealthy, privileged and imperious older woman; Mr. Sevenhampton, an importer of European sporting goods; and Tommy Ross, Miss Margindale's manservant, are all arrested, but Castang is once again unable to stand "simply" on the side of offended innocence: "He, too, after years and years of blacks, whites, and judicial greys, was beginning to discover colours. The tones and tints and hues of light and shadow. A part in these deaths."

In *Cold Iron* (1986) Commissaire Richard retires, leaving Castang with a new superior officer, Terranova, who wants to hire a staff more in keeping with his conservative values. Sensing the delicacy of his position, Castang asks to be transferred with a "step" to principal commissaire in an area in the Lille region. The climate is cold and rainy, the architecture is commonly thought to be dreary, but Castang and Vera like the grim brickwork and slightly dilapidated quality of the place: "It is . . . the metaphysical part of a pretty materialist country."

With his promotion comes a whole new staff, all of them predictably suspicious of their new chief: Castang's work is made more difficult by the secretiveness of his two principal inspectors, Campbell and Steelpath, and by the "indisciplined insolence" of his one "girl," Veronique Varennes, whom he quickly learns to call "VV" or "The Big Maid" because of her solid build. VV proves to have common sense and sensitivity as well as muscle, and Castang grows to appreciate her as they work together on a double homicide that leaves a family dynasty in shambles: they must figure out what has happened to Marguerite Lecat, the wife of a local business magnate, who has found her smothered to death in her bed. As Castang begins his inquiry he fights back confusion, for Lecat's friends and staff will answer specific questions but not offer more general information. When Castang remains without material evidence or ideas for an uncomfortably long time, Freeling draws on his experience as a chef to make an analogy between police work and cooking a superb dinner: both require patience and the ability to let the subject "simmer." Before Castang can come up with any solid hypothesis Lecat is found bludgeoned to death near his swimming pool.

The first break in the wall of silence that surrounds this family comes when Castang finds a small hoe that could have inflicted Lecat's head wound. With the suspects and witnesses "ripe" with anxiety, he begins a second round of questions. Persistant bluffing gets him his second break, for the gardener and Aurelie, an assistant in Lecat's winery, flee in terror that Castang has discovered their guilt. It is the escape itself that gives them away, but Castang persuades them to tell their story anyway. Lecat had been a thoroughly nasty man, corrupted by power and ready to corrupt others for his own pleasure. When he proposed setting up Aurelie as his mistress in Amsterdam, Jean-Baptiste, the gardener, had smacked him on the head with a garden hoe. Castang immediately understands the emotions involved: the swing of the hoe had been the only action available to a poor, uneducated man in defense of the honor of his woman; he had possessed no other way to combat Lecat's power. Knowing that Lecat had other mistresses in the town, Castang remains hopeful that Jean-Baptiste's crime of passion will meet with lenient punishment.

He is left with untangling the original homicide, a task complicated by local politics. Everyone would like to believe that Lecat killed his wife: it is an economical solution which leaves the remainder of the ancient, aristocratic family at peace. But Castang, like the gardener, has his own ideas of honor and persists in his inquiry. What he suspects turns out to be close to the truth, and the story is confessed: the husband of Marguerite's sister, a well-respected army gen-

eral, had been sleeping with Marguerite. His own wife, unable to bear the sordidness and humiliation of her private situation, had smothered her sister in the name of justice, honor, God–all the forces of conservatism that had been betrayed.

The "cold iron" of the book's title refers to the feel of handcuffs on a prisoner's wrists. But Freeling uses the tangible situation of the captured criminal to identify the realities of European life in a more general way. For in Castang's world, people are often "manacled" by daily necessities: money must be made, jobs attended to, greed and corruption faced, trivialities accepted. In the course of digging out criminals, Castang must live through his own "cold iron" circumstances. He is never exalted, never honored as brilliant nor rewarded for heroic behavior. But in serving the state, he reveals to readers the warmth and honesty that can temper the cold iron cast of modern European existence. As he and Vera and their two children figure out how to live without greed or corruption, they present Freeling's vision of the honor that remains possible in private life.

As quoted on the dust jacket of the American edition, Stanley Ellin, writing about this book, says: "Nicolas Freeling's new Henri Castang story, *Cold Iron*, is a powerhouse of a novel. Identification with Castang is immediate and intense, the view of his troubled and troublesome world made brilliantly vivid. And there is that unique writing style . . . that the author has honed to perfection as the instrument for getting into the marrow of every character he creates. *Cold Iron* is a triumph . . . a masterwork not to be missed."

References:

Jane S. Bakerman, "Arlette: Nicolas Freeling's Candle against the Dark," *Armchair Detective*, 16 (Winter 1983): 348-353;

Carol Shloss, "The Van der Valk Novels of Nicolas Freeling, " in *Art in Crime Writing: Essays on Detective Fiction*, edited by Bernard Benstock (New York: St. Martin's, 1983), pp. 159-173.

Andrew Garve
(Paul Winterton)
(12 February 1908-   )

Mary Helen Becker
Madison Area Technical College

BOOKS: *A Student in Russia*, as Paul Winterton (Manchester: Co-operative Union, 1931);

Russia—with Open Eyes, as Winterton (London: Laurence & Wishart, 1937);

Death beneath Jerusalem, as Roger Bax (London: Nelson, 1938);

Mending Minds: The Truth about Our Mental Hospitals, as Winterton (London: Davies, 1938);

Red Escapade, as Bax (London: Skeffington, 1940);

Eye-Witness on the Soviet War-Front, as Winterton (London: Russia Today Society, 1943);

Report on Russia, as Winterton (London: Cresset, 1945);

Disposing of Henry, as Bax (London & New York: Hutchinson, 1946; New York & London: Harper, 1947);

Blueprint for Murder, as Bax (London & New York: Hutchinson, 1948); republished as *The Trouble with Murder* (New York: Harper, 1948);

Inquest on an Ally, as Winterton (London: Cresset, 1948);

Came the Dawn, as Bax (London: Hutchinson, 1949); republished as *Two if by Sea* (New York: Harper, 1949);

No Tears for Hilda, as Andrew Garve (London: Collins, 1950; New York: Harper, 1950);

No Mask for Murder, as Garve (London: Collins, 1950); republished as *Fontego's Folly* (New York: Harper, 1950);

A Grave Case of Murder, as Bax (London & New York: Hutchinson, 1951; New York: Harper, 1951);

Murder in Moscow, as Garve (London: Collins, 1951); republished as *Murder through the Looking Glass* (New York: Harper, 1952);

A Press of Suspects, as Garve (London: Collins, 1951); republished as *By-Line for Murder* (New York: Harper, 1951);

A Hole in the Ground, as Garve (London: Collins, 1952; New York: Harper, 1952);

Paul Winterton, whose pen names include Andrew Garve, Roger Bax, and Paul Somers (photograph by Paddy Eckersley)

The Cuckoo Line Affair, as Garve (London: Collins, 1953; New York: Harper, 1953);

Death and the Sky Above, as Garve (London: Collins, 1953; New York: Harper, 1954);

The Riddle of Samson, as Garve (London: Collins, 1954; New York: Harper: 1955);

The End of the Track, as Garve (London: Collins, 1956; New York: Harper, 1956);

The Megstone Plot, as Garve (London: Collins, 1956; New York: Harper, 1957);

The Narrow Search, as Garve (London: Collins, 1957; New York: Harper 1958);

The Galloway Case, as Garve (London: Collins, 1958; New York: Harper, 1958);

Beginner's Luck, as Paul Somers (London: Collins, 1958; New York: Harper, 1958);

Operation Piracy, as Somers (London: Collins, 1958; New York: Harper, 1959);

A Hero for Leanda, as Garve (London: Collins, 1959; New York: Harper, 1959);

The Shivering Mountain, as Somers (London: Collins, 1959; New York: Harper, 1959);

The Far Sands, as Garve (New York: Harper, 1960; London: Collins, 1961);

The Golden Deed, as Garve (London: Collins, 1960; New York: Harper, 1960);

The Broken Jigsaw, as Somers (London: Collins, 1961; New York: Harper, 1961); as Garve (London: Collins, 1966);

The House of Soldiers, as Garve (New York: Harper, 1961; London: Collins, 1962);

Prisoner's Friend, as Garve (London: Collins, 1962; New York: Harper, 1962);

The Sea Monks, as Garve (London: Collins, 1963; New York: Harper & Row, 1963);

The Ashes of Loda, as Garve (London: Collins, 1963; New York: Harper & Row, 1965);

Frame-up, as Garve (London: Collins, 1964; New York: Harper & Row, 1964);

Murderer's Fen, as Garve (London: Collins, 1966); republished as *Hide and Go Seek* (New York: Harper & Row, 1966);

A Very Quiet Place, as Garve (London: Collins, 1967; New York: Harper & Row, 1967);

The Long Short Cut, as Garve (London: Collins 1968; New York: Harper & Row, 1968);

The Ascent of D-13, as Garve (New York: Harper & Row, 1968; London: Collins: 1969);

Boomerang, as Garve (London: Collins, 1969); republished as *Boomerang: An Australian Escapade* (New York: Harper & Row, 1970);

The Late Bill Smith, as Garve (London: Collins, 1971; New York: Harper & Row, 1971);

The Case of Robert Quarry, as Garve (London: Collins, 1972; New York: Harper & Row, 1972);

The File on Lester, as Garve (London: Collins, 1974); republished as *The Lester Affair* (New York: Harper & Row, 1974);

Home to Roost, as Garve (London: Collins, 1976; New York: Crowell, 1976);

Counterstroke, as Garve (London: Collins, 1978; New York: Crowell, 1978).

OTHER: Andrew Garve, "The Man Who Wasn't Scared," in *A Choice of Murders*, edited by Dorothy Salisbury Davis (New York: Scribners, 1958; London: Macdonald, 1960), pp. 225-230;

Garve, "Who Would Steal a Mailbox?," in *John Creasey's Mystery Bedside Book 1969*, edited by Herbert Harris (London: Hodder & Stoughton, 1968);

Garve, "Line of Communication," in *Ellery Queen's Mystery Parade* (New York: New American Library, 1968; London: Gollancz, 1969);

Garve, "A Case of Blackmail," in *John Creasey's Mystery Bedside Book 1972*, edited by Herbert Harris (London: Hodder & Stoughton, 1971);

Garve, "A Glass of Port," in *Winter's Crimes*, edited by George Hardinge (London: Macmillan, 1975);

Garve, "The Last Link," in *John Creasey's Crime Collection 1981*, edited by Harris (London: Gollancz, 1981).

Paul Winterton, British journalist and author, has written forty crime and suspense novels since 1938 under the pseudonyms Roger Bax, Paul Somers, and Andrew Garve, the name by which he is best known. He has amazed critics and reviewers by producing many different types of fiction, displaying a mastery of the detective story, espionage, police procedural, adventure, and romantic suspense. His special knowledge of the Soviet Union, of journalism, and of sailing are put to good use in many of the Garve novels, all of which are written in clear and literate prose that is a pleasure to read. Millions of readers have come to expect the sympathetic characters, ingenious plots, and fascinating backgrounds that comprise his entertaining thrillers.

Born in Leicester, England, 12 February 1908, Paul Winterton is the son of Ernest Winterton, who was also a journalist and served as a member of Parliament. He attended Purley County School in Surrey and the London School of Economics, from which he received a B.S. in 1928. After graduation he went to Russia on a traveling scholarship. In the foreword to *Report on Russia* (1945), he wrote of that experience: "I lived in the Ukraine with a Russian family for nearly a year and learned to speak the language with reasonable fluency. Since then I have made many visits, and always with the aim of keeping abreast of developments, collecting *facts*, and then attempting to interpret them in the light of Russian history, Russian temperament, Russian aspirations and Soviet politics." In 1931 his first book, *A Student in Russia*, based on his travels from 1928 to 1929, was published. In 1929 he took a job on the staff of the *Economist*. He moved to the *London News Chronicle*, a daily, in 1933 and worked as reporter, editorial writer, and foreign correspondent. In 1937 his book *Russia–with Open Eyes* was released. *Mending Minds: The Truth about Our Mental Hospitals*, his study of the mental health system in Great Britain, was published in 1938. The *London News Chronicle* assigned him to Moscow as special correspondent from 1942 to 1945, where he also did radio broadcasts for the BBC, reporting, as he said in the foreword to *Report to Russia*, "only nice things. Criticism was impossible." Upon his return to London, Winterton gave a factual report on the Soviet Union in *Report on Russia* and *Inquest on an Ally* (1948), which are still fascinating reading. He left newspaper work in 1946. A member of the Society of Authors, P.E.N., the Detection Club, and Mystery Writers of America, he was also a founding member of the Crime Writers' Association, serving as one of the organization's first joint secretaries.

Winterton has kept his personal life private, not revealing much of himself even in his writing. What is apparent in his fiction is expertise on subjects that are of particular interest to him, as well as certain qualities of courage, optimism, and good humor. While it is possible to consider a chronology of his books, looking for changes in style and subject matter, it is also appropriate to look for recurring themes and subjects and to note the variations he plays upon them. Many of his best books combine several of these interests, always presented in a new and different pattern.

By the time he wrote his first suspense novel, *Death beneath Jerusalem*, published in 1938 under the name Roger Bax, Winterton was already an accomplished stylist, experienced and skilled in his chosen craft. His hero, a foreign correspondent–interestingly named Philip Garve–is in Palestine, reporting on the unrest there and investigating an Arab plot against the British. His employers are anti-Arab, an attitude not shared by Garve. Garve and Hayson, an archaeologist (whose name is really Hussein), are both interested in Esther Willoughby, a lovely but naive English girl who subsequently is kidnapped and held hostage. The action unfolds underground, beneath the city, in Hezekiah's tunnel and Solomon's quarries. This book contains detailed information about the archaeology of Jerusalem

set within an exciting story and a charming romance–components of many of Winterton's thrillers that would follow. Long out of print, it should be reissued to entertain a new generation of readers. Fifty years later, the author's observations about the Middle East do not seem out-of-date.

Other books written as Roger Bax include *Disposing of Henry* (1946) and *Blueprint for Murder* (1948; published in the United States as *The Trouble with Murder*), both fairly traditional crime novels which contain well-drawn characters. *Blueprint for Murder* features a villain who has survived the horrors of Russia and Poland at the end of World War II and who is an intrepid sailor, like many of Winterton's heroes. *Came the Dawn* (1949; published in the United States as *Two if by Sea*) is an adventure set in 1947 in which two Englishmen, one a foreign correspondent who speaks Russian, sail across the Baltic in a small boat, the *Dawn*, to rescue the Russian wives they married during the war and were forced to leave behind. Filmed as *Never Let Me Go* (1953), starring Clark Gable, the book has recently been reprinted. *A Grave Case of Murder* (1951), a detective story set in East Anglia, is the last book published as Roger Bax. It followed the appearance of two works by Andrew Garve. Winterton once said that he took the name Garve from a village he noticed while driving in Scotland and he thought the name Andrew went well with it.

No Tears for Hilda (1950), the first book published by Andrew Garve, is something of a masterpiece, widely praised for the author's uncanny ability to evoke sympathy for murderer and amateur sleuth alike. In *A Catalogue of Crime* (1971) Jacques Barzun and Wendell Hertig Taylor call it "solid work, which can be reread at intervals with greatest pleasure. The detection is adroitly divided, or doubled (as one may want to look at it), so that the business of being on both sides of the hunt does not produce the usual disintegration of suspense. The hero and heroine are likable, and so is the murderer. Garve writes with economy and color–another rare combination." In their *A Book of Prefaces to Fifty Classics of Crime Fiction, 1900-1950* (1976), Barzun and Taylor say, "The plight of the accused man is really hopeless. Logic insists that the murderer would never have been found. But by sheer literary power, by deceptively terse and transparent description and dialogue, the miracle happens; and among other hard-edge depictions it leaves the reader with the unforgettable portrait of Hilda the unwept."

Dust jacket for the first edition of one of Winterton's favorites among his works

The Garve protagonist is often a newsman. *Murder in Moscow* (1951; published in the United States as *Murder through the Looking Glass*, 1952) is one of Winterton's favorites among his works. It is also one of the finest Garve books. George Verney, who tells the story, is a British journalist sent back to Moscow in 1951 to report on changes since his assignment there during World War II. From Warsaw, Poland, the train on which he is traveling is occupied by a group of Western Communist sympathizers, "peace" delegates, and a typical British workingman, all led by an obnoxious clergyman known as "Red" Mullett. When Mullett is murdered during the delegation's tour of Russia, some solid detection by British and American journalists forces the Soviet authorities to revise their politically easy and expedient frame-up of the hotel's valet. Anthony Boucher (*New York Times Book Review*, 27 April 1952) wrote that "Mr. Garve never allows political satire and significance, both present in dexterous

doses, to interfere with lively storytelling, sound detective work, or a very real affection for Russia itself." Of *By-Line for Murder* (1951; published in Great Britain as *A Press of Suspects*), set in a newsroom, Boucher wrote (19 August 1951) that "the lively intelligence of the writing and the satirically heightened realism of the London newspaper background make this an item not to be missed by any literate reader." In *The Ashes of Loda* (1963) the hero is a journalist stationed in Moscow. On leave in London Lord Quainton of the *Sunday Recorder* becomes engaged to the daughter of chemist Dr. Stefan Raczinski, Polishborn survivor of the Loda concentration camp. When a newspaper clipping is found which accuses Raczinski of war crimes allegedly committed while interned in the camp, his daughter breaks off her relationship with Quainton. Hunted by the Soviet police, Quainton struggles to survive in the frozen countryside. Praised by critics on both sides of the Atlantic, the story was serialized in *Argosy* before its publication in Britain.

Winterton's interest in archaeology has been put to use in several of his most intriguing Garve tales, including *The Riddle of Samson* (1954), set in the Isles of Scilly, in which the plans of an archaeologist conflict with those of smugglers, but most notably in *The House of Soldiers* (1961). Set in Ireland at the Hill of Tara, the site of King Cormac's mead hall, *The House of Soldiers* features newsman Sean Connor and archaeologist James Maguire. In the *New York Times Book Review* (10 September 1961) Boucher said of this book: "The slow, quiet and fascinating start of the novel deals with plans for a splendid pageant recreating the days of Ireland's kings on the very site of Tara. Later developments are quite as breathtakingly suspenseful as anyone could ask."

Winterton's research skills are exceptional, enabling him to set stories in exotic locations or in specialized surroundings which always seem authentic and based on personal knowledge. *No Mask for Murder* (1950; published in the United States as *Fontego's Folly*), for example, which takes place in a leprosarium in a colony in the tropics, shows his ability to create a community disrupted by murder. The social structure and politics within the group are memorable. *A Hole in the Ground* (1952) offers a character study of a left-wing politician determined to blow up a nuclear power plant and a vivid picture of the cave where he is carrying out the plan. Another fine adventure story is *The Ascent of D-13* (1968). After a plane crash in the mountains on the border between Turkey and the Soviet Union, Bill Royce, a British mountain climber, and Varya Mikhailovna, a Russian woman, undergo incredible difficulties as they attempt to reach Ankara. The novel contains a passionate justification for mountain climbing and an eloquent defense of democracy as well as a pleasant love story. *Boomerang* (1969; published in the United States as *Boomerang: An Australian Escapade*, 1970) opens in England where gambler and financier Peter Talbot, in Wormwood Scrubs prison for drunk driving, plans with his cell mates to recoup his losses with an audacious scheme in Australia. The action moves to the wilds of Australia in a comic caper reminiscent of some of the tales of John Boland.

Winterton has liked to write in winter, saving the summer for travel, boating, and exploring the waterways of the east coast of England; boats and the sea are favorite themes and are woven into many of his books. *The Cuckoo Line Af-*

fair (1953), a first-rate detective story with fine characters, depends for its solution on railway timetables and tidal charts in a coastal region. *The Megstone Plot* (1956), which was filmed as *A Touch of Larceny*, is a story of seafaring and attempted extortion. Boucher enthusiastically recommended the book in the *New York Times Book Review* (7 April 1957): "With lively understanding and irony, plus the open-air vividness which is so much his own, Garve constructs a short novel of high tension without resorting to murder or indeed to any overt crime–a connoisseur's item, unclassifiable and welcome."

The Narrow Search (1957) is set on the inland waterways of England and the canal boats that move along them. Most of the action in *A Hero for Leanda* (1959) takes place in a small craft on the Indian Ocean. An intrepid sailor has been hired to transport the leader of a liberation movement from his British island prison to the coast of Africa. *The Sea Monks* (1963) is a memorable thriller set in a lighthouse in the English Channel. Four young thugs invade the lighthouse, killing one of the keepers. The resourcefulness of the other keepers and a violent storm even the odds. *The File on Lester* (1974; published in the United States as *The Lester Affair*) is an ingenious tale of a plot against James Lester, a politician whose chance to become prime minister is threatened by children's nurse Shirley Holt, who claims to have had an affair with him aboard his yacht. How Lester deals with repercussions in the press in the week in which he is demonstrating that he could not have met her is fascinating.

Between 1958 and 1961, during which time five books were published under the Garve name, Winterton wrote four books under the pseudonym Paul Somers. *Beginner's Luck* (1958) introduces courageous novice reporter Hugh Curtis. Sent to Sussex to investigate a seemingly trivial story, he encounters Mollie Bourne, crime reporter for a rival paper. Their adventures and romance are quite enjoyable; and they meet again in *Operation Piracy* (1958), a thriller in which Curtis investigates the armed attack at sea of a tycoon's yacht. The story features scuba diving and salvage operations. The last adventure featuring Curtis and Bourne is *The Shivering Mountain* (1959), a case involving the kidnapping of a government scientist. *The Broken Jigsaw* (1961), the final book bearing the name Somers and reprinted (1966) as by Garve, is a complicated murder mystery with a writer as hero.

Dust jackets for the first edition of two of Winterton's many books with nautical settings

Too many of Garve's later books have been called "slender," "slight," or "short," by critics, somehow implying that length and bulk might somehow be preferable. For example, *Frame-Up* (1964), called "a slender affair" by Barzun and Taylor, was termed "a flawless specimen of the most classic form" by Boucher (19 April 1964), who added, "This is a lively, tight, murder puzzle with (apparently) only two suspects, splendid manipulation of alibis and other contradictory evidence and long, well-reasoned discussions of the case . . . a modern gem in the grand old genre." *Murderer's Fen* (1966, published in the United States as *Hide and Go Seek*) is a simple, uncluttered, and quite satisfactory mystery. Engaged to rich Susan, Alan Hunt nevertheless seduces Gwenda. He arranges a successful alibi for a crime that is not committed but then plans a real murder. Of *The Long Short Cut* (1968), which is the story of confidence man Michael Bliss's biggest project, Barzun and Taylor say: "Short and slick. Garve's excellent storytelling carries the reader along, but at the end one feels as if dropped into an air pocket." The *New York Times Book Review* (28 April 1968), on the other hand, said it is "exquisitely plotted and written with a dry wit and delightful understatement." *Home to Roost* (1976), in which two men with solid alibis confess to murder, is a complex murder mystery involving a mystery writer, his unhappy wife, and her lover. In Garve's last book to date, *Counterstroke* (1978), the wife of a member of Parliament is kidnapped, and a terrorist's release is the ransom demanded. Robert Farran, an actor, prepares to impersonate the terrorist. Critics considered the ending to be abrupt and disappointing after an intriguing buildup, but readers will find much to enjoy despite the quibbles of the critics.

On 24 April 1960 Boucher wrote retrospectively about Andrew Garve in the *New York Times Book Review*: "Frankly, I do not see how a man can write fourteen crime novels in a little over ten years without ever repeating himself in any way–consistently coming up with fresh characters

Counterstroke—28—RM
Mr Farran . . . Let us hope these bizarre activities will
prove justified.'

23

Though undoubtedly impressed by the outcome of the
trial, George still seemed reluctant to take a final view,
and I didn't quarrel with that. The success of the experiment had naturally increased my own confidence, but I
wasn't yet entirely satisfied. The conditions in the cell
had favoured me. The light had been adequate, but not
bright. A severer test might well lie ahead. The eye
problem still worried me – and of course there was the
danger of the missing mole. Obviously I couldn't count on
keeping my right forearm covered in all circumstances. I
discussed the matter again with George – in a rather more
serious vein than on the first occasion. As a result he made
an appointment for me at some place he described as a
private clinic, and the next afternoon he drove me there.
It was out in the country, somewhere in Sussex not far
from Lewes. Evidently it was a *very* private clinic, because
the sign outside said/ 'British Chemicals Ltd. Positively
No Entry', and there was a guard on the gate.

[handwritten marginal note: a big sign warned against unauthorised entry, and there was a guard on the gate.]

  The staff inside were friendly, matter-of-fact and un-
inquisitive. No names were asked for, or given. George
had brought along a full-face 'still' of Lacey, and I pointed
out to the surgeon the slight upward tilt of the eye setting,
which I said I would like him to copy as far as possible.
He didn't seem at all surprised by the request, and after
a brief examination he told me what he proposed to do.
He would make an incision on each side of the forehead
under the hairline, remove a little skin, and sew up the
gap. In fact, put in George's 'tuck'. With a local anaes-
thetic, he said, the small operation would be quite pain-
less; and the after-effects would be negligible. Naturally
it would slightly alter my appearance – that being the
object of the exercise – but if later I didn't like the way I
looked, new skin could be grafted and the operation
reversed. As for the missing mole, that was a trifling
matter. I said 'Okay – fine!' and he led the way into a
small operating theatre and, with the assistance of a
nurse, got to work.
  All went smoothly, and in a little over an hour I was
ready to leave. I had a piece of plaster on my right forearm in the spot I'd marked X, and a patch of gauze on
each side of my forehead, and that was all. George drove
me back to Pimlico, and we had a beer together in the
flat. He said he'd be calling again some time next day,

Revised galley for Winterton's last Garve novel, Counterstroke *(courtesy of the author)*

in a fresh scene, with a fresh theme and startlingly fresh plot-construction. But such is the record of Andrew Garve." The author was to keep up his pace, producing many more first-rate suspense novels. With the exception of the three novels featuring Hugh Curtis and Mollie Bourne, Winterton did not write series stories. His characters are civilized men and women caught up in extraordinary circumstances. He writes romance without explicit sex, crime without coarseness, and his sailors do not often swear—such is his literary skill that he does not need those props to evoke heart-stopping suspense. What his readers can depend on are intelligent, witty, well-written tales told by a master storyteller. Truly versatile in plot and characterization, even in genre, Paul Winterton has produced some of the finest thrillers published in the last century.

References:

Melvin Barnes, *Best Detective Fiction* (London: Bingley, 1975);

Jacques Barzun and Wendell Hertig Taylor, *A Book of Prefaces to Fifty Classics of Crime Fiction 1900-1950* (New York: Garland, 1976);

H. R. F. Keating, *Whodunit? A Guide to Crime, Suspense & Crime Fiction* (New York: Van Nostrand Reinhold, 1982);

John E. Kramer, Jr., and John E. Kramer III, *College Mystery Novels* (London: Garland, 1983);

Bill Pronzini and Marcia Muller, *1001 Midnights* (New York: Arbor House, 1986);

Myron J. Smith, Jr., *Cloak and Dagger Fiction: An Annotated Guide to Spy Thrillers*, revised and enlarged edition (Santa Barbara & Oxford: ABC-Clio, 1982);

Julian Symons, *Mortal Consequences: A History from the Detective Story to the Crime Novel* (New York: Harper & Row, 1972).

Michael Gilbert
(17 July 1912-   )

James Gindin and Joan Gindin
University of Michigan

BOOKS: *Close Quarters* (London: Hodder & Stoughton, 1947; New York: Walker, 1963);

They Never Looked Inside (London: Hodder & Stoughton, 1948); republished as *He Didn't Mind Danger* (New York: Harper, 1949);

The Doors Open (London: Hodder & Stoughton, 1949; New York: Walker, 1962);

Smallbone Deceased (London: Hodder & Stoughton, 1950; New York: Harper, 1950);

Death Has Deep Roots (London: Hodder & Stoughton, 1951; New York: Harper, 1952);

Death in Captivity (London: Hodder & Stoughton, 1952); republished as *The Danger Within* (New York: Harper, 1952);

Dr. Crippen (London: Oldhams, 1953);

Fear to Tread (London: Hodder & Stoughton, 1953; New York: Harper, 1953);

Sky High (London: Hodder & Stoughton, 1955); republished as *The Country-House Burglar* (New York: Harper, 1955);

Be Shot for Sixpence (London: Hodder & Stoughton, 1956; New York: Harper, 1956);

The Claimant (London: Constable, 1957);

Blood and Judgment (London: Hodder & Stoughton, 1959; New York: Harper, 1959);

The Bargain [play] (London: Constable, 1961);

A Clean Kill [play] (London: Constable, 1961);

After the Fine Weather (London: Hodder & Stoughton, 1963; New York: Harper & Row, 1963);

The Shot in Question [play] (London: Constable, 1963);

Windfall [play] (London: Constable, 1963);

The Crack in the Teacup (London: Hodder & Stoughton, 1966; New York: Harper & Row, 1966);

Game without Rules (New York: Harper & Row, 1967; London: Hodder & Stoughton, 1968);

The Dust and the Heat (London: Hodder & Stoughton, 1967); republished as *Overdrive: A Novel* (New York: Harper & Row, 1968);

The Etruscan Net (London: Hodder & Stoughton, 1969); republished as *The Family Tomb* (New York: Harper & Row, 1970);

Michael Gilbert (© Jerry Bauer)

Stay of Execution, and Other Stories of Legal Practice (London: Hodder & Stoughton, 1971);

The Body of a Girl (London: Hodder & Stoughton, 1972; New York: Harper & Row, 1972);

The Ninety-Second Tiger (London: Hodder & Stoughton, 1973); republished as *The 92nd Tiger* (New York: Harper & Row, 1973);

Amateur in Violence, edited by Ellery Queen (Frederic Dannay and Manfred B. Lee) (New York: Davis, 1973);

Flash Point (London: Hodder & Stoughton, 1974; New York: Harper & Row, 1974);

The Night of the Twelfth (London: Hodder & Stoughton, 1976; New York: Harper & Row, 1976);

The Law (Newton Abbot, U.K. / North Pomfret, Vt.: David & Charles, 1977);

Petrella at Q (London: Hodder & Stoughton, 1977; New York: Harper & Row, 1977);

The Empty House (London: Hodder & Stoughton, 1978; New York: Harper & Row, 1978);

Death of a Favourite Girl (London: Hodder & Stoughton, 1980); republished as *The Killing of Katie Steelstock* (New York: Harper & Row, 1980);

The Final Throw (London: Hodder & Stoughton, 1982); republished as *End-Game* (New York: Harper & Row, 1982);

Mr Calder and Mr Behrens (London: Hodder & Stoughton, 1982; New York: Harper & Row, 1982);

The Black Seraphim (London: Hodder & Stoughton, 1983; New York: Harper & Row, 1984);

The Long Journey Home (London: Hodder & Stoughton, 1985; New York: Harper & Row, 1985);

Trouble (London: Hodder & Stoughton, 1987; New York: Harper & Row, 1987);

Young Petrella (London: Hodder & Stoughton, 1988; New York: Harper & Row, 1988).

OTHER: "Technicalese," in *The Mystery Writers' Handbook*, edited by Herbert Brean (New York: Harper, 1956), pp. 57-65;

Crime in Good Company: Essays on Criminals and Crime Writing, edited by Gilbert and others (London: Constable, 1959);

Best Detective Stories of Cyril Hare, edited by Gilbert (London: Faber & Faber, 1959; New York: Walker, 1961);

"The Invisible Bond," in *Murder Ink*, edited by Dilys Winn (New York: Workman, 1977), pp. 154-157;

The Oxford Book of Legal Anecdotes, edited by Gilbert (Oxford & New York: Oxford University Press, 1986).

The long and continuing literary career of Michael Gilbert (he published his first detective novel, *Close Quarters*, in 1947) illustrates both his diversity of occupational and institutional interests and many of the varieties possible within the form of detective fiction. He has written plays, television, and radio dramatizations, and three to four hundred short stories, in addition to his more than twenty detective novels. He was a founding member, in 1953, of the Crime Writers' Association. He has written a study of the fa-

mous murderer Dr. Crippen (Hawley Harvey Crippen) and edited *The Oxford Book of Legal Anecdotes* (1986). Although an Inspector Hazelrigg figures in a number of the early novels and a Detective Sergeant Patrick Patrella figures in some later novels and stories, Gilbert has no consistent series detective. More appropriately for his perspective, the focus is on the police as an institution, working out or contributing to the uncovering or consequences of crime in society. In some novels the principal agent discovering or opposing crime and corruption is a member of another profession–for example, a doctor, businessman, or insurance investigator. His fiction also varies in form. While most of the novels are studies of the revelation and resolution of crime, some are thrillers, and some have elements of the spy stories that, for example, dominate the volume *Game without Rules* (1967). In his searching treatments of contemporary social and institutional problems, Gilbert offers sharply and cogently written detective fiction of considerable range and complexity.

Michael Francis Gilbert was born in Billinghay, Lincolnshire, on 17 July 1912, to Bernard Samuel Gilbert, a writer, and Berwyn Minna Cuthbert Gilbert. He attended St. Peter's, Seaford, and Blundell's School and he received an LL.B. from the University of London in 1937. He worked as an articled clerk in London from 1938 to 1939, subsequently joining the Royal Horse Artillery. He served in North Africa and Italy during World War II and was captured in January 1943. He escaped in September 1943 and rejoined his regiment in time for the Battle of Cassino. In 1947 he joined Trower, Still & Keeling, a law firm in which he became a partner. He married Roberta Mary Marsden on 28 July 1947, and they have seven children.

Gilbert first became prominent as a writer with the publication of his fourth novel, *Smallbone Deceased* (1950). It is a deft and frequently comic treatment of conventional detective themes and techniques. The comedy is underlined in the elaborate systems of organizations within a law firm, such as the storage of papers of significant clients in individual large boxes, in one of which the corpse of Smallbone has reposed for six or eight weeks before discovery. Although the novel reveals particular forms of business and legal chicanery in both the present and the past, much of the plot relies on ideas and processes conventional to detective fiction. The suspects are logically confined to members of the

Dust jacket for the first American edition of Gilbert's first short-story collection

law firm; the placing of significant clues and possibilities in a rigid time frame provides both possible mistakes and solutions for the process of deduction. A second murder both underlines and complicates the clues provided from the first, and an understanding of the firm's hidden past is necessary in order to discover the crimes of the present. Young lovers, suspected because of their concealment, are finally proved innocent. The traditional clue of left-handedness is both played with and used centrally, for the criminal is a champion golfer who has developed a strong, steady left hand to balance her right-handed swing so that, when she strangles the victims with a cord, it looks as if particular pressure has been applied with the left hand. In all these elements, as in its process of deduction by careful elimination, *Smallbone Deceased* is a conventional detective novel distinguished by deft writing and by Gilbert's ability to combine comedy and suspense.

Insofar as Gilbert's fiction is social and historical commentary, World War II is crucially important as the central and defining experience of Gilbert's own generation. This influence is visible in almost all the early fiction. *They Never Looked Inside* (1948; published in the United States as *He Didn't Mind Danger*, 1949) is an Inspector Hazelrigg novel set in the corrupt postwar world, in which the criminal is a former commando who desperately needs an outlet for talents that were necessary and praiseworthy during the war. *Death Has Deep Roots* (1951) centers on a firm of lawyers allied to members of the French Resistance, connecting current crime to necessary wartime deception. *Death in Captivity* (1952; published in the United States as *The Danger Within*) deals with the escape of British prisoners of war in Italy, reflecting some of Gilbert's own experience. In *After the Fine Weather* (1963), fascism also persists after the war. The Nazis rise again in a small community in the Tyrol and, in a corrupt world, are defeated only by the courage and honesty of an English girl from a prim, virtuous boarding-school background. As Gilbert's fiction has developed and deepened, however, the influence of the war has been most carefully explored within English society. One of Gilbert's best and most significant novels, *The Body of a Girl* (1972), illustrates this on several levels. In one way local society has changed. What once was the small autonomous English village, Stoneferry, not very far from London, has become "Sinferry," a convenient spot for "men living with other people's wives" or "little bits of fluff tucked away in bungalows down the river." A preoccupation with immorality and deception has replaced class as the issue that dominates English social life. On a deeper level both the principal criminal and local garage owner, Jack Bull, and the complex detective, Mercer, have been through the war and injured by experience. Bull has lost an arm while in a "Special Service battalion" of parachute troops and now thinks he was a fool to have "been a good little boy . . . [who] followed the rules." He is determined to get recompense. Mercer can understand and sympathize, but he has chosen, both as a man and as a policeman, to establish his own new and much more difficult rules. The world in which they operate is also very different from the English world before the war, one full of Jack Bulls in varying degrees, of people accustomed to danger and dishonesty who can justify exclusive concentration on their own self-interest. It is a world full of menace and the implicit threat of violence.

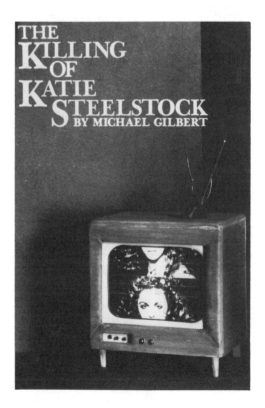

Dust jackets for the first American editions of four of Gilbert's novels that present contemporary society as permeated with corruption

This sense of menace and fear, often brilliantly described, pervades Gilbert's fiction of the last fifteen years or so. *The Night of the Twelfth* (1976) begins with a scene of a missing young boy, the local constable telling his mother not to worry because he does not know what else to say. Within a few pages, a pair of lovers in a roadside enclave at night touch "something cold," "a naked human foot," belonging to the murdered boy. This is the third child murder within the area, and the fear soon spreads to the nearby public school, a fear magnified with political ramifications in that the son of the Israeli ambassador threatened by Arab terrorists is a student at the school. A detective named Manifold poses as a teacher both to protect the Israeli boy and to uncover the crime. None of the students at the school has yet been a victim, but clues seem to settle around the school and the sense of fear is overwhelming. Although Manifold saves the Israeli boy from a threatened abduction, the political is finally less the threat than the perverse in the midst of what is apparently ordinary, humane English life. The criminals are the ostensible lovers on the staff. One is an engaging and popular master, a good cricketer, who is revealed as a pathologically weak and depraved man who will do anything to satisfy his sadistic mistress, an apparently competent matron's assistant who is sexually aroused only by watching her lover dismember young human flesh. The novel finally is a frightening depiction of contemporary society: what, on the surface, seems so open and attractive is cruel and senselessly destructive. Other Gilbert novels are also full of the sense of menace, such as the world of casual dockyard violence, drugs, and theft in *The Final Throw* (1982, published as *End-Game* in the United States). Ironically, in *The Night of the Twelfth* one of the novel's least attractive characters, the headmaster's jealous, sex-starved, demanding, and unpleasant wife, is the only one who suspects the criminals before the evidence is fully revealed. In reversing the function of the young lovers in detective fiction, Gilbert overturns one of the form's principal conventions of reassurance.

Most detective story writers are referential, recalling characters or references from other fiction both within and apart from detective fiction. Gilbert, with his insightful cleverness, both uses and disavows literary reference, sometimes simultaneously. In *Smallbone Deceased* the description of one of the legal partners recalls Charles Dickens's *The Life and Adventures of Nicholas Nickleby* (1837-1839) and nonliterary observation: the character is said to be "in appearance two-thirds of Charles Cheeryble to one-third of Lord Beaverbrook." *Death of a Favourite Girl* (1980; published in the United States as *The Killing of Katie Steelstock*) has a character who impersonates P. G. Wodehouse's Jeeves, a reference that signals a lightening, in this instance temporary, of the serious tone. *The Night of the Twelfth* has a character named Tennyson, explicitly not related to the poet. Mercer, in *The Body of a Girl*, trying to establish himself as a new and different kind of detective, replies, when another character talks of a book he's been reading, "I don't read a lot myself." In *The Empty House* (1978), set on the cliffs of North Devon, one of the characters incongruously combines references to R. D. Blackmore's *Lorna Doone* (1869) with those to Matthew Arnold's poetry, a kind of reference that is an example of one of Gilbert's stylistic characteristics. He is likely to play references, scenes, or themes against each other in quick, sharp bursts. Cleverly, a scene or reference bursts out, is picked up and turned around in contrast or repeated with a contrasting implication in tone, seriousness, or theme. In *The Empty House* an insurance investigator named Peter Manciple goes down to Devon to look into the apparent suicide of a scientist who has presumably driven his car over a cliff. Peter talks lightly of his paranoid mother who sees "little" men following her. In the next scene, when the missing scientist's sister talks of her brother being followed, Peter thinks irrelevantly of his mother and is brought up sharply by the sister because the scientist really had cause to fear pursuers. The whole novel tracks the causes and consequences of the scientist's legitimate fears (his apparent death is a masquerade, finally unsuccessful because he is eventually killed by an Israeli agent, herself frightened by pursuers), but a later scene returns to Peter's mother who ineptly shoots at the policemen who have come to inform her that Peter, whom she had then thought drowned in Devon, is alive and well. The themes of fear and paranoia, comic or lethally serious, intersect in a world in which the human being is seldom able to judge with accuracy or clarity. A similar technique is visible in *The Black Seraphim* (1983). The novel centers on the conflict in a cathedral town (which resembles Salisbury, but is called Melchester, which was Thomas Hardy's fictional name for Salisbury) between the dean, who would preserve church property against the encroachments of commercial developers, and the archdeacon, who would sell the property to pay off church debts and support worthy causes. The dean's daughter, Amanda, first introduces a reference to coffee. She tells James Scotland, the doctor who is finally the novel's central investigator, an anecdote of her and her father's previous life at a mission in Ethiopia: "When we were in Ethiopia, we got our supplies up about once every two months. Daddy used to put all the coffee into one of his socks. When we wanted a drink, we used to boil up a saucepan of milk and dip the sock into it and give it a little squeeze. That way we made it last. I must admit it did taste a bit peculiar toward the end." The next time Amanda tells James of their experience in Ethiopia she relates the horror story of their servant massacred, themselves only saved by the fact that the marauding terrorists ate the chunks of meat laced with cyanide as a bait for foxes. The two different scenes of Ethiopian consumption of food are combined in striking recall when the archdeacon is poisoned by what is apparently cyanide (although it turns out to be distilled nicotine) in his coffee at the dean's fete and Amanda is wrongfully suspected. Gilbert's structure of parallels and contrasts quickly and ingeniously develops his themes.

Most of Gilbert's novels have an institution or profession in the contemporary world in central focus. Most often the institution is that of the police, as in a number of police procedurals and the early police documentary, *Blood and Judgment* (1959), in which the imminent retirement of the incompetent local chief shows why drastic reform is necessary. An equally lazy and evasive chief who wants only to retire (and, unfortunately, is killed in the dangerous pursuit he wanted to avoid) is in conflict with Mercer in the more complex treatment of the police in *The Body of a Girl*. Mercer's zeal for expunging "filth" and righting the moral wrongs of Stoneferry, his habit of looking up old cases that were apparently solved, and his willingness to associate with all the people in the town earn him the "disrepute" of both the local chief and his supervisors in London, who had sent him down to Stoneferry to help revive a moribund force. At one point, he is shadowed, suspected of murder or blackmail himself. The police can be as complacent as any other social institution, but Mercer is finally both justified and heroic in his insistence that the police represent a moral force as humanity's only defense against a totally corrupt society. *Death of a Favourite Girl* takes place in a similar and equally cor-

rupt town, the product of the changes in postwar English industry and life, after the murder of Katie, a local girl who has become a television celebrity. The institution of the police is examined through an ambitious outsider sent down from London. Anxious to gain a quick and obvious conviction that will further enhance his career he settles on the most obvious suspect, Jonathan, Katie's former lover, a truculent young man who cares for the young boys who worship him and defies all authority, especially the police. For a time, the novel almost becomes a legal procedural rather than a police procedural, going through all the meticulous steps that will help the inspector from London make his case. Yet, slowly, evidence mounts that Jonathan is not guilty, including facts about Katie's rather open and superficially unsavory life as a London television success. The killer is discovered to be a highly moralistic local policeman, McCourt, originally from Scotland, who thought Katie and her contemporary companions were depraved by the London life he himself could not stand. He has even articulated earnestly the usual Gilbert judgment about the police, that "If we don't play the rules, who is going to?"–in this instance no one. Some of the police, like the inspector, distort or are corrupted by career; some, like McCourt, turn criminal because they cannot stand or assimilate the strains of modern life. Jonathan, too, is no hero, for, learning that McCourt has killed Katie and has inadvertently caused her brother (whom Jonathan really loved) to commit suicide, Jonathan shoots McCourt. In this novel the police are as complicated, as corrupt, and as violent as is the rest of society.

Other institutions are also characterized carefully in Gilbert's fiction. *The Black Seraphim* anatomizes the clergy in its relation to the modern world and deals to some extent with science through the investigations of James Scotland, supposedly on a peaceful holiday, whose knowledge and assistance at the autopsy establishes a murder in the first place and finally discovers the poisoning agent. James even debates the role of science with an old canon, each able to disrupt the stereotypical view the other holds of his profession. A profession at its best, in Gilbert's world, honestly establishes procedures and rational forms of inquiry that, within carefully limited areas, can discover some forms of truth and avoid the complete chaos of accepting whatever is in the modern world. Yet, the professions themselves are invariably flawed–in this novel, various

Dust jacket for the first edition of Gilbert's 1971 short-story collection (courtesy of Otto Penzler)

members of the clergy are bribable, corruptible, too anxious to be accepted by or to oppose intransigently the changes in the modern world. The struggle between the archdeacon and the dean, as an issue of clerical principle, is meaningless. In practical terms in the novel the dean wins because the archdeacon is dead, and James wins Amanda. But the dean's victory is hardly moral in that one of his followers, himself corrupted by need for money and his own incapacity to assimilate the strains of the world, has done the killing. James and Amanda still see science and its prerogatives in very different lights. Corruption permeates Melchester, and the police commissioner has avoided identification with it, this time, only by the chance mistake of a middle initial. Town councils, in Gilbert's world, are frequently themselves corrupt. In *Sky High* (1955; published in the United States as *The Country-House Burglar*) a local town councillor, who had profiteered on the black market in the past, is blackmailed, beginning a network of corruption in local government that affects the whole society. *The Crack in the Teacup* (1966) depicts dishonest collusion between a town council and land developers. In this novel a naive young solicitor exposes both corruption and local police brutality. Although his side wins the election and temporarily alleviates the evils, the book asserts that the intersection of politics with personal financial interest invariably brings private profit to someone at public expense.

In all Gilbert's more recent novels the corruption of the modern world is endemic, reflected in institutions that are, at the same time, the ostensible and established safeguards against various evils. Sometimes, the best of the institution is represented only by some loner, like Mer-

Dust jacket for the first American edition of Gilbert's 1983 novel

cer, virtually denounced by the institution itself; or some obsessive truth seeker, like the young lawyer in *Flash Point* (1974), who wants to prove that a local politician is a thief before the politician rises to power nationally. *Flash Point* is full of established society's dirty tricks calculated to snare the truth seeker. Yet martyrdom is never Gilbert's answer. In *The Final Throw*, amidst all the violence of the docks and other displaced industries, which are directly connected with the financial schemes of company takeovers and high finance, two parallel characters work their way to the discovery of the truth. At the very beginning Susan and David, who have been living together, split publicly over what is apparently her anger at his feckless drinking and irresponsibility. On the surface a charming con man, he works his way down from an accountant's office that specializes in tax avoidance to a travel agency that is a front for international drug-running, and finally to a society of drug-taking tramps. He is apparently following the career of a forerunner named Moule (pro-

nounced "Mole"), a drug addict who reveals the location of significant papers just before he is murdered. Susan's movement is in the opposite direction, demonstrating her business capacity and sagacity about complex financial negotiations in ways that elevate her from one position to another, ever closer to the corruption at the center of established society. They discover the truth and expose the worst of the criminals. Readers learn late in the novel that they are working with each other and for the police. But the police as an institution barely appear, except at the end; rather, the focus of the novel remains on the lonely and apparently unlikely process of discovering truth, the alternate burrowing and escalating, movement down and movement up, that with circumspection is the only means available for understanding the complicated connections of modern society. A similar agent acting alone is the self-made millionaire in *The Long Journey Home* (1985) who sells his computer company to an international cartel and impulsively gets off a plane on the way to New Zealand (his instincts are sound–the plane crashes) to walk through Italy, fixing machinery, on the way home. He sees, at firsthand, the contemporary workman's problems of violence, unions, and Mafia organizations, and, with his skill, is able to use blackmail to keep violence out of a portion of the industrial structure. But, evil as the corporation is, nothing else can provide jobs, and Gilbert implies that sheer survival requires man to deal as well as he can with the corrupt structures he has invented. Although his novels vary in tone and in the degree of lightness or fear with which they face contemporary society, Gilbert's world seems to have grown more grim and its problems more irresolvable over the years; no lovers now can avoid the corpse of *Smallbone Deceased*.

Not all of Gilbert's fictions depict the world with the complexity of interlocking interests visible in *The Body of a Girl*, *The Black Seraphim*, *Death of a Favourite Girl*, and *The Final Throw*. Sometimes, as in a novel like *The Empty House*, with its combination of insurance investigation, science, deceptive sexuality, and the Arab-Israeli conflict, the issues Gilbert suggests seem to spin away from any coherent focus. The novel's metaphorical connection, dependent on the fact that the missing scientist had once written a paper linking Israel with a physical organ placed in the body so inappropriately that it is dangerous to the entire organism, and that this has been misinterpreted as a gesture in the current Arab-Israeli conflict, is less one of Gilbert's striking seriocomic parallels than a sort of painfully irrelevant stretching for coherence. As Gilbert is more global he seems to become less convincing, and his characters' international expeditions are likely to be sprinkled with the high and unconvincing adventurousness and technology one associates with Ian Fleming's James Bond. Italy, for Gilbert, seems to function consistently as an extreme version of corruption and lawlessness, from *Smallbone Deceased*, in which every Italian is both a former partisan and a genial thief, to *The Final Throw* and *The Long Journey Home*, in which a combination of criminals, terrorists, and the Mafia control every aspect of Italian life. Gilbert is at his strongest and most searching in his direct and scathing treatments of contemporary English life. He is particularly effective in the depiction of institutions over a fairly large number of novels, especially the police and the law, those institutions which should help make the society itself more rational and humane. Few, if any, contemporary writers of detective fiction see these institutions with such range, depth, and intensity. His best works are police procedurals in the broadest sense, the fullest possible account of the ranges of the nature, activity, and humanity of the police. In a number of the novels, too, as in *The Body of a Girl*, he demonstrates a partial identity between criminal and detective. As Mercer recognizes, the differences between him and Jack Bull are minimal. They have the same background of poverty and deprivation, the same faith in their own intelligence, the same response to the horror of the war they have survived, and "the same sort of outlook on life." They differ only in that Bull decides to stand to the side of the hero while Mercer finds it is "easier, and a lot safer" to go along with the rules of the society's myth about itself. Venetia, Mercer's educated girlfriend (and differences in education are the only remnants of class left in Gilbert's Britain), is appalled that "easier" and "safer" are his only reasons for supporting the society, but Mercer, despite all his honest zeal for social justice, gives it no metaphysical sanction or warrant, no status as truth. He just holds to it, defensively, for there is nothing else. The police, legality, and the authority of social structure, imperfect and corrupt as all of them may be and often are, are man's only counters to the bestiality and corruption of the modern world. Even in *Death of a Favourite Girl*, in which the policeman (advocate of rules as giving man some degree of meaning) is himself the killer, no freedom or separation from social structure provides even as much meaning. Men and women, in Gilbert's world, can come closest to giving themselves identity and coherence by living within the far from perfect social and professional structures they have designed as a defense against encroaching chaos.

Reference:

Jacques Barzun and Wendell Taylor, "Preface to *Smallbone Deceased*," in *A Book of Prefaces to Fifty Classics of Crime Fiction, 1900-1950* (New York: Garland, 1976), pp. 53-54.

Geoffrey Household
(30 November 1900-4 October 1988)

Gina Macdonald
Loyola University in New Orleans

BOOKS: *The Terror of Villadonga* (London: Hutchinson, 1936); revised and republished as *The Spanish Cave* (Boston: Little, Brown, 1936; London: Chatto & Windus, 1940);

The Third Hour (London: Chatto & Windus, 1937; Boston: Little, Brown, 1938);

The Salvation of Pisco Gabar, and Other Stories (London: Chatto & Windus, 1938); expanded edition (Boston: Little, Brown, 1940);

Rogue Male (London: Chatto & Windus, 1939; Boston: Little, Brown, 1939); republished as *Man Hunt* (New York: Triangle, 1942);

Arabesque (London: Chatto & Windus, 1948; Boston: Little, Brown, 1948);

The High Place (London: Joseph, 1950; Boston: Little, Brown, 1950);

A Rough Shoot (London: Joseph, 1951; Boston: Little, Brown, 1951);

A Time to Kill (Boston: Little, Brown, 1951; London: Joseph, 1952);

Tales of Adventurers (London: Joseph, 1952; Boston: Little, Brown, 1952);

The Exploits of Xenophon (New York: Random House, 1955); republished as *Xenophon's Adventure* (London: Bodley Head, 1961);

Fellow Passenger (London: Joseph, 1955; Boston: Little, Brown, 1955); republished as *Hang the Man High* (New York: Spivak, 1957);

Against the Wind (London: Joseph, 1958; Boston: Little, Brown, 1959);

The Brides of Solomon, and Other Stories (London: Joseph, 1958; Boston: Little, Brown, 1958);

Watcher in the Shadows (London: Joseph, 1960; Boston: Little, Brown, 1960);

Thing to Love (London: Joseph, 1963; Boston: Little, Brown, 1963);

Olura (London: Joseph, 1965; Boston: Little, Brown, 1965);

Sabres on the Sand (London: Joseph, 1966; Boston: Little, Brown, 1966);

The Courtesy of Death (London: Joseph, 1967; Boston: Little, Brown, 1967);

Prisoner of the Indies (London: Bodley Head, 1967; Boston: Little, Brown, 1967);

Dance of the Dwarfs (London: Joseph, 1968; Boston: Little, Brown, 1968); republished as *The Adversary* (New York: Dell, 1970);

Doom's Caravan (London: Joseph, 1971; Boston: Little, Brown, 1971);

The Three Sentinels (London: Joseph, 1972; Boston: Little, Brown, 1972);

The Lives and Times of Bernardo Brown (London: Joseph, 1973; Boston: Little, Brown, 1974);

The Cats to Come (London: Joseph, 1975);

Red Anger (London: Joseph, 1975; Boston: Little, Brown, 1975);

Escape into Daylight (London: Bodley Head, 1976; Boston: Little, Brown, 1976);

Hostage, London: The Diary of Julian Despard (London: Joseph, 1977; Boston: Little, Brown, 1978);

The Last Two Weeks of Georges Rivac (London: Joseph, 1978; Boston: Little, Brown, 1978);

The Europe That Was (Newton Abbot, U.K.: David & Charles, 1979; New York: St. Martin's, 1979);

The Sending (London: Joseph, 1980; Boston: Little, Brown, 1980);

Capricorn and Cancer (London: Joseph, 1981);

Summon the Bright Water (London: Joseph, 1981; Boston: Little, Brown, 1981);

Rogue Justice (London: Joseph, 1982; Boston: Little, Brown, 1983);

Arrows of Desire (London: Joseph, 1985; Boston: Atlantic Monthly, 1985);

The Days of Your Fathers (London: Joseph, 1987).

PERIODICAL PUBLICATIONS: "Prisoners of the Plain," *Saturday Evening Post*, 223 (21 October 1950): 22-23;

"Rescue Mission," *Saturday Evening Post*, 223 (3 March 1951): 20-21;

"Run from the Hangman," *Saturday Evening Post*, 223 (10 March 1951): 17-19, 123-128; (17 March 1951): 42-43, 59-68; (24 March 1951): 45-62; (31 March 1951): 43, 81-89;

"Hut," *Atlantic Monthly*, 188 (December 1951): 17-19;

Geoffrey Household

"Magnificent Thief," *Saturday Evening Post,* 224 (15 December 1951): 20-21;

"Escape by Starlight," *Saturday Evening Post,* 227 (2 April 1955): 31;

"Drug for the Major," *Atlantic Monthly,* 197 (April 1956): 48-50;

"Treasure Hunt," *Saturday Evening Post,* 230 (20 July 1957): 20-21;

"Eye of a Soldier," *Vogue,* 130 (15 November 1957): 126-127;

"Sabres on the Sand," *Saturday Evening Post,* 231 (17 January 1959): 22-23;

"Escape by Passport," *Atlantic Monthly,* 203 (April 1959): 117-119;

"Deadly Torrent," *Saturday Evening Post,* 232 (25 July 1959): 20-21;

"Twilight of a God," *Atlantic Monthly,* 204 (October 1959): 52-58;

"Thief in the Cathedral," *Saturday Evening Post,* 232 (7 November 1959): 22-23;

"Escape Artist," *Saturday Evening Post,* 232 (5 December 1959): 28-29;

"Lost Continent," *Saturday Evening Post,* 233 (3 September 1960): 14-15.

For almost half a century Geoffrey House-
hold turned out adventure novels characterized by old-fashioned virtues: charm and wit, an erudite appreciation of the historical and the literary, a sense of irony and humor, and a depth of feeling for nature. His style, usually communicated by a first-person narrator who is a cosmopolitan man of decency and honor, is Edwardian, Etonian–the bemused speech of a gentleman, full of classical allusions and eclectic facts and details that were the commonplace knowledge of upper-middle-class Englishmen before World War I. Although his work includes reenactments of significant historical events, picaresque novels, science-fiction satire, and nature studies, he is most famous for writing about the manhunt, usually told as a confession in which the psychology of hunter and hunted is laid bare. A sense of chivalry and sportsmanship imbues Household's hunts with an ironic counterpoint: the violence and savagery of life and death struggles, "Nature tooth and claw," is played off against an assumption of sporting rules and civilized values. Household externalizes and makes understandable the psychology of men who are shocked by the discovery of the animal beneath their own civilized

veneer, who fear a loss of control, a shedding of personal and human identity in their struggle for survival and for vindication, and yet who are spurred on to acts of violence by their righteous indignation and their sense of justice. Even amid the insanities of the world of espionage and villainy, his heroes maintain a firm grip on reality, though at times they understand more easily the psychology of a good horse, a wily fox, or a sinister cat than that of the human animal who stalks them or whom they stalk.

Household's canon is uneven in quality and effectiveness, but it is always interesting. He is particularly good at making the bizarre seem credible, at delving into the motives and reasoning of a decent man trapped in circumstances beyond his control who learns to make the best of his situation. His understanding of psychology is broad, and he demonstrates convincingly how reality can be distorted and how gentle men can be forced into violent acts.

Born 30 November 1900 into what he himself is quoted on some of his dust jackets as calling "a conventional and mildly cultured environment" in Bristol, England, Geoffrey Edward West Household was the son of Horace W. Household, the secretary of education for Gloucester, and his wife, Beatrice. Household attended Clifton and Magdalen College, Oxford, where he received first class honors in English literature in 1922. Between 1922 and 1935 he engaged in international commerce, first as a confidential secretary for a bank in Romania, an experience he talks about in "traveller," the first part of his autobiography, *Against the Wind* (1958). Some of his dust jackets report that "one day he jammed his umbrella into the grillwork of the bank's gate, placed his bowler on the handle, and boarded a night train for Madrid," an incident that is not narrated in the autobiography. There he says that in 1926 his mother got him a position with Elders & Fyffes, banana importers, who sent him to France. He stayed with Elders & Fyffes, mostly in Spain, until 1929. He went to Los Angeles, in part in pursuit of an American-Romanian Jewish woman he had met in Bucharest. From Los Angeles he followed the woman, whom he calls "Marina" in his autobiography, to New York. It was the Depression, and the best job he could get was as a writer for a children's encyclopedia and later as a writer of radio plays for children. He married Marina in the early 1930s. From 1933 to 1939 Household sold printing ink for John Kidd in Scandinavia, Greece, Italy, Portugal, Spain, the

Dust jacket for the first edition of Household's second book (courtesy of Otto Penzler)

Middle East, Romania, Poland, Latin America, and Mexico. His experiences during these travels provided the background for his writing.

The success of his short stories led the *Atlantic Monthly* (which had published many of them) to encourage Household to write professionally. In 1935 he gave up commerce altogether and devoted himself full time to a literary career. His first book, *The Terror of Villadonga* (1936; revised and republished as *The Spanish Cave*), is a work for children. In 1939 he separated permanently from Marina soon after he entered the British military. Household served in the Intelligence Corps until 1945, an experience he relates in "soldier," the second part of his autobiography. During that time he was a security officer in Romania, Greece, Syria, Iraq, Palestine, and Germany; he rose to the rank of lieutenant colonel, was awarded the Territorial Decoration, and was mentioned in dispatches for his services as a special agent in the Near East. His most famous work,

Rogue Male (1939; republished as *Man Hunt*, 1942), came out while he was serving as an intelligence officer in Romania. He speaks of the gestation of *Rogue Male* in "craftsman," the third part of his autobiography:

> One day in December 1938 I wrote the opening pages of a novel–a habit of which I was growing very weary. But these seemed exciting, and eventually I let them go to the printer with hardly a change. To what incidents these pages were to lead I did not know, but the whole of the story was inherent in them, and *Rogue Male* began, week after week, to live. I observed, faintly protesting, that whereas I had intended a picaresque story in which Fear would supply the suspense, what I was really writing had some affinity to Buchan without his coincidences and with the cry of human suffering unsuppressed. But who was I to complain of inspiration? I could have wished the angel less prepossessed with violence, but if that was what it wanted I was prepared to place my craft at its disposal.

In 1942 Household married Ilona Zsoldos-Gutman, a Hungarian. The couple had three children.

Household's forte is his control of first-person narrative, not only to plunge one into action but to make his psychological study of man under pressure trying to come to terms with his experiences through self-analysis an experience readers can share. The narrator of *Rogue Male* expresses empathy with his captors as the novel opens by saying, "I cannot blame them. After all, one doesn't need a telescopic sight to shoot boar and bear; so that when they came on me watching the terrace at a range of five hundred and fifty yards, it was natural enough that they should jump to conclusions. And they behaved, I think, with discretion." He examines his motivation: "To preserve my sanity it is necessary that I take things in their order. That is the object of this confession: to tell things in their order, reasonably, precisely: to recover that man [he once was] with his insolence, his irony, his ingenuity. By writing of him I become him for the time." In *Rogue Justice* (1982), its sequel, this same protagonist begins in despair, "My first thought was that in a world where there was any mercy I should have been killed cleanly then and there, for I had no doubt that a more protracted death after days and nights of agony awaited me." He contemplates life's absurdist choices, to squeal vainly in protest to an indifferent universe or to kill himself and thereby end a world of torment, but

when unexpectedly given an out, he blindly but determinedly seizes it and returns to his doomed struggle against injustice, challenged to "outthink the enemy," the "sewer rats" who wipe out whole peoples and centers of culture like Cracow. Dr. Owen Dawnay, in *Dance of the Dwarfs* (1968; republished as *The Adversary*, 1970), notes a recent "tendency to talk" to himself and defines his goal: "I want to marshal the facts of my relationship to my environment and compel myself to think about them. I also need to be able to turn back time and feel what sort of person I was two or three months before." Through self-analysis Dawnay tries to come to terms with the horror that has transformed him and which will destroy him. In *Watcher in the Shadows* (1960) the narrator looks back on his course of action as lunacy: "and yet at the time it seemed the only way out. . . . One can never quite escape from one's ancestors." In *Fellow Passenger* (1955; republished as *Hang the Man High*, 1957) the narrator takes "satisfaction in being in the Tower of London," and hence set "in the company of the great" and contemplates how his behavior as a product of Latin American upbringing differs from that of those of pure English birth, arguing that he is "too much in love with the world as it is to bother about what it ought to be" and going on to demonstrate that in his narration.

Through his narrators Household projects a love of the earth and, generally, an appreciation of its restorative virtues. At the end of *Rogue Male* the exhausted narrator, who has been committed to suicidal action, feels "relief and certainty" in a "valley between . . . sun-dried hills, where the water trickled down the irrigation channels from one hand-dug, well-loved terrace to another, and no light showed but the blazing stars." He sleeps until dawn: "my face in the short grass by the water's edge, my body drawing strength from that warm and ancient earth." In *Rogue Justice* the tiny group of survivors from German torture find peace and the "illusion of safety" among the reeds, where "the peace of sky and birds and water" sinks into them, restoring them after much carnage and despair. *The Lives and Times of Bernardo Brown* (1973) eulogizes "willows and reeds, birds and buffaloes and wine, the low chant of the rivers as they glided from the rim of Transylvania to the Danube." In *A Rough Shoot* (1951) "the life of grass and hedgerow," the "copse and downland stretching away . . . till the folds of England vanished into a mist of gray and green," are "too busy satisfying hunger to be on guard." But in foreign territory nature might turn against man, as in *Dance of the Dwarfs*, which is set in a "no man's land between savannah and forest; the last, forgotten, blind alley of grass . . . bounded by darkness" to the west and south, and "empty under the blazing sun" to the north, a land where the vast emptiness of the plain oppresses as much as the sinister, closed horizons of the forests.

Household's language abounds in erudite allusions to history, literature, animal behavior, and psychology. A face, bruised and battered, all pallor and angles, is "like that of a Christian martyr in a medieval painting" (*Rogue Male*). A badly injured man laughs at himself "as Moses in the bulrushes" as his friends bathe him in the icy Vistula (*Rogue Justice*). Later his rescuer holds watch over a dead body, under an "icon of St. Michael, whose drawn sword . . . promised a day of reckoning." A villain in *A Rough Shoot* "was like the men in the Bible. He had fallen on his sword." The narrator of *Fellow Passenger* says, "I shall emulate Sir Walter Raleigh and Archbishop Laud. Like me, they were innocent of High Treason but thoroughly deserved the accusation"; later he muses, "I have never been able to believe those delightful fourteenth-century stories where the hero takes the place of husband or lover in the dark," but, after an amusing interlude, repents by saying, "It seemed as if Boccaccio must be right after all." His characters' voices echo Dr. Johnson's, their prophecies those of William Morris. In *Hostage, London: The Diary of Julian Despard* (1977) the narrator describes man, "the successor to the dinosaurs," as "a running ape which can question its motives and use paw and pencil to resolve them," and as "still enough of an animal to be far more keenly observant when he is in danger or engaged in illegalities." The protagonist of *Watcher in the Shadows* finds the police in the position "of a hunter who is trying to protect some terrified native village from a man-eater. It is no use to cordon the place and post a rifle up every tree. The man-eater simply observes the whole preparation–tempering its disappointment with contempt–and goes away until everyone is sick of the whole business. Then it returns."

Household's first novel for adults, *The Third Hour* (1937), a three-part adventure, has been praised for its unusual mix of rich humor, lively adventure, and serious philosophical implications. Basil Davenport, in *Saturday Review of Literature* (2 September 1939), found it "a remarkable combination of the adventure story and the novel of ideas." It tells of a Spanish adventurer, Manuel Vargas, who takes advantage of the revolution in Mexico to steal a fortune in gold from a wrecked train and bury it away in the desert, only to find himself in exile with a price on his head. In South America he meets and allies himself with an English salesman, Toby Manning, who agrees to recover the gold for a percentage and then proceeds to do so. The final section theorizes about the potential utopian order which might well be financed with the recovered gold. Critics such as E. B. C. Jones in the *Spectator* (10 September 1937) and Olga Owens in the *Boston Transcript* (8 January 1938) found some of the theorizing too preachy and sometimes difficult to take seriously (as in the speculation about nobles and their monastery), but the characterization is effective and the storytelling skilled.

Rogue Male is clearly Household's most popular work and one of his finest books, the one which has made his reputation. It has been called "a deft, neat book, written with unusual distinction . . . an impeccable narrative of action" (Kate O'Brien, *Spectator*, 1 September 1939), "one of the most original adventure tales of recent times . . . intelligent dramaturgy . . . exciting to consume . . . (William Soskin, *Books*, 17 August 1939), and "an almost overpowering *tour de force*" (Katherine Woods, *New York Times*, 27 August 1939). It is spare and tense and fast-paced; its plot is ingenious; it makes the incredible seem ordinary and right. Its dry humor, its lyricism, and its drama elevate it above the ordinary adventure story. An unnamed English sportsman from a reputable and well-to-do family determines to shoot an unnamed central European dictator, obviously Hitler, in revenge for the death of his fiancée at the hands of his secret police. He is a formal, tight-lipped narrator, literate and civilized, an English gentleman who reflects the inbred values of his nation and class: hiding amid cabbages in a muddy field, he thinks of "Monmouth's troops . . . flying from Sedgemoor, floundering their horses in that awful plough-land, . . ." Yet his terse first-person narration reveals his fortitude, courage, and strength of body, mind, and will. He is realistic about nature and the hunt and believes firmly in the justice and morality of retribution. After serious thought he had purposefully crossed the Polish frontier and stalked the dictator, only to be captured when he hesitated to pull the trigger–he had been told from childhood never to point his gun at a human being. Just before the story opens he has been brutally tortured and then flung over a cliff to make his death seem accidental. He is a tenacious man who uses his knowledge of nature and the hunt to survive. He returns to England and then goes underground both literally and figuratively to evade his pursuers. Under stress, his reactions are instinctive and primitive. In hiding, he shares his hole and provisions with Asmodeus, a stray cat, and looks for signs of demoralization, of loss of humanity, as he finds common cause with the fox. His imagery reflects these fears as he describes himself "creeping like a Nocturnal caterpillar," moving as quietly and sleeping as lightly as a dog-fox: "Living as a beast, I had become a beast" at the price of deprivation "of ordinary human cunning." He is hunted, the search led by Major Quive-Smith, a man as cunning as he is, until the final sequence. Household's hero is a fastidious man who, after two necessary murders, is anxious for the record to exonerate the innocent and his government, but who firmly believes the ethics of revenge are "the same as the ethics of war." There is a postscript in the novel in the form of a letter to the narrator's solicitor, who has power of attorney, in which he says he wants the manuscript published and declares his intention to begin another hunt for the dictator, but this time in man's natural habitat, a town. The motion picture *Man Hunt*, based on *Rogue Male* and starring Walter Pidgeon and Joan Bennett, was released in 1941; a 1975 television motion picture starring Peter O'Toole retained Household's title.

Household's *Arabesque* (1948) is a World War II novel of intrigue about gunrunning in the Middle East. Providing romance and adventure while skillfully capturing the labyrinth of Middle Eastern politics, of interracial and intercultural conflicts between French, English, Jew, and Arab, it builds on Household's personal knowledge of people and politics from his military service as an intelligence officer in the area. Its descriptive details paint a vivid picture of place and character: military bureaucrats, single-minded and totally indoctrinated gunrunners, political maneuvering, and chicanery. The heroine, Armande Herne, of French-English descent, finds herself caught up in an Arab-Jew arms conflict when she attempts to secure arms from an Arab sheikh, only to have them diverted by the British to the Jews. She must be rescued by a laconic British intelligence officer, Sergeant Dion Prayle, with whom she falls in love. The book did not do well in England but was popular in the United States.

In his autobiography Household calls *The High Place* (1950) a failure. Pat Frank (*Saturday Review of Literature*, 12 June 1950) praised its authenticity, its vivid depiction of the cold-blooded deceptions of espionage and politics, its satire "like a controlled whip lash," but attacked it for its improbabilities, its "Levantine runaround." Roger McDonough (*Library Journal*, 1 May 1950) called it "a serious novel of ideas which never quite comes off." The book combines spy hunt and dialectics in a compact story of an Englishman, Eric Amberon in Syria. Amberon is torn between his love for Elisa, the leader of an international anarchist group, and his abhorrence of the methods the anarchists espouse to stop state encroachment on individual liberty, methods which could foment World War III. Amberon chooses to act on his convictions, though it might cost him his beloved.

Shoot First, a 1953 United Artists film, was based on Household's *A Rough Shoot*, another spy-chase novel that does not quite come off. It begins excitingly enough with the narrator accidentally killing a trespasser in his fields and then covering it up to avoid legal retribution at the expense of his family. This protagonist, a retired colonel, now a gentleman-farmer and quarry agent, lives with his wife and two sons in a small Dorset village. His initial anguish is at deceiving his wife for her own protection, but later, as the repercussions of his acts prove strangely unpredictable, he begins to suspect that respectable upper-middle-class neighbors, knowledgeable about country ways and proud of their ancestry, are really traitors, fascists in disguise, and his rough shoot a landing ground for subversives. When this is confirmed by a Polish general chasing down a particularly nasty German agent who has gone to ground in England, the two join forces to expose the conspirators. There is much running around hillsides in the dark, attacks and counterattacks, but overall the situation is artificial, the villains not terribly menacing. The chase scenes, as the *Times Literary Supplement* reviewer described them (2 November 1951), are more like "a Keystone cops comedy than a serious pursuit." The hero of *A Rough Shoot*, Roger Taine, continues his pursuit of traitors in a sequel, *A Time to Kill* (1951). This time the scheme is to use ticks to spread disease among England's cattle, though no explanation of why is given. When Taine begins to investigate, Russians kidnap his children, and he in turn kidnaps the German scientist (a Communist) responsible for the ticks, sails up-

1.

I cannot blame them. After all one doesn't need a

telescopic sight to shoot boar and bear; so that when they

came on me watching the terrace at a range of 500 yards

it was ~~likely~~ _{natural} enough that ~~they wouldzdrawxtheir~~ _{should jump to} conclusions.

And they behaved, I think, with discretion. I ~~wasn't~~ ^{am not} an obvious

anarchist or ~~xxxxxxx~~ ^{fanatic}, and I didn't look as if I took any

interest in politics. I might_^ ^{perhaps} have sat for an agricultural

constituency in the south of England, but that hardly counts

as politics. I had a British passport, and if I had ~~walkedxup~~ ^{been caught}

~~toxthe~~ _{walking} up to the house instead of watching it, I should

probably have been asked to lunch. It **was** a difficult problem

for angry men to solve in an afternoon.

They must, of course, have wondered whether I was, ~~as~~

~~it~~ were, on_^ an official mission, but I think they turned that

down. No government, and least of all ours, permits assassination.

Then was I a free lance ? That must have seemed very ~~probable~~ ^{unlikely}

~~(though inexplicable)~~. Or was I ~~completely~~ innocent_^ and exactly

what I claimed to be - a sportsman who had always given way

to the temptation to stalk the impossible ? ~~That might be true~~

and after an hour or two I could see I had them shaken. But ~~if~~

~~it were true, it~~ made no difference; I couldn't be allowed to

live, ~~for~~ by that time I had, of course, been knocked about

very considerably. My nails are growing back, but my left eye

is still pretty useless. I wasn't a case you could turn loose

with apologies. The only solution was to make ~~it~~ appear an

accident and express official regret. They would probably have

given me a funeral

~~putzupxaxmonument~~ ^{and} with huntsmen firing volleys and sounding

horns and (all the big-wigs present in fancy dress, and put up

a stone obelisk to the memory of a brother sportsman. They do

Pages from the revised typescript for Rogue Male, *Household's best-known work (courtesy of the Manuscript Department, Lilly Library, Indiana University, Bloomington, Indiana)*

80.

supported a foot above the ground. Later on, when I stole some

bricks from a tumbledown barn and propped up my poles in the

middle, it was as strong and dry as a floor of laths.

On this same night I began the ~~mixingxthatxI~~

work on the rabbit holes

~~that I hoped would eventually provide~~ me with shelter from the

rain, with a hearth, and ~~with a bolt-hole~~. In a few hours I had

made a hollow long enough to receive my body, and about two feet

in diameter. The roof was of earth and the bottom of sandstone;

in theory it should have been dry and warm; in practice it acted

as a drain. I came across no recent traces of rabbits. They too

the bank was not habitable

must have discovered that ~~itxwasxnozplacexforxholex~~ during a wet

summer.

To burrow into the sandstone, soft though it was, would

have been an interminable job, but I found that it was easy to

scrape away the surface and thus lower the floor of my hole

inch by inch. In a week I had a shelter to be proud of. The

drip

roof had a high vault, packed with clay. The ~~water~~ trickled down

the sides and was caught on two projecting ledges~~xhxxmx~~ which

ran the length of the burrow and were channelled to lead the

water into the lane. The floor was three fet below the level

of the ledges and crossed by short faggots of ash which kept

my bed ~~xhxxx~~ from resting on damp stone. ~~Here is a cross section~~

~~of the entrance:~~

I passed another tranquil week, waiting for my beard and

moustache to grow. It was ~~really~~ a tranquil week. ~~I was a deal~~

~~better off than the majority of the combatants in the last war,~~

No human being came near me and

~~and~~ the weather was warm. My only danger was from dogs. There

were three on my ground. The first was a collie who worked the

sheep on the down to the east. He was too staid and busy to annoy

Dust jacket for the first edition of Household's 1939 novel (courtesy of Lilly Library, Indiana University, Bloomington, Indiana)

river to the home of the key villain, rescues his children, exposes the plot, and thereby thwarts the malefactors. In his autobiography Household says that his publishers encouraged publication of *A Rough Shoot* though he thought it was too ephemeral.

Fellow Passenger, praised for its craftsmanship, comedy, and thrills, follows the picaresque adventures of Claudio Howard-Wolferstan, an amusing, charming, enterprising Anglo-Ecuadorian, an accomplished cricket player, sent by his dying father's request to recover unnamed family assets supposedly hidden inside an attic chimney in the former family mansion, now a hostel for atomic scientists. He is captured and imprisoned. MI 5 and Scotland Yard, thanks to the folly of his student days when he called for European unity under Communist banners, are convinced he is a traitor. He escapes from the police only to discover that Russian agents think he might be on their side. Howard-Wolferstan must decide whether to deal with the Russians to save his life or face possible capture and hanging as a spy. Howard-Wolferstan tells his story with wit and humor and constantly contrasts English and Latin American perceptions and behavior. He wonders if his normal social gaiety has been mistaken for insolence "in so ancient and traditional a country as England" where "there is a proper manner for every situation, and one knows it or should know it by instinct." He notes that "A

Latin American functionary would wear his uniform all night in any cafe or public place as a matter of course," while "nothing would persuade an Englishman to do so—once he had passed the age of ten," and argues that it is "unEnglish to take drastic action when its outcome could not be prophesied, but the political instinct of the Latin has always been to blow up what exists and then profit by the falling fragments." Discovering hidden talents, he becomes a master of disguise, changing his hairstyle and attire, posing as a bohemian artist, an elephant trainer, a banana-boat seaman, a chimney sweep, a strolling minstrel, and an oriental prince to keep one step ahead of his pursuers. He escapes from a Russian freighter only to be trapped on a buoy off the coast of Kent. Eventually he encounters a burglar-friend of his father and learns the truth of his heritage, returns to the manor house, and finds a fortune, only to lose part of it temporarily in a romantic venture. A delightful and mildly satiric spoof of a type much like Graham Greene's *Our Man in Havana: An Entertainment* (1958), this book goes well beyond the limits of the traditional spy novel.

Watcher in the Shadows (1960) is an intriguing and highly successful reversal of the concept in *Rogue Male*. Herein a vengeful monomaniac, determined to serve justice on surviving officials of Buchenwald, pursues a former Austrian Graf, Charles Dennin, a quiet English zoologist, who did indeed serve in Buchenwald, but as a British

There is a satisfaction in being imprisoned in the
Tower of London. It seems to set one [a man], however undeservedly, in
the company of the great. I wonder if criminals feel the same
about Dartmoor. It's likely. After all, a sentence of twenty
years, served in Dartmoor, does mean that one has reached the
summit of one's profession.

I wish I could claim that the ~~grand~~ blackness of my guilt
was worthy of the grandeur of my prison, ~~but~~ the fact is that I
do not know whether I am guilty of High Treason or not. Nor does
a somewhat embarrassed state. That suits all parties. The
government is in no hurry to decide what to do with me. I, so long
as they continue to keep me safe from newspaper reporters, am in
no hurry to leave. The food, while uninteresting, is at least
as good as that of the average English hotel, and the service
suggests a club ~~admittedly~~ in which the rules are somewhat
too stringent and the servants a little too ceremonious in
manners and dress

There are [is] also the blessings of leisure, as well
as a strong tradition for its use. And as I have always wanted
to write a book, I shall emulate Sir Walter Raleigh and Archbishop Laud. Like me they were innocent of high treason, but
thoroughly deserved the accusation. That, I think, is a combination which lends itself to literature.

I ~~don't~~ [do not] propose to justify myself, ~~For one thing, I~~
~~can't. For another,~~ I don't feel in the least ill-used. If I
had been brought up in England and ~~could bring myself to feel~~ [shared]

Page from the revised typescript for Fellow Passenger, *Household's comic novel about a reluctant spy (courtesy of Manuscript De-*
partment, Lilly Library, Indiana University, Bloomington, Indiana)

undercover agent. Since police protection will only postpone the inevitable attack, Dennin stakes himself out as bait to trap this "mad tiger." As is typical of Household at his best, this novel is characterized by a thrilling manhunt whose stalkings, ruses, and pursuits are recounted with an eye for the details of terrain and a deep-seated feeling for the English countryside and its inhabitants, both wild and human. The image of the man-tiger runs throughout it until eventually Dennin calls up "the tiger on ground of " his "own choosing" and engages in a life and death duel in the woods at night. The plot is simple but electric, with a precise Edwardian style with chivalric overtones. The critics praised it highly. V. P. Hass (*Chicago Daily Tribune*, 26 June 1960) said: "Were the evidence not before me, I would not have believed that Geoffrey Household could ever again rise to the brilliance of his celebrated *Rogue Male*. But the evidence is here." Anthony Boucher (*New York Times Book Review*, 3 July 1960) called the book "A thriller of the highest quality, always credible, well written, solidly grounded in locale and character." Its humor and suspense, its gentle, discreet romance, its tribute to the English horse, its mixture of the savage and the genteel, its running battle focused on the psychology of man against man, and its final image of forgiveness and expiation mark *Watcher in the Shadows* as one of Household's best works.

Thing to Love (1963) creates a mythical troubled Latin American republic, Guayanas, which has no middle class and is dominated by the military. Outside pressure from both the United States and Russia, and an ambitious president willing to ride roughshod over the populace, inevitably cause a revolution. The book is an ironic and distanced study of pretences and tactics from the perspective of a professional soldier, a Czechoslovakian refugee from communism who feels loyalty to his adopted state but contempt for its present leader. His loyal troops could decide the outcome of civil war. Household's detached refusal to take a stand allows him to make an objective study of Latin American political conflicts.

The structural and narrative complexity of *Olura* (1965) is, to a great extent, responsible for its literary success. In it Philip Ardower, a wandering comparative philologist, finds himself helping an unlikely pair (a black prime minister and an alluring young girl, Olura) dispose of a murdered corpse, and in so doing gets caught up in erratic chases and hair-raising duels involving both the Spanish police force and dangerous right-wing French forces. *Olura* has a triple narrative perspective: that of Olura's godfather who frames the tale, that of Olura, and then that of Philip as narrated through manuscripts in the godfather's possession. The godfather's comments punctuate the narratives of the other two. The reviewer for the *Times Literary Supplement* (17 June 1965) called *Olura* commendable and "highly original," but unduly "complicated" by the triple telling of the plot. D. B. Hughes (*Book Week*, 17 October 1965) called it the best of all his books, including *Rogue Male*. He praised its supporting characters as "superbly done," and its political comments as "provocative" and "supreme." The multiple perspectives, the suspense, the deft handling of political climate, and the irony of the deus ex machina ending mark this book as indeed vintage Household.

The Courtesy of Death (1967), one of Household's less inspired tales of hunter and hunted, is narrated by Yarrow, a mining engineer whose charitable assistance to a seemingly befuddled man arouses his curiosity. Carefully disguised attempts on Yarrow's life, kidnapping, and incarceration in one of the secret caves revered by a maniacal religious organization follow. Set in the valleys and caves of the Mendip Hills near Glastonbury, this novel verges on the mythic and surreal, as its plot turns on the existence of prehistoric paintings that inspire a tradition of apologies for killing. The action and motivations lack credibility, and the final cover-up is vaguely dissatisfying, though the images of terror, of being trapped in the dark and pursued by vicious Doberman pinschers, are certainly striking.

Set where llano and jungle meet in up-country Colombia, *Dance of the Dwarfs* is a peculiar tale of jungle creatures that appear in time of drought. They are labeled malevolent spirits by the superstitious, pygmies by the more civilized; but the creatures are, in fact, deadly mustelids. Anglo-Argentine field agronomist, Dr. Owen Dawnay, enamored of a simple but affectionate young Peruvian girl, must deal with a drunken Indian shaman, local Marxist guerillas with whom he has an uneasy truce, and officers of the Colombian National Liberation Party while he seeks the terrifying truth of the "duendes." The ending is poignant and terrible as hunter becomes hunted, and beast outwits man. The psychology of an outsider who seeks to explain all in rational, scientific terms, categorizing his world, only to find the limits of his logic, is the heart of the book.

Doom's Caravan (1971) is set in the same spirit as the 1962 film about T. E. Lawrence, *Lawrence of Arabia*. A World War II British Intelligence officer deserts, goes native, and passes as an Arab. But, despite Household's clear knowledge of the area–its terrain and its people–the book is less successful than Household's books with English settings. Its narrator, a security officer, tracks the deserter down and, despite his admiration for the deserter's firm convictions, forces him to act as a spy and aid in a private war to stop a 1942 Nazi takeover in the Middle East. At this point the book degenerates into the predictable conventions of spy fiction–bearded disguises and bombing raids.

Set amid oil fields on the west coast of South America, *The Three Sentinels* (1972) was called a "sophisticated thriller, an intricate moral confrontation" by Martin Levin in the *New York Times Book Review* (18 July 1972). It focuses on the psychology of a labor dispute involving an oil company whose improved technology has meant labor reduction. Troubleshooter Matthew Darlow is sent to establish rapport and arbitrate with the dissident forces: the company, the state, the union, and the workers. Although he represents the company, Darlow is not a company man, a fact significant in the final confrontation between Darlow and the key leader of the workers, Cabo Desierto.

The picaresque *Lives and Times of Bernardo Brown*, an old man's reminiscences of his youth, traces the madcap peregrinations of Brown, an unassuming and innocent young Anglo-Hispanic shipping clerk whose attempts to avoid involvement in a shooting plunge him headlong into an Austro-Hungarian intrigue involving Empress Zita, as he flees the police of half a dozen countries. Experiencing the feeling "that he had lost all personality in a world no more controllable than a dream," he finds himself caught up in international plots, forced to pose as Romanian, Hungarian, Belgian, and English. He is accused of murder, espionage, forgery, theft, and pandering and is seduced by a cabaret dancer, a mysterious Baronin, and a Russian girl (whom he later marries) with an unusual anatomy. He is aided by Sephardic Jews, Romanian Gypsies, and Bucharest prostitutes among others. As Brown endures multiple travails he makes a voyage of discovery about people and commitments and about his own resourcefulness. He careens from mishap to mishap with wit, charm, and dexterity until he comes full circle. This book is an interesting

blend of traditions: satire and romance, picaresque and Arabian fantasy, travelogue and international intrigue. It abounds in witty lines, such as "all the best people are international criminals."

In *Red Anger* (1975) a young English bank clerk, Adrian Gurney, a product of Romanian and Egyptian education, fakes his own suicide to escape his boring job and a blackmailing employer. He disguises himself as a Romanian refugee from a Russian trawler fleet (alias Ionel Petrescu), never thinking the trawlers could be less-than-innocent fishing boats. Recruited by a friendly Romanian to take a message to the eccentric aunt of a political fugitive, Alwyn Rory, he finds himself pursued by KGB, CIA, and MI 5. Joined by Rory, who has been framed for treason by a girlfriend with Russian connections, he dons a number of disguises and, aided by Rory's sister and a pet ferret, forces a confession from the girlfriend. Later he and Rory are chased down amid the fields and estuaries of the West Country, and his friend's sacrifice allows him to reassume his true identity. Set against idyllic, evocative descriptions of rural England and its ancient heritage (Roman earthworks and Arthurian legend), this story mocks the conspiratorial attitudes of espionage agencies and eulogizes the flexibility and idealism of youth, the rebel nature of the aged who remain true to their youthful ideals, and the endurance of the countryside, "the deep green womb" of nature. Its ultimate lesson is "that the end never justifies the means."

Hostage, London: The Diary of Julian Despard is the account of an idealistic university lecturer intellectually attracted to the idea of a "New Revolution" but ultimately shocked by what it entails. The plan is to blackmail Downing Street with threats to detonate an atomic bomb in downtown London. Despard's experiences make him all too aware of his limitations: "The obscenities of the society I seek to destroy are definite, while the beauty which I may destroy with them is unknown and unlimited.... Preserve the blossom and your insecticide destroys the bees. Control the flooding and you pollute the estuary. We can never foresee the appalling damage done by long-range good intentions and I suspect that the Cosmic Purpose cannot foresee it either, that it is in fact a Cosmic Experimenter." When he uses his insider's knowledge to try to find and defuse the bomb, he finds himself pursued as a terrorist by Scotland Yard and as a turncoat by his former associates, the ruthless and anarchistic Magma

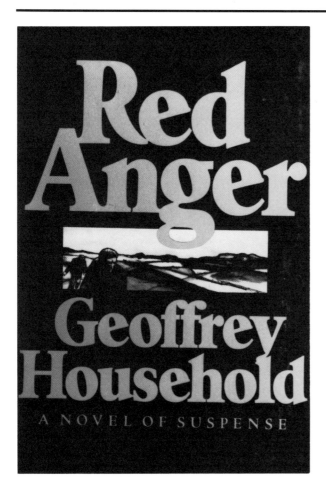

Dust jacket for the first American edition of Household's 1975 thriller

International. Fleeing over Cotswold hills and down London streets, this coolheaded protagonist, considering action "within the bleak uplands and tangled undergrowth" of his own mind, analyzes his folly, his obligations, and his chances in an objective, self-possessed manner that heightens the suspense as the seconds and minutes on the bomb tick away. The doomed city is described as "a trapped animal," but Despard, spurred by pangs of conscience for an evil for which he feels responsible, saves London, kills the head of the anarchists, and charges the police in a suicidal act to expiate his guilt.

The Last Two Weeks of Georges Rivac (1978) is a lighthearted tale of a young innocent, Georges Rivac, who, much like Bernardo Brown, becomes unexpectedly caught up in espionage. A fervent advocate of a united Europe, given his Spanish mother, French father, and English grandmother, Rivac, an import agent in Lille, France, is entrusted by Karel Kren, a Czech businessman,

with two seemingly harmless brochures for London delivery. When the Czech dies at sea under suspicious circumstances, Rivac becomes the object of pursuit by foreign agents and English police, discovers his inner resources, and leads a merry chase along the Thames, through Wallingford, and over the Berkshire Downs. In the process he becomes entangled with a debonair young Hungarian, Zia Fodor, a horsewoman with a complexion "like a young lioness married to a peach," who makes his pursuit more tolerable.

The Europe That Was (1979) is a collection of stories about discovery and loss: the loss of innocence, of youth, of illusion, and even of limbs; the discovery of courage, of values, of man- or womanhood, of kindness, of knowledge. In "Kindly Stranger" a curious and disobedient youngster years later continues to blame himself for two wars because Gabriel Princip, assassin of the Archduke Ferdinand in Ruritania, used him (a harmless, well-bred foreign lad) to bluff his way near enough to make his fatal shot. "Roll Out the Barrel" involves another sort of bluff, one that saves a life and teaches a cook about the quick-thinking merit of her employer. "Give Us This Day" records the extreme sacrifice a poor peasant makes to avoid military duty for the sake of his hungry children. "Low Water" focuses on six female entertainers who must face hard truths about their future potential and give up their dreams of stardom for the reality of fish. In "Sabres on the Sand" an Englishman's careless insult to a Romanian Captain requires an illegal duel to prove his breeding, in what proves a dangerous but creditable affair for all concerned. In "The Cook-Runner" a Londoner, desperate for gourmet Bucharest cooking, penetrates the Iron Curtain in a fractionating column to bring his favorite cook back alive, only to return with the cook's whole family, a bevy of Communist ministers (including his ambitious godson), and a missing foot. "Tell These Men to Go Away" and "The Picket Lines of Marton Hevessay" both deal with strong-willed individuals who stand up to authority. In the first a little old lady backs down the SS; the second is a most unusual character reference for a Hungarian with the courage to make moral choices: to become a Jew as the Nazis invade, to force the courts of Communist commissars to legally recognize his right to a title of baron, and to pass himself as a possible Communist in the America of 1951.

The Sending (1980), like *Dance of the Dwarfs* and *The Courtesy of Death*, partakes of the occult.

Based on anthropological myth, the story follows longtime celibate Alfgif Hollaston, who, after the apparent murder of a friend, experiences a "sending," a paranoic fear of danger originated by a sorcerer. Aided by his neighbor, Rita, a beautiful Oxford don whom he secretly adores, he seeks to find and develop his psychic powers. When Rita also is stricken by a sending, Alfgif tracks down the sorcerer, Izar Odaga, in Basque country. He defeats Odaga more through cunning than magic in one of the book's best episodes. In the last part of the book Hollaston develops his powers and learns lessons about life and love. He takes the name "Robin" to signify his greatest gift, the ability to heal animals, and is himself healed of his need for celibacy and unites himself with Rita.

Summon the Bright Water (1981), set along the River Severn in the Thornbury area, takes advantage of the Roman and pre-Roman past of the area to build an imaginative tale of a modern voyage into an unknown past: a Paleolithic mine where ancient mariners left valuables long hidden by the treacherous Severn. In it, Piers Colet, a student of ancient economies on a walking search of the Severn for evidence of pre-Roman ports, stays at a rural commune of farmers and metalworkers who see themselves as the hope of the future; expecting the collapse of urban civilization but believing in the transmigration of the soul and the value of druidical rites, they are mastering the crafts of the Dark Ages, skills they hope to carry with them into the darkness to come. Their charismatic but enigmatic leader, Simeon Marrin, is obsessed with gold: with creating it alchemically, with possessing it, with crafting it into simulations of the Holy Grail. Colet's specialized knowledge of history and anthropology, his inquiring mind, his close observation of details, and his skin-diving skills threaten Marrin's secret, a buried treasure trove whose priceless art is being melted down for personal profit. The novel begins with Colet, thought safely drowned, shadowing Marrin from his forest hiding place. He joins forces with Marrin's lovely niece Elsa, with whom Colet has become enamored, and with the eccentric Major Matravers-Drummond, a fanatical and informed Arthurian who fears Marrin's perversion of the Holy Grail. With their assistance, though he inadvertently causes two deaths, Colet unravels Marrin's secret and makes an unprecedented archaeological find but chooses love and mystery over fame and fortune. *Summon the Bright Water* is vintage Household.

Forty years after the publication of *Rogue Male*, with its lasting appeal, Household finally wrote its sequel, *Rogue Justice*. After a short prologue, it begins with the narrator of the original now identified as Raymond Ingelram, in shock, "slinking along . . . like a beast through a line of beaters." Ultimately he crawls out of the rubble of a German prison decimated by an RAF bombing raid and begins again his vengeful hunt for his fiancée's killer. Donning a dead German officer's uniform, he takes command of a group of prisoners being shipped to Auschwitz, finds common cause in their spirit of resistance, endurance, and hatred of German inhumanity, and helps them and himself cross out of German territory. Chased by the Gestapo, as well as other security forces, they in turn pick off German soldiers one by one in the marshes, plains, and mountain forests of central Europe, "practising the stealthiness and camouflage of a leopard among rocks." Aided by priests and partisans, good-hearted simple people who deplore Nazi atrocities, they journey through Sweden, Poland, Czechoslovakia, Romania, Turkey, and Greece, until they finally reach Palestine. There Ingelram leaves his friends and goes on to Egypt, Kenya, and finally to the Belgian Congo, ever the courageous loner. His final embrace of death and his beloved, his "lioness of the twilight," is a mystical end to a heritage Ingelram traces back to the heroes of Waterloo, Agincourt, and the Crusades.

Ingleram is a romantic with strong notions of right and wrong, waging what is for the most part a single-handed battle against forces of evil and reexamining his values and motivations to decide what defines justice. In this attitude, and in his ability to survive, he is very much the same character he was in *Rogue Male*. The reviewer for *Harper's* (February 1983) found Household's first-person narrator "old-fashioned" in speech and attitudes and the book "as darkly melodramatic as its hero . . . suffused with the apocalyptic atmosphere of forty years ago, when it seemed that the civilized world was ending."

Household's twenty-second novel, *Arrows of Desire* (1985), is both a tribute to England and a satire that comments on British troubles and the difficulties of the Thatcher government. The Irish situation, the immigrant problem, the welfare state, and problems with the common market are all issues in the novel. Although it is set in a mythical future, seven hundred years after "the Age of Destruction," in the days of "the last few British," it treats concerns that have been a part of Household's repertoire from his earliest books: freedom versus tyranny, the ethics of political violence, and a love of the cantankerous and eccentric British character. In it British settlers who insist on patriotism and self-rule are denounced by Ali Pretorius, high commissioner of an international welfare state, the Euro-African Federation. In fact world opinion labels the British barbarous, their values "venomous," and their pleasures (riding horses and drinking beer) subversive. Nonetheless, the high commissioner sends his daughter, Thea, to treat with the enemy, one Humphrey of Middlesex, a formidable forest dweller, a "barbarian prince." The story exists more for its engaging dialogue about the nature of humanity, of political conflict, and of civilization than for the plot itself. It is a benevolent, though ironic, patriotic eulogy to British values and England herself–her land, her beauty, and her mystic qualities.

Household's short stories in general are lively and entertaining, written with the smooth urbanity and the sense of intrigue and humor that mark his other works. Crisp, vivid, and fast-paced, they are placed against a variety of backgrounds from South American jungles to worldwide fighting fronts and are filled with insightful glimpses of human nature. Household's third published book, *The Salvation of Pisco Gabar, and Other Stories* (1938), has convincing settings and a fascinating concern with the strange and the bizarre as well as with human absurdity. The reviews of the book were mixed. F. T. Marsh (*New York Times*, 14 April 1940) quipped, "The title story is the most deft; 'Delilah of the Back Stairs' has the most depth; 'Taboo' is the most daft; 'El Quixote del Cine' has the best idea; 'Dionysus and the Pard' is the most amusing of the raconteur pieces ... for its breezy humor of expression; ... 'An Irishman and a Jew' is the most sentimental; 'Estancia la Embajada' is the most disappointing, for it contains some of the best things in the book but doesn't amount to anything as a tale." *The Brides of Solomon, and Other Stories* (1958) includes tales of Vichy France and Nazi Greece, Resistance fighters, soldiers, and sailors, with "The Case of Valentin Lecormier," the story of a French deserter who becomes a Syrian brigand, being among its best. Although many of these tales are dated, their depiction of man as an adventurer engaged in travel and intrigue, their adroit simplicity, their underlying values of manhood and fairness and old-fashioned gallantry, their inventiveness, and their occasional

surprises are typical of Household. *Tales of Adventurers* (1952) blends comedy and tragedy with irony, subtlety, and gruesome humor. "The Hut" tells of a French traitor, untouchable legally, kidnapped by English patriots who plan to execute him but find him so insufferably humble and polite that they have difficulty doing so. In "Women in Love" a Romanian girl on her way to marry in Sweden is so genuinely excited that she forgets to burn the secret information she has memorized but ironically is so ebulliently above suspicion that all goes well. In "Debt of Honor" an Anglican archdeacon to an African parish pays a witch doctor to bring rain while he is on leave to England, and in "Three Kings" an English geologist searches deep into the bleak Iranian desert to find a legendary luminous mountain, followed by a Russian opportunist inspired by uranium; their conversation over the body of a fugitive priest atop a radioactive, but worthless, metallic mass is the heart of the tale. In his autobiography Household says that his publishers completely sold out of *Tales of Adventurers*. He calls it "the book by which I should wish to be judged, since it could not possibly have been written by anyone else. Original work, upon which he need not even put his name or trade-mark, is all any craftsman can claim. How far it is aesthetically pleasing he cannot know, for the eye of affection forgives too much."

The Days of Your Fathers (1987) contains fourteen short stories, only one of which, "Keep Walking," is an adventure tale of the hunter-hunted variety. In it a lone and heroic female spy, spotting a tail, strives to outwit the tenacious opponents who pursue her in a suspenseful and action-packed eight pages. The concept unifying the rest of the stories is that of a humorous optimism about the past, whether revealed through a shrewd and diplomatic clergyman interceding between Heaven and Hell, a genial Irish vet whose drunken advances calm a pair of frightened Austrian Jews, or a Spanish Conde and various privileged young men like him caught up in farcical escapades. Colin Greenland, in the *New Statesman* (6 March 1987), calls these tales "comic but civilised romps and sombre but tranquil meditations on the gulfs that are fixed between race and race, or, at times, between individuals."

Household's works for juveniles are exciting, challenging, realistic tales that make historical setting, values, and life-styles come alive for the young reader. *The Exploits of Xenophon* (1955; republished as *Xenophon's Adventure*, 1961), for example, is a fine retelling of Xenophon's *Anabasis* through a brisk, first-person narration that captures the heroism of defeated Greeks retreating home through Persian territory to the Black Sea. *Prisoner of the Indies* (1967), an uncompromising historical adventure, which challenges young readers to deal maturely with complex material, builds on the true, first-person account of Miles Philips, who left Plymouth at age thirteen as cabin boy for one of John Hawkins's ships and returned fifteen years later, having survived on a vessel plagued by famine and fever, enslavement by the Spanish, trial by the Inquisition, and hostile Indians, Moors, and pirates. The book provides a clear understanding of such trades as weaver, gunner, pikeman, silver-mine superintendent, and construction supervisor.

A Household work is synonymous with international adventure, cosmopolitan attitudes, and images of hunter and hunted. Household is intrigued by the psychology of man under pressure and the heroism of the common man; he is moderately scornful of authority in any form, but most particularly of intelligence agencies that let national interests outweigh common human-

ity. He sympathizes with idealistic rebels but scorns the self-inflated pretensions of those who would remake society in their own image. His works reflect a closeness to nature, a mystic unity with land and beast, that affects his imagery and his portrait of man himself. The pattern of his work, like that of Greene, who for many years shared with Household the title of British spymaster, moved from international suspense and intrigue to a deeper concern with why savagery has continued in the West, a world now theoretically at peace.

References:

Michael Barber, "The Life and Times of Geoffrey Household," *Books and Bookmen*, 19 (January 1976): 40-42;

Leroy L. Panek, *The Special Branch: The British Spy Novel, 1890-1980* (Bowling Green, Ohio: Bowling Green University Popular Press, 1981), pp. 155-170.

Papers:

Household's papers are held at the Lilly Library, Indiana University, Bloomington, Indiana.

P. D. James
(Phyllis Dorothy James White)
(3 August 1920-)

Bernard Benstock
University of Miami

BOOKS: *Cover Her Face* (London: Faber & Faber, 1962; New York: Scribners, 1966);

A Mind to Murder (London: Faber & Faber, 1963; New York: Scribners, 1967);

Unnatural Causes (London: Faber & Faber, 1967; New York: Scribners, 1967);

The Maul and the Pear Tree: The Ratcliffe Highway Murders, 1811, by James and T. A. Critchley (London: Constable, 1971; New York: Mysterious, 1986);

Shroud for a Nightingale (London: Faber & Faber, 1971; New York: Scribners, 1971);

An Unsuitable Job for a Woman (London: Faber & Faber, 1972; New York: Scribners, 1973);

The Black Tower (London: Faber & Faber, 1975; New York: Scribners, 1975);

Death of an Expert Witness (London: Faber & Faber, 1977; New York: Scribners, 1977);

Innocent Blood (London: Faber & Faber, 1980; New York: Scribners, 1980);

The Skull beneath the Skin (London: Faber & Faber, 1982; New York: Scribners, 1982);

A Taste for Death (London: Faber & Faber, 1986; New York: Knopf, 1986);

Devices and Desires (London: Faber & Faber, 1989).

OTHER: "Ought Adam to Marry Cordelia?," in *Murder Ink: The Mystery Reader's Companion*, edited by Dilys Winn (New York: Workman, 1977), pp. 68-69;

"A Fictional Prognosis," in *Murder Ink: The Mystery Reader's Companion*, edited by Winn (New York: Workman, 1977), pp. 339-342;

"Dorothy L. Sayers: From Puzzle to Novel," in *Crime Writers* (London: British Broadcasting Corporation, 1978), pp. 64-75.

PERIODICAL PUBLICATION: "A Series of Scenes," in "How I Write My Books," compiled by H. R. F. Keating, *Writer's Digest*, 63 (October 1983): 26-27.

P. D. James (photograph by Nigel Parry)

The coming-of-age of a mature crime fiction in England, to which P. D. James has contributed prominently, can be attributed to a variety of disparate causes: the rapid changes in a society that had appeared for so long as monolithic; the end of the death penalty; the reaction of writers of fiction against experimentation; the shift of emphasis in psychology from science to a study of the human enigma; the persistence of inexplicable evil; the demise of the pure puzzle mystery; and the necessity that British detective fiction confront the presence of violent action that had become so much a characteristic of the American thriller. In her writings P. D. James expresses aspects of all of these factors, and since the first appearance of her fiction in 1962 she has established a major reputation in Britain and only to a slightly lesser extent in America, rivaled only by that of Ruth Rendell. According to dust-jacket blurbs, James and Rendell are the queens of contemporary detective fiction, just as were Dorothy L. Sayers and Agatha Christie of the previous generation. Furthermore, journal reviews praise James as a masterful writer and storyteller, even though her work is considered popular rather than serious. James has been instrumental, along with other writers of the last three decades, in narrowing the gap between crime fiction and serious fiction, between what Sayers had separated as "literature of escape" and "literature of expression."

The James canon of eleven novels is by no means homogenous: a progression of changes in style, mood, and scope can be discerned along the way, as well as variations in the investigative focus of her novels. Adam Dalgliesh (spelled *Dalgleish* in the first book, but not thereafter), whom she created as her New Scotland Yard inspector, remained her primary detective for the first four books, but her fifth introduced a young woman as private investigator. The more romantic book reviewers quickly predicted a love affair in the future for the twenty-two-year-old Cordelia Gray and Dalgliesh (twice her age), reading between the lines of their closing confrontation in *An Unsuitable Job for a Woman* (1972). The next two novels return exclusively to Adam Dalgliesh; Cordelia Gray is barely mentioned. A new departure is taken in the eighth novel, in which neither of the two plays any part: *Innocent Blood* (1980) is a psychological crime thriller without a detective even peripheral to the action, much less as the central focus. But Cordelia Gray returns as the operative in the ninth novel, Adam Dalgliesh in the tenth—and the sentimental reviewers and readers have remained frustrated in their anticipation of romance. James's outspoken admiration for Sayers might have had a hand in the assumption of a love affair imitating that of Lord Peter Wimsey and Harriet Vane, but she has persisted in her established separation of Adam and Cordelia. Her two characters do share a love for church architecture and for natural flow-

ers, but in a short piece in *Murder Ink: The Mystery Reader's Companion* (1977) entitled "Ought Adam to Marry Cordelia?" James remains noncommittal, commenting: "I can only say that I have no plans at present to marry Dalgleish [*sic*] to anyone. Yet even the best regulated characters are apt occasionally to escape from the sensible and controlling hand of their author and embark, however inadvisably, on a love life of their own."

P. D. James is the pen name of Phyllis Dorothy James White, who was born in Oxford, England, on 3 August 1920, the daughter of Sidney and Dorothy May Hone James. (In *Innocent Blood* the main character is a young potential writer who combined for her own pen name, "Phillippa Ducton," the first name given to her by her adoptive parents and the surname that she has eventually learned is actually hers—a hybrid that suggests an aspect of P. D. James's choice for herself.) Her father was an official of the Inland Revenue, and the family moved to Cambridge where she attended the Cambridge High School for Girls. At the age of sixteen James went to work in a tax office, but a few years later she became an assistant stage manager at the Festival Theatre in Cambridge. (*The Skull beneath the Skin* [1982] is her only work to date with some aspect of a theatrical setting.)

In 1941 Phyllis James married Ernest Conner Bantry White, a physician who served in the Royal Army Medical Corps during World War II. White returned to England in 1945 a mental invalid and remained so until his death in 1964. In 1949, when her daughters were five and seven years old, Mrs. White became the main financial support of the family, working for the newly established National Health Service and eventually being promoted to the position of hospital administrator. Medical administration became her career and would prove valuable for clinical settings in many of her detective novels: *Shroud for a Nightingale* (1971) is situated in a teaching hospital for nurses; *A Mind to Murder* (1963) in a London psychiatric clinic; *The Black Tower* (1975) in a home for the critically disabled. *Death of an Expert Witness* (1977) is located in a forensic laboratory, reflecting the author's subsequent career. In 1968 she entered the Home Office after being selected from an open competition for senior-level applicants: she served as a principal first in the Police Department and later in the Criminal Policy Department, experiences that constantly made their way into the verisimilitude of her fiction.

Dust jackets for the first American editions of two of James's novels from the 1970s

She has also served as a magistrate in inner London. She retired in 1979 and has been devoting herself full-time to her writing, a factor that does not reflect itself in any greater frequency of publication but in the larger format of her books since that time.

The extended format also allies James with Sayers, whose *Gaudy Night* (1936) purposely offended the traditions of the genre with its length and sustained intensity. Unlike Sayers, James does not avoid making her mystery contain a murder: the 454-page *A Taste for Death* (1986) begins with the discovery of two throat-slashed corpses and ends with violence and death as well. The fully mature James novel opens into the lives of its characters with depth and analytical insight, including the police officials along with the victims and the suspects. American reviewers in particular have balked at this superseding of the purity of the genre. The reviewer of *A Taste for Death* in the *New York Times* (23 October 1986), who credits the author with "demonstrating an increasing

grasp of emotions and themes that normally lie beyond the genre of the detective thriller," finds "a falling off " in *The Skull beneath the Skin* and is perplexed by the "plot complication, thematic digression, character articulation and details, details, details" of *A Taste for Death*. That James creates a vast and intricate cross section of English life in the 1980s and probes the hidden corners of various characters may well be the achievement of this novel rather than its limitation.

In becoming a critically acclaimed and publicly acknowledged master of the detective novel James has achieved a popularity that exceeds that of her detectives (unlike the creators of Sherlock Holmes, Lord Peter Wimsey, and Inspector Maigret). Not that Dalgliesh and Gray are inconsequential personalities, but they do not have the eccentric touches that had once been considered essential for the detective hero of fiction, until at least the 1930s. Instead of providing Adam Dalgliesh, for example, with an initial set of outré characteristics to be repeated as the givens of his personality throughout the novels, James presents him and sustains him as something of an enigma, rationally understandable perhaps but nonetheless enigmatic in his private self. The Dalgliesh story as such evolves through the eight books in which he appears (although only as a disturbing afterthought in *An Unsuitable Job for a Woman*). At the Dalglieshian center may reside the fact that his wife and son died in childbirth in the early years of his career, disclosed to the reader in *Cover Her Face* (1962) as Dalgliesh's private recollection. In that initial novel Detective Chief Inspector Dalgliesh is a proven veteran of the Metropolitan CID, whose "first big case" had been seven years ago. He pursues his investigation with cold precision: "I'll see the body first. The living will keep" are his first words. He is intent on uncovering all hidden secrets remorselessly, insisting that a murder investigation takes precedence over all private affairs (of course keeping the privilege of his own privacy intact). But he can also be extremely gentle with the suffering and even sympathetic with the murderer, in this case a particularly fine person.

Not all the "facts" about Dalgliesh are permanent: the "30-foot sailing boat" that serves as relaxation after the case in *Cover Her Face* has been solved never surfaces again; perhaps it was sold along with an Essex cottage mentioned in *A Mind to Murder*. In the recent novels he lives in a flat "high above the Thames in the City," which is never described in detail. James's *A Mind to Murder*, her second novel, opens at a sherry party given by Dalgliesh's publisher, and only because a murder has been committed across the square is Dalgliesh involved. In having to leave the party he has to drop his plan to ask a young woman to dinner, a woman whose mother he had arrested three years before (in *Cover Her Face*). Only when the new case is solved, not particularly to Dalgliesh's credit, does he pick up where he had left off and make the phone call. In *Unnatural Causes* (1967) he is torn by his commitments to the woman, who has been his mistress for a while, and he goes off to contemplate whether to ask her to marry him. What had been intended as a meditative holiday evolves into a nasty murder case that almost costs him his life. At its conclusion he writes a poem to the woman, but it never gets sent since her letter arrives telling him that she is leaving for America. Sharing his life proves difficult for Adam Dalgliesh, and his unstinting commitment to his profession bars any rival commitment. In the succeeding books he remains un-

married but has a vague series of sexual affairs along the way. The pull of the past is particularly pointed in *A Mind to Murder:* on "the anniversary of his wife's death, Dalgliesh called in at a small Catholic church behind the Strand to light a candle. His wife had been a Catholic."

The professional Dalgliesh is succinctly delineated in *A Mind to Murder*, from the opening statement that "he had never yet known the taste of defeat" to the concluding humility after tracking the wrong murderer (whom he nonetheless apprehends in the act of attempted murder): "If this case doesn't cure me of conceit, nothing will." *A Mind to Murder* is a rare instance in which he does not adhere to his stated methodology, the time-honored caution not to theorize in advance of the facts. Dalgliesh particularly prides himself on the speed with which he solves his cases, and when this one seems somewhat bogged down, he feels impatient: James narrates, "There followed a hiatus in the investigation, one of those inevitable delays which Dalgliesh had never found it easy to accept. He had always worked at speed. His reputation rested on the pace as well as the success of the cases. He did not ponder too deeply the implications of this compulsive need to get on with the job. It was enough to know that delay irritated him more than it did most men." An inherent contradiction begins to show itself in Adam Dalgliesh: the stolid policeman respectful of the facts and doggedly determined to "get on with the job" undercut by the impatient perfectionist with a strong belief in his instinctive powers–the man of conceit.

In James's third novel, *Unnatural Causes*, Dalgliesh not only returns to full form but does so despite the apparent evidence that the victim has died a natural death. He then describes himself as "stupidly persistent, blindly following his hunch in the teeth of the evidence." It leads him into physical danger as he confronts the murderer ("It was at that moment that he sensed a warning, the unmistakable instinct for danger. It was as much part of his detective's equipment as his knowledge of firearms, his nose for an unnatural death. It has saved him time and time again and he acted on it instinctively").

The biographical information on Dalgliesh accumulates from volume to volume: whereas in the first Chief Inspector Dalgliesh's ten-year-old sorrow is the basic piece of biography, in the second Superintendent Dalgliesh's career as a publishing poet becomes germane, while in the third he has published his second volume of verse, and

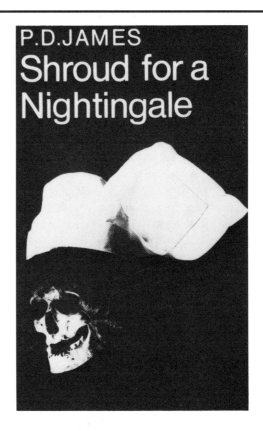

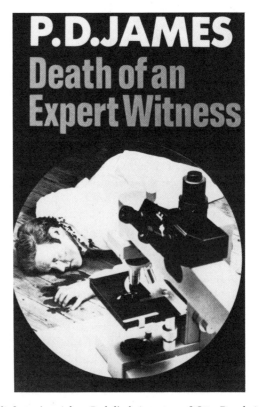

Dust jackets for the first editions of four of James's novels featuring Adam Dalgliesh (courtesy of Otto Penzler)

readers learn that he is a parson's son. It is as the son of a cleric that he finds himself involved in a series of murders in *The Black Tower*, murders well disguised as suicides or natural deaths. On convalescent leave he responds to a call to visit a sickly old priest who had been his father's curate, only to find him dead. The grim series of deaths obsesses him, and as he attends one of the funerals he remembers the funeral of a fourteen-year-old contemporary, a friend who had murdered his family and killed himself. Only Dalgliesh and the curate had been at the grave; Dalgliesh's own parents were away on holiday, and the townspeople were hostile toward the young parricide. This shared experience at age fourteen had established a bond with his father's curate that Dalgliesh hopes to continue in his frustrated inquiries into the events surrounding his death. No stranger to churches, and indeed an enthusiastic surveyor of church architecture, he nonetheless confesses to being an unbeliever: "All these problems are easier for people who believe in God," he comments. "Those of us who don't or can't have to do the best we can. That's what the law is, the best we can do. Human justice is imperfect, but it's the only justice we have."

In *Shroud for a Nightingale* Dalgliesh is chief superintendent; in *The Black Tower* he has become a commander, and his rise in prestige has made him something of a legend at New Scotland Yard, while the people that he encounters in his cases know him as a poet. ("The Yard's wonder boy," comments a character in *Death of an Expert Witness*, "descends from the clouds. Well, let's hope that he works quickly.") Yet in *A Taste for Death* readers learn that he has not written poetry for some time, and he is even twitted for the failure of his muse. His self-dissection is even more mordant: he calls himself "the poet who no longer writes poetry. The lover who substitutes technique for commitment. The policeman disillusioned with policing." That disillusionment reaches its nadir in *The Black Tower*. Dalgliesh has recovered from an illness that mistakenly had been diagnosed as terminal and had made his decision to resign from the force. His obsession with the old curate's death, however, makes his an active investigation despite himself. Although both his physical strength and his will prove to be weak, his success against the odds is achieved. "The truth is, he thought, that I don't know what, if anything, I'm investigating, and I only spasmodically care. I haven't the stomach to do the job properly or the will and courage to leave it alone." Self-analysis can become very much a part of his personality, and he despairs of getting the case officially opened since he has no facts to present to the police: "He couldn't say: I, Adam Dalgliesh, have had one of my famous hunches—I disagree with the coroner, with the pathologist, with the local police, with all the facts." Only the murderer respects Dalgliesh's hunches and attempts to kill him, but not until he learns that Dalgliesh has decided to remain on the police force. Dalgliesh cunningly plans ways to make sure that if he is killed his death will be laid at his murderer's door, and he succeeds in sending the murderer to his death instead. Now hospitalized for a flesh wound, Dalgliesh hallucinates the hospital stay with which the novel opens. Physical danger has become a hallmark from the third book on and is no respecter of gender: Cordelia Gray comes close to death in both her cases. James has opted out of the genteel puzzle mystery in favor of American preferences for violence and danger at the resolution.

Very much his own person and insisting on a privacy that is close to total aloofness, Dalgliesh is seen in different ways by the women with whom he comes in contact. In *A Mind to Murder* a woman psychiatrist blushes after noting that "He's about forty, I should think. Tall and dark. I liked his voice and he has nice hands." A senior nurse in *Shroud for a Nightingale* muses: "Probably he would be thought handsome by most women, with that lean bony face, at once arrogant and sensitive. It was probably one of his professional assets, and being a man he would make the most of it." But a beautiful and rather coldhearted woman in *Death of an Expert Witness* sums him up in a discussion with her brother, who asks:

> "Was Dalgliesh offensive?" ·
>
> "No more offensive than I to him. Honours even, I should have said. I don't think he liked me."
>
> "I don't think he likes anyone much. But he's considered highly intelligent. Did you find him attractive?"
>
> She answered the unspoken question.
>
> "It would be like making love to a public hangman."

Dalgliesh indeed solicits such occasional negative responses, especially from some of the more unlikable people whom he meets. But it is the reaction of those who have to work with him that proves to be the most diagnostic—and caustic.

In James's first two novels, which are rather benign considering the sinister qualities of their successors, Dalgliesh's working relationships disclose very little. His sergeant in both is a man named Martin who is "ten years older than his chief and it was unlikely now that he would gain further promotion." All that readers learn is that "Dalgliesh and Martin worked together for too many years to find much talking necessary and they moved about the flat almost in silence," searching for clues. When the nondescript Sergeant Martin is replaced by Sergeant Masterson in *Shroud for a Nightingale*, particular judgments are made: "Masterson respected him. . . . He thought him very able. . . . he disliked him heartily. He suspected that the antipathy was mutual." Dalgliesh occasionally displays a fondness for good food and in this context wins some points with Masterson, who "thought that they never got closer to liking each other than when they were eating and drinking together." But there is hardly enough there for friendship, and Masterson eventually feels the brunt of Dalgliesh's wrath. Masterson's case against him is later summed up: "Dalgliesh who was so uncaring about his subordinates' private life as to seem unaware that they had any; whose caustic wit could be as devastating as another man's bludgeon."

Death of an Expert Witness introduces Detective-Inspector the Honourable John Massingham as Commander Dalgliesh's assistant, the rank reflecting the new system at the Metropolitan Police. He is the son of a peer who has made the odd choice of the police force instead of the army. Massingham does not like his superior any better than did his predecessors, and he is surprised when other people seem to like Dalgliesh ("God knows why. At times he's cold enough to be barely human"). Dalgliesh's own verdict at the end of the case is that he "wished never to see Massingham again. But he would see him again and, in time, without even caring and remembering." Oddly enough, he chooses Massingham for his special squad in *A Taste for Death*, along with a female assistant, Kate Miskin, who has heard a great deal about her boss and sums up the conclusion at New Scotland Yard: "He's a bastard, but a just bastard." Dalgliesh's brief appearance in *An Unsuitable Job for a Woman* brings him into contact with his superior, the assistant commissioner, and the verdict there is presented with ironic humor: "The two men disliked each other but only one of them knew this and he was the one to whom it didn't matter."

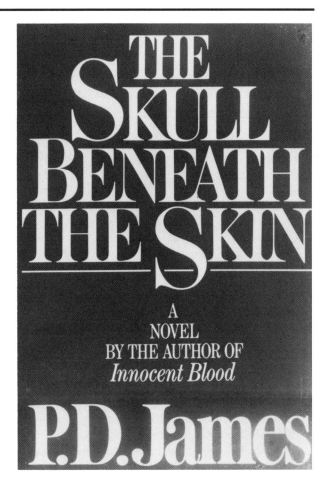

Dust jacket for the first American edition of one of two James novels featuring Cordelia Gray; the other is An Unsuitable Job for a Woman.

Locating the essentials of Adam Dalgliesh, the inner man concealed so deftly by the professional personality, has not been easy for James's readers, although there have been some clues along the way. As early as *Unnatural Causes*, in which he is battling his own doubts between his job and a possible marriage and at best interfering with the local inspector on a case that is not his own, he has a moment of self-doubt: "Suddenly he felt again some of the uncertainties and the inadequacies which had tormented the young Detective Constable Dalgliesh nearly twenty years ago." In *Shroud for a Nightingale*, in a moment of frank conversation with a sympathetic listener, he is prodded into admitting that "I can't interest myself in anything which I not only don't understand but know that I have no prospect of ever understanding." The degree to which self-doubt determines his temporary decision to resign, as he half-unconsciously pursues an uninvited inquiry in *The Black Tower*, careful not to tread on the toes of the local police, can only be gauged by his ultimate success and decision not to leave his job, but to "get on with it." Now, with his extended appearance in *A Taste for Death*, where readers learn that his mother died when he was fifteen, there are additional clues, particularly as he associates himself with the victim, someone he had known and about whom he becomes almost as obsessional as he had over the dead priest. "We're alike even in this," Dalgliesh muses: "If he had a splinter of ice in the heart, then so have I." At a fairly leisurely moment he contemplates the escapism of a self-indulgent couple and realizes that he, too, has "his own contrivances for keeping reality at bay." The conflict between his job and his self, the basic contradiction, perhaps, between the poet (now lapsed) and the policeman (dominant, but never quite certain–Massingham ranks his interests as "his poetry, his job and his privacy. And probably in that order"), never resolves itself. At a low moment he thinks: "And if I tell myself that enough is enough, twenty years of using people's weakness against them, twenty years of careful non-involvement, if I resign, what then?" Between arrogant self-confidence fostered by his success, and moments of despondency when he realizes the futility of life, Adam Dalgliesh makes his balanced observations, not without a touch of irony: "It was odd, he sometimes thought, that a man morbidly sensitive about his own privacy should have chosen a job that required him to invade almost daily the privacy of others." In *Devices and Desires* (1989), James's latest novel, she continues to develop Dalgliesh's character.

The Cordelia Gray narratives weave their way through the later Dalgliesh narratives as well: as a private investigator she is significantly distanced from the New Scotland Yard man yet inadvertently influenced by him at every turn. At the opening of *An Unsuitable Job for a Woman* she finds that she has inherited the detective agency where she had started as a typist and quickly been made a partner by her boss, Bernie Pryde, who prides himself at having learned his trade from Dalgliesh at the CID–from which he had been sacked (by Dalgliesh). Pryde idolizes his former boss and passes on words of wisdom constantly, to Cordelia Gray's silent anger:

> Sometimes she had wondered whether this paragon had actually existed or whether he had sprung impeccable and omnipotent from Ber-

nie's brain, a necessary hero and mentor. It was with a shock of surprise that she had later seen a newspaper picture of Chief Superintendent Dalgliesh, a dark, sardonic face which, on her closer scrutiny, disintegrated into an ambiguity of patterned micro dots, giving nothing away. Not all the wisdom Bernie so glibly recalled was the received gospel. Much, she suspected, was his own philosophy. She in turn had devised a private litany of disdain: supercilious, superior, sarcastic Super; what wisdom, she wondered, would he have to comfort Bernie now.

Pryde commits suicide, and Dalgliesh never acknowledges his death. Cordelia claims her legacy as a responsibility and the only job she had, not quite realizing that she also inherits Dalgliesh's "wisdom" through a dead intermediary.

Cordelia's life is as open a book as Dalgliesh's is a closed one. Her past is established in the opening sections of *An Unsuitable Job for a Woman:* her mother died just after her birth; her father, a militant radical engaged in clandestine politics, has her fostered out to various families; a mistake of identity has her educated in a Catholic convent; the opportunity to attend Cambridge is vetoed by her father, who claims her; she has two sexual affairs with young comrades; her father's death frees her to return to London, where she goes to work for the Pryde Agency. Only in *The Skull beneath the Skin*, published ten years later than the first book in which she is featured but allowing only for a gap of less than a year in Cordelia's life, are readers informed that her father was a famous Marxist lecturing from university platforms. The sale of his Paris apartment provides enough money for Cordelia's new flat on the Thames, inadvertently making her Dalgliesh's neighbor (she is aware that "they shared the same river").

In both novels Cordelia Gray finds herself investigating murders when her initial assignments were decidedly less demanding than that, and despite her inexperience, not to mention her gender, her investigations are successful. In both cases, however, the solutions are not neat, textbook resolutions: in the first she finds herself concealing the killing of the murderer she had unmasked, and in the second she faces an uphill court battle if the murderer is ever to be convicted. (In the interim her agency deals with hunting down lost pets.) In both cases the slight twenty-two-year-old Cordelia is nearly murdered–in a well and in a cave–and each time she employs strategy, determination, and physical courage to survive. In the well she realized that she "was alive and capable of thought. She had always been a survivor. She would survive," and in the cave "she fought like a desperate and cornered beast. The sea was death, and she struggled against it with all she could muster of life and youth and hope." These qualities immediately and permanently identify Cordelia Gray.

As a young woman engaged in a profession reserved for mature and physically powerful men, Cordelia comes under everyone's scrutiny. In *The Skull beneath the Skin* the police even treat her as a suspect until Dalgliesh disabuses them of that opinion: thereafter she is only suspected of being an impressionable female with an unchecked imagination. Various people inform her that hers is "an unsuitable job for a woman," a comment she ignores. Nonetheless, the cynical murderer in *An Unsuitable Job for a Woman*, positive that Cordelia could never find the evidence to have him arrested, scoffs even after she has proven her courage and her deductive powers, and even a woman she aids in the process misunderstands her motives: "I thought you might have acted in the service of justice or some such abstraction." Cordelia Gray responds, "I wasn't thinking of any abstraction. I was thinking about a person," a young unfortunate who, like Cordelia, had been orphaned.

A sympathetic male character in *The Skull beneath the Skin* provides the most objective evaluation of Cordelia. In observing her he realizes that "despite those candid, almost judgemental eyes, the disconcerting honesty, the impression of controlled competence, she was at heart a sensitive child," noting also "how sweet she was, with that gentle, self-contained dignity." The local police sergeant, on the other hand, is far more wary: "She's attractive. Like a cat.... Self-contained and dignified." In *An Unsuitable Job for a Woman* Dalgliesh interviews her, knowing full well what she has done in her cover-up (she had used his methods, following a hunch as she knew he would have, and consequently he is able to follow her lines of thought as if they were his own). When the murderer for whom Cordelia perjured herself is killed in a road accident, Dalgliesh's concern in his job of uncovering is moot. She had withstood his interrogation well: "She had resisted the momentary temptation to change her story. Bernie had been right. She recalled his advice; the Superintendent's advice; this time she could almost hear it spoken in his deep, slightly husky voice: 'If you're tempted to crime, stick to your

original statement.'" To his superior Dalgliesh reports that his investigation is closed, indicating, "I don't think that young woman deludes herself about anything. I took to her, but I'm glad that I shan't be encountering her again." He is, of course, theorizing in advance of the facts: when he is hospitalized Cordelia sends him flowers that she had picked, fresh flowers rather than the cut flowers he detests, and in his delirium at the end of *The Black Tower* he worries over not having thanked her for them.

There is no evidence for a long time that their paths have ever crossed again, but he is obviously in her thoughts: she tries unconvincingly to dismiss her attraction by labeling him a father-surrogate. When she knows that the police are investigating her and her agency she tries to imagine that it is Dalgliesh climbing her stairs but knows that he is too important these days for so menial a job: "From the rarefied and mysterious heights of hierarchy which he now inhabited, any such chore was unthinkable. She wondered whether he would read about the crime, whether he would learn that she was involved." The local inspector is quite caustic in identifying Commander Dalgliesh: "The Commissioner's blue-eyed boy, darling of the establishment," but he nonetheless acknowledges Dalgliesh's impressive accomplishments ("He could have had his own force by now . . . if he hadn't wanted to stick to detection"). His transmittal of Dalgliesh's assessment of the suspect is highly revealing of the personal evaluation concealed in his professional one:

> He knows the girl, Cordelia Gray. They tangled together in a previous case. Cambridge, apparently. No details offered and none asked for. But he's given her and that agency a clean bill. Like him or not, he's a good copper, one of the best. If he says that Gray isn't a murderess, I'm prepared to take that as evidence of a sort. But he didn't say that she's incapable of lying, and I wouldn't have believed him if he had.

(In *A Taste for Death*, when gossip reaches Dalgliesh about "Adam Dalgliesh, poet-detective, with Cordelia Gray at Mon Plaisir," the commander merely comments: "Your readers must lead very dull lives if they can find vicarious excitement in a young woman and myself virtuously eating duck à l'orange.")

As forceful and delightful as her two detectives are, they do not overshadow the fictions in which they are central, and with the publication

Book 4 section 7

responds as if I were the one doing the favour. What is it about

this job that makes people grateful that I can act like a human

being?'

The two men waited in silence, but the tea came very quickly.

So that, he thought, accounted for the delay in opening the door.

She had hurried at his knock to put on the kettle. They sat ~~round~~ *at*

raised himself *stiffly from*

the table in stiff formality waiting while Albert Nolan ~~had~~ edged *his chair*

and

his way painfully into his seat. The effort set up a new spasm of

Without speaking his wife poured his tea and set the cup before him.

shaking/ He didn't grasp ~~his cup~~, but bent his head and slurped

it

his tea noisily from the side. His wife didn't even look at him.

There was a half-cut cake which she said was walnut and marma-

lade, and she smiled again when Dalgliesh accepted a slice. It

was dry and rather tasteless, rolling into a soft dough in his

mouth. Small pellets of walnut lodged in his teeth and the

occasional sliver of orange-peel was sour to the tongue. He

washed it down with a mouthful of strong, over-milked tea. Some-

where in the room a fly was making a loud intermittent buzz.

He said:

'I'm sorry that I have to trouble you, and I'm afraid it may be

painful for you. As I explained on the telephone, I'm

investigating the death of Sir Paul Berowne. A short time before

he died he had an anonymous letter. It suggested that he might

have had something to do with your granddaughter's death. That's

why I'm here.'

Mrs Nolan's cup rattled in her saucer. She put both hands under

the table like a well-behaved child at a party. Then she glanced

at her husband. She said:

'Theresa took her own life. *I thought you'd know that, sir.*

Page from the revised typescript for A Taste for Death *(courtesy of the author)*

in 1980 of *Innocent Blood* James wrote her only nondetective novel to date, proving that she could sustain a long narrative without a detective as its focal point. Nor is *Innocent Blood* a traditional crime novel: a murder *had* taken place, but that was ten years in the past; a vengeance killing is being planned, making the novel in part a type of inverse crime novel, but it misfires when the knife is plunged into the neck of the victim who had already committed suicide. As James has explained, one of the inspirations for the novel came from the passing of the "Legislation for Children Act of 1975," which "gave eighteen-year-old adoptive children in England and Wales the right to set out on the journey of exploring who their real parents were by having access to their birth certificates." James's eighteen-year-old is a young woman not unlike Cordelia Gray, rebelling against her unloving adoptive parents and persistent in finding out her own identity. That her father died in prison, convicted of having raped a twelve-year-old girl, and her mother was soon to be released from prison, having killed the rape victim, seems to bother her less than the news that her mother had violently mistreated her as a child, necessitating her adoption *before* the rape and murder. The father of the dead girl meanwhile stalks the released murderer, who now lives with her daughter. All the elements of the crime novel are there, and all the motifs, techniques, and individual touches of a James mystery are there as well. "I think it shows the influence of the detective story," James has commented, "in that it is a book which does in fact have clues–clues to personality, clues to events that have happened."

There are numerous characteristics that make a James mystery recognizable, the most prominent being the setting, what James has called a sense of place. Few of her books are located in London. Until such late works as *Innocent Blood* and *A Taste for Death*, only *A Mind for Murder* was set in London, with no real incorporation of the city ambience; the two recent books, however, powerfully evoke the areas around Paddington, Notting Hill, and West Kensington, particularly the Holland Park section where James now lives. The scene of her first novel is rather conventional, an Elizabethan manor house in an Essex village, but that was before James began to realize her potential for Gothicism. Only with the third book does the Gothic become a vital, though never controlling, element in her fiction. *Unnatural Causes* is situated in the East Anglian

region that James particularly loves, from childhood summers and her own Southwold cottage, and she has even written an article for one of the posh Sunday newspapers in which she traces the routes and scenes of that novel. The Dorset coast provided the mood setting for her starkest novel, *The Black Tower*, where an asylum for the dying crippled, staffed by attendants in monks' habits, is claustrophobically sequestered from the nearby sea. Also in the same area is the setting for *The Skull beneath the Skin* but in this case in a restored castle on a forbidding island off the coast. The location of the hospital in *Shroud for a Nightingale* is of less importance than the doomed building itself, while the wild fen country plays its atmospheric role in *Death of an Expert Witness*. By contrast, *An Unsuitable Job for a Woman* is very much a nostalgic evocation of the beauties of Cambridge, but not without its stark outposts and byroads.

Once she realized her talent and taste for the Gothic, James has never relented in using it, although she employs it judiciously. She evokes the sounds of smugglers' horses along coastal roads and the bells of long-drowned churches causing the "stirring of an atavistic fear of darkness and the unknown" in *Unnatural Causes*, a work that begins with a drifting dinghy containing the body of a neatly dressed corpse whose hands have been hacked off at the wrists. (The grisly opening also proves potent in later James novels–Cordelia finding Bernie Pryde's dead body in the office when she arrives for work; an elderly spinster and a ten-year-old boy finding two corpses with throats slashed in the church vestry–a contrast to some of the openings of her more genteel mysteries.) In *Unnatural Causes* a storm that rages along the East Anglian coast terrifies a crippled woman in her vulnerable cliff-side cottage as she arms herself against what she believes is a murderous intruder, although she herself is the murderer.

James has a keen eye for architectural structures and reads them as emblematic of the lives of their inhabitants; a concern in her fiction is the impact of the past on the present and the violation of the past by the present. The Gothic effect is immediate for the convalescent Dalgliesh as he approaches the area of the black tower: "He sensed something strange and sinister in its emptiness and loneliness which even the mellow afternoon sunlight couldn't dispel." Two recent deaths and three that follow them are reinforced by the legend of the death of the builder of the tower who while alive immured himself within it awaiting the Second Coming but tore his fingers to the bone attempting to undo his interment. The ghostly sounds emanating from the tower frighten even Dalgliesh, but he uses the sound of the rasping torn branches to good advantage when he is in a death struggle with the murderer. A grisly death in the island castle cave also sets a precedent in *The Skull beneath the Skin*, for it claims a new victim at the resolution of the novel–and almost claims Cordelia as well. Like *The Black Tower*, *Shroud for a Nightingale* also begins with an approach to a "Castle Perilous," although the building is merely a hospital that had been created out of a country house. A dark and rainy early January morning finds the visitor driving toward Nightingale House: "She felt strangely isolated in the dim quietness and suddenly she was touched with an irrational unease, a bizarre sensation of journeying out of time into some new dimension, borne onwards towards an uncomprehended and inescapable horror." (Within the hour she will witness the violent death by poisoning of a nurse during a demonstration of intragastric tube feeding.) The house itself is the basic Gothic structure. After the three murders, as well as the bludgeon attack on Dalgliesh, the walls of this House of Usher are doomed to fall. The architectural structure had been desecrated in its transition into a hospital, for which it was quite unsuited, and when the visitor returns after the case has been resolved, she finds that the "house looked as if it had been clumsily cut into two by a giant's claw, a living thing wantonly mutilated." The building is being pulled down, for the nurse's training school has been relocated. The murderer's cottage in *Unnatural Causes* is perceived by Dalgliesh as "an ugly building, as uncompromisingly square as a doll's house," and it is destined to be tumbled into the sea by violent nature–a nature as violent but without the same purposeful maliciousness as its occupant.

Both Adam Dalgliesh and Cordelia Gray have an eye for architecture and decor, as does Phillippa in *Innocent Blood*, as they evaluate their surroundings. They are able to appreciate a house that is "simple but strongly formalized in design," a room that is beautifully proportioned, a row of cottages that displays "unity of age, architecture and height," but each cottage "charmingly individual." A solicitor's office building may display "solid affluence, tradition and professional rectitude," but his own office mirrors the man himself: the room is "poky, stuffy and untidy." In James such contrasts often are diagnostic of a vio-

lation, a falling-off, a failure to keep faith. The death cottage in *An Unsuitable Job for a Woman*, in which Cordelia camps out during her investigation, has been superstitiously neglected but was in the process of being rescued and restored when its occupant was killed ("It was, she thought, a curious place, heavy with atmosphere and showing two distinct faces to the world like facets of a human personality"). Dalgliesh encounters the same dichotomy when he arrives at the forensic laboratory that a nineteenth-century benefactor has made from his own manor house. As he admires the "excellent example of late seventeenth-century domestic architecture," his escort comments, "Agreeable, isn't it? But wait till you see what the old man did to some of the interior." What he sees is a despoliation of the contours for pragmatic purposes, making makeshift work space out of elegance, proportion, and spaciousness, a compromise noted in many professional buildings that he enters, even those of the government in Whitehall. Whereas the old buildings with "Gothic splendour" he assumes were "infuriating and uncomfortable to work in," the new ones reveal an intention "to express confident authority tempered by humanity," but "he wasn't sure that the architect had succeeded. It looked more suitable for a multinational corporation than a great Department of State."

For the cheerful and sanguine Cordelia Gray the viewings of the three dwellings are diagnostic, including the two-faceted cottage in which she takes refuge. The main house to which the cottage belongs is a "large Victorian edifice of red brick," and she wonders why "anyone should have wanted to build such an intimidatingly ugly house, or, having decided to do so, would have set down a suburban monstrosity in the middle of the countryside.... Even the rock plants burgeoned like morbid excrescences." Major ambiguity is found in a house in which the victim had been reared and where his father, his murderer, still lives and runs a major laboratory:

> The house was obviously Georgian, not perhaps the best Georgian but solidly built, agreeably proportioned and with the look of all good domestic architecture of having grown naturally out of its site. The mellow brick, festooned with wisteria, gleamed richly in the evening sun so that the green of the creeper glowed and the whole house looked suddenly as artificial and unsubstantial as a film set. It was essentially a family house, a welcoming house. But now a heavy si-

 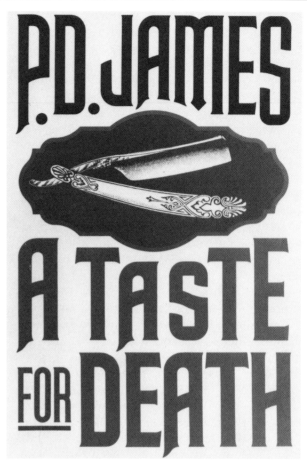

Dust jackets for the first British edition and the first American edition of James's 1986 novel (courtesy of Otto Penzler)

lence lay over it and the rows of elegantly proportioned windows were empty eyes.

A constant undercutting of the potentially positive delineates an important aspect of the James novels. There are frequent negative descriptions of ugly edifices, the smug bourgeois, and the insipid poor, but the subtle undermining of a manor house is particularly characteristic of James.

While regarding the Victorian dwelling Cordelia wonders if "perhaps it had replaced an earlier more agreeable house," and indeed many of the buildings that serve as the central stage of the Jamesian dramas have been converted from something else, and each is either in the process or in potential danger of being reconverted, abandoned, or demolished. Numerous indications of an old order having changed, and now in the flux of changing once again, with a loss of continuity and a greater degree of depersonalization, permeate the mood of her novels generally, but nowhere as subtly as in *Death of an Expert Witness*.

The new employee, a bright woman of eighteen, is impressed that the forensic laboratory has a long and unbroken history, but the new director has replaced the portrait of the founder with a modern painting intended to discomfort his staff. (Paintings hung in residential dwellings and offices are carefully scrutinized by each of the James protagonists and are significant indicators throughout–when Phillippa of *Innocent Blood* leaves her adoptive home for the flat she rented for her real mother, she takes with her only a valued and valuable painting.) The disruption within the administration of the forensic lab is making its effects known, and a new structure is in the process of being built on the grounds. At present it is a dangerous area, with warning signs to the staff not to use it as a shortcut. Yet when she finds herself in danger, Brenda Pridmore, a young employee, cuts through it in the dark and manages to terrify herself to the extent that she rushes into the chapel for succor–only to discover a hanging corpse. She survives her experience but does not return to her job.

Two architectural creations loom large in *A Taste for Death*, both by famous nineteenth-century designers but fictionalized by James for her particular settings: a Romanesque church in Paddington credited to Arthur Blomfield and a four-story residence on Campden Hill Square attributed to Sir John Soane. The church has as its vicar an unkempt priest who has lost his faith to the same extent as the church has lost its parishioners, and yet it is here that one of the victims has had a religious conversion and is brutally murdered, along with a tramp who used it as a haven. The house, greatly admired by Dalgliesh, is nonetheless assessed by him as a dwelling in which none of the residents, except for the eighty-two-year-old grande dame, has endowed it with any element of individual personality. These buildings declare their elegance as architectural achievements but not as reflections of their constituent humanity. In her work James strongly implies that only those places in which someone has devoted time and effort, a measure of love and attention (transferred intact from builder to resident), an indication of an individual personality or the shared love of the occupants, have a human resonance and an element of beauty. The destructive defeat caused by poverty, the aesthetic indifference derived from bourgeois complacency, or the callous results of narrow ambition can turn any residence into a demeaning hovel or an architectural horror, relentlessly reflecting the lives within.

Her variants on Edgar Allan Poe's House of Usher theme seem representative for her of either fine traditions fading out or obsolete traditions still dug in, of ugly buildings retained or beautiful buildings cannibalized. Stables that once housed fine horses have either been sold off (*Cover Her Face*) or converted into garages (*The Black Tower*) or laboratories (*An Unsuitable Job for a Woman*). Renovations, when they do suggest an element of progress, are inefficacious, as in the London address of one of the shadier suspects in *Unnatural Causes*:

> The cobbled entrance was uninviting, ill-lit and smelt strongly of urine.... The premises had apparently once been the headquarters of a driving school and a few tattered notices still clung to the garage doors. But they were dedicated now to a nobler purpose, the improvement of London's chronic housing shortage. More accurately, they were being converted into dark, under-sized and over-priced cottages soon, no doubt, to be advertized as "bijou town residences."

The basic milieu of the James mysteries is unmistakably that of the upper middle class, particularly among those of professional status, physicians and scientists, writers and technicians, and even a member of Parliament, but the sociological perspective is often much broader. When Phillippa in *Innocent Blood*, reared in upper-middle-class comfort, begins her trek in search of her parents, a train takes her eastward from London, and she views "rows of drab houses with blackened bricks and patched roofs from which sprang a tangle of television aerials, frail crooked fetishes against the evil eye; layered high-rise flats smudged in a distant drizzle of rain; a yard piled high with the glitter of smashed cars in symbolic proximity to the regimented crosses of a suburban graveyard; a paint factory; a cluster of gasometers; pyramids of grit and coal piled beside the track; wastelands rank with weeds; a sloping green bank rising to suburban gardens with their washing lines and toolsheds and children's swings among the roses and hollyhocks."

In describing and analyzing the social scene in England, using her skills as a former employee of the Criminal Policy Department and her expertise in the juvenile courts, James nonetheless has no fixed political perspective as such, and one can believe her statement to Julian Symons (in a review of *A Taste for Death*) that at various times she has voted Conservative, Labour, and Liberal: a strong humanitarian thrust is tempered by a sense of tradition and a mood of caution. Nor does the professional sociologist necessarily fare particularly well, especially in *Innocent Blood*, where Phillippa's adoptive father, a famous professor of sociology and a television debater, is viewed by her as cold and unloving (he depicts himself as "invincibly arrogant in the high renaissance of the heart")—although she not only returns to him but goes to bed with him. Scrutiny of the social scene is balanced, and even undercut, by James's fascination with aberrant psychology, particularly in her later works. The *New York Times* reviewer of *A Taste for Death* may have balked at the book's resolution, which not only shifts from the detective format to an inverse crime story but also has as its revealed murderer a "psychopath" (also dismissed as an "erratic madman"), yet the murderer becomes so psychologically authenticated as he discloses his motivations that the charge of authorial arbitrariness seems unfounded. James rarely opts for the *surface* motives for murder, although enough suspects have them, but more and more often finds motivation within the realm of hate and love, within the personal rather than the social realm. Human fallibility, instead of greed, ambition, or desire, is frequently at the core of the crime. In *Shroud for a Nightingale* the matron exonerates a nurse who considers herself guilty of theft ("Every one of us has some incident in our lives that we're ashamed and sorry about"); soon after, Dalgliesh exonerates the matron on the basis of a valid alibi, and she responds: "I know it's foolish to feel such relief at not being under suspicion when one knows anyway that one is innocent. Perhaps it's because none of us is innocent in any real sense." What she is concealing is that she had stood trial for war crimes at Nuremberg, and she knows that her close associate has killed a nurse who knows this fact. The associate has murdered and will murder again, as well as attack Dalgliesh, out of love, a love that she has used as blackmail in her demanding friendship with the matron. She is discovered to have killed herself, but Dalgliesh knows—although he is unable to prove—that she has been murdered by the matron, who eventually does commit suicide. In its profound and perverse manifestations, love often proves to be potentially dangerous in James's novels.

It is interesting to note that the first four James books have a woman as the murderer (there are two murderers in *Shroud for a Nightingale*), although there is also a male accomplice in one instance and a male attempting murder in another. That women are not exempt from criminality in her work is particularly underscored by the fact that she presents women as having strong capacities for emotional commitment and emotional frustration. James's nicest murderess is the mother in *Cover Her Face* (she is also the nicest of all the suspects); she throttles an infuriatingly disruptive element in her household, a maid who threatens the sanctity of the family. When Dalgliesh has eliminated all of the other suspects she quietly confesses, having waited until her terminally ill husband has died so that she could be free to be imprisoned. Although no one had apparently suspected her as such, there was a reluctance among the family and friends to encourage the police in their investigation, as if the necessity to bring the murderer to justice was in itself an aberration of human justice. "Then why not leave it to the police?" one of the most perceptive suspects comments; "Their greatest difficulty will be to get enough evidence to justify a charge."

In James's fiction, that a murder is sometimes not so much an antisocial act as a corrective undercuts the concept that society must avenge every homicide and protect itself from anyone with homicidal tendencies. Dalgliesh muses on the idea that "Every death benefited someone, enfranchised someone, lifted a burden from someone's shoulders, whether of responsibility, the pain of vicarious suffering or the tyranny of love. Every death was a suspicious death if one looked only at motive, just as every death, at the last, was a natural death." Yet in *Cover Her Face* five murders have been committed—and the murder of Dalgliesh is attempted—by a murderer protecting his acquired affluence, attained through illicit drug trafficking. The "tyranny of love" is hardly operative in *The Black Tower* as it is in *Shroud for a Nightingale*, *A Mind to Murder*, and *A Taste for Death*: the need to assure the comfort of a terminally ill mother by preventing a change in a will and the obsessive dependence on a sister's love produce two very different kinds of killers. In controlling her narratives James opts for the modernist tendency of allowing her suspects to reveal their thoughts to the reader without precipitously revealing their guilt, so that the mother in *Cover Her Face* can reveal her "honest mind" as she "explored . . . this revelation that a loyalty which the family had all taken for granted had been more complicated, less acquiescent than any of them had suspected and had at last been strained too far." In effect, this is a confession but only apprehended by a reader exploring psychological motivations instead of the more traditional ones.

Twice in the James canon a four-element package of motives is presented as all-inclusive: in *Unnatural Causes* Dalgliesh remembers his "old chief" insisting on the "four L's—love, lust, loathing and lucre" and concludes that "superficially that was true enough." The key element in this case is loathing, the least traditional of the four and the one that eventually explains the ghastly murder and mutilation. Hate hides itself more successfully than love, but few writers of detective fiction would ever feel secure enough in using it as a motive for murder unless they could provide the psychological portraits that have become James's particular strength. To educate her readers on the potency of hatred she has the most innocent of the suspects turn on one of the more obvious ones and declare, "I don't think you hated him that much." The murderer herself is even more precise in her taped confession, when she gloatingly states that "it was convenient that there should be at least two people at Monksmere, both spiteful, both aggrieved, both with an obvious motive." When Dalgliesh in *A Taste for Death* reiterates the verdict of "an old detective sergeant," there is a new emphasis (perhaps intended to both lead and mislead the reader): "Love, Lust, Loathing, Lucre, the four Ls of murderer, laddie. And the greatest of these is lucre." The complexity of *A Taste for Death* is such that both the murderer and the woman who provides him with an alibi harbor hatred and love—the latter invariably misdirected—but that securing wealth for his beloved sister also means securing it for himself as well. In effect, all four L's are operative, given the various lies and concealments practiced by the suspects. One of them Dalgliesh dismisses as displaying "arrogance, aggression, sexual jealousy. . . . But not hate." Dalgliesh has developed a sixth sense about hate, noting that "this murderer didn't kill from expediency. There had been hatred in that room. Hate isn't an easy emotion to hide." Conversely, in *Death of an Expert Witness* Dalgliesh again quotes his mentor ("the first detective sergeant I worked under") as saying: "They'll tell you that the most destructive force in the world is hate. Don't you believe it, lad. It's love. And if you want to make a detective you'd better learn to recognise it when you meet it."

The conventional notion, which is propagated through most of the history of detective fiction either explicitly or implicitly, has been the assumed redressing of balance with the apprehension of the murderer, especially in the years of capital punishment (an eye for an eye, a death for a death, returns the world to normality). Yet the problem has been complicated by the two persistent extremes: the victim more heinous than the murderer and the murderer, usually the multiple murderer, who is particularly vile. James deals with both extremes, the first in *Cover Her Face* and *Death of an Expert Witness*, and the second in *The Black Tower* and *A Taste for Death*, as she investigates an intricately unpleasant society, uncovering the "sad sludge of a dead world." Dalgliesh is aware of the dangers of such uncoverings: in *Death of an Expert Witness* he is told by the retiring controller of the Forensic Science Service, "You chaps usually bring as much trouble with you as you solve. You can't help it. Murder is like that, a contaminating crime. Oh, you'll solve it, I know. You always do. But I'm wondering at what cost." The same observation is made with bitterness by the murdered man's mistress in *A Taste for Death*, again to Dalgliesh: "but what about your victims? I expect you'll catch

Paul's murderer. You usually do, don't you? Does it ever occur to you to count the cost?"

Despite the precision with which James practices her craft, no rational or scientific touchstone is applied to the society she dissects, and, as with many other writers of the genre, she reveals a fascination with death, a vision of "the skull beneath the skin," a phrase from Renaissance revenge tragedian John Webster which has been transmitted in the present century with a quasi-religious note by T. S. Eliot. (Even before using it as the title of her ninth novel, James employs the phrase in *The Black Tower*, and she uses it again, in *A Taste for Death*.) Religion plays an important role in all of James's novels, from the love of English church architecture shared by her two protagonists, though neither professes to being religious, to the sham religion of *The Black Tower* and the persistence of the religious in *A Taste for Death*. In *Death of an Expert Witness* a lovely Wren chapel is used for fornication and later for a murder, and in *A Taste for Death* the throat slasher strikes again and shoots the vicar. The book ends with the devout parishioner, who found the dead bodies in the church, trying to pray, despite her realization that she had probably lost her faith. James told Symons that she was an Anglican, and "quite a religious person," but the most pervasive aspect of the religious in her novels is the underlying persistence of evil, stronger throughout than even the most dire of sociological causes and the most pronounced of psychological causes. Few of the books are without some speculation that evil or wickedness is an entity in itself and basically at the bottom of the homicidal horror. Even before the murder in *Cover Her Face* has been discovered, the perpetrator of the crime has a feeling that "the imminence of evil took hold of her and she had to pause for a second before she could trust her voice." Yet it is the need to care for her dying husband that keeps her from immediately confessing to the crime of manslaughter.

Whatever role unmitigated evil has been allowed to play in the detective subgenre, where hardheaded and logical deduction has been expected to hold sway despite an almost supernatural atmospheric aura at times, it has been given prominence as the result of criminal tendencies rather than the cause. On occasion in a James novel it is that aura that pervades, perhaps suggesting something more, as when Dalgliesh senses that "no corner of Nightingale House was free of the oppressive atmosphere of evil; the very plants seemed to be sucking their manna from the tainted air" and has his sensation corroborated at the end when the visitor watches it being demolished: "It was a horrible house; an evil house. It should have been pulled down fifty years ago." In the tradition of the Gothic tale a house is imbued with evil, and the act of demolition is also the act of exorcism. Dalgliesh feels the same emanations in the dead priest's cottage where he takes his temporary residence (as Cordelia did in the dead youth's cottage): "He could almost believe that he smelt the presence of evil." As a detective he mistrusts the nonrational ("It was an alien factor which he half resented and almost wholly distrusted"), yet it leads him to the conclusion that the priest had been murdered. Cordelia comes to the same conclusion about the presumed suicide victim whose cottage she inhabits: "Evil existed–she hadn't needed a convent education to convince her of that reality–and it had been present in this room. Something here had been stronger than wickedness, ruthlessness, cruelty or expedience. Evil." (Her convent education parallels Dalgliesh's parsonage childhood.) Cordelia discovers that the murder was done with ruthlessness and cruelty and for expediency, and the murderer taunts her with her own human complicity: "If you are capable of imagining it, then I'm capable of doing it. Haven't you yet discovered that about human beings, Miss Gray? It's the key to what you would call the wickedness of man."

Gray is naturally more receptive than Dalgliesh to the concept of evil as it is embodied in an evil human being. In *The Skull beneath the Skin* she examines poison-pen letters and considers their effect on the receiver, both the maliciousness of the intender and the vulnerability of the intended: "in all societies there was an atavistic fear of the malevolent power of a secret adversary working for evil, willing one to failure, perhaps to death. There was a rather horrible and frightening intelligence at work here"–the closest she comes to accepting a demonic presence. Later she discusses evil with the dying man who befriended her, specifically in religious terms, acknowledging to herself that "it was when she had finally stared into the face of his murderer [that of the youth in *An Unsuitable Job*] that she had known about evil." Ironically, the writer of the poison-pen letters does not intend death as his result but covers up someone else's inadvertent murder and now finds himself in the process of attempting to murder the slayer (and Cordelia) to keep him quiet. Aware of multiple ironies, he ex-

plains that he was being blackmailed and staked everything in keeping the money that he inherited despite his violation of the tax laws that would deprive him of all his gains. It was a charitable act that had brought him back from tax exile, and that act of charity was now resulting in his criminal acts. It was "a simple act of filial kindness," and yet it was the germinating cause of malevolence and murder: "Evil coming out of good, if those two words mean something to you." In *Innocent Blood* Phillippa hears her mother describe her father's rape of the twelve-year-old girl and thinks, "He had made use of what was good and kind in her to destroy her. If evil existed, if those four letters placed in that order had any reality, then surely here was evil."

With eleven novels James is at the zenith of her career. She is probably the most complex writer of detective fiction in England today, and her achievements have been appropriately acknowledged. Four of her books have been made into television films; she was awarded an OBE in the Queen's Birthday Honours in 1983; and in 1985 she was elected a Fellow of the Royal Society of Arts and an Associate Fellow of Downing College, Cambridge. She has written her first play, *A Private Treason* ("there is a crime within it," she has acknowledged, "although it is not a mystery story as such"), produced in Watford in April 1985. Her most interesting departure, however, is *The Maul and the Pear Tree: The Ratcliffe Highway Murders, 1811* (1971), coauthored with her then supervisor at the Home Office, T. A. Critchley. In it they examine an old case that excited incredible interest in England at the time, including questions in Parliament. Bloody crimes were committed for which a suspect was arrested, but he died by his own hand instead of that of the executioner. To James and Critchley it remains an unsolved crime, and they investigate the documents in the case with careful scrutiny, unsatisfied with the reported result but still unable to determine the total facts of the case. It is both a history and a condemnation of archaic police methods and of inhumane behavior toward others. Published in England in 1971, it has only recently been published in America, attesting to James's newly acquired stature on this side of the Atlantic.

James's commitment to the detection format, which had been put in question by the writing of *Innocent Blood* and the speculation that she might join her rival and admirer Ruth Rendell in some sort of alternation of detective and nondetective fiction, seems to remain firm after the publication of the latest Cordelia Gray and Adam Dalgliesh books. When she was pointedly asked about that commitment, she told Symons, "I write detective stories. I hope they're novels, too, and I don't see any contradiction in that. But if I felt there *was* a contradiction, if the detective element got in the way of the novel and I had to sacrifice one or the other, then the detective element would have to go. I hope and believe I shan't have to make such a choice." Her sense of what she is doing as a detective novelist can best be viewed in what she wrote in *The Skull beneath the Skin*, where the case under investigation can be read to pertain to the novel under construction:

> Murder, the unique and ultimate crime, was seldom the most interesting forensically or the most difficult to solve. But when you did get a good one there was no excitement like it: the heady combination of a manhunt with a puzzle; the smell of fear in the air, strong as the metallic smell of blood; the sense of randy well-being; the fascinating way in which confidence, personality, morale, subtly changed and deteriorated under its contaminating impact. A good murder was what police work was about. And this promised to be a good one.

Despite her professed preference for what she terms "literary realism" and the exacting verisimilitude of her settings and details, James is instinctively aware of the gap between real life and good fiction, and the murders she plots are invariably replete with excitement and the qualities she lists. A good murder is what her novels are about.

Interviews:

Barbara Bannon, "PW Interviews: P. D. James," *Publishers Weekly*, 209 (5 January 1976): 8-9;

Patricia Craig, "An Interview with P. D. James," *Times Literary Supplement*, 5 June 1981, p. 4079;

Dale Salwak, "An Interview with P. D. James," *Clues*, 6 (Spring-Summer 1985): 31-50;

Rosemary Herbert, "A Mind to Write," *Armchair Detective*, 19 (1986): 340-348.

References:

Jane S. Bakerman, "Cordelia Gray: Apprentice and Archetype," *Clues*, 5 (Spring-Summer 1984): 101-114;

Bakerman, "From the time I could read, I always wanted to be a writer," *Armchair Detective*, 10 (1977): 55-57, 92;

Bernard Benstock, "The Clinical World of P. D. James," in *Twentieth-Century Women Novelists*, edited by Thomas F. Staley (London: Macmillan, 1982), pp. 104-129;

SueEllen Campbell, "The Detective Heroine and the Death of her Hero: Dorothy Sayers to P. D. James," *Modern Fiction Studies*, 29 (Autumn 1983): 497-510;

M. Cannon, "Mistress of Malice Domestic," *New York Times Book Review*, 27 April 1980, p. 50;

S. L. Clark, "*Gaudy Night*'s Legacy: P. D. James's *An Unsuitable Job for a Woman*," *Sayers Review*, 4 (1980): 1-11;

Lillian De La Torre, "Cordelia Gray: The Thinking Man's Heroine," in *Murderess Ink*, edited by Dilys Winn (New York: Workman, 1977), pp. 111-113;

Richard B. Gidez, *P. D. James* (Boston: G. K. Hall, 1986);

Donald Goddard, "The Unmysterious P. D. James," *New York Times Book Review*, 27 April 1980, p. 28;

Bruce Harkness, "P. D. James," in *Essays in Detective Fiction*, edited by Benstock (London: Macmillan, 1983), pp. 119-141;

Erlene Hubly, "Adam Dalgliesh: Byronic Hero," *Clues*, 3 (Fall-Winter 1982): 40-46;

Hubly, "The Formula Challenged: The Novels of P. D. James," *Modern Fiction Studies*, 29 (Autumn 1983): 511-521;

Nancy Carol Joyner, "P. D. James," in *Ten Women of Mystery*, edited by Earl F. Bargainnier (Bowling Green, Ohio: Bowling Green University Popular Press, 1981);

Thomas Lask, "Another Aspect of a Mystery Writer," *New York Times*, 8 February 1980, p. 27;

Norma Siebenheller, *P. D. James* (New York: Ungar, 1981);

Patricia A. Ward, "Moral Ambiguities and the Crime Novels of P. D. James," *Christian Century*, 101 (16 May 1984): 519-522;

Robin W. Winks, "P. D. James: Murder and Dying," *New Republic* (31 July 1976): 31-32.

H. R. F. Keating

(31 October 1926-   )

Mary Jean DeMarr
Indiana State University

BOOKS: *Death and the Visiting Firemen* (London: Gollancz, 1959; Garden City, N.Y.: Doubleday, 1973);

Zen There Was Murder (London: Gollancz, 1960);

A Rush on the Ultimate (London: Gollancz, 1961; Garden City, N.Y.: Doubleday, 1982);

The Dog It Was That Died (London: Gollancz, 1962);

Death of a Fat God (London: Collins, 1963; New York: Dutton, 1966);

The Perfect Murder (London: Collins, 1964; New York: Dutton, 1965);

Is Skin-Deep, Is Fatal (London: Collins, 1965; New York: Dutton, 1965);

Inspector Ghote's Good Crusade (London: Collins, 1966; New York: Dutton, 1966);

Inspector Ghote Caught in Meshes (London: Collins, 1967; New York: Dutton, 1968);

Inspector Ghote Hunts the Peacock (London: Collins, 1968; New York: Dutton, 1968);

Inspector Ghote Plays a Joker (London: Collins, 1969; New York: Dutton, 1969);

Understanding Pierre Teilhard de Chardin: A Guide to "The Phenomenon of Man," by Keating and Maurice Keating (London: Lutterworth, 1969);

Inspector Ghote Breaks an Egg (London: Collins, 1970; Garden City, N.Y.: Doubleday, 1971);

Inspector Ghote Goes by Train (London: Collins, 1971; Garden City, N.Y.: Doubleday, 1972);

The Strong Man (London: Heinemann, 1971);

Inspector Ghote Trusts the Heart (London: Collins, 1972; Garden City, N.Y.: Doubleday, 1973);

Bats Fly Up for Inspector Ghote (London: Collins, 1974; Garden City, N.Y.: Doubleday, 1974);

The Underside (London: Macmillan, 1974);

A Remarkable Case of Burglary (London: Collins, 1975; Garden City, N.Y.: Doubleday, 1976);

Murder Must Appetize (London: Lemon Tree, 1975; New York: Mysterious, 1981);

Filmi, Filmi, Inspector Ghote (London: Collins, 1976; Garden City, N.Y.: Doubleday, 1977);

A Long Walk to Wimbledon (London: Macmillan, 1978);

H. R. F. Keating (© Universal Pictorial Press & Agency, Ltd., London, England)

Inspector Ghote Draws a Line (London: Collins, 1979; Garden City, N.Y.: Doubleday, 1979);

Sherlock Holmes: The Man and His World (London: Thames & Hudson, 1979; New York: Scribners, 1979);

The Murder of the Maharajah (London: Collins, 1980; Garden City, N.Y.: Doubleday, 1980);

Go West, Inspector Ghote (London: Collins, 1981; Garden City, N.Y.: Doubleday, 1981);

The Lucky Alphonse (London: Enigma, 1982);

Great Crimes (London: St. Michael, 1982; New York: Harmony Books, 1982);

The Governess: A Novel, as Evelyn Hervey (Garden City, N.Y.: Doubleday, 1983; London: Weidenfeld & Nicolson, 1984);

The Sheriff of Bombay: An Inspector Ghote Novel (London: Collins, 1984; Garden City, N.Y.: Doubleday, 1984);

Mrs. Craggs: Crimes Cleaned Up (London: Buchan & Enright, 1985; New York: St. Martin's Press, 1985);

The Man of Gold, as Hervey (London: Weidenfeld & Nicolson, 1985; Garden City, N.Y.: Doubleday, 1985);

Under a Monsoon Cloud (London: Hutchinson, 1986; New York: Viking, 1986);

Into the Valley of Death, as Hervey (London: Weidenfeld & Nicolson, 1986; Garden City, N.Y.: Doubleday, 1986);

Writing Crime Fiction (London: Black, 1986; New York: St. Martin's Press, 1987);

The Body in the Billiard Room (London: Hutchinson, 1987; New York: Viking, 1987);

Crime and Mystery: The One Hundred Best Books (London: Xanadu, 1987; New York: Carroll & Graf, 1987);

Dead on Time (London: Hutchinson, 1988; New York: Mysterious, 1989);

The Bedside Companion to Crime (London: O'Mara, 1989);

Inspector Ghote: His Life and Crimes (London: Hutchinson, 1989).

OTHER: *Blood on My Mind: A Collection of New Pieces by Members of the Crime Writers' Association about Real Crimes, Some Notable and Some Obscure*, edited by Keating (London: Macmillan, 1972);

Agatha Christie: First Lady of Crime, edited by Keating (London: Weidenfeld & Nicolson, 1977; New York: Holt, Rinehart & Winston, 1977);

Reginald Hill and others, *Crime Writers: Reflections on Crime Fiction*, edited by Keating (London: British Broadcasting Corporation, 1978);

Whodunit?: A Guide to Crime, Suspense and Spy Fiction, edited by Keating (London: Windward, 1982; New York: Van Nostrand Reinhold, 1982);

G. K. Chesterton, *The Best of Father Brown*, edited by Keating (London: Dent, 1987).

Best known for his creation of Ganesh Ghote (pronounced "Go-tay"), a Bombay policeman who is both an effective investigator and an appealing man, H. R. F. Keating has been instrumen-

tal in widening the boundaries of the mystery novel. In the forefront of those who have introduced social concerns, local color, and depiction of particular ethnic groups into the genre, he has also been a warm and supportive encourager of the talents of others and has published incisive criticism about the field of the detective story.

Born in St. Leonards-on-Sea, Sussex, on 31 October 1926, Henry Reymond Fitzwalter Keating has claimed in *Contemporary Authors* (1976) that his second name was given its unusual spelling because it would look better on the spines of the books he was expected to write. His father, John Hervey Keating, a schoolmaster, and mother, Muriel Marguerita Clews Keating, both came from bookish families, but their son, always called "Harry," professes ignorance as to the origins of the literary ambitions that he long resisted out of modest uncertainty of having anything to say. His wife finally challenged him to forswear a career as a journalist and attempt to write detective fiction, since he was so fond of the genre and since they both believed, erroneously, he later discovered, that mysteries did not say anything.

Of Anglo-Irish background, Keating was educated at the Merchant Taylor's School, London, and at Trinity College, Dublin (B.A., 1952). He served in the British army from 1945 to 1948, having been inducted on the day of the end of the war with Japan. He married Sheila Mary Mitchell, an actress, on 3 October 1953. The couple has three sons and one daughter. His diffidence about the originality of his talents led him into a career as a journalistic subeditor for newspapers in Wiltshire and London from 1952 to 1960. When his crime novels began to succeed he was able to leave journalism, although he reviewed mysteries for the *London Times* from 1967 to 1983.

His literary career began slowly. His first two novels failed to achieve publication; the third, however, was *Death and the Visiting Firemen* (1959). Initial notes for a story set in 1953, using as background some of the pageantry connected with the coronation of Elizabeth II, later seemed to Keating to be vivid in their immediacy and suggested the verbless style that distinguishes the narrative portions of this novel. After making the rounds of publishers, it had the good fortune to be accepted by Gollancz and to confirm Keating in the career to which he felt destined.

Six more crime novels followed within the next half decade. Each novel was an experiment of a different sort, and together they show

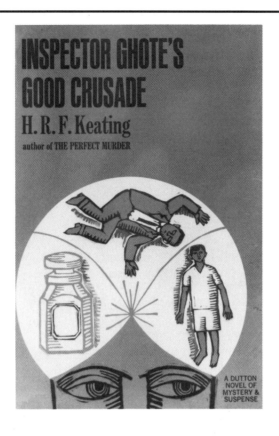

Dust jackets for the first American editions of three of Keating's novels from the 1960s featuring Inspector Ganesh Ghote

Keating feeling his way toward his own idiom and beginning to discover that the mystery form need not be empty of thematic content. The first four of these novels are particularly varied. *Zen There Was Murder* (1960) anticipates the interest in the East that Keating was later to develop through his Inspector Ghote series. Here he wished to take advantage of the current fashionable interest in Zen Buddhism. Murder occurs during an adult-education conference on Zen led by a Japanese Zen master. Characters represent varied types and attitudes: an Anglican clergyman and a police inspector contrast most markedly with the Zen master, both of them being unable to comprehend the paradoxes he sets them or the detachment which enables him to find the truth even while denying its meaning or importance. A rather conventional puzzle, the novel is interestingly constructed.

A *Rush on the Ultimate* (1961) and *Death of a Fat God* (1963) make witty and amusing use of croquet and opera, respectively. Keating has commented in volume 8 of the *Contemporary Authors Autobiography Series* (1989) that the former is about violence and the latter about pride. *Death of a Fat God*, which derives its title from an opera being produced by a fictional provincial opera company, has for its Holmes and Watson a pair of charwomen whose constant access to all parts of the opera house enables them to play detective. Keating returned to these characters in *Mrs. Craggs: Crimes Cleaned Up* (1985), a later collection of witty and comic short pieces, several of which originated as sketches to be read over the radio by his actress wife.

The Dog It Was That Died (1962) is an interesting variation on the spy novel. Two refugees from a secret militaristic establishment in England are at work in Dublin at a humanistic institute; one is murdered, and the other spends most of the novel fleeing those who desire to use his linguistic knowledge for propaganda purposes. The brainwashing attempt he undergoes after his capture is well depicted.

Three other nonseries crime novels, written after Keating had become known primarily for the creation of Inspector Ghote, deserve special mention. *Is Skin-Deep, Is Fatal* (1965), the earliest of these, coming between the first two Ghote novels, is a variation on the first-person narrator-murderer technique with which Agatha Christie had shocked the mystery-reading world in *The Murder of Roger Ackroyd* (1926), except that Keating uses a third-person narrative method. In-

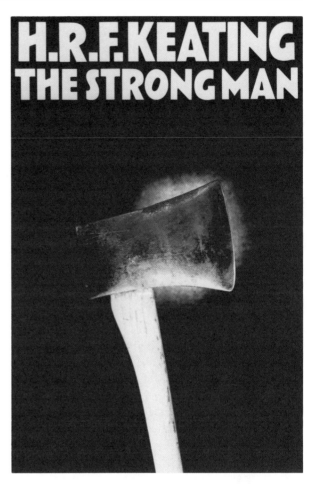

Dust jacket for the first edition of one of Keating's novels from the early 1970s that does not feature Inspector Ghote

deed, Keating said in the *Contemporary Authors Autobiography Series* that the plot is "blatantly pinched" from Christie. Police Constable Peter Lassington, the central consciousness of *Is Skin-Deep, Is Fatal*, is revealed in the book's last pages to have been a double murderer. Earlier, he had followed his former friend, a detective constable, and a police superintendent as they sought to solve crimes set around a nightclub whose murdered owner-manager had run sleazy beauty contests. Although his insensitivity is revealed by the narrative, Peter appears a conscientious police officer and readers trust him largely because they see events through his eyes. Suspicions are for a time directed to Peter's friend, and Peter's distancing himself from that friend adds to the reader's sense of his reliability. However, the clues given by Peter's resentments and lack of sympathy for others subtly prepare the reader to accept his guilt when it is finally revealed. The novel, while not one of Keating's strongest, is a skillfully crafted tour de force.

Ten years later, after the Ghote series was well established, Keating returned to the English scene and to another nonseries novel with *A Remarkable Case of Burglary* (1975). This is one of only two historical mysteries by Keating, although he has used the Victorian period in several other pieces. Set in 1871 and climaxing with a thwarted burglary, the novel is concerned primarily with a group of lower-class characters who become enmeshed in both criminality and sexual passion. Val Leary, an unemployed ne'er-do-well, entices a young maid in a wealthy household to learn essential details about the house so he may sell them to a "putter-up," a mastermind of burglaries. But then he falls in love with another young woman, and the jealous passions roused by his involvement with the two women lead to the bungling of the burglary. None of the characters is willing or able to take responsibility for his or her actions; as he is carried off, wounded, Val blames the burglary's failure on chance. The novel makes interesting use of a central military metaphor–the prospective burglars and the household they wish to victimize become an army besieging a fortress. Class hatred is strikingly stressed: the maid, Janey, bitterly hates the butler who is the primary instrument of oppression that she meets on a daily basis, and the master of the house is portrayed as cruel, heedless, neurotically fearful of burglary, and totally insensitive to the feelings of the servants. Indeed, he seems to consider them almost of a different species from himself and his family. The historical background, particularly the life of servants and members of the criminal class, is well presented.

One other non-Ghote novel, a historical crime novel set in India, is worth special mention. The action of *The Murder of the Maharajah* (1980) occurs in 1930 on the opulent estate of the ruler of Bhopore. It begins on April Fools' Day, and the joke-loving Maharajah's pranks soon turn serious. A house party which includes a variety of guests is involved, and the novel becomes a variant of the English country-house murder motif. An Anglo-Indian policeman investigates, soon making friends with the resident Schoolmaster; they establish a Holmes-Watson relationship, although it is not always completely clear who plays which part, and the last lines of the novel reveal that the Schoolmaster, never previously named, is to be the father of a future policeman whom Keating's readers know as Inspector Ghote. The novel's representation of the

sumptuous world of Indian rulers during the Raj is compelling, with the brief treatment of the world of purdah, of the secluded women, being particularly striking. *The Murder of the Maharajah* won the Crime Writers' Association's Gold Dagger Award in 1980.

None of the early nonseries novels found publishers in the United States before 1966, a major financial obstacle for a writer who wished to support himself and a growing family by his pen. As the problem seemed to be that his work was too parochially English, Keating cast about for a device that would enable him to reach an American audience, and in so doing he happened upon a setting and a character that were to become uniquely his own and upon a greater thematic depth that was to enrich and strengthen his fictions as novels. The first Ghote novel, *The Perfect Murder* (1964), succeeded beyond his relatively modest expectations of an American edition; warmly reviewed, in 1964 it received the Crime Writers' Association's Gold Dagger Award, and in 1965 it was given a special Edgar by the Mystery Writers of America.

The theme of the imperfect, of the tension between an unreachable perfection and a practical if defective reality, had long attracted Keating, and when India struck him as an obvious and effective symbol for the flawed, the basis for *The Perfect Murder* was present. Although he had not yet visited India, he read as much as he could about the country and called upon the advice of a new and serendipitous acquaintance, an experienced India-hand, to help him avoid howlers. The title, an obvious play on a convention of the mystery genre, is ironic. Keating had been delighted to learn that "Perfect" was actually a name occurring within the Indian Parsi community, giving him his title and the name of his victim. However, no murder actually occurs, a failed attempt being only one of a number of examples of imperfection within the novel. The main plot concerns what the Bombay press insists upon referring to as the "Perfect Murder," an attack on Mr. Perfect, who was not only not killed but was also the wrong man, attacked by mistake. A subplot centers around the apparent theft of one rupee from a wealthy man, in a variant on the conventional locked-room mystery. But just as there was no murder, it turns out that there has been no theft, only a test for the police concocted by the purported victim. A dramatic chase after the wrong man occurs near the end of the novel, making the actual solution almost anticli-

Dust jacket for the first American edition of Keating's 1982 reference book for crime-fiction enthusiasts

mactic and adding to the examples of the faulty in the novel.

Bombay policeman Inspector Ghote in this first appearance is already the familiar diffident figure who prevails almost in spite of his sense of his own fallibility. Carrying on the theme of imperfection, he solves the "murder" plot almost by accident–the solution is triggered by the onset of the monsoon–but he works out the answer to the "theft" plot by conventional logic. Throughout the novel he is accompanied by a Swedish UNESCO representative who is in India to study police methods. Initially Ghote finds the Swede a burden and a bother, but eventually they become friends and the Swede is a true help to Ghote. A touching scene occurs when the Swede is involved in an automobile accident in which a child is injured and Ghote stays to comfort and help him at the risk of missing an urgent appointment. Keating uses the Swede's point of view, as an outsider, to give perspective on the imperfec-

tions of Indian life and society and to contrast Eastern and Western thought and attitudes toward life. But the final estimation of the problem of imperfection is left to Inspector Ghote's point of view. In the novel's last pages he meditates, "The Perfect Murder had in fact been all a mistake, a simple mistake in the dark. He should have expected as much in this land of imperfections: to be confronted with a very imperfect murder, with a victim who was not meant to have been a victim at all and an attack that had, naturally, been bungled. He might have known it would be like this all along, a triumph of the incompetent." Typically for Ghote, after considering his own imperfection and possible complicity in making things worse, he finally concludes, "It's all a great muddle. . . . But perhaps after all muddle is the only possible thing."

There has followed *The Perfect Murder*, at approximately yearly intervals, a series of novels using Inspector Ghote as their central character. Each novel tends to add information about the protagonist, but his presentation has remained remarkably consistent. He has grown, but the directions of the growth have always seemed implicit in the earlier characterizations. Keating has said simply that he has continued to make new discoveries about his protagonist. Constantly in the background, though infrequently depicted directly, are Ghote's much-loved though sometimes sharptongued wife, Protima, and his young son, Ved. By giving Ghote a home and family, hostages to fortune, Keating helps make particularly poignant Ghote's frequent fears of failure and underlines the ordinariness of the man. Keating has said in the *Contemporary Authors Autobiography Series* and elsewhere that there is much of himself in Ghote, in his modesty and very human insecurities as well as in his shrewdness.

Keating's study of India has enabled him to place his fictions among various groups and settings in that complicated and diverse land. He conveys the flavor of Ghote's Indian English effectively in his dialogue, particularly through the manipulation of progressive verb forms, through skillful placements of the adverb "only," through repetitions of words and phrases for emphasis, and through careful use of Anglo-Indian vocabulary. Other varieties of Indian English, spoken by members of other classes and ethnic groups, as Meera T. Clark (1984) has pointed out, are equally well represented and are carefully distinguished from each other. In an interview in *Contemporary Authors* (1986) Keating commented on his sensitivity to language: "I have this [attunement to the subtleties of expression] to a fair degree," he said, "so by reading novels and seeing films, by seeing even the subtitles on Hindi films, which are translated often not into English English but what they call Indian Variant English, I got a lot of it. And . . . I got hold of a splendid publication written in India with the object of telling Indians who speak English fairly well the differences between IVE, as they call it, and English English. . . . So I was able to use that in reverse; it's got a list of expressions which mean different things in the two 'languages.' " Thus, Keating learned to effectively convey the special cadences of English as spoken by Indians.

But it is not only in their use of the language that the Ghote novels are effective as local-color stories. Keating includes characters of various classes and ethnic groups, and his descriptions of places and events are filled with well-chosen details which convey a sense of life in India and of Indian cultures. Readers regularly learn of the ethnic or linguistic backgrounds of individual characters; Ghote himself is Maharashtrian, and his wife is Bengali. Sometimes, as in *The Perfect Murder*, the device of the outside observer helps create both distance from and an intimate introduction to the Indian scene. Some novels depict particular aspects of the society, as for instance, *Filmi, Filmi, Inspector Ghote* (1976), which studies the Bombay film industry, and *The Sheriff of Bombay: An Inspector Ghote Novel* (1984), an examination of prostitution in Bombay which Keating said in the *Contemporary Authors Autobiography Series* was based on the "subjectivity of our way of looking at things." Even *Inspector Ghote Caught in Meshes* (1967), a rather incredible tale of atomic spying, nevertheless reminds the reader of India's membership in the group of nations with the capability of fighting atomic war and studies the problem of conflicting loyalties, as Ghote is forced to balance his commitment to the police work which gives him his identity against his love for his country.

It was only in 1974, after the publication of over a half-dozen Ghote novels, that Keating was able to visit India. He was pleased to discover many things that he had gotten right along with some that he had missed, and he returned home with notebooks filled with details and ideas for future books. However, as Clark has suggested, those novels Keating has written about alien scenes he has recently visited tend to be more specifically and shallowly satiric and less believably

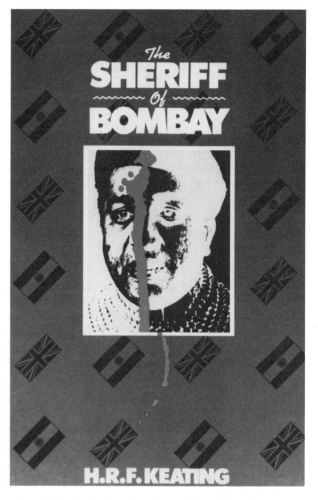

*Dust jacket for the first American edition of Keating's 1984
Inspector Ghote novel*

real and persuasive than those created more wholly from his imagination; examples in point are *Filmi, Filmi, Inspector Ghote* and *Go West, Inspector Ghote* (1981), the former written after that Indian tour and the latter after a trip to the United States.

Keating presents his policeman as dedicated, indeed unable to imagine any other sort of life. He is a disciple of Hans Gross's *Criminal Investigation*, which is frequently referred to as his companion and guide. His major investigative technique is stubborn, persistent plodding, as he follows clues, always doubting that he is understanding the clues rightly or pursuing them correctly. He sums it up himself in an early Ghote novel, *Inspector Ghote Plays a Joker* (1969): "The way to deal with a murder case is to find out who had the opportunity to kill the victim, where he was killed and when and exactly how, and then the identity of the killer is often plain enough.

And *bas.* Enough. Make sure of every step of your evidence and get him into court." Yet his successful solutions of crimes often result from intuitive leaps made at the inspiration of some apparently irrelevant observation: the onset of the monsoon in *The Perfect Murder*, the accidental viewing of some peacocks in *Inspector Ghote Hunts the Peacock* (1968), or the sight of the joker in a pack of cards in *Inspector Ghote Plays a Joker*, for instance. Keating balances logic and intuition with each other particularly effectively in these novels, each having its place, but with logic sometimes presented as an illusion and with intuition more reliably leading to truth.

Twice Keating took Inspector Ghote abroad, in novels that are interesting for their comment on cultural differences although they have not been considered among the most effective of the Ghote novels. *Inspector Ghote Hunts the Peacock* takes him to London, while thirteen years later *Go West, Inspector Ghote* is set in California. In both novels Ghote's Indian eyes are startled and, in varying degrees, horrified by much of what he observes about life in the West. The American novel is particularly astringent; here Ghote observes life on an American ashram—and what he sees seems to him to be a vulgarized misunderstanding of Hindu religious belief. Ironically, however, his major discovery is of the fakery of a Hindu holy man venerated by his American followers. In passing, the novel also looks with a jaundiced eye at California life in general; to Ghote it is shallow, materialistic, fast, and ugly, with the freeways being particularly nightmarish. He discovers, however, that one feature which he finds especially distasteful, the hot tub, makes him feel better. Keating indicated to Dale Salwak (1984) that, ironically, he was able to transpose materialism and mysticism, "so that in fact California represents the mystic and India represents the materialist." This is certainly true of the plot: Ghote comes to California on behalf of a worried Indian parent to rescue a young woman from a spiritual community that the father distrusts and fears. But the spirituality turns out to be a fake, and thematically the contrast between materialism and mysticism largely follows the expected pattern. One symbolic—and amusing—representation of the difference between the materialism of the West and the humanity of the East comes in methods of distinguishing truth from falsehood. Ghote is appalled by the very idea of the polygraph, but he finds that his own way of recognizing a truth teller, by the way the speaker's toes

are curled, is ineffective in a place where most feet are clad in shoes.

A more successful novel, *Inspector Ghote Hunts the Peacock* centers on the traditional theme of illusion and reality. Here the illusion is Ghote's expectation of what England will be like—a preconception based on his Indian colonial education. Ghote is sent to London to attend an international conference on drug trafficking. Typically, he is only third choice: his superior could not attend and, refusing to choose between two more-likely candidates as substitutes for fear of offending one of them, he sends Ghote. But to Ghote this trip is a dream come true.

From the moment of disembarking from the plane in Heathrow Airport, Ghote looks with wonder at everything he sees, trying to make it all fit into his preconceptions of England. And from the beginning his observations lead to a mixture of romantic delight and disillusioned regret. The "calm, order and dignity" he first observes agree perfectly with his expectations, and he is especially pleased by his first English bobby: "The figure in front of him really seemed to be exactly as he would have expected. He was all the pictures he had seen over the years come to life. Tall, loftily calm, helmeted, grave, clad from head to foot in dignified blue, he stood surveying the crowd before him with quiet aloofness." Ghote is delighted to muse that they are brothers, both policemen descended from a long and noble tradition.

But, as happens repeatedly throughout the novel whenever Ghote is moved by admiration for things British, he is rudely recalled to his own humble Indian self; his wife's cousin's husband hurls himself upon him and immediately plunges him into a family crisis. Thus, though Ghote has come to England on a police assignment of some importance, he finds himself occupying his time there largely in using his investigative skills to solve the mystery of the disappearance of a young family connection of his wife's.

Ghote discovers that his wife's London relatives, who run an Indian restaurant, are vociferously anti-British. In fact, in the way of many exiles, they self-consciously exaggerate their Indianness. To Ghote, with his respect for English traditions, especially English law, this is rather startling—and distasteful. At first he tries to place some distance between himself and his Indian connections. However, they do persuade him to undertake a search for the missing young woman, nicknamed "the Peacock" because of her flashy

under 1

1

Inspector Ghote had been ~~expecting~~ ^{awaiting} it for a week or more. But

when ~~a peon from the Commissioner's office brought him~~ the stiff

^(was brought into the) ^{experienced} ^{as}

white sealed envelope he ~~felt~~ a thud of despair/plummeting as

^{the message}

if ~~it~~/had been altogether a surprise. Yet without opening the

envelope he could have recited ~~word for word~~ more or less to the word the

^{words}

the ~~memo~~ it would contain.

The tingling oppressiveness of the pre-monsoon heat, ~~heavy in~~ hardly stirred by

the squeaking fan in

~~t~~ his little office, suddenly struck at him as if until now it had

not existed.

Automatically, with the envelope ^(surreptitiously, intent,) ~~sweat~~-stained from the ~~peon's~~

of the peon who had delivered it

fingers/still lying squarely in front of him, he reached down to

the bottom-most drawer of his desk for the ~~small~~ towel he kept there

perspiration

and ~~with it~~ mopped at the heavy bulbs of ~~sweat~~ that had sprung up

all over his face and neck.

Then, ~~unable to control a trembling in his hands~~, he roughly &

tore open the envelope.

inside

The memo/ as he had known it would be, was brief.

From the Commissioner of Police, Bombay

To: Inspector G.V. Ghote

I have considered the events alleged to have occurred at

Vigatpore P.S. on the night of June 24 last and I must request

a full account of your part therein. I require to have the

Dating OK

aforesaid account before me by ~~Xxxxx~~ 0900 hours on Monday, June ~~24~~.

He felt sick. Sick as if he had become suddenly stricken by food poisoning.

Inspector Ghote felt from the first a sullen anger at his abrupt

transfer to take charge of Vigatpore Police Station. He knew that

he should not let the feeling persist. He ought to be tackling

this assignment, whatever the circumstances it had been handed down

Page from the revised typescript for Under a Monsoon Cloud *(courtesy of the author)*

beauty. And these investigations take Ghote into parts of London and of British life that he would never have penetrated had he, as he originally wished, stayed in a London hotel and spent all his time attending the conference and seeing the conventional tourist attractions.

As he observes more and more of English life and people, Ghote becomes more and more disillusioned. Keating selects the miniskirt as Ghote's principal symbol of the differences between the shameless Western lack of inhibition, even decadence, he observes and the Indian decorum whose value he comes consciously to recognize by contrast. And gradually, with both regret and relief, he realizes that he is out of place in England, that being a colonial from a society much influenced by British culture only makes it more difficult for him to fit in, for the resemblances he finds reassuring turn out to be deceptive and only send him into greater confusion.

In the *Contemporary Authors Autobiography Series* Keating has described this novel as centering around the "problem of pride, how much you should have of it," and it is surely no accident that in it this constitutionally humble man meets with even greater embarrassments than usual. Undertaking to follow a suspect, he undergoes a series of humiliations which include being shouted at and bested by several small street urchins and which climax with his standing under a grate from which a dog bathes him from head to foot with urine. His dreamed of–and feared–moment of public recognition, presenting his superior's paper, also turns into a moment of shame, as he repeatedly loses his place, repeats himself, and generally turns the paper into gibberish as he sneezes his way through it.

In his usual way, however, Ghote finally prevails–and in prevailing comes to a more balanced and realistic view of England and the English. In his moment of deepest despair and humiliation, he sees some real peacocks–gloriously beautiful and yet greedy–and through a typical sleight of intuition finds things suddenly falling into place. He realizes the truth about the disappearance of the human Peacock and turns his wife's cousin's husband in to the English police as a murderer. Though "the Peacock" had worn the hated miniskirt, symbolizing her corruption by British society and alienation from Indian culture, her death, he realizes, was caused by a combination of evils from both societies: she had learned that her foster parent was a taker of opium and had attempted to blackmail him, and

thus she had instigated her own murder. Even the scorned miniskirts come, in Ghote's final reconciliation to the land which had so disillusioned him, to seem almost benign: he observes some young girls wearing them and thinks that they after all "breathe an air of half-innocent enjoyment of the gifts nature had given them. They were no doubt much the same as young girls anywhere else, only with more confidence." And he goes off to buy for Protima a china teapot he had earlier looked at and angrily rejected.

Inspector Ghote Hunts the Peacock was an experiment, inspired by the frequent requests of readers that Keating take Ghote to England. Although Keating was not particularly happy with the result, it is an effective presentation of some aspects of London life in the 1960s, made sharp by their being seen from the perspective of a naive outsider with exaggerated and romantic schoolboy notions of England and the English. It is effectively built around the theme of appearance and reality through both its mystery plot and Ghote's fluctuating responses to the England he observes. It is worth noting that in both this novel and in *Go West, Inspector Ghote*, Keating's protagonist is taken abroad on errands for Indian superiors (to deliver his chief's paper; to discover the whereabouts of a young Indian woman of good family who has been studying in California), and while abroad he discovers transplanted Indians who have been corrupted both by their assimilation into and their rejection of the West. Keating's use of the naive yet perceptive viewpoint of Ghote enables him to comment trenchantly on aspects of British life, even while the contrast between East and West, seen through Ghote, reflects the imperfections of India as well.

Prior to the publication of *Under a Monsoon Cloud* (1986), the warmest and most profoundly humane of the Ghote novels was *Inspector Ghote Trusts the Heart* (1972). The theme of this novel is the conflict between intellect and emotion, its title indicating the bias of the novel. The small son of a rich man's tailor is kidnapped by mistake, and the kidnappers then demand a ransom from the employer. The tailor's anguish is wrenchingly though briefly depicted; a more detailed and complex portrait is that of Mr. Desai, the rich man, who vacillates between denying any responsibility and risking his own life to save the child. Ghote's conflict is between his obligation to obey the orders of his superior and his sympathy for the child and his father, since that tenderness directs him to disobey and to follow unorthodox

Keating on the cover of Bombay *magazine, 1987 (*Bombay, The City Magazine, *Bombay, India)*

methods. Duty and compassion are set at odds. Finally, Ghote solves the mystery and rescues the boy as a result of obeying his heart, against orders, and though he expects to be accused of disobedience to a superior officer and, ironically, of risking the rescue mission, he feels the conclusion of the case is "satisfactory" because the child is safe. Keating refuses to surrender to the implicit temptation to romanticize any of his characters here: Mr. Desai, despite his occasional flashes of heroism, is basically materialistic and selfish, and the child, when readers finally see him at his rescue, has been so brutalized by his experience that he seems little more than an animal with whom even Ghote finds it difficult to sympathize.

To date, the most startlingly innovative of the Ghote novels is *Under a Monsoon Cloud.* Here Inspector Ghote, the devoted policeman, himself becomes a criminal, and his primary dilemma is the conflict between his duty as a policeman and his conviction that in the long run he can best serve the law and justice by an illegal act. What he does is instigate and carry through the cover-up of a homicide, because the killer is a superior

whom he respects most highly, and he therefore believes that his mentor's life of dedication–and promise of continued future service–outweighs a nearly accidental killing done in a moment of great anger. Almost from the moment of manufacturing a fake drowning to conceal the facts of the killing, however, Ghote is tormented by guilt. And when his guilt causes him to let slip a piece of truth that will undoubtedly lead to the revelation of both the crimes and the cover-up, his mentor commits suicide, leaving Ghote with an even heavier burden of guilt.

Protima, Ghote's wife, plays a more prominent role in this novel than in most, and she here represents practicality. When Ghote confides in her, she urges him to continue the lie, and through much of the novel he vacillates, unable either to make a firm decision to reveal his complicity in crime and accept the consequences for himself (and for his wife and son) or to continue in a lie which denies his entire previous life. Finally, however, after having perjured himself in court, he does confess in a police inquiry and is found guilty. The Presiding Officer at first says he will recommend that which Ghote had most feared, his dismissal from the police force, but then he refuses to sign the papers: underlining the seriousness of the dilemma presented by the novel, he expresses sympathy for Ghote's motives.

Thus it all seems to have blown over, and the final scene shows Ghote with Protima and Ved relaxing at the beach. Readers observe that at least Ghote has learned to control his anger, not waste it as his mentor had in the killing which began the novel's chain of events. The central problem which Keating examines might be restated as that of ends and means, and the final solution somewhat ambiguously reinforces the principle that good ends must not be tainted by corrupt means. Ghote has undergone a testing of greater depth and seriousness than in any of the earlier novels. He is still the same humble, self-effacing, insecure man, but he has learned lessons of a profundity that should make him both a finer man and a more humane policeman.

In addition to his crime fiction, Keating has written several "mainstream" novels and has written and edited several books about the mystery form and mystery writers. *Sherlock Holmes: The Man and His World* (1979) won an Edgar in 1980. His youthful conviction that the crime novel had no worldly implications has long since evaporated. His practice of centering each mystery around some philosophical theme or dilemma (violence, the lie, loyalties, head and heart, pride, and so on) is excellent evidence against that naive conception, which Keating has recently been at pains to deny, in such publications as *Contemporary Authors Autobiography Series*.

In his introduction to *Whodunit? A Guide to Crime, Suspense and Spy Fiction* (1982), Keating defines crime fiction as "fiction that is written primarily as entertainment and has as its subject some form of crime, crime taken in its widest possible meaning. Crime writing is fiction that puts the reader first, not the writer." Pleasing the reader, then, is the first obligation accepted by the mystery writer, and the inclusion of a message, of "telling the reader something," is secondary, although Keating's own mysteries generally begin with a philosophical idea. He notes that the mystery writer has a "whole bag of goodies that the literary novel often goes without"–such as the puzzle, the happy ending, action and violence, as

well as "beauty of form" and the knowledge "that, however it looks in the horrid world, justice will eventually be done."

Keating stands at the forefront of those writing in the vein of the traditional mystery today, both for his use of conventional forms and motifs and for his originality within the constrictions of the genre. His understanding of his form is penetrating, and his practice has been skilled. His creation, Inspector Ghote, may not be of equal stature with Sherlock Holmes, Lord Peter Wimsey, and Hercule Poirot, but he is more human than any of these great predecessors. His very fallibility and humility make him a refreshing contrast to his literary ancestors. But most particularly, Keating's use of the mystery novel simply as a novel which tells a story and says something about the human condition places him among the leaders of his craft.

In his autobiographical statement for *Contemporary Authors Autobiography Series*, Keating summed up his understanding of the contribution of his Ghote novels. "One of the things I have come to realize the Ghote books do is to show us our common humanity through emphasising the differences in the relatively less important areas of life between the Indian way (say, arranged marriages) and the Western (love matches). The books show, I hope, that the real fundamentals, the actual love of one human being for another, the anger that comes to us all wherever we live, the yearning for perfection that can bloom in an Indian as easily as in a Briton or an American, are what we all share. And in showing that, I trust, they earn their keep in the world." Indeed they do.

Interviews:

Meera T. Clark, "H. R. F. Keating: An Interview," *Clues: A Journal of Detection*, 4 (Fall/Winter 1983): 43-65;

Dale Salwak, "An Interview with H. R. F. Keating," *Clues: A Journal of Detection*, 5 (Fall/Winter 1984): 82-92.

Reference:

Meera T. Clark, "H. R. F. Keating," in *Twelve Englishmen of Mystery*, edited by Earl F. Bargainnier (Bowling Green, Ohio: Bowling Green University Popular Press, 1984).

John le Carré
(David John Moore Cornwell)
(19 October 1931-)

Joan DelFattore
University of Delaware

BOOKS: *Call for the Dead* (London: Gollancz, 1961; New York: Walker, 1962); republished as *The Deadly Affair* (Harmondsworth: Penguin, 1964);

A Murder of Quality (London: Gollancz, 1962; New York: Walker, 1963);

The Spy Who Came In from the Cold (London: Gollancz, 1963; New York: Coward-McCann, 1964);

The Looking-Glass War (London: Heinemann, 1965; New York: Coward-McCann, 1965);

A Small Town in Germany (London: Heinemann, 1968; New York: Coward-McCann, 1968);

The Naive and Sentimental Lover (London: Hodder & Stoughton, 1971; New York: Knopf, 1971);

Tinker, Tailor, Soldier, Spy (New York: Knopf, 1974; London: Hodder & Stoughton, 1974);

The Honourable Schoolboy (London: Hodder & Stoughton, 1977; New York: Knopf, 1977);

Smiley's People (London: Hodder & Stoughton, 1980; New York: Knopf, 1980);

The Little Drummer Girl (New York: Knopf, 1983; London: Hodder & Stoughton, 1983);

A Perfect Spy (London: Hodder & Stoughton, 1986; New York: Knopf, 1986);

Vanishing England, by le Carré and Gareth H. Davies (Topsfield, Mass.: Salem House, 1987);

The Russia House (London: Hodder & Stoughton, 1989; New York: Knopf, 1989).

OTHER: Bruce Page, David Leitch, and Phillip Knightley, *The Philby Conspiracy*, introduction by le Carré (Garden City, N.Y.: Doubleday, 1968), pp. 1-16.

PERIODICAL PUBLICATIONS: "Dare I Weep, Dare I Mourn," *Saturday Evening Post*, 240 (28 January 1967): 54-56, 60;

"What Ritual Is Being Observed Tonight?," *Saturday Evening Post*, 241 (2 November 1968): 60-62, 64-65.

John le Carré (photograph by Stephen Cornwell)

John le Carré (pseudonym of David John Moore Cornwell) is the author of realistic spy stories resembling those of Eric Ambler and Graham Greene. His best-known novels are *The Spy Who Came In from the Cold* (1963) and the George Smiley trilogy: *Tinker, Tailor, Soldier, Spy* (1974), *The Honourable Schoolboy* (1977), and *Smiley's People* (1980). Le Carré was born in Poole, Dorset, on 19 October 1931. His father, Ronald Thomas Archibald Cornwell, had left school at the age of fourteen and embarked upon a series of financial speculations which were often unsuccessful and occasionally illegal. As le Carré later remarked (*Time*, 3 October 1977), "He was like Gatsby. He lived in a contradictory world. There was always credit, but we never had any cash, not a penny. My father would occupy a house and default, then move to another one. He had an amazing, Micawber-like talent for messing up his business adventures." When le Carré was still a child, his father was convicted of fraud and sentenced to his first prison term. Shortly afterward le Carré's mother, the former Olive Glassy, left her husband and moved in with one of his business associates. Cornwell later divorced her and remarried twice, and le Carré did not see his mother again until he was twenty years of age. He and his brother, Tony, spent some time with relatives who refused to discuss either parent, and le Carré later claimed that his earliest experience of espionage was his attempt to piece together, from the little that he and his brother managed to overhear, some explanation for his mother's desertion and his father's frequent absences. He concluded at one point that his father must be a spy, called away to perform dangerous missions for the good of his country.

As a result of his family's frequent moves le Carré never settled into one school or felt at home with one group of friends. At first he had the companionship of his brother, two years his senior, upon whom he was very dependent; but later their father, deciding that his sons should be more self-sufficient, sent them to boarding schools thirty miles apart. Although the two boys usually spent Sundays together, bicycling to a point halfway between the two schools, le Carré felt abandoned. This sense of isolation, which he experienced through most of his childhood and youth, is reflected in the loneliness and alienation of his fictional protagonists.

Le Carré's last preparatory school was Sherborne, in Dorset (scene of the musical film *Goodbye, Mr. Chips*). There he was a reasonably successful student, and at the age of sixteen he won his first award for literature, the school prize for English verse. However, at this point he decided that he had had enough of school life, and he informed the headmaster that he would not return to Sherborne for his final year. Thoroughly annoyed, his father sent him to Switzerland, where they had relatives, in order to spend a year studying German language and literature at the University of Bern.

Dust jacket for the first edition of le Carré's 1963 best-seller featuring George Smiley

On his return to England in 1949 le Carré joined the army and was assigned to the intelligence corps. Because of his proficiency in German he was sent to Vienna, where he encountered Eastern European refugees who had been imprisoned by both the Axis and the Allies. He also encountered Royal Air Force officers who, having bombed Berlin four years earlier, had returned to assist with the airlift and relief programs. The ironic inconsistencies of political institutions, and the ruthless disregard of those in power for the rights and well-being not only of their enemies and victims but also of their own agents, made a lasting impression on le Carré and became the major themes of his best work. "It was," he observed in *Time*, "like reading the right book at the right time. I saw the right *things* at the right time."

When he left the army le Carré was persuaded by his father to resume his university studies. Despite, or perhaps because of, his own legal difficulties, Cornwell wanted both of his sons to be lawyers. Le Carré's brother had read law at Cambridge and had been called to the bar, but he had left immediately afterward for North America. (He eventually became one of the directors of a Manhattan advertising agency.) Le Carré himself, who had no interest in the law, read modern languages at Lincoln College, Oxford. In 1954, while he was still at Oxford, le Carré married Alison Ann Veronica Sharp, daughter of a field marshal in the Royal Air Force. Shortly after his marriage he accepted a teaching position at Millfield Junior School in Glastonbury, Somerset, but after a year he returned to Oxford, where he took a degree in modern languages in 1956.

After taking his degree le Carré spent two years at Eton as a tutor in French and German. As he told *Current Biography* (1974), his reactions to Eton were mixed: "In some ways, those who knock the upper classes have no idea how awful they are. Eton, at its worst, is unbelievably frightful. It is intolerant, chauvinistic, bigoted, ignorant. At its best, it is enlightened, adaptable, fluent, and curiously democratic." He left Eton in 1958 and attempted to make a living as a painter and illustrator, but without success. He had no desire to return to teaching, so when he saw an advertisement for late entrants into the Foreign Office, he answered it. Largely because of his proficiency in French and German he was accepted.

While commuting by train between the Foreign Office in London and his home in Great Missenden, Buckinghamshire, le Carré wrote his first novel, *Call for the Dead* (1961; republished as *The Deadly Affair*, 1964). It introduces George Smiley, the brilliant, prosaic spy who was to become le Carré's series protagonist. Le Carré's conception of the character is clear and virtually complete in the introductory chapter of *Call for the Dead:* he is a nearsighted, unobtrusive middle-aged man, deceptively mild and painstaking to the point of genius. Smiley is the antithesis of the glamorous spy-hero epitomized by Ian Fleming's James Bond. A timid and inexpert driver, he wears expensive but ill-fitting clothing and is often cuckolded by his wife, who addresses him as "my darling teddy-bear" or "toad." His hobby, like le Carré's, is doing scholarly research on obscure seventeenth-century German poets.

Although Smiley is a member of the British Secret Service, *Call for the Dead* is essentially a detective story rather than a spy story. Smiley, having cleared a member of the Foreign Office, Samuel Arthur Fennan, of the charge of being a

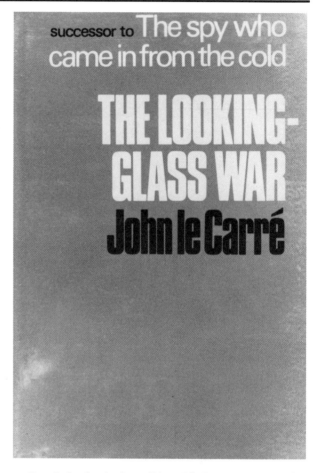

Dust jacket for the first edition of le Carré's 1965 novel

Communist sympathizer, learns that Fennan is believed to have committed suicide and soon suspects that he has been murdered. The chief clue is suggested by the title of the novel: the dead man had requested a wake-up telephone call for the morning following his supposed suicide. With the help of Peter Guillam and Inspector Mendel, who also appear in later stories, he identifies both Fennan's murderer and the head of an East German spy ring. However, in his single-minded determination to solve the case, Smiley commits an act of ruthlessness which appears to him, upon reflection, to have been a betrayal of his principles and of his humanity. In order to avoid further conflicts between his duty and his honor, he resigns from the Secret Service. *Call for the Dead* thus includes a comparatively simple and straightforward version of themes which were to appear in le Carré's later novels in increasingly elaborate and sophisticated forms: the tension between man and his institutions, the sacrifice of truth to expediency, and the loss of humanity in the drive for efficiency. Further, Smiley's personal dilemma and the corresponding conflicts of supporting characters in the novel illustrate le Carré's tendency to incorporate into the traditional suspense-story format an unusual depth of characterization, not by endowing his characters with a wide range of personal quirks or external mannerisms, but by identifying in them a consistent and complex philosophical or ethical viewpoint.

In 1967 *Call for the Dead* was filmed under the title *The Deadly Affair*, with James Mason in the role of Smiley, who is for no apparent reason renamed Charles Dobbs. Simone Signoret, Maximilian Schell, and Lynn Redgrave also appear. Sidney Lumet directed the film, which is a reasonably faithful adaptation of the novel, although it is an uneven production, wavering between suspense and fast-paced action on one hand, and pointless, didactic conversation on the other.

When *Call for the Dead* was accepted for publication, its author had to choose a pseudonym because members of the Foreign Office were not encouraged to publish fiction under their own names. He used one of his middle names and a name he claims to have appropriated from a sign in a London shop window. Since "le carré" means "the square," the name may have suggested a slangy pun on his realistically unglamorous portrayal of life in the Secret Service, as opposed to the gimmicks-girls-and-guns approach of Fleming, whose James Bond books were approaching the height of their popularity when le Carré wrote *Call for the Dead*.

In 1961 le Carré was posted to the British embassy in Bonn, where he served as second secretary; and, while commuting between his home and his office, he wrote his second novel. Like many second novels, it is not quite as good as the first. *A Murder of Quality* (1962) is a detective story in which Smiley, having resigned from the Secret Service, investigates at the request of a friend the murder of a schoolmaster's wife. The murder victim, like Daphne du Maurier's Rebecca, is first portrayed as having been an exemplary woman and then, gradually, is exposed as having been a scheming virago; and her murderer is, in a sense, her victim. As he does in *Call for the Dead*, Smiley persists in seeking answers to seemingly unimportant questions upon which, in the end, the solution rests. However, because he possesses, in the words of one of his former superiors, "the cunning of Satan and the conscience of a virgin," Smiley is unprepared for the human consequences of his professional success. Having applied himself single-mindedly to solving the

murder puzzle, he realizes as he confronts the murderer that he does not want to hand this man over to be hanged, but the realization comes too late.

Le Carré, who had been a schoolmaster himself, was praised for his trenchant portrayal of the British public school community which serves as the background for this novel. However, although—or perhaps because—many of the characters in it are based on single individuals rather than on composites or types, they are more shallow than the supporting characters in le Carré's earlier novel. Further, because Smiley faces no convincing personal dilemma until the end of the story, it lacks the sustained internal conflict of le Carré's best work.

Both *Call for the Dead* and *A Murder of Quality* enjoyed a reasonable degree of critical and commercial success, but le Carré, who by the mid 1960s had three sons, found it impossible to give up his position in the Foreign Office to become a full-time writer. Therefore, his third novel, like its predecessors, was written when he could spare the time from his official duties. When *The Spy Who Came In from the Cold* was published, le Carré, who was then a British consul in Hamburg, is said to have laughingly instructed his accountant to inform him if his bank balance ever reached twenty thousand pounds, the sum he felt that he had to have in reserve before he could afford to resign. Much to his surprise the book was a best-seller. His balance rose far above the required figure, and in February 1964 he became a full-time writer.

The Spy Who Came In from the Cold received the most enthusiastic reviews accorded to any novel of espionage since Eric Ambler's *The Mask of Dimitrios* (1939). Graham Greene, with whom le Carré is often compared, called it "the best spy novel I have ever read"; J. B. Priestley wrote that it is "superbly constructed with an atmosphere of chilly hell"; and Anthony Boucher declared that it places le Carré "beside Ambler and Greene in the small rank of writers who can create a novel of significance, while losing none of the excitement of a tale of sheer adventure." Le Carré also received the Crime Writers' Association's Gold Dagger Award for 1963 and the W. Somerset Maugham Award for 1964. The commercial success of the book was as great as its critical success, and within ten years the worldwide sales of *The Spy Who Came In from the Cold* had reached twenty million copies.

Dust jacket for the first American edition of le Carré's 1968 novel

Unlike le Carré's earlier work, *The Spy Who Came In from the Cold* is not a detective story but a novel of espionage. It introduces the recurrent character of Control, the unscrupulous and unfeeling head of the Secret Service, which Smiley is eventually prevailed upon to rejoin. Smiley is not, however, the protagonist of this novel, although he appears briefly. Its protagonist is Alec Leamas, former head of the British spy network in East Germany. Leamas is requested by Control to take the leading role in an attempt to discredit Hans-Dieter Mundt, head of operations for the East German Abteilung, who was responsible for the elimination of all the agents who had made up Leamas's network. Leamas willingly undertakes the destruction of Mundt, whom he regards not only as a professional target but also as a personal antagonist. He finds, however, that the plan does not proceed as Control had said it would; and then he realizes, gradually and reluc-

tantly, that Control had never intended that it should. Leamas is caught in a magnificently conceived multiple-cross: not only does he find himself in a situation in which nothing outside himself is as it seems to be; not only does he, in carrying out orders which he believes will lead to one result, unwittingly and unwillingly contribute to bringing about its opposite; but, in the very act of disobeying Control's orders and taking steps to abort his plan, Leamas completes the plan, because by defying Control at that particular point he does exactly what Control had expected and hoped he would do. However, although Control succeeds in double-crossing his opponents by triple-crossing his own agent, Control appears only briefly in the novel and is seldom even mentioned. As a result, the novel centers almost exclusively on characters who have no means of determining or even of anticipating the effects of their own actions. The novel thus projects the vision of a Hardyesque, absurd universe in which free will is negated by ignorance, self-determination is an illusion, and trust is an act of insanity.

Le Carré solved the enormous technical problems involved in presenting a story of this complexity by focusing very closely on the character of Leamas, so that the reader views events through Leamas's eyes and usually penetrates a particular layer of plot only when he does. As a result, although *The Spy Who Came In from the Cold* is occasionally bewildering, the confusion does not concern what is happening, but why it is happening; and that confusion is in itself an integral part of the story's meaning. Further, the close identification of Leamas's perceptions with the plot itself and with the reader's experience of the story contributes to the psychological depth which le Carré, like Ambler and Greene, succeeded in incorporating into an essentially cerebral form of literature.

The film rights to *The Spy Who Came In from the Cold* were purchased by Paramount shortly after the novel was published, and in 1965 the film was released. It stars Richard Burton as Alec Leamas, with Claire Bloom, Oskar Werner, Sam Wanamaker, Cyril Cusack, and Bernard Lee in supporting roles. This film, which is extremely faithful to the book, was made in grainy black and white to emphasize the harsh realism of the story. The absence of color and the comparative slowness of the action also serve to underline the contrast between this film and the romantic spy films epitomized by the James Bond series. Al-

Dust jacket for the first American editions of le Carré's 1974 novel in which Smiley comes out of retirement to locate a mole in the Circus and its 1977 sequel

though it was not a box office success when it was first released, *The Spy Who Came In from the Cold* is considered by most critics to be a landmark in the development of the realistic spy film. The screenwriters, Paul Dehn and Guy Trosper, were nominated for the Writers Guild Award.

The success of *The Spy Who Came In from the Cold* catapulted le Carré into the celebrity circuit, where he was distracted by people who wanted to lionize, interview, photograph, gush over, or shake hands with him. He promptly withdrew to Crete, and then to Vienna, to work on his next book.

Le Carré's fourth novel repeats the central themes of *The Spy Who Came In from the Cold*, but it lacks the complexity and the brilliance of its predecessor. *The Looking-Glass War* (1965) concerns a minor and almost extinct branch of the British Secret Service, whose chief, Leclerc, tries to revitalize his department and to bolster his own ego by sending an agent into East Germany

to investigate a rumor of Russian troop activity. The mission is quite unnecessary from an operational point of view, but Leclerc is anxious to assert his right to run agents, thus challenging the monopoly of the Circus, the branch of the Secret Service run by Control. In an apparently uncharacteristic burst of generosity, Control provides Leclerc with a radio set and crystals to be used by the agent, Leiser. However, the set is twenty years out of date, and Leiser, poorly trained and poorly equipped, has almost no chance of survival. As he crosses into East Germany he finds it necessary to kill a young border guard, which focuses the attention of the police on the area and unnerves Leiser himself. Upset by the police activity and by his own guilt for having killed the guard, Leiser not only broadcasts very slowly, but also forgets to change crystals and frequencies when communicating with his superiors, who have remained on the West German side of the border. When Control learns, through connections in the Foreign Office, that the East German police have picked up Leiser's signal and are ready to arrest him during his next broadcast, he delightedly sends Smiley to West Germany to inform Leclerc and his associates that they must abandon Leiser. Control's continued monopoly over the running of agents is thus assured.

In *The Looking-Glass War* le Carré abandoned the single narrative viewpoint of *The Spy Who Came In from the Cold* to portray a variety of responses to the central themes of treachery, duplicity, and abandonment. Leclerc, like Control, is concerned with the success of the mission only as it affects his own prestige and that of his department; he abandons Leiser with a shrug of the shoulders and sets about salvaging what he can of his department's importance. An alternative point of view is provided by Leclerc's naive young associate, Avery, who, horrified by Leclerc's casual abandonment of Leiser, weeps for Leiser and for his own lost ideals. Smiley, too, abhors the callous indifference with which the men in power view individual agents, but his understanding of the duplicity involved is much more sophisticated than Avery's. He realizes that the service's breach of faith with Leiser goes much deeper than simple abandonment because he knows that Control, in addition to providing an antiquated radio set, had deliberately warned the East German police to listen for Leiser's signal. He also realizes that it is futile to respond to such duplicity, as Avery does, by trying to obstruct it or by weeping over it. Leiser never quite understands what has happened to him but retains his humanity and performs his futile mission with genuine, if misguided, courage.

Although *The Looking-Glass War* provides the complexity of a variety of viewpoints, it is in some respects a short story padded into a novel. Individual episodes, such as Leiser's period of training, are stretched far beyond the requirements of plot, theme, or effect; and conversations whose only purpose is the exploration of moral or ethical concepts slow the action of the novel and give it an undertone of didacticism. However, despite its faults *The Looking-Glass War* is an entertaining novel which explores, from a complicated and technically demanding perspective, the mechanism of betrayal. The book received mixed reviews, but, aided perhaps by the momentum from *The Spy Who Came In from the Cold*, it became a best-seller, and le Carré received the Mystery Writers of America Edgar Allan Poe Award for 1965.

Dust jacket for the first edition of le Carré's 1980 Smiley novel

In 1970 *The Looking-Glass War* was made into a film by Columbia Pictures, starring Christopher Jones, Pia Degermark, Ralph Richardson, and Anthony Hopkins. Unlike the film of *The Spy Who Came In from the Cold*, the film of *The Looking-Glass War* is quite different from the novel on which it is based. Leiser, who is a nondescript middle-aged man in the novel and whose age and appearance are an important part of his characterization, appears in the film as a conspicuously handsome young man who is frequently seen shirtless. The screenplay was written by the director of the film, Frank R. Pierson, who inserted a number of action scenes which serve no apparent purpose except to provide opportunities for stunt work. The film is confusing and episodic, exaggerating the faults of the novel and bypassing its virtues.

In a few of the scenes in *The Looking-Glass War*, such as those relating to the domestic situations of the characters involved in the plot, le Carré introduced elements of the "straight" novel as opposed to the thriller. He moved further in this direction in his next book, *A Small Town in Germany* (1968), in which the defection of Leo Harting, a minor official in the British embassy in Bonn, is considered from several viewpoints. Like *Call for the Dead* and *A Murder of Quality*, *A Small Town in Germany* involves a great deal of detective work, but here the detective and espionage genres are more integrated, as an investigator from the Security Department in London attempts to discover what has become of Harting and of the top-secret file that disappeared with him. These composite thriller elements are wedded to the "straight" novel by means of the emphasis that le Carré places upon the personal and, in some cases, romantic motivations underlying activities which appear, on the surface, to be purely political. For example, Harting has a personal grudge against Karfeld, leader of a German antiparliamentary movement, whom he hopes to destroy by means of the circumstances of his own defection. Meadowes, an embassy official, is at odds with investigator Alan Turner because of an extremely unpleasant incident involving Meadowes's daughter; and the reaction of the head of chancery, Bradfield, to Harting's defection is influenced by Bradfield's knowledge that Harting has been his wife's lover. The personal motivations thus revealed add depth to the characters and poignancy to otherwise uninteresting episodes and contribute to the plausibility of the story by creating the illusion of a behind-the-scenes look at a real-life political news item. Further, the emphasis that le Carré places on personal motivations makes it clear that the action of the novel is not based on the characters' responses to events impinging on them, as is often the case in pure thrillers, but on conflicts created by the interplay of the characters themselves. However, the continuity and the total effect of *A Small Town in Germany* suffer from le Carré's failure to blend rather than alternate the literary genres he was combining. Much of the novel is presented as a series of dramatic action scenes followed by explanations of their personal or romantic background, which has the effect of superimposing on the genuine complexity of the story an element of unnecessary and unproductive structural confusion.

A Small Town in Germany became a bestseller, although neither this novel nor *The Looking-Glass War* enjoyed the success of *The Spy Who Came In from the Cold*. Critical response to *A Small Town in Germany* was mixed. Some reviewers felt that le Carré's own experience as a consul in Bonn, where his responsibilities had included reporting on political movements within Germany, contributed greatly to the plausibility and sophistication of the political background of the story; and that, in addition to sustaining interest as a spy story, *A Small Town in Germany* provided interesting and valid sociological commentary on British institutions and customs. Others, however, felt that the novel lacks excitement, and that in combining several fictional genres it fails to do justice to any. Malcolm Muggeridge, one of the severest of these critics, condemned the entire book as "remarkably silly."

After moving steadily in the direction of the "straight" novel in his first five books, le Carré finally abandoned the thriller genre altogether in his sixth book to write a psychological/romantic story, *The Naive and Sentimental Lover* (1971), based in part on a short story, "What Ritual Is Being Observed Tonight?," which he had published in the *Saturday Evening Post* in 1968. Some critics believe that *The Naive and Sentimental Lover* is a roman à clef, responding to *Some Gorgeous Accident*, a novel written by a friend of le Carré's, James Kellavar.

Le Carré told *Current Biography* that both the title and the central conflict of *The Naive and Sentimental Lover* are based on Friedrich von Schiller's observation that "a poet either *is* nature, and naive, or *seeks* nature, and is sentimental." The sentimental lover in the novel is Aldo Cassidy, a successful manufacturer of baby carriage accessories; the naive lover is Shamus, an unconventional and highly colorful artist. Both men are in love with a woman aptly named Helen. Although it is not a thriller, *The Naive and Sentimental Lover* expresses many of the same themes as le Carré's earlier work, particularly with reference to the conflict between individuals and the institutions that trap and betray them. Nevertheless, the novel was critically and commercially unsuccessful. The reviewer for the *Times Literary Supplement* (24 September 1971) called the book "a disastrous failure," and the reviewer for the *Spectator* (6 July 1974) called it "appalling." Shortly after the publication of *The Naive and Sentimental Lover* le Carré and his first wife were divorced, and both promptly remarried. Le Carré's second wife, Valerie Jane Eustace, had been an editor employed by the publishing firm of Hodder and Stoughton in London. Their son, Nicholas, was born in 1972.

After the negative reception of *The Naive and Sentimental Lover* le Carré decided to return to a combination of the "straight" novel and the thriller, and to his original protagonist, George Smiley. In *Tinker, Tailor, Soldier, Spy* Smiley, having been forced to retire from the Circus because of a change of administration following the death of Control, is drawn back into the world of British espionage when Oliver Lacon, a civil servant acting as liaison between the Secret Service and the appropriate ministries in Whitehall, asks him to investigate a rumor that the security of the Circus has been breached by an Englishman acting as a Russian agent-in-place: in espionage jargon, a "mole." The plot was suggested by the scandal which had erupted in 1963 when Kim Philby, a senior and highly placed member of British intelligence, escaped to Moscow after years of unsuspected treachery.

The presence of the mole, whose code name is "Gerald," is suggested to Control by fragmentary but highly suspicious bits of evidence. Further, the nature of the mole's activities and the quality of the material to which he evidently has access make it clear to Control that the mole must be one of five people: Percy Alleline, a Circus official who would become chief after Control's death, code-named Tinker; Bill Haydon, head of London Station, code-named Tailor; Roy Bland, code-named Soldier; Toby Esterhase, head of the Acton Lamp-lighters organization (couriers, overseas supplies, communications), code-named Poorman; or Smiley himself, code-named Beggarman. Smiley is eliminated from the list of suspects because of the circumstances surrounding his enforced retirement from the Circus after Control's death; and, with the help of Peter Guillam, still in the Circus but in disfavor with the new administration, Smiley sets out to track down the mole.

Because Smiley's search for the mole, Gerald, takes the form of painstaking, often tedious burrowing through Circus records and through the sometimes rambling recollections of former Circus employees, and because it involves a limited number of clearly identified suspects, *Tinker, Tailor, Soldier, Spy* is an excellent example of the blending of detective-fiction conventions into a novel of espionage. Further, in this novel le Carré finally succeeds in effectively incorporating elements of "straight" fiction into a thriller plot. *Tinker, Tailor, Soldier, Spy* is, in many respects, a novel of manners centering around the inhabitants of Britain's secret world, detailing their habits of dress, speech, and social intercourse. Because these observations are actually clues to the

identity of Gerald, however, they not only provide human interest but also further the plot. Similarly, Smiley's relationship with his unfaithful wife, Ann, closely parallels his experience with the Circus, which simultaneously attracts and betrays him. It also parallels Gerald's relationship with the country of his birth and with his Russian masters, and it serves as an integral part of the plot against England. This plot was conceived by Karla, head of the branch of Soviet Intelligence which corresponds to the Circus, and carried out by Gerald. Unlike *The Looking-Glass War* and, to a lesser degree, *A Small Town in Germany*, which merely add elements of "straight" fiction to a thriller plot, *Tinker, Tailor, Soldier, Spy* is a thriller which is, equally and inseparably, a "straight" novel.

The structure of *Tinker, Tailor, Soldier, Spy* resembles that of a set of Russian dolls, each opening up to reveal a smaller doll inside. Each layer of the plot thus presented reveals not only new factual material, but also new insight into the philosophical or ethical basis of the novel. Unlike le Carré's earlier work, notably *The Spy Who Came In from the Cold* and *The Looking-Glass War*, *Tinker, Tailor, Soldier, Spy* comes to grips with some of the fundamental ideological distinctions between the Communist world and the free world. It also explores the fact that these distinctions do not cease to exist even when the men who control the free-world institutions are themselves ruthlessly ambitious. As Smiley confronts the trapped mole at the end of the novel and listens to his poorly presented and entirely unconvincing assertions about the moral superiority of the Eastern monolith over the crass commercialism of the West, Smiley's own vaguely humanitarian liberalism begins to harden into the conviction that, although many of Gerald's criticisms of the West are accurate, his final evaluation is not. Gerald, having exploited, on Karla's orders, Ann's infidelity to Smiley, describes Smiley's continued love for Ann as his one point of vulnerability, "the last illusion of the illusionless man." By introducing into the conflict between Smiley and Karla the opposition between love, vulnerability, and human decency on one hand, and ruthlessly rational and perhaps irresistible efficiency on the other, le Carré sets up the terms for the continuing rivalry between Smiley and Karla which forms the basis of his next two novels.

Most of the reviews of *Tinker, Tailor, Soldier, Spy* were wildly enthusiastic, applauding its suspenseful complexity and its depth of characteriza-

Cambridge Circus, London, site of the Circus

tion and comparing it favorably with *The Spy Who Came In from the Cold*. Predictably most of the negative or mixed reviews focused on the novel's ideological and social commentary, accusing the novel of superficiality and of mongrelizing the genre; but these represented the reactions of a small minority of readers. Although le Carré's work had always been realistic–or at least plausible–*Tinker, Tailor, Soldier, Spy* was particularly noted for this quality. An official of the Central Intelligence Agency is quoted in *Time:* "We know that our work plays havoc with our personal lives. We know that an awful lot of what we have to do is slogging through file cards and computer printouts. Poor George Smiley. That's us."

Although *Tinker, Tailor, Soldier, Spy* is much too intricate to be adapted into a two-hour film, it was produced as a miniseries by London Weekend Television. The producer of the series, Richard Bates, was adamant in his insistence on retaining the grimly realistic spirit of the novel and avoiding all temptations to glamorize the story for television. The series, starring Alec Guinness in a superbly underplayed performance as Smiley, won both critical and popular acclaim.

The story begun in *Tinker, Tailor, Soldier, Spy* is resumed in *The Honourable Schoolboy* in which Smiley, now caretaker chief of a demoralized and largely ineffectual Circus, seeks to restore its prestige by undertaking a long and intensive search whose object is to determine what materials have been falsified or destroyed by Gerald, thus revealing the areas of Circus intelligence regarded by Karla as sensitive enough to require suppression, even at the risk of Gerald's exposure. The paper-chase and interview methods of *Tinker, Tailor, Soldier, Spy* are repeated here, yielding at last the knowledge of a "gold seam"– a series of secret Soviet payoffs. Smiley sends Jerry Westerby, a reporter who occasionally works for the Circus and who appeared briefly in *Tinker, Tailor, Soldier, Spy* as one of Gerald's victims, to investigate rumors of a connection between the Russian payoffs and a Hong Kong millionaire, Drake Ko.

Beneath Smiley's determination to restore the prestige of the Circus is a growing personal rivalry between him and Karla, his opposite number in the Russian secret service. Smiley rejects completely what he regards as Karla's absolutist and antihumanitarian methods, but he finds himself faced with the alternatives of displaying a certain degree of ruthlessness himself or of losing to Karla. He compromises gradually, becoming withdrawn and secretive, balancing professional priorities against the rights and well-being of individuals, reassuring himself that it is necessary to be "inhuman in defence of our humanity . . . harsh in defence of compassion . . . single-minded in defence of our disparity." Smiley does in fact retain a surprising amount of gentleness and compassion, even as chief of the Circus. The narrative voice, whose interruptions constitute one of the novel's chief stylistic flaws, repeatedly assures the reader that Smiley is doing as well as anyone could do under the circumstances, and that his critics in the service and in Whitehall fail to understand the pressures with which he must deal. Nevertheless, Smiley himself is dissatisfied with his own performance, and in a letter to his estranged wife, he writes, "I honestly do wonder, without wishing to be morbid, how I reached this present pass. . . . Today, all I know is that I have tried to interpret the whole of life in terms of conspiracy. That is the sword I have lived by, and as I look round me now I see that it is the sword I shall die by as well. These people terrify me, but I am one of them. If they stab me in the back, then at least that is the judgment of my peers." His peers do indeed stab Smiley in the back; and, despite the success of the Hong Kong operation, he is ousted from the Circus once again by an ungrateful ministry.

The Honourable Schoolboy sustains the level of characterization set in *Tinker, Tailor, Soldier, Spy*,

Dust jacket for the first American edition of le Carré's 1983 novel

particularly in its depiction of Westerby, the title character. He is, in some respects, a foil for Smiley: unintellectual but instinctively shrewd and emotionally vital, he respects the judgment of those he calls "the owls"–Smiley and the other upper-level policymakers in the Circus–acknowledging their superior grasp of the total operational picture. He is, however, too empathetically imaginative to carry out their orders when faced with the actual human beings whose weaknesses and failings he has been sent to exploit. If Karla resembles one side of Smiley in his brilliance, dedication, and persistence, Westerby resembles Smiley's benignly humanitarian side. Although he does not condemn Smiley himself, because he recognizes Smiley's essential decency and realizes that he himself does not understand the reasons for Smiley's orders, Westerby rejects Smiley's position, as Smiley once rejected Control's. Inevitably Westerby's simplistic and sympathetic approach to the complex and ruthless world in which he moves costs him his life; and, in view of Smiley's action in le Carré's next novel, it is possible to see in Westerby's death the impending compromise of Smiley's own humanitarian ideals.

Since much of the action in *The Honourable Schoolboy* takes place in Southeast Asia, le Carré made five visits to that area to collect background material for his book. On one occasion, exposed to automatic weapons fire in Cambodia, he rolled under a truck and lay there making notes of his sensations on index cards. Although much of this firsthand material provides the novel with color and immediacy, le Carré included so much background description that parts of the book read like a travelogue. He also wrote a lengthy and largely unnecessary opening sequence, apparently for the sole purpose of creating the character of Old Craw, a reporter, modeled on a real-life journalist, Dick Hughes. These scenes, together with the often didactic interruptions of the narrative voice, are no more than padding for an already overly long novel.

Largely because of its verbosity and its consequent loss of focus, *The Honourable Schoolboy* did not enjoy the enthusiastic reception which had been accorded to *Tinker, Tailor, Soldier, Spy*. Further, several reviewers pointed out specific examples of overwriting and mixed metaphors. Clive James, for example (*New York Review of Books*, 27 October 1977), mentions le Carré's description of a conversation between Smiley and a former Circus employee, Sam Collins: " 'Now at first Smiley tested the water with Sam—and Sam, who liked a poker hand himself, tested the water with Smiley.' Are they playing cards in the bath?" Nevertheless, most reviewers noted the fine interplay of characters and the sustained suspense which are the novel's strongest points. *The Honourable Schoolboy* became the Book-of-the-Month Club selection for October 1977, and it superseded *Tinker, Tailor, Soldier, Spy* as the highest-grossing espionage novel ever written. Le Carré received two major awards for *The Honourable Schoolboy*: The Black Memorial Award and the Crime Writers' Association's Gold Dagger Award.

In the final volume of the trilogy, *Smiley's People*, Smiley discovers that his opponent, Karla, has an emotionally disturbed daughter whom he has secretly sent out of Russia to avoid the political embarrassments which her condition would cause him if she remained there. In the course of establishing and maintaining her false identity in Switzerland, Karla orders the deaths of several people, including Smiley's friend and former

agent, Vladimir. Called out of retirement to investigate Vladimir's murder, Smiley grasps this opportunity to accomplish the utter defeat of Karla: his enforced defection to England. However, in bringing about this result Smiley is forced to exploit Karla's love for his daughter even more ruthlessly than Karla once exploited Smiley's love for his wife. Although Smiley repeatedly bolsters his resolution by recalling the horrors which Karla, in his single-minded ambition, has ordered, he cannot escape the realization that if what Smiley condemns in Karla were all of Karla, Smiley would not have been able to defeat him. It is not Karla's cruelty, but the one vestige of affection which redeems him from utter inhumanity that leads to his destruction.

By the time he wrote *Smiley's People* le Carré had become so adept at combining the detective, espionage, and "straight" fictional genres that most readers had ceased even to take note of it. Many of the events in *Smiley's People*, like those in *Tinker, Tailor, Soldier, Spy* and *The Honourable Schoolboy*, are based on the conventions of detective fiction: a paper chase, interviews, the discovery and investigation of clues, and the pursuit and eventual capture of the prey. On the other hand, Smiley's uncertainty about the purity of his motives and the right-mindedness of his actions adds to the externally oriented suspense of the conventional thriller a dimension of internal tension usually associated with the "straight" novel. Moreover, the action of *Smiley's People*, like that of its predecessors, is generated by the interplay of rounded characters rather than by a series of more or less implausible or unexpected external events.

Le Carré's next novel, *The Little Drummer Girl* (1983), was a significant departure from his earlier work. Asked why he had abandoned Smiley, he said that Guinness's portrayal of the character in the television adaptations of *Tinker, Tailor, Soldier, Spy* and *Smiley's People* had been so convincing that he could no longer envision Smiley apart from Guinness. As a number of reviewers observed, however, a more obvious explanation is that the Smiley story had run its course, at least for the moment. Le Carré's first female protagonist, Charlie, is an intelligent, sensitive, but somewhat scatterbrained young actress who is active in a variety of political movements that she barely understands. As befits her profession, she not only engages in an elaborate charade but also falls in love with a succession of masks. Recruited by Israeli intelligence to infiltrate a Pales-

Dust jacket for the first edition of le Carré's first novel to be serialized in the Soviet Union

tinian terrorist organization, she finds that neither cause nor individual has only one face.

Like earlier le Carré novels, *The Little Drummer Girl* blurs the distinction between "them" and "us," between action and motivation, and between honor and betrayal. The substitution of a comparatively naive and idealistic protagonist for the cynical Smiley recalls Leamas and Westerby, but Charlie has less chivalry and a correspondingly better chance of survival. Like Leamas and Westerby, she is occasionally victimized by her employers; and, like them, she is aware that she is playing a role but unaware of its real dimensions and goals. Nevertheless, her responses to her gradual disillusionment include not only anger, but also some recognition of the inevitable ambivalence that underlies political interactions. Despite

her initial political shallowness, Charlie becomes, in some ways, one of the most instinctively perspicacious of le Carré's characters. She never sees the clear outlines within which other characters in the novel move, but the novel opens the possibility that her multilayered, affective, frequently muddled visions of reality may not be altogether removed from the truth.

Le Carré's next novel, *A Perfect Spy* (1986), is written in an ironically autobiographical mode that features flashbacks detailing the relationship between the protagonist, Magnus Pym, and his father. Like le Carré's father, Ronald Thomas Archibald Cornwell, Richard Thomas Pym is a charmingly manipulative swindler who never quite understands why good intentions are not a fully acceptable substitute for reliable behavior. Taught from childhood that betrayal is not inconsistent with love, Magnus Pym becomes a natural betrayer—first a spy and then, in an inevitable progression, a double agent. All of le Carré's novels include layers of betrayal, but *A Perfect Spy* is truly an anatomy of betrayal, dwelling in detail on its origins, progression, distinguishing characteristics, and consequences. Le Carré's plotting has never been simple, but *A Perfect Spy* is one of his most complex novels. The narrative alternates between a long apologia that Magnus Pym is writing to his son, Tom, and an account of the search for Pym that the British and the Czechs are conducting. In the epistolary segments Pym seeks an understanding of himself; in the rest of the novel others seek an understanding of him. Eventually, these internal and external searches, which initially seek to explain how he has arrived at his present point in life, focus on the reasons he must now die. Since *A Perfect Spy* is the most intimate of le Carré's novels, this gradual perception of the inevitability of Pym's death should elicit a much more vivid affective response than is characteristic of most spy fiction. The absence of such a response is, perhaps, the most serious consequence of the novel's major flaw: like all of le Carré's novels, this one is word-heavy.

Even in the love scenes, apparently intended to be evocative and touching, words pile up dauntingly. For example, this paragraph occurs early in the description of Pym's relationship with his wife, Mary: "He is watching her and when she catches sight of him he bursts out laughing and shuts her mouth with passionate kisses doing his Fred Astaire number, then it's upstairs for a full and frank exchange of views, as he calls it. They make love, he hauls her to the bath, washes her, hauls her out and dries her, and twenty minutes later Mary and Magnus are bounding across the little park on the top of Dobling like the happy couple they nearly are, past the sandpits and the climbing-frame that Tom is too big for, past the elephant cage where Tom kicks the football, down the hill towards the Restaurant Teheran which is their improbable pub because Magnus so adores the black-and-white videos of Arab romances they play for you with the sound down while you eat your couscous and drink your Kalterer. At the table he holds her arm fiercely and she can feel his excitement racing through her like a charge, as if having her has made him want her more." The line between poetry and verbosity may be hard to define in the abstract, but there can be little doubt about the side of that line on which passages like this one fall. As Bruce Allen observed in his *Christian Science Monitor* review, "This may be a major novel that nobody will be able to finish."

A Perfect Spy was made into a television miniseries that portrays Magnus Pym as a basically good-natured but befuddled betrayer. Like the production of *Tinker, Tailor, Soldier, Spy*, the adaptation of *A Perfect Spy* is faithful to the novel in its setting and tone as well as in its characterizations and plot. It is particularly effective in capturing the experience of physical wandering and psychological wandering that is so essential to the sense of Pym's story.

Although some readers believed that *The Little Drummer Girl* and *A Perfect Spy* had signaled the end of le Carré's Soviet plots, those readers were proven wrong when, in 1989, le Carré's *The Russia House* was published. The protagonist of this novel, Barley Blair, is a marginally successful publisher who often travels to the Soviet Union because his company's book list includes some works by Soviet authors. Blair resembles Eric Ambler's best-known protagonists in that he is a nonprofessional who suddenly finds himself caught up in espionage and counterespionage. Le Carré had been slowly progressing in this direction, beginning with the journalist-courier Westerby in *The Honourable Schoolboy* and continuing with the actress-recruit Charlie in *The Little Drummer Girl*. Blair is an entirely innocent bystander until the secret world is literally thrust upon him in the form of a package sent to him by a dissident Russian scientist and author nicknamed "Goethe," with whom he had once shared a drunken Sunday outside Moscow. Embedded in the rambling literary manuscript is information on how the So-viet Union's weapons systems work–or, more precisely, on how they fail to work. In sending this information to the West, Goethe envisions slowing down the arms race by disillusioning the British and American political establishments about the strength of the Russian military threat. In a sense this is the obverse of le Carré's earlier theme that the West is as morally impoverished as the East. Now the message is that the East is as technologically impoverished as the West.

Once the information is in British and American hands, there is a mad scramble to confirm it, deny it, get more of it, and/or bury it, all at once. Of particular concern are certain American politicians described as "Bible-belt knuckle-draggers who take it into their heads to pillory Goethe's material because it endangers Fortress America." Mimicking such politicians, who are described as having hair between their toes, one of Blair's interrogators drawls, "This li'l ole planet just ain't big enough for two super-powers, Mr. Brown. Which one do *you* favor, Mr. Brown, when poo-ush comes to sheu-uve?" ("Mr. Brown" is Blair's code name.) This novel thus adds to le Carré's recurrent themes of personal ambition, international rivalry, and interservice bickering a new element of deliberately preserved ignorance based on xenophobia and mindless militarism. The point that the novel is making on this issue is suggested by its first epigraph, a quotation from Dwight David Eisenhower: "Indeed, I think that people want peace so much that one of these days governments had better get out of their way and let them have it."

Amid all these waves of conflict, Blair struggles to maintain his balance, his humanity, and his concern for Katya, Goethe's politically naive courier. As the plot of *The Russia House* develops, echoes of le Carré's earlier novels, especially *The Spy Who Came In from the Cold* and *The Looking-Glass War*, become evident. For example, the narrator of *The Russia House*, Palfrey, plays much the same role in the plot of this novel that Smiley plays in *The Looking-Glass War* and, to a lesser extent, in *The Spy Who Came In from the Cold*. Like Smiley, Palfrey is a scholarly middle-aged man with an unsuccessful love life and a correspondingly low level of self-esteem and interpersonal trust. Despite the cynicism that results from that description, Palfrey, like Smiley, represents the voice of sanity, reason, and humanity in a world that contains very little of these qualities. Smiley does not narrate any of the novels in which he appears, as Palfrey narrates *The Russia House*, but it

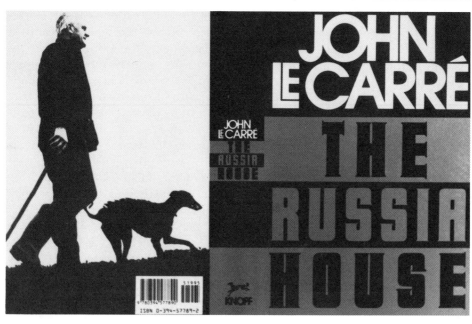

Dust jacket for the first American edition of le Carré's 1989 best-seller

seems as if le Carré has need of a character of this type to provide the light by which the actions of others can be evaluated. Further, just as Smiley is often on the fringes of the espionage world–retired, resigned, about to resign–Palfrey serves in the rather tangential role of legal advisor to the secret service. This allows le Carré to comment on the action of the novel by means of a character who, while remaining involved enough to know what is going on, is independent of direct lines of authority and does not quite represent the establishment.

The ending of *The Russia House* can be read as an upbeat revision of *The Spy Who Came In from the Cold*, at least from the point of view of the main character, since he avoids the traps set for him by the secret service of his own country and saves the woman he loves. If he betrays his country to accomplish this, which is left unclear, perhaps in the world of this novel that country deserved to be betrayed. In any case, this novel, unlike *A Perfect Spy*, deals with some elements of human triumph rather than with unredeemed betrayal.

The Russia House will, in accord with Mikhail Gorbachev's policy of openness, be serialized in the Soviet Union in the magazine *Ogonyok*, and an Australian director is already negotiating film rights for a script to be filmed on location in Moscow. A *New York Times* feature article (22 May 1989) focused on the relationship between the improvement of East-West relations and le Carré's

novel, which clearly transcends the cold-war themes of his earlier work. In a rare interview, le Carré observed, "We had no contingency plan for the end of the cold war. . . . The notion that peace should break out was one that was never seriously contemplated. We really have to make the choice of whether we're going to help them out of the ice or stamp them on their fingers every time they try to crawl out." The same ideas appear at greater length in a cover article in *Newsweek* (5 June 1989). There, le Carré is quoted as opposing Margaret Thatcher's "chauvinistic revival," stating, "I'm deeply pessimistic about what Mrs. Thatcher has done to our national soul." As these examples indicate, one of the few things about *The Russia House* that is entirely unambiguous is its political relevance.

The *Newsweek* article, by Tom Mathews, describes *The Russia House* as being "faster and leaner than anything le Carré has done in years," while a *New York Times* (18 May 1989) book review by Christopher Lehmann-Haupt objects that "there's a little too much emphasis on language." *The Russia House* is certainly less bulky, physically and syntactically, than its immediate predecessors, and it contains some effective and blessedly brief descriptions. Of Blair, for example, Palfrey says, "He has people inside himself who really drive him mad" and "his mind leaves the room and you wait on tenterhooks to see whether it will come back." The novel even includes a few examples of le Carré's infrequent use of humor;

for example, Goethe describes himself to Blair by saying, "I'm a moral outcast. . . . I trade in defiled theories." "Always nice to meet a writer," Blair replies. Nevertheless, as the *New York Times* review indicates, this novel exhibits le Carré's almost indefinable tendency toward a quality that most reviewers see as verbosity.

In the course of le Carré's publishing career, which has spanned a quarter of a century, he has moved from writing comparatively plot-oriented detective spy stories to producing complex political and psychological novels that qualify him for consideration as a "serious" author. This development is discernible not only in his writing in general, but also in the evolution of his best-known character, George Smiley. In *Call for the Dead* Smiley is a rather fuzzily portrayed detective/spy; in *Smiley's People* he approaches the level of a tragically flawed character who has sold his soul but does not quite know when or how it happened. The post-Smiley novels continue le Carré's trend toward writing "serious" novels in which characters happen to be spies, as the characters created by other authors happen to be psychiatrists or airline pilots. The greatest drawback to his writing is, as critics and reviewers have repeatedly pointed out, the insistent heavy-handedness of his style. Although this quality is modified significantly in *The Russia House*, his persistence in writing lengthy novels that include verbose and ap-

parently pointless descriptive passages, innumerable tangents, and a plethora of poorly defined minor characters is intriguing if not perverse. It is as if he is convinced that this style will work if he can only get it right–and, considering the unquestionable success of his books, that may be true. In any case, this combination of brilliance and diffusiveness makes a final assessment of le Carré's work difficult. What is certain, however, is that he occupies a place among the most commercially–and, on the whole, the most critically–successful writers of espionage fiction, and deservedly so.

References:

Tony Barley, *Taking Sides: The Fiction of John le Carré* (Philadelphia: Open University Press, 1986);

Eric Homberger, *John le Carré* (London & New York: Methuen, 1986);

Peter Lewis, *John le Carré* (New York: Ungar, 1985);

David Monaghan, *The Novels of John le Carré: The Art of Survival* (New York: Blackwell, 1985);

Monaghan, *Smiley's Circus: A Guide to the Secret World of John le Carré* (London: Orbis, 1986);

Peter Wolfe, *Corridors of Deceit: The World of John le Carré* (Bowling Green, Ohio: Bowling Green University Popular Press, 1987).

Peter Lovesey

(10 September 1936-)

James Hurt
University of Illinois

BOOKS: *The Kings of Distance: A Study of Five Great Runners* (London: Eyre & Spottiswoode, 1968); republished as *Five Kings of Distance* (New York: St. Martin's Press, 1981);

The Guide to British Track and Field Literature 1275-1968, by Lovesey and Tom MacNab (London: Athletics Arena, 1969);

Wobble to Death (London: Macmillan, 1970; New York: Dodd, Mead, 1970);

The Detective Wore Silk Drawers (London: Macmillan, 1971; New York: Dodd, Mead, 1971);

Abracadaver (London: Macmillan, 1972; New York: Dodd, Mead, 1972);

Mad Hatter's Holiday (London: Macmillan, 1973; New York: Dodd, Mead, 1973);

Invitation to a Dynamite Party (London: Macmillan, 1974); republished as *The Tick of Death* (New York: Dodd, Mead, 1974);

A Case of Spirits (London: Macmillan, 1975; New York: Dodd, Mead, 1975);

Swing, Swing Together (London: Macmillan, 1976; New York: Dodd, Mead, 1976);

Goldengirl, as Peter Lear (London: Cassell, 1977; Garden City, N.Y.: Doubleday, 1978);

Waxwork (London: Macmillan, 1978; New York: Pantheon, 1978);

The Official Centenary History of the Amateur Athletic Association (Enfield: Guinness Superlatives, 1979);

Spider Girl, as Lear (London: Cassell, 1980; New York: Viking, 1980);

The False Inspector Dew (London: Macmillan, 1982; New York: Pantheon, 1982);

Keystone (London: Macmillan, 1983; New York: Pantheon, 1983);

Butchers and Other Stories of Crime (London: Macmillan, 1985; New York: Mysterious, 1987);

Rough Cider (London: Bodley Head, 1986; New York: Mysterious, 1987);

Bertie and the Tinman: From the Detective Memoirs of King Edward VII (London: Bodley Head, 1987; New York: Mysterious, 1988);

On the Edge (London: Bodley Head, 1989; New York: Mysterious, 1989).

Peter Lovesey, mid 1970s (photograph by Keith McDavid)

TELEVISION: *The Detective Wore Silk Drawers*, Granada, 1980;

Something Old, Something New, by Lovesey and Jacqueline Lovesey, Granada, 1980;

The Horizontal Witness, by Lovesey and Jacqueline Lovesey, Granada, 1980;

The Hand That Rocks the Cradle, by Lovesey and Jacqueline Lovesey, Granada, 1981;

The Choir That Wouldn't Sing, by Lovesey and Jacqueline Lovesey, Granada, 1981;

Murder Old Boy, by Lovesey and Jacqueline Lovesey, Granada, 1981;

256

The Last Trumpet, by Lovesey and Jacqueline Lovesey, Granada, 1981.

OTHER: "The Bathroom," in *Winter's Crimes*, edited by Virginia Whitaker (London: Macmillan, 1973);
"The Historian: Once upon a Crime," in *Murder Ink: The Mystery Reader's Companion*, edited by Dilys Winn (New York: Workman, 1977), pp. 475-476;
"The Locked Room," in *Winter's Crimes*, edited by Hilary Watson (London: Macmillan, 1978);
"How Mr. Smith Traced His Ancestors," in *The Mystery Guild Anthology* (London: Constable, 1980);
"A Man with a Fortune," in *Best Detective Stories of the Year, 1981*, edited by Edward D. Hoch (New York: Dutton, 1981);
"The Virgin and the Bull," in *John Creasey's Crime Collection, 1983*, edited by Herbert Harris (New York: St. Martin's Press, 1983);
"The Secret Lover," in *Winter's Crimes*, edited by George Hardinge (London: Macmillan, 1985).

PERIODICAL PUBLICATIONS: "Becoming a Novelist," *Writer*, 88 (August 1975): 21-23;
"Have You Tried Murder?," *Writer*, 96 (April 1983): 9-11;
"Dr. Crippen and the Real Inspector Dew," *Armchair Detective*, 17 (Summer 1984): 244-248.

Novels sometimes contain scenes that, while remaining a credible part of the narrative, also seem to point past the immediate fictional situation to the book in which they appear. One such moment in the fiction of Peter Lovesey is a scene in *Mad Hatter's Holiday* (1973). Sergeant Cribb and Constable Thackeray are on their way down from London to Brighton to look into an especially grisly murder. Thackeray is eager to see the famous Brighton pier, but Cribb tells him:

I want you to make sure you get a look at that pier you're talking about. There's two of 'em where we're going, paper-doily things, with fancy iron-work all white and smelling of fresh paint. When you've had your eyeful of the scrubbed decks and the dapper little buildings, take a look underneath, right under the pier. I'll tell you what you'll see. Girders festering with barnacles. Slime and weed and water black as pitch lurching and heaving round the under-structure fit to turn your stomach. That's part of your pier, too. Just as slums and alleys and back-

streets lie behind the nobby hotels along the seafront.

Thackeray, his stomach predictably turned, replies, "Don't, Sarge."

Cribb's speech points to the immediate situation—a young woman's dismembered body has been found beneath the pier—but it also metaphorically anticipates the action of the rest of the book, which consists of an extended look at the horrors that lie beneath the surface tranquility and order of an apparently respectable Victorian family. The passage also points toward the complete work of Lovesey, in which recurringly a charmingly nostalgic, usually comic surface action overlies depths of personal and cultural perversity.

Lovesey practices the art of the historical detective story; he is best known for the Sergeant Cribb novels, set in Victorian England, although he has moved up to 1920s England in *The False Inspector Dew* (1982), to 1915 Hollywood in *Keystone* (1983), and even to World War II England in *Rough Cider* (1986). His novels are full of vivid, often offbeat historical details: the "paper-doily things" of the pier. They are not pastiche, as they have sometimes been called; Lovesey makes no attempt to imitate a Victorian style or use Victorian narrative forms. His are modern novels about the past, not attempts to resuscitate past forms. Lovesey can imitate past styles when he wants to, and he exhibits such linguistic exotica as Victorian sports writing and legal language and the slang of pioneer Hollywood with the same relish he displays in more material artifacts. But the crisp, contemporary style of the central voice in the Lovesey novels sets a distance between past and present time; the past is being examined, not recreated. The charm of the historical detail never becomes merely quaint, because it has a foundation in Lovesey's keen, realistic sense of the contradictions and ambiguities in his colorful societies and in his power to trace the psychological effects of those contradictions upon his vivid, complexly imagined characters, perhaps especially the criminal ones. The Sergeant Cribb novels are sophisticated while remaining light, predominantly comic entertainments.

Peter Lovesey was born 10 September 1936 in Whitton, Middlesex, to Richard Lear and Amy Strank Lovesey. He was educated at Hampton Grammar School and the University of Reading, where he earned a B.A. in English literature in 1958. On 30 May 1959 he married Jacqueline

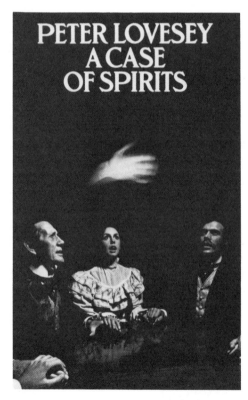

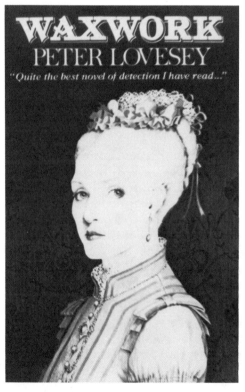

*Dust jackets for three of Lovesey's nine novels featuring Sergeant Cribb and Constable Thackeray
(courtesy of Otto Penzler)*

Ruth Lewis. The couple have two children. In 1969 he became head of the General Education Department at London's Hammersmith College for Further Education. His career as a writer began when he happened upon a copy of the *Sporting Chronicle Annual for 1898* in a secondhand bookshop in Charing Cross Road. The book contained a picture of Deerfoot (Lewis Bennett, 1828-1897), an American Indian who went to England in 1861 and set a record (which he held for thirty-four years) for the greatest distance covered in one hour. Lovesey, who had an interest in track and field dating from childhood, became interested in Deerfoot, whose career he reconstructed from the newspaper files of the British Museum. His research led him to write a series of articles about the history of running and, eventually, to two books, *The Kings of Distance: A Study of Five Great Runners* (1968; published in the United States as *Five Kings of Distance*, 1981) and *The Guide to British Track and Field Literature 1275-1968* (1969).

Lovesey made the transition from sports historian to mystery writer in 1969, when he read an advertisement in the *London Times* for the Macmillan / Panther First Crime Novel Award, which carried a prize of one thousand pounds. He had recently been reading in another Victorian sports annual about a bizarre sort of endurance race (rather like the marathon dancing of later years) in which contestants ran, or "went as they pleased," around an indoor track for six days and nights. Lovesey was not a mystery reader, but he asked his wife Jacqueline, who was, if she thought one of these "wobbles," as they were called, would make an interesting background for a crime story. She was enthusiastic and immediately suggested the title used for *Wobble to Death* (1970). Lovesey completed the novel in three months, won the prize, and was launched on his career as a mystery writer.

Wobble to Death has been followed by eight more mysteries featuring detectives Sergeant Cribb and Constable Thackeray. These novels form a coherent sequence, in which Lovesey both established limits of style and content for himself and successively explored the possibilities of development within those limits. They can therefore best be considered sequentially. *Wobble to Death* established the lines along which the Cribb novels were to develop: the traditional complementary detectives, Cribb and his assistant Thackeray (the third, equally traditional recurring figure, the pompous, obstructionist inspector, Jowett, would

not join them until Lovesey's second novel, *The Detective Wore Silk Drawers*, 1971); a setting in the 1880s, built around some curiosity of Victorian social history; a violent, passionate crime which Cribb solves through his shrewd understanding of human nature; and a gallery of Dickensian comic secondary characters, as well as more sinister figures, including bewitching but perverse women and monomaniacal men.

Lovesey has described the Cribb novels as "Victorian police procedural novels," and if this description omits the important strain of social comedy, it does properly emphasize the novels' grounding in the history of the Victorian police. The precise time of the novels is important. *Wobble to Death* takes place in 1879, and the rest of the Cribb novels are set in successive years of the decade of the 1880s, skipping only 1883, 1886, and 1887. In an interview with John C. Carr, Lovesey has described the 1880s as something of a low point in British law enforcement, just before the professionalization of the police and the rise of forensic science that took place in the 1890s, which are reflected in Arthur Conan Doyle's Sherlock Holmes stories. The police in the 1880s were largely untrained, worked under harsh conditions, and were widely distrusted and ridiculed by the public. The system was administered largely by retired military men who had little understanding of police work and offered little support to the working policeman. The Turf Fraud Scandal of 1877, which led to the establishment of the Criminal Investigation Department, eroded public confidence; it is reflected in the *The Detective Wore Silk Drawers*. Bloody Sunday, in which the London Metropolitan Police brutally and clumsily put down an 1887 demonstration of the unemployed, forms part of the background of *Waxwork* (1978).

Lovesey's description of the books as Victorian police procedural novels must be taken in the context of the criminology of the day. Cribb has a police laboratory available to him–the "Bunsen and beaker brigade," he calls it–but it can do only simple tests such as identifying poisons. Even fingerprint identification remains in the future, and none of the novels uses technical material in any important way. Cribb relies upon an orthodox working through of "suspects, means and opportunity, and possible motives." His chief asset is his understanding of human nature and his chief weapon the interview. "There was more to detective work than clues and statements," he reflects in *Waxwork*. "It involved people, their ambi-

SUNDAY, ~~MARCH 15~~ 15th APRIL ①

~~ONE~~

There was nothing shifty ~~about~~ James Berry's eyes. No inward
glance or drooping lids. They were wide ~~open~~ and steady ~~fixed~~. The
~~Yorkshire~~ Telegraph had called them codfish eyes once. ~~Soon after~~ After that
he had changed to the Graphic.

The eyes scanned
~~He read~~ it line by line, column by column, ~~paragraph by paragraph~~
~~reading~~. The reports on criminal matters, headed Police Intelligence,
interested him most. Over the mantelpiece in the front room
of his house in ~~Clayton~~ Bilton Place, Bradford, were two ~~gilt~~ frames,
each filled with eight small photographs of men and women, mounted on best
Bristol board. He ~~was proud of~~ prized them. ~~Everyone~~ Each was a convicted
murderer.

a select bunch.
They were ~~not riff-raff~~. They all came in the carte-de-visite
size, which showed they were not riff-raff. Two were doctors. ~~Only~~
~~a decent class of person had his photograph done in a studio.~~

This ~~April~~ Sunday evening in 1888 his wife was ~~going to talk~~ talking
~~to him~~ about them. 'I believe I could ~~bear~~ stand that lot hanging
over my front room mantelpiece if there was ~~something~~ summat else up
there beside them.'

He looked over his paper. 'What ~~have~~ did you have in mind ~~my dear~~?'
'A picture of you, ~~my~~ love.'
It had never occurred to him to put himself up there.

~~Come to~~ Now that he considered it,
~~Certainly~~, he would not ~~half~~ look ~~so~~ bad in sepia. At thirty-six
he still had most of his hair. ~~His was the sort of face~~ face ~~with the~~ manly ~~it was~~ broad enough broad and
powerful, with a good growth of black beard. There was a ~~long~~ deep scar
down the right cheek, but the beard covered most of it. He had a
notion that his wife liked the scar. She had never enquired how
he came by it, but there were times when she traced it with her
fingertip. Ever so lightly.

He told her she was talking rubbish and went back to
the Graphic. There was a case of poisoning in Kew.

She said the rogues' gallery made her flesh creep. She
wanted to look up from her sewing once in a while and see an

Corrected manuscript pages from the beginning of Waxwork *(courtesy of the author)* honest, God-fearing face.

He knew why she mentioned the Almighty. They both took a pride in the lay-preaching. ~~he did all which~~ Folk sat up in ~~their pews~~ chapel when James Berry ~~~~ went ~~~~ to the pulpit. ~~for the wicked. ~~~~ he could speak with authority on the wages of sin.

"There's that elegant studio in Bridge Street," she went on. "You know — with velvet at window? I've seen what he can do. Beautiful likenesses. You ~~~~ can wear your chapel suit and butterfly collar. You'll make a grand picture, Jim!"

He told her straight that he did not hold with photography. She said it was no sin so far as she was aware. There was nothing about it in the Good Book that she could recollect.

He did not hold with sarcasm either. If it had not been ~~Sunday~~ the Sabbath he would have cuffed her for that. He told her so. She went out to make ~~~~ the cocoa.

The Graphic had a lot to say about the Kew murder. It seemed ~~~~ the suspect was a young married woman. Her ~~people were~~ ~~~~ well-to-do. ~~~~ ~~~~ ~~counsel~~ They would see she was well represented at the trial. Someone of the calibre of Clarke or Russell was expected to lead the defence. A classic trial was in prospect.

~~~~

When she reappeared with his mug and a biscuit he told her why he had no intention of going to the studio in Bridge Street. "In my sort of work you don't go out of your way to be recognised. You get enough of that, without photographs. If I had my picture took in Bradford, inside the hour it would be in t'shop window with James Berry, Public Hangman in large letters under it."

She was unimpressed. "We've no cause to be ashamed, Jim. If folk round here want to see your likeness, why not let them?"

tions and fears, innocence and guilt. You needed solid evidence to determine the truth, but you could divine a lot by meeting them face to face." Cribb's characteristic posture, while investigating a crime, is sitting quietly (while he assigns the long-suffering Thackeray prodigious feats of leg-work). He is a masterful interrogator, and although he can spring into physical action when required, often he arrives at the truth of a crime by simply talking with all concerned, probing quietly for the dynamics of human motivation behind the events.

Lovesey's major characters in his Cribb novels are distinct personalities. He initially conceived Cribb, he told the interviewer Carr, as simply "a working Victorian policeman of the time, quite different from a Sherlock Holmes character." In *Wobble to Death*, set in 1879, he is said to be "in his forties" (perhaps forty-one, since in *Waxwork*, set in 1888, he is fifty). He is tall, thin, and birdlike–"he moves his head with birdlike suddenness"; and he has an unusually long nose and a luxuriant set of side-whiskers, "Piccadilly Weepers." He served in the army and became a detective sergeant in 1878; he seems permanently fixed in that rank, partly through the jealousy of Inspector Jowett, partly because of his own sharp tongue and unwillingness to cultivate friends in high places. In *Waxwork* he is described as "sharp, too, in speech, quick to spot deceit. His sense of irony kept him tolerant of others in most situations. He often fumed, rarely erupted." Cribb undergoes considerable development in the course of the stories. He retains his gruffness and his rough speech, but he mellows considerably, especially in his treatment of Thackeray and in his judgments of human nature. Edward Thackeray, "a burly, middle-aged man with a fine grey beard," is steady and reliable, "a tower of strength at exhumations." He has a healthy respect for Sergeant Cribb, but their relationship is strictly professional. (Both are married but appear to be childless, and their wives and private lives never appear directly in the novels.) Cribb often uses him as a sounding board: "He liked to affect ignorance with Thackeray. It brought out the constable's best qualities, and often encouraged a point worth taking up." But Thackeray's deductions are invariably wrong, a lame parody of Cribb's own mental processes. Inspector Jowett is a former fellow sergeant who has been repeatedly promoted over Cribb, not through competence but through currying favor with his superiors:

What was Jowett? A sandwich-man without boards, with a new message each time you met him. He was one of the few at the Yard who emerged unscathed from the Turf Fraud Scandal of 1877, when the Detective Department's three Chief-Inspectors stood in the dock at the Old Bailey accused of conspiracy, and two were convicted. Heads had rolled in plenty after that. Not Jowett's though. Who knew what he stood for?

Wobble to Death introduces the method of using period details that Lovesey was to pursue and develop in his succeeding novels. On the first page, readers are transported to the great Agricultural Hall in Islington, the setting in the 1860s and 1870s of royal balls, animal shows, bullfights, and evangelical meetings, and now, in November 1879, of a "Go As You Please" or "Wobble" race, the creation of Sir John Astley the previous year. In the course of the novel Lovesey gives his readers a complete education in Victorian footracing–the competitors, the training practices, the advertising, the forms of competition. He does this indirectly; "In writing period fiction," Lovesey wrote in his essay "Becoming a Novelist" (*Writer*, August 1975), "one must avoid introducing gratuitous information. You know the sort of thing–a reference to horse-drawn cabs in an era when nobody would think of commenting on the horse because all cabs worked that way. . . . I have come to the conclusion that it is best to assume an understanding with the reader that when he picks up the book, he steps into the period with you."

Wobble to Death presents a broad gallery of well-developed secondary characters, but the most striking secondary figure introduces a type that is to figure very importantly in subsequent Lovesey novels: the passionate, imperious woman who manipulates men through her sexuality and draws them to disaster. Cora Darrell floats into the Agricultural Hall in the third chapter of the novel to inspect her husband's accommodations, and all activity immediately begins to revolve around her seductive figure. The resolution of the novel turns around Cribb's realization of the nature of the power she holds over at least three of the men associated with the race. She is a type of *belle dame sans merci* that haunted the Victorian imagination.

The endurance race itself becomes a lightly ironic metaphor for Victorian values. "The public likes these events," proclaims the oleaginous promoter Sol Herriott. "Endurance, persistence, the will to conquer–these are the qualities of our

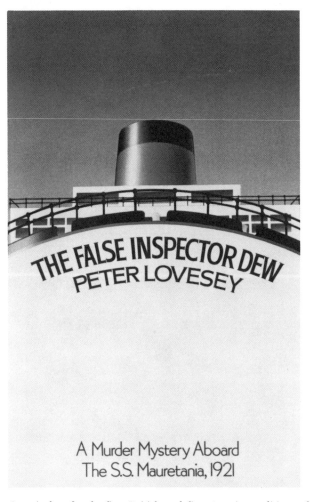

Dust jackets for the first British and first American editions of Lovesey's mystery novel which won the Crime Writers' Association's Gold Dagger Award in 1982 (courtesy of Otto Penzler)

time, gentlemen." The racers themselves make up a little model of Victorian society, from the aristocratic Oxfordian and captain of the Guards Erskine Chadwick, M.A., through his working-class opponent Charles Darrell, and down to the desperate rabble doomed to failure on the outside track.

In the 1985 edition of *Bloody Murder,* his history of crime fiction, Julian Symons wrote that *Wobble to Death* itself showed "occasional wobbliness in plotting." This is perhaps more a clever than a just judgment; the novel maintains movement and suspense, and the resolution is well prepared for though surprising. The choice of the wobble race as a setting was probably a good one for a beginning novelist, since it provided a sort of ready-made structure. The action takes place entirely within the Agricultural Hall, and the sections of the novel are labeled with the successive

days of the six-day race. But a price is paid in a certain stiffness in the construction and a lack of variety in atmosphere. Lovesey was never to return to such extreme unity of time and place.

Lovesey (in "Becoming a Novelist") noted that "there is an obvious danger when using the same detectives of becoming stereotyped in one's writing and producing the same plot dressed a little differently each time. I try to avoid this–and keep my own interest fresh–by varying the form of the books." Indeed the most striking feature of the eight Cribb novels that follow *Wobble to Death* is the number of changes Lovesey is able to bring within the general pattern he had set for himself. *The Detective Wore Silk Drawers,* for example, renounces the almost claustrophobic confinement of *Wobble to Death* and takes Cribb and Thackeray out of London to the fields and villages of rural Essex for an investigation into the murders

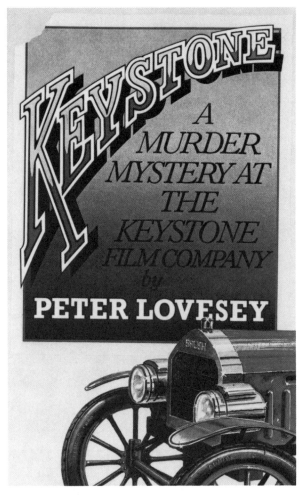 

Dust jackets for the first British and first American editions of Lovesey's 1983 mystery novel set in 1915 in Hollywood (courtesy of Otto Penzler)

of a series of headless corpses fished out of the Thames, and ultimately into the world of illegal bare-fisted pugilism. The narrative structure of the second Cribb novel is also more complicated than that of the first. The center of the action moves back and forth between Cribb and Thackeray (in London and the countryside) and Constable Jago, who is undercover within sinister Radstock Hall, where he is investigating a criminal ring while being groomed to fight bare-fisted. There is a grisly second murder late in the book, and the plot climaxes in a sustained chase scene, with Cribb and Thackeray trying to get to the fight scene in Kent before Jago is maimed or killed by his opponent, Sylvanus Morgan, a giant, black, bare-fisted pugilist.

The details of Victorian boxing–training, gambling, ring procedure, and the slang of the sport–are re-created in great detail; but perhaps the most memorable feature of *The Detective Wore*

Silk Drawers is the creation of Isabel Vibart, a Victorian vampire lady in the line of Cora Darrell, but vastly elaborated from her. Isabel operates Radstock Hall, ruling over the household: Robert D'Estin, her violent and half-crazed trainer and former lover; Edmund Vibart, her agent, brother of her dead husband, and a church organist; and Sylvanus Morgan, "The Ebony." Isabel wears black, less in mourning for her dead husband than for its sinister connotations. On her neck is a pendant of a cobra poised to strike. She revels in her collection of Indian art, dominated by a life-sized bronze statue of the Hindu goddess Kali, who "is said to dance among the slain on the battlefield and eat their flesh." Isabel uses the fighters in her stable for perverse sexual gratification, delighting in imposing cruel and unnecessary torments on them while she watches them through a peephole. After a success, she gives the fighters highly sensual massages, culminating either in copulation or cruel scratches from her long fingernails. In a brutal and shocking scene, D'Estin rapes her, but even after the rape, she cows him into submission by her self-possession and scorn. Her foil is Lydia Boltover, the proper young lady engaged to Constable Jago. Jago must struggle comically in moments of weakness with the lure of Isabel by holding fast to the image of his Lydia. Like the sinister woman Isabel, the virtuous woman Lydia is to have successors in later Cribb novels.

A Victorian music hall is the setting for *Abracadaver* (1972). The formal innovation in the novel is that it is told entirely from the point of view of Thackeray, from the moment he is rescued from hated "educational classes" at Paradise Street Police Station by a summons from Cribb to the climactic burning of the Paragon music hall. The precipitating crime here is not murder but a series of accidents, only apparently coincidental, to music-hall performers, none of which results in serious injury, but all of which expose the performers to ridicule and ruin their careers. This absence of a corpse becomes a running joke through the early part of the novel until a real murder is committed. "We've taken on some odd cases, I know," exclaims Thackeray at one point, "but there's always been a corpse to make the whole thing worth while." This line fairly represents the broad comedy of the entire novel, which is, appropriately, of a rough, knockabout, music-hall variety, and many of the characters, including Cribb and Thackeray, seem at times like characters from music-hall sketches. The novel places them in a series of situations as ridiculous as anything on the stage: Thackeray is a scene-shifter, dressed in bright yellow kneepants, during an obscene music-hall performance and Cribb fights off the advances of the eccentric Mrs. Body in her private theater-box. Such scenes have a touch of the self-referential: scenes shaped like music-hall sketches in a novel about music halls. Lovesey's rejection of pastiche in the Cribb novels does not bar him from including parody among his comic tools, a device he returns to in *Invitation to a Dynamite Party* (1974; published in the United States as *The Tick of Death*), which imitates a Victorian "dynamite thriller," and in *Swing, Swing Together* (1976), which is closely, though ironically, modeled on Jerome K. Jerome's *Three Men in a Boat (To Say Nothing of the Dog)* (1889).

The most grotesque figure in *Abracadaver* is that of Mrs. Body, mistress of Philbeach House for retired and distressed music-hall performers. Mrs. Body is a tiny, doll-like figure with childlike blond curls, whose drawing room contains painted heads on the wallpaper, plaster heads on the sideboard, and eggshell heads on the piano, all arranged to create the illusion of a music-hall audience as seen from the stage. Mrs. Body is another Lovesey villainess, given a comic, music-hall treatment. She seduces men in her theater-box / boudoir, but as private detective Major Chick shrewdly realizes, she is attracted only to men with obvious weaknesses: "It's the runt of the litter that lady fancies, I can tell you." The foil to Mrs. Body is Ellen Blake, who enters the novel singing "Fresh as the New-Mown Hay." By the novel's end Blake turns out to be a complex version of the Victorian virgin. Once again, Sergeant Cribb's keen intuition of feminine psychology is the key to his solution of the case. "What makes a young woman [Blake] as vicious as that, do you think?," asks Jowett, with uncharacteristic respect for Cribb's opinions. "A strong streak of Puritanism," replies Cribb. "And infatuation for a young man. A powerful combination, sir."

All the Cribb novels are comic, to varying degrees, but the comedy is broader in *Abracadaver* than in any other Lovesey novel, except perhaps for *Swing, Swing Together*. Lovesey perhaps felt in both cases that he was in danger of broadening the characters and situations to the point of losing credibility, for in both cases he followed the comic novel with one more serious in tone, *Waxwork* in the case of *Swing, Swing Together* and *Mad Hatter's Holiday* in the case of *Abracadaver*.

Mad Hatter's Holiday explores the possibilities of the detective-story form in the direction of the modern novel. Lovesey has said of this book (in "Becoming a Novelist"), "I experimented with pace, giving a slow, teasing build-up to the murder, and only introducing my detectives halfway through." He gives the novel a Jamesian quality through an adroit manipulation of point of view and the use of well-worked-out symbols. *Mad Hatter's Holiday* is the first Cribb novel told primarily from the point of view of a character other than Cribb or Thackeray; Albert Moscrop is a notably subjective and obtuse observer. The theme of perception introduced by this use of limited point of view is further reinforced by a number of subtle and effective symbols.

The date is September 1882, and Moscrop, manager of a London optical shop and a telescope hobbyist, is in Brighton for his solitary holidays. His delight is in peering at life through his

Dust jacket for the first American edition of Lovesey's only short-story collection

telescopes and binoculars, and within hours he has fixed upon a striking young woman as the object of his attentions, once removed. She turns out to be Zena Prothero (wife of the much older Dr. Gregory Prothero, stepmother to the precocious fifteen-year-old Guy Prothero, mother of little Jason Prothero, and employer of the nursemaid Bridget). Moscrop, who feels most at home when he is "invisible" in a large crowd, gradually insinuates himself into the Prothero party, alternately observing them safely through his binoculars and telescopes and arranging carefully staged meetings. New Scotland Yard becomes involved when a young woman's dismembered body is found on the beach under the promenade; the subsequent death, apparently natural, of Guy Prothero of an acute asthma attack further complicates matters.

The book features a wealth of historical detail–including the vogue for telescopes and binoculars in the 1880s and a description of

Brighton in 1882–and nowhere in the Cribb novels is historical material better integrated. The optical instruments become a metaphor for perception itself. Cribb refuses to use them because they blind a person to what is near at hand; a man with a pair of binoculars is a perfect victim for a pickpocket, he points out. Moscrop is no Peeping Tom–he would not stoop to surveying the ladies' bathing machines, for example–but he uses his instruments as a way of preserving his own detachment from life, which he rationalizes as "scientific objectivity." But his view of life is intensely subjective, and he misinterprets everything he sees, while it is Cribb who can, with his naked eyes, see beneath surface appearances to the truth.

The truth that lies behind appearances is usually monstrous in this book, as are the slime and weeds that underlie the scrubbed decks of the pier. Crocodiles are an image of the violence beneath the tranquil surface of Brighton and of

Victorian England. Readers first see Guy holding the infant Jason over the crocodile tank in the aquarium with a teasing cruelty, the tank where a severed hand is later found. Moscrop later buys Jason a wooden crocodile; and a fireworks display celebrating the triumphant return of the British army from Egypt features a set piece of a crocodile, representing Egypt. "What cheers there were as the sparks spent themselves and the enemy was exposed as a charred and smoking ruin! Marvellous to be British, and in Brighton, and secure from such monsters!"

Two murders are well integrated into the novel; both are outbreaks of a monstrous reality that crack the facade of a carefully manipulated illusion. Zena, when the nature of the first murder is revealed, acknowledges her part in maintaining an illusion of a happy and tranquil household, shielding herself with sleeping draughts from acknowledgment of her husband's infidelities and her stepson's homicidal violence. But now there will be "no escape from the truth. . . . I do not know whether the removal of our illusions is the best thing." And the climax of the novel–the solution of the second murder–involves Cribb in a decision whether to reveal the truth or to collaborate in maintaining a comforting facade.

The character of Cribb is considerably deepened in *Mad Hatter's Holiday* as readers see him for the first time contemplating problematic questions of moral, rather than strictly legal, justice. The book has its moments of comedy, especially in Constable Thackeray's adventures with Dr. Prothero's mistress, Samantha Floyd-Whittingham, who has an appetite for older men. But the general effect of the book is very far from the knockabout comedy of *Abracadaver*, and it represents an antithetical direction of development of the Cribb material from the preceding book.

There is nothing in the least Jamesian in *Invitation to a Dynamite Party;* it is, in Lovesey's words (from "Becoming a Novelist"), an "attempt to write a thriller–with the standard ingredients of kidnappings, secret organizations, beautiful women, dynamite and double-crossings–in the Victorian idiom." It would be difficult even to call *Invitation to a Dynamite Party* a detective story; Cribb's problem here is not who the criminals are but how to stop them from carrying out their plans. And the plot, while slightly tongue-in-cheek, is genuinely thrilling. The book is set against the background of the Irish bombing campaigns in London in 1884 and 1885, and Lovesey based it closely on a Victorian memoir entitled

Twenty-five Years in the Secret Service (1892), written by a police informer named Henri Le Caron, who had infiltrated an organization of Irish bombers much as Cribb does in the book. Thackeray has unwittingly encountered the dynamite gang and been kidnapped by them, and Cribb infiltrates in the guise of a paid adventurer. The dynamiters plan to blow up a pier at Gravesend while the Prince of Wales is on it, a feat to be accomplished by a Holland submarine packed with dynamite. The book is structured around a series of cliff-hanging crises and narrow escapes, and culminates in an escape by Cribb and Thackeray from the underwater craft and an aquatic chase scene after the escaping criminals.

The characters in *Invitation to a Dynamite Party* have a quality of whimsical parody. Chief among them is Rossanna McGee, head of the dynamite gang, whose behavior suggests an equation between passion and dynamite. She holds her position through the circumstance of her father, Daniel McGee, having been horribly mutilated in an explosion. Most of his face has been blown away, and he wears a black silk mask to hide the horrid remains. Rossanna, who ostensibly acts as his interpreter to the gang, swings between cold-blooded cruelty and a rather voracious sensuality, reminiscent of Isabel Vibart. She shoots Malone, a weak comrade, in cold blood and takes part in torturing Thackeray, but she also conceives a passion for Cribb and attempts to seduce him. She has Samantha Floyd-Whittingham's "copper-colored" hair and her taste for older men as well. Cribb attacks her sternly for shooting Malone and is surprised to find that she responds amorously. He concludes that "she was one of those unusual members of her sex uninterested in young men, preferring to submit to the authority of older, more masterful partners." *Invitation to a Dynamite Party*, modeled as it is on the Victorian thriller, perhaps approaches pastiche more nearly than the other Cribb novels. But its tone is very different from the actual thriller novels of the Victorians in that it is crisp and ironic without sacrificing genuine excitement. It is a contemporary author's loving but slightly bemused tribute to a popular art of a vanished age.

A Case of Spirits (1975) presents Sergeant Cribb wrestling with a locked-room mystery. The year is 1885; Cribb and Thackeray are called in to investigate two burglaries that have occurred during séances. The case turns into a murder investigation when Peter Brand, a fraudulent medium, is electrocuted during a séance in which he sat in an electrified chair, maintaining a low-voltage electrical circuit with his hands in order to guarantee that he did not move during the séance. The problem is how the apparently safe mechanism suddenly transmitted a fatal shock and who manipulated it to do so. Cribb solves the problem with a classic "re-enactment of the crime" and a gathering of all concerned to hear his solution. As the *New York Times* reviewer (15 February 1976) commented, "Traditionalism can go no further."

A Case of Spirits is an impeccably plotted novel with a number of curious and well-developed characters; especially prominent roles for Thackeray and Jowett (who becomes more and more a major comic creation); and a wealth of Victoriana, including not only the "spiritualist" movement, but the novelty of electricity, the feminist movement, and genteel pornography as well. But what unifies the novel is not the ingenious plotting or the historical lore, but the well-developed character relationships and motives. These turn, in *A Case of Spirits*, around Victorian sexuality and family life. The Proberts are a classic Victorian family. Cribb fails to notice the self-effacing Mrs. Probert when he first comes to the Probert establishment. "There is no need to apologize," she tells him. "My husband has failed to notice me for years now. I am quite resigned to it." Dr. Probert is a pompous, domineering Victorian father; Cribb thinks that "the single thing in favor of the man was that his house had been burgled." Probert opens his first conversation with Cribb bluntly: "I don't propose to beat around the bush. My wife misunderstands me." As for their daughter, Alice, she seems to be in strenuous training to become an angel of the house, spending her time in good works. "To see young Alice striding down the Hill with a marrow under her arm in search of a destitute family is a stirring sight, I promise you," boasts her fond father.

Reality is somewhat at odds with this prim facade. The unobtrusive Mrs. Probert, while she is supposed to be reading the collection, *Notable British Sermons*, in her room, is really passing the time with a gentleman caller and a bottle of gin. Dr. Probert comforts himself with a gallery of pornographic paintings, and young Alice, once down the hill with her marrow, hastens to an artist's studio to pose in the nude.

The starting point of *Swing, Swing Together* is the 1889 craze for Jerome's whimsical novel *Three Men in a Boat*. "Jerome's book really was

the best seller of the day," Lovesey explained in a 1983 interview with John C. Carr:

> And after that, everybody wanted a trip up the river. There really were groups of three people with a dog going up the river in a boat. So it seemed to me quite conceivable and quite amusing that we would have two bunches, two sets of people, who appeared to be suspects making their way up the river in that way. The chance to actually do the trip place by place was quite amusing and I had some fun myself. I walked up the riverbank and called in at the pubs and so on and got to know the route.

Even the form of Lovesey's novel follows *Three Men in a Boat*, structured around a picaresque river journey from Henley to Oxford and divided into forty short chapters, all with Jeromeian chapter headings ("Original use of butter," "River scene with figures," "Something rather horrid," etc.). Harriet Shaw, a student at Elfrida College for the Training of Female Elementary Teachers near Henley, joins two fellow students for a surreptitious nude midnight swim in the Thames, and they see three men and a dog in a boat. The innocent schoolgirl lark turns into a murder case when a body is fished out of the river the next day, and Harriet is called to give evidence about the mysterious party in the boat. She joins Cribb, Thackeray, and the attractive young Buckinghamshire constable Roger Hardy in a pursuit of the mysterious suspects up the Thames. (Lovesey has fun with the names in the novel; when Cribb temporarily leaves the boat to continue the chase by train, the three left in the boat are Thackeray, Hardy, and Shaw.) The Thames is swarming with vacationers re-creating the excursion in Jerome's book. Cribb and his party encounter one such group, with the fine names of Humberstone, Gold, and Lucifer, and they become major suspects. And, of course, Cribb's own group consists of three men in a boat (to say nothing of the girl).

Swing, Swing Together is the sunniest and most genial of the Cribb novels, a wonderful excursion into Victorian whimsical comedy. Much of its charm radiates from the character of Harriet, whose point of view shapes the novel. Harriet is a genteel young lady of eighteen, her head full of girlish fantasies: her first impression of Cribb is that "he had reached what her mother called the dangerous time of life." But she is also remarkably shrewd and resourceful; she takes an active part in solving the crime and pursues Constable Hardy with as much determination as she does the criminals, though with different motives.

The charm of *Swing, Swing Together* is all the more effective for the shadows in the book. The book's double vision of Victorian whimsy is suggested by the title, both a quotation from the "Eton Boating Song" and a reference to hanging. The Jack the Ripper murders, which occurred during the same period as the fad for *Three Men in a Boat*, form an important part of the background. The private sadism of the Ripper murders is matched by the approved, institutionalized sadism of Victorian penology. At one point in the novel, Cribb goes to the Coldbath Fields House of Correction and sees the prisoners being "exercised" on the treadmill and the crank, a sight that disperses "any thoughts Cribb might have entertained of a career in the prison service." The three men (not all in a boat) ultimately revealed as the book's murderers are driven by motives that suggest the inverted passions possible in a society that was capable of producing both Gilbert and Sullivan and Jack the Ripper.

Waxwork is in many ways the most complex Cribb novel. Lovesey continues his practice of varying the form of each novel by taking on a retrospective plot in the manner of Agatha Christie. By the time Cribb enters the case, Miriam Cromer has made a full, detailed confession of the poisoning murder of the assistant of her photographer-husband, has pleaded guilty at her trial, and has been sentenced to death by hanging. An anonymous communication to the home secretary has brought out one discrepancy in her confession, however, and Jowett assigns Cribb to conduct a detailed reexamination of the crime in the eleven days remaining before the execution. The whimsical gaiety of *Swing, Swing Together*, Lovesey's previous novel, is replaced in *Waxwork* by a dark, sinister quality. Even the comic office politics of Jowett become in *Waxwork* a cynical conspiracy to protect the reputation of those in high places even if it means hanging an innocent woman. The private crime of Miriam Cromer is tacitly contrasted with the public one of the commissioner of the Metropolitan Police, Sir Charles Warren, notorious for having put down a demonstration of the unemployed the previous year with a force of four thousand police and six hundred guardsmen, with needless brutality and taking of life. The sardonic irony of the novel is heightened by the counterpointing of three plot threads. Against Cribb's slow progress toward the solution of the crime are set an account of the prison routine in Newgate, as Miriam is prepared for execution, and the preparation of James Berry, public hangman, to come up to London for the "job."

Cribb characteristically pursues his inquiry through a series of interviews. (He is alone: this is the only Cribb novel in which Thackeray does not appear.) Miriam's confession is a straightforward, fairly simple account of the crime, but once Cribb pulls one thread, the entire fabric begins to unravel, revealing a background of complex and perverse motives. If Harriet Shaw is Lovesey's finest ideal woman, Miriam Cromer is his best-realized manipulative woman, driven by compulsive desires and acting with icy cruelty. Her husband, Howard Cromer, is equally complex and equally perverse. He carries Albert Moscrop's tendency to keep life at a distance by viewing it though a lens to the point of madness; Cribb recognizes that Miriam "was more real to this man as a series of photographs than a wife."

The climax of the novel comes when Cribb finally wins permission to interview Miriam herself in her prison cell. He has known all through the case that he will ultimately have to see her in person: "Understand the woman, see her, hear her, and he would get to the truth." When he does interview her, he is well armed with facts uncovered by patient investigation and with a theory of how the crime was committed. But finally, it is not facts but personalities that reveal the truth: "people, their ambitions and fears, innocence and guilt."

Lovesey's double vision of Victorian life, its charm and the repressed forces by which that charm was maintained–the Brighton pier and its slimy underside–is summed up in the title *Waxwork*. The "waxwork" alluded to Madam Tussaud's museum, where the hangman Berry is having his statue made and to whom he intends to sell Miriam Cromer's clothing. But more generally the title refers to all the "images" in the novel, not only the wax figures at Madam Tussaud's, objects of a prurient Victorian preoccupation with crime and punishment, but also the photographic images into which Howard Cromer has retreated, and even the mental images that Miriam has pursued in her misguided life. The climax of the novel comes when Cribb looks into Miriam Cromer's face and sees "no longer the face in the photograph" but a real human face.

Many Cribb novels were reborn on television in 1980 and 1981 on Granada in England

and PBS in the United States. Lovesey did the adaptation of *The Detective Wore Silk Drawers;* seven other Cribb novels were dramatized by other writers. In addition, Lovesey has written, in collaboration with his wife Jacqueline Lovesey, six original Cribb television mysteries. The novels, with their vivid, colorful settings and their wealth of comic dialogue, have turned out to be well suited to television.

Lovesey's Cribb novels stand as a major achievement of modern British mystery fiction. Their freshness and originality lie in their way of dealing with the past within the mystery form, not merely as a gimmick or as a source of vague atmosphere but as their central content. His exploration of Victorian England is not especially profound, but it is continuously interesting and is fully dramatized rather than merely providing a period backdrop. The books are also memorable for their humor, perhaps a better word than comedy, since their laughter, though sometimes broad, is always genial and kind. Cribb, Thackeray, and Jowett are creations worthy of Dickens, and the secondary characters constitute a great gallery of humors comedy. The books sometimes deal with grim topics—the slime beneath the pier—but they temper the grimness with healthy laughter, a combination that is perhaps their most truly "Victorian" quality.

Lovesey described to Carr what led him to write two nonmystery thrillers, *Goldengirl* (1977) and *Spider Girl* (1980), and to publish them under the pseudonym Peter Lear:

> When I became a full-time writer–I'd been a teacher and decided, I think in 1975, that the time had come to take the plunge and drop the job and write full time–I thought then I couldn't carry on with Sergeant Cribb indefinitely, that I ought to try to widen my range. It was sensible to look for a different market and write an up-to-date book, and I didn't think that my Cribb readers would particularly appreciate a book about the modern Olympic games.

Clearly the upcoming Olympic games also figured in Lovesey's choice of subject for *Goldengirl,* written in 1977 but set at the 1980 Olympic games in Moscow. The topicality of the subject also probably prompted the producers of the 1979 film of the book, starring Susan Anton. (Neither Lovesey nor the filmmakers, of course, could have foreseen the U.S. boycott of the Moscow games.)

Goldengirl is told from the point of view of Jack Dryden, a British expatriate who runs a successful sports promotion agency in California. A few months before the 1980 Olympics, he is drawn into a secret consortium of businessmen who plan to unveil a brilliant but unknown woman runner, have her win three gold medals at the games, and make a fortune on her endorsement of various commercial products. The leader of the consortium is a physiologist named William Serafin, and the prospective "golden girl" is his adopted daughter Goldine Serafin. Dryden investigates Serafin and learns that Goldine is actually Dean Hofmann, the third-generation product of Nazi eugenics experiments. Orphaned at two, she has been adopted by Serafin, who tracked her down as part of his research in genetics. Her six-foot, two-inch height and her extraordinary athletic skills are not, however, the result of her "Aryan" heritage but of Serafin's injections of a growth hormone during childhood, extensive plastic surgery, and a nightmarish, neo-Pavlovian training regimen. Just before the Olympics it is discovered that Goldine has diabetes, triggered by the growth hormones. Even more severe are her emotional problems, which take the form of a split between her normal identity as "Goldine" and an arrogant, megalomaniacal fantasy identity as "Goldengirl." At the climax of the novel, Goldine rises above her diabetic symptoms and wins her three gold medals but collapses psychologically to become locked into her frightful "Goldengirl" persona forever.

The protagonist of *Spider Girl* is Sarah Jordan, a graduate student in a New York university whose specialty is arachnology, the study of spiders. She appears in an educational-television documentary about phobias and is such a success that she is engaged as a narrator for another documentary about spiders, which employs human actors enacting arachnid behavior on giant webs. The experience of playing a spider–and the ill-considered advice of a consultant psychiatrist with the television company that she approach her role by identifying spiderlike characteristics in herself–lead to her gradual retreat from reality into the role of "Spider Girl," a role reinforced by media exploitation of her overnight success. At the climax of the novel she murders a man in her spider persona and almost commits a second murder before she dies in an accidental fall.

Goldengirl and *Spider Girl* are interesting experiments. For one thing, Lovesey experiments in them with becoming an American writer. Both have American settings and are written in an almost aggressively American idiom. It is true that in *Goldengirl* Lovesey provides a safety net by making his protagonist a naturalized Englishman. But the net is really unnecessary; Lovesey has an uncanny ear for American–even Californian–speech, and the language of both novels rings true. He also experiments in the two novels with a contemporary setting, giving up the charming nostalgia of the Cribb novels for the comparatively harsh light of the present. The two novels do have a contemporary feel and engage topical issues. But there remain certain links with the Cribb novels in the way they use research into specialized areas. *Goldengirl* provided an opportunity to use the knowledge of the history of track that had inspired *Wobble to Death;* threaded through the book is a history of the Olympics, especially emphasizing the history of women's participation. Lovesey also uses his expert's knowledge of contemporary training techniques and the political history of the Olympics to raise troubling questions about the contemporary meaning of the games. Can the high-minded idealism of amateur athletes from all over the world meeting in peaceful competition be sustained in the light of Orwellian training methods and the politicization of the games? Goldine's chief competitor is an East German runner named Ursula Krüll, and Dryden at one point remarks:

> Krüll is the prestige vehicle of an ideology. She's running in the name of Marx and Lenin. Since she's running well, those ideologues can put enormous pressure on the coaches to try her for the triple. What do they care if she's a spent husk at the end of it?

The irony here, which Dryden can't see, is that Goldine Serafin is the product of an ideology too, that of technological capitalism. Created by chemicals and conditioning and presold as a commodity even before she runs a single race, she is the expression of a system as inhuman in its own way as the Nazi human engineering which lies in her background.

Spider Girl provides a short course in arachnology, as well integrated and as unobtrusively introduced as the Victorian lore in the Cribb novels. But the central theme of the novel is not spiders but the media and its exploitation of the individual in its quest for hype. At the end of the novel Havelock Sloane, the producer, makes the monstrous proposal that a documentary be made

of Sarah's troubled life. Her friend Don Rigdon, in the last speech of the novel, agrees but bitterly demands that the documentary assign full guilt to those who were implicated in her death, including "you, Mr. Sloane, the guy who makes the big decisions, like putting that confused girl on a web and telling her to become a spider." The scene recalls the ending of *Goldengirl*, in which Jack Dryden is forced to confront his own complicity in Goldine's madness, when he declined an opportunity to prevent her obsessive, self-destructive pursuit of the three gold medals.

The False Inspector Dew, which won the British Crime Writers' Association's Gold Dagger Award in 1982, is Lovesey's masterpiece thus far and one of the best mysteries ever written, one that opens up new possibilities for the genre. Subtitled "A Murder Mystery Aboard the *S.S. Mauretania*, 1921," it takes as its starting point the famous Crippen murder case of 1910. Dr. Crippen, a London dentist, fell in love with his nurse, Ethel Le Neve, murdered his wife and buried her in the cellar, and fled to Canada with Ethel, who dressed as a boy and posed as his son. The ship's captain saw through the disguises and wired Scotland Yard. Inspector Walter Dew boarded a faster ship to Canada and was waiting to arrest them when they disembarked in Toronto. Crippen was convicted of the murder and hanged.

Lovesey's novel deals directly, however, not with the historical Crippen and Le Neve but with a couple who determine to emulate them. A dentist named Walter Baranov falls in love with Alma Webster, one of his patients. Baranov is married to a vain, domineering, unsuccessful actress upon whom he is completely dependent financially. He and Alma determine to copy Crippen and Le Neve but to avoid their mistakes. Lydia Baranov is sailing to America, where she thinks her acquaintance with Charlie Chaplin will gain her entrée to the movies. Baranov and Alma plan to go on board, chloroform Lydia and push her through a porthole, and sail on to America in bliss, leaving behind no telltale body. At first all seems to go as planned, but Baranov has made the mistake of booking his passage under the name "Walter Dew," as a private joke with Alma. When an unrelated murder occurs on the ship, he is identified as the famous Inspector Dew and recruited to investigate it. The results are a dazzling series of surprises and reversals, completely unexpected but meticulously plotted.

The False Inspector Dew, as a historical mystery, obviously has much in common with the Cribb novels. The *Mauretania* itself is meticulously visualized down to the last detail, and life on board the liner is re-created very amusingly and convincingly. Prohibition, the Chaplin craze, and other 1920s phenomena unobtrusively fill the background, without being pointed up as self-conscious "period detail." As in the Cribb novels the historicity of the book extends beyond concrete artifacts to value systems. The crime itself is quintessentially a 1920s crime, one that involves a bursting of traditional constraints, testing boundaries, and trying on unfamiliar roles, themes that are echoed in many ways throughout the novel. In one amusing scene, for example, the important secondary character Barbara Cordell comes out of her studious shell and becomes a flapper.

The chief structural difference between the Cribb novels and *The False Inspector Dew* is the absence of the detectives. And the reader senses that Lovesey's feeling of liberation is almost as exhilarating as Barbara's. Amusing as Cribb and Thackeray were, they impose certain structural limits on the novels in which they appear. Without this obligatory limited point of view Lovesey can construct a much more complex and open narrative. *The False Inspector Dew* is cast as a documentary; a foreword claims that the pages that follow are a "reconstruction" of the incident of the false Inspector Dew based on a recently discovered file in the Cunard Company archives. The novel itself is structured in six parts, each made up of several short numbered episodes. In the short sections an omniscient Lovesey adopts the point of view of several different characters: Baranov and Alma, the Cockney pickpocket Poppy Duke, one or another member of the wealthy Livingstone Cordell family, the playboy Paul Westerfield, the cardsharper Jack Gordon, and others.

The structure of *The False Inspector Dew* is based on the principle of doubling. Lovesey had used this device for comic purposes in *Swing, Swing Together*, in the proliferation of boats with three men and a dog; here he carries it to its logical extreme. There are two of everything, not only a false Inspector Dew and a real Inspector Dew, but also a true and false Dr. Crippen and Ethel Le Neve, a false body and a real one, a false love for both Baranov and Alma and true ones. The *Mauretania* itself is doubled by its sunken sister ship the *Lusitania*, and there is even a false Charlie Chaplin (at a shipboard costume party) to set beside the true one. There is a certain brittle, gamelike quality about the artificiality, but doubling is basic to Lovesey's themes. The ultimate true-false pairings are within the selves of the protagonists. The paradox of Baranov's masquerade as the false Inspector Dew is that it becomes true. When Alma, late in the novel, congratulates him for having deceived the authorities into thinking he was solving the mystery, he is offended: "My dear, I have solved it. I know who committed the murder and I know why. That's what I'm saying. I'm a very good detective." Put to the test, the weak, easily dominated Baranov discovers depths in himself he did not know existed. He discovers, for one thing, that he was not cut out to be a Crippen; his role in the drama is Dew, and he ultimately becomes a true Inspector Dew.

Alma undergoes a similar initiation and rebirth. A London Gerty McDowell, she has dreamed away her youth reading the romances of Ouida and Ethel M. Dell and ordering her reality after the pattern of those books. She is able to propose murder to Baranov only because murder lacks reality for her. When she thinks of the Crippen case, she ignores the dead woman and thinks only of the presumed glamour of the lovers: "She had tried to decide whether she, too, could have faced that moment with dignity. Love, and love alone, must have fortified them." But when Baranov actually kills Lydia (or when Alma thinks he has), her haze of illusion begins to dissipate. She finds that she is no more an Ethel Le Neve than he is a Crippen and finds a real lover to replace her fantasy one.

It is tempting to call *The False Inspector Dew* a postmodern mystery, an elegant verbal structure whose real subject is the genre itself. As a detective novel with a false detective at its center, it demystifies the whole convention of the Holmesian detective. "I thought it would be difficult at first," Baranov tells Alma, "but it wasn't. I didn't need to ask clever questions or discover hidden clues. Being a detective is just a matter of getting other people to talk." There is an ironic, purloined-letter quality to the solution of the final puzzle, too. Readers are given the key on the first page and insistently reminded of it throughout, and yet it is a dazzling surprise when it is explained in the final section. And it is appropriate that it turn around the figure of Charlie Chaplin, who practices the actor's art of finding the truth by means of falsity. A recurring ambition of mystery writers is to "transcend the genre," to achieve the substantiality of serious fiction within the conventions of mystery fiction. And yet a common difficulty is that when the genre is thus transcended, the result is often a rather old-fashioned realistic novel, as in, for example, P. D. James's otherwise admirable *A Taste for Death*. *The False Inspector Dew* offers an alternative strategy. Rather than chafing under the conventions of the genre, it joyfully embraces them and makes them its subject. The result is a lightness, a joy, a delight in its own fictionality that suggests comparisons not with Dickens or William Makepeace Thackeray but with Jorge Luis Borges, Gabriel García Marquez, and Milan Kundera.

The new direction in Lovesey's work marked by *The False Inspector Dew* was extended and confirmed by his next novel, *Keystone*. Set in Mack Sennett's Keystone Studios in 1915, it is a comic mystery which explores a vivid historical setting. But the determination Lovesey has shown in the Cribb novels not to let a method become a formula is equally clear in the progression from *The False Inspector Dew* to *Keystone*. This novel, Lovesey's twelfth, is the first written in the first person. In it he gives up the openness and contrapuntal complexity of his omniscient third-person point of view in *The False Inspector Dew* for the compression and concentration of the point of view of a single character, a Keystone Cop named Warwick Easton, nicknamed, by Mack Sennett himself, "Keystone."

Keystone is an English vaudevillian stranded in California at the end of an American tour. He takes a job at the Keystone Studios and, on his first day, witnesses an apparent accident, a fatal fall of a Keystone Cop from a roller coaster. The accident begins to look like murder when the mother of an actress named Amber Honeybee, with whom Keystone falls in love, is bludgeoned by an intruder who searches her home. When Keystone himself is attacked and Amber is kidnapped he is forced to turn detective and track down the killer inside the studio. The novel ends in a literal cliff-hanger when Amber, bound and dressed as a Keystone dummy, is about to be pushed over a cliff in a Keystone wagon; Keystone races to intercept the wagon in a car.

Lovesey's forays into the American movie industry with *Goldengirl* and the televised Cribb series may have had some influence on his choosing as his protagonist an Englishman bemused by the bizarre ways of Hollywood. Keystone himself is an engaging character, whose English reserve contrasts comically with the Keystone flamboy-

ance. The gross, tyrannical Sennett finds him hilarious when he interviews him. Midway through the novel, Keystone pauses to analyze his own character:

> I knew I was not good at making friends. Most of my life, people had described me as stand-offish and aloof. That was my temperament, though. I preferred to call myself reserved. Oddly, it had proved an asset in the music-halls. I was a natural straight man. In America, with my British ways and accent, I was even more of an outsider. I provoked amusement and occasionally derision.

In *Keystone* Lovesey has done his historical homework. Not only Sennett but Mabel Normand and Roscoe "Fatty" Arbuckle as well are major characters, and Lovesey's characterizations of them are historically accurate. Fascinating technical details of early moviemaking and distribution are introduced with Lovesey's characteristic skill and tact. The historical setting provides not only color but also a central theme in the book. In the background of the novel is World War I; England is already at war, and Keystone is determined to earn his passage home to join the army. On the one hand, Sennett and his moviemakers seem irresponsible, if amusing, cynics, cranking out foolish mass entertainment while the world is poised on the edge of a cataclysm. On the other hand, the war seems to have invaded the studios, and both seem to be built upon the same values. Sennett remarks at one point, "Movie comedy is like war. People get hurt." In another scene Keystone, having finished a day of filming a silly seaside comedy, pauses on a hill above the beach and looks down on the film crew, contrasting their behavior with the battlefields of Europe.

As occasionally in Lovesey's earlier comic novels, in *Keystone* part of his subject seems to be comedy itself. Sennett's Keystone comedy, innocent as it seems, has an undercurrent of aggression and violence. "One thing was real," Keystone remarks. "In the so-called fun factory of Keystone lurked violence and malice." He is directly referring to the murders, but there are also violence and malice in the films themselves, as the descriptions of the ones under production make clear. The Keystone Cops, off-camera, are addicted to cruel and humiliating practical jokes (such as running an electric current to Charlie Chaplin's urinal), and Sennett, whose sensibility the films express, is crude, boorish, and tyrannical. The book implies that Keystone comedy is a veiled expression of the violence of America on the threshold of world war.

Life often imitates art in Lovesey's novels, as when an investigation into a gang of dynamiters turns into a Victorian "dynamite thriller" (*Invitation to a Dynamite Party*) or when Baranov and Alma shape their lives along the lines of accounts of the Crippen case (*The False Inspector Dew*). Keystone's adventures in the Mack Sennett studios gradually take on the contours of a Mack Sennett film. Cast in a seaside comedy, Keystone and Amber have a private love scene on the beach. And the climax of the novel is a Keystone chase scene along the cliffs, incorporating a real police car as well as a Keystone wagon.

Keystone is a worthy successor to *The False Inspector Dew*. If it seems somewhat less rich in texture and ideas, that is probably because of Lovesey's decision to use a smaller canvas than the broad, panoramic one of the earlier novel. Successors of *Keystone* to date have been *Rough Cider*, *Bertie and the Tinman: From the Detective Memoirs of King Edward VII* (1987), and *On the Edge* (1989), varied novels which are linked by Lovesey's sense of history and comic touch.

In his *Bloody Murder* (1974) Julian Symons divides his chapter on contemporary crime novelists into two sections–"Serious Crime Novelists" and "Entertainers"–and places Lovesey (whose work he praises) firmly in the second category. This is probably just, though the dividing line between "serious" and "entertaining" is not so clear (and one would hope not so absolute) as Symons makes it. Lovesey's chief contribution to the current resurgence of British mystery writing has been his gift for developing rich comic characterizations within a traditional puzzle framework and thus humanizing a too often sterile form. To say that his novels are light is not to denigrate them but to identify their central virtue. At his best (and he is often at his best) Lovesey has brought a comic lightness to the mystery novel that has expanded its possibilities in new and unexpected ways.

Interview:

John C. Carr, "Peter Lovesey," in *The Craft of Crime: Conversations with Crime Writers* (Boston: Houghton Mifflin, 1983), pp. 258-288.

Reference:

James Hurt, "How Unlike the Home Life of Our Own Dear Queen: The Detective Fiction of Peter Lovesey," in *Essays on Detective Fiction*, edited by Bernard Benstock (London: Macmillan, 1983), pp. 142-158.

Gavin Lyall

(9 May 1932-   )

Carol Simpson Stern
Northwestern University

BOOKS: *The Wrong Side of the Sky* (London: Hodder & Stoughton, 1961; New York: Scribners, 1961);

The Most Dangerous Game (New York: Scribners, 1963; London: Hodder & Stoughton, 1964);

Midnight plus One (London: Hodder & Stoughton, 1965; New York: Scribners, 1965);

Shooting Script (London: Hodder & Stoughton, 1966; New York: Scribners, 1966);

The War in the Air 1939-1945: An Anthology of Personal Experience, edited by Lyall (London: Hutchinson, 1968); republished as *The War in the Air: The Royal Air Force in World War II* (New York: Morrow, 1969);

Venus with Pistol (London: Hodder & Stoughton, 1969; New York: Scribners, 1969);

Blame the Dead (London: Hodder & Stoughton, 1972; New York: Viking, 1973);

Judas Country (London: Hodder & Stoughton, 1975; New York: Viking, 1975);

Operation Warboard: Wargaming World War II Battles 20-25 mm Scale, by Lyall and Bernard Lyall (London: Black, 1976; New York: McKay, 1977);

The Secret Servant (London: Hodder & Stoughton, 1980; New York: Viking, 1980);

The Conduct of Major Maxim (London: Hodder & Stoughton, 1982; New York: Viking, 1983);

The Crocus List (London: Hodder & Stoughton, 1985; New York: Viking, 1986);

Uncle Target (London: Hodder & Stoughton, 1988; New York: Viking, 1988).

MOTION PICTURE: *Moon Zero Two, with Others,* screenplay by Lyall, Frank Hardman, and Martin Davison, Hammer, 1969.

Gavin Lyall writes two types of thrillers: tales of high adventure, told in the first person, structured around an unusual mission, and usually featuring a former military pilot or hired bodyguard as protagonist; and tales of the British intelligence services, narrated in the third person, structured around a national or interna-

Gavin Lyall (photograph by Fay Godwin)

tional crisis, and featuring a serial protagonist, Major Harry Maxim. The high-adventure novels belong in the tradition of Geoffrey Household and Raymond Chandler. Chandler lends the tough-guy style, the heavy reliance on dialogue to carry the tale, and the careful use of place to suggest the moral dimensions of the story as well as to provide a vivid sense of scene. Lyall's landscapes mirror the condition of society, and his plots are well crafted. The adventure novels are romantic and somewhat sentimental at the same time. They feature protagonists in the manner of Chandler's Marlowe and Norman Mailer's hero in *Tough Guys Don't Dance.* Lyall's spy thrillers evolve from his earlier writing but represent two interesting departures: the invention of a compelling serial protagonist enables him to offer a more subtle, less formulaic hero, and it frees him from the requirements of first-person narration. The world of spying and bureaucratic rivalries among the branches of British intelligence lend themselves to the creation of rich geographical settings for his novels and enable him to offer elaborate moral and political commentary. Lyall has earned the Crime Writers' Association's Silver Dagger Award on two occasions. Two of his novels on Major Maxim have been adapted for television and were popularly received in England. He is an able writer, most skilled in his handling of landscape and situation, and capable of creating compelling heroes.

Gavin Tudor Lyall was born in Birmingham, Warwickshire, England, on 9 May 1932, to Joseph Tudor and Ann Hodgkiss Lyall. He was educated at King Edward VI School, Birmingham, from 1943 to 1951. From 1951 to 1953 he served in the Royal Air Force, becoming a pilot officer in 1952. He attended Pembroke College, Cambridge, from 1953 to 1956, earning a B.A. in English (with honors) in 1956 and editing the college newspaper. From 1956 to 1957 he served as a reporter for *Picture Post* magazine. In 1958 he married Katherine E. Whitehorn, a writer who has served as a columnist and fashion editor for the *London Observer* since 1960 and who became associate editor for the paper in 1980. From 1958 to 1959 Lyall was a film director for the news with BBC television, London. He joined the *London Sunday Times* serving as a reporter and air correspondent and finally as an aviation editor during the period from 1959 to 1963. In 1963 he resigned his editorship to devote himself full time to the writing of suspense and adventure stories. Lyall has edited *The War in the Air 1939-1945: An Anthology of Personal Experience* (1968) and coauthored a book of rules for warboard games, *Operation Warboard: Wargaming World War II Battles 20-25 mm Scale*, with his brother in 1976. He has drawn on his experiences as a staff journalist to Europe, Libya, India, Pakistan, Persia, Nepal, the United States, and Australia for the rich, descriptive detail and the exotic climes of some of his novels. Lyall's wife is the author of numerous how-to-survive books (*How to Survive in a Hospital; How to Survive Children; How to Survive in the Kitchen*; and *How to Survive your Money Problems*), and undoubtedly she has provided him with some of the domestic detail and fashion descriptions which figure in

his novels, particularly in *The Secret Servant* (1980), *The Conduct of Major Maxim* (1982), and *The Crocus List* (1985). Since 1979 Lyall has served on the Air Transport Users Committee, in 1985 becoming an honorary consultant; and since 1986 he has served as a member of the Air Travel Commission. He was chairman of the Crime Writers' Association from 1966 to 1967. Recreationally, he enjoys travel, cooking, military history, guns, model-making, cats, and beer. By religion he is a Quaker.

Lyall began his literary career as a writer of adventure and suspense novels. The landscape of these novels ranges over Britain, the Mediterranean, Greece, Cyprus, Israel, North Africa, and Europe. The protagonists in his first seven novels share certain common resemblances: they tend to live on both sides of the law; often they reminisce about their war experiences; they are usually loners, men's men, with a public-school code of honor and a love of blood sports. One is a Resistance hero turned gunman, another is a security adviser turned bodyguard, and another is an expert in old weapons and a gun smuggler. Several are pilots. His plots are cunning, taut, nicely delineated, and entertaining. Lyall revels in creating memorable backgrounds for his stories. He also researches his novels thoroughly. Whether he is describing army weaponry, the fraud practiced in the art world, the illegal traffic in stolen jewels, or the financing, finagling, and takeover of a Liechtenstein corporation, he makes the subject matter insinuating and flatters his readers with those moments of self-congratulation which come when the unfamiliar seems familiar. His first seven novels derive from the romantic tradition of adventure writing. They recall the writings of Household, particularly *Rogue Male* (1939). Like Household, Lyall exploits the chase and hunt. He places his heroes in predicaments of extreme physical difficulty. In *The Most Dangerous Game* (1963), it is man who is stalked and hunted in the remote regions of northern Finland, along the forbidden zone of the Russian frontier, where the landscape is as inhospitable as the hunter. As the action becomes ever more desperate, two wounded men, locked in a life-and-death struggle, rely on their tenacity and animal cunning until only one survives. Lyall places his protagonists in extremis, moving them to frontiers which permit him to peel away the veneer of civilization and probe the nature of man's identity and moral character. In *The Wrong Side of the Sky* (1961), the protagonist forms a sinister intimacy with nature and with his human prey before his journey ends.

In Lyall's four Maxim novels he introduces one central protagonist, Major Maxim, an SAS man assigned to the British prime minister to handle sensitive intelligence missions which fall under the control of neither MI 5 or MI 6, but involve both. The landscape includes Northern Ireland and North America in addition to London, the British countryside, and the Continent. The widowed major is permitted some love interest with the competent Agnes Algar of MI 5, and readers are given glimpses of his more private family life with his son, who has been cared for by Maxim's parents since the violent death of his wife in the Persian Gulf states of the Middle East. The Maxim novels provide Lyall an opportunity for extended character delineation and for political commentary. To capture the world of espionage and probe a more complex protagonist, he uses third-person narration and relies heavily on filmic techniques. At present, it seems likely that Lyall will stay with his serial protagonist and the espionage novel, working in the manner of John le Carré but with less brilliance and cynicism. His Maxim novels follow the tradition of Joseph Conrad and Graham Greene. They trace the collision of the private man, at his best, with his highest intelligence and with physical courage, against man as he is organized in the highly structured, bureaucratic units of government. In this context the individual's conduct can be elevated to the genre of tragedy. Conrad and Greene almost achieve the tragic moment. Lyall does not; his protagonist acts out of the highest motives, and he does kill rather than be killed, but his suffering is not elevated to tragic proportions, nor does he die. Nonetheless, it is useful to consider Lyall's works in the tradition of the realist spy novel, where man at his best is helpless to control his fate, is a puppet manipulated by governments and spy rings, is a kind of Corialanus facing an Aufidius, both men very much alike, both forced to be enemies. Major Maxim is like Smiley's Control in le Carré's novels. Like Smiley, he has to learn "to be inhuman in defense of our humanity . . . harsh in defense of compassion . . . singleminded in defense of our disparity" (*The Honourable Schoolboy*).

Lyall's first three novels, *The Wrong Side of the Sky*, *The Most Dangerous Game*, and *Midnight plus One* (1965) are structured around dangerous missions and treasure hunts. They are characteristic of the genre of high adventure and suspense in the twentieth century. Written in a context where culture is a commodity, where the genre of suspense and mystery writing is a product of middle-class society in an age of mechanical reproduction, these books reflect society's fascination with technology, its preoccupation with the individual, and its lack of faith in the political state. Naturally, the books also derive some of their entertainment value from society's faith in property; its vicarious appetite to see men's greed and ambition fueled, even if it ultimately will be checked; and its nostalgic view of World War II and the breakdown of British colonialism. In *The Wrong Side of the Sky*, Jack Clay, a former army pilot flying a Dakota, transports illegal cargo for a Greek agent of whom one does not ask too many questions. His work leads him in search of the lost jewels of an Indian Nawab, which had been stolen more than ten years earlier and had resurfaced in Beirut, and it reunites him with Ken Kitson, his old wartime flying buddy. Clay and his friend had participated in a misguided mission during India's partition, which cost them their flying licenses and put them on "the wrong side of the sky" for the rest of their careers, but Clay still dreams of a time when he can fly for the big airlines. The reader is asked to believe that this dream of a fresh start is sufficient to account for the risks he takes and the men he kills in order to get a cut of an extremely valuable cache of jewels. Clay and Kitson are legendary fliers, men who were the best, but their ill judgment and high ambition left them outsiders for the rest of their lives. In *The Most Dangerous Game*, Lyall again tells the tale from the vantage of a free-lance pilot. Bill Cary, the protagonist, once a worker for a Finnish mining company, is chartered by an American hunter to fly him into a remote region of Finland in search of the Volkof treasure abandoned during the Russian Revolution of 1917. Soon Cary is piloting far into the Arctic Circle, discovering a sabotaged aircraft, and becoming involved in a plot engineered by a Finnish counterespionage organization. *Midnight plus One* is structured around a race against time as an industrial mogul, Maganhard, attempts to reach Liechtenstein in time for a business board meeting which he must attend if he is to protect his company from a hostile takeover. To meet the midnight deadline he hires an old Resistance fighter to escort him across France. Together they try to evade both the French police, who are after Maganhard on trumped-up charges, and Galleron, leader of the takeover, who is determined to prevent his ar-

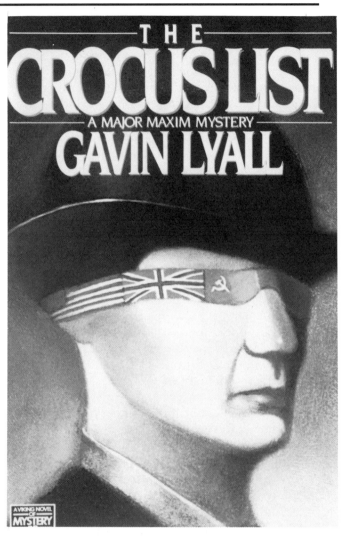

Dust jackets for the first British and American editions of Lyall's third Major Maxim novel (courtesy of Otto Penzler)

rival; all is resolved in a fine conclusion.

Lyall's first three novels depend heavily for their success on his skillful and technically precise descriptions of how a series of obstacles is overcome, enabling the protagonist to chase down his quarry. *The Most Dangerous Game* belongs purely to the genre of hunter and hunted. The other two novels also show men in extremis; in one case the final human hunt is set on the old Resistance route from World War II. The descriptions are precise, juxtaposing the particulars of man's close knowledge of the hazards posed by the environment. In *Midnight plus One*, Lyall shows off his extensive knowledge of military history. In all three of the novels, the protagonist demonstrates his consummate skill at either flying or driving, and Lyall provides a richly visual sense of the story's landscape. Lyall's descriptions, of a crashed "Dak," or of its cockpit in air, or of the

steps to be followed to fly it beneath a storm front of cumulus clouds, make the reader believe in the place and the reality of the situation. In each novel the protagonist is brought into contact with his past and with traumatic and decisive moments which define moral character. Although his protagonists are outsiders in the peacetime world, they are men of conscience despite the fact that they often live on the wrong side of the law. They are disillusioned idealists. Tough guys in their manner, they are men who witness their veneer of civilization stripped away as they journey and finally encounter the darker regions of their own souls and question who they are, what friends are, and why men kill.

Venus with Pistol (1969), *Shooting Script* (1966), and *Judas Country* (1975) continue in the manner of Lyall's first three novels, but his control as a writer becomes more secure, his plots more complex, and his tone more cynical. *Venus with Pistol* involves the world of art forgery and the doings of Doña Margarita Umberto, who has come to Europe with her entourage from Nicaragua in order to spend several million dollars creating an art museum for her country. "Venus with Pistol" is the $2,500,000 painting she is after; whether it is by Giorgione or a fraud is the question that determines its worth and who lives or dies in the novel. *Shooting Script* revolves around the adventures of another pilot, Keith Carr, who flies a camera plane for a film company on location in the Caribbean. *Judas Country*, again involving a pair of former military pilots, Roy Case and Ken Cavit, is a tale of smuggling, blackmail, a bankrupt hotel chain, and a quest for the sword of Richard Coeur de Lion. Like *Venus with Pistol* it also involves an acquisitive, conniving woman from the art world—an American curator—who hopes to purchase the sword legally and at an advantageous price. Set in Cyprus, Damascus, and Jerusalem, *Judas Country* is a novel of betrayal played against the backdrop of the political turmoil of the Middle East. In *The Wrong Side of the Sky*, the loner protagonist finally confronts his friend, of whom he was suspicious from the onset, preparing the reader for a final break; Ken bows to Clay's will, and the two men understand each other. In *Judas Country*, the grim betrayal is more direct and final. Case's flying partner of more than twenty years turns on him. Unwilling to serve another stint in prison as the necessary punishment for their illegal gains, he flees with the sword only to be killed moments later. Case is left to serve the prison term. Lyall handles the final betrayal skillfully, managing to quiet the reader's suspicions, so much so that the reader is surprised when the predictable scene occurs. It is his deft handling of dialogue and narration and the complexity of the plot that keep the reader in suspense. The protagonists in these novels are moral, but the world of these books is more cynical than that of the earlier ones, and some of the romanticism is less overt.

Blame the Dead (1972) is a transitional novel, setting the stage for Lyall's movement away from novels of adventure into those of espionage. It opens with a one-paragraph, second-person narration in which the reader relives with Jim Card the moment just before his client Martin Fenwick—a man whom he was hired to guard—is shot down at a meeting place in Arras. When Card returns to England he determines to learn why his client, a managing director of a Lloyd's of London syndicate in marine insurance, has been killed and why he, Card, is now being hunted. His quest takes him to the ports of Norway and into an investigation into a maritime collision. The plot involves a lengthy car chase along the fjords of Norway, and the theme of personal betrayal recurs. On the surface, this novel seems to follow the formula of Lyall's previous adventure tales, but a closer examination of some of its elements reveals that he is stretching the genre. The other novels were all told through first-person narration, and each began with the narrator's description of a place and a situation. The exposition was often quite technical in the early pages of each novel, describing the technology of airplanes and the hazards of a mission. Lyall allowed himself several chapters to introduce his hero and the antagonists in the story. In *Blame the Dead*, as in the four Major Maxim novels, Lyall opens immediately with a scene of violence told in a manner which withholds as much information as it offers. He abandons first-person narration in the Maxim series to enable himself to capture the complexity of the intelligence service from a perspective other than Maxim's. In *Blame the Dead* Lyall has not yet moved away from the first-person tale of a lonely adventurer outside of a social context, but he does experiment with point of view, offering the snippet of second-person narration told actually by the first-person narrator, but alluding to himself in the second person. The cameralike, cinematic-zoom effect of the second-person narration is a technique Lyall extends in his later novels. In addition, in *Blame the Dead*, Lyall delves at length into the workings of the syndicates at Lloyd's of London, and he brings his hero, James Card, to the attention of the Ministry of Defense. His descriptions of the workings of the ministry, Special Branch, the Foreign Office, and an agent in civil counterintelligence, together with his belittling references to James Bond, anticipate the much more elaborate introduction to the world of espionage in his later novels. Lyall's earlier loner-protagonists had many close calls with customs officials, they had occasional brushes with the intelligence services of foreign governments, and they often were fleeing the police. The difference in *Blame the Dead* is one of degree. Card's background as a major in the army, as a captain who has served a short stint in the Ministry of Defense, and as a man with a code of honor which requires him to risk danger in order to satisfy his sense of order and honor all prefigure Lyall's creation of Maxim.

Chronologically, *Blame the Dead* precedes the writing of *Judas Country*. The latter novel is a return to Lyall's familiar style, but its cynicism anticipates the movement to a more sinister world of espionage and the more complicated moral predicaments it carries with it.

Lyall's *The Secret Servant* introduces Maxim. In all four Maxim novels, *The Secret Servant, The Conduct of Major Maxim, The Crocus List,* and *Uncle Target* (1988), the protagonist is called upon to handle a sensitive matter which is potentially damaging to the prime minister and Britain. *The Secret Servant* revolves around Maxim's efforts to prevent Britain from being seriously compromised during talks on nuclear strategy to be held in Germany. A learned Cambridge don and a former military hero, John White Taylor, a man with a horrible secret in his past which involves cowardice and cannibalism, has been chosen to represent Britain in the talks. Gerald Jackaman, an intelligence man with MI 5, has committed suicide, leaving a damaging letter that both the Russians and the British want to secure. Maxim has been brought to number 10 Downing Street to probe Jackaman's death, secure the letter, and protect England's interests at the peace table. As in the other three Maxim novels, the major's army past makes him appear trigger-happy in the minds of MI 5 and MI 6. The two agencies squabble with each other, often running interference with Maxim's missions, while the Ministry of Defense, chiefly through the figure of George Harbinger, continues to rely upon Maxim for his outside-of-the-law missions. In *The Conduct of Major Maxim* an upheaval in the East German cabinet and the presence of Gustave Eismark as the new East German general secretary threaten to destabilize the relationship between Britain and the Soviet Union unless MI 6, in its customary manner, can find a secret in Eismark's past which will enable them to blackmail and control him. At the beginning of the novel Maxim is called upon by his old friend, Jim Caswell, a former sergeant, who wants his assistance in bringing Ron Blagg, a deserting corporal, back into the army's fold. Blagg's story is one of counterespionage and blunders. Mistakenly believing he was assisting a covert effort, he had gone to East Germany with a female agent of MI 6. The agent was killed, and Blagg killed her assailant and fled. Maxim's efforts to bring Blagg back into the good graces of the army lead to an exchange of gunfire with Russian agents and with the men of MI 6, who are tailing the Russians, Blagg, and Maxim. The plot rap-

idly thickens with interagency quarrels. Maxim journeys to East Germany to reconstruct the scene of the agent's death. He discovers that Eismark has been guilty of incest, a secret which makes him liable to blackmail. The novel concludes in England with the kidnapping of Eismark's sister, a woman who has defected more than a decade earlier, and the daring rescue mission led by Maxim, which leads to the exposure of Eismark's secret. *The Crocus List* involves the uncovering of the identities, the motives, and the names of the men on the Crocus List and of their leader, a man who is unwilling to carry out the orders to shut down his undercover group and leave security matters to British intelligence and the CIA. This tale opens with what appears to be an assassination attempt upon the U.S. president during a visit to London. Maxim's attempt to discover the truth behind the attack takes him to the CIA, a small town in St. Louis, a country estate in the Cotswolds, and finally to East Berlin, where an assassination attempt upon an archbishop's life is to be made. This novel is Lyall's most complex. Both Agnes and Maxim are forced to make a moral accounting of their acts. Agnes's business requires that she use her wits and body to effect her ends. In one scene she ponders why her body, which had seemed such a willing accomplice when she slept with a high CIA official, should be so reluctant and unsatisfied when she sleeps with Maxim, a man she is growing to love. In another, both she and Maxim taste their own corruption, realizing that their promises of a safe exit and protection have driven a woman to run wildly to her violent death. In *Uncle Target* Maxim is called upon to rescue Colonel Katbah, a Jordanian held hostage in a London hotel by members of a rebel Jordanian group bent upon learning the location of a high-tech tank prototype lent by the British to the Jordanian government. The rescue mission fails and Katbah is killed. As the tale progresses, Maxim discovers he must destroy the tank, which has become an object of interest not only of the rebel Jordanian group but also the governments of United States, Great Britain, Saudi Arabia, and Syria. The tank is the Uncle Target of the title: a target of opportunity in the lingo of the arms trade.

In his four Maxim novels Lyall's journalistic skills add richness. Whereas many writers of spy tales have little real sense of place, despite the fact that their books are set in Berlin, or Paris, or London, Lyall's descriptions of place could come out of a Michelin guidebook, and his sense of a

239

In the commander's seat again, he pressed to transmit on their
own channel. "Cactus, this is Harpoon. Over."

"Harpoon, copy."

"Cactus, can you give me distances of units to the west? Over."

"Harpoon, hold." Aerial radio procedures were far terser than
Army ones; he had noticed that before. They left out a lot of 'overs'
and 'outs' - though maybe, zooming around the uncluttered sky, they
were used to far sharper reception than somebody trying to send a message
from the bottom of a ditch at the foot of a hill covered in trees.

"Harpoon, two units 260 from your position approximately one
thousand yards." Of course, the Americans hadn't gone metric yet. Still,
call that under one thousand . metres. "Other units approximately
1200 yards on bearings..."

~~The bearing from the west would be the personnel carriers. The~~
~~back in the dunes. When the they had approached~~
~~the fort, it had been 600 of several about 800 metres, hadn't they?~~
~~T~~ ~~where they'd debus. But still a chance...~~

"Alec, start up." The tank shuddered and rumbled.

Al-Hamedi said: "They are speaking on the radio. 17th Armoured."

"What?"

"They say we must release Major Zyadine or they will attack."

~~Oh God, he~~ ~~But he had to keep~~
~~g~~ing. "Say yes, we're releasing him now. Where do they want him to
go?" ~~The~~ idiots, still showing doubts by their subtleties. Opening
themselves to...

Zyad~~in~~e was tied up in a corner and was going to stay there.
"Ahmed - " he had~~n~~'t called Al-Hamedi that b~~ef~~ore; it might work or it
might alienate him; ~~~~ load sabot and pre pare for a range of about
800. We're going to go o~~ut~~, turn rig~~ht~~, right again around the fort
and fire at the personnel ca~~rriers~~. Alec, did you get that? Then adva~~n~~ce."

Was the beast still ~~w~~o~~r~~king, the whole nastiness of it?

Could he make the beast w~~o~~rk again, in all its beastliness,
a second and last ti~~m~~e?

They rock~~ed~~ and slewed through ~~the~~ doorway, crunching stone,
swiping a bit mo~~r~~e out of one side, offering~~ a~~ brief sight of their
thin-armoured backside to the tanks up north, t~~hen~~ rocking to a stop
beside the fort and facing west.

He snapped the PVD onto 260 degrees and there ~~w~~as a bright
~~sp~~ot ~~o~~n the infra-red. "Gunner, on. Fire."

A moment's pause, then: "Firing n-- " and the tank wh~~a~~cked
~~b~~ackwards. A dot on the screen diminished away from him, seemed ~~to~~

Page from the revised typescript for Uncle Target, *Lyall's 1988 novel (courtesy of the author)*

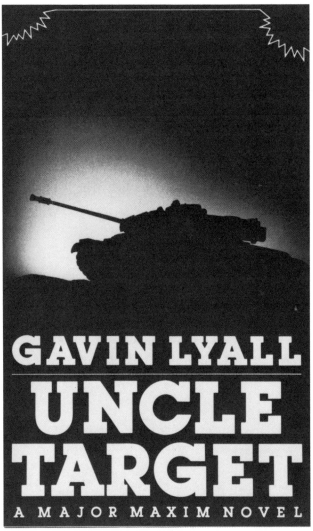

Dust jacket for the first American edition of Lyall's
1988 novel

country or city's ethos provides the greater particularity which makes his sense of locale real. In *The Crocus List*, his descriptions of a small town in midwestern America, its diners, its library, the expressways and smaller roadways that lead to it, and its people are authentic. Similarly, his descriptions of London, Washington, D.C., and New York City also evoke the architectural landmarks of these places and capture their rhythms. Usually it is left to novelists, not thriller writers, to make a place real. Lyall, like Graham Greene, is an exception. Finally, the plot in *The Crocus List* is the most intricate that he had devised to the date of its publication. He still uses the quest for a secret to structure it, but the action resonates and grows as the story progresses, and the motives of the secondary characters are more interesting than usual. In addition, the series of clues he

plants, which move the story forward, are more varied than in his previous work. Not only does he rely on the familiar devices of letters, photographs, personal reminiscences, and newspaper documentation to lead his protagonist to the truth he is seeking, but he also becomes more comfortable with the paraphernalia of the espionage novel, with its moles, its information acquired through bugging, its systems of coding, its relish of scandal, and its stereotyped responses to homosexuality and blackmail.

Lyall's four Maxim books have strengthened his reputation as a writer of thrillers and spy tales. The critical reception of his writing since his first novel has been generally favorable, but the most recent criticism is the strongest. In an early review of Lyall's writing appearing in the *London Times* (20 December 1969), H. R. F.

Keating found his tales entertaining and exciting, but missed a sense of the writer's "view of the world or insight into human nature." Later, Keating became rather taken with Lyall's journalistic richness but missed in some of the novels, notably *Venus with Pistol*, a sense of excitement. Keating praised *The Secret Servant* as Lyall's "best effort to date" but argued that it lacked a "steel-compressed intensity." Both Keating and Tim Heald (*London Times*, 16 May 1985) were most praiseworthy of *The Crocus List*. Heald wrote affectionately of the portrait of Maxim, calling him an "instantly recognizable character with warts we love to know."

Lyall's reputation as a writer of novels of suspense and of espionage is secure. He knows how to tell a tale; his interest in moral dilemmas steers the course of his plots, bringing his protagonists to their decisive moments. The British stamp on his novels is marked. They are tame sexually. Although they are marked with violence, it is of a British sort and takes its cues from military experience. He is interested in the furniture of his novels–the offices at number 10 Downing Street, the lace-curtained windows of rooming houses and unostentatious flats, and the more sumptuous accoutrements of country manors. He also takes a passing interest in costume–what Agnes Algar wears, the dress of an intelligence agent, an arms sergeant, or a British boxer. And he writes by borrowing techniques from film–using close-up shots, a wide-angle lens, and a collage of images–which permit him to tell his tale synchronistically in a narrative mode that is heavily diachronic. Finally, in addition to being adept at constructing the situations which shape his work, his recent novels reveal his strengths as a writer of character. Maxim, Agnes, George, and Annette are real people, not stereotypes.

Helen MacInnes

(7 October 1907-30 September 1985)

Gina Macdonald

Loyola University in New Orleans

BOOKS: *Above Suspicion* (Boston: Little, Brown, 1941; London: Harrap, 1941);

Assignment in Brittany (Boston: Little, Brown, 1942; London: Harrap, 1942);

While Still We Live (Boston: Little, Brown, 1944); republished as *The Unconquerable* (London: Harrap, 1944);

Horizon (London: Harrap, 1945; Boston: Little, Brown, 1946);

Friends and Lovers (Boston: Little, Brown, 1947; London: Harrap, 1948);

Rest and Be Thankful (Boston: Little, Brown, 1949; London: Harrap, 1949);

Neither Five Nor Three (New York: Harcourt, Brace, 1951; London: Collins, 1951);

I and My True Love (New York: Harcourt, Brace, 1953; London: Collins, 1953);

Pray for a Brave Heart (New York: Harcourt, Brace, 1955; London: Collins, 1955);

North from Rome (New York: Harcourt, Brace, 1958; London: Collins, 1958);

Decision at Delphi (New York: Harcourt, Brace & World, 1960; London: Collins, 1961);

The Venetian Affair (New York: Harcourt, Brace & World, 1963; London: Collins, 1964);

Home Is the Hunter: A Comedy in Two Acts (New York: Harcourt, Brace & World, 1964);

The Double Image (New York: Harcourt, Brace & World, 1966; London: Collins, 1966);

The Salzburg Connection (New York: Harcourt, Brace & World, 1968; London: Collins, 1969);

Message from Málaga (New York: Harcourt Brace Jovanovich, 1971; London: Collins, 1972);

The Snare of the Hunter (New York: Harcourt Brace Jovanovich, 1974; London: Collins, 1974);

Agent in Place (New York: Harcourt Brace Jovanovich, 1976; London: Collins, 1976);

Prelude to Terror (New York: Harcourt Brace Jovanovich, 1978; London: Collins, 1978);

The Hidden Target (New York: Harcourt Brace Jovanovich, 1980; London: Collins, 1980);

Helen MacInnes

Cloak of Darkness (New York: Harcourt Brace Jovanovich, 1982; London: Collins, 1982);

Ride a Pale Horse (New York: Harcourt Brace Jovanovich, 1984; London: Collins, 1984).

OTHER: Otto Kiefer, *Sexual Life in Ancient Rome*, translated by Helen MacInnes Highet and Gilbert Highet (London: Routledge, 1934; New York: Dutton, 1935);

Gustav Mayer, *Friedrich Engels: A Biography*, translated by Helen MacInnes Highet and Gilbert Highet (New York: Knopf, 1936; London: Chapman & Hall, 1936).

Helen MacInnes was the author of twenty-one spy novels, which have sold more than twenty-three million copies in the United States alone. Her work has been translated into more than twenty-two languages, and four of her novels have been made into films. She has been called the "queen" or "the doyenne" of international suspense, "a grand old professional," "one of the most topical of all spy novelists": "her name . . . synonymous with superior thrillers." Her novels are riveting, lively, informative, literate, and entertaining. She ranks among the most successful of modern women writers and made the best-seller lists with every novel. Her books, political analyses of contemporary world events, pit believable, ordinary men and women of decency and fortitude against the faceless agents of totalitarian regimes: the Nazis in the 1940s, the Communists and their terrorist compatriots thereafter. In so doing, MacInnes was strongly influenced by George Orwell, whose works she admired and whose warnings she took seriously. Her interest in the jargon of espionage, the euphemisms that hide the grim reality of betrayal, is a linguistic extension of Orwell's premises. Her writings also reflect an affinity for Arthur Koestler and Rebecca West, with their strong opposition to any form of tyranny and totalitarianism. Her romances are restrained; her action violent; her moral convictions firm. She may sometimes lapse into sermonizing, but never into the obscene or the tasteless. Her characters may despair, but the ultimate thrust of her works is optimistic: goodwill prevails, with time.

Helen MacInnes was born in Glasgow, Scotland, in 1907 to Donald and Jessica McDiarmid MacInnes. She was reared in the Scots Presbyterian tradition and educated at Glasgow University (M.A., 1928) and University College, London (Diploma in Librarianship, 1931). MacInnes married scholar Gilbert Highet 22 September 1932 and during the 1930s worked with him on translations to help finance their summers spent traveling in Europe.

Before Highet accepted an invitation to teach at Columbia University in 1937, MacInnes served as special cataloger for the Ferguson Collection at the University of Glasgow, helped the Dunbartonshire Education Authority select books for county libraries, and acted with the Oxford University Dramatic Society and with the Oxford Experimental Theatre. During that time she played tennis, went to concerts, and read avidly, particularly in paleography and the history of the English novel. Her grounding in the arts inevitably shows up in the backgrounds and conversations of her characters (especially her love of music and concerts).

Dust jacket for the first edition of MacInnes's 1963 novel

MacInnes's personal observations of events during the 1930s and 1940s, common sense, and intimate contact with a World War II British intelligence officer (husband Gilbert) provided her with a special insight into the nature and realities of Nazi tyranny and espionage. In fact, it was her husband who, after reading her notebook analyses and predictions based on newspaper stories of Nazi activities, encouraged her to attempt her first novel, *Above Suspicion* (1941). It was his interest in the classics that led to her two-act play, *Home Is the Hunter* (1964), a comedy about Ulysses returning from the Trojan War, but it was her interest in the conflict between the quiet homebody and the aggressive invader he must oust that gave it its focus as a portrayal of what an ancient resistance movement might be like.

MacInnes and her husband divided their time between New York City and East Hampton until Highet's death in 1978. It was upon moving to New York that MacInnes, inspired by events around her and by her husband's support, began writing seriously, and she continued doing so until her death in 1985. She and her husband visited most of the places she wrote about, he for his research, she for her stories, but they went most often to the Dolomites, to the Salzburg Festival, and to Vienna. In 1966 she received the Columbia Prize in Literature from Iona College, New Rochelle, New York.

MacInnes is perhaps best known and most highly praised for her exotic, romantic settings—usually European. Critics call them "classic travelogues" with the added spice of romance, adventure, and espionage; and indeed her works are memorable for their strong evocations of place, though they are certainly more than mere travelogues. Her firsthand experience (extensive travel throughout Europe), combined with careful research into the historical, cultural, political, religious, and geographic nature of an area, provided her novels with a detailed, accurate sense of place that lends her stories an integrity and an interest independent of plot, whether the background be Switzerland or Granada, Brittany or Venice, Vienna or the American Southwest. Her pleasure in reading maps, timetables, and guidebooks translates itself into the type of detailed description that fascinates readers and disturbs critics. Often she includes maps that give a sense of territory covered; always she makes concrete reference to food and drink, architecture, culture, and landscape to re-create setting vividly in an authentic way. Sometimes even the names and details of streets, restaurants, markets, shops, and bars are genuine. For example, *Assignment in Brittany* (1942) captures the rebellious spirit of Nazi-occupied Brittany, and its evocation of Mont-Saint-Michel is vivid. The details of the Breton countryside, the seacoast villages, and the behavior of their inhabitants are typical of the precision of her description. Her lovingly drawn portrait of St. Deodat, with its ironic motto, "Nothing changes," is characteristic of her technique: it is a collage of details from actual fourteenth-century castles in Brittany. The setting of *The Snare of the Hunter* (1974) moves from Vienna's opera house to gourmet dining at Grinzing, from the grim Czechoslovakian border to the mountain wonders of Italy and Switzerland. For *Decision at Delphi* (1960), set in Sicily and Greece, MacInnes tracked down and interviewed World War II partisans to find out precise details of battles and locales. For *Prelude to Terror* (1978) she verified the one-way streets of

Venice to make sure her characters' movements were accurate.

John Baker, in an interview with MacInnes (*Publishers Weekly*, 17 June 1974), reports that her portrayal of the Polish Resistance to the Nazis in *While Still We Live* (1944; published in Great Britain as *The Unconquerable*, 1944) was so convincing that she was called to Washington to reveal her sources. *Horizon* (1945) explores the dangerous confusion of the South Tyrol after the surrender of Italy and includes graphic details of mountain climbing, a sport MacInnes engaged in firsthand. *Friends and Lovers* (1947) moves between Scotland, London, and Oxford; *Rest and Be Thankful* (1949) depicts an easterner's encounter with the West, particularly Wyoming, where MacInnes had vacationed for several months. *Neither Five Nor Three* (1951) centers on New York City, *I and My True Love* (1953) on Washington, D.C. Her final set of books involves pursuits that sweep across the map: *The Hidden Target* (1980) and *Ride a Pale Horse* (1984) are played out across three continents; *Cloak of Darkness* (1982) catapults from London to New York City, Washington, Paris, Chamonix, Amsterdam, Zurich, and Djibouti, Ethiopia.

Typically MacInnes's settings are the backdrop for fast-paced, intriguing action in which young innocents get caught up in the Machiavellian machinations of international politics and learn the hard way that espionage, intrigue, and terror are an inescapable part of modern life. MacInnes's earliest adventure-suspense novels grew out of World War II action and portray undercover agents in enemy territory (*Above Suspicion, Assignment in Brittany, While Still We Live*, and *Horizon*). In fact, *Assignment in Brittany* so brilliantly evokes the difficulties of undercover work that the military used it to train Allied personnel to help the French Resistance. Her postwar adventures deal with explosive World War II secrets that continue to threaten a world recuperating from international trauma (*Pray for a Brave Heart* [1955] and *The Salzburg Connection* [1968]). Her later works concern Communist threats and deadly cold war games (beginning with *I and My True Love*). As the length of her novels increased, so too did the complexity of her plots. While her first two novels gained a strength and a conviction from her personal horror at disruptive political change in regions she considered home, her later novels inevitably reflect a greater maturity and a more polished control of organization, style, and character. Her early works are based

Dust jacket for the first British edition of MacInnes's 1968 novel

on a simple premise and move single-mindedly forward; her middle works, in contrast, involve more complicated plots, more fully developed characters, and a more complex interplay of illusion and reality. In her last few books the complications and black-and-white messages dominate, and the sense of real people in real places dealing with genuinely threatening situations is lost in a morass of characters and subplots and ingenious interconnections. Despite the weaknesses of these final efforts, her works remain compelling. Always her protagonists undergo a process of maturation, one that involves a discovery of political realities. Dangerous complications and narrow escapes are integrally bound up with her warning to the naive American to beware: one cannot ignore politics; one must be ready to defend what one believes in; idealism must be tempered by knowledge and wisdom; the unknown, unseen enemy, deadly, dedicated, unscrupulous, and driven, is there, waiting to use and abuse the gullible. Motives must be questioned; even "facts" are suspect. Her final books deal, in particular, with

terrorism and with disinformation, the distortion of facts for political motives. As her character Bristow muses in *Ride a Pale Horse:* "There had always been that danger: the victors wrote the history books. But today—with the far reach of television and radio, of instant news—future victors wouldn't even need to win a war before they wrote the history books. They'd manipulate minds and emotions, outsmart an unwitting world." MacInnes's world is one of clear-cut moral values, one in which freedom and responsibility, humanistic obligations and personal integrity go hand in hand; consequently, despite initial confusion about the position of one character or another, evil is eventually exposed, and, after much difficulty, good is vindicated. Her basic formula is to throw together a young couple in a romantic foreign setting, to involve them in espionage and intrigue for reasons of patriotism, and to make them endure misunderstandings, kidnappings, hair-raising escapes and pursuits, and even murder, in order ultimately to make the world a little safer for democracy.

Highet was a fellow at St. John's College, Oxford University, from 1932 to 1938. MacInnes's first novel, *Above Suspicion*, tells of Frances and Richard Myles, a young Oxford couple, much like MacInnes and Highet, who regularly pass their summers in the Tyrol, in the Dolomites, and who go for one last look at Europe in peacetime; as such they are "above suspicion" and hence ideal to be used as amateur agents whose mission is to contact the underground and find the whereabouts of a British anti-Nazi agent. Their wit, good humor, and courage help them through trying encounters with people who are powerless in the grip of "the new order." MacInnes makes the menace of Nazism come alive. For example, at one point, thinking nostalgically of the Europe she had once loved, Frances is brought back to ugly reality by the entrance of a detachment of German troops, their faces expressionless: "Men who marched like that, who dressed like that, whose faces held the blankness of concentration and dedication, were a menace, a menace all the more desperate because of the hidden threat." The couple finds literate, sophisticated friends from past visits dedicated to the Nazi cause and others–ordinary, simple people– unable to accept that new order and willing to fight against it on a personal level. The heroine repeatedly voices MacInnes's own sentiments: "It's only when you think of history as blood and tears that you can ever learn from it"; at the end of the novel she says, "knowing evil could be worse than guessing. When you guessed, you could always hope that evil things might not be so bad as your worst fears. But when you knew, then there was no hope left." Aided by the underground, after a rugged climb through the Dolomites, their mission finally accomplished, the young couple returns to England, much sadder but now firmly dedicated to battle the vindictive and cruel Nazi regime. Critics praised the "technical smoothness" of this work, its "subtle" humor, its "feminine insights," its "pervading atmosphere of suspense," but criticized its "simplified black and white portraits." M-G-M produced a film version of *Above Suspicion* in 1943 starring Joan Crawford and Fred MacMurray, but MacInnes was dissatisfied with all film versions of her novels, feeling they so twisted character and plot that both became incomprehensible.

Assignment in Brittany is as exciting and convincing as MacInnes's first book. In fact, critic Rose Feld, in "Brittany Parachute Adventure" (*New York Herald Tribune Books*, 12 July 1942),

called it "more complex and ambitious," written with "finesse and subtlety and reality" as she captures the "restless ferment of a proud people . . . only temporarily conquered." A British agent named Matthews is parachuted into Brittany in the summer of 1940 after the Nazi occupation of France. His mission is to impersonate a Breton Nationalist, Corlay, whom he closely resembles. He is to feign shell shock to explain away lapses of memory, and in this way gather detailed information about fortifications and military activity to help the Allies determine German intent. However, while he has convinced the family servants and even Corlay's mother, he finds himself in the awkward position of falling in love with Corlay's betrothed, Anne, just when she has decided to break their forced engagement, and he is stuck with Corlay's mistress, a French Mata Hari. The plot becomes more complicated as he shelters an American escapee from the Nazis, then discovers Corlay's double-dealing as a Nazi-sympathizing traitor. His knowledge allows Matthews to cold-bloodedly use Corlay's connections to facilitate his mission, and a deadly game of bluff and counterbluff ensues. It is thanks to the courage of the unyielding Bretons, the love of Anne, and his own wits that Matthews makes his final rendezvous. M-G-M's 1943 movie version starred Susan Peters and Jean-Pierre Aumont.

In *While Still We Live* MacInnes examines the Nazis from the perspective of the Polish Resistance. Although critics found this work more strained and less convincing than her previous efforts, they admit that the hunter / hunted drama and the detailed account of the Polish underground's day-to-day operations make it well worth reading. The problem is that a melodramatic story could not compete with the real-life tragedy of Poland, and that the numerous plot shifts necessary to cover all fronts reduced credibility. The heroine is Sheila Matthews, a British girl on holiday who decides, out of idealism, outrage, and curiosity about her dead father's past, to stay and help the Poles on the eve of the German invasion. In so doing she gets caught up in the nightmare violence of the war. Contact with a German representative of her uncle's firm leads to her first being accused of spying for the Germans. When truly contacted by German agents she plays a double game to help the Poles capture a murderous German agent, Kordus, a man responsible for the destruction of whole villages and the burning alive of children. Tossed back and forth from Germans to Poles, she ends up

Dust jackets for the first American editions of three of MacInnes's novels from the 1980s

with the Resistance and with the Pole she loves, shares their suffering and heartache, and, thanks to special knowledge gleaned from her German experiences, identifies a traitor in their midst. Overall the incredible twists and turns of this plot cannot detract from the overriding sense of menace and outrage that dominates it.

Horizon recounts the bravery of a young English painter, Peter Lennox, who, after a daring mass escape from an Italian prison camp engineered with the aid of a Tyrolese, is ordered to head for the Dolomites and await further orders. Just when he has begun to feel totally useless, however, Germans disguised as Americans appear, and Lennox has a chance to act decisively and truly aid the Allied cause. As in her preceding books, MacInnes is intrigued by the heroic efforts of underground resistance to totalitarian oppression and aggression. Critics found *Horizon* disappointingly limited and uneventful but agreed that the descriptions of scenery are memorable, as is the study of POW psychology.

In her next two novels, following the advice of critics and publishers, MacInnes broke her traditional patterns to focus not on plot and suspense but on human relationships, expressed almost entirely in dialogue. The first, *Friends and Lovers*, is a love story, at least partly autobiographical, about two students, David and Penny, who test themselves, each other, and their families as they build a firm foundation on which to rest marriage and careers; inevitably it ends with reconciliations and marriage, and a first night together on the Scottish Express. In the second, *Rest and Be Thankful*, a harried New York writer, Margaret Peel, takes a much-needed vacation in Wyoming, where eastern literati meet western cowpokes in a sharp, but good-natured, satire on both. The ironic contrast between hardworking wranglers, worried about day-to-day practicalities and contemptuous of "dudes" who are physically inept, and the posing, egocentric easterners, with their pretentious literary allusions, their conversations about the nature of art, and their snobbish amusement at what for the cowboys is serious business is intensified by Margaret Peel's memories of the changes wrought in Europe, the old days gone, the old friends dead or imprisoned or embittered by postwar politics, by her fears of Communist propaganda undermining democratic values, and by her sense of being a stranger in her own country. The book follows her process of discovery as she reevaluates past values and present friends, is impressed by the simple humanity of Wyoming

country folk, and becomes more and more disillusioned with the superficiality and artificiality of would-be artists, posing drones who lack genuine artistic sensibility. It concludes with Indians tracking down a hysterical easterner, a marriage of East and West, and a big-time rodeo with a couple of "dudes" finally proving their physical prowess. Ultimately, however, this book is disappointing; it is restful, but not challenging. It received little critical acclaim, for, where it could be biting, it pulls back from any final statement that, as George Conrad pointed out in "World Travelers in Wyoming" (*New York Herald Tribune Weekly Book Review*, 7 August 1949) would "reach the bedrock of reality." After these two not-so-successful forays into alternative forms MacInnes wisely returned to the topics and patterns that made her career: espionage and patriotism.

Her next suspense novel, *Neither Five Nor Three*, a product of the Communist scares of the 1950s, explores Communist infiltration of New York's sophisticated world of publishers, writers, and artists. Recently demobilized Paul Haydn, returning to his old newspaper position, learns that his wartime replacement, Blackwood, has been discreetly fired for distorting stories to present a Communist line; that his prewar flame, Rona Metford, is engaged to a man who is a fast friend of Blackwood and the friend of a teacher who uses the classroom for Communist propaganda; and that his old circle of friends has been subtly influenced by distortions in news stories. The novel emphasizes the difficulty of proving a case, with freedom-of-speech guarantees protecting men who attack the American press as corrupt, the FBI as a menace, and draft laws as warmongering. It claims that a free press allows one to talk of witch-hunting, but never to mention purges in Eastern Europe; to attack intolerance, but not "the Believe-and-Obey rules of Communism"; to talk of peace, while "fighting a war in secret." The novel condemns those who "take our good will and turn it as a weapon against us." Haydn, his publisher, and some of his friends take it upon themselves to show the misrepresentations and lies for what they are, and to ferret out men like Blackwood, who abuse position and power for propagandistic purposes. Rona Metford is used to represent the typical American reaction to contact with the Communist threat: incredulity, dawning awareness, horror and disgust, then a decision to act. The results of her disillusioned awakening to the truth about her new fiancé are personal threats, violence, courageous action, and death.

I and My True Love is a poignant, tragic love story. It focuses on the heartaches and torn loyalties of Sylvia Pleydell. Once in love with a Czechoslovakian war hero, Jan, who was imprisoned and presumed dead, she is now married to an ambitious State Department consultant, who played falsely on her sympathies to win her hand, who destroys any letters that make it through the Iron Curtain, and who now guards her jealously as a possession, not a lover. When she learns that Jan not only survived the war but is on a mission to Washington—to find her and possibly to defect to the West—she is forced to face the emptiness of her marriage, wealth and power without love. The lovers find themselves trapped by forces beyond their control because Jan's family is held as security for his behavior. The picture of Georgetown scenes and figures is skillfully drawn: quiet dinner parties and state affairs; the aging bachelor, so suave and debonair; the self-effacing Korean War hero; the gossip; and diplomacy as a cover for espionage. Critics like Constance Morgan found the emotional dilemmas overdone, but praised MacInnes's lucid demonstration of how injurious a tiny information leak can be, her ability to "invest a shabby room off lower Connecticut Avenue with the menace of an occupied country," and her "terse recital" of the heroine's final acts.

Pray for a Brave Heart is a short thriller in which hunter becomes hunted. Despite the chattiness of its characters, it is action packed, with chance encounters, secret messages, dangerous blondes, kidnapped scientists, precocious youngsters, Bulgarian thugs, and hit-and-run murder. Acting on a tip from a professional intelligence officer, members of several intelligence services pool information to find Nazi diamonds being used to finance Communist operations. Professionals and amateurs alike (an American couple, a wartime friend of the murder victim, and a young woman involved in the underground railroad from behind the Iron Curtain) converge on a Swiss mountain cottage for a daring rescue. This book has little time for character development or even explanations, but it is fast-paced and flashy.

North from Rome (1958) is based on genuine Interpol and United Nations reports on narcotics smuggling in Europe. Writer Bill Lammiter, mistaken for an American secret agent, is drawn into Rosana DiFeo's amateurish investigation of her brother's death, an investigation that uncovers a drug ring run by the Communists and their quisling allies, one of whom is an Italian count engaged to Lammiter's former girlfriend. After another murder and a kidnapping, Lammiter, with help from Italian and American agents, exposes the villains, rescues his former girlfriend, and learns how expendable people are to the professional Communist. The portrait of an Italian princess, who faced down Mussolini and survived, and then dealt in-house with the traitorous acts of her son, is memorable.

In *Decision at Delphi* free-lance architect Ken Strang, commissioned to sketch Greek ruins, learns too late that he is the pawn in a murderous assassination plot. Unbeknownst to him, his luggage is used to smuggle into Greece photographic evidence accumulated by his old friend, Stefanos Kludos, to identify Kludos's brother Niko, a former guerrilla fighter, code-named Odysseus, as head of an anarchistic Greek minority party bent on political upheaval. At the center of a flurry of activity, Ken has a series of "accidental" encounters, followed by enigmatic conversations clearly designed to extract information from him. His friend Aleco Christophorou, an intelligence officer with a journalistic cover, helps him make contact with the right authorities, but, a romantic idealist at heart, Strang cannot avoid involvement. He had unknowingly witnessed Stefanos's kidnapping aboard the yacht *Medea*, and, spurred on by his anger at being searched, his fears for his friend, and his sense of justice, he makes contact with World War II Greek guerrilla fighters to try (aided by a lovely American photographer) to bring to justice those responsible for past terror, the kidnapping of thousands of children at the close of the war, and the massacre of villagers. The indiscreet chatter of the wife of a stuffy diplomat makes secrecy difficult, and one by one those who can identify Niko Kludos are eliminated. Friendship is betrayed, and Strang learns all too well "the horror of nihilism."

The Venetian Affair (1963), with its stern warnings about the dangers of communism, its evocative descriptions of Piazza San Marco, Venetian canals, and shadowy alleyways, its intricately baroque plot, and its romance amid dangers, is typical of MacInnes. Critics thought the sermonizing, the emotional entanglements, and the purple passages could well have been cut, but they are as vital to her worldview as the sense of conspiracy and threat amid the deceptively innocuous. The book argues that "the basic reality of power poli-

Gilbert Highet, MacInnes's husband (photograph by Fabian Bachrach)

tics" is "who is going to control your life—you or your enemy," positing that if you evade or ignore that question "you have lost." The plot concerns the manipulation of the Algerian OAS for Communist purposes. Bill Fenner, drama critic turned amateur sleuth, is the hero. The heroine is Claire Langley, the widow of a victim of terrorism in Saigon. His raincoat being switched at an airport and her courageous decision to pursue her husband's executioners bring them together to expose a terrorist organization and to stop the further loss of innocent lives in the name of political expediency. The plot is complicated by the fact that Fenner's former wife works for the opposition. The book builds on traditional espionage lore (as do all MacInnes's later works): boutonnieres for identification, cyanide gas in pens, microphones in flowers, secret villas, and final betrayals. It is courage, intelligence, and persistence in the face of personal danger that ultimately defeat the enraged fanatic, Kalganov, a twisted man without conscience.

Allied agents from *The Venetian Affair* reappear in *The Double Image* (1966), a complicated story based on a 1960s newspaper report of the empty grave of a Nazi war criminal. An eminent archaeologist, survivor of Auschwitz, testifies at the Frankfurt trials and, upon leaving, identifies a supposedly dead Nazi death camp director as alive and well in Paris. Pursued by that Nazi, now a Soviet agent, he confides in a former student, John Craig, a newspaperman. Craig's embassy connections plunge him into the midst of a hunt that will expose a far-flung Soviet espionage apparatus. The professor's suicide / murder leads American, British, French, and Greek counterintelligence agents on the one hand and Nazi-Soviet agents on the other to engage in careful fencing with disguises, elaborate feints, and backtracking. The opposition fastens on Veronica Clark, a young lady who had attracted Craig's interest, to use her as unwitting bait to get him to Mykonos where danger awaits him. But he overwhelms them in his daring rescue of her. While critics praised the authentic background details, the sense of ambience, they found the interagency communication difficulties a bit dated. One senses that, despite MacInnes's study of real espionage strategies, she is most at home with the patterns and conflicts of World War II.

The Salzburg Connection again interconnects Nazi and Communist, this time through a secret list of important collaborators, sunk in a remote Austrian lake and still guarded by a ring of fanatical agents: the Nazis, the KGB, the Austrians, the British, and the Americans compete for the list. Two young Americans, a lawyer and a publisher's representative, get caught up in the action and despite kidnappings and murder manage to save the day—but only after an intricately woven, riveting adventure.

Message from Málaga follows the traditional MacInnes pattern: a handsome, well-meaning, young patriot, athletic, loyal, and relatively uncomplicated, stumbles into international intrigue (CIA, KGB, New Left activists, Maoists, and so on) in Spain and, amid the sounds of castanets and the fragrance of bougainvillea, defends American values. The story begins with the murder of a wine merchant who is really an undercover CIA agent. Since he and the dead man were pilots together in Korea, Ian Ferrier, a U.S. Space Agency executive on vacation in Spain, feels compelled to join forces with his dead friend's partner, Favita, a beautiful flamenco dancer, to help CIA agents hide a Cuban defector from KGB Department 13, which is devoted to training terrorists and assassins. Pursued by spies, assassins, and double agents, shot at by cyanide guns, they race around the countryside of Málaga and Granada, giving speeches about what is right and wrong with America, until finally the myriad enemy is defeated. Despite the predictability of the plot and the confusing number of minor characters, MacInnes's careful description and clear-cut exposition make the action somehow seem credible and the ending compelling. Her Americans are often refreshingly brighter than her Europeans, and her treatment of local color (like flamenco dancing) is accurate and charming.

In retrospect *The Snare of the Hunter* is startlingly evocative (before the pattern became commonplace) of real-life situations of Soviet intelligentsia (such as Aleksandr Solzhenitsyn in exile). She told Baker that its conception was based on *New York Times* reports on the plight of Czech writers coupled with her viewing of the movie *The Confession*, both of which made her speculate on the disrupted lives and allegiances of writers in exile. Music critic turned amateur agent David Mennery is persuaded to identify an old flame (Irina Kusak), who is escaping from Czechoslovakia to the West, but in so doing endangers her famous author-father, Jaromir Kusak, whose controversial notebooks she carries. As Anglo-American agents try to reunite father and daughter in his Swiss hideaway, they discover the whole escape has been carefully orchestrated by the secret police, who step-by-step eliminate all who aid Irina. The couple flee with Soviet agents in pursuit. After a terrifying chase scene, the disparate forces converge on a single point, and the victims turn on their attackers. The doubts and fears, schemes and stratagems of all involved are intensified by MacInnes's stream-of-consciousness narrative, which roams the minds of villains and heroes alike. This technique increases the emotional depth of her characters but sometimes reveals motivations and plans too soon to maintain suspense. However, MacInnes feels that "in international intrigue, suspense is not achieved by hiding things from the reader." For her the important question is not what is going to happen, but when and how it will happen, so that, as she pointed out, "A reader may know everything, but still be scared stiff by the situation" (Herbert Mitgang, "Behind the Best Sellers," *New York Times Book Review*, 7 December 1978).

In *Agent in Place* (1976) an amateur agent (Tom Kelso) and a professional agent (British

Tony Lawton) both deal with sinister double and triple agents, all in pursuit of a secret NATO memorandum. The question of the newsman's moral obligation to publish versus his obligation to protect security information is raised, as a foolish and idealistic reporter leaks some top-secret information, only to lose the rest to a Soviet agent. Their security breached, English, French, and American intelligence agencies combine efforts to outwit their sinister East European opponents. This novel captures the terror of a private home violated and raises questions of short-term expediency versus long-term policy.

In *Prelude to Terror* New York art consultant Colin Grant, in Vienna to bid on a valuable painting, becomes caught up in conspiracy, murder, and terrorism. The heroine voices the book's argument: "There's a job to be done, a necessary job. Someone has to do it; we can't all sit back and watch the totalitarians take over. . . . Or else we'll all end up regimented nonentities, scared to death to step out of line. . . ." Directed by professional intelligence officers, Grant helps unravel a plot to divert money from rich art investors to a Communist slush fund: rare paintings, sold in rigged auctions for huge sums, are then replaced by fakes and their buyers executed. Bookstores and art centers prove fronts for villainy. A sense of tragic waste pervades this book: art is perverted for evil causes and innocent lives are wasted. The novel is pervaded with a sense of loss: in the beginning Grant's wife is the victim of senseless murder; toward the conclusion his new beloved becomes the victim of cold war intrigue.

Most critics agreed that MacInnes's next book, *The Hidden Target*, was one of her least persuasive efforts, because it adhered too closely to her formula, strained credulity, and attempted too much for any one part to be truly memorable. Two young terrorists, with some Russian backing, take a group of six young people on a camping tour of Europe and Asia as cover while they finance and recruit terrorists across the map. Somehow they manage to skip the traditional tourist traps and end up in spots little traveled or rarely suggested by tourist agents—such as the Bombay red-light district. There are secret drops, code names, innumerable alternative plans and cover strategies; the final murder weapon is a cyanide pen. At the close of the book the lovely heroine is saved from the main villain, Erik, and the misguided tourists, stunned by their naive acceptance of such hardened terrorists, promise future caution. Robert Renwick, MacInnes's hero, voices the book's key point: "We have all been idiots at one time or another. It's the human condition. . . ."

The Hidden Target ends with the establishment of Interintell, International Intelligence Against Terrorism. Its sequel, *Cloak of Darkness*, begins with Interintell's search for Erik in Africa, acting for corporations dealing in illegal arms and assassinations. Renwick returns to warn people on an assassination list, to protect Nina (from the previous book), to find an informer, and to capture a second list of the rich sponsors of terrorist activities. There is a great deal of travel, which ends up at the chateau of one of the key villains. The novel is generally overdone, with little to make characters or action stand out. Critics have called this MacInnes's weakest work ever, and Michele Slung has a particularly stinging review of it, "Good Guys, Bad Guys," in the *New York Times Book Review* (26 September 1982).

In *Ride a Pale Horse* Karen Cornell, a journalist promised an important interview at an international peace convocation in Prague, agrees to carry top-secret documents to Washington for would-be defector Josef Vasak to help prevent "an end to Western alliances. . . . a hideous war." When they prove to be letters of skillfully contrived disinformation and Vasak is linked with an active Soviet file, Farrago, agent Peter Bristow commandeers her aid in countering Soviet plans, negating the letters' effectiveness, and bringing Vasak in. But all is not as it seems, for there are moles at work in the CIA, and Vasak has used KGB and CIA for ulterior motives that endanger Karen and Bristow and lead to breathtaking action. In this, her final book, MacInnes returned to the skilled plotting that characterized her most popular novels.

Helen MacInnes's work has been criticized for not belonging to the hard-boiled school. She makes no attempt to capture the nuances of street talk. Her characters, good and bad, are educated: they have read widely, have a historical sense, and speak refined English. Her agents make erudite allusions to Shakespeare, Dante, and other literary greats and feel at home discussing the merits of Vermeer, Turner, or Dali. Characters are defined by their taste in music, the decor of their rooms, the quality of their tailors. Jests are genteel. Her novels might include chatty

biographical vignettes from the lives of great artists as well as detailed summations of political events in a particular area over a decade.

Anatole Broyard, in "Adverbs are Deadly Weapons" (*New York Times*, 6 September 1971), has criticized her use of adverbs (for example, sharply, bitingly, curtly, caustically, grimly, eyes blazing, flashing, or wary; head held high) as being too formulaic, too exaggerated, or too impossible to pin down, and her descriptive detail as too effusive: a CIA agent not only says he will see someone to the door but adds that he will lock it afterward. Others find her plots overcomplicated, convoluted, and predictable; her logic limited; her characters underdeveloped, simplistic, and interchangeable. MacInnes has been criticized for being too analytical, too discursive, too long-winded, too determinedly old-fashioned. Her Nazis and her Communists blend together; they all are vicious, ruthless, manipulative, clever, and dangerous. They are rarely humanized. Their methods and technology overlap.

Yet her novels were clearly successes. Perhaps their popularity can be best attributed to MacInnes's good eye for detail, conflict, and action. She was particularly skillful at exploring the nuances of human interaction that lead to suspicion or trust, love or loathing. She was at her best at mise-en-scène and at presenting characters with conflicting ideologies. She developed her characters with compassion and understanding; her action is well paced and absorbing. Over the years she polished her style and complicated her plots, increased the amount of action and the amount of internal speculation and self-analysis. Nevertheless her earliest books were the most powerful. She attacked regimes that (as she told Mitgang) see "men and women not as human beings but as instruments," and she held no sympathy for "neutrals" who let themselves be used by antihumanistic forces in the name of objectivity. Her work was dedicated to exposing the secret advocates who spend time and effort creating credible facades behind which to work against freedom, democracy, and human rights. Her philosophy struck a sympathetic chord in readers and allowed them to ignore what was overdone or unrealistic in their desire to find out what happens and how, and to gain satisfaction from seeing ruthlessness undone.

Peter O'Donnell
(11 April 1920-   )

Michael J. Tolley
University of Adelaide

BOOKS: *Modesty Blaise* (London: Souvenir, 1965; Garden City, N.Y.: Doubleday, 1965);

Sabre-Tooth (London: Souvenir, 1966; Garden City, N.Y.: Doubleday, 1966);

I, Lucifer (London: Souvenir, 1967; Garden City, N.Y.: Doubleday, 1967);

A Taste for Death (London: Souvenir, 1969; Garden City, N.Y.: Doubleday, 1969);

The Impossible Virgin (London: Souvenir, 1971; Garden City, N.Y.: Doubleday, 1971);

Pieces of Modesty (London: Pan, 1972; New York: Mysterious, 1986);

The Silver Mistress (London: Souvenir, 1973; Cambridge, Mass.: Archival, 1982);

Last Day in Limbo (London: Souvenir, 1976; New York: Mysterious, 1985);

Dragon's Claw (London: Souvenir, 1978; New York: Mysterious, 1985);

Modesty Blaise: In the Beginning (London: Star, 1978);

Modesty Blaise: The Black Pearl and The Vikings (London: Star, 1978);

The Xanadu Talisman (London: Souvenir, 1981; New York: Mysterious, 1984);

The Night of Morningstar (London: Souvenir, 1982; New York: Mysterious, 1987);

Mr. Fothergill's Murder: A Play in Two Acts (London: English Theatre Guild, 1983 [?]);

Dead Man's Handle (London: Souvenir, 1985; New York: Mysterious, 1985);

Mister Sun (London: Titan, 1985).

PLAY PRODUCTION: *Murder Most Logical*, Windsor, Theatre Royal, 1974.

MOTION PICTURE: *The Vengeance of She*, screenplay by O'Donnell, Fox, 1968.

OTHER: "Becoming Modesty," in *Murder Ink: The Mystery Reader's Companion*, edited by Dilys Winn (New York: Workman, 1977), pp. 158-160.

Peter O'Donnell

Peter O'Donnell's fantastic characters, Modesty Blaise, Willie Garvin, and their associates, have so large a popular following that it is probably correct to accord them modern mythic status. He is adroit at mingling insouciant comedy with grim, sardonic cruelty. In a 1986 *Contemporary Authors* interview O'Donnell said the 1966 translation of Modesty Blaise to film was not successful, but she persists as the cartoon-series character from which she originated in the *Evening Standard* (May 1963), and she has qualities which, one might think, could readily be converted into a successful film or television series. O'Donnell has perhaps been most praised for his success in providing ingenious and seemingly original methods for getting his characters out of tight situations; his hero and heroine rely more on physical skills and improvisation than on high technology. Like Ian Fleming's James Bond, Modesty is a legend in her own lifetime inside the series of books about her; it is because of the legend that she is employed as a spy in the first novel. As the series has developed, she has acquired a circle of interesting characters about her, a sort of family group, some of whom seem to exist primarily for the purpose of being rescued, although each has a unique talent, sometimes one that might fairly be called fantastic. This fantastic quality is also given to many of the larger-than-life and exceptionally odious villains in the saga. Modesty is not spared the cruelties of her antagonists; she is, for instance, raped several times. Her special relationship with Willie, who never makes love to her but spends much time wrestling with her, gives the pair a mystique; both have active love affairs outside their friendship, which is in other respects closer than friendship or even the most intimate working partnership. Unlike, say, Donald Hamilton's Matt Helm, both Willie and Modesty have the Achilles' heel of loyalty; they will not knowingly injure or betray a friend. This knowledge becomes widespread in the characters' fictional world, and adversaries increasingly use it against them in the series. O'Donnell tells the story of his creation of the heroine in his essay "Becoming Modesty." He explains that, unlike the creator of a hero such as Bond or Leslie Charteris's the Saint, the maker of such a "king-sized heroine" has to explain how she got that way. He found his inspiration for her beginning among the urchin refugees he met in 1942 while a soldier in northern Persia: "They have survived, somehow, living off the land like little animals, and they will continue to survive. You can see it in their old-young faces." In an interview he said the name "Modesty" hit him when he mistyped "modestly": he had found "the antithesis of a dramatic name. 'Blaise' followed quickly because I was studying the Arthurian legends at the time, and Blaise was the master of Merlin, so the name had a touch of magic as well as flowing nicely from 'Modesty.' "

O'Donnell was born in Lewisham, near London, 11 April 1920, and was educated at Catford Central School, London. Before World War II he was in the Territorial Army. He served in the Royal Signal Corps from 1938 to 1946. Probably his most exciting experience during the war was sailing toward France while the Dunkirk evacuation was proceeding, as part of a British Expeditionary Force project to establish a line of communication. As his group was not allowed to land, new orders took him to Northern Ireland for a year. Signalman O'Donnell married Constance Doris Green in November 1940. The couple's first baby lived for only two days, and three days after that he was posted overseas, not getting any

more news of his wife for four months. He served in Iran, Iraq, Syria, Lebanon, Palestine, Egypt, Italy, and Greece (all settings used in the Modesty stories). When he was reunited with his wife, they had not seen each other for four years. The couple and their two daughters presently reside in the Brighton area.

O'Donnell has been very prolific and eclectic in his writing. Even before the war, after an unsuccessful attempt to get a job on a national newspaper, he worked for Amalgamated Press (now Fleetway Publications), writing for such children's comics as *Comic Cuts*, *Chips*, *Joker*, *Jester*, *Rainbow*, *Tiger Tim*, *Puck*, and *Sparkler*. This work, which often involved the need to provide plausible solutions to cliff-hanger situations week after week, was clearly an ideal preparation for his work as an adult novelist. His Fleet Street ambitions (now partly fulfilled by his having an office there) were aroused by his father, Bernard O'Donnell, a successful crime reporter. In a 1966 interview in *Woman's Mirror*, O'Donnell said that his father "covered 320 murder trials in his time. He was a marvellous reporter and could get on with anyone. He was always bringing murderers' wives and underworld characters to the house, and Katie, my mother, would feed them and find them a bed." After the war, O'Donnell found life as a freelance writer tough going: he made £250 in his first year, then joined a small publishing company, writing articles for a wide range of magazines and helping produce such annuals as *The Boy's Book of Sport* and *The Boy's Book of Scotland Yard*. In the early 1950s he was keeping six or seven boys' series going simultaneously: they included Jack Keen, Master Detective; Willy Wizard, Lord of Sherwood; Billy the Kid; Mick the Moonboy; and the Mishaps of Merlin. He has remained a painstaking worker, at his desk in businessman's fashion from nine to five.

When O'Donnell took over writing the famous Garth comic strip in 1952, a new phase of his career began, and he was soon able to drop the boys' series and specialize in comics for adults. Garth and Romeo Brown (which he began writing in 1956) had not originated with him, although he had made the strips more romantic (for example, Garth got a steady girlfriend, the goddess Venus). When Romeo Brown was dropped in 1962, O'Donnell had the time and incentive to devise the Modesty Blaise comic strip. He defined her characteristics and then worked backward to give her a life history. He obtained the services of Jim Holdaway, one of the best artists in the comics industry, to do the drawings. (Holdaway died in 1970, and Badia Romero took over the artwork.) The Modesty Blaise series was a huge success. By 1977 it was syndicated to newspapers in forty-two countries.

Publishers wanted to hire someone other than O'Donnell to write a Modesty Blaise novel, not appreciating that a cartoon-strip writer could also work at novel length, but O'Donnell insisted that he could do it. He had written a screenplay for the *Modesty Blaise* film (which was not used), and he adapted it for a novel. *Modesty Blaise* (1965), which introduces many of the regulars in the Modesty Blaise novels, remains fresh and brilliant in style and construction. The frame-by-frame quality of the cartoon-series writer is evident from the beginning of the slow but absorbing first chapter, which proceeds in short paragraphs, with brief exchanges of dialogue punctuated by careful descriptions of setting. Jack Fraser and Sir Gerald Tarrant prepare to visit Modesty in the hope of persuading her, a rich woman recently retired from a successful life as a career criminal in charge of the Network syndicate, to do a job for them. Tarrant, a spymaster, observes everything, Fraser as much as Blaise. He is also a shrewd decision-maker, who will note his lieutenant's advisory hand signals but ignore them when his better wisdom dictates. In later novels, Tarrant's obsession with Modesty will seem voyeuristic (though this is perhaps too strong, because he is also a father-substitute for her), and his role as observer (the reader's surrogate) makes his own modesty more noticeable when she appears unclad (he looks away because he is the one who is most aware that looking is immoral). In the series Tarrant is the foil for Willie, whose obtrusive cockney speech is almost an affectation of classlessness. Tarrant and Fraser first come upon Modesty engaged in her hobby of gem-carving; when, later, they enter Willie's sanctum, the gym and workshop behind his country pub, The Treadmill, he is working on various gadgets, both lethal and ornamental.

Willie and Modesty can do almost everything, though each is given a careful modicum of imperfection, and their talents are complementary; she is a better shot with a gun, he is more accurate with a knife, for instance. That Willie, himself a superhero, should be content to serve her platonically is scarcely credible to her macho lover, Paul Hagan, who is part artist, part agent. Hagan is used in *Modesty Blaise* partly to exemplify the difference between the professional and the amateur approach to an "operation" (he is intensely irritated by her shunning of sexual intercourse and her withdrawal from him into yoga exercises before beginning an investigation). Hagan is also used as a concession to the reader's expectation that Modesty will enjoy the sexual act, even if only at the rest-and-recreation level; readers may, however, wish her taste in partners was less peccable. Both for Modesty and for Willie, though, the supreme excitement is found in the dance with death. Another concession is Modesty's secret indulgence of tears following an operation (a secret only Willie can share with the reader); this stands in contrast to her ability to undergo sexual assault in a self-induced state of unconsciousness. O'Donnell skips lightly over the difficulty of preserving the life-affirming character of his heroes despite the brutality of their chosen line of work.

In the first novel Modesty and Willie become the captives of supercriminals directed by a villain named Gabriel in order to foil their plot to steal a huge shipment of diamonds being sent from South Africa to a Middle Eastern potentate, Sheik Abu-Tahir (who turns out to be one of Modesty's admirers). As the book opens, Tarrant tells Modesty that Willie, bored with retirement, has engaged in a banana-republic revolution and, captive, awaits execution. She rescues him. The first phase of the campaign to stop Gabriel requires Modesty to tangle with Pacco, one of her own former criminal lieutenants, who is in the south of France where Hagan is Tarrant's agent-in-place. Pacco assumes that Modesty is trying to take over the syndicate again and reacts violently. Modesty and Hagan, taken by surprise, manage to alert Willie, who is in bed with Pacco's disaffected girlfriend, Nicole. Later Nicole, overconfident of being able to pump Pacco about Gabriel, is killed by him on Gabriel's instructions. The suddenly grim mood of the novel is not altogether lightened by the way Willie uses Pacco's overt sentimentality (he can weep for the girl he has had murdered) in executing him. (O'Donnell's villains usually are brutally indifferent to life.) After Modesty and Willie have allowed themselves to be captured by Gabriel and he has discussed the manner of their disposal, one of the villains, McWhirter, expresses the wish to see a hanging. His wish is granted ironically when this happens to Mrs. Fothergill, Gabriel's killing machine, just when she seems about to win a fight with Modesty. The seizure of the diamonds (Willie has to do the main work, cutting into the ship's hold

"When I've made a quarter of a million I retire" said Modesty Blaise. And did.

A twelve-year-old girl tramping across war-ravaged Europe, through refugee camps, across the Middle East knowing hunger, rape, despair —this was the making of Modesty Blaise. She wanted the security of money and got it. In every worth-while place she organised The Network, a crime organisation, efficient, deadly. She took a degenerate Willie Garvin from the gutter and turned him into her right-hand aide—a man as deadly and as professional as herself.

They made their money and retired. But where was the excitement in pretty clothes, jewels or running a pub on the Thames? Now on the right side of the law for once they pit themselves against a vicious schemer who played for very high stakes ruthlessly. Their story is one of tension and excitement. We see the blazing gun, feel the thud of steel against flesh and sicken at the paralysing Karate blow. This is the first of what every reader will want to be a very long series.

PETER O'DONNELL

MODESTY BLAISE

SOUVENIR PRESS

PETER O'DONNELL

Dust jacket for the first edition of O'Donnell's initial Modesty Blaise novel

from below, while in a diving bell) and the prolonged escape sequence are carefully considered set pieces. Modesty and Willie use the elaborate equipment they have smuggled inside their clothing and even inside a large sheet of plastic skin; enemies are usually more careful in later adventures. O'Donnell slides over the simple actions that might have been taken by the authorities to prevent the robbery (there is a time when Gabriel with his key personnel could simply have been arrested on his yacht and detained), but such sleight of hand is almost always required in his plots.

Despite the mediocrity of the film, it must have helped the paperback sales of *Modesty Blaise*, which were approaching the half-million mark as *Sabre-Tooth* (1966) was published. *Sabre-Tooth* concerns an attempt to take over Kuwait. The supervillain this time is Karz, a Mongolian brute who commands an army of four hundred "hard, cold, self-confident men," each a proven expert in his chosen trade of killing. Karz's assistant is Liebmann, "fair, with a thin ascetic face and the

voice of a fallen angel," a man whose emotions have been burnt out of him, save for the frisson of fear he feels in the presence of Karz. Karz's special weapon is a pair of Siamese twins, Lok and Chu, who hate each other except when they are working as a precision instrument of murder; readers see them at their exercise in the first chapter. Following a hunch of Tarrant's, Modesty and Willie eventually pretend to join Karz's guerilla army in the Hindu Kush so as to thwart Karz and rescue Willie's adopted daughter, Lucille, from him. Modesty has to fight the twins; she is also raped by several people. This upsets Tarrant, but Willie explains, by drawing an analogy between Modesty's misfortune and the scar of a partially completed initial on the back of his own hand, that the incident occurred in the past and is over now. One of Modesty's past lovers returns in the book (one of three who have taken her to the heights of sexual love); he betrays her, and she has to shoot him. John Dall, an extremely wealthy American businessman with CIA connections, appears for the first time in this novel; he is often present in other adventures.

In *I, Lucifer* (1967) the Seffs, a criminal couple, have enlisted Lucifer (who can foretell death) to blackmail people, and Garcia (who can control dolphins) to collect the loot. Modesty's new lover, Stephen Collier, a mathematician and statistician who is expert in psychic research, is called in by the Seffs to improve Lucifer's talent. The Seffs have an executioner, Jack Wish, who rigs visual magician's tricks to enhance Lucifer's confidence in his own power. Modesty and Collier are both fitted with "death-capsules" that can be remote-activated by transmitter; when Willie comes to their rescue, he has to be "killed" by her in a duel. Expert parachuting figures in the action, and the climax features an escape from the roof of a burning building. Lucifer, who is an innocent in his way, is given his first sexual experience by Modesty. It is given to him to kill his persecutor, Seff, by throwing him from a great height. In researching this book, O'Donnell spent much time with a dolphin specialist at the Natural History Museum in England.

A Taste for Death (1969) introduces a blind woman with fantastic powers of divination, Dinah Pilgrim. Collier falls in love with her (and later marries her), and their courtship is a refreshing ingredient in O'Donnell's novels. Gabriel, who resurfaces here, needs Dinah's talent in a quest for treasure, but he and his majordomo McWhirter are relatively minor figures in the action compared with a giant, ironically named Delicata, who once nearly killed Willie in a previous encounter. Modesty's principal antagonist is Wenczel, a master swordsman, whom she faces in a fencing match, stripped to her briefs, while he is protected by a mesh jacket, in the arena of a Saharan city built by a Roman tribune. Modesty has to accept a wound in the arm in order to defeat Wenczel, and her arm swells up with poison. She is thus helpless to intervene in another duel between Delicata and Willie. Delicata kills Gabriel and McWhirter, apparently on the orders of a wealthy villain, Presteign, who is pulled into a watery grave by Modesty (wearing scuba gear for the occasion) just as he thinks he is escaping. O'Donnell spent a week with the Amateur Fencing Association before he worked out the details of the engagements for the book; two fencing masters then acted out the moves he had written and confirmed that they were quite possible and technically correct.

The Impossible Virgin (1971) introduces Giles Pennyfeather, a simple healer with surprising tal-

Dust jacket for the first American edition of O'Donnell's only Modesty Blaise short-story collection

ents. The story begins when a Russian studying satellite reports discovers a gold seam in Africa. He is tortured by the man with whom he hopes to deal but gets as far as Pennyfeather's mission hospital and reveals the map coordinates to the physician before dying. Modesty rescues Pennyfeather from torture and begins a struggle against the dwarfish villain, Brunel, whose henchmen are Adrian Chance and Jack Muktar. Brunel has a slave-mistress, Lisa, who is controlled by voices in her head from a transmitter embedded in a tooth. Brunel decides to enslave Modesty also and captures her, dropping Willie from an airplane at three thousand feet while en route to his African plantation. Also recaptured is Pennyfeather, who is tortured by Chance. However, Chance is ambitious for his boss's job; he learns the secret of Brunel's control of Lisa and uses it against her master. Willie, who has survived the fall from the plane by landing on a snow-covered slope, comes to the rescue, escaping with Modesty, Pennyfeather, and Lisa (who is suffering from appendicitis) to the "Impossible Virgin," a natural formation that includes a valley filled with wasps. Pennyfeather helps Modesty get out of a gorilla's cage and performs an operation on Lisa. There are strong pragmatic touches as well as near-fanciful ones in the action, as when papers in Brunel's safe in a guarded house are stolen by brute force, the wall broken by an iron ball and the whole safe removed by a fork-lift, while barbed wire is draped over doors and windows to prevent egress of the defenders. The novel was well received by reviewers in Britain and America.

Pieces of Modesty (1972) collects six stories. In "A Better Day to Die," set in South America, Modesty, Jimson (a pacifist missionary), and a busload of schoolgirls are captured by rebels. The rebels rape one of the girls and undoubtedly will continue with the others (Modesty is being saved for their chief) when Willie appears, and he and Modesty attack them. The rebels retreat to a defended position and throw a grenade. The grenade, which will almost certainly maim Jimson, is caught by him and thrown back at the rebels, killing all of them. The "Giggle Wrecker" is a story about how to get someone across the Berlin Wall by circus cannon. "I Had a Date with Lady Janet" is unusual in having Willie as first-person narrator; here he rescues Modesty from a Scottish castle where she is being held by an old enemy, Rodelle. The title refers to Lady Janet Gillam, Willie's girlfriend when he is at home at The Treadmill. In "A Perfect Night to Break Your Neck," set in the Riviera and concerning Collier, Modesty uses a water ski to board silently an enemy's yacht at night. "Salamander Four" is set in Finland, where Modesty is posing nude for a statuette for John Dall; she gets involved with industrial spies, and again there is a pacifist character, the sculptor Alex Hemmer, to offset the Modesty Blaise-Willie Garvin ethos of violence. In "The Soo Girl Charity" Modesty and Willie seek vengeance on a sadistic financier. When they invade his home, they find his Asian wife on the point of committing suicide because he has found a new woman to torture. Later she murders her husband, and Modesty sends her to her parents.

In *The Silver Mistress* (1973) Tarrant is granted his long-expressed wish to see Modesty in action. This is very much Tarrant's book and, despite that (he can be irritating), is one of the best in the series. The title describes Modesty, naked and glistening with oil, as she appears to Tarrant when about to engage in mortal combat, alone in a cavern with "the golden master" of unarmed combat, the suave, sadistic, incredibly fast and powerful Mr. Sexton. Her one advantage is the choice of ground. Tarrant has been held captive by a gang of blackmailers in a Gothic castle in the Pyrenees. The villains are nasty; they include the inhuman Colonel Jim with his loathsome mistress, Lucy, and the vicious, murdering Angel (Angelica), whose weapon is piano wire. On Modesty's side, but caught with her in the same trap, are Willie and Lady Janet (Janet's false leg provides the means of escape), as well as a new chum, Quinn, who witnesses the kidnapping of Tarrant from a cliff ledge and knows the cave route into the castle. The *Times Literary Supplement* reviewer called this "another splendid bag of tricks" and proclaimed that "Peter O'Donnell is our current master of get-me-out-of-here, with his outstanding ingenious use of 'what lies to hand.'" The Archival Press edition has twenty full-page illustrations.

Last Day in Limbo (1976) is somewhat similar to *The Impossible Virgin* in outline. Mad Aunt Benita has her own slave plantation, Limbo, in the Guatemalan jungle. Her slaves are rich people kidnapped in such a way that they are believed dead. The story begins with Benita's failed attempt to add Modesty and Dall to her collection. A female spy, Maude Tiller, joins the protagonists as Willie's girlfriend; she has had a nasty experience with Benita's nephew Paxero and his friend Damion, who like to cooperate in systematic sexual humiliation. Danny Chavasse, who is also part of Modesty's extended family from the days of the Network (he has a special "magic" with women), is used as the witness of life in Limbo. Modesty is horrified to find that Dinah Collier, the sensitive blind girl, has been kidnapped to Limbo while accompanying her husband on an archaeological expedition. She is in imminent danger of death, scheduled for sacrifice to a Mayan god. In order to rescue her, Modesty allows herself to be kidnapped. Willie and Maude approach Limbo from the jungle. There is no big set piece duel for Modesty or Willie in this book, but good teamwork. Reviewing it in the *Evening Standard*, Kingsley Amis affirmed that he "was gripped from the start and stayed gripped."

Dragon's Claw (1978) is a simply structured story where the fine details matter in particular episodes. The villains, Beauregard Browne, Clarissa de Courtney-Scott (nymphomaniac and expert at murder with a bicycle spoke), and the Reverend Uriah Crisp (self-styled Hammer of God, executioner with a lightning-draw pistol), are coordinated by an Australian media millionaire, Sam Solon. They are based on Solon's island, Dragon's Claw, in the Tasman Sea, where art experts are brought to admire his stolen art collection before being killed. Solon would prefer to avoid killing his admirers and enlists a Dr. Feng to induce amnesia in them, but Feng's first patient, top painter Luke Fletcher, escapes before his memory is quite destroyed and is rescued from the sea by Modesty, who is on a solo yacht trip to New Zealand. Beauregard's gang proceeds to steal a Ming chair from Amsterdam and put Modesty, Willie, and Luke under surveillance. Luke, now Modesty's lover, is kidnapped so that she and Willie may be blackmailed into stealing a "Jade Princess" from Burlington House; another friend of theirs, Dick Kingston, is killed to prove the gang's seriousness, and Luke is also killed when his full memory returns. Modesty and Willie pursue the villains to Australia, but Solon, posing as a friend, deceives them, drugs them, and delivers them to the island for execution. There they kill the villains in a rousing finale, employing among other things a homemade hang glider, to escape by night from a trap on a plateau.

In 1978 two Star paperbacks were published of cartoon-strip adventures. *Modesty Blaise: In the Beginning* comprises "La Machine," which offers an alternative version of the story of Tarrant's original recruitment of Modesty and Willie, and "The Long Lever," wherein Modesty allows sentiment to override duty during an attempt to rescue a kidnapped millionaire. *Modesty Blaise: The Black Pearl and The Vikings* provides two more adventures with the bonus of a convenient sketch of Modesty's early life. "The Black Pearl" requires Modesty and Willie to bring a bear out of Tibet; "The Viking" has them rescuing a foolish former Network man, Olaf Nilsen, from a gang run by a demented, ax-wielding neo-Viking.

Using what looks at first like somewhat unpromising low-key villains, O'Donnell constructs in *The Xanadu Talisman* (1981) an excellent story with several nice ironic and humorous touches, as well as adequate violence. The talisman of the title is the fabulous peacock crown that belonged to the Shah of Iran before being stolen by the French husband of Tracy June. Two brothers, Jeremy and Dominic, are under the control of

their nanny, Miss Prendergast, who disciplines them by withholding sexual favors. Although they are a nasty pair who run a Mediterranean gang called El Mico (the Monkey), readers are not surprised that Modesty should humiliate them both in an arena combat; this, however, is followed by a more dangerous encounter between Willie and a panther. By then matters have become serious, as Modesty and Willie become trapped in Xanadu, a sheik's fortress in the Atlas Mountains. Assisted by Giles Pennyfeather, they rescue the captive, now-widowed Tracy June from the sheik. But she is vociferously ungrateful for the favor: Xanadu was a paradise for her.

In a *Times Literary Supplement* review, "The Ravages of Time," Robert Bernard Martin says of *The Xanadu Talisman* that "over the years Peter O'Donnell has shifted his emphasis from the high camp descriptions of Modesty's *haute couture*, brand-name cars and drinks, elegant houses and cod language to non-stop action, a camp considerably further down the mountain." He adds that "somewhere along the line," Modesty has learned to use naughty words, as she never used to do, and it takes her nearly three hundred pages to get into basic black jersey and pearls, with her hair and fingernails in tolerable order. It's still good fun, but it's unlike the girl we used to know." Some of his observations are correct, even if his plot synopsis is incorrect in places. Detailed descriptions of Modesty's nude body are not as prevalent in the more current books, and O'Donnell seems to relax more frequently with humor at his heroine's expense, but this was present even in the first adventure with the litany of what Modesty could not do well. Martin's charge that Modesty more frequently uses vulgar language is untrue. One of her most vicious comments occurs in chapter 1: "She seldom swore, but now she shook her head and said softly, wondering, 'Bloody hell ... why me?'" This comment comes after six minutes in which she has encountered "an earthquake, entombment, a fight with a killer, and an attempt to save a stranger from bleeding to death."

The Night of Morningstar (1982) begins with an episode from Modesty's past, the time of the winding up of the Network when Hugh Oberon, an unpleasant and ambitious young man, was dismissed, an incident he never forgot. When he becomes an important agent in a Russian-paid terrorist group, the Watchmen, and their paths cross again, Oberon makes it a personal issue. There are several main episodes: the freeing of some

Dust jackets for the first British and first American editions of O'Donnell's twelfth and thirteenth Modesty Blaise novels

white slave girls (Modesty joins the girls in order to achieve this); the foiling by Willie of an attempt to murder Tarrant, for which Polish twins, who use only their bare hands to kill, have been employed by Oberon; a relatively light-hearted extraction of information from Oberon's go-between for the killer, fixer Bernie Chan; and a highly unpleasant Watchmen exercise in which Modesty accidentally gets involved by blowing the cover of Ben Christie, a CIA agent who has pretended to join them. Modesty manages to save the Golden Gate Bridge from destruction, although Christie loses his life in saving hers. The book's climax is the foiling of an elaborate plot to kill four national leaders at a summit conference held in the Madeira Islands. Individually, the villains are not especially outrageous, although the wife of one of them, Victoria, Countess St. Maur, is in the tradition of Miss Prendergast: she literally rides her lovers (and is ridden by them). The chief villain, Golitsyn, unusual in O'Donnell, is given a sense of humor.

Dead Man's Handle (1985) breaks no new ground but makes for pleasant reading. It is especially clear in this novel that the Modesty Blaise-Willie Garvin circle has become an extended family, as O'Donnell makes a point of bringing in most of the surviving members from earlier escapades. He also recalls earlier adventures in the narrative, particularly *Last Day in Limbo*. Dinah and Stephen Collier figure prominently, and Salamander Four, who were used in the story "Salamander Four" in *Pieces of Modesty*, are here employed as a threat to blackmail Modesty. The prelude recounts Willie's rescue of Molly Chen's grandfather from a mainland Chinese prison ten years before the main action. The prelude is important for reinforcing the idea that Willie's self-esteem is fragile and dependent on Modesty (see also chapter 2 of *Modesty Blaise*) and because the main plot has Willie believing (through drugs and hypnosis) that he is in the Network again, Modesty is dead, and he must avenge her killing by eliminating "Delilah" (who looks like her). This crazy scenario is organized primarily for the entertainment of Dr. Thaddeus Pilgrim, the insane leader of a sham religious group, the Hostel of Righteousness, a criminal organization that answers prayers by killing or otherwise dealing with people obstructing those who might be wealthy enough to reward the group. The villains also engage in scams for big profits; Pilgrim would like to recruit Modesty and Willie to help with one of these, especially when they kill his best assassins,

Sibyl Pray and her lover Kazim, in gladiatorial combat (after the plot to have Willie kill Modesty on sight has failed). The main action takes place on a small Greek island, Kalivari, where Pilgrim has his headquarters. Both Pilgrim—a disgusting villain with a circumlocutory style of speech—and his sycophantic, spider-like henchwoman, Mrs. Ram (a lesbian who worships him), are eventually killed by one of the more decent members of their gang. The title of the novel refers to Pilgrim's plan to secure Modesty and Willie to his service by exploiting their major weakness, friendship; the Colliers will be murdered by Salamander Four if Pilgrim does not talk with the assassins twice a day. However, Modesty manages to get a message through Weng to Tarrant to protect the Colliers and to frighten off Salamander Four. In using the shortwave radio on a stormy night, however, she is struck nearly dead by lightning, and Willie has to carry her down a cliff to hide in a cave; by then he is rehabilitated, though she has had to wean him from the shock of discovering that he had almost been induced to kill her. There is a relaxed, amusing final chapter in which the Colliers and the other friends learn that the adventure happens to have brought in much money.

In unpublished correspondence O'Donnell has explained that his 1974 play, *Murder Most Logical*, is not a whodunit but "how-are-they-going-to-do-it-and-will-it-work?" When it went on tour, the title was changed to *Mr. Fothergill's Murder* (published 1983), a reference to the one line which survived (mangled) from the original script O'Donnell wrote for the *Modesty Blaise* film. The tour, he says, was a great success, but in the West End it ran only five weeks, having been "slaughtered by the national critics"; "House Full" notices were being achieved by that time, but another play had been booked.

For a summary of the character and merits of the Modesty Blaise books, one can hardly better the assessment of Kingsley Amis in his review of *Last Day in Limbo* (*Evening Standard*, 21 May 1976). He credits the thriller series with "ingenious ideas, . . . a sharply-twisting story-line, varied locations, a really formidable criminal project to be foiled, lots of healthy violence, nasty villains, well-sketched minor characters, expert grading of tension, and above all the bond of faith and respect between Modesty and Willie Garvin, her lieutenant. Theirs is one of the great partnerships in crime fiction, bearing comparison with (though necessarily different from) that of Sherlock Holmes and Dr. Watson." He defends himself against any idea that this last remark is absurdly or shamefully inflated by pointing out that the novels, whatever the cartoon-strip might show, reveal that "she's neither a joke nor a titillation device and that her exploits, though naturally and properly sensational, aren't sensationalist in the vicious meaning of the term. On the contrary, her moral universe is in many respects a satisfyingly old-fashioned one, founded on loyalty, obligation and the keeping of promises, even on patriotism and the belief that our side is actually better than their side." However, in view of Amis's own reputation for being "old-fashioned," one should perhaps add Mary Beth Pringle's assessment of the sources of Modesty's appeal: "My conclusions are that Modesty Blaise is a prototypical, twentieth-century, fantasy heroine and that the pattern of her heroism is especially (in ways, uniquely) appealing to females. Modesty's mysterious past, physical appearance, present lifestyle, current vocation, and relationships with people appeal to each of our childish, adolescent and adult fantasies / mythologies about ourselves. In addition, her origins and her existentialist characteristics link her to male (and, rarely, to female) quest heroes in detective and other types of fiction. Both cartoon strips and novels portray her as a potent fantasy heroine; the film version . . . does not."

Interview:
Woman's Mirror (8 January 1966): 14-15.

References:
Mary Beth Pringle, "*Modesty Blaise*: Fantasy Heroine," *Cartonaggio*, 3 (July-September 1980): 1-9;
Michael J. Tolley, "Modesty Blaise and Other Heroines," Unit 6, of *The Hero in Popular Fiction* (Adelaide, Aus.: University of Adelaide, Radio University 5UV, 1976);
Richard West, "Modesty Blaise: Checklist of Strip Stories," *Cartonaggio*, 3 (July-September 1980): 48-51.

Ruth Rendell
(17 February 1930-   )

Susan Resneck Parr
University of Tulsa

BOOKS: *From Doon with Death* (London: Long, 1964; Garden City, N.Y.: Doubleday, 1965);

To Fear a Painted Devil (London: Long, 1965; Garden City, N.Y.: Doubleday, 1965);

Vanity Dies Hard (London: Long, 1966); republished as *In Sickness and in Health* (Garden City, N.Y.: Doubleday, 1966);

A New Lease of Death (London: Long, 1967; Garden City, N.Y.: Doubleday, 1967); republished as *Sins of the Fathers* (New York: Ballantine, 1970);

Wolf to the Slaughter (London: Long, 1967; Garden City, N.Y.: Doubleday, 1968);

The Secret House of Death (London: Long, 1968; Garden City, N.Y.: Doubleday, 1969);

The Best Man to Die (London: Long, 1969; Garden City, N.Y.: Doubleday, 1970);

A Guilty Thing Surprised (London: Hutchinson, 1970; Garden City, N.Y.: Doubleday, 1970);

No More Dying Then (London: Hutchinson, 1971; Garden City, N.Y.: Doubleday, 1972);

One Across, Two Down (London: Hutchinson, 1971; Garden City, N.Y.: Doubleday, 1971);

Murder Being Once Done (London: Hutchinson, 1972; Garden City, N.Y.: Doubleday, 1972);

Some Lie and Some Die (London: Hutchinson, 1973; Garden City, N.Y.: Doubleday, 1973);

The Face of Trespass (London: Hutchinson, 1974; Garden City, N.Y.: Doubleday, 1974);

Shake Hands Forever (London: Hutchinson, 1975; Garden City, N.Y.: Doubleday, 1975);

The Fallen Curtain, and Other Stories (London: Hutchinson, 1976; Garden City, N.Y.: Doubleday, 1976);

A Demon in My View (London: Hutchinson, 1976; Garden City, N.Y.: Doubleday, 1977);

A Judgement in Stone (London: Hutchinson, 1977; Garden City, N.Y.: Doubleday, 1978);

A Sleeping Life (London: Hutchinson, 1978; Garden City, N.Y.: Doubleday, 1978);

Make Death Love Me (London: Hutchinson, 1979; Garden City, N.Y.: Doubleday, 1979);

Means of Evil, and Other Stories (London: Hutchin-

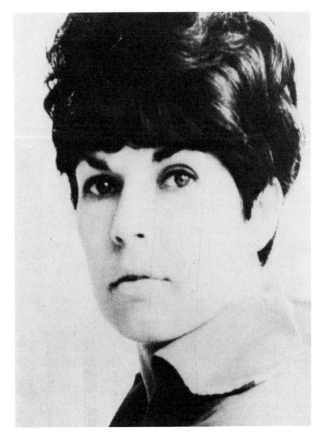

Ruth Rendell

son, 1979; Garden City, N.Y.: Doubleday, 1980);

The Lake of Darkness (London: Hutchinson, 1980; Garden City, N.Y.: Doubleday, 1980);

Put On by Cunning (London: Hutchinson, 1981); republished as *Death Notes* (New York: Pantheon, 1981);

Master of the Moor (London: Hutchinson, 1982; New York: Pantheon, 1982);

The Fever Tree, and Other Stories (London: Hutchinson, 1982; New York: Pantheon, 1983);

The Speaker of Mandarin (London: Hutchinson, 1983; New York: Pantheon, 1983);

The Killing Doll (London: Hutchinson, 1984; New York: Pantheon, 1984);

The Tree of Hands (London: Hutchinson, 1984; New York: Pantheon, 1984);

The New Girlfriend and Other Stories (London: Hutchinson, 1985; New York: Pantheon, 1986);

An Unkindness of Ravens (London: Hutchinson, 1985; New York: Pantheon, 1985);

Live Flesh (London: Hutchinson, 1986; New York: Pantheon, 1986);

A Dark-Adapted Eye, as Barbara Vine (London: Viking, 1987; New York: Bantam, 1987);

A Fatal Inversion, as Vine (Harmondsworth: Viking, 1987; New York: Bantam, 1987);

Heartstones (London: Hutchinson, 1987; New York: Harper & Row, 1987);

Talking to Strangers (London: Hutchinson, 1987); republished as *Talking to Strange Men* (New York: Pantheon, 1987);

The Veiled One (London: Hutchinson, 1988; New York: Pantheon, 1988);

The House of Stairs, as Vine (London: Viking, 1988; New York: Harmony, 1989);

The Bridesmaid (London: Hutchinson, 1989; New York: Mysterious, 1989).

Ruth Rendell has in recent years established herself as a major force in modern detective fiction, having won such prestigious awards as the Edgar Allan Poe Award from the Mystery Writers of America, the *Current Crime* Silver Cup for the best crime novel, and the Crime Writers' Association's Gold Dagger Award (twice). Although all of her nearly thirty novels display the intricacies of plot characteristic of the genre, Rendell has brought to it a sophisticated emphasis on both the psychology of the criminal mind and the psychology of those who are committed to justice, as well as an attentiveness to contemporary British life. Rendell's own keen interest in things literary is also apparent in her graceful style, her penchant for literary allusions (which Robert Barnard, who talks about her "storyteller's gift," calls "the dreaded quotation habit"), and her attention to the place of language and books within her fictional worlds.

Rendell's novels are of two kinds: those in a series centered around Inspector Reginald Wexford and those novels which take as their subject the criminal or emotionally disturbed mind. Although most of her works are set in Kingsmarkham, a village about an hour from London,

they offer two very different and often contradictory visions of the universe. The fourteen Wexford novels have a moral center and present an optimistic view of the possibilities for personal growth, love, and responsible choice, generally embodied in the characters of Wexford, his subordinate Michael Burden, and their families, whose stories comprise an ongoing subplot. These are novels which Jane S. Bakerman (April 1978) says explain Rendell's "real center of interest: a varied and compelling examination of friendship and love–and their too frequent companion, selfishness." Rendell's other novels, which exist individually rather than as parts of a series, suggest an altogether different world, one in which individuals are psychologically flawed, morally callous, and often capable of easy murders. These works have no Wexford or Burden to redeem them or to offer hopes: "It is," as Julian Symons (*London Sunday Times*, 12 April 1981) observes, "the frustrations and absurdities of ordinary people that Ruth Rendell notes like an uncensorious Recording Angel." At the same time she is, says Douglas Johnson (*London Review of Books*, 7 March 1985), "meticulous in describing the details of everyday life, the food that is bought from the supermarket, the geography of the buses and tubes around North London, the plants and flowers that surround the houses." Indeed, as he argues, "the precise emphasis on the real and ordinary makes the eruption of the fantastic all the more terrible." Rendell has also published three novels under the pseudonym of Barbara Vine.

Ruth Grasemann Rendell was born in London on 17 February 1930. Although her parents, Arthur and Ebba Elise (Kruse) Grasemann, had named her "Ruth," Mrs. Grasemann's Scandinavian parents were, according to Rendell, unable to pronounce the name. The result was that Rendell's mother called her "Barbara" while, for a time at least, her father called her "Ruth." Eventually, Rendell writes, "since this sort of duality was impossible in one household, my father finally started calling me Barbara too." However impossible the duality was in Rendell's childhood home, it has persisted in her adult life, leading her to combine the name "Barbara" with that of her paternal great-grandmother's maiden name, "Vine," as a pseudonym. It may also account for the two very different perspectives offered in her fiction: the hopeful one of the Wexford novels and the bleaker one of the others.

After graduating from Loughton High School in Essex, Rendell (who continued to be called both "Ruth" and "Barbara") spent several years as a reporter and subeditor with the *Express* and *Independent* newspapers of West Essex. During this period, in 1950, she married Donald Rendell, whom she divorced in 1975 and remarried in 1977. The Rendells have one son, Simon. The couple live in North London and spend weekends in their cottage in Suffolk. Rendell is also an avid reader and a self-taught student. She has, for example, learned both Greek and German on her own.

Rendell's first novel, *From Doon with Death* (1964), reveals some of the themes that recur throughout her fiction. Specifically, the novel explores the ways in which seemingly ordinary people are driven to acts of violence by secret passions. It also focuses on the complexities of relationships between people, the ways in which childhood moments shape adult behavior, and the impact of social class on individual attitudes and actions. *From Doon with Death*–with literary epigraphs for every chapter–evinces Rendell's reliance on literary allusions as a means of suggesting the universality of the events she dramatizes, a reliance which has become more subtle through her career. But perhaps most importantly, the novel introduces Wexford and Burden, providing a baseline against which their growth as individuals and their deepening relationship can be measured.

The plot is straightforward. A prim and ordinary former schoolteacher, Margaret "Minna" Parsons, is found murdered. Wexford and Burden, in attempting to identify her killer, come to learn that murderous passion can lie latent in the most unlikely of people. In this case, the murderer (who thinks of herself as "Doon") is a beautiful socialite and the wife of a successful solicitor. Obsessed for the past twelve years by an unrequited schoolgirl crush on Margaret, Doon has chosen a celibate marriage. Her celibacy in turn prompts her husband to engage in a series of destructive extramarital affairs.

As will be true of many of her subsequent novels, the values of Rendell's characters are revealed through their attitudes toward books. For example, Doon lives surrounded by books that she loves. Her husband, bound to her despite theirs being a "strangely sexless communion," remains proud of his wife's knowledge of literature. In contrast, Doon's beloved "Minna" keeps the beautifully bound books Doon had given her

Dust jacket for the first edition of Rendell's eighth novel featuring Inspector Wexford

hidden in an attic trunk; Minna's husband reads only books on crime and tells Wexford, "I never want to see another book as long as I live"; and Minna's first boyfriend (whom she chose over Doon) reads only paperback thrillers and *Reader's Digest*. Even Burden shares in this anti-intellectualism, telling Minna's husband, "It's all those books you read. . . . It's not healthy." Such attitudes prompt the well-read Wexford to tease Burden that he probably should not have read a book on psychology and crime because it was leading Burden into the realm of amateur psychological analysis.

But it is the presentation of Wexford and Burden, both as individuals and in relation to one another, that is the novel's most interesting feature. Wexford is described as being "taller than Burden, thick-set without being fat, the very prototype of an actor playing a top-brass policeman." Burden is not described at all. Until the final pages, their relationship is almost impersonal. In fact Wexford tends to be hard on his assistant, speaking to him sarcastically and chastising him with such expressions as "Have you gone raving mad, Burden?," "Be your age," and "You make me puke." Burden for his part quietly accepts Wexford's imperiousness. Able to sleep through crises and a believer in having "a sense of proportion," Burden seldom experiences, much less understands, the passions that motivate those he investigates. Nevertheless, by the end of the novel the two men have grown more intimate, and Burden has become more tolerant of human frailty. Although he is still "a little sick" at the notion that Doon and her husband may never have consummated their marriage, he comes to feel sympathy for Doon's husband. He also joins with Wexford in reconstructing the events leading up to the murder and then in reading Doon's unsent love letters to Minna. The last line of the novel both denotes their new closeness and foreshadows Burden's growing interest in the written word: "Then they pulled their chairs closer to the desk, spread the letters before them and began to read."

A New Lease of Death (1967; republished as *Sins of the Fathers*, 1970), like *From Doon with Death*, explores the ways in which individual lives are influenced by childhood events, the power of passion within relationships, and Wexford and Burden's developing relationship. To this mix Rendell also introduces the question of whether people are shaped more by their heredity or their environment. The novel centers around the growth of Rev. Henry Archery. Early in the novel Archery has dedicated himself to disproving that his son's fiancée's (supposed) father, Harry Painter, was a murderer. Content in his own marriage and believing that respectability and genetic purity are more important than love, Archery had initially opposed the engagement. But through his growing awareness of his own weaknesses and his deepening regard for his prospective daughter-in-law, Tess, Archery comes to favor the marriage, regardless of Tess's parentage. His softening in great part stems from his attraction to Imogene Ide, the granddaughter-in-law of the murder victim, a former model who was once "the most photographed face in Britain." Indeed, in a moment in which Archery nearly succumbs to his desire, he thinks, "he must be going mad, for he could not understand

that twenty years of discipline could fall away like a lesson imparted to a bored child."

Tess's parentage is only one strand in a weaving of parental relationships that form the texture of the novel. For example, Tess's childhood friend Elizabeth Crilling was endowed at birth with all the advantages that a middle-class childhood provided. Yet, because Elizabeth had found the body of the person Tess's father is accused of killing and, even more importantly, because her mother had refused to allow her to discuss her feelings about what she had seen, the girl's childhood was dismal. She failed as a student, was unable to hold a good job, became a drug addict, killed someone while driving drunk, and eventually murdered her own mother in a moment linked to her recurring flashbacks to the original murder scene in which she was threatened by the murderer. Tess's childhood should have been just as psychologically damaging to her. Her natural father was a poet who died after Tess had been conceived but before he and her mother were married. Her mother's first husband, whom Tess has believed to be her father, was the murderer whose conviction had stood in the way of Archery's approval of his son's marriage. Tess's salvation has come by way of her mother's second husband, a man of cheerful spirit who had the "rare quality" of being "interested in all things." Thus, despite the complexities of her heritage and her upbringing, Tess has become a productive, intelligent, graceful, and generous adult.

Rendell does not resolve the nurture versus nature question, attributing Tess's loveliness both to the environment her stepfather provided her and the genes she inherited from her natural father. Even so, she suggests that communication is more important than either one's genetic makeup or one's environment. For example, had Tess's mother been able to transcend her need for respectability, she would have told the girl that she was a love child. And had she done so, Tess would have grown up without the trauma of believing her father to be a murderer. Or, had Tess's stepfather been able to draw his wife out about her past, Tess would have been spared the anguish over whether she was fit to marry. Similarly, had Elizabeth's mother listened to her daughter, Elizabeth might well have come to terms with the terrible moment of discovering a murder and then being threatened by the murderer.

A New Lease of Death presents both Wexford and Burden more fully. Wexford is now described as "a big man with big features and a big intimidating voice" whose gray suit was "shabby and wrinkled," which suited him because it was "not unlike an extension of his furrowed pachydermatous skin"; while Burden is seen as "lean as a greyhound, his face thin and acute," characteristics which match his "hound's instinct for scenting the unusual coupled with a man's eager imagination." Wexford has softened in this novel, and Burden has come to accept his superior's foibles: "In his five years as Wexford's right hand man, Burden had grown immune to his teasing. He knew he was a kind of safety valve, the stooge perhaps on whom Wexford could vent his violent and sometimes shocking sense of humor." Burden even understands that Wexford's vulgarisms are meant to horrify him. At the same time, Wexford is more fully identified with "The law incarnate," as a man totally incorruptible who radiates strength, while Burden, despite his uxoriousness, his "stolid stick-in-the-mud nature and a certain primness of outlook," learns that he (like Archery) can be tempted if only momentarily by physical desire. Attracted to Elizabeth Crilling, he is aware that: "For a split second he felt what his rather prudish nature told him was vile, then that nature, his duty and a swift suspicion took over."

Wolf to the Slaughter (1967) has an especially complicated plot, one of Rendell's hallmarks. Although Wexford and Burden know that someone has been murdered, it is only in the final pages of the novel that they learn that the man they had assumed to be the murderer is the victim while the person they had thought to be the victim has simply been away on holiday. The novel focuses mainly on distorted love relationships between men and women. The apparent murderer is a sadist whose passion is aroused only after he has drawn blood from his lovers' necks with a knife and who is compelling enough to young women that they will engage in such games with him. His obsession is matched by that of Drayton, an ambitious young police officer who falls in love with Linda, the daughter of a pornography-peddling shopkeeper. Drayton's obsessions are initially more socially acceptable, leading him to "carry out all Wexford's instructions meticulously, absorbing the Chief Inspector's homilies, lectures, digressions and pleasantries with courteously inclined head," to model himself on Wexford so that he reads only works on psychology and forensic medicine and an occasional novel "but nothing lighter than Mann or Durrell," and

to want to "marry the right wife, someone like Mrs. Wexford, good-looking, quiet and gracious." However, Drayton's passion for Linda leads him to betray his profession. Knowing that "His ambitions had no place in them for such a girl . . . " and that "Not even a single rung of his ladder could be spared to bear her weight," he gives in to his desires only to learn that Linda–who ironically turns out to have committed the murder, albeit in self-defense–has never cared for him and was only using him.

Burden and Wexford become more likable in *Wolf to the Slaughter*. Initially Burden is described as a man who "had no temptations, few dreams," and who has a contempt for modern paintings he does not understand. Wexford even chides his partner, "You remind me of that remark of Goering's. . . . Whenever I hear the word culture I reach for my gun." But as the novel progresses, Burden gains some of Wexford's compassion for people who give way to temptation or who are dreamers. For example, even as he is pleased to be thought as tough as Wexford and even as he knows he does not understand the love affair between a petty thief and a woman who rents her home out to illicit lovers, Burden chooses to behave with kindness toward them. He also earns Wexford's admiration when he chooses to learn something about modern art. As Wexford puts it, "Instead of reaching for his gun, Burden had evidently reached for a reference work." Wexford sheds some of his earlier harshness. For instance, when Burden offers the rather pious maxim "a man who'll commit [adultery] once will commit it again," Wexford responds with a smile and a rather gentle "Thus speaks the stern moralist . . . I don't know that I'd go along with that." And although Wexford himself knows he has been deceived and disappointed by Drayton, he is gentle toward him as well; aware that "he had forgotten what it was like to be in love," Wexford nevertheless feels tender toward the young man. In fact, as he accepts Drayton's resignation he thinks, "He had no son, but from time to time it is given to every man to be another's father."

Wolf to the Slaughter marks a distinctive movement by Rendell to a more subtle use of literary allusion. While *From Doon with Death* relies on epigraphs mainly drawn from nineteenth-century British and American poetry and each chapter of *A New Lease of Death* points to a verse from *The Book of Common Prayer*, this novel incorporates unacknowledged literary allusions as part of the reg-

Set 67 lines 11/6 a 13/6 Pilgrim
22 em
plus set 2 folios 22 and 23
mark off all lines

18pt ital

2 line drop

When Quentin Nightingale left home for London each

morning his wife was always still asleep . His housekeeper

served him with breakfast , opened the front door for him

and handed him his hat and his umbrella , while the <u>au pair</u>

girl fetched his newspaper . Next to speed him on his way

were the two gardeners , saluting him with a respectful

' Good morning , sir ' then perhaps his brother-in-law ,

hurrying to the sequestered peace of his writer's haven

in the Old House . Only Elizabeth was missing , but if

Quentin minded he never showed it . He walked briskly and

confidently towards his car like a happy man .

On this particular morning in early September everything

was just as usual except that Quentin didn't need his

umbrella . The gardens of Myfleet Manor lay half-veiled

by a golden mist which promised a beautiful day . Quentin

came down the stone steps from the front door and paused

Page 1, 'A Guilty Thing Surprised'
Ruth Rendell

Page from the typescript for A Guilty Thing Surprised *(courtesy of the author)*

ular text. For instance, in the early pages of the novel Burden offers an unknowing nod to T. S. Eliot's opening lines in *The Waste Land* when he thinks, "Unlike his superior, Chief Inspector Wexford, he was not given to quotation but he would have agreed on this bitter Thursday morning, that April is the cruelest month, breeding, if not lilacs, grape hyacinths out of the dead land."

In *The Best Man to Die* (1969) two of the main characters, the murdered Charlie Hutton and his friend Jack Pertwee, are likened from the opening pages to the biblical Jonathan and David. The reference is an ironic one, for although Jack echoes David's grief in 2 Samuel for his lost comrade, neither Jack nor Charlie achieve any of the stature of his biblical counterpart. Although in this novel Rendell again explores the hidden motives that characterize relationships between men and women, it is the friendship between Jack and Charlie that opens the novel and ends it; Rendell is explicit that societal constraints prevented the two men from articulating and perhaps even acknowledging what their friendship meant to them. As she puts it, "If Charlie had been a different man, a cultivated man or effeminate or living in a bygone age when tongues were more freely unloosed, he might now have embraced Jack and told him from a full heart how he entered wholly into his joy and would die for his happiness." But because these circumstances do not pertain, both men accept the convention that "love was between a man and a woman, love was for marriage, and each would have died before admitting to anything more than that they 'got on well' together."

As with the other novels in the Wexford series, *The Best Man to Die* revolves around Wexford and Burden's search for a murderer and, at least initially, for the identity of the victim. In the process they come face to face with a series of unhappy relationships: the Fanshaw marriage, in which the now-deceased Jerome Fanshaw had bribed his wife with money and material goods to tolerate his love affairs; his daughter Nora's engagement to a handsome man whose attention she is buying with the money she has inherited from her father; and Charlie's marriage which was based on his ability through blackmail to provide his wife and friends with possessions far beyond their means.

These relationships are set in sharp counterpoint to Wexford's family life, for his relationship to both his wife and his daughter Sheila are

based on love and candor. In fact, when Fanshaw's daughter tells Wexford about her father, Rendell writes, "In [a] flash of unusual sentimentality, Wexford thought he would rather be dead than be the man about whom a daughter could say such things." Wexford and Burden also come to acknowledge what their friendship means to one another. For example, Wexford recognizes that despite his impatience with Mike from time to time, he "had amiable, sometimes distinctly fond feelings" for him. Sheila Wexford rhetorically asks Burden, "You really care about poor old Pop, don't you."

In *A Guilty Thing Surprised* (1970) Rendell turns to incest between a brother and sister orphaned and separated in their teens and reunited as lovers in their early twenties. Determined to keep their relationship secret, the beautiful and wealthy Elizabeth Nightingale and her brother, schoolteacher and author Denys Villiers, present to the public a face of mutual hatred. However, because Denys has cultivated a relationship with Elizabeth's husband, the brother and sister meet easily and regularly. Eventually, their relationship is destructive to them and their spouses. Elizabeth's indifference to her husband leads him to an affair with their au pair while Denys's second wife, on observing the brother and sister in an embrace, becomes so jealous that she murders Elizabeth.

The novel makes an especially sophisticated use of subplots. Burden's teenage children, John and Pat, are locked in an intense sibling rivalry which provides an ironic counterpoint to Elizabeth and Denys's love affair. Elizabeth's fear of growing old and losing her beauty is matched by Wexford's own anger at aging. For example, desirous of being thought twenty rather than forty, Elizabeth spends hours every day "conserving her beauty," while Wexford, faced with his attraction to the au pair, is also enraged that he is no longer young:

> A passionate longing, bitter and savage, to recapture for one hour the youth he had lost engulfed Wexford. And suddenly growing old seemed the only tragedy of life, the pain beside which every other pain dwindled into insignificance. Mature, wise, usually philosophical, he wanted to cry aloud, "It isn't fair!"

In counterpoint to Denys's wife, Wexford begins to understand jealousy. Despite his growing closeness to Burden, he is uneasy that Burden is the one who seems to be doing most of the effective work on the case. Thinking that he, like T. S. Eliot's Gerontion, is "An old man in a dry month," Wexford returns to his office to discover Burden sitting casually in his superior's chair eating his lunch. For the unhappy Wexford, Burden's innocent act seems one of usurpation.

The parallels in the two plots of *A Guilty Thing Surprised* are limited, for, as Wexford understands, the difference between the sane and the insane mind is that "between fantasy and reality a great gulf is fixed." Or to put it another way, he recognizes that the sane mind is able to choose deliberately not to act on impulse, whether the impulse is to passion or to violence, while the insane mind will act. And so, even though Wexford longs for the "rejuvenation" that an affair with the au pair might bring him, he decides, "And that which seems possible, reasonable, felicitous, when conjured in the mind, dissolves like smoke in a fresh wind when its object is present in words and solid flesh."

Literary allusion plays a particularly important role in this novel, for it is Wordsworth's relationship with his sister that has led Denys Villiers to devote his life to a study of the poet. Villiers's study in turn provides Wexford with the clue to the cause of Elizabeth's death. Wexford is also explicit in this novel about his love of literature and learning, thinking, "he needed instruction and knowledge because the purpose of education is to turn the soul's eyes toward the light."

Rendell's next Wexford novel, *No More Dying Then* (1971), is focused on Michael Burden. Widowed within the year by the unexpected death of his beloved Jean, Burden is beside himself with grief and sexual longing. He has moved from gentleness to nastiness and from familial devotion to avoiding his children and his sister-in-law housekeeper. In this state of mind he is vulnerable to Gemma Lawrence, the mother of a missing child. Her unconventional nature makes her the antithesis of Jean and all that Burden values in women. Although eventually Gemma ends the relationship by telling him, "I'm not conventional enough for you, not respectable, not good enough if you like," she has "given him his sentimental education" and in the process has softened him and taught him a new compassion. He will, for example, no longer equate a woman's housekeeping abilities with her ability to be a loving mother. He will no longer judge women so readily by their dress and their sexuality or expect that women will spoil him by "serving him food on dainty china from trays covered with lace cloths."

Burden's obsession with Gemma has its negative mirror image in the relationship of mother and stepfather of another missing child, Stella Rivers. Whereas Gemma places her child before her lover, Wexford believes that Stella's mother "would have sacrificed a dozen children to keep" her second husband. Here too, however, Burden learns new understanding, for there are moments when his own "powerful black jealousy" of Gemma's missing child nearly overwhelms him. Because Burden is sane and ultimately in control, he does not give way to those feelings. He also has learned how much he values his own children, that he can finally live with grief and loss, and that a woman like Grace, his sister-in-law, can be his friend.

Burden's loss of Jean, his affair with Gemma, and his struggles with his sense of the world first put him at odds with Wexford, who both worries about and is impatient with his younger colleague. The two men come to a new closeness, however, in a touching scene in which Wexford confronts Burden with his anger: "Mike, I have to say this. It's time I said it. I'm tired. I'm trying to solve this case all on my own because I can't count on you any more. I can't talk to you. We used to thrash things out together, sift the muck, if you like. Talking to you now— well, it's like trying to have a rational conversation with a monkey." Wexford's words lead Burden to break down and confide his grief and fears to Wexford. In tears and fearful of his supervisor's derision, Burden experiences the compassion Wexford had advocated earlier as Wexford puts his "heavy hand on his shoulder" and says, "Mike, my dear old friend. . . ." It is a moving scene that marks personal growth for both.

Murder Being Once Done (1972) focuses on Wexford's new sense of vulnerability. Victim of a mild thrombosis, he accepts his doctor's orders, goes on a strict diet, gives up all alcohol, and takes a forced holiday in London. He also gives himself over to self-pity. For example, he believes himself useless to his nephew Howard Fortune, a detective superintendent in the London police force. His wife and Howard's wife both treat him as an invalid and prepare for him only non-fattening foods which he hates. Eventually, however, Wexford declares his independence and involves himself in the mystery surrounding the murder of an unidentified young woman. After an embarrassing false start, Wexford discovers

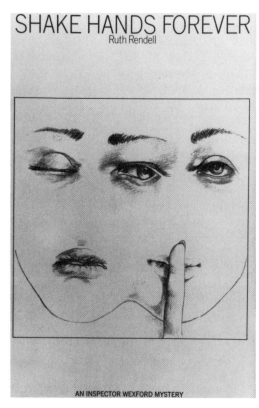

Dust jackets for the first American editions of three of Rendell's Inspector Wexford novels

both the identity of the girl and of her murderer. But the novel's real life comes from its examination of Wexford's struggle with his mortality. At first he enters into an unseemly competition with his nephew's embittered assistant, Michael Baker. He is also condescending to his wife and niece. For example, Rendell notes his dismissiveness toward Dora in a moment of unhappiness by writing, "Dora's manner . . . was injured and distrait, but the Chief-Inspector had been married for thirty years and had seldom permitted petticoat government." Later he even lies to Dora about his activities so that she will not worry about him. He also finds himself committing "the very sin he had laid at Baker's door, that of formulating a theory and forcing the facts to fit it. Fame had been more important to him than truth."

Eventually, after excursions into the world of a religious sect, Children of Revelations, Wexford sorts out the unhappy circumstance of the murder, but his pleasure at doing so is distasteful to both Wexford and the reader. Nevertheless, his success also leads him to throw off the constraints imposed by his doctor and his wife. He decides to embrace a life with some pleasures in it rather than a death-in-life of total denial. As he puts it, "No one but a fool follows a regimen that debilitates him while moderate indulgence makes him feel good." In fact, he recognizes that staying up all night in the service of solving a crime, having a double scotch on occasion, and walking miles in the rain all reinvigorate him. He also makes amends with Baker. His revelation in this regard is also in sharp contrast to the life-denying, rigid qualities of the Children of Revelations.

In *Some Lie and Some Die* (1973) Wexford and Burden's role is to solve the mystery rather than to be actors within it, or, as Wexford asserts facetiously, to "ask, deduce, to conclude and to catch." It is nevertheless worth noting that Burden has moved from his earlier, if temporary, indifference to his children to an overprotective and indulgent posture. The person Wexford and Burden hope to catch is the murderer of Dawn Stonor, a London waitress who had delusions of grandeur. Their investigation leads them into the world of a rock star, Zeno Vedast (born Harold Goodbody), who was a childhood friend of Dawn's. Vedast has in the years since he knew Dawn become rich, famous, jaded, and exploitative. The most public manifestation of his amorality is his menage à trois with Nell and Godfrey

Tate, a couple whom he has psychologically enslaved. It is out of this same mentality that he decides to play a practical joke on Nell's first husband and Dawn Stonor, a joke that leads the husband to a moment of temporary insanity in which he murders Dawn.

In contrast to Vedast's self-concerns, African student Louis Mbowele intends to become the leader of his country, for he is dedicated to giving his people a better life. Mbowele's conversations with Wexford deal with the question of control and even enslavement on another level, however, for Louis believes that his country would benefit from a benevolent totalitarian rule, for a time at least. Wexford, aware of the dangers inherent when individuals give up their freedom to others, whether in a personal or a political setting, tells him, "Oh, Louis . . . that's what they all say."

In *Shake Hands Forever* (1975) the focus is again on Wexford, whose obsession with proving that Robert Hathall has had a part in murdering his wife runs parallel to his infatuation with Hathall's neighbor, Nancy Lake. For Wexford devotees, the detective's struggle with his attraction to Lake will hold more interest than his struggle to put to rest his belief in Hathall's guilt. The novel begins with Hathall's mother finding the body of a young woman she believes to be her estranged daughter-in-law, Angela. Although Wexford's "feelings" tell him from the beginning that Hathall is guilty, his superior takes him off the case because he does not wish to create negative publicity for his department. For the next year the outraged Wexford continues his investigation privately, spending both his vacation time and his money on the case. Wexford's wife, Burden, and the man Wexford hires to follow Hathall all warn him that his obsession is putting him off balance, something he too recognizes. Eventually, his intuition that Hathall is the murderer proves valid. What Wexford does not know, until the very end of the novel, is that the victim was not Angela Hathall. Rather, Angela and her husband together conspired to murder a woman who apparently had learned that they were defrauding Hathall's company. They also had deliberately created the perception that Angela had been the victim.

Wexford is more successful at keeping in perspective his strong attraction to Lake, a beautiful and warm woman who tries to seduce him. His diet in *Murder Being Once Done* was successful, and he is proud of his new physique. Neverthe-

Rendell, 1989

less, he still feels keenly that he is growing old. Lake, on the other hand, seems to him like Cleopatra, "one of those rare creatures whom time cannot wither or stale or devitalize." During their initial meetings, Wexford is able to resist the temptation that Lake offers. When a vision of Lake "threatened to develop into a fantasy," he "shook it off." Recognizing that he would like to make love to her, he resists, thinking that it was a shame that "work and convention and prudence" prevented him from doing so. And when Lake pursues him to a restaurant after he had turned down her invitation for lunch, Wexford's guilt at how pleasant the encounter was leads him to decide that "he would see her no more. If necessary, he would eat his lunch in the police canteen, he would avoid her, he would never again be alone with her, even in a restaurant." Wexford keeps all aspects of that vow for a year and then, engaged still in the Hathall investigation, goes to Lake's home for tea. After hours of conversation, she offers herself to him. Although the text at first glance seems ambiguous about whether Wexford this time gives in to his passion, it ultimately suggests that he behaved as a "man of sense," acting "according to his own standards and what was right for him." Although he knows that another man might have justified an affair by invok-

ing "what was right for him," Wexford recognizes that he has throughout his life made choices that serve an ethical standard. He puts it this way: "So he had to decide what he should do, whether to go or stay. Gather ye rosebuds, while ye may? Or be an old man, dreaming dreams and being mindful of one's marriage vows? The whole of his recent life seemed to him a long series of failures, of cowardice and caution. And yet the whole of his recent life had also been bent towards doing what he believed to be right and just. Perhaps, in the end, it came to the same thing."

The final scene of the novel seems to reaffirm Wexford's choice of family. At home with his beloved daughters, his grandchildren, his wife, his nephew with whom he has grown even closer through the Hathall case, his nephew's wife, and Burden and his children, Wexford is again content, freed of all his obsessions and temptations. He has also again affirmed what he has believed all along, that the difference between the sane and the insane person is not desire but action.

A Sleeping Life (1978) marks Rendell's growing attentiveness to feminism. In this novel Wexford begins to confront the ways in which societal changes affect not only the women he investigates but the women in his own family. His oldest daughter, Sylvia, provides the subplot of the novel. Married at a young age and the mother of two children, Sylvia decides that her role as wife and mother offers her little more than dependence. Although both her parents love her, neither is sympathetic to her concerns. In fact, in a moment bound to distress Wexford's feminist admirers (and one which validates Barnard's criticism that Rendell's "level of [feminist] comment is quite superficial, embarrassingly so"), the chief inspector asks his daughter "if she didn't think that to be a woman had certain advantages"; the advantage he cites is the likelihood that if she has a flat tire, a man will almost certainly stop to help her.

Wexford's relationship to his oldest daughter Sylvia may prove disconcerting to his readers on another count: it demonstrates his unabashed favoritism toward Sheila, his other daughter. Indeed, early in the novel he admits to himself that he "loved both his daughters dearly, but Sheila, the younger, was his favourite." Even so, during the course of the novel he comes to a new understanding of Sylvia's needs, and it is that new understanding which leads him to solve the murder he is currently investigating. Specifically, in another example of Rendell's intricate plots, the murder victim, Rhoda Comfrey, also turns out to be Wexford's major suspect, the writer Grenville West. It is Wexford's new sympathy to the difficulties facing women who wish independence and productivity in British society that leads him to understand why Comfrey assumes the identity of a man.

A Sleeping Life also explores the psychology of some of the major characters: the dependent young woman Pauline (or Polly) Flinders; the newly self-confident Dora Wexford; and Wexford himself, whose tendency to become obsessive about cases leads him to make serious errors of judgment. Ultimately Wexford is successful on all counts: he appeases an unhappy superior, helps Sylvia restore her marriage, threatened by her new feminism, and—despite his ability to break some of the rules—he sees that justice is accomplished even though in this case he feels (perhaps for the first time) great sympathy for the murderer.

In *Put On by Cunning* (1981; published in the United States as *Death Notes*) Wexford again becomes obsessed with a case but in a much milder way than in *Shake Hands Forever*. Mindful of Wexford's tendencies in this way, Burden warns

him early in the case, "I don't want to speak out of turn and no offence meant . . . but this could be the kind of thing you get–well, you get obsessional about." This time Wexford's intuition is wrong, for he has believed that the woman posing as the daughter of the famed flutist Manuel Carmargue is an imposter who arranged for Carmargue's murder. By the end of the novel Wexford learns that the woman is Natalie Carmargue after all and that, while she profited from her father's murder, she did not arrange it.

Wexford's relationships with his wife and his daughter Sheila serve as foils for the relationships of those he is investigating. His momentary jealousy of his wife's childhood sweetheart mirrors the jealousy of those he is investigating. In time, however, Wexford comes to terms with his jealousy and through the process gains a renewed appreciation for his wife: "Wexford marvelled at his wife. . . . Instead of allowing herself to be a passive encumbrance, she had made him absurdly jealous and had hoodwinked him properly. . . . And like Trollope's Archdeacon of his wife, he wondered at and admired the greatness of that lady's mind."

Wexford also gains new respect for Burden, who is now happily married to his second wife, Jenny, a history teacher who has interested him in literature, art, and music: "Admiration was not something Wexford had often felt for the inspector in the past. Sympathy, yes, affection and a definite need, for Burden had most encouragingly fulfilled the function of an Achates or a Boswell, if not quite, a Watson. But admiration? Burden was showing unexpected powers that were highly gratifying to witness, and Wexford wondered if they were the fruit of happiness or of reading aloud from great literature in the evenings."

For the first time in the series, Wexford's investigations take him out of England, first to California (a trip he pays for himself since the case had stalled in England) and then to the south of France. Although the change in setting really does little to forward the plot, it anticipates Rendell's interest in her next Wexford novel, *The Speaker of Mandarin* (1983), in exploring cultural differences.

The opening part of *The Speaker of Mandarin* is set in China, where Wexford finds himself victim of his own hallucinations. Although he later comes to understand that his reliance on green Chinese tea had triggered his visions of a small Chinese woman with bound feet, during the experience itself he begins to question his own sanity. For example, after one hallucination he wonders, "Perhaps he was going mad. Presumably if you developed schizophrenia–which was quite possible, there was such a thing as spontaneous schizophrenia coming on in middle age– presumably then you had hallucinations and didn't know they were hallucinations and behaved, in short, just as he had." Ultimately, the China trip is merely a prelude for the events of the novel, which concern Wexford's quest to discover the murderer of one of the other British travelers on his China tour, Adella Knighton. Wexford had not known the victim well but was aware of her own indifference during the trip to the death by drowning of a young Chinese. Specifically, when Wexford had asked her who had gone overboard, Mrs. Knighton had replied "with indifference, 'Not one of us. A Chinese.' " The China experience also provides the substance of one of the novel's subplots, the relationship between an antique dealer, his new wife, and their Chinese neighbor.

The novel has a convoluted plot that is characteristic of Rendell. Adam Knighton, a successful lawyer who desires to marry another woman (the mother-in-law of the antique dealer), believes he has initiated his wife's murder and so commits suicide. The pathological Silver Perry, determined to repay a twenty-year-old debt to Knighton, intended to accomplish what he thought was Knighton's bidding to kill his (Knighton's) wife but was beaten to the murder by another member of the Knighton family, who is driven solely by greed. But as much as the novel teases the reader with questions about what happened, it also explores the psychology of some of the key characters, particularly Knighton in his guilt, Perry in his belief that his gratitude to Knighton justifies murder, and the antique dealer in his fear that his fraudulent action in taking precious items out of China will be discovered.

For Rendell readers who have become attached to Mike Burden's new sensibilities, *The Speaker of Mandarin* is a disappointment, for Burden here seems to have lost much of the tolerance and compassion he had gained in *No More Dying Then*. He now is presented as "a conventional conservative man who believed passionately in law and order. The slightest offence against those principles irked him and he loathed crime." In fact, "he was insensitive and he lacked sympathy." Margaret Cannon (*Maclean's*, 20 June 1983) faulted the novel, saying, "this coincidental

and boring tale is unworthy of Rendell. . . . The best thing to be said about *Mandarin* is that Rendell must have wanted to write a travelogue."

An Unkindness of Ravens (1985) restores to Burden his more attractive qualities as he and his new wife, Jenny, assume prominent roles. Jenny's much-desired pregnancy becomes a crisis for her when she believes that the child she is carrying is a girl. Her growing belief that she does not wish to have a daughter runs counter to her earlier feminism. It also throws Jenny into an uncharacteristic depression and strains the marriage seriously. "In vain [Burden] had asked her why this prejudice against girls, she who was a feminist, a supporter of the women's movement, who expressed a preference for her friends' small girls over their small sons, who got on better with her stepdaughter than her stepson, who professed to prefer teaching girls to boys." Burden even comes to believe that the pregnancy "had driven her mad" and horribly was bringing him "to hate the unborn child himself and to wish it had never been conceived."

The Burdens' story serves as a subplot to the main narrative, the story of Rodney Williams's bigamous double life, the relationship between the daughters and eventually the wives of his two marriages, and the radical feminist group Arria. Once again, Rendell begins to explore the psychology of her main characters, particularly the factors that led the two daughters to "*folie à deux*, a kind of madness that overtakes two people only when they are together and through the influence of each on the other."

In the end Rendell resolves the Burden plot too facilely. Jenny's amniocentesis had been wrong: the baby turns out to be a boy, and Jenny's distress subsides. Burden even goes so far as to rationalize Jenny's original feelings and her recovery: "Jenny says it taught her a lot about herself. It's taught her she's not what you might call a natural feminist and now she has to approach feminism not from an emotional standpoint but from what is–well, right and just."

Rendell's Wexford novel *The Veiled One* (1988) has many of the characteristics of her psychological novels, focusing as it does on the effects of obsessiveness on seemingly ordinary people. What makes the novel unique, however, is that the character obsessed to the point of destructiveness is Michael Burden. Mistakenly believing that Clifford Sanders, an unhappy young man who lives at home with his mother, is the murderer of a woman whose body has been found in

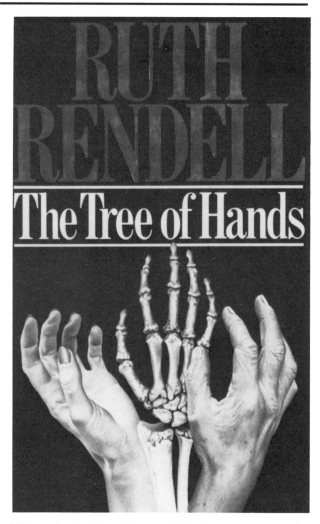

Dust jackets for the first editions of two of Rendell's novels which do not feature Wexford

a shopping center parking lot, Burden sets up interview after interview with the suspect. These interviews drive Sanders first to a psychological transference in which he becomes dependent on Burden (whom he calls and visits despite Burden's rejection of him) and then to murder his own mother.

The subplot of the novel focuses on Wexford's favorite daughter, Sheila, who, Burden and Wexford believe, is the victim of murder attempts because of her public stand against nuclear weapons. In fact, at one point Sheila's car is bombed, injuring not Sheila but her father, who is driving it. This episode leads Wexford to recognize his self-protective tendencies, that "what he would have liked was to shut her up somewhere for ever and stand guard over the door." On edge, he also has a serious quarrel with Burden over his obsession with Sanders, recognizes how "wrong" it is of him to love one of his children

more than the other, and sympathizes with a Holocaust survivor who tells him, "Everything in the garden is *not* lovely. There is a snake in the bush and worms under the stones and half the plants are poisonous."

In the end, Sheila turns out to be able to be both true to her beliefs and safe from terrorism. Burden and Wexford are reconciled although Burden needs Wexford's help in coming to terms with his behavior toward Sanders. The novel ends on an optimistic note as Wexford realizes that his house, destroyed in the car bombing, is now–as is his life–in the process of being rebuilt.

The Rendell novels which do not focus on Wexford evidence the same qualities of intricate plotting, attention to the psychology of the characters, and exploration of relationships of husband and wife, brother and sister, parent and child, and friends. The first of these, *To Fear a Painted Devil* (1965), focuses on a group of unhappy people living in an upper-middle-class development in London, but particularly on the beautiful but unfaithful Tamsin Selby, her handsome and unfaithful husband Patrick, their lovers Oliver Gage and his overbearing wife Nancy, Freda Carnaby and her insecure twin brother, Edward, and the writer manqué Crispin Marvel. With few exceptions all these characters are motivated by selfishness or greed. The only genuinely attractive characters in the novel are the physician Max Greenleaf and his wife Bernice. Their valuing of themselves and their children and their awareness as Jews of the genuine atrocities of the Holocaust set them apart from the pettiness and self-serving nature of the rest of the community. Indeed, in many ways Greenleaf fulfills a Wexford-like role, for it is he who attends to Patrick Selby the night before he dies, who later recognizes that Selby had been murdered, and who eventually discovers the identity of the murderer.

In her next two novels that do not feature Wexford, *Vanity Dies Hard* (1966; published in the United States as *In Sickness and in Health*) and *The Secret House of Death* (1968), Rendell focuses on the psychology of female protagonists who find themselves in relationships with men whom they believe they love but of whom they become fearful. Both women, although initially trapped by their growing emotional dependence on these relationships, come to new knowledge of the men they love as well as new self-knowledge, and it is this new knowledge that allows them to regain their independence and mental health. Alice Whittaker Fielding in *Vanity Dies Hard* is obsessed with finding her friend Nesta, who has suddenly disappeared. Although she is happy in her new marriage to Andrew, a handsome man nine years her junior, Alice convinces herself that Nesta had been poisoned and that whoever murdered Nesta may now be poisoning her. Her suspicions turn finally on Andrew and then on Harry, her physician and longtime friend. Although Alice learns that she has not been very perceptive about either Nesta or herself (for example, she did not know that because of an illness Nesta had false lashes and a false hairpiece nor did she know about Nesta's promiscuity) and although all those around Alice warn her that she is becoming somewhat mentally unstable, she persists in believing her own version of the world. But at the moment when Alice is sure first that her husband and then that Harry are trying to murder her, Rendell resorts to a deus ex machina: Nesta returns alive, well, and engaged to a man with a

Jaguar. As importantly, Alice learns that her own hysteria had been brought on by a pregnancy she longed for but had thought impossible. Andrew for his part turns out to be a genuinely loving husband. In short, Rendell offers not a sinister mystery but a somewhat implausible romance after all.

The Secret House of Death, on the other hand, offers no such benign solutions. Susan Townsend, abandoned by her husband for another woman, is struggling to stabilize her life and that of her six-year-old child. For that reason, she resists being drawn into the neighborhood gossip about the rumored love affair between her immediate neighbor Louise North and a central-heating salesman, Bernard Heller. She also rejects Louise's overtures of friendship. However, when she finds the two of them dead on Louise's bed, she is drawn into a relationship with Louise's apparently distraught husband Bob North. The twist in the plot is that the presumed lovers–Louise North and Bernard Heller–turn out to be "two mild and gentle people" murdered by their mates. They were not lovers, as the neighborhood and papers initially believe, or victims of a murder-suicide pact. Even more than the details of the murder, it is Susan's growing relationship with Bob North that is at the heart of the novel. Although Susan recognizes Bob North's potential for violence almost immediately and although she knows he is unstable, she allows herself to be drawn to him out of her own loneliness and her awareness of his need. She does not, however, ever lose sight of herself and soon recognizes that all they have in common is Louise and Bernard's deaths. Rendell ends this novel, as well, as though it were a romance. David, a young set designer and acquaintance of Bernard Heller, becomes obsessed with the case and–through his own investigation–discovers the evidence which points to the murder conspiracy.

Like many of Rendell's other novels, *The Secret House of Death* offers a series of minor characters who are even more memorable than the protagonists: for example, Susan's first husband, Julian, a newspaper columnist who is not on "nodding terms" but "sneering terms" with others; Julian's second wife, Elizabeth, who shares her husband's passion for food; Susan's cleaning woman, Mrs. Dring, who is critical of everyone but her husband, of whom she insists, "There's nothing that man doesn't know"; and Bernard Heller's twin brother, the ponderous Carl.

Front cover from 18 May 1985 issue of Bookseller

One Across, Two Down (1971) focuses on Stanley Manning, a man who fails at everything but making and solving crossword puzzles. At odds with his mother-in-law Maud and contemptuous of his hardworking and long-suffering wife Vera, Stanley finally causes the deaths of both Maud and her closest friend, Ethel. Counting on Vera's inheritance from Maud, he becomes a partner with a disreputable antique dealer who begins to pressure him for promised money. As Stanley's worries about money grow, so do his obsessions with puzzles and an eye twitch that at times spreads to his entire body. Indeed, his obsession with crossword puzzles is so extravagant that, in time, for Stanley "words were the meaning of existence, the panacea for all agony." Although much of the novel's effectiveness stems from the effectiveness of Stanley's crossword clues, in the end his actions become more powerful than words. In this novel, like those preceding it, Rendell offers a romantic relationship as the means to happiness for her victims. Here, it is Vera's renewed relationship with James, the man her mother had hoped she would marry, that of-

fers her a future. Also in the spirit of a romance, the novel's subplot has happy rather than sinister consequences. Specifically, Vera learns that her father and Ethel, unbeknownst to her mother, had been lovers and that Ethel had given birth to a child. This news, rather than being a source of torment, brings to Vera a new set of nurturing familial relationships.

The Face of Trespass (1974) presents a more sinister and tormenting world. Gray Lanceton, whose only successful novel "was obviously autobiographical, about a sort of hippie Oedipus," comes to terms with his mother's marriage to the French writer Honoré but learns that the woman he loves, Drusilla Janus, is aptly named. Although she presents a loving face to Gray, the duplicitous Drusilla is in fact using him because she wants him to murder her affluent husband. When Gray ends the relationship rather than accede to Drusilla's wishes, he comes close to suffering a breakdown. He is unable to write, sees almost no one, and refuses to answer his phone. The novel ends with a series of typical Rendellian twists. The death of Gray's mother leads him to understand that love between a man and a woman can exist and be enduring. Fortified with this new knowledge, he believes Drusilla when she tells him that she has abandoned her scheme to murder her husband and that she will come and live with him. But once again Drusilla is presenting a false face; she murders her husband and sets up Gray so that the police assume he is the murderer. It is only through a series of fortuitous coincidences that Gray is freed from prison and vindicated.

A Demon in My View (1976), too, is located in a sinister world. Arthur Johnson, twenty-year resident of a boardinghouse in London, keeps in check his murderous tendencies by periodic assaults on a female dummy he keeps hidden in the basement. His controlled life changes when an alter ego, Anthony Johnson, moves into the same house in order, ironically, to complete his doctoral thesis on "Some Aspects of the Psychopathic Personality." Although Anthony has a relationship with a married woman, he shares some of Arthur's anger toward women. For example, provoked by one of the other boarders, he is aware of "a surge of angry misogyny" and contemplates striking or at least pushing her. In addition, when Anthony comes across Arthur's dummy, "he wanted to knock it down and leave it to lie on the sooty floor, but he restrained himself and turned quickly away." It is such restraint, of course, that distinguishes the sane from the insane in Rendell's world. Arthur, unable to control his emotions, turns to human victims when his surrogate victim, the dummy, is destroyed. Ultimately, Anthony is reconciled with his girlfriend, who leaves her husband, himself a psychopathic personality. Her decision drives her husband to violence, and he becomes an unwitting and ironic instrument of justice. Believing Arthur to be Anthony, the distraught husband murders the wrong man, who, of course, himself is a dangerous murderer.

In Rendell's *A Judgement in Stone* (1977) illiteracy is the driving force behind murder. In fact, the opening line of the novel makes the point: "Eunice Parchman killed the Coverdale family because she could not read or write." Rendell carries the motif another step, for had the Coverdale family not been so literate and cultured themselves, their housekeeper might not have been driven to the extreme of murdering them. Eunice Parchman has become like a stone because of her illiteracy. As Rendell puts it, "Illiteracy had dried up her sympathy and atrophied

her imagination. That, along with what psychologists call *affect*, the ability to care about the feelings of others, had no place in her make-up." In an effort to hide her inability to read, she has totally suppressed all human emotions and is unconnected to those around her until she enters into a folie à deux with the religious fanatic Joan Smith. Even after the two of them have murdered George and Jacqueline Coverdale and George's daughter Melinda and Jacqueline's son Giles, Eunice is unmoved: "No pity stirred her, and no regret. She did not think of love, joy, peace, rest, hope, life, dust, ashes, waste, want, ruin, madness, and death, that she had murdered love and blighted life, ruined hope, wasted intellectual potential, ended joy, for she hardly knew what these things were. . . . She thought it a pity about that good carpet getting in such a mess, and she was glad none of the blood had splashed onto her."

Make Death Love Me (1979) suggests that as illiteracy stifles humanity, literacy can provide life with meaning, although in this case the end result is as tragic. The protagonist, Alan Groombridge, is a bank manager who has for the thirty-eight years of his life "lived in a world of dreams," dreams that themselves had their origin in the fiction he read voraciously. For example, even though he is married and the father of two teenage children, it was fiction, not life, that had taught him "that there is such a thing as being in love." Sadly, other than his books, his only genuine excitement comes from secretly fondling the money in the bank safe when his assistant Joyce goes out for lunch. As Rendell puts it, "With the kind of breathless excitement many people feel about sex—or so he supposed, he never had himself—he looked at the money and turned it over and handled it. Gently he handled it, and then roughly as if it belonged to him and he had lots more." Joyce, in contrast, is a young woman grounded in the reality of her daily life and impending marriage.

A bank robbery changes both their lives. Joyce is kidnapped by the unhappy Marty and Nigel. Alan Groombridge finds himself in possession of three thousand pounds and the freedom to re-create his life. Much of the rest of the novel deals with Joyce's relationship with her kidnappers, Nigel's fantasies of dominating both his partner and Joyce, Groombridge's adoption of a new identity, and his creation of a new life (itself constructed on a fantasy) with a woman he comes to love. Eventually Groombridge's sense of responsi-

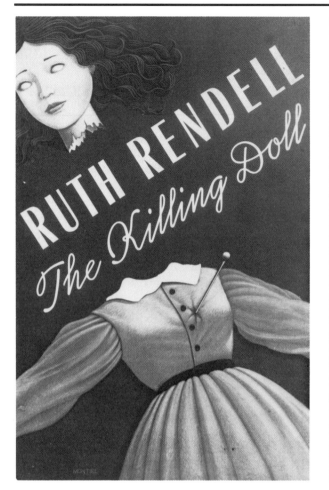
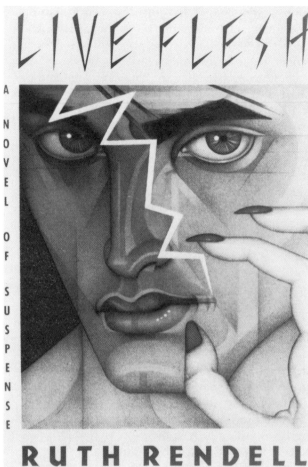

Dust jackets for the first American editions of two of Rendell's novels from the 1980s

bility for Joyce leads him to rescue her. It also brings him to the harshest reality of all: his own hero's death. As Barnard has noted, the novel also "displays with particular brilliance Rendell's gift for social observation, and her rendering of the contemporary scene has an almost Dickensian relish for the grotesque."

Martin Urban, the protagonist of *The Lake of Darkness* (1980), like Alan Groombridge, initially lives his life vicariously. A rather staid accountant, he has almost no friends other than the newspaper reporter Tim, and no romantic relationship in his life. When he wins more than a hundred thousand pounds in the football pools, his life changes dramatically. He decides to give half of it to people in need. The other half he gives to his new girlfriend, Francesca. But Martin's charity has ironic results. Most of those to whom he gives are ungrateful, while one man actually dies of shock when he learns about Martin's bequest. His romance with Francesca, too, does not turn out to be what he hoped. In reality, she

is Tim's common-law wife and the two of them have set Martin up. But in the novel's most devastating sequence, another recipient of Martin's charity, the hired murderer Finn, kills Francesca in a deliberate hit-and-run accident, believing that Martin's gift to his mother is really payment for Francesca's death.

As with other Rendell novels, *The Lake of Darkness* explores the criminal mind. Finn treats his murders-for-hire as a profession. Feeling no remorse, he seeks to hide his crimes only out of love for his mother, whose own sanity has been broken by her knowledge of Finn's first murder. Tim and Francesca's crime of defrauding Martin is the result of Tim's desire for revenge and Francesca's wish for material possessions. In her presentation of these relationships Rendell also explores Martin's repressed homosexuality, which in a Lawrentian scene emerges in his wrestling match with Tim at the end of the novel. But Martin's self-knowledge comes too late: Francesca is dead, and Tim's wish for friendship has turned to contempt. Martin's death, although an accident, nevertheless comes at Finn's hands and is the direct result of Martin's learning of his own unwitting part in the girl's murder.

Master of the Moor (1982) is equally chilling. Stephen Whalby, believing his mother to be the illegitimate daughter of a famous writer, is obsessed by the moor adjacent to his home. Although by trade he helps his father restore furniture, by avocation he writes a newspaper column about the moor and spends most of his free time walking it. Thwarted emotionally by his mother's abandonment of him and his father, Dada, for a new husband, Stephen's marriage is a celibate one.

In time, Stephen's repressed misogyny comes to the fore. Drawn to his mythical friend Rip, who he believes has committed several murders of young women with long blonde hair, Stephen in time becomes a murderer as well. He is so distant from his own reality that for a time he even mistakenly believes that his victim is his wife (who has by now left him for another man). But in the end Stephen comes to new knowledge. He learns that his mother was neither the daughter of the famous writer nor the lovely woman of his fantasies, and he learns that his fellow murderer is none other than his own father.

As distressing as these novels are, Rendell's next novel not featuring Wexford, *The Killing Doll* (1984), is one of her most disturbing, focusing unrelentingly on the disintegration of two minds: the lonely Dolly, whose life has been thwarted by a facial birthmark; and Diarmit Bawne, whose split personality leads him to murder. The novel also explores the power of the occult on the unstable mind. In what is nothing more than a childhood game, Dolly's brother Pup in "the winter before he was sixteen . . . sold his soul to the devil." But while Pup outgrows what he considers white magic, the alcoholic Dolly becomes obsessed with what she believes to be her brother's power. Certain that he is responsible for their stepmother's death and their father's success as a novelist, she turns to him to murder a friend's husband and to eliminate her birthmark. Pup, of course, refuses, and so, overwhelmed by her hallucinations about her dead mother and stepmother and feeling betrayed by Pup's refusal to use his magic to do her bidding, Dolly takes matters into her own hands. In an effort to preserve what she believes is her only friendship, she murders someone only to learn that she has selected the wrong victim. The

Diarmit subplot offers an equally disturbing portrait of the schizophrenic and disintegrating mind. In his sane moments Diarmit assumes the identity of the sane Conal Moore, who can hold a job and enter into the world. In his Diarmit identity he is instead a paranoid man who seldom ventures out-of-doors and, when he does, is inclined to murder. In fact, at one point Diarmit decides, "I kill, therefore I am." Although Dolly and Diarmit do not meet until the end of the novel, their unhappy fates seem ordained from the beginning. Indeed, Rendell ends the novel, "Everything that had happened to them had inexorably led to this end, and as they closed together with the knives between them, each gave an equal cry of fear."

The Tree of Hands (1984) is different from other Rendell psychological novels in that the protagonist, Benet, is essentially both moral and sane. The author of a best-selling novel and single mother of a twenty-one-month-old boy, Benet has found contentment for herself. A visit from her mother, Mopsa, a woman prone to depression and in the past to schizophrenic breaks, disrupts her routine, but it is the death of her son, James, that truly devastates her. The novel's action, however, really begins when Mopsa kidnaps another two-year-old to substitute for James. Benet, driven by a desire to protect her mother and aware that the two-year-old in her care has been physically abused by his own family, procrastinates in telling the police about the kidnapping. In time, she decides that she will keep the boy, whom she now calls Jay, and raise him as if he were her own son. That choice requires her to end her relationship with a young physician with whom she has fallen in love, for she knows he would never conspire with her in her deception.

Rendell's presentation of the other characters in Benet's world suggests that she is justified in her actions. Jay's mother, Carol, herself an abused child, is an indifferent mother to all three of her children and ultimately cruel to her young and devoted lover Barry. Carol's family and neighbors lead equally impoverished lives on a spiritual and emotional as well as financial level. Edward, the father of Benet's child, is a cold man who commits psychological violence toward those close to him. But, as in so many of these novels, the denouement depends on acts of physical violence as well. Carol and Edward get together because Edward hopes to buy Jay from Carol, but they are murdered by one of Carol's lovers, leaving the way open for Benet to carry out her decep-

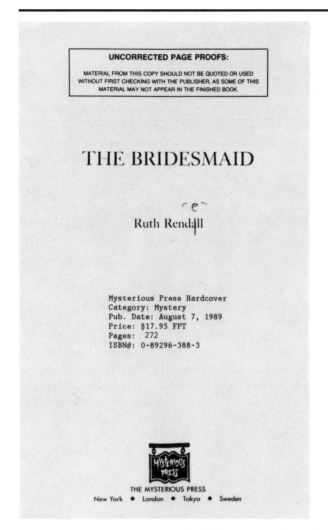

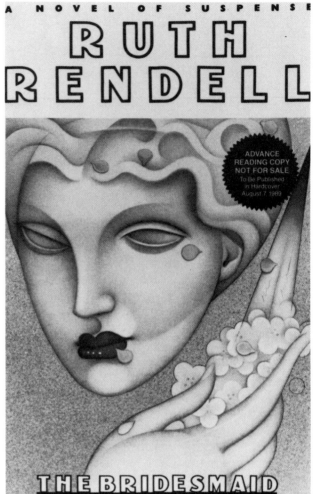

Front wrapper for proofs and dust jacket for bound copies sent to reviewers before publication of the American edition of Rendell's thirty-seventh book (courtesy of Mysterious Press)

tion that Jay is truly her son. The novel ends nevertheless on a hopeful note, for Benet's actions are motivated by a nurturing love. Jay's life with Benet is already centered around trips to the library and being read to. As Carol Kennedy (*Books and Bookmen*, February 1985) notes, "Love and fulfillment of a kind win through in an ending that is both bleak and a hopeful relief, like a winter dawn."

In *Live Flesh* (1986) former police officer David Fleetwood, a quadriplegic after being shot while trying to free a hostage, and his assailant, Victor Jenner, become locked in a relationship after Victor's release from prison. Their need at first is mutual: David desires to understand what happened in the moment that destroyed his life, and Victor wants to justify his actions. But as the novel proceeds, Victor begins to lose his grasp on reality. He invents not only the scenario that led

up to his shooting David but also key aspects of his relationship with Clare, David's fiancée. Victor, too, is unable to assume responsibility for his own actions and is convinced that David has "inflicted" a "great injury" on him and that David, despite his paralysis, "had nothing to worry about, no awful past to forget, uncertain future to dread. He didn't need a job, he would have a nice fat pension, and growing older wouldn't make much difference to him." Victor's failure to assume responsibility for his own actions pervades his narrative. For example, he thinks "that no one was responsible, that it was fate, the force of circumstances and destiny which had inflicted such terrible injury" upon David. He also distances himself from the rapes he has committed and those he desires to commit, justifying his dreams about rape by thinking, "A man was not responsible for dreams, they were something else."

The novel ultimately requires the reader to suspend disbelief, however, and accept as plausible that David and Clare would enter into a social relationship with Victor and, even more incredibly, that Clare would take Victor as her lover. As John Gross (*New York Times*, 22 August 1986) writes, "for David and Clare to accept Victor so readily, and then positively warm toward him, argues something rather kinky about them, or at any rate something more complicated than anything we are shown." But in the world of this novel, victim and victimizer do enter into such a relationship, and Clare spends a night with Victor. Her subsequent rejection of Victor pushes him over the edge: he attempts to rape another woman; he torments Clare and David with phone calls; he murders his affluent aunt from whom he has been stealing since his release from prison; and finally, he dies from a wound suffered in his final rape attempt. The last line of the novel suggests that Victor's physical and psychological assaults on David and Clare will have persistent consequences. Sitting on his patio in the dark, David watches "a big white moth" which "had spread its wings flat on the house wall, waiting for the outside lights to come on, waiting to burn itself to death on the sizzling glass." And when Clare responds to David's request to turn the lights on, the moth, a metaphor for them both, "fluttered off the wall and came to the light to burn its tender white feathery wings."

In *Talking to Strangers* (1987; published in the United States as *Talking to Strange Men*) Rendell for the first time touches, albeit lightly, on political matters. A group of public-school boys establishes a spying game which suggests just how dangerous such espionage games can be both to the players and to innocent bystanders. Indeed the game becomes an obsession first to Mungo and then later to his schoolmate Charles Mabledene. But it is Mungo's older brother Ian who early in the novel notes the dangers, telling Mungo, "visionary, that's what you are . . . or else it's schizophrenic."

The world that Rendell portrays in this novel is indeed a schizophrenic one and, as the protagonist of the important subplot, John Creevey, realizes, a threatening one: "He saw the world as a dangerous place, the seemingly ordinary men who lived in it as dangerous, and himself as potentially so." Tormented both by the death eighteen years earlier of his beloved sister Cherry and by his abandonment by his wife, Jennifer, Creevey tries to provide meaning in his life

through routine. As his sister's former lover, Mark Simms, tells him, "You are a very conventional person, aren't you, John? Not to say routine-driven. You'd sacrifice real living to a principle of going to bed at the right time and getting up at the right time. Life will always pass you by because your petty rituals are more important to you than your own or other people's pain or happiness." The novel is a process of John's coming to awareness: that Cherry was promiscuous, not chaste as he had assumed, that Mark was lying to him that he had murdered Cherry, and that Jennifer had been happy as his lover. But John remains ignorant that his involvement with the spy games has real and serious consequences. For example, it leads to the death of Jennifer's lover, the pederast Peter Moran, and to the growing coldness of Charles Mabledene. Indeed, Charles Mabledene, whose code name is Dragon, is at the age of fourteen a ruthless young man, adept at deception, willing to cross the line into immoral action, and–although in self-defense–a murderer who has come to accept and justify his actions. His plan to develop a ring of public schoolboys who will later assume positions of political power seems both plausible and terrifying.

In *The Bridesmaid* (1989) Rendell again explores the potential for violence which (the novel suggests) is inherent in all people. Although the novel begins with Philip Wardman's awareness of his "phobia for murder and all forms of killing, the wanton destruction of life in war, and its senseless destruction in accidents," he comes to recognize not only his own capability for violence but "that we are all capable of almost anything." Philip has also come to question the relationship between truth and fantasy and his ability to distinguish between the two.

What precipitates Philip's unhappy evolution is his love affair with the beautiful, silver-haired Senta Pelham, who asks Philip to prove his love for her by murdering someone. In turn, Senta promises she will murder someone as reciprocal proof of her love for him. Philip, believing himself to be desperately in love with the girl and persuaded that she is interested only in fantasies about murder, first promises her that he will kill someone and then fabricates a story for her that he has committed murder. Shortly after that, Senta tells him that she has murdered a former beau of Philip's mother, Gerard Arnham, because she believes Arnham was Philip's "enemy." Although the reader suspects that Senta is telling the truth, Philip persists in believing that the

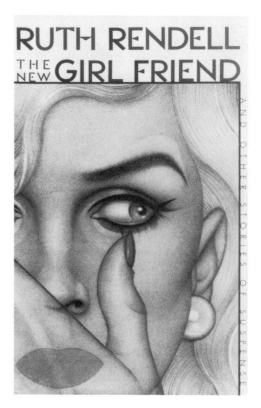

Dust jackets for the first American editions of Rendell's three short-story collections

girl's talk of murder is merely fantasy, a belief reinforced by his encountering Arnham alive on the street. In time, however, Philip learns that Senta has in fact murdered two people: the young girl Rebecca Neave, who was dating a man Senta desired; and a neighbor of Arnham's whom Senta mistakenly believed to be Arnham. When Philip finally acknowledges to himself that Senta has murdered and that he has contributed to her doing so, he loses all control. Although he knows "he had been the man who hated violence, who couldn't imagine himself performing any brutish act," he begins to beat her before he realizes what is happening: "Her shoulders were in his hands, grasped with the nails digging in, and he was crashing her body up and down on the bed, pounding the frailness of her into the mattress, the flimsy ribcage, the bird's bones." Philip now understands that Senta is mad and that her purpose in establishing the murder pact was to "set the two of them apart, to make them unfit for other company." With this new knowledge comes the end of all Philip's desire. He now no longer equates Senta with the lovely marble statue, Flora, that has been so important to his family but rather thinks of the girl first as "some decaying drowned thing or a sack of garbage" and then with extreme pity.

Philip's blindness about Senta is matched by his blindness about his mother and sisters, all of whom he loves. It has not occurred to him that his mother could have taken Arnham as a lover. Later he mistakenly believes that his mother has a new girlfriend when in reality the person she has been seeing is a man whom she is likely to marry. He is unaware for a long time that his sister Cheryl, who has the same addiction to gambling that their deceased father did, is in trouble. He also inflates his own importance in the company for which he works until his boss, in a moment of anger, calls him "a little squirt on the bottom rung of the ladder."

Despite his ability to be deceived and to deceive himself, Philip has some redemptive qualities, as do his mother and his sisters. These are people who love and care for one another. They are people who do their best, and although their best is often flawed, at times it is comically so. For example, whereas Senta's house is tainted by the odor of the corpse of Rebecca Neave, which Senta has hidden on the upper level of the house, Philip's home is permeated by the slightly unpleasant but benign odor of the permanents his mother gives in her kitchen to earn money.

But even as this comic vision balances the more tragic and frightening one offered by Senta, the novel ends with a desolate Philip holding the girl he now knows is insane, waiting for the police to arrive to arrest them both.

Rendell's novels are increasingly popular, produced quickly in paperback versions and prominently displayed in American bookstores. In her portrayal of all classes of British society, she has created a fictional microcosm of modern British life. In her attentiveness to relationships, the meaning of truth, the importance of individual and societal perceptions, and the nature of sanity, and in her questioning of the possibilities for individual volition and responsible choice and action, she also touches on the human dilemmas that characterize not only Britain but life in contemporary, developed societies. In her Wexford novels she has created an enduring set of reassuring, if sometimes flawed characters who deepen as they grow older. In her psychological novels, with what Barnard has called her "talent to disturb," she has created characters most of her readers would rather forget. It is in the balance of her two different worldviews, however, that her achievement as an artist is most apparent.

Interviews:
Jane S. Bakerman, "Rendell Territory," *Mystery Nook*, 10 (August 1977): 1-6;
Lesley Adamson, "It May Not Be Art but it Entertains," *Guardian*, 10 May 1978, p. 14.

References:
Jane S. Bakerman, "Explorations of Love: An Examination of Some Novels by Ruth Rendell," *Armchair Detective*, 11 (April 1978): 139-144;
Bakerman, "Ruth Rendell," in *Ten Women of Mystery*, edited by Earl F. Bargainnier (Bowling Green, Ohio: Bowling Green University Popular Press, 1981), pp. 126-149;
Bakerman, "The Writer's Probe: Ruth Rendell as Social Critic," *Mystery FANcier*, 3 (September-October 1979): 3-6;
Robert Barnard, "A Talent to Disturb," *Armchair Detective*, 16 (Spring 1983): 146-152;
Michele Field, "Ruth Rendell / Barbara Vine," *Publishers Weekly*, 235 (26 May 1989): 46-47;
Don Miller, "A Look at the Novels of Ruth Rendell," *Mystery Nook*, 10 (August 1977): 8-10.

George Sims

(3 August 1923-   )

Nancy Pearl

BOOKS: *Poems* (London: Fortune, 1944);

The Immanent Goddess (London: Fortune, 1947);

A Catalogue of Letters, Manuscript Papers and Books of Frederick Rolfe, Baron Corvo (Harrow: Sims, 1949);

The Terrible Door (London: Bodley Head, 1964; New York: Horizon, 1964);

Sleep No More (London: Gollancz, 1966; New York: Harcourt, Brace & World, 1966);

The Last Best Friend (London: Gollancz, 1967; New York: Stein & Day, 1968);

The Sand Dollar (London: Gollancz, 1969);

Deadhand (London: Gollancz, 1971);

Hunters Point (London: Gollancz, 1973; New York: Penguin, 1977);

The End of the Web (London: Gollancz, 1976; New York: Walker, 1976);

Rex Mundi (London: Gollancz, 1978);

Who is Cato? (London: Macmillan, 1981);

The Keys of Death (London: Macmillan, 1982; Bath, U.K.: Chivers / South Yarmouth, Mass.: Curley, 1983);

Coat of Arms (London: Macmillan, 1984);

The Rare Book Game (Philadelphia: Holmes, 1985).

OTHER: "The Charlie Adams Affair," in *Pick of Today's Short Stories 7*, edited by John Pudney (London: Putnam's, 1956).

George Sims (photograph by Vivienne)

Most significant for his excellent characterization, George Sims takes advantage of his experiences with manuscripts and rare books in creating the settings and protagonists of many of his novels. The world of the British rare-book dealer is well presented: the auction houses, the collectors of poetry and pornography, the large country-house sales all come across to the reader as true to life. Sims's love of literature is also evident in the many authors he either quotes or refers to in his novels. In *Sleep No More* (1966), for example, there are quotations from, or references to, Carolus Linnaeus, Samuel Taylor Coleridge, Samuel Johnson, the Bible, Mark Twain, William Shakespeare, Omar Khayyam, Robert Browning, Henry James, and Lewis Carroll, among others.

George Frederick Robert Sims was born in Hammersmith, London. He attended John Lyon's School, Harrow, Middlesex, from 1934 to 1940. Before joining the British army, in which he served from 1942 to 1947, he was a junior reporter for the London Press Association. Sims worked for a year for an antiquarian bookseller, then opened his own shop, G. F. Sims (Rare Books), in 1948 in Harrow. In 1954 he moved his business to Hurst, Berkshire, where he lives in a seventeenth-century cottage with his wife and three children.

Sims is interested in exploring, in all its facets, the reality behind the illusions men and women present to the world. At the end of *Sleep No More*, Sims has one of his characters describe what can be said to be the general theme of his novels, that people are seldom what they appear. Jeffrey Wilson, who had hoped to write a biography of William Beaumont, a film star, says that the "motif [of the biography] . . . has been the discovery of the face behind the mask." The masks that are worn by Sims's characters may be actual ones, used to hide a grotesque deformity, as in *The Keys of Death* (1982), or to disguise a character's identity, as in *The End of the Web* (1976). Or, the masks may be those of attitude, such as the mask of conventional manners and morality used to disguise murderous plans, as in *Sleep No More*. The mask may be the face presented to the world to hide deep-seated feelings. As Ed Buchanan says of himself in *Hunters Point* (1973), he was " 'posing' rather than being." Garve, a character in *Hunters Point* who hides behind his highly successful business in order to plot other men's deaths, is yet another example of the theme of masks in Sims's novels.

Another theme which runs through Sims's novels is that of the emptiness and sterility of life experienced by men in their forties. Their jobs, their marriages, their situations in life no longer bring them satisfaction or pleasure. In order to escape their fears of old age and death, his protagonists search for excitement and romantic love in relationships with much-younger women. Even while they know that these entanglements are not the answers to their problems, they are loath to give them up because the affairs give some meaning to an otherwise dismal existence. As character Robert Seldon says in Sims's first novel, *The Terrible Door* (1964) (and he as much speaks for the main character in *The Last Best Friend*, 1967; *The Sand Dollar*, 1969; *Deadhand*, 1971; and *Rex Mundi*, 1978), "My inability to enjoy the present seemed to me my biggest defect. I wondered if I was doomed always to slide through situations, not making the most of them, and then spend hours thinking about them."

While the protagonists in Sims's novels are generally alike (with the exception of *Sleep No More*, which has a multitude of characters but no real hero), the main characters in *The Terrible Door*, *The Last Best Friend*, *The Sand Dollar*, and *Deadhand* are virtually indistinguishable from one

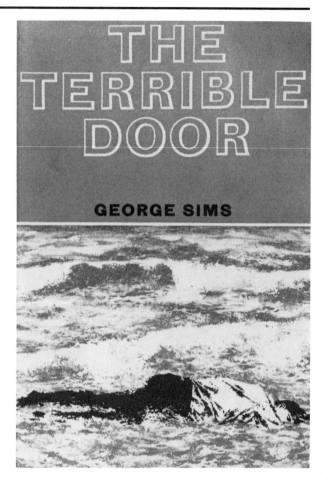

Dust jacket for the first edition of Sims's first novel

another. Their similarities include a love of music, their breakfast cereal, and their profession of bookseller and/or antique dealer. The only differences among these men are the adventures in which each man finds himself and the young woman with whom he is involved. In *The Terrible Door* Robert Seldon is asked to be the executor of a fellow bookseller's will. The dead man was disguised in life as a "dull, rather boring Yorkshire man" when in fact his complicated life and a collection of letters lead Sheldon into the path of a psychopath who hires thugs, or "professional frightener[s]" (the expression is first used in *The Sand Dollar* and reappears in other novels) to fight for him. Edward Balfour, in *The Last Best Friend*, hears from his estranged wife that Sam Weiss, an old friend and fellow book dealer, has seemingly committed suicide. In his attempts to disprove the suicide verdict Balfour learns not to trust the surface appearance even of people he thinks he knows well. In *The Sand Dollar* Nicholas Howard searches for a young woman, a friend of his dead wife, who has disappeared. Howard's wife was a supposed suicide, and Howard's guilt over the lack of sympathy he had had for his wife's apparent problems drives him in his quest for the young woman. His search brings him into conflict with Curtis Mahon, a midget, whose only interests are high-class pornography, drugs, chess, and women. In *Deadhand*, Ralph Neville receives a letter from a man, now dead, who had saved his life during World War II. Neville is asked for a favor which he feels honor-bound to do.

Two novels, *Hunters Point* and *The End of the Web*, feature the same hero. In *Hunters Point* Ed Buchanan, a member of the Special Branch of the London Police Department, is sent to California to investigate the activities of a suspected radical involved in terrorist activities in Berkeley and San Francisco. Buchanan sees "the cruelty and chaos which lay underneath the surface appearance." He reappears in *The End of the Web*, one of Sims's most compelling novels. The reader is introduced to Leo Selver, unhappily a womanizer, owner of an antique shop, who has become involved with two other antique dealers in a dangerous situation that has gotten to be too much for him. The reader sees Selver's indecision and fear quite clearly. He is a sympathetic character, who thinks retrospectively that "before embarking on dangerous escapades one should consider whether one had the courage to face them out." Selver and his most recent girlfriend are found dead in the woman's apartment. Buchanan, who resigned from the Special Branch after his experiences in *Hunters Point*, is asked by Selver's wife to investigate the verdict of murder and suicide. In this novel the reader gets a clear picture of Sims's view of a psychopath. He is a man who "always felt intensely alone, as if he was the only man alive in a world otherwise peopled by phantoms." Sims's strengths are evident in *The End of the Web*. The minor characters are all well presented and interesting. His descriptions of the Brixton area of London, with its Rastafarians, reggae music, and West Indian life, are painted with fondness and accuracy.

Rex Mundi and *Who is Cato?* (1981) are poorly plotted. In *Rex Mundi* Harry Gilmour, while on vacation in Corfu, becomes involved in a hunt for treasure which turns on the connection between the Albigensians, a religious group that flourished in the late Middle Ages, and a walled house on Corfu. The connection is extremely tenuous, and the resolution of the story is filled with coincidence. *Who is Cato?* is peopled with stock characters in typical situations. Wid-

Dust jacket for the first American edition of Sims's novel which features Ed Buchanan, who is also the investigator in Hunters Point *(1973)*

ower William Marshall (his wife died in an automobile accident), an art dealer, is asked by an old friend from World War II to take part in a secret mission, part of which involves Marshall's young girlfriend, Gwen, and her husband.

Two of Sims's novels stand out, *The Keys of Death* and *Sleep No More*. *Sleep No More* is the story of William Beaumont, an American actor, still recovering from the shocking death of his wife in a flaming automobile accident which he survived. His life is falling apart: he is uninterested in working on any films; he is having a pointless affair with the wife of his publicity agent; and worst of all, he is being subjected to a campaign of mental and physical destruction by an unknown person, for unknown reasons. Drugs are added to his drinks, newspaper clippings about people being burned to death are sent to him, and someone breaks into his flat and leaves a butcher's hook on his bed. How Beaumont learns who is tormenting him and comes to terms with his wife's death are the subjects of this novel, yet

Dust jackets for the first editions of two of Sims's novels from the 1980s

a plot description would not do justice to Sims's ability to portray the supporting characters, so that each of Beaumont's supposed friends becomes real. These people may not be wholly admirable, but the reader knows them well, from Beaumont's publicity agent, to the agent's secretary, to the young American academic who is hoping to write Beaumont's official biography.

The reality beneath everyday routine is a focus of *Sleep No More*. The psychopathic potential murderer is described as a compulsive eater in private who presents himself as a constant dieter in public. He is a man "who has settled in life for a routine performance of daily, monotonous tasks . . . while being kept going by a secret, imaginative existence." As one minor character says, obviously speaking for the author, "When you get up close and look behind the mask everybody is just the same. There's always a small guy, hidden in back, worried about his health, sex life,

his past, or something." Sims very effectively presents the growing terror and disruption making up Beaumont's life, and even though the reader knows the identity of the psychopath tormenting Beaumont long before the end of the book, the novel does not lose its strength or appeal.

The Keys of Death is an ingenious novel of suspense. The reader is first introduced to Catherine O'Driscoll as she is being physically assaulted, "brutalised in a casual, semi-joking manner that was somehow more frightening than any blows she had known delivered in anger." After Catherine disappears (she is found dead at the end of the book), her married lover, Jack Quinn, sets out to discover what has happened to her. In the course of his investigation, Quinn learns that two people have been murdered by the same man, a "professional frightener," a psychopath who thinks of himself in the following way: "F. B. Gurnard vs. the hostile world." A very effective technique used by Sims is to have each of the people murdered or threatened by Gurnard tell their own story of the encounter. Quinn learns that the murders were ordered by a grotesquely facially deformed man, Tristram, who always wears a mask in public. After Tristram kills himself rather than be revealed as the mind behind the murders, Quinn's need to avenge Catherine's death turns to pity for Tristram.

Sims's plotting is the weakest aspect of his books. The novels often peter out lamely, with no real conclusion and often, as in *Who is Cato?*, with no real point. Whatever working out of a puzzle is done is by coincidence or luck, not by logical deduction. The lack of coherent plots leads Sims into using complicated, farfetched situations. This gives him the opportunity to write about fascinating bits of information garnered from a life well-filled with literature, as in the long description of the Hell-Fire Club in *The Keys of Death*. These seldom add much to the plot, however.

What Sims excels at is characterization. Even though his books are filled with many characters who have nothing to do with the plot, who seem to be only an indulgence of the author's, they are so well drawn, so real, that readers forgive Sims his indulgences. The middle-aged man whose life has become constrained and dull is exceptionally well portrayed. Sims is also able to put the reader inside the mind of both the victim and the villain of his novels so that both are understandable.

Julian Symons

(30 May 1912-   )

Larry E. Grimes
Bethany College

BOOKS: *Confusions about X* (London: Fortune, 1939);

The Second Man (London: Routledge, 1943);

The Immaterial Murder Case (London: Gollancz, 1945; New York: Macmillan, 1957);

A Man Called Jones (London: Gollancz, 1947);

Bland Beginning (London: Gollancz, 1949; New York: Harper, 1949);

A. J. A. Symons: His Life and Speculations (London: Eyre & Spottiswoode, 1950);

The Thirty-First of February (London: Gollancz, 1950; New York: Harper, 1951);

Charles Dickens (London: Barker, 1951; New York: Roy, 1951);

Thomas Carlyle: The Life and Ideas of a Prophet (London: Gollancz, 1952; New York: Oxford University Press, 1952);

The Broken Penny (London: Gollancz, 1953; New York: Harper, 1953);

The Narrowing Circle (London: Gollancz, 1954; New York: Harper, 1955);

Horatio Bottomley: A Biography (London: Cresset, 1955);

The Paper Chase (London: Collins, 1956); republished as *Bogue's Fortune* (New York: Harper, 1957);

The Colour of Murder (London: Collins, 1957; New York: Harper, 1957);

The General Strike: A Historical Portrait (London: Cresset, 1957; Chester Springs, Pa.: Dufour, 1957);

The Gigantic Shadow (London: Collins, 1958); republished as *The Pipe Dream* (New York: Harper, 1959);

The Progress of a Crime (London: Collins, 1960; New York: Harper, 1960);

A Reasonable Doubt: Some Criminal Cases Re-examined (London: Cresset, 1960);

The Thirties: A Dream Resolved (London: Cresset, 1960; Westport, Conn.: Greenwood, 1973; revised edition, London: Faber & Faber, 1975);

Murder! Murder! (London: Fontana, 1961);

Julian Symons (photograph by Mark Gerson)

The Detective Story in Britain (London: Longmans, Green, 1962; expanded, 1969);

The Killing of Francie Lake (London: Collins, 1962); republished as *The Plain Man* (New York: Harper & Row, 1962);

Buller's Campaign (London: Cresset, 1963);

The End of Solomon Grundy (London: Collins, 1964; New York: Harper & Row, 1964);

The Belting Inheritance (London: Collins, 1965; New York: Harper & Row, 1965);

England's Pride: The Story of the Gordon Relief Expedition (London: Hamilton, 1965);

Francis Quarles Investigates (London: Panther, 1965);

The Man Who Killed Himself (London: Collins, 1965; New York: Harper & Row, 1965);

Critical Occasions (London: Hamilton, 1966);

Crime and Detection: An Illustrated History from 1840 (London: Studio Vista, 1966); republished as *A Pictorial History of Crime* (New York: Crown, 1966);

The Man Whose Dreams Came True (London: Collins, 1968; New York: Harper & Row, 1968);

The Man Who Lost His Wife (London: Collins, 1970; New York: Harper & Row, 1970);

Bloody Murder: From the Detective Story to the Crime Novel (London: Faber & Faber, 1972); republished as *Mortal Consequences: A History from the Detective Story to the Crime Novel* (New York: Harper & Row, 1972); revised as *Bloody Murder* (Harmondsworth: Penguin, 1974; revised again, 1985);

Notes from Another Country (London: London Magazine Editions, 1972);

The Players and the Game (London: Collins, 1972; New York: Harper & Row, 1972);

The Plot Against Roger Rider (London: Collins, 1973; New York: Harper & Row, 1973);

The Object of An Affair, and Other Poems (Edinburgh: Tragara, 1974);

A Three Pipe Problem (London: Collins, 1975; New York: Harper & Row, 1975);

Ellery Queen Presents Julian Symons' How to Trap a Crook and 12 Other Mysteries, edited, with an introduction, by Ellery Queen (Frederic Dannay and Manfred B. Lee) (New York: Davis, 1977);

The Blackheath Poisonings: A Victorian Murder Mystery (London: Collins, 1978; New York: Harper & Row, 1978);

The Tell-Tale Heart: The Life and Works of Edgar Allan Poe (London: Faber & Faber, 1978; New York: Harper & Row, 1978);

Conan Doyle: Portrait of an Artist (London: Whizzard, 1979; New York: Mysterious, 1988);

The Modern Crime Story (Edinburgh: Tragara, 1980);

Sweet Adelaide: A Victorian Puzzle Solved (London: Collins, 1980; New York: Harper & Row, 1980);

Critical Observations (London & Boston: Faber & Faber, 1981; New Haven, Conn.: Ticknor & Fields, 1981);

The Great Detectives: Seven Original Investigations (London: Orbis, 1981; New York: Abrams, 1981);

A. J. A. Symons to Wyndham Lewis (Edinburgh: Tragara, 1982);

Drawing of Symons by Wyndham Lewis, 1938 (courtesy of Julian Symons)

The Detling Murders (London: Macmillan, 1982); republished as *The Detling Secret* (New York: Viking, 1983; Harmondsworth & New York: Penguin, 1984);

The Tigers of Subtopia, and Other Stories (London: Macmillan, 1982; New York: Viking, 1983);

The Name of Annabel Lee (London: Macmillan, 1983; New York: Viking, 1983);

1948 and 1984 (Edinburgh: Tragara, 1984);

The Criminal Comedy of the Contented Couple (London: Macmillan, 1985); republished as *A Criminal Comedy* (New York: Viking, 1986);

Dashiell Hammett (San Diego: Harcourt Brace Jovanovich, 1985);

Two Brothers (Edinburgh: Tragara, 1985);

Makers of the New (London: Deutsch, 1987; New York: Random House, 1987);

The Kentish Manor Murders (London: Macmillan, 1988; New York: Viking, 1988).

Collections: *The Julian Symons Omnibus*, introduction by Symons (London: Collins, 1966);

The Julian Symons Omnibus (Harmondsworth: Penguin, 1984).

OTHER: *An Anthology of War Poetry* (Harmondsworth & New York: Penguin, 1942);

Between the Wars: Britain in Photographs (London: Batsford, 1972);

"Progress of a Crime Writer," in *The Mystery and Detection Annual*, edited by Donald K. Adams (Beverly Hills, Cal.: Adams, 1974), pp. 238-243;

Verdict of Thirteen: A Detective Club Anthology, edited by Symons (New York: Harper & Row, 1979);

Tom Adams, *Agatha Christie: The Art of Her Crimes*, commentary by Symons (New York: Everest House, 1981).

Poet, biographer, historian, novelist, criminologist, and critic, Julian Symons, president of the Detection Club since 1976, is heir to the kingdom of crime literature previously presided over by G. K. Chesterton, E. C. Bentley, Dorothy L. Sayers, and Agatha Christie. He has argued persuasively in *Bloody Murder: From the Detective Story to the Crime Novel* (1972; published in the United States as *Mortal Consequences: A History from the Detective Story to the Crime Novel*) that crime writing has changed greatly since World War II. Author of more than twenty crime novels, three histories of the genre, two collections of detective stories, and numerous articles and reviews of crime fiction published in the *London Times* and elsewhere, Symons has both mapped and colonized new territories.

Born in London on 30 May 1912, Julian Gustave Symons is the youngest son of Morris Albert Symons, an immigrant probably of Jewish origin, who was a shopkeeper, and Minnie Louise Bull Symons, his English wife. A demand for secondhand goods during World War I pushed the Symons family into the middle class after years of marginal existence. The new money bought a car, four racehorses, and in 1919 a large Victorian house in Cedars Road, Clapham. The family's hold on its newfound wealth and status was not firm, however. Only the house and four pounds remained of Morris Albert Symons's fortune when he died in 1929.

Julian Symons's formal education ended in 1927 when he completed study as a shorthand typist at commercial school and soon after began work at Victoria Lighting and Dynamos. From 1927 to 1939 Symons lived a double life. Part of his time was spent working at Victoria Lighting and Dynamos so that he might devote the rest to his true interests–games and literature. He and his brother Maurice were noted table-tennis players. When he was not working or playing he was

Dust jacket for the first American edition of a novel that embodies a frequent theme in Symons's fiction: when real life is sterile, games and fantasies give meaning to existence

busy fleshing out his literary education, which he describes in his memoir *Notes from Another Country* (1972): "Things go together: and what went on in my life was the daily journey by 26 or 28 tram to Victoria, the fingers tapping a typewriter in the service of Mr. Budette . . . the reading of books, the writing of poems, the dream of a literary magazine. . . . The young man who worked away in the evening at improving his forehand drive, spent part of the day discovering with astonishment the violent emotions not only felt but expressed by people in *The Brothers Karamazov*."

Symons was greatly influenced by his brother A. J. A. Symons, best known for the classic of modern biography, *The Quest for Corvo: An Experiment in Biography* (1934), a life of Frederick Rolfe that contains some of the conventions of the detective story. Julian Symons profiled his brother in a 1950 biography, *A. J. A. Symons: His Life and Speculations*. Between the ages of seventeen and twenty-two Julian Symons read widely

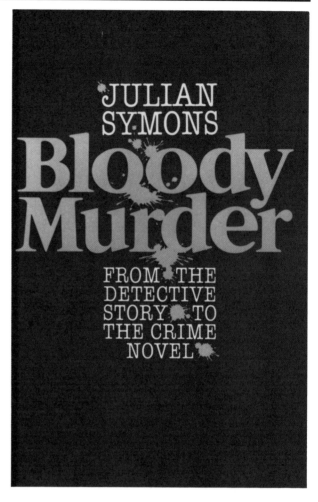

Dust jackets for the first American edition and the second revised edition of Symons's history of mystery fiction

in contemporary literature, including James Joyce's *Ulysses*, T. S. Eliot's poems and essays, Ezra Pound's early cantos, and the work of Wyndham Lewis. Deeply involved in London's literary scene, he was an avid reader of the "little magazines." He paid his respects to the early moderns in an excellent study of the period, *Makers of the New* (1987), which concerns the "revolution in literature" occurring between 1912 and 1939. John Gross (*New York Times*, 6 November 1987) called *Makers of the New* a "lively and engaging book" and said that Symons is to be praised for not overstating the influence of Wyndham Lewis, whom Symons has called "the most original thinker about art and society, and the most remarkable stylist of the twentieth century" (*Contemporary Authors: Autobiography Series*, 3, 1986).

In 1937 Symons began publication of a literary magazine, *Twentieth Century Verse*, which published work by Dylan Thomas, Roy Fuller, George Woodcock, Wallace Stevens, and Gavin

Ewart, among others. World War II brought an end to this phase of Symons's literary life. *Twentieth Century Verse* folded in 1939, and his years of work at Victoria Lighting and Dynamos came to a halt. He held out as long as he could against the war, filing for exemption as a pacifist. His radical brief against what he saw as a capitalist war was rejected, and he was called to service, but not before marrying Kathleen Clark in October 1941. Mustered out of the army in 1944 due to the discovery of a benign tumor on his arm, a botched operation to remove it, and subsequent tendon transplant surgery, Symons eventually took a job writing advertising copy. He worked at Humble, Crowther, and Nicholas until 1947 when, with Kathleen's support, he quit to be a full-time writer.

His career as a novelist began when Kathleen discovered in a drawer the 1939 manuscript of *The Immaterial Murder Case* (1945), a parody of the detective novel featuring Inspector

Bland and amateur Sherlockian Teake Wood. She encouraged its publication. A second detective story, *A Man Called Jones*, was published in 1947. *Bland Beginning* (1949) was his first work as a full-time writer. It lacks the social critique and complex psychological base of his best fiction, but this story of murder and literary fraud has finely sketched characters (particularly two eccentric bibliographic experts) and is dressed out by expert knowledge of the bibliographic field.

An assessment of Symons's place in the world of crime literature must include a discussion of his comments as critic and historian of the genre, for his important reviews, historical surveys, and critical biographies provide a perspective which is useful to the critic of his fiction. His most important contribution to the study of the genre is his assertion that much of the focus in crime writing in the twentieth century has changed. In the period before World War II, he writes in *The Detective Story in Britain* (1962), "there was a belief that human affairs could be ruled by reason and that virtue, generally identified with the established order of society, must prevail in the end. The post-war writers did not identify themselves with such a point of view. They saw, instead, a world in which German force had been defeated only by the greater force employed by the Allies, and in which concentration camps and the atomic bomb mocked a liberal dream of reason. The new writers have not wished to create locked room puzzles. They have turned instead to stories which, while often retaining a puzzle element, are primarily concerned with crime in relation to character and motive." Affirming that the rise of what he calls the crime novel has not meant the demise of the classical detective story, Symons defines the crime novel in contrast to it. In *Bloody Murder* he says that the detective story is built around a great detective and upon a plot of deception. It places great emphasis on crime clues and methods, is socially conservative, and often takes its power from the puzzle which the crime poses. The crime novel, on the other hand, often has no detective, is based on the psychology of its characters, uses the lives of those characters (not methods, clues, and puzzles) as the basis of the story, stresses the pressures of a particular way of life on a person who commits a crime, and often makes a radical critique of the social order.

The modern shift to the crime novel has freed crime literature, according to Symons, from the chains of formula, allowing it to be

Dust jacket for the first American edition of Symons's 1973 mystery novel

taken seriously as both social criticism and as art. He chastens those who criticize realism in the crime novel, saying it is necessary. As he has noted, "to exclude realism of description and language from the crime novel in a period when it has been accepted as normal in other fiction is almost to prevent its practitioners from attempting any serious work." Because it is free from the restrictions of the detective story, the crime novel can have "symbolic interest and value for our time." In short, Symons thinks that crime writing must be taken seriously as literature, although he concedes that "the crime novel must, even in its highest reaches, always be a work of art of a peculiar, flawed kind, since an appetite for violence and pleasure in employing a conjurer's sleight of hand seems somehow always to be blended with the power in delineating character and analyzing event that in the end make any novel worth reading."

Symons's first crime novel is *The Thirty-First of February* (1950). The novel, organized by calendar dates, opens with the death of "Andy" Anderson's wife, which a coroner declares "death by accident." Demands from the marketplace force the traumatized Anderson back to work without a period of mourning. Slowly, under the unrelenting pressure of "business as usual," Anderson is drummed out of Vincent Advertising, physically pained by a new shaving cream he must test and subjected to mental torture by a team of policemen who are convinced that he is guilty of murdering his wife. The result is that Anderson, who is never proven guilty, is pushed all the way from the fourth of February to insanity—the thirty-first of February. The novel presents the often radical social attitude essential to the crime novel, an attitude based on a belief that society is under great stress. As Symons posits in *Critical Occasions* (1966): "the license to kill that has always been granted to soldiers in war, the right to exterminate inferior beings assumed by the Nazis, the necessity to kill civilians involved in large-scale air raids . . . : all these things, as we have absorbed them into our own knowledge and emotional understanding, have imposed a strain on the fabric of our lives."

After a brief excursion into the world of the spy thriller (the excellent 1953 novel, *The Broken Penny*), Symons returned to the crime novel format with the publication of *The Narrowing Circle* (1954). As in *The Thirty-First of February*, Symons sets his novel in the world of work. This time he plots his action from inside a pulp publishing company. The novel opens with David Nelson, the protagonist, hoping to beat out rival Willie Strayte for the position of section editor of Gross Enterprises' newest endeavor, *Crime Magazine*. Strayte gets the nod and then is murdered. Inspector Crambo is assigned to the case, and he hounds Nelson, reminding him that the police have only to put a noose lightly on the shoulders of the guilty and their investigations will tighten it. But it is not the noose of law that chokes Nelson. He is cleared of murder, only to continue the money race and thereby choke off his ability to be human and know love.

Besides the biography of his brother, Symons wrote three other biographies in the 1950s. In *Charles Dickens* (1951) Symons examines his work in terms of his thesis that Dickens exhibited "marked manic-depressive traits throughout his life." Harvey Curtis Webster (*New York Times Book Review*, 9 November 1952) said *Charles Dickens* was "one of the best short critical studies in English." *Thomas Carlyle: The Life and Ideas of a*

Prophet (1952) was also well received. Donald Barr (*New York Times Book Review*, 5 October 1952) said that while it added nothing to the mass of documentation about Carlyle's life it was "an excellently written account." *Horatio Bottomley: A Biography* (1955) is a life of the English journalist, financier, and swindler who held wide popular support until his imprisonment in 1922 for misappropriation of funds.

Symons's next significant novel, *The Colour of Murder* (1957), won the Crime Writers' Association's Crossed Red Herrings Award for the best crime novel of the year. This novel of crime in the workplace, set in a large Oxford Street department store, is composed of three parts. Part 1 is a psychoanalyst's transcript of John Wilkins's first-person narrative of his life before the death of his fancied lover, Sheila Morton. The second part (told in third person) recounts events following the murder. Here Symons introduces the barrister Magnus Newton, a series character who reappears in some of Symons's best books, including *The Progress of a Crime* (1960) and *The End of Solomon Grundy* (1964). Part 3 is a short epilogue wherein Newton provides evidence which suggests that Wilkins, convicted of Sheila's murder, is in fact innocent. There is no question, however, of an appeal that could benefit Wilkins, who has become insane.

Symons's influence on crime literature increased after the publication of *The Colour of Murder*. He served as chairman of the Crime Writers' Association from 1958 to 1959 and began his tenure as a reviewer for the *London Sunday Times* in 1958. His new duties did not diminish the quality of his literary work. *The Progress of a Crime* received an Edgar Allan Poe Award from the Mystery Writers of America. In *The Progress of a Crime* Symons exploits his knowledge of working-class life as he had done in *The Colour of Murder*. This time, instead of placing characters in the Clapham of his youth, he moves them to a nameless city in the provinces where he explicitly treats a theme central to his work, the struggle of human beings to free themselves from traps which restrict and diminish their lives. Almost always these traps are created by middle-class values and aspirations. The novel has as its center three young lives. Leslie Winter is one of six gang members arrested in connection with a Guy Fawkes Day murder which receives wide publicity in the London papers. Local reporter Hugh Bennett sees in the murder a chance for advancement, and the *London Banner* exploits his am-

Dust jacket for the first American edition of Symons's brief illustrated biography of Arthur Conan Doyle

nocent world of children's game songs. The resulting characterization of a Nietzschean superman is a chilling picture of a disordered world. The theme is an extension of character: in a criminal world one must either become a criminal or remain a hypocrite. Solomon Grundy, adman and cartoonist, commits murder. His crime almost frees him from the hypocritical games of his caste and class until suburban do-gooder neighbors, aided by Magnus Newton, gain his acquittal. He is forced to kill again in order to obtain justice—to act and be responsible for his actions.

In *The Man Who Killed Himself* (1965) Symons varies the theme he used in *The End of Solomon Grundy*—when real life is sterile and bankrupt the fantasies and private games human beings play are what make life worth living. Meek and mild Arthur Brownjohn lives out his fantasy life in the guise of "Major Easonby Mellon." Brownjohn kills his wife for freedom's sake; then Easonby Mellon "kills" Brownjohn. The twists and turns of his metamorphosis tease the reader as much as any detective story plot and reveal more. For Easonby / Brownjohn has plotted a perfect murder, not for murder's sake, but for the sake of freedom from an imperfect world.

The Players and the Game (1972), the most literary of Symons's novels, brings all of his major themes together. Two excellent stories are intertwined. The first story is contained in a mysterious journal kept by a person known only as Count Dracula. It records the bizarre exploits he undertakes with his accomplice, "Bonnie Parker." The journal is the record of fantasy become reality, of crime as sane behavior in a criminal society. It ends with Dracula renouncing his vampire self and declaring that he is Friedrich Nietzsche. Running counterpoint to Dracula's story is that of the decline and fall of Paul Vane, a business executive struggling for success and status in modern, capitalist society. While Dracula's diary of madness crescendos, Vane (as his name suggests) stumbles blindly but certainly toward failure and destruction. For Symons the problems facing weak, morally bankrupt human beings who have an urge for social success can be resolved only through strength, moral courage, and personal integrity. Symons's next two novels, *The Plot Against Roger Rider* (1973) and *A Three Pipe Problem* (1975), are not of the quality of *The Players and the Game*, although *A Three Pipe Problem* is interesting because it is a successful experiment in writing a comic crime novel.

bition. Hugh, in turn, puts his growing relationship with Winter's sister, Jill, to personal use. The result is that the *Banner* agrees to bear the cost of Leslie Winter's defense in exchange for exclusive rights to his life story. Magnus Newton is hired for the defense, and everything goes well until Leslie Winter, just acquitted, hangs himself. It then becomes clear that the crimes which have been in progress throughout the novel go beyond the murder which Leslie and his cohorts actually did commit. Culpable are police who obtain information by using brute force, lawyers who are only concerned with the drama of the courtroom, and newspapers that see in human lives only profitable copy. Hugh and Jill see the trap which surrounds them, quit their jobs, and walk off into an uncharted future.

The End of Solomon Grundy is an excellent example of a serious crime novel. Symons again makes use of his advertising experience, this time contrasting that cutthroat environment with the in-

DOCUMENTS IN THE CASE (i)

(1937?) Daily Banner, Wed 10 August 1936.

MYSTERY OF THE VANISHING POET.

Friends tonight said they were concerned about the whereabouts of Mr Hugo Headley, the novelist and poet. Mr Headley's car was seen on Tuesday morning, parked on a patch of shingle near the beach outside the Kent resort of Littlestone-on-Sea, and Miss Ellen Corliss, a resident, noticed clothing piled on the back seat and assumed the owner had gone for a swim. The car being still there on the following morning, she notified the police. Police are enquiring into the matter, but there are no treacherous currents locally, and they regard a bathing accident is unlikely. Mr Headley is known to be an eccentric character, and it is thought possible he was suddenly afflicted with the divine afflatus, and wandered away in pursuit of a poem.

Daily Banner, Fri. 12 August 1936

THE MISSING POET: A TRAGIC ACCIDENT?

Nothing more has been heard of Mr Hugo Headley, the writer who left his car on the shingle beach near Littlestone-on-Sea last Monday and police are now seriously concerned that he may have been the victim of underwater currents. "Most of the beach is safe enough," according to local fishermen, "but there are strong currents in the area where the car was left." Inspector Lynton of the local constabulary says that while he is still inclined to the view that Mr Headley is possibly some other explanation of Mr Headley's disappearance is likely, the possibility of a tragic bathing accident cannot now be ignored.

Daily Banner Tues 23 August 1936

THE HEADLEY MYSTERY
MYSTERY OF THE MISSING POET
SUICIDE, MURDER, ACCIDENT, — OR PLANNED DISAPPEARANCE?
By our Special Reporter

The little Kentish seaside village of Chimpstone is buzzing with rumours about the disappearance nearly two weeks ago of the bohemian poet Hugo Headley. It was at first thought that Mr Headley had gone for a late night swim, and been caught in one of the currents known to local fishermen, and drowned. But no body has been recovered from the sea, and Inspector Lynton told me some of the unexplained aspects of the affair that lead him to doubt whether this strange disappearance

Page from the manuscript of Symons's current work in progress, "What Happened to Hugo Headley?" (courtesy of the author)

Both *The Blackheath Poisonings: A Victorian Murder Mystery* (1978) and *Sweet Adelaide: A Victorian Puzzle Solved* (1980) are fictional representations of actual crimes set in historically accurate Victorian surroundings. A third Victorian crime novel, *The Detling Murders*, appeared in 1982. The best of Symons's Victorian re-creations is *Sweet Adelaide*. For the first time in his fiction, the protagonist is a woman. Adelaide and her spiritually weak clergyman lover conspire to murder Adelaide's dull and boorish shopkeeper husband. Both Adelaide and the Reverend Dyson are romantics who prefer fantasy to reality. Adelaide, a true Nietzschean, wills that her fantasy exist and assumes both the burden and the consequences of projecting her personal vision onto a dreary world.

In both his fiction and nonfiction Symons has shown a great interest in courtroom drama. Court transcripts seem to tease his imagination. They offer the allure of the intellectual puzzle and provide detailed reflections of violent human behavior, a cracked mirror of the human self in conflict with the social order. In *A Reasonable Doubt: Some Criminal Cases Re-examined* (1960), Symons applies the tools of the crime-writing trade to an analysis of several actual cases. Through careful review and dissection of court transcripts, case commentaries, and other available documents, he probes motive and character in an effort to set right the facts of each case. It is his deep and abiding concern for character which most informs his opinions.

Nowhere in Symons's corpus is the distinction between fiction and nonfiction blurred more than in *The Great Detectives: Seven Original Investigations* (1981), a work handsomely illustrated by Tom Adams. Symons uses a character named Julian Symons to shed light on the lives of seven great fictional detectives. His knowledge of the genre and his playful wit are evident on every page as he provides readers with a very believable pastiche of Sherlock Holmes's last case, a case which may have been undertaken at the request of Agatha Christie's Miss Marple in her salad days. This is followed by the voice of the Reverend Leonard Clement, retired vicar of St. Mary Mead, who ambles and rambles through his memories of life with Miss Marple. Rex Stout's Archie Goodwin is interviewed by Symons, and he refuses to rule out the possibility that Nero Wolfe may still be alive. Writing in the voice of Julian Symons, literary critic, Symons then explores the Ellery Queen corpus for internal evidence which

Dust jacket for the first edition of Symons's 1988 mystery

will prove the thesis that there were, in fact, two Ellery Queens. Symons turns his attention to Georges Simenon's Jules Maigret and Christie's Hercule Poirot, and he speculates as to the identity of the person on whom Raymond Chandler's Philip Marlowe was based. Each excursion into the life of a great detective demonstrates that he knows the territory of crime literature inside out.

The Tell-Tale Heart: The Life and Works of Edgar Allan Poe (1978), a critical biography, is meant for a nonacademic audience and does not pretend to extend the boundaries of Poe scholarship. Symons contents himself with trying to make clear two contradictory sides of Poe's life and work: Logical Poe and Visionary Poe: "The two are as nearly as possible identical. He had no subject except himself, and there are no characters in any of his serious stories except the fears, hopes, and theories of Edgar Allan Poe. Several stories express his fear of madness, others are inhabited only by Logical Poe. All the women are specters, idealized images drained of blood. The narrators sometimes embody the point of view of Logical Poe while the action is carried through by Visionary Poe, but there are few stories other than the merely trivial in which he is able to dispense with a narrator. As an artist he worked always in the first person, looking again at his personality in a glass that often gave back frightening reflections. Concerned wholly with the depths he discerned in the mirror image, Poe was altogether incapable of imagining what other people felt or believed. . . ." This passage is significant because the mirror metaphor is central to Symons's own crime fiction. The Poe of his biography appears as a character familiar to readers of Symons's novels. Here one is faced with a puzzle. Is Symons's Poe biography flawed because he presents Poe as very much like one of Symons's characters, or does the parallel between Poe and Symons's characters merely reveal a deep and lasting influence? The biography was generally well received, although Daniel Hoffman (*New York Times Book Review*, 9 July 1978) faulted Symons for dismissing recent American Poe scholarship.

Symons's other important and problematic literary biography of a crime writer is *Dashiell Hammett* (1985). It is quite different from the Poe volume largely because it offers no special point of view. Indeed, Symons goes out of his way to avoid interpretation. Hammett is presented as a serious fiction writer. For example, Hammett the stylist is compared favorably to Hemingway; his complex narrative technique, Symons suggests, makes use of theory expounded by T. S. Eliot; and his comic strategy can be compared with that of Evelyn Waugh. In short Hammett is cataloged consistently as a significant writer among significant writers.

Symons's *The Criminal Comedy of the Contented Couple* (1985; published in the United States as *A Criminal Comedy*, 1986) is among his very best novels. It confirms the wisdom of those who, in 1982, made him the fourth person to win the Grand Master Award of the Mystery Writers of America. Not only is it a crime novel of the first order, it is also a biting social comedy, a fine puzzle, and a narrative tour de force. The germ for the novel is found in the short story "A Theme for Hyacinth," which first appeared in *Ellery Queen's Magazine* in 1967 (republished in *The Tigers of Subtopia, and Other Stories*, 1982).

The short story, set in Yugoslavia, introduces a beautiful young travel courier named Gerda, who seduces Robin Edgley, an older man, then frames him for the murder of her husband.

Her husband dead, Gerda is free to live her life with a younger man. The story makes explicit reference to poems by Wallace Stevens ("Le Monocle de Mon Oncle") and T. S. Eliot (*The Waste Land*), thus calling attention to the work's overt modernist concerns. Personalities are fragmented; the drive to action is brute instinct; and beauty, manners, and accomplishment are all facade. What is left as real and certain are aging and death. Edgley attempts to revive within himself the young man he once was, but he cannot. In *The Criminal Comedy of the Contented Couple* Gerda is a former travel courier married to Charles Porson, the coowner of PC Travel. The setting is Headfield, a London suburb, and Venice. The revision complements the modernist theme with modernist narrative technique, for it is a collage of narratives: newspaper articles, third-person narration, excerpts from a private journal, and a third-person epilogue. No real attempt is made to harmonize the parts. Instead the reader is left with fragments which suggest a whole.

Perhaps the novel is a comedy; a claim is made in the title and on the opening page of the narrative where the lives of "Derek and Sandy and Charles and Gerda" are associated with "some consciously light and bright American film." Derek Crowley and Charles Porson are partners in PC Travel. Sandy is Derek's wife. Off in the wings, recording this little comedy in his journal, is Derek's lifelong Prufrockian friend, Jason Durling. Letters purporting that Derek and Gerda are lovers flood the bedroom suburb of Headfield. Charles and Derek quarrel over Derek's proposal to offer tours of the Orient. Derek's rich uncle asks Jason to haul Derek back from the edge of scandal, something Jason has done more than once before. Then, in Venice, Charles is killed. The police consider Derek to be the prime suspect, though readers believe him to be innocent of both murder and adultery. Given the tension between the perceptions of the police and the reader, what this criminal comedy demands is an ending which exonerates the innocent and sets the social order right.

The novel is parodic, and parody is most evident in the epilogue, which is set on the island of Elba. As expected in a comedy, it is here that the lovers come together to live, without impediment, the sweet dream of their love. Then comes the reversal. Jason Durling tracks Gerda, freed from her swinish husband by his murder, to her love bower. There he is surprised when a man, coming toward the terrace upon which he stands with Gerda, takes off his hat, for the "man" is Sandy, Derek's recently divorced wife, with her hair cut short. This is hardly the triumph of nature, the celebration of wedded bliss, proper to comic endings.

Through Jason Durling's role in the novel and the place of his journal in the narrative structure, Symons keeps the reader permanently in doubt about "who did it and why." Jason is a closet homosexual who has loved Derek since childhood. Further, as a closet academic he is humiliated and "scooped" in his lifelong attempt to write the literary biography of a minor novelist. Prufrock-like, Jason has sat at the edge of his life tying bow ties for decades. Yet during the time of these events he comes to life; he wills to live, and perhaps his willing to live includes murder. Derek could have committed the murder. His profit motive is strong, and the adultery charge against him is never completely disproved. The British government could have killed Charles to protect clandestine activities and undercover agents. Sandy and Gerda may have killed him to make space for their lesbian affair. In modernist fiction it is difficult indeed to find the story, for in such fiction the telling is the thing.

No individual has done more in the postwar period to make crime stories into serious literature as has Julian Symons. He has documented a historical change in the crime-and-mystery genre, proposed a theory to account for the change, and subjected his theory to the test of writing. His many excellent novels and stories support the theory.

References:

Steven R. Carter, "Julian Symons and Civilization's Discontents," *Armchair Detective*, 12 (January 1979): 57-63;

Ellery Queen (Frederic Dannay and Manfred B. Lee), Introduction to *Ellery Queen Presents Julian Symons' How to Trap a Crook and 12 Other Mysteries*, edited by Queen (New York: Davis, 1977).

Papers:

Symons's papers are held at the Humanities Research Center, University of Texas at Austin.

Checklist of Further Readings

Adey, R. C. S. *Locked Room Murders and Other Impossible Crimes.* London: Ferret, 1979.

Aisenberg, Nadja. *A Common Spring: Crime Novel and Classic.* Bowling Green, Ohio: Bowling Green University Popular Press, 1979.

Albert, Walter. *Detective and Mystery Fiction: An International Bibliography of Secondary Sources.* Madison, Ind.: Brownstone Books, 1985.

Altick, Richard D. *Victorian Studies in Scarlet.* New York: Norton, 1970.

Atkins, John. *The British Spy Novel: Studies in Treachery.* London: Calder, 1984.

Ball, John, ed. *The Mystery Story.* San Diego & Del Mar: University of California Press, 1976.

Bargainnier, Earl F. *Comic Crime.* Bowling Green, Ohio: Bowling Green University Popular Press, 1989.

Bargainnier and George N. Dove, eds. *Cops and Constraints: American and British Fictional Policemen.* Bowling Green, Ohio: Bowling Green University Popular Press, 1986.

Barnes, Melvyn. *Best Detective Fiction: A Guide from Godwin to the Present.* London: Bingley/Hamden, Conn.: Linnet, 1975.

Barnes. *Murder in Print: A Guide to Two Centuries of Crime Fiction.* London: Barn Owl, 1986.

Barzun, Jacques, and Wendell Hertig Taylor. *A Book of Prefaces to Fifty Classics of Crime Fiction, 1900-1950.* New York: Garland, 1976.

Barzun and Taylor. *A Catalogue of Crime,* second impression, corrected. New York, Evanston, San Francisco & London: Harper & Row, 1974.

Benstock, Bernard, ed. *Essays on Detective Fiction.* London: Macmillan, 1983. Republished as *The Art of Crime Writing: Essays on Detective Fiction.* New York: St. Martin's Press, 1983.

Benvenuti, Stephano, and Gianni Rizzoni. *The Whodunit: An Informal History of Detective Fiction.* Translated by Anthony Eyre. New York: Macmillan, 1980.

Borowitz, Albert. *Innocence and Arsenic: Studies in Crime and Literature.* New York: Harper & Row, 1977.

Bourgeau, Art. *The Mystery Lover's Companion.* New York: Crown, 1986.

Breen, Jon L. *What About Murder? A Guide to Books about Mystery and Detective Fiction.* Metuchen, N.J. & London: Scarecrow Press, 1981.

Carr, John C. *The Craft of Crime: Conversations with Crime Writers.* Boston: Houghton Mifflin, 1983.

Cassidy, Bruce, ed. *Roots of Detection.* New York: Ungar, 1983.

Cawelti, John G. *Adventure, Mystery, and Romance: Formula Stories as Art and Popular Culture.* Chicago: University of Chicago Press, 1976.

Champigny, Robert. *What Will Happen: A Philosophical and Technical Essay on Mystery Stories.* Bloomington: Indiana University Press, 1977.

Charney, Hannah. *The Detective Novel of Manners: Hedonism, Morality and the Life of Reason.* Rutherford, N.J.: Fairleigh Dickinson University Press, 1981.

Cook, Michael L. *Mystery, Detective, and Espionage Magazines.* Westport, Conn.: Greenwood Press, 1983.

De Vries, P. H. *Poe and After: The Detective Story Investigated.* Amsterdam: Bakker, 1956.

Eco, Umberto, and Thomas A. Sebeok, eds. *Dupin, Holmes, and Pierce: The Sign of Three.* Bloomington: Indiana University Press, 1983.

Edwards, P. D. *Some Mid-Victorian Thrillers: The Sensation Novel, Its Friends and Its Foes.* St. Lucia, Queensland: University of Queensland Press, 1971.

Gribbin, Lenore S. *Who's Whodunit: A List of 3218 Detective Story Writers and Their 1100 Pseudonyms.* University of North Carolina Library Studies, no. 5. Chapel Hill: University of North Carolina Press, 1968.

Grossvogel, David I. *Mystery and Its Fictions: From Oedipus to Agatha Christie.* Baltimore: Johns Hopkins University Press, 1979.

Haining, Peter. *Mystery! An Illustrated History of Crime and Detective Fiction.* London: Souvenir Press, 1977.

Harper, Ralph. *The World of the Thriller.* Cleveland: Press of Case Western Reserve University, 1969.

Haycraft, Howard. *Murder for Pleasure: The Life and Times of the Detective Story,* enlarged edition. New York: Biblio & Tannen, 1968.

Haycraft, ed. *The Art of the Mystery Story: A Collection of Critical Essays.* New York: Simon & Schuster, 1946.

Herman, Linda, and Beth Steil. *Corpus Delecti of Mystery Fiction: A Guide to the Body of the Case.* Metuchen, N.J.: Scarecrow Press, 1974.

Hubin, Allen J. *Crime Fiction, 1749-1980: A Comprehensive Bibliography.* New York & London: Garland, 1984.

Hughes, Winifred. *The Maniac in the Cellar: Sensation Novels of the 1860s.* Princeton: Princeton University Press, 1980.

Johnson, Timothy W., and Julia Johnson, eds.; Robert Mitchell, Glenna Dunning, and Susan J. Mackall, assoc. eds. *Crime Fiction Criticism: An Annotated Bibliography.* New York & London: Garland, 1981.

Kalikoff, Beth. *Murder and Moral Decay in Victorian Popular Literature.* Ann Arbor: UMI Research Press, 1986.

Keating, H. R. F. *Crime and Mystery: The 100 Best Books.* New York: Carroll & Graf, 1987.

Keating. *Murder Must Appetize*. London: Lemon Tree Press, 1975.

Keating. *Whodunit? A Guide to Crime, Suspense & Crime Fiction*. New York: Van Nostrand Reinhold, 1982.

Keating, ed. *Crime Writers*. London: BBC, 1978.

La Cour, Tage, and Harald Morgensen. *The Murder Book: An Illustrated History of the Detective Story*. Translated by Roy Duffell. London: Allen & Unwin, 1971.

Lambert, Gavin. *The Dangerous Edge*. London: Barrie & Jenkins, 1975.

The Lilly Library, Indiana University. *The First Hundred Years of Detective Fiction, 1841-1941, By One Hundred Authors. On the Hundred Thirtieth Anniversary of The First Publication in Book Form of Edgar Allan Poe's "The Murders in the Rue Morgue," Philadelphia, 1843*, introduction by David A. Randall. Bloomington, Ind.: Lilly Library, 1973.

Mandel, Ernest. *Delightful Murder: A Social History of the Crime Story*. London: Pluto, 1984.

Mann, Jessica. *Deadlier than the Male. Why Are Respectable English Women So Good At Murder?* New York: Macmillan, 1981.

McCleary, G. F. *On Detective Fiction and Other Things*. London: Hollis & Carter, 1960.

McCormick, Donald. *Who's Who in Spy Fiction*. New York: Taplinger, 1977.

McSherry, Frank D., Jr. *Studies in Scarlet: Essays on Murder and Detective Fiction*. San Bernardino, Cal.: Borgo, 1985.

Meet the Detective. London: Allen & Unwin, 1935.

Menendez, Albert J. *The Subject Is Murder; A Selective Subject Guide to Mystery Fiction*. New York: Garland, 1986.

Merry, Bruce. *Anatomy of the Spy Thriller*. Dublin: Gill & Macmillan, 1977.

Modern Fiction Studies, special "Detective & Suspense" issue, 29 (Autumn 1983).

Most, Glen W., and William W. Stowe, eds. *The Poetics of Murder: Detective Fiction & Literary Theory*. New York: Harcourt Brace Jovanovich, 1983.

Murch, A. E. *The Development of the Detective Novel*. London: Owen, 1958.

Nevins, Francis M., Jr., ed. *The Mystery Writer's Art*. Bowling Green, Ohio: Bowling Green University Popular Press, 1970.

Olderr, Steven. *Mystery Index: Subjects, Settings and Sleuths of 10,000 Titles*. Chicago: American Library Association, 1987.

Oleksiw, Susan. *A Reader's Guide to the Classic British Mystery*. Boston: G. K. Hall, 1988.

Osborne, Eric. *Victorian Detective Fiction: A Catalogue of the Collection Made by Dorothy Glover & Graham Greene*. London, Sydney & Toronto: Bodley Head, 1966.

Ousby, Ian. *Bloodhounds of Heaven: The Detective in English Fiction from Godwin to Doyle.* Cambridge, Mass.: Harvard University Press, 1976.

Palmer, Jerry. *Thrillers: Genesis and Structure of a Popular Genre.* London: Arnold, 1978.

Panek, Leroy L. *An Introduction to the Detective Story.* Bowling Green, Ohio: Bowling Green University Popular Press, 1989.

Panek. *The Special Branch: The British Spy Novel, 1890-1980.* Bowling Green, Ohio: Bowling Green University Popular Press, 1981.

Panek. *Watteau's Shepherds: The Detective Novel in Britain, 1914-1940.* Bowling Green, Ohio: Bowling Green University Popular Press, 1979.

Pate, Janet. *The Book of Sleuths: From Sherlock Holmes to Kojak.* London: New English Library, 1977.

Pate. *The Book of Spies and Secret Agents.* London: Gallery Press, 1978.

Peterson, Audrey. *Victorian Masters of Mystery.* New York: Ungar, 1983.

Phillips, Walter C. *Dickens, Reade and Collins, Sensation Novelists.* New York: Columbia University Press, 1919.

Prager, Arthur. *Rascals at Large: Or, The Clue in the Old Nostalgia.* Garden City, N.Y.: Doubleday, 1971.

Pronzoni, Bill, and Marcia Muller, eds. *1001 Midnights: The Aficionado's Guide to Mystery and Detective Fiction.* New York: Arbor House, 1986.

Quayle, Eric. *The Collector's Book of Detective Fiction.* London: Studio Vista, 1972.

Queen, Ellery. *The Detective Short Story: A Bibliography.* Boston: Little, Brown, 1942.

Queen. *Queen's Quorum: A History of the Detective-Crime Short Story as Revealed in the 106 Most Important Books Published in This Field Since 1845,* new edition, with supplements through 1967. New York: Biblio & Tannen, 1969.

Reilly, John M., ed. *Twentieth-Century Crime and Mystery Writers,* revised and enlarged edition. New York: St. Martin's Press, 1985.

Routley, Erik. *The Puritan Pleasures of the Detective Story: A Personal Monograph.* London: Gollancz, 1972.

Skene Melvin, David, and Ann Skene Melvin. *Crime, Detective, Espionage, Mystery and Thriller: Fiction and Film: A Comprehensive Bibliography of Critical Writing through 1979.* Westport, Conn.: Greenwood Press, 1980.

Smith, Myron J., Jr. *Cloak and Dagger Fiction: An Annotated Guide to Spy Thrillers,* revised and enlarged edition. Santa Barbara & Oxford: ABC-Clio, 1982.

Smyth, Frank, and Myles Ludwig. *The Detectives: Crime and Detection in Fact Fiction.* Philadelphia & New York: Lippincott, 1978.

Steinbrunner, Chris, Charles Shibuk, Otto Penzler, Marvin Lachman, and Francis M. Nevins, Jr. *Detectionary: A Biographical Dictionary of the Leading Characters in Detective and Mystery Fiction*, revised edition. Woodstock, N.Y.: Overlook Press, 1977.

Steinbrunner and Penzler, eds., with Lachman and Shibuk. *Encyclopedia of Mystery and Detection*. New York, St. Louis & San Francisco: McGraw-Hill, 1976.

Stewart, R. F. *... and Always a Detective: Chapters on the History of Detective Fiction*. Newton Abbot, U.K. & North Pomfret, Vt.: David & Charles, 1980.

Symons, Julian. *Bloody Murder*, revised edition. New York: Viking, 1984.

Thomson, H. Douglas. *Masters of Mystery: A Study of the Detective Story*. London: Collins, 1931. Republished, with an introduction and notes by E. F. Bleiler. New York: Dover, 1978.

Watson, Colin. *Snobbery with Violence: Crime Stories and Their Audience*. New York: St. Martin's Press, 1971.

Winks, Robin W. *Modus Operandi: An Excursion into Detective Fiction*. Boston: Godine, 1982.

Winks, ed. *Detective Fiction: A Collection of Critical Essays*. Englewood Cliffs, N.J.: Prentice-Hall, 1980.

Winn, Dilys. *Murder Ink: The Mystery Reader's Companion*, revised edition. New York: Workman, 1984.

Winn. *Murderess Ink: The Better Half of the Mystery*. New York: Workman, 1979.

Woeller, Waltraud, and Bruce Cassidy. *The Literature of Crime and Detection: An Illustrated History from Antiquity to the Present*. Translated by Ruth Michaelis-Jena and Willy Merson. New York: Ungar, 1988.

Contributors

Mary Helen Becker ....*Madison Area Technical College*
Bernard Benstock ....*University of Miami*
David A. Christie ....*Ken Gardens, New York*
Joan DelFattore ....*University of Delaware*
Mary Jean DeMarr ....*Indiana State University*
James Gindin and Joan Gindin..*University of Michigan*
Larry E. Grimes...*Bethany College*
James Hurt...*University of Illinois*
Andrew F. Macdonald...*Loyola University in New Orleans*
Gina Macdonald ....*Loyola University in New Orleans*
Susan Resneck Parr...*University of Tulsa*
Nancy Pearl..*Tulsa, Oklahoma*
Carol Shloss ....*West Chester University*
T. R. Steiner ....*University of California, Santa Barbara*
Carol Simpson Stern ....*Northwestern University*
Michael J. Tolley ....*University of Adelaide*

Cumulative Index

Dictionary of Literary Biography, Volumes 1-87
Dictionary of Literary Biography Yearbook, 1980-1988
Dictionary of Literary Biography Documentary Series, Volumes 1-6

Cumulative Index

DLB before number: *Dictionary of Literary Biography*, Volumes 1-87
Y before number: *Dictionary of Literary Biography Yearbook*, 1980-1988
DS before number: *Dictionary of Literary Biography Documentary Series*, Volumes 1-6

B

D

F

G

H

K

M

Cumulative Index

O

Thoughts on Poetry and Its Varieties (1833), by John Stuart Mill DLB-32

Thurber, James 1894-1961 ....DLB-4, 11, 22

Thurman, Wallace 1902-1934 ....DLB-51

Thwaite, Anthony 1930- DLB-40

Thwaites, Reuben Gold 1853-1913 ....DLB-47

Ticknor, George 1791-1871 ....DLB-1, 59

Ticknor and Fields DLB-49

Ticknor and Fields (revived) DLB-46

Tietjens, Eunice 1884-1944 ....DLB-54

Tilton, J. E., and Company DLB-49

Time and Western Man (1927), by Wyndham Lewis [excerpts] DLB-36

Time-Life Books DLB-46

Times Books DLB-46

Timothy, Peter circa 1725-1782 ....DLB-43

Timrod, Henry 1828-1867 ....DLB-3

Tiptree, James, Jr. 1915- DLB-8

Titus, Edward William 1870-1952 ....DLB-4

Toklas, Alice B. 1877-1967 ....DLB-4

Tolkien, J. R. R. 1892-1973 ....DLB-15

Tolson, Melvin B. 1898-1966 ....DLB-48, 76

Tom Jones (1749), by Henry Fielding [excerpt] DLB-39

Tomlinson, Charles 1927- DLB-40

Tomlinson, Henry Major 1873-1958 ....DLB-36

Tompkins, Abel [publishing house] DLB-49

Tompson, Benjamin 1642-1714 ....DLB-24

Tonks, Rosemary 1932- DLB-14

Toole, John Kennedy 1937-1969 ....Y-81

Toomer, Jean 1894-1967 ....DLB-45, 51

Tor Books DLB-46

Torberg, Friedrich 1908-1979 ....DLB-85

Torrence, Ridgely 1874-1950 ....DLB-54

Toth, Susan Allen 1940- Y-86

Tough-Guy Literature DLB-9

Touré, Askia Muhammad 1938- DLB-41

Tourgée, Albion W. 1838-1905 ....DLB-79

Tourneur, Cyril circa 1580-1626 ....DLB-58

Tournier, Michel 1924- DLB-83

Tousey, Frank [publishing house] DLB-49

Tower Publications DLB-46

Towne, Benjamin circa 1740-1793 ....DLB-43

Towne, Robert 1936- DLB-44

Tracy, Honor 1913- DLB-15

Train, Arthur 1875-1945 ....DLB-86

The Transatlantic Publishing Company DLB-49

Transcendentalists, American DS-5

Traven, B. 1882? or 1890?-1969? DLB-9, 56

Travers, Ben 1886-1980 ....DLB-10

Tremain, Rose 1943- DLB-14

Tremblay, Michel 1942- DLB-60

Trends in Twentieth-Century Mass Market Publishing DLB-46

Trent, William P. 1862-1939 ....DLB-47

Trescot, William Henry 1822-1898 ....DLB-30

Trevor, William 1928- DLB-14

Trilling, Lionel 1905-1975 ....DLB-28, 63

Triolet, Elsa 1896-1970 ....DLB-72

Tripp, John 1927- DLB-40

Trocchi, Alexander 1925- DLB-15

Trollope, Anthony 1815-1882 ....DLB-21, 57

Trollope, Frances 1779-1863 ....DLB-21

Troop, Elizabeth 1931- DLB-14

Trotter, Catharine 1679-1749 ....DLB-84

Trotti, Lamar 1898-1952 ....DLB-44

Trottier, Pierre 1925- DLB-60

Troupe, Quincy Thomas, Jr. 1943- DLB-41

Trow, John F., and Company DLB-49

Trumbo, Dalton 1905-1976 ....DLB-26

Trumbull, Benjamin 1735-1820 ....DLB-30

Trumbull, John 1750-1831 ....DLB-31

T. S. Eliot Centennial Y-88

Tucholsky, Kurt 1890-1935 ....DLB-56

Tucker, George 1775-1861 ....DLB-3, 30

Tucker, Nathaniel Beverley 1784-1851 ....DLB-3

Tucker, St. George 1752-1827 ....DLB-37

Tuckerman, Henry Theodore 1813-1871 ....DLB-64

Tunis, John R. 1889-1975 ....DLB-22

Tuohy, Frank 1925- DLB-14

Tupper, Martin F. 1810-1889 ....DLB-32

Turbyfill, Mark 1896- DLB-45

Villard, Oswald Garrison 1872-1949 ....DLB-25

Villarreal, José Antonio 1924- DLB-82

Villemaire, Yolande 1949- DLB-60

Villiers, George, Second Duke
    of Buckingham 1628-1687 ....DLB-80

Viorst, Judith ?- DLB-52

Volkoff, Vladimir 1932- DLB-83

Volland, P. F., Company DLB-46

von der Grün, Max 1926- DLB-75

Vonnegut, Kurt 1922- DLB-2, 8; Y-80; DS-3

Vroman, Mary Elizabeth circa 1924-1967 ....DLB-33

W

Waddington, Miriam 1917- DLB-68

Wade, Henry 1887-1969 ....DLB-77

Wagoner, David 1926- DLB-5

Wah, Fred 1939- DLB-60

Wain, John 1925- DLB-15, 27

Wainwright, Jeffrey 1944- DLB-40

Waite, Peirce and Company DLB-49

Wakoski, Diane 1937- DLB-5

Walck, Henry Z. DLB-46

Walcott, Derek 1930- Y-81

Waldman, Anne 1945- DLB-16

Walker, Alice 1944- DLB-6, 33

Walker, George F. 1947- DLB-60

Walker, Joseph A. 1935- DLB-38

Walker, Margaret 1915- DLB-76

Walker, Ted 1934- DLB-40

Walker and Company DLB-49

Walker, Evans and Cogswell Company DLB-49

Walker, John Brisben 1847-1931 ....DLB-79

Wallace, Edgar 1875-1932 ....DLB-70

Wallant, Edward Lewis 1926-1962 ....DLB-2, 28

Walpole, Horace 1717-1797 ....DLB-39

Walpole, Hugh 1884-1941 ....DLB-34

Walrond, Eric 1898-1966 ....DLB-51

Walser, Martin 1927- DLB-75

Walser, Robert 1878-1956 ....DLB-66

Walsh, Ernest 1895-1926 ....DLB-4, 45

Walsh, Robert 1784-1859 ....DLB-59

Wambaugh, Joseph 1937- DLB-6; Y-83

Ward, Artemus (see Browne, Charles Farrar)

Ward, Arthur Henry Sarsfield
    (see Rohmer, Sax)

Ward, Douglas Turner 1930- DLB-7, 38

Ward, Lynd 1905-1985 ....DLB-22

Ward, Mrs. Humphry 1851-1920 ....DLB-18

Ward, Nathaniel circa 1578-1652 ....DLB-24

Ward, Theodore 1902-1983 ....DLB-76

Ware, William 1797-1852 ....DLB-1

Warne, Frederick, and Company DLB-49

Warner, Charles Dudley 1829-1900 ....DLB-64

Warner, Rex 1905- DLB-15

Warner, Susan Bogert 1819-1885 ....DLB-3, 42

Warner, Sylvia Townsend 1893-1978 ....DLB-34

Warner Books DLB-46

Warren, John Byrne Leicester (see De Tabley, Lord)

Warren, Lella 1899-1982 ....Y-83

Warren, Mercy Otis 1728-1814 ....DLB-31

Warren, Robert Penn 1905- DLB-2, 48; Y-80

Washington, George 1732-1799 ....DLB-31

Wassermann, Jakob 1873-1934 ....DLB-66

Wasson, David Atwood 1823-1887 ....DLB-1

Waterhouse, Keith 1929- DLB-13, 15

Waterman, Andrew 1940- DLB-40

Waters, Frank 1902- Y-86

Watkins, Tobias 1780-1855 ....DLB-73

Watkins, Vernon 1906-1967 ....DLB-20

Watmough, David 1926- DLB-53

Watson, Sheila 1909- DLB-60

Watson, Wilfred 1911- DLB-60

Watt, W. J., and Company DLB-46

Watterson, Henry 1840-1921 ....DLB-25

Watts, Alan 1915-1973 ....DLB-16

Watts, Franklin [publishing house] DLB-46

Waugh, Auberon 1939- DLB-14

Waugh, Evelyn 1903-1966 ....DLB-15

Way and Williams DLB-49

Wayman, Tom 1945- DLB-53

Weatherly, Tom 1942- DLB-41